PENGUIN

THE PORTABLE ARTHUR MILLER

ARTHUR MILLER was born in New York City in 1915 and studied at the University of Michigan. His plays include *All My Sons* (1947), *Death of a Salesman* (1949), *The Crucible* (1953), *A View from the Bridge* and *A Memory of Two Mondays* (1955), *After the Fall* (1964), *Incident at Vichy* (1965), *The Price* (1968), *The Creation of the World and Other Business* (1972), and *The American Clock* (1980). He has also written two novels, *Focus* (1945) and *The Misfits*, which was filmed in 1960, and the text for *In Russia* (1969), *In the Country* (1977), and *Chinese Encounters* (1979), three books of photographs by Inge Morath. His most recent works include a memoir, *Timebends* (1987), the plays *The Ride Down Mt. Morgan* (1991), *The Last Yankee* (1993), *Broken Glass* (1994), and *Mr. Peters' Connections* (1999), *Echoes Down the Corridor: Collected Essays, 1994–2000*, and *On Politics and the Art of Acting* (2001). He has twice won the New York Drama Critics Award, and in 1949 he was awarded the Pulitzer Prize.

HAROLD CLURMAN, an internationally known stage director and former executive consultant for the Repertory Theater of Licoln Center for the Performing Arts, previously published *Lies Like Truth*: *Theatre Essays and Reviews*. He died in 1980.

CHRISTOPHER BIGSBY has published more then twenty books on British and American culture. His works include studies of African-American writing, American theater, English drama, and popular culture. He is the author of two novels, *Hester* and *Pearl*, and has written plays for radio and television. He is also a regular broadcaster for the BBC. He is currently professor of American Studies at the University of East Anglia, in Norwich, England.

The Portable
Arthur Miller

Original Introduction by
HAROLD CLURMAN

Revised Edition Edited with an Introduction by
CHRISTOPHER BIGSBY

PENGUIN BOOKS

PENGUIN BOOKS

Published by the Penguin Group
Penguin Group (USA) Inc., 375 Hudson Street, New York, New York 10014, U.S.A.
Penguin Books Ltd, 80 Strand, London WC2R 0RL, England
Penguin Books Australia Ltd, 250 Camberwell Road, Camberwell, Victoria 3124, Australia
Penguin Books Canada Ltd, 10 Alcorn Avenue, Toronto, Ontario, Canada M4V 3B2
Penguin Books India (P) Ltd, 11 Community Centre, Panchsheel Park, New Delhi – 110 017, India
Penguin Books (N.Z.) Ltd, Cnr Rosedale and Airborne Roads, Albany, Auckland, New Zealand
Penguin Books (South Africa) (Pty) Ltd, 24 Sturdee Avenue, Rosebank, Johannesburg 2196, South Africa

Penguin Books Ltd, Registered Offices: 80 Strand, London WC2R 0RL, England

First published in the United States of America by The Viking Press 1971
Published in Penguin Books 1997
Updated edition published in Penguin Books 1995
This edition published 2003

1 3 5 7 9 10 8 6 4 2

Copyright © Arthur Miller, 1995
Copyright © Christopher Bigsby, 1995
Copyright © The Viking Press, Inc., 1971
All rights reserved

LIBRARY OF CONGRESS CATALOGING IN PUBLICATION DATA
Miller, Arthur.
The portable Arthur Miller / edited, and with an introduction, by
Christopher Bigsby : original introduction by Harold Clurman.
p.   cm.
Includes bibliographical references.
ISBN 0 14 24.3755 7
1. United States—Social life and customs—20th century—Drama.
2. Salem (Mass.)—History—Colonial period, ca. 1600–1775—Drama.
3. Witchcraft—Massachusetts—Salem—Drama.   I. Bigsby, C. W. E.   II. Title.
PS3525.I5156A6   1995
812'.52—dc20   95-9485

Printed in the United States of America
Set in Bembo

CONTENTS

BIOGRAPHICAL NOTES

FROM THE 1970 EDITION, EDITED BY HAROLD CLURMAN

There can be no doubt at this point in our literary and theatrical history as to Arthur Miller's position in it. Among the playwrights since the emergence of Eugene O'Neill only Lillian Hellman, Clifford Odets, and Tennessee Williams are at all comparable to him. Hellman's and Odets's writing does not possess so wide a formal range, nor has it extended over so long a period. Only Williams has been more prolific. Miller is the author of nine plays, a screenplay, numerous short stories and essays, a novel, occasional poems, reportage, and, most recently, commentary on a trip to the Soviet Union which accompanies Inge Morath's photographs assembled under the title *In Russia. Death of a Salesman,* which won the Pulitzer Prize in drama in 1949, has been produced in virtually every one of the world's capitals and has been read in book form by several million people who have never seen it performed—unusual for a contemporary play.

When he was asked recently in what way his plays were related to the events of his life, Miller replied, "In a sense all my plays are autobiographical." The artist creates his biography through his work even as the events of his life serve to shape him.

He was born on 112th Street in Manhattan on October 17, 1915. He is one of three children. He has an elder brother in business, a sister on the stage. The Millers were unequivocally middle-class and Jewish. His mother, no longer living, was born in the United States; his father, a manufacturer of women's coats, was born in what before the First World War was part of the Austro-Hungarian empire. Until the Depression of the 1930s the Millers were a moderately well-to-do family. Arthur attended grammar school in Harlem and went to high school in Brooklyn.

By the time he finished high school, his parents could no longer afford to send him to college. His grades were not sufficiently high to qualify him for entry into the school of his choice, the University of Michigan. He found two ways out of this dilemma. He got himself a job in a warehouse on Tenth Avenue and 60th Street as a "loader" and shipping clerk, and saved a sum sufficient to pay his tuition. He also wrote a letter to the president of the university and asked for a chance to prove his merit within the first year of his studies. If he failed to distinguish himself he would quit. He did very well and stayed on to take his degree of Bachelor of Arts in 1938.

In his boyhood Arthur was neither particularly bright nor very well read. He was a baseball fan. He began to read while working at the warehouse. He is probably the only man who ever read through *War and Peace* entirely on the subway, standing up. At college he also began to write—plays. Several of them were awarded the University of Michigan's Jule and Avery Hopwood prizes. One of them won a prize of $1,250 given by the Theatre Guild's Bureau of New Plays. With money from these prizes and $22.77 a week from the Federal Theatre Project, Miller was able to support himself during the early years of his career. He was living at Patchogue, Long Island, at the time and had to check in every day at the project office in Manhattan, fifty-seven miles away, to collect his wage. He wrote a play about Montezuma which was submitted to the Group Theatre, as well as to others, no doubt, and which the editor of the present volume, then the Group Theatre's Managing Director, found several years later in his files— unread!

In 1944, a diary Miller had kept while visiting Army camps in the United States, researching for a film, *The Story of G.I. Joe* (the war life of the journalist Ernie Pyle), was published under the title *Situation Normal*. In

1945, as a reaction to the activities of a fascist organization known as the Christian Front, Miller wrote his only novel, *Focus,* which attracted considerable attention. Its subject was anti-Semitism.

Also in 1944 came the production of Miller's first play in the professional theatre, *The Man Who Had All the Luck,* which had no luck at all: there were only four performances. Still, Miller was launched! One critic, Burton Rascoe, recognized a potentially powerful playwright. More important, several producers, including myself, got in touch with Miller, requesting him to submit his next play. That was *All My Sons,* which was produced by Harold Clurman, Elia Kazan, and Walter Fried on January 29, 1947. It was a box-office success and was voted the Best Play of the Season by the Drama Critics' Circle. The dates and circumstances of his other plays will be found in the Introduction.

Along with his life as a playwright, Miller has been an engaged public figure. He has lectured widely, written articles on the theatre and its relation to world affairs, and participated in liberal movements of the day. In 1956, when he appeared before the House Un-American Activities Committee, he refused to name people who had attended a meeting to which he had been invited as a guest, some of whom he surmised were members of the Communist Party. On this account he was convicted of contempt of Congress in 1957, a conviction which was reversed by the Supreme Court in 1958. In 1965 Miller was elected international president of P.E.N., the worldwide society of poets and playwrights, essayists and editors, novelists and nonfiction writers. Though nonpolitical by its charter, P.E.N. was momentarily torn by conflicting national interests. His presidency was so successful in the causes of international understanding through literature and of freedom for writers everywhere that he was unanimously elected to a second term.

Arthur Miller has been married three times. His first marriage—to Mary Slattery, a sometime social worker—took place in 1940. Two children, a boy and a girl, were born of this marriage, which ended in divorce in 1956. His second marriage took place the same year, to Marilyn Monroe, the actress. They were divorced in 1960. In 1962 he married the photographer Inge Morath, Austrian-born and educated in France and Germany, where she had lived through the Hitler regime and the war. A daughter was born of this union. The Millers now live in a country place in Connecticut.

                                                                    —H.C.
                                                                June 1970

• • •

Writing in 1970, Harold Clurman listed nine produced plays (ten, if he had included *They Too Arise,* performed by the Federal Theatre). By 1995 this figure had risen to twenty-four. Clurman's comparison of Miller, at that time, with Lillian Hellman and Clifford Odets, has long since been proved inappropriate. The range and impact of his work is such that today no living playwright could be said to be his equal. Not a day passes without a production of a Miller play somewhere in the world. Those who do not see his plays frequently read them. The Penguin paperback sales of just two of his plays (*Death of a Salesman* and *The Crucible*) amount to some ten million copies in the last two decades alone.

Arthur Miller has continued to be an international presence. His book on Russia was followed by one on China, again jointly produced with his wife, the Magnum photographer Inge Morath. Harold Pinter recalls with some pride how Miller joined him when he was thrown out of the United States embassy in Turkey, following a political disagreement. In the 1980s he was one of a group of writers who met with Mikhail Gorbachev as the Soviet empire began its spectacular collapse. But before that he had met with dissident writers in Czechoslovakia and elsewhere, and has frequently sought to defend writers against censorship and imprisonment. More parochially he was instrumental in securing the release of a young man falsely accused of murder in his own community. Justice is not a concern only in his plays.

The young daughter referred to by Harold Clurman has grown up to be an artist, an actress, a screenwriter, and a film director. Miller and his wife continue to live in the same Connecticut township where, when not writing plays, he works with wood, and has fashioned the table at which he dines and the bed in which he sleeps. Today, according to his friend and neighbor William Styron, he "looks like a Jewish Abraham Lincoln," if only a Jewish Abraham Lincoln would occasionally choose to dress with a "gentleman farmer's rumpledness." His typewriter has been exchanged for a computer, and a FAX machine now unspools messages from around the world, but in other respects he remains un-changed. At eighty he is even more prolific than he was at fifty or, indeed, forty. He plays tennis, swims in his own pond, and, against his own better instincts, works in the garden. But most of all he writes plays, or novellas, or films, or short stories, or articles.

Every now and then he fires off laconic proposals to *The New York Times*, in which he calls for public executions or the privatization of Congress, in the hope that satire will accomplish what politics cannot. In 1968 he was a Eugene McCarthy delegate at the Democratic National Convention in Chicago. It follows that if he has a personal saint it is probably Saint Anthony, patron saint of lost causes. But as a Jewish writer he undoubtedly dispenses with saints in favor of a moral conscience, a powerful awareness of irony, and a sense of humor, of which his plays provide ample evidence.

Edward Albee has said of him, as a writer, that "his plays and his conscience are a cold burning force." Peter Ustinov has said of him, as a friend, that he is "quite simply, fun." From the point of view of an actor, he is the author of some of the most affecting, convincing, and moving characters in world theater. As Dustin Hoffman has remarked, "You can usually tell if a writer loves actors or not by the parts he gives them. He gives you tap dances. He gives you arias." And from the point of view of the audience? As David Mamet remarked, after seeing *Death of a Salesman*, "it was our story that we did not know until we heard it."

C.B.
March 1995

INTRODUCTION
TO THE ORIGINAL EDITION

Reading Arthur Miller's plays and stories in sequence reminded me of an anecdote I heard told about Einstein. A reporter interviewing him asked if any "new ideas" had occurred to him lately. "You know," Einstein answered, "one has only one or two ideas in a lifetime."

There is considerable variety in Miller's work but, viewing it as a body, we soon come to discern its essential unity. All his ideas are parts of one Idea. This does not make his writing "ideological," nor does it render it monotonous. One test of an artist's excellence is the degree to which he is capable of giving his idea constantly renewed or enriched embodiment.

If we follow Miller's career from the reportage of *Situation Normal*, written in 1944 when he was twenty-eight, and his only novel, *Focus*, written a year later, to his most recently produced full-length play, *The Price* (1968), we are struck by the wide range in subject matter which his idea assumes. We may also observe how the theme in one play or book becomes the seed of still another. Each new work may be likened to a function or an organ of the growing corpus.

The incident which opens *Focus* resembles the point of departure in Camus' *The Fall*, written eleven years after Miller's book. In *The Fall* a respected lawyer hears the splash of a body as it strikes the Seine. He does not turn back to find out if a woman he has just seen as he was crossing the bridge has attempted suicide and what he might do about it.

This momentary lapse of conscience causes a crisis of self-examination which turns to self-accusation. In the Miller novel a humdrum citizen asleep in bed one night is awakened by the agonized cry of a woman in the street calling, "Police! Police!" He rationalizes his failure in responsive action and goes back to sleep, apparently forgetting all about the momentary disturbance. But later, under very different circumstances, when his own safety is threatened, the woman's wild appeal for help resounds in his consciousness and prods him into an awareness of his connection with it.

We are all part of one another; all responsible to one another. The responsibility originates on the simplest, almost animal level: our immediate kin. But this vital attachment to the family—father, mother, children, brothers and sisters—is germinal and with the maturing of the person extends beyond its initial source.

In *Situation Normal* (Miller's first published book) there is the "story" of Watson, a soldier who is under close observation while a candidate in officers' training after a period of efficient and brave service in Japan. What troubles him is that his backwardness in the required mathematics may lead to his rejection for a commission as an officer. This would seem to him like a betrayal of his company companions, to whom he has become deeply attached. (The expression of this bond among "brother" combatants in the Army is echoed in a speech in *All My Sons*.)

On reflection about Watson's "case," Miller asks himself to what sort of folk Watson will feel similarly devoted when he returns to civilian life. Will that interdependence, that strength which comes from helping to sustain and being sustained by a group such as the Army company, be found again in the postwar world? Miller hopes that this may be so, but his fear that the contrary may be true is apparent in the quasi-patriotic concluding pages of his report.

Basic elements of Miller's feeling may be deduced from these two instances: a sense of responsibility for our fellow creatures, and belief in the need for a common goal which validates the act of responsibility. Irresponsibility, in Miller's view, is the root of sin. Without profoundly nurtured belief, the concept of responsibility becomes null and void.

I speak of "sin." It is an unfashionable word nowadays and Miller rarely uses it. He is, as we shall see, sufficiently imbued with the skepticism of modern thought to shy away from the presumptions implicit in it. But that Miller is willy-nilly a moralist—one who believes he knows what sin and evil are—is inescapable.

Along with the moral conflict—one of the attributes that give Miller's work its dramatic tension—we find, too, an ever-increasing awareness that there is arrogance and even menace inherent in the moralist's posture. Sue Bayliss, the doctor's wife in *All My Sons* (Miller's first successful play), says of its "hero," "Chris makes people want to be better than it's possible to be." When asked, "Is that bad?" she flashes back with "I resent living next door to the Holy Family. It makes me look like a bum." Sue's quite understandable challenge is keenly felt by Miller himself. Even though in *All My Sons* he brings wrath to bear on the sinner, it is mitigated by the fact that the sinner in this case may possibly have recognized his misdeed and punished himself for it. But I venture to suggest that it is the moral stance in Miller, with its seemingly punitive bent, which causes a certain resistance to his work in some quarters.

More often than not the moralist posits a god. God is the father. The father in Miller's work is a recurrent figure regarded with awe, devotion, love, even when he is proved lamentably fallible and when submission to him becomes painfully questionable. The father is a godhead because he is the giver and support of life; he is expected to serve as an example of proper conduct, of *good*. He therefore inspires and confirms *belief*, informing all our most significant actions, and fosters our reason for living. He gives identity and coherence to our being, creates value.

"A father is a father," the hard-pressed and culpable Joe Keller shouts in *All My Sons* and defends his malfeasance perpetrated on behalf of his family. To which his wife replies, referring to their son, Chris, "It doesn't excuse it that you did it for the family." Keller counters with, "It's got to excuse it." Then the mother says, "There's something bigger than the family to him." Keller retorts, "Nothing is bigger." The mother again: "There is to him." And we gather that Miller believes this too.

In the crucial confrontation with his father, Chris reveals himself (and Miller) by exclaiming, "I know you're no worse than most men but I thought you were better. I never saw you as a man. I saw you as a father." In this he has moved beyond the realm of common sense and speaks of fatherhood in a religious sense.

The family is pivotal, but beyond the family is the family of mankind. The family has its extension in the community, the social body—the *polis*, as it was once named. Here, then, is where Miller locates the focus of responsibility. This may become an evasion where "society" is so generalized a concept as to be dehumanized, faceless. God, whether it be the head of the family or the *polis*, cannot be reified. Miller does not write what in the 1930s we dubbed "social plays." Our relation to society is particularized in immediate and close contact with neighboring individuals.

Connection with others—the need to feel others as part of ourselves and ourselves as part of them—is not an intellectual matter. It is an impulse native to all of us, an almost universally recognized intuition, indeed a fact. We call people without it "sick." Yet we see this prime impulse constantly being impeded and crippled. Miller's work is largely devoted to the dramatization and depiction of the forces that induce impediments to responsibility—which is based on mutuality. Like all moralists, he seeks to expose the sin.

Everywhere today, and most glaringly in America, what diverts us from our responsibilities is the heartless functionalism of the marketplace, of *practicality*. "The cats in the alley are practical," Chris protests. "This is a zoo, a zoo!"

Practicality too has its god: it is success. In Miller's first and now out-of-print play, *The Man Who Had All the Luck* (produced in 1944), the central figure is a boy who fears success when it is not founded on work or merit. In that play there is a father who presses his son toward success, regardless of its origins. Five years later the destructive role played by the consecration of or fixation on success (shall we call it *Dementia Americana*?) was to be given its amplest and most affecting expression in *Death of a Salesman*.

Willy Loman believes wholeheartedly in the operative ideal of his fellow countrymen. Being a kindly man, he speaks not of success so much as of being "well liked." The crass vibrations implied in the more general term take on an aspect of smiling benevolence. He has forsworn his modest gift for carpentry to become a salesman because it promises a brighter future of ease and affluence. By turning away from himself he becomes an utterly confused person. He is now only half a man, a blind man, always in contradiction to himself, even to the smallest details of his existence. He dreams the American legend—the brother who walked into the jungle and when he was twenty-one came out of it rich. He sees everything in its light: the boss's good will, the business contacts, advertisements, publicity, bigness, gladhanding, being "impressive." He has misplaced and can no longer recognize his own reality.

So Willy Loman wreaks havoc on his own life and on that of his sons. The blight of his own confusion is visited upon them. Unaware of what warped his mind and behavior, he commits suicide in the conviction that a legacy of twenty thousand dollars is all that is needed to save his beloved but almost equally damaged offspring. This may not be "tragic," but such distorted thinking maims a very great number of folk in the world today.

Dramatically absorbing in itself, *The Crucible* may be viewed as a transitional piece if we consider it in the context of Miller's later development. Using a historical subject, the play shows how a materialistically instigated social trauma may fester into a sadistic fever to which an entire community succumbs. It leads it to superstitious hysteria and to the abandonment of all moral scruple and intelligence. (A similar theme stimulated Miller to undertake the adaptation of Ibsen's *An Enemy of the People*.) The fear and frenzy of the McCarthy era is plainly the fire which ignited *The Crucible*. "Is the accuser always holy?" is its key line. But there is something more to the play than "propaganda."

It contains two features which time and further experience magnified. One of them has to do with marital relationships. There is a certain Puritan coldness in Elizabeth, *The Crucible*'s heroine. She forgets nothing, and forgiveness comes hard to her. Her husband, Proctor, admonishes, "Learn charity, woman." Perhaps it is this forbidding quality in her which has betrayed him into a momentary adultery. It is a fall from grace in his eyes. Despite his plea for compassion, he finds it difficult to forgive himself. "The magistrate sits in your heart that judges you," she says. "I never thought you but a good man, only somewhat bewildered." She is right, and the web of their intimate struggle with each other anticipates some of the marital complexities in the thematic material of *After the Fall*.

A note first struck in *All My Sons* is developed in *The Crucible*, and in another vein in *Incident at Vichy* and again in *The Price*, where it leads to a sort of impasse. It may be isolated in a phrase from *All My Sons* in which a character refers to "the star of one's honesty." But something more than "honesty" is involved. Proctor chooses to die in *The Crucible* rather than live and besmirch his "name." Von Berg in *Vichy* chooses to face punishment (possibly death) to save a man he hardly knows. Victor Franz [in *The Price*] chooses to give up his education to aid his fault-ridden father. Apelike Tony Calabrese in the short story "Fitter's Night" decides to risk his neck doing a job for which there is neither obligation nor recompense. What is manifest in all these instances is a sort of gratuitous heroism—determinations without "rational" imperative. Even the "mixed-up" and not at all admirable Eddie Carbone in

A View from the Bridge pleads to preserve his "name" (or honor) and virtually commits suicide because this is not granted to him. It is just this sort of drive in men, almost as integral to them as the sheer animal impulse to self-preservation, in which Miller finds the glory as much as the mystery of life.

A moralist stops at nothing in his pursuit of virtue. If he is honest he is driven to sit in judgment upon himself. Pressed by this self-induced compulsion, he can hardly forbear from self-accusation and self-condemnation. To recover from what must surely prove a debilitating or destructive sense of guilt, he gropes toward self-rehabilitation. This process is most vividly traced in *After the Fall*.

That there is an autobiographical base to this drama is undeniable, but to enlarge upon it is to miss the play itself. What anyone who carefully studies *After the Fall* must recognize is that Miller does not exculpate his *alter ego*, Quentin. "I don't know if I have lived in good faith," he confesses. He examines the evidence that has aroused his suspicion.

His mother planted in him the notion that he would be a bright star, "a light in the world." His successful career as a liberal lawyer seemed to substantiate the prophecy. He became convinced of being in the right and of his ability to help the less favored, even to guide them. His failures in marriage undermined the foundations of his self-esteem. He begins to doubt the subjective authenticity of all his former benefactions. His first wife, whom he reproaches for being hard, may simply be a reflection of his own moral rigor. But after his second wife accuses him of not knowing how to relate to a woman, he remembers that this is exactly what his first wife had said.

Quentin's conceit has led him to believe he could shape Maggie's (the second wife's) innocent, trusting, tormented soul and transform it to splendor. The girl is a victim both of her unwholesome background and of the image of herself created by the gaudy environment into which she has been promoted. Torn and wounded by the enormousness of his ambition in regard to her, Quentin comes to realize that his noble design may have been little more than the mask of his sensual desire and, much worse, a bent toward power. The stern humanist he believed himself to be, the judge and scold of others, the apostle of justice, lacks the gift of love. And where love is missing, the urge to power always steps in.

There was a flaw, he now burningly suspects, in all his attitudes. His principles so staunchly maintained, so haughtily proclaimed, were not altogether sound—that is, organic to his nature. Abstract principles are delusive. That is why he turns for sustenance to the German woman, whose knowledge of the Nazi horror is personal. She understands its complexity, its relevance to all our blindness and failures. It is her "uncertainty," the absence of spiritual arrogance, he now blesses. She doesn't seem to be looking, he says, for some "goddamned moral victory." Recognizing that the lofty posture of his earlier days was a species of hypocrisy, he is impelled to seek a new direction. "To admit what you see," he muses, "endangers principles."

Yet he cannot live without them. "I can't be a separate person!" he exclaims, still another formulation of Miller's root idea. This very need for connection makes him understand his tie with the evil he abhors. The Nazis were killers, but we are all, to some degree, killers. All of us, through lack of self-knowledge, have contributed to the building of concentration camps and the gas chambers, those monuments of human depravity.

How may we resolve this appalling contradiction? We must recognize the quotient of the murderous within ourselves, the base egotism which lingers in all but the saintly; it is imperative that we strive with all our forces to master it, no matter how difficult this may be. This in the end can be accomplished only through the fortitude of love, which is also innate in us. Thus Quentin has reason to hope that he will cast off the garment of a spurious sanctity, to go forward again with a consciousness of his own all too human fallibility.

Surviving this test of conscience without nihilistic bitterness, achieving skepticism without its becoming the excuse for a pretentious or cynical passivity, Miller writes a stark morality play, *Incident at Vichy*. The play is not just another dramatization of the Hitler holocaust; it is a fresh statement of the main theme in nearly all his previous plays, whether they deal with the crime of delation, as in *A View from the Bridge*, or with cooperation among poor folk, as in *A Memory of Two Mondays*.

The spokesman in *A View* decries the demand for "absolute justice" by saying that "one settles for half and I like it better," which Miller at the time of its writing (1955) was hardly able to do, for then he thought of the "squealer" Eddie Carbone as largely villainous. In *A Memory*, the gentlest of Miller's plays, all the warehouse fellows sense their kinship with their alcoholic comrade broken by the conditions that obtain there, and they try to protect him.

What *Incident at Vichy* reiterates is our proclivity to evade troublesome facts so that confrontation with evil and hence our responsibility for it are avoided. Miller sees in the emergence of Hitler not simply a historical calamity but evidence of the absence of operative ideals, of a truly binding faith everywhere in our time. In such a period "what we used to conceive a human being to be will have no room on this earth."

In this play the ones who stand fast against the prevailing brutalization are the orthodox Jew; the Communist worker (who is mistaken in his interpretation of the situation); the adolescent boy made staunch by his devotion to his mother; the embittered doctor, who finds no alleviation through what we ordinarily term "human nature"; and the Catholic aristocrat, who has few ideas and acts mindlessly, that is, without a reason he might be able to explain or "sensibly" defend. The others are to die abjectly.

A choice is made; and that is freedom. When, as previously noted, Calabrese is asked by the naval captain to undertake the perilous job described in "Fitter's Night," he feels that "for the first time . . . it was entirely up to him with no punishment if he said no, nor even a reward if he said yes, gain and loss had collapsed, and whatever was left standing was a favor asked that would profit nobody"—and Calabrese chooses to do it. Here again I am reminded of a character in Camus: in *The Plague*, the doctor who stoically chooses to remain in an infected city and tend to the sick, though he hardly expects to save them by his efforts. There is an inner compulsion in the making of such decisions which is no less real for not having an honored name.

Choice entails a price. It does not come easily where there is no identifiable measure, cash value, or public blessing. There are two brothers in *The Price*, as in several of Miller's plays (emblematic of the tensions within him): one aggressive and lucky, the other loyal and obscure. The first is the more "realistic," the second the somewhat foolish and perhaps defeated. Miller is no longer prone to plead for one against the other. Nowhere else in his work are these opposites so evenly matched or so closely studied as in *The Price*. Both are justified. One has given up "golden" opportunities which might have led to a success equal to that of his more resolutely practical brother. He did so on behalf of a father who was hardly worth the sacrifice. The son speaks of love within the family. But his brother challenges him to ascertain whether there really has been so much love in their home. Who, then, was the "winner"?

Some critics have gone so far as to suggest that in this ambiguity, given the futility of the idealistic brother's choice, we may read a retreat from radical struggle against the "establishment" of Miller's beginnings, a surrender. But if we look closely we see that the failure, the presumably defeated brother, is the play's Victor.

In the final reckoning it is perhaps Solomon, the almost ninety-year-old Jewish furniture dealer, who possesses something like wisdom. His is the existential conclusion that life is enough, provoking laughter as well as tears. Yet even he takes a stand and calls the contestants to account, demands moral commitment: "What is the matter with you people! . . . Nothing in the world you believe, nothing you respect—how can you live? You think that's such a smart thing? That's so hard, what you're doing? Let me give you a piece advice—it's not that you can't believe nothing, that's not so hard—it's that you still got to believe it. *That's* hard. And if you can't do that, my friend—you're a dead man!"

It is hardly necessary at this point to expatiate on the fluency and rhythm of Miller's dialogue, coupled with his superb sense of play structure. But there is another aspect of his writing, less often noted, that bears consideration here.

In describing the setting for *Death of a Salesman*, Miller speaks of it as "a dream rising out of reality." This may be equated with his aesthetic aim. His plays are always firmly planted in specifically rendered environments. (The very color of the walls in the improvised police station is noted in *Incident at Vichy*.) Yet it would be hasty to set these plays down—with the possible exception of *All My Sons* and *A Memory of Two Mondays*—as wholly naturalistic.

"I prize the poetic above all else in the theatre," Miller writes. An artist's declared intention is not always proof of its accomplishment. But I believe Miller's plays move toward poetry. I refer not to language but to conception and intensity. The poetry in Miller's plays and in several of his stories is that of the impassioned moralist who, as in a parable, seeks to convey not so much a thought as an emotion which goes beyond the factual material employed. Virtually all the artists who have devised settings for the Miller plays have been aware of their transcendence of the naturalistic and have expressed this awareness through designs of a semi-abstract or symbolic character.

What is unmistakably convincing and makes Miller's theater writing hold is its authenticity in respect to the minutiae of American life. He is a first-rate reporter; he makes the details of his observation palpable. There is excellent descriptive writing in "The Misfits," the story that provided the basis for the screenplay in which Marilyn Monroe and Clark Gable starred. Miller knows our lower middle class as very few other dramatists do. In this he does not strain, as so many other writers do, for comic stage effect. He understands people through his sympathy for them.

Willy Loman is his supreme character creation. Loman is a pathetic fool, but so is Gaev in *The Cherry Orchard*. It does not make the Russian a more notable figure that he apostrophizes a bookcase while Loman extols (or curses) his car. Willy Loman is more recognizable as well as more generally meaningful—to laugh at, commiserate with, or deplore—than Babbitt.

Moralists are usually humorless. There is an abundance of humor in the portrayal of Solomon in *The Price*, both charming and hilarious. In fact, a vein of humor runs through most of Miller's work.

Miller's women are usually shadowy characters, rarely as fully realized as even some of the secondary men. The exceptions are the women in *After the Fall*: the mother, Elsie, Holga. Here too we find the helpless Maggie, one of the most perceptively delineated women in all of American drama. (When she hurls the epithet "Judgey" at Quentin, she delivers the *coup de grâce* to all his pretensions.) Miller values her far more than he does his mouthpiece, Quentin. Maggie is woman, redemptively sensual, intuitive, captivating, tormented and tormenting, the glamour girl as victim, of which our society offers too many examples.

Surprisingly in a dramatist of the urban middle class, there is a remarkable feeling for the outdoors in Miller's writing. This is not merely a yearning, as in various passages of *Salesman*, but something both fresh and eloquent as in "The Misfits." Even the battered car in that story takes on a poetic aura as it rarely does for drivers in the big cities: it is made to seem part of nature. It is alive with the impulse toward movement in the restless American who seeks a home, not just a house. The men in this story, once pioneers, are now "misfits." They don't like to work for wages.

The writer of plays, unlike the novelist, has a medium other than merely the printed word between himself and his audience. His understanding of that medium is obviously a part of his effectiveness. I feel impelled to add a note about Miller's contribution through his presence prior to and during the rehearsal periods of his plays. As the director of national companies of both *All My Sons* and *Death of a Salesman* and as the director of the original production of *Incident at Vichy* at the Repertory Theatre of Lincoln Center—and adviser in the production there of *After the Fall*—I have firsthand evidence.

He is a most meticulous craftsman. Hardly any revisions are demanded of him by his producers because, except for occasional cutting, as in the case of *After the Fall*, his plays are virtually complete in every detail by the time he submits his scripts to them. I remember that some clarifications were requested for *Death of a Salesman*. Miller consented to make them. But when these clarifications were written, the producers acknowledged that they were redundant. No "fixing" had been needed.

Miller is extremely respectful of his producers and directors and, though he is sometimes uncertain or hesitant in the matter of casting actors, he is usually glad to abide by his theater collaborators' final choice. He likes to read his plays to the acting company, which he does convincingly. He leaves the actual staging—placement and movement of characters, or what in theater parlance is called "business"—almost entirely to the director. His reflections on the acting and direction are in the main judiciously helpful.

If there is a fault in Miller's theatrical habit, it is his impulse to expatiate to the acting company too elaborately, sometimes too intellectually, on the motivations of his writing. Actors are seldom stimulated as actors by this sort of exegesis. Their insights in performance rarely arise from critical verbalization. Their intuitions have to be set in motion by indirect suggestions, a process which is a bit of a "mystery" and best left to the skills of the director.

There can be no question that Miller has a sure sense of what he has written and what he would like to see conveyed in the productions of his plays. Still, he always stands ready to be gratifyingly astonished. Both these attributes are highly appreciated by all who take part in the creation of the completed stage event.

Let me conclude with a word about Miller's role in the world of the theater today. Europeans prefer Miller to any other American playwright. His plays always register ("get across") in New York, Paris, Berlin, London, Vienna, Rome, Tel Aviv, and almost everywhere that modern drama is performed. He is popular and respected among us, but he means something special to the European.

We are enveloped in a mood of chaotic rage and negation. We are apparently so disappointed in ourselves, so distraught and disgusted by the shortcomings of our civilization, so frustrated by the fact that our "know-how" has left us bereft of a knowledge of how to live, that we seem to resent any affirmative counter-statement. Anything which remotely resembles a generalization, a panacea, an encouraging word, has virtually become taboo, a sop for suckers. Europeans have for a long time now given voice to this mood, with considerable artistic ingenuity and poignancy. (We imitate this with less skill and genuineness.) Now they are sick of their own sickness, because, sick or not, they must live. The basic health of Miller's plays, not to be categorized as "edifying," is something Europeans crave as much as a man in the desert craves water. While they appreciate and applaud Miller's criticism of America, what stirs them subliminally is precisely the vigorous, courageous, optimistic moral concern which is one of the most enduring contributions of our American heritage.

Harold Clurman
May 1970

INTRODUCTION
TO THE REVISED EDITION

The first *Portable Arthur Miller* appeared twenty-five years ago, in 1970, with an introduction by Harold Clurman (page xiii). I would not dissent from a word of it. He identified thematic concerns that have continued to fascinate Miller, moral commitments that he has sustained throughout his life, and issues that exercised critics in the 1970s and that continue to exercise them today, from his supposed realism to his popularity with European audiences.

Miller has written more plays since 1970 than he had before. The world has changed and Miller with it, since he has always been acutely conscious of the social, political, and cultural tone of his age. If there are continuities, therefore, there are also differences.

This new *Portable* expands Miller's career in two directions, back to a play written in the late 1930s, and forward, to his plays of the 1990s. In those sixty years he has engaged in a debate with America and its values, and staged the struggle of men and women anxious to understand their lives and to insist on their significance in what Tennessee Williams once called "times inimical to man."

Miller has written plays in every decade of this century since the 1930s. They add up to an alternative history of a troubled century. It is a history told through the lives of those who have endeavored to make sense of themselves as much as of the period in which they have lived. Indeed his concern for those individual lives, and his belief that they hold a clue to the nature of public experience, is in itself an indication of his own moral commitment and dramatic strategy.

It may not have required a particularly sensitive seismograph to register the cataclysm of the Depression, whose aftershocks were to disturb the American psyche for decades to come, but Miller has, throughout his career, proved acutely aware of the shifting ground beneath his feet. *All My Sons* (1947) and *Death of a Salesman* (1949) addressed the empty materialism that existed at the heart of postwar America, indeed at the very center of an animating American myth. *The Crucible* (1953) and *A View from the Bridge* (1955) acknowledged the corrosive psychological and social impact of betrayal at a time when the price of inclusion in the American dream was a denial of responsibility to oneself and to others. *After the Fall* (1964) and *Incident at Vichy* (1965) explored the implications of tearing up the contract that commits us to the idea of a mutually supportive society. These last two plays looked back to the Second World War but had echoes in a society then battling with racism at home and launched on a bitter and divisive war abroad. Miller's observation with respect to the latter play, indeed, could be said to apply, in general terms, to all of his works, however precisely they appear to be located in time: "The occasion of the play is the occupation of France but it's about today. It concerns the question of insight—of seeing in oneself the capacity for collaboration with the evil one condemns. It's a question that exists for all of us—what, for example, is the responsibility of each of us for allowing the slums of Harlem to exist?"[1]

By the same token, *The Archbishop's Ceiling* (1977) examined the psychological and social coercions of a totalitarian state but extended its concerns to question the nature of the reality we imagine ourselves to serve. *The American Clock* (1980), though set in the 1920s and 1930s, implies a parallel between the hedonism of the 1920s and that of the 1970s and 1980s, while *The Ride Down Mount Morgan* (1991) further explored aspects of Nixon and Reagan's America. *Broken Glass* (1994), set in 1938, bore directly on a contemporary world in which, once again, genocide was a present fact.

It is hard now to understand the impact of the Depression. Henry Luce had declared this the American century, but the century seemed to have lasted barely thirty years when it came to an abrupt halt. American capitalism, with its promise to pay the bearer not only money but happiness, seemed invalidated by history. The pieties of a culture suddenly stood exposed as simply that and no more. If America had meant anything, it meant amelioration, perfectibility. It alone possessed the future. The past was for other people. Then, in 1929, time stopped. Debts were called in. The past exercised its presumptive rights. In the land of plenty people starved while milk was poured down drains and crops were destroyed to keep prices high. Bankers called for nationalization of the banks. Officials of the Stock Exchange jumped out of windows or were taken off to jail. If the dead had walked untenanted from their graves, people could hardly have been more surprised or dismayed. The American clock stopped.

Miller's first plays concerned strikes, the need for prison reform, corrupt manufacturers. He seemed, in other words, a pure product of his times. But the fact is that he arrived at the end rather than the beginning of things. If 1935 marked a high point of American theatrical radicalism, with the production, by the Group Theatre, of Clifford Odets's *Waiting for Lefty* and *Awake and Sing,* within a few years that radicalism had collapsed of its own internal contradictions. Odets was seduced by Hollywood, along with many other members of the Group Theatre. Orson Welles, for whose Mercury Theatre Miller briefly worked, took the same route, while the Federal Theatre, a Works Progress Administration venture established under the New Deal and on which Miller had pinned his hopes of production, was closed down for supposed Communist influence—but not before the Detroit branch had staged *They Too Arise,* a rewritten version of his first play, originally entitled *No Villain.*

They Too Arise is based, in part, on Miller's own family. The father, like his own, is a manufacturer of coats. One son, Ben, has given up college to help his father; the other, Arnold, has not and takes sides with the workers in a strike. The play sounds conventional enough, and is certainly touched with 1930s melodrama, including, in one version, an epigraph from Engels. It is written, however, with genuine passion and wit, and there are elements that foreshadow Miller's later work. Thus one draft of the play anticipates Willy Loman's attitude toward his sons as the father insists, "I wanna leave ya with . . . a name . . . with a clean name and a . . . healthy business,"[2] while in another he says, "I wanna see you on top. . . . It ain't fair that I should give my life up like this and go out—with nothing."[3] In the final version, by then called *The Grass Still Grows,* Ben, now a would-be writer, confesses that he cannot "appreciate evil. I don't know what to do when it confronts me"[4]—a dilemma that became the basis for the play that he started in the same year: *The Golden Years.*

In his 1970 introduction Harold Clurman refers to a play about Montezuma and Cortés that Miller submitted to the Group Theatre and that he discovered, unread, in the Guild files many years later. It was neither published nor performed. Many years later I came across a copy of this play at the University of Texas and spent an afternoon reading a work that seemed entirely worthy of production. It compared, it seemed to me, more than favorably with Peter Shaffer's *The Royal Hunt of the Sun*. The problem was that it required a cast of over twenty, and few, if any, American theaters could contemplate a production on that scale. The loss of the Federal Theatre had proved crucial at the time, and the scope of the work still made production difficult in the 1980s. I did, however, persuade the BBC in England to mount a radio production in 1987. The success of this led to a television version.

Though set in sixteenth-century Mexico, *The Golden Years* (1939–40) was a response to events in Europe in the 1930s. Miller was fascinated and appalled by the political and moral paralysis that had afflicted European powers faced with the rise of Hitler. Appeasement was simply a word to describe the response of those who allowed themselves to be disabled, mesmerized by the sheer fact of Adolf Hitler. At a time when they could still have acted, they watched, with a kind of stunned fascination, the process of their own destruction, believing that disinterest might buy immunity and partly aware of their own responsibility for creating the man who now confronted them. So Montezuma had watched the slow approach of Cortés, the man who would destroy him, transfixed not by his power but by his sheer implacability and by the myth that attached itself to a man who seemed to be an agent of destiny. Conscious of his own culpability, in a society itself edging toward dissolution, he stares into the sun of this man who apparently has neither doubts nor conscience. As Miller remarked in 1960, speaking of *The Crucible* but with relevance to *The Golden Years* and, indeed, virtually all of his plays, "it was an attempt to create the old ethical and dramaturgic order again, to say that one couldn't passively sit back and watch his world being destroyed under him even if he did share the general guilt. In effect I was calling for an act of will. I was trying to say that injustice has features, that the amorphousness of our world is so in part because we have feared through guilt to unmask its ethical outlines."[5]

Montezuma's poetic language, his natural resort to metaphor, breaks on the rock of Cortés's blunt prose. They speak to each other across more than a linguistic divide. Cortés makes a religion out of ambition, pride, and rapacity. There is no transcendence in his world, merely pragmatic deference to a religion that is itself little more than a cover for imperial expansion and material greed. Yet Montezuma's transcendent world has a thirst for human blood. His cosmic end is profoundly tainted by its material means. His cultivated world, which generates beauty, poetry, music, secures its own salvation, maintains its own purity, by destroying others. The eclipse of the sun that occurs in the play has symbolic force to Montezuma but it has, too, for Miller. For as the 1930s turned into the 1940s the Holocaust followed its deadly logic and witnessed the eclipse of human values. Several of his other wartime plays, unperformed and unpublished, reflect this deepening anxiety, which he was to address in later plays: *The Crucible, After the Fall, Incident at Vichy, Broken Glass.*

The Detroit production of *They Too Arise* aside, Miller's public career began, as Clurman notes, disastrously with a play that lasted a mere four days. *The Man Who Had All the Luck* (1944) was scarcely a lucky debut. However, over forty years later, it was restaged in Britain by the Bristol Old Vic, where it proved both powerful and successful, and was transferred to London. The initial production and not the play, it seems, resulted in the disaster. At the time, though, the effect was to turn Miller aside to write a novel, *Focus,* which dealt with the question of anti-Semitism in America and which was itself a considerable success, selling ninety thousand copies in hardback. But the theater drew him back, and the success of *All My Sons,* in 1947, marked the real beginning of his career in the theater. It also served to distort critical response to him as a writer. As he later lamented, "I began to be known really by virtue of the single play I have ever tried to do in completely realistic Ibsen-like form."[6] Given the experiments with style and form in *Death of a Salesman, A View from the Bridge,* and *After the Fall,* it is a little difficult to understand the persistence of this error, which Clurman felt obliged to address in his 1970 introduction. From the perspective of the 1990s, after *The American Clock, Two-Way Mirror,* and *The Ride Down Mount Morgan,* it is even more bewildering to hear the same description repeated.

Casually dismissed as a realist, in fact Miller has quite consciously experimented with form and pressed character to the point at which it begins to dislocate and dissolve. The language that his characters speak is often far from realistic, not least because of his habit, particularly in his early work, of writing speeches first in verse. Indeed he followed *All My Sons* with a play that itself represented a radical break with tradition in its approach to dramatic structure, character, and mise-en-scène.

In *Death of a Salesman* (1949) Miller created a fluid staging that reflected the state of mind of his protagonist. The past infiltrates the present as memories are summoned up by present need. For Willy Loman the real has always been insubstantial, a shadow cast backward by a receding future. The set, designed by Jo Mielziner, reflected this, simultaneously as solid as Willy's prosaic existence and as intangible as the memories that haunt him. A single change of light serves to collapse time and space to create those aching ironies that so torment Willy as the rural simplicity of his youth dissolves into a threatening modernity. Thematic concern and psychological truth find a correlative in form. As Miller observed in a notebook entry, generalizing on the basis of *Death of a Salesman,* "Life is formless . . . its interconnections are concealed by lapses of time, by events occurring in separated places, by the hiatus of memory. . . . Art suggests or makes these interconnections palpable. Form is the tension of these interconnections, man with man, man with the past and present environment. The drama at its best is a mass experience of that tension."[7]

Death of a Salesman mimics the processes of the human mind. Willy is no schizophrenic, peopling the world with visions and voices that are the product of a malfunctioning brain. He is a man, blindly aware of some insufficiency, who searches for the key to his sense of incompletion and failure; he is a failed actor, trying to get by on a smile and a shoe shine, playing out a drama whose text he can neither clearly see nor understand.

It is not that Willy Loman has no values. It is just that he believes that his spiritual needs can be satisfied with material goods. As Miller remarked in 1959, "In our big car civilization we still clutch to our breasts these chromium-plated iron hulks in the hope that they are salvation."[8] Willy's icons are a refrigerator and a car. Advertisements have become the articles of his secular faith. He is a salesman who has been sold a guarantee of satisfaction that can never be redeemed. A gap has opened up between the claims of his society and its reality, just as a gulf has opened up between his image of himself and the truth that he glimpses from time to time. As Miller has said, "Every man has an image of himself which fails in one way or another to correspond with reality. It's the size of the discrepancy between illusion and reality that matters."[9]

Willy Loman feels temporary. Personal and social meaning are endlessly deferred. In the notebooks that Miller kept while writing the play that feeling is made explicit: "I tell you the truth, Ben, for a long time I felt that as soon as Pop came back I'd be ready to get started, somehow. But he's *never* come. I still feel kind of temporary about myself . . . I'm never sure it's what I ought to be. Ben will find Pop, and a great change will happen."[10] He waits, like Beckett's Vladimir and Estragon, for something that will make sense out of a life in whose inner coherence he can no longer believe. It is the essence of the dream he takes for reality that it should retreat before him even while he is drawn ever more, in his mind, back toward a moment before failure and guilt had tainted that dream. It is a double movement that recalls F. Scott Fitzgerald's Gatsby. Together, they beat on, "boats against the current, borne back ceaselessly into the past."[11]

In a play that Miller wrote for CBS radio, and which was published in 1941, the central character makes a statement that goes to the heart of his work: "The one thing a man fears most next to death is the loss of his good name. Man is evil in his own eyes, my friends, worthless, and the only way he can find respect for himself is by getting other people to say he's a nice fellow." But some men, he adds, "don't need the respect of their neighbors and so they aren't afraid to speak the truth."[12] This is the distinction between Willy Loman and the protagonist of Ibsen's *An Enemy of the People,* which Miller adapted for a 1950 Broadway production, and between Willy Loman and John Proctor in *The Crucible.*

The millenarian beliefs of a Willy Loman, for whom the promises that America made were as real as the needs that prompted them, lie, too, at the heart of *The Crucible.* For Willy Loman they took material form; for the Puritans of seventeenth-century New England they took spiritual form: a new Jerusalem, a City on a Hill, purged of sin and void of ambiguity.

Miller had been aware of the story of the Salem witchcraft trials for many years, but it was the fact of the anti-Communist hysteria of the 1950s, led by the House Un-American Activities Committee chaired by Senator Joseph McCarthy, which made him understand something of their inner procedures. The parallels between New England and 1950s America seemed persuasive: the same air of hysteria, the same doubtful evidence, the same requirement of confession followed by betrayal, the same guilt by association, the same insecure authority anxious to consolidate its power, the same surrender of justice to prejudice, of principle to pragmatism, and of humanity to expediency. It seemed so much a play of its time, indeed, that its reception was clouded by the politics of the age. Today the ashes of those passions are cold, and no one now needs to recall that curious and painful era in order to understand *The Crucible,* a play that, beyond the immediate issue of McCarthyism, is a study of power and authority. *The Crucible* explores the potentially disabling nature of guilt and the price of refusing to accept responsibility for one's actions. It identifies the ease with which we betray others in order to survive or simply to sustain the idea of our own innocence. It has proved Miller's most produced play not because of an abiding interest in anti-Communist hysteria but because its concerns remain central. Betrayal, private and public, is a constant. The coercive authority of dogma, ideology, and myth is no less powerful at the end of the second millennium than it was in 1692.

Miller followed *The Crucible* with *A View from the Bridge,* a play in which, apart from anything else, he tries to understand the psychology of the informer, the impulses that lead a man to sustain a sense of his own innocence by pointing the finger of accusation at others. But he wrote the play when society had other priorities. As he has said, "The production of *A View from the Bridge* clinched a growing feeling that the work I was doing was regarded as unimportant . . . I felt I was a kind of entertainer, succeeding in drawing a tear or a laugh, but it seemed to me that what was behind my plays remained a secret . . . I decided that either the audience was out of step or I was. There seemed to be no resolution and yet I felt that there must be one."[13] *A View from the Bridge* ran a mere 149 performances. The next year Miller found himself called before the House Un-American Activities Committee and sentenced to prison for refusing to become an informer; the sentence subsequently was quashed on appeal.

For nine years no new play by Arthur Miller opened in America. When he returned to the theater it was with a play of almost frightening temerity, a drama in which major events of public history were refracted through the mind of a man in a state of crisis. On the verge of a third marriage, Quentin, an attorney who appears before the court of his own conscience, struggles to understand how and why the contract between people can have proved so fragile. He is acutely aware, too, of a similar breaking of charity on a wider scale, with the Holocaust and the House

Un-American Activities Committee confronting him with the fact of human betrayal on a more profound level.

The theme in some senses determines the theatrical form as experiences distant in time and space are brought together, and as memories are invoked in an attempt to make order out of the apparently random. So, figures appear for a few seconds, caught at a moment of revelation; the tower of a concentration camp is briefly lit to underscore the connection between private duplicity and public horror. As Miller remarked, "The way I see life is that there are no public issues; they are all private issues. We have gotten divided . . . I can't see the separation . . . the attempt, in *After the Fall,* was to unify both worlds, to make them one, to make an embrace that would touch the concentration camp, the Un-American Activities Committee, a sexual relationship, a marital relationship, all in one embrace, because that's really the way it is."[14]

The irony of this most adventurous of Miller's plays is that critical response paid little attention to such concerns, preferring to dwell on the connection between the figure of Maggie, Quentin's third wife, and Marilyn Monroe, who had been Miller's second. The costuming of Barbara Loden, who played Maggie, in a blond wig seemed to underscore that link. Meanwhile, the circumstances of the play's first production—Lincoln Center's theater was not yet ready to receive it, and a temporary building was constructed on West Fourth Street—meant that the fluidity of presentation, the instantaneous linking of separate elements, became difficult to attain.

Subsequent productions have revealed a different play—especially in Europe, where the Monroe connection never seemed of critical significance. Indeed a National Theatre production in London cast a black actress, Josette Simon, in the part of Maggie, surely one of the most powerful women's roles in any of Miller's plays. Time has restored the proper balance.

The characters in *After the Fall* are more abstract than in Miller's other works, more prone to declare their motives, announce their anxieties, confess their guilt. Here he works through image and symbol. The apparently remote and dissimilar are brought together until, in being struck against one another, they create a spark of meaning. It is not a realistic play. It operates, Miller has said, in the way a mind would go in quest of meaning. It works by a kind of moral logic as its central character endeavors to sustain a coherent vision that will enable him to function.

In the end he comes face to face with his own culpability and with the deeply flawed nature of the world he inhabits, but acknowledges, too, a surviving instinct to proceed, a refusal to capitulate to despair. What Miller has said of *Incident at Vichy,* the play with which he followed it, could be said, too, of *After the Fall:* "In this play the question is what is there between people that is indestructible. The concentration camp is the final expression of human separateness and its ultimate consequence. It is organized abandonment . . . the logical conclusion of contemporary life."[15] Yet to surrender to such moral entropy is to accept its authority. To his mind the theater of the absurd did precisely that.

In essays and interviews he has repeatedly rejected a theater in which the individual is isolated from causality and moral concern. He has also resisted an absurdist vision that presents that individual as no more than cosmic victim—a perspective that, for all its intellectual clarity, transforms the self into a detached observer of its own annihilation. Miller responded uneasily, therefore, in the 1950s and 1960s as the theater of the absurd seemed to occupy the theatrical high ground. It increasingly seemed to him that, viewed from this perspective, the Holocaust, for example, could too easily be viewed as no more than a practical manifestation of a metaphysical irony. For Miller, Jews were not killed by irony; they were killed by men and women who could be called to account only if the moral world they had dismantled as a means of denying their own culpability were reconstructed. In an absurdist world there is no guilt, no contract to be denied, no responsibility to shun. The writer's duty, therefore, was to reconstitute that moral world through tracing the roots of what we choose to call evil to their origin in the human psyche. *After the Fall, Incident at Vichy,* and *Playing for Time* addressed these issues directly but they are also at the center of *The Golden Years, The Crucible, Broken Glass,* and, indeed, many of Miller's other plays insofar as he sees a flawed society as an extension of a deeply fallible human nature.

Following *The Price* (1968), a highly successful play in which two brothers are forced to reexamine the past and their own manipulation of it, and following, too, *The Creation of the World and Other Business* (1973), a jeu d'esprit with a serious concern, in which human violence is tracked to its lair, Miller wrote a subtle play, set in Eastern Europe, called *The Archbishop's Ceiling* (1977). The action takes place in an old archbishop's palace in which there may or may not be microphones concealed in the ceiling. The result is a work in which the characters are turned into actors by their circumstances, unsure whether they are overheard, performing their lives, uncertain as to the substance of what they take to be real. The original American production was based on an inferior text and, despite its relevance to an America whose president bugged his own office and endeavored to bug other people's, was not well received. I recall sitting in Miller's study and comparing the original version, which he had sent me, with the revised performance script. As a consequence of this conversation a British publisher agreed to print the original, with an Escher drawing on the front cover to emphasize those metaphysical conundrums that had somehow disappeared from the later version. A similar treatment was given to two excellent one-act plays, which had originally been produced under the title *Two by A.M.* and which, with Miller's approval, if some bafflement, I rechristened *Two-Way Mirror* for the purposes of the British publication. Both of these plays have now been widely and successfully produced.

In 1980 Miller turned back to the period of his youth with *The American Clock*. If it seemed odd to be revisiting the Depression, in an age of material prosperity, it did not seem such to its author. He wrote the play, in the late 1970s, because he had a sense of "living in . . . a kind of oblong blur."[16] He wrote it, he explained, out of an urge to tell people, "This is when there was such a thing as necessity. . . . People didn't know what was necessary anymore and I was tempted by the idea of telling them that underneath all this prosperity there is a skeletal structure of human relations which is still there but is covered up by all this prosperity. And I wanted to show them how when it collapses you can find it."[17]

If this had proved his last work there would have been a neat symmetry, for *The American Clock* returns to the world of his first play, and the Baum family is clearly based on his own. The play takes us back to a moment when the fate of the individual and the state of society were manifestly and undeniably related, a time when necessity forced a rediscovery of fundamental values based on the reality of human need. For Miller, writing at the turn of the decade, America had lost touch with that reality and those values.

The American Clock is about survival and in that sense is celebratory. It is, he insists, a vaudeville and as such consists of a series of scenes connected with music. Forty years earlier he would have written it as an earnest social drama. That drama is there but almost as postmodern quotation. Now it becomes an impressionist epic, a pointillist landscape, a series of tableaux, a mural, as he restages the past for the benefit of the present. He has said, "I think the job of the artist . . . is to remind people of what they have chosen to forget."[18] Forget or deny. More than a decade later, in *Broken Glass* (1994), denial became his central concern.

There is a tendency for writers to turn to the past late in their careers. It was true of Eugene O'Neill and Tennessee Williams, as it has proved of Edward Albee. What takes them back is unfinished business. In Miller's case he turned back to 1938 and Kristallnacht, the apocalyptic night when Jewish property was destroyed and Jews were attacked all over Germany, because he saw the conditions of that time being re-created. Not merely have we witnessed the return of fascism, but the same paralysis that Miller had noted in *The Golden Years* once again seemed to afflict a world that stood by and watched starvation and genocide in Africa and ethnic cleansing in Europe. *Broken Glass*, hailed in England as a major work of the American theater, creates a metaphor for that paralysis in the person of Sylvia Gellburg. It also explores, with compassion yet unblinking clarity, our capacity to deny that which we would rather not confront. *Broken Glass* is not "about" Kristallnacht, nor what might pass as its contemporary parallels. Like Miller's other plays it is about men and women who struggle with their own contradictory impulses. In another powerful and moving 1990s play, *The Last Yankee*, those contradictions had to do with the coercive power of that very American myth that had led Willy Loman to his death. In *Broken Glass* they concern a desperate wish to refuse responsibility for one's life while insisting on one's right to respect from others. Denial has driven man and wife apart as it has driven races, societies, and nations. It has alienated people from themselves. It is finally, therefore, not simply the horrific and bewildering mystery of Nazi atrocities that appalls, crimes seemingly remote from our own experience and, indeed, from human nature, but their more terrifying familiarity, their roots in impulses as undeniably human as those that must be mobilized to oppose them.

Broken Glass is not unrelenting. It stages a battle that has its victories. Here, and in *The Last Yankee*, redemption is a possibility, for Miller is no more ready to give up on the future of the race now than he has ever been. But neither is he ready to retract his demand that we acknowledge our responsibility for the world that we have made.

That, then, is the shape of Arthur Miller's career to date, though with three new plays in the first four years of the 1990s, this remains a provisional report. Twenty-five years from the publication of the first *Portable* his reputation has grown still further. It remains true, however, that, respected as he is in America, Europeans like to claim him as their own. In part this is because the full range of his plays is staged there. The British have encountered excellent productions of *The Golden Years* and *The Man Who Had All the Luck,* from the early part of his career, and of *The Archbishop's Ceiling, Two-Way Mirror, The Last Yankee,* and *Broken Glass* from the later, usually performed by major companies. *The Ride Down Mount Morgan* even received its world premiere in London and, at the time of this writing, has yet to reach New York. In America, with its high production costs, high ticket prices, negligible subsidy, peremptory reviews, and an acting profession effectively forced to choose between the theater and movies, his plays, particularly his later ones, seem rarely to command major stages. But beyond that there is something about Miller's drama that Europeans respond to perhaps even more directly than Americans.

William Dean Howells once remarked that what the American public really wanted was a tragedy with a happy ending. Edith Wharton later expressed doubts whether a play with "a sad ending" and a "negative hero" could ever get a hearing from an American audience. Though this is plainly overstating the case, Eugene O'Neill came to much the same conclusion. Miller has always been concerned with the tragic sensibility, and this in a country whose central myths have to do with recoverable innocence and perfectibility. Europe has quite other myths and a history that offers a different vision of human nature. The past, indeed, bears more directly and obviously on the present than it does in an America in which rejection of history was a motivational force in its settlement and seems to remain a central article of faith. In Europe, the corpse of the past is never far beneath the surface, as the events of the 1990s remind us. America leans into the future. It pursues a dream. Thus, when one of Miller's characters announces that the past is holy, he makes a statement in tune with European experience but in some ways at odds with America, where the past is sentimentalized, transformed into icon, domesticated into theme parks, but not seen as the key to private and public experience.

Arthur Miller's models were and are European. He finds in them a double commitment that is central to his own work, a commitment to the theater as a social art and to the past as the key to present experience. As he has said, "I've come out of that playwrighting tradition which is

Greek and Ibsen where the past is the burden of man and it's got to be placed on the stage so that he can grapple with it. That's the way those plays are built. It's *now* grappling with *then,* it's the story of how the birds come home to roost. Every play."[19]

The fact is, though, that Arthur Miller is a playwright for all seasons and all nations. Nor is there any doubt about his commitment to continuing the debate with his culture that he initiated sixty years ago. It could be said of him what he has said of Mark Twain, another American writer who chose to challenge his own society in the name of the very values that it had itself proclaimed: "He is not using his alienation from the public illusion of his hour in order to implicitly reject the country as though he could live without it, but manifestly in order to correct it."[20]

If his plays are ineluctably social it is because he cannot conceive of the individual outside of a social context or of a society that does not reflect the values of those who constitute it: "You live in the world even though you only vote once in a while."[21] But behind the social issues, beyond the particularities of time and place, transcending, even, his engagement with American possibilities and disappointments, he has been concerned to explore the essence of a human nature that has, on occasion, led us to the brink of apocalypse but has also made us resist its logic. He writes not out of moral certainty but a conviction that we must confront ourselves, stripped of the evasions, the denials, the self-justifications that threaten the self we would thereby protect. "The challenge," he has said, "is still the Elizabethan one, the public address on the street corner."[22] The theater is, after all, the most public of the arts, mimicking the community it addresses in its own collaborative methods.

Beyond that, its transformations—as Lee J. Cobb becomes Willy Loman and a blank stage another time and place—suggest the possibility of change. Perhaps that is no longer the direct social and political change Miller had looked for in the 1930s, but it is a transformation that stands as a justification of his own drama and of the theater itself: "On the stage a man must act, and against a background of human values. In our time, when futility has overwhelmed the spirit, when a deadly inaction threatens the heart, it is good that we possess a form whose very existence demands action." At a time when there is "a widespread disbelief in the power of men to affect their own situation," the theater, he insists, by its very nature, demonstrates the opposite. The challenge is "to discover an interior order deeper than paralysis . . . the life even in death."[23]

The fact that Miller's plays travel so easily, translate so well, suggests the degree to which they address fundamental issues that transcend the particularities of the moment. That he writes with such understanding and humor is undoubtedly a part of his fascination. That he has charted so accurately the shifting mood of his times has, indeed, made him a kind of moral historian to whom we can look for understanding of the chaos that so often seems to confront us. But, ultimately, his achievement lies not so much in his carefully honed language, a language that never transcends the sensibility of the character who speaks it, nor even really in his power to move, instruct, and entertain, but in his ability to create characters, from salesmen and farmers to dockers and doctors, whose lives are wholly credible but who stand as images of our own betrayals, uncertainties, and even triumphs. He creates metaphors, without ever forgetting that the power of those metaphors rests on the human commitment of his audiences to the lives that generate them. He creates characters without ever forgetting that if they are to transcend the immediate circumstances of their own existence their lives must have metaphoric force.

In 1989 he was asked what had given him the greatest pleasure as a writer. His reply can stand both as a description of his work and as a statement of the faith that brought it into being:

All these years later when I see a play of mine that I wrote thirty-five years ago, and I see that the audience is screwed into it in the way they were in the first place, I like to believe that the feeling that they have is that man is worth something. That you care about him that much is a miracle, I mean considering the numbers of ourselves that we have destroyed in the last century. I think art imputes value to human beings and if I did that it would be the most pleasant thought I could depart with . . . I guess the other thing is the wonder of it all, that I'm still here, that so much of it did work, that the people are so open to it, and that we sort of grasped hands somehow, in many places and many languages. It gives me a glimpse of the idea that there is one humanity. . . . And I think it's a sort of miracle.[24]

Christopher Bigsby
March 1995

NOTES TO THE
INTRODUCTION

1. Matthew C. Roudané, *Conversations with Arthur Miller*. Jackson: University of Mississippi, 1987, p. 80.
2. Arthur Miller, *They Too Arise*, typescript. Humanities Research Center, University of Texas, Austin.
3. Ibid.
4. Arthur Miller, *The Grass Still Grows*, typescript. Humanities Research Center, University of Texas, Austin.
5. Roudané, p. 61.
6. Ibid., p. 102.
7. Arthur Miller, Manuscript notebooks. Humanities Research Center, University of Texas, Austin.
8. Roudané, p. 55.
9. Ibid., p. 7.
10. Manuscript notebooks.
11. F. Scott Fitzgerald, *The Great Gatsby*. Harmondsworth, England: Penguin, 1954, p. 188.
12. Arthur Miller, *The Pussycat and the Expert Plumber Who Was a Man*, in *One Hundred Non-Royalty Plays*, William Kozlenko, ed. New York: Greenberg, 1941, pp. 27, 29.
13. Roudané, p. 81.
14. Christopher Bigsby, ed., *Arthur Miller and Company*. London: Methuen, 1990, p. 139.
15. Roudané, p. 108.
16. Bigsby, p. 199.
17. Ibid.
18. Ibid., p. 200.
19. Ibid., p. 201.
20. Arthur Miller, introduction to *The Oxford Mark Twain*, Shelley Fisher Fishkin, ed. New York: Oxford University Press, 1996.
21. Roudané, pp. 100–101.
22. Ibid., p. 64.
23. Arthur Miller, "World Theater Day: A Message from Arthur Miller," typescript.
24. Bigsby, p. 233.

The Portable

ARTHUR
MILLER

TIMEBENDS: A LIFE

THE VIEW FROM THE FLOOR IS of a pair of pointy black calf-height shoes, one of them twitching restlessly, and just above them the plum-colored skirt rising from the ankles to the blouse, and higher still the young round face and her ever-changing tones of voice as she gossips into the wall telephone with one of her two sisters, something she would go on doing the rest of her life until one by one they peeled off the wire and vanished into the sky. Now she looks down at me looking up at her from the foyer floor, bends over and tries to move me clear of her foot. But I must lie on her shoe, and from far up above through skirt and darkness I hear her laughing pleasantly at my persistence.

Then, later, a slightly more elevated view, from about two and a half feet above the floor: she sits at a sixth-story window that overlooks Central Park, her profile emblazoned against the afternoon sun, hair still long but gathered in a bun, her full arms pressing against the gauzy cotton of her shirtwaist sleeves above a shorter skirt now and velvet pumps. Both hands rest on an open book in her lap as she listens intently to a young man with a pipe, thick glasses, and a short beard, a student from Columbia to whom she pays two dollars an afternoon each week simply to come and talk with her about novels. She knows hardly anyone in or out of the family who has ever read a book, but she herself can begin a novel in the afternoon, pick it up again after dinner, finish it by midnight, and remember it in detail for the rest of her life. She also remembers the names of the entire British royal family and their German cousins. But her secret envy, made evident by her contempt, is for Madame Lupescu, the Jewish paramour of King Carol of Rumania, and also, she believes, his brains.

Still later, there is the view from about five feet above the floor: from here she is in high heels with rhinestone buckles, a black beaded knee-length dress, and a silver-and-black cloche hat over her bobbed hair. Her lips are red with lipstick. She is high-busted and round-armed, already in the habit, whenever she dresses up to leave the house, of drawing her upper lip down in order to slim her pudgy nose. There are diamonds on her fingers, and she trails a silver fox across the floor as she promises to bring home the sheet music of the show they are off to see, Kern or Gershwin or Herbert, which she will play the next morning on the Knabe baby grand, and sing in the happy, slightly hooting soprano so proper and romantic and fashionable. She is holding her head high to flatten the double chin but also out of the insecure pride of moving alongside him, a head taller than she, blue eyes and skin so white it is nearly translucent, reddish blond curly hair enhancing his innocent alderman's look, a fellow whom policemen are inclined to salute, head-waiters to find tables for, cab drivers to stop in the rain for, a man who will not eat in restaurants with thick water glasses, a man who has built one of the two or three largest coat manufacturing businesses in the country at the time and who cannot read or write any language.

A still later view: in the little Brooklyn house where she shuffles about in carpet slippers, sighing, cursing with a sneer on her lips, weeping suddenly and then catching herself, in the winters feeding the furnace with as scant a shovelful of coal as will keep it burning, making meal money at high-stakes professional bridge games all over Midwood and Flatbush, which are sometimes raided by the police, whom she talks into letting her go home to prepare supper. She had arrived at the bottom of the Depression, when to get arrested for trying to make a buck was not the total eclipse of respectability it so recently would have been. My mother moved with the times.

This desire to move on, to metamorphose—or perhaps it is a talent for being contemporary—was given me as life's inevitable and rightful condition.

FROM

THE GOLDEN YEARS
(A Play)

ACT ONE

Scene One

A night in Autumn, 1519.

Tenochtitlan (now Mexico City), Capital of the Aztec Empire.

This is the Mountain House of Montezuma, King of the Aztec Nation, Emperor of the World. Over the left half of the stage the open sky is seen. A night sky thick with stars. The roof covers only the right half. On a medium level, at its center, is the large throne, built square and low with a high slanting back, and carved with the jagged Aztec design. Up above it two torch lamps burn. In the background the faint outline of mountain peaks at the edge of the sky.

On the rise, the room is lighted only by the torches and the greenish glare of the moon. Montezuma sits deep in the throne, flanked on a lower level by his council, the Lords: Guatemotzin, a man of twenty-four and built lithely for war; Cuitlahua, about forty and of slower movement; Cagama, solid, stocky, about forty-five. Montezuma, standing, is watching the Astronomer who, charts in hand, is rapidly calculating the stars which he looks up to frequently. On this lowest level, but at the far right, Tapaia stands watching Montezuma for the slightest command. Beside the Astronomer, Talua, a boy, stands studying the stars and comparing them with a stone-covered book he holds open in his arms.

★   ★   ★

There is no movement, but the Astronomer's, for a moment, the Lords and the King watching him as though waiting for him to say something. Montezuma glances at the moon, rises slowly, and walks left and stops when he is abreast of the Astronomer but above him.
All men—deep sonorous chant in background.

MONTEZUMA, *looking up:* My star seems bleeding.

ASTRONOMER, *intent on charts:* The sun is on it, my lord, from around the world.

MONTEZUMA, *pause. To Astronomer:* When will you be finished with your charts and numbers?

ASTRONOMER: A moment more.

Montezuma looks at the sky. Pause.

GUATEMOTZIN, *nervously takes a few steps:* The air . . . the air is growing heavier, Uncle. How much longer before the moon dies?

Astronomer lifts hand for silence. Guatemotzin feels the air.

GUATEMOTZIN: The air seems to be filling with water.

CUITLAHUA: No wind is a good sign. The flame of the sacrifice may easily rise to the moon.

GUATEMOTZIN: Is this the way the world ends? Not with battles, but waiting like old men? Uncle, what are your thoughts now?

MONTEZUMA: My life and the meaning of it . . . when will you speak?

ASTRONOMER: The calculations are done, my lord.

All come toward him anxiously—humming stops.

ASTRONOMER: Look there, the Eastern Star . . .

MONTEZUMA: To the point, how long have we . . . ?

ASTRONOMER: Depending on that star, my lord. It is dropping fast, and when it falls behind the horizon, the speckled moon will ride into eclipse and . . .

CUITLAHUA, *points up:* What's that!

ASTRONOMER: There it is, my lord, the black tip of the shadow . . .

MONTEZUMA: I see it now . . .

Distant single drum beat.

ASTRONOMER: It will move across the moon, and if your sacrificial fire does not burn it off, the world is dead this quarter hour.

MONTEZUMA: A quarter hour?

ASTRONOMER: She's black within a quarter, my lord, no longer.

MONTEZUMA, *slight pause. Nervously:* Perhaps an error . . . ?

ASTRONOMER: Impossible. You see, the earth turns on this orbit I have drawn. *Shows him chart.* . . . and when the sun revolves . . .

MONTEZUMA: Enough, enough. *Comes away from him towards center.* Tapaia. Bring the sacrifice to me. *Pause.* Is my judge dead yet?

TAPAIA: He is being taken to the block now, my lord.

MONTEZUMA: Bring him here . . . hurry. And remember, they must keep an eye on the high road. I am expecting a courier.

Tapaia bows . . . starts out.

CUITLAHUA: Tapaia, wait a moment.

Tapaia stops.

CUITLAHUA, *to Montezuma:* My lord, I think it would be wise for you to send a proclamation to the people.

MONTEZUMA: The people? What can I say to the people?

CUITLAHUA: This year was filled with terrors for them, and now the moon,—your word might calm their hearts . . .

MONTEZUMA: Their hearts must not be calmed. They must be terrified tonight, and we, we must be wondrous and searching, not calm. The meanings in this moon we will not read at our ease, but suffering! The sacrifice, Tapaia, hurry.

Exit Tapaia.

CUITLAHUA, *as Montezuma goes up a level:* You are strange tonight, my lord.

MONTEZUMA: I am all questions, Cuitlahua. *Looks upward.*

Drum stops.

CUITLAHUA: And I.

CAGAMA, *anxious, nervous:* When you brothers speak together, I hear. But it's another language, secret between you. Am I dull, my lord? I am not afraid to die.

Silence. No answer.

CAGAMA: When there was a war to fight, I fought. A kingdom to knock down, I was ready with the blow . . . I am not afraid now. I have lived honorably. *No answer.* Montezuma, you are wiser, closer to the gods than I. Tell me why I should be afraid. What do you see that I am blind to? The Spaniards, my lord? If you've proof now that they're gods I'll be happy to join you in welcoming them . . .

CUITLAHUA: Cagama . . .

CAGAMA: No, let me speak if my lord will let me. The time is very short. Montezuma, I am rich and if the Spaniards are proven gods, I'll give them my wealth with all my heart. But I cannot be expected to exult. Not when I know the towns they've wrecked, the countryside they've burned, the black destruction they bring wherever they march. And you've done nothing to stop them, my lord. I confess, they are nearing the city and my mind is uneasy . . . What do you see in the moon, my lord? Montezuma, I will not be arrogant! What do you see that I cannot!

MONTEZUMA: I see only what any man might who will open eyes. I tremble under this menacing sky, remembering the hostile shudderings of the earth this year. How the lakes overflowed. Why? . . . without reason; how lightning would strike silently, thunderless; and the stars that fell in the afternoon,—what were the gods striving to tell us? Are we so strong, so proud and tall that when volcanoes fill the air with fiery stones and comets fall like rain we may go our ways indifferent, saying it will be well, we are too great to fall? And now the moon, the moon is shrouding over while striding inward from the East a band of white-faced strangers, unknown to mankind, from out of the sunrise they come calling *my* name. And what am I advised? What wisdom do we draw from such miracles? Pray God for the moon, you say!—we must not die! Slaughter the Spaniards, they've come to conquer! I say the world is agonized, profligate with signs that point to some cancer in the heart of the state: the gods roar warnings in our ears that something must be changed and we're blind and deaf to the signs!

GUATEMOTZIN: But the signs meant the ending of the world.

MONTEZUMA: And more, Guatemotzin—more a thousandfold than the ending of the world!

Sounds—enter Parach and Boy Sacrifice.

PARACH: My lord, our offering to the Gods approaches your Majesty.

MONTEZUMA: May the weight of your step on my threshold bring a blessing to this house.

BOY SACRIFICE: My lord, my great King!

MONTEZUMA: How beautiful you've grown.

PARACH: He must be on the mountain soon.

MONTEZUMA: I want him here a moment. *To Boy, smiling:* You shall hear strange questions in this room. Listen and carry them to heaven in the flame; and I pray you, beg the gods to send us an answer. Roses . . . *Touches Boy Sacrifice.* You're lovely as the flowers you wear . . . *To Lords:* A god to walk with the gods. *To Boy Sacrifice:* Are you sad tonight?

BOY SACRIFICE: It has been such a happy year for me, great King.

MONTEZUMA: And you'll not forget how you drank of oldest wine? How you fed on succulent meat? And the concubines we lay at your side on the couch of down, and the perfumed air, you'll not forget?

BOY SACRIFICE: Oh, my Lord, in the flame, in the wind, in the clouds beyond the sun, I will remember this holy year!

PARACH: His pyre is ready, the wood is dry. We stand talking, talking, the moon withers . . .

MONTEZUMA: He will carry a question to the gods.

PARACH: Questions? A priest answers questions. Only a priest . . .

Sound of chains. Enter fettered Judge with Tapaia.

JUDGE: Why am I dragged here from the block?

PARACH: Now the Emperor even confers with criminals!

MONTEZUMA: Tapaia, bring the courier to me as soon as he arrives.

Tapaia disappears.

MONTEZUMA: Old friend . . .

JUDGE: A judge may claim the privilege of death.

MONTEZUMA: I do not take you from the block to spare you. Nor am I sad that you die a criminal.

JUDGE: I *will* die, Montezuma.

MONTEZUMA: So will all of us perhaps.

JUDGE: But the world will *live* if the flame goes high. And I must not be here when tomorrow comes. I'll kill myself!

MONTEZUMA, *slight pause:* I must know why you're afraid to live. You took a bribe, a rich man, a rich and honored man—a bribe that would not buy him a sandal for his foot. Why? What calamity is wracking my world that my greatest judge must debase himself?

JUDGE: Let me die . . .

MONTEZUMA: What is your secret? In all our history, no judge has ever been corrupt. We have no penalty in law for such a crime. How is it possible! Speak!

Judge pauses. He cannot bear to look at the King.

JUDGE: I have only horrors to tell you, my lord, let me go!

MONTEZUMA: I have seen horrors this year. I can bear another!

JUDGE: My lord, you fought your last war a year ago. When that war finished, I looked out on the world. There is hardly a rise of ground left for you to conquer, Montezuma.

MONTEZUMA: Aye, all horizons are garrisoned.

JUDGE: Then where is the further glory? What step can you take but downward?

GUATEMOTZIN: The man is mad, my lord! Take him away!

MONTEZUMA: No. Let him speak!

JUDGE: Then I saw the waters rising. I saw the silent lightning, and the comets falling. I could not sleep, what did they mean? I walked the streets of your cities, listened to the people, the potter, the jeweler, the monger, and the fisherman. "The price is high," they said, "I am a poor man." "Crops are good," they say, "but I starve for food." "I had a son, they took him for the wars." Whispering, the cities of empire sullen, whispering: "Montezuma? He lives like a god and we suffer." "How long? How long? How long? How long?"

GUATEMOTZIN: Stop it!

JUDGE: Would the gods I could! But between the lips of both oceans the empire is cracking!

The Lords are furious.

GUATEMOTZIN: Insolent man!

MONTEZUMA: Leave him! *Quiet.* He sees it too.

CAGAMA, *astounded:* Sees what, my lord?

MONTEZUMA: The empire is cracking, Cagama. *Pause.* The gods are loitering here, let the truth confront them. *To the Judge:* And you thought, how the situation might be saved?

JUDGE: I did, until that dawn three months ago, when the Spaniards landed on the Eastern coast.

MONTEZUMA, *to Boy:* Hear it, Holy Boy, hear it now! *To Judge:* And what did you think then?

JUDGE: You wove the tapestry of Mexico but now the threads run out.

GUATEMOTZIN: How can you listen to him, Uncle?

MONTEZUMA, *rapidly:* You've seen it from below; what will mend the cracking? How would you mend the state if you were king?

GUATEMOTZIN: Troops made it and troops will mend it! The whip will shut their mouths!

MONTEZUMA: Aye, and for how long, how long, Guatemotzin?

GUATEMOTZIN: Until they whisper again, then whip again!

MONTEZUMA: And if it only cracks wider still?

Pause.

JUDGE: Now you are wise! You have reached the hour where force no more will rule the state . . .

MONTEZUMA: Yes . . .

JUDGE: And force will not bind up its rotting limbs.

MONTEZUMA: Hear it. *To Boy:* Holy Boy, hear it, a question for the gods!—This is the horror I see rising on the state, the question that the writhing universe has thrown up in my brain;—how shall I rule if not with the sword!

JUDGE: Die with me now, Montezuma!

MONTEZUMA: Die!

JUDGE: Now, at the zenith of your glory, die as you lived; Emperor of the World, or you'll crumble furious in storms.

CAGAMA: He dare not . . . !

GUATEMOTZIN and LORDS: Kill him! Kill the madman!

JUDGE, *to Lords:* You are the madmen! Fools! Mad with power and the riches you hold! Your day is over. The people are reaching for arms! Him they'll follow, but where? Can he lead them to conquer the oceans? If you love this King let him die in glory!

MONTEZUMA: Enough!

JUDGE: My lord . . . !

MONTEZUMA: I would die with you now for I see the same horror. But I'll not believe that all I've built, my golden cities, my roads, my gardens, aqueducts and spires, my state, my Aztec state unparalleled on earth before—I'll not believe they rose out of the earth for spiders to devour.

JUDGE: Everything dies!

MONTEZUMA: Not this! This will end only with the world! There must be a way to govern that does not end in ruins!

JUDGE: But if you can't rule by force can you rule without it? Therefore the thing is finished!

CAGAMA: I don't understand! My lord, are we all mad? How can you govern except by force?

ASTRONOMER: My lord, the shadow is moving quickly!

All look up at the moon.

MONTEZUMA, *still looking up. It is quiet:* Parach, will the sacrificial flame soar so high?

PARACH: Emperor, what is turning in your mind? How can you rule without force?

MONTEZUMA: Parach, will the world go on?

PARACH: I pray for a tall flame.

MONTEZUMA: Then I bid you, Holy Boy, tell this to the gods in heaven. I, Montezuma, made this nation in the way I knew—and war was enough for a king to know. But what the sword has won the sword alone cannot keep safe. But I am not sad; I know that my thoughts come to me from heaven, although I do not always understand them. But I have imagined rivers of flowing brass where swords and shields have melted, and I often think of times before our fathers, and their fathers before them—when the world was young and a man-god lived on this ground we love, and he ruled here with a soft voice and never touched weapons. You know his name, Holy Boy, our Quetzalcuatl god, gentle Lord of the moving wind, the white god who walked into the sunrise and with his going, murder burst on the world, and war. But he promised to return one day . . .

GUATEMOTZIN: These Spaniards are murdering . . . !

MONTEZUMA: "I will return!" he said, "and the Golden Years will shine again from my outstretched hands."

GUATEMOTZIN: How could *they* be . . . ?

MONTEZUMA, *to Boy Sacrifice:* The Spaniards are white, and they came from the sunrise! It's true they've come calling commands, ruthless; but I've not stopped them and I will not raise a hand until I know; are they God's children, or mortal strangers coming for conquest? Go now; beg the spirits, send this King a sign to go by; in the trees, in the sky, brand them with a name! Are they men or gods? They're close now. If I must kill again, it must be soon. Take him, Parach, take him to the mountain top. And may the flame of your strong body burn us onward to a stronger year! Farewell, Holy Boy.

BOY SACRIFICE: I will ask the spirits to send my lords a sign; farewell.

ASTRONOMER: The time is short, my lord!

MONTEZUMA: Hurry, Parach, and let the flame climb heavenward from his burning heart!

Parach and the Boy go out. There is a pause.

CAGAMA: I understand nothing . . .

GUATEMOTZIN: My lord . . . is war . . . my life and all I've learned and worshipped . . . suddenly to be despised?

MONTEZUMA: Try to understand . . . and you, Cagama . . . *Breaks off angrily.* I am not mad; a better time has never been for gods to return . . . Brother, my lords, does not one prince tremble with me! The gods may have returned!

CUITLAHUA: I am ready to believe.

MONTEZUMA, *eagerly:* You have received a sign, Cuitlahua?

CAGAMA: My lord, I see only *your* eyes. All my cities and I will travel by the clear conviction of those stars.

MONTEZUMA: That is good. And you, Guatemotzin, your cities?

GUATEMOTZIN: If there is a sign . . . then I'll bow to Spaniards. But how a peaceful god can sack your towns . . .

CUITLAHUA: But the people resist, they must be put aside . . .

GUATEMOTZIN: Put aside, and raped! Uncle, I know I am too young to understand, but if they're men, we're opening the gates to conquerors, and . . .

MONTEZUMA: *Four hundred* conquerors. I can muster eighty thousand troops this hour. Be sure of it, Guatemotzin, if they're men they'll die as all my enemies have died!

Enter Tapaia, hurrying.

TAPAIA: The courier is in sight, my lord, coming down the high road from the East.

ASTRONOMER: The moon is almost covered! The stars are fading!

MONTEZUMA: Hurry, bring him to me!

Exit Tapaia. A man laughs quietly.

MONTEZUMA, *startled*: Ah!

Man laughs again.

MONTEZUMA: I had forgotten you.

JUDGE: But death forgets no one, my lord.

MONTEZUMA: Spare me your wisdom. Go—take him!—Go, and be a good example for the country; die bravely, as befits one of Montezuma's judges.

JUDGE: I will die with my memories of Aztec hands building a world. The stones now are dropping from the walls . . . I see dust rising . . .

Enter Tecuichpo.

TECUICHPO: Don't let him say any more, Father!

MONTEZUMA: Tecuichpo.

TECUICHPO: Take him away!

JUDGE: I pray the Montezuma king will not outlive his honor.

MONTEZUMA: Take him.

Exit Judge.

TECUICHPO: There is some spirit here; making us mad, Father . . . I must not keep it from you—I have prayed in the Temple . . . it came upon me suddenly to pray . . . that they will come here to us.

GUATEMOTZIN: You prayed in the Temple for Spaniards?

TECUICHPO: It was like a great hand on my back, pressing me up-ward . . .

GUATEMOTZIN: She has prayed for your death, Uncle!

TECUICHPO: No. Not death, Guatemotzin! . . . for the coming-to-life of my dreams!

MONTEZUMA: You dreamed . . . ?

GUATEMOTZIN: They've poisoned the air we breathe!

MONTEZUMA: Tell me what you dreamed!

TECUICHPO: A thousand dreams, Father, since the hour they touched the coast they have walked into my nights; brightly, brightly, Father, like the sun on wet rock, and I must see them now, how they move, and how they talk . . . I want to touch their eyes . . . !

GUATEMOTZIN: And if it's conquerors you've prayed for!

MONTEZUMA: What did they say, did they speak?

TECUICHPO: Like rivers, with the voices of rivers . . . last night they gave me a white swan . . . *Recalling:* and it died in my hands . . . I had—

MONTEZUMA: A swan died . . . ?

TECUICHPO, *seeing their fright:* What does that mean? Oh, Father, I can't have prayed for conquerors! Guatemotzin, there *will* be a wedding in the Spring! *Sees they draw from her.* Why do you turn from me? Then attack with your armies; I don't want them here—who will forgive my wicked heart!

A slight pause. Montezuma turns to Cuitlahua, wonderingly.

MONTEZUMA: I have never known such a dream . . . a white swan, and it died . . .

Sudden booming of drums in distance.

ASTRONOMER: The stars are gone!

GUATEMOTZIN: The drums!

As they all start towards the open sky, enter Tapaia supporting Courier. Montezuma rushes to him.

TAPAIA: Here is the courier from the coast, my lord.

MONTEZUMA: Speak. Have you seen the Spaniards!

COURIER: A great battle is preparing, my lord. In Tlascalla, fifty thousand troops are facing the Spaniards!

CAGAMA, *joyously:* Fifty thousand! Tlascalla is standing up to them!

MONTEZUMA: You left before the battle started?

GUATEMOTZIN: Tlascalla will wipe them out!

MONTEZUMA, *to Courier:* But you saw no fighting?

COURIER: No, my lord. But I thought you should see this before the moon goes dark . . . I stole it from their camp as you commanded . . .

He hands Montezuma a cloth-covered object.

MONTEZUMA: This . . . this is . . .

Montezuma uncovers it in silence but for the rising drumbeats in the distance. All eyes glued to it . . . as the cloth falls from it, the drums suddenly get louder and . . .

COURIER: His helmet, my Lord. Cortez wore it on his head.

ASTRONOMER: Montezuma . . . the moon is black!

MONTEZUMA: Tapaia, the torch! *Still eyeing the helmet.* Now we'll know what they are . . .

CAGAMA: What does it mean . . . ?

TECUICHPO: Look at all the people on the mountain!

MONTEZUMA: On the head of the Quetzalcoatl god who stands in the Temple is the metal helmet he left behind, when he departed into the sun . . .

CUITLAHUA: Compare them!

ASTRONOMER: A falling star! Signal the mountain, Montezuma! Burn the Holy Boy!

MONTEZUMA: My Lords . . . if the moon returns and lights up the world again we'll go to the Temple, compare this with the headpiece of the god, and if they match!—The gods have come; we . . .

TECUICHPO: Oh, Father, I'm afraid now!

GUATEMOTZIN: And if they do not match!

ASTRONOMER, *frenzied:* They're waiting for the signal! My lord, the torch . . .

MONTEZUMA: Signal the mountain to start the sacrifice!

An Aztec horn is blown which echoes through the atmosphere.

GUATEMOTZIN: My lord, if they are not at all the same!

TECUICHPO: The sky is lower!

CUITLAHUA: They're lighting the pyre!

MONTEZUMA: Pray God to return us the world; we attack tomorrow if they're not the same. And the waiting's done, and we'll drive the Spaniard back to the sea!

The sky reflects a rising fire.

CUITLAHUA: The flame! Look, the mountain is burning!

GUATEMOTZIN: The smoke leaps to heaven!

The drumming becomes louder.

CUITLAHUA: It's reaching for the shadow! Like morning!

TECUICHPO: The sky is closer! The world is burning!

CUITLAHUA: The flame is red! The Boy is burning now, my lord!

GUATEMOTZIN: Look at the mountain, bright as the sunrise!

Pause.

CAGAMA: Why doesn't it move?

TECUICHPO: The shadow's not moving from the moon . . . oh, my wicked heart!

ASTRONOMER: The world is standing still! It is the end!

The wind rises suddenly during the invocation. There is humming behind his invocation.

MONTEZUMA, *calls up to the heavens:*
      I call to the lightning!
      Strike out of slumber!
      Crack open the tomb!
      I call to the stars;
      Light on the world again!
      Thunder in the clouds again!
      On mountains we burn, burning the beautiful,
      I call to all gods, and the god of all;
      Return us the light,
      Resurrect the shrouded moon! . . .

ASTRONOMER, *hushed:* My lord . . . the wind!

MONTEZUMA, *feeling it:* Wind?

CUITLAHUA, *alarmed:* . . . . Suddenly . . .

GUATEMOTZIN, *opening his palm to it:* . . . . Feel it . . . how swift . . .

ASTRONOMER, *fearful:* My lord, the moon is not moving . . .

Pause.

CAGAMA, *the fright grows:* It's flattening out . . .

GUATEMOTZIN: The people are running away!

CUITLAHUA: Brother, the flame's blowing out!

MONTEZUMA: No!

ASTRONOMER: My lord, the end!!

MONTEZUMA, *rushes out to the sky, throws his arms out, and roars:* Stop the wind! STOP THE WIND!

CUITLAHUA: It's out! The fire is out!!

They stand fixed, staring at the black sky, Montezuma's hands rigid over his head. A long silence when the faintest greenish light sprays the sky and their faces. Montezuma's arms come down slowly to his sides. The others survey the sky, mystified.

CUITLAHUA, *softly, struck:* The flame did not rise.

CAGAMA: How can it be . . . ?

TECUICHPO: The stars . . . !

GUATEMOTZIN, *facing the moon:* The moon is shining again . . . why . . . how . . . ?

Guatemotzin turns to Montezuma with the others. Montezuma turns slowly from the moon to the helmet which gleams brightly in the moonlight. They follow his eyes. He goes softly, lifts it as though it were alive. All are entranced by it. He turns it over in his hands again, then raises his eyes to them. They return the look wide-eyed and transfixed with fearful wonder as the light fades into complete darkness.

DEATH
OF A SALESMAN

*Certain Private Conversations in Two Acts
and a Requiem*

THE CAST
(in order of appearance)

WILLY LOMAN	Lee J. Cobb
LINDA	Mildred Dunnock
BIFF	Arthur Kennedy
HAPPY	Cameron Mitchell
BERNARD	Don Keefer
THE WOMAN	Winnifred Cushing
CHARLEY	Howard Smith
UNCLE BEN	Thomas Chalmers
HOWARD WAGNER	Alan Hewitt
JENNY	Ann Driscoll
STANLEY	Tom Pedi
MISS FORSYTHE	Constance Ford
LETTA	Hope Cameron

*Directed by Elia Kazan; produced by Kermit Bloomgarden and Walter Fried. Opened
February 10, 1949, Morosco Theatre, New York City.*

The action takes place in Willy Loman's house and yard and in various places he visits in the New York and Boston of today.

Throughout the play, in the stage directions, left and right mean stage left and stage right.

ACT ONE

(An Overture)

A melody is heard, played upon a flute. It is small and fine, telling of grass and trees and the horizon. The curtain rises.

Before us is the Salesman's house. We are aware of towering, angular shapes behind it, surrounding it on all sides. Only the blue light of the sky falls upon the house and forestage; the surrounding area shows an angry glow of orange. As more light appears, we see a solid vault of apartment houses around the small, fragile-seeming home. An air of the dream clings to the place, a dream rising out of reality. The kitchen at center seems actual enough, for there is a kitchen table with three chairs, and a refrigerator. But no other fixtures are seen. At the back of the kitchen there is a draped entrance, which leads to the living room. To the right of the kitchen, on a level raised two feet, is a bedroom furnished only with a brass bedstead and a straight chair. On a shelf over the bed a silver athletic trophy stands. A window opens onto the apartment house at the side.

Behind the kitchen, on a level raised six and a half feet, is the boys' bedroom, at present barely visible. Two beds are dimly seen, and at the back of the room a dormer window. (This bedroom is above the unseen living room.) At the left a stairway curves up to it from the kitchen.

The entire setting is wholly or, in some places, partially transparent. The roof-line of the house is one-dimensional; under and over it we see the apartment buildings. Before the house lies an apron, curving beyond the forestage into the orchestra. This forward area serves as the back yard as well as the locale of all Willy's imaginings and of his city scenes. Whenever the action is in the present the actors observe the imaginary wall-lines, entering the house only through its door at the left. But in the scenes of the past these boundaries are broken, and characters enter or leave a room by stepping "through" a wall onto the forestage.

21

From the right, Willy Loman, the Salesman, enters, carrying two large sample cases. The flute plays on. He hears but is not aware of it. He is past sixty years of age, dressed quietly. Even as he crosses the stage to the doorway of the house, his exhaustion is apparent. He unlocks the door, comes into the kitchen, and thankfully lets his burden down, feeling the soreness of his palms. A word-sigh escapes his lips—it might be "Oh, boy, oh, boy." He closes the door, then carries his cases out into the living room, through the draped kitchen doorway.

Linda, his wife, has stirred in her bed at the right. She gets out and puts on a robe, listening. Most often jovial, she has developed an iron repression of her exceptions to Willy's behavior—she more than loves him, she admires him, as though his mercurial nature, his temper, his massive dreams and little cruelties, served her only as sharp reminders of the turbulent longings within him, longings which she shares but lacks the temperament to utter and follow to their end.

LINDA, *hearing Willy outside the bedroom, calls with some trepidation:* Willy!

WILLY: It's all right. I came back.

LINDA: Why? What happened? *Slight pause.* Did something happen, Willy?

WILLY: No, nothing happened.

LINDA: You didn't smash the car, did you?

WILLY, *with casual irritation:* I said nothing happened. Didn't you hear me?

LINDA: Don't you feel well?

WILLY: I'm tired to the death. *The flute has faded away. He sits on the bed beside her, a little numb.* I couldn't make it. I just couldn't make it, Linda.

LINDA, *very carefully, delicately:* Where were you all day? You look terrible.

WILLY: I got as far as a little above Yonkers. I stopped for a cup of coffee. Maybe it was the coffee.

LINDA: What?

WILLY, *after a pause:* I suddenly couldn't drive any more. The car kept going off onto the shoulder, y'know?

LINDA, *helpfully:* Oh. Maybe it was the steering again. I don't think Angelo knows the Studebaker.

WILLY: No, it's me, it's me. Suddenly I realize I'm goin' sixty miles an hour and I don't remember the last five minutes. I'm—I can't seem to—keep my mind to it.

LINDA: Maybe it's your glasses. You never went for your new glasses.

WILLY: No, I see everything. I came back ten miles an hour. It took me nearly four hours from Yonkers.

LINDA, *resigned:* Well, you'll just have to take a rest, Willy, you can't continue this way.

WILLY: I just got back from Florida.

LINDA: But you didn't rest your mind. Your mind is overactive, and the mind is what counts, dear.

WILLY: I'll start out in the morning. Maybe I'll feel better in the morning. *She is taking off his shoes.* These goddam arch supports are killing me.

LINDA: Take an aspirin. Should I get you an aspirin? It'll soothe you.

WILLY, *with wonder:* I was driving along, you understand? And I was fine. I was even observing the scenery. You can imagine, me looking at scenery, on the road every week of my life. But it's so beautiful up there, Linda, the trees are so thick, and the sun is warm. I opened the windshield and just let the warm air bathe over me. And then all of a sudden I'm goin' off the road! I'm tellin' ya, I absolutely forgot I was driving. If I'd've gone the other way over the white line I might've killed somebody. So I went on again—and five minutes later I'm dreamin' again, and I nearly— *He presses two fingers against his eyes.* I have such thoughts, I have such strange thoughts.

LINDA: Willy, dear. Talk to them again. There's no reason why you can't work in New York.

WILLY: They don't need me in New York. I'm the New England man. I'm vital in New England.

LINDA: But you're sixty years old. They can't expect you to keep traveling every week.

WILLY: I'll have to send a wire to Portland. I'm supposed to see Brown and Morrison tomorrow morning at ten o'clock to show the line. Goddammit, I could sell them! *He starts putting on his jacket.*

LINDA, *taking the jacket from him:* Why don't you go down to the place tomorrow and tell Howard you've simply got to work in New York? You're too accommodating, dear.

WILLY: If old man Wagner was alive I'd a been in charge of New York now! That man was a prince, he was a masterful man. But that boy of his, that Howard, he don't appreciate. When I went north the first time, the Wagner Company didn't know where New England was!

LINDA: Why don't you tell those things to Howard, dear?

WILLY, *encouraged:* I will, I definitely will. Is there any cheese?

LINDA: I'll make you a sandwich.

WILLY: No, go to sleep. I'll take some milk. I'll be up right away. The boys in?

LINDA: They're sleeping. Happy took Biff on a date tonight.

WILLY, *interested:* That so?

LINDA: It was so nice to see them shaving together, one behind the other, in the bathroom. And going out together. You notice? The whole house smells of shaving lotion.

WILLY: Figure it out. Work a lifetime to pay off a house. You finally own it, and there's nobody to live in it.

LINDA: Well, dear, life is a casting off. It's always that way.

WILLY: No, no, some people—some people accomplish something. Did Biff say anything after I went this morning?

LINDA: You shouldn't have criticized him, Willy, especially after he just got off the train. You mustn't lose your temper with him.

WILLY: When the hell did I lose my temper? I simply asked him if he was making any money. Is that a criticism?

LINDA: But, dear, how could he make any money?

WILLY, *worried and angered:* There's such an undercurrent in him. He became a moody man. Did he apologize when I left this morning?

LINDA: He was crestfallen, Willy. You know how he admires you. I think if he finds himself, then you'll both be happier and not fight any more.

WILLY: How can he find himself on a farm? Is that a life? A farmhand? In the beginning, when he was young, I thought, well, a young man, it's good for him to tramp around, take a lot of different jobs. But it's more than ten years now and he has yet to make thirty-five dollars a week!

LINDA: He's finding himself, Willy.

WILLY: Not finding yourself at the age of thirty-four is a disgrace!

LINDA: Shh!

WILLY: The trouble is he's lazy, goddammit!

LINDA: Willy, please!

WILLY: Biff is a lazy bum!

LINDA: They're sleeping. Get something to eat. Go on down.

WILLY: Why did he come home? I would like to know what brought him home.

LINDA: I don't know. I think he's still lost, Willy. I think he's very lost.

WILLY: Biff Loman is lost. In the greatest country in the world a young man with such—personal attractiveness, gets lost. And such a hard worker. There's one thing about Biff—he's not lazy.

LINDA: Never.

WILLY, *with pity and resolve:* I'll see him in the morning; I'll have a nice talk with him. I'll get him a job selling. He could be big in no time. My God! Remember how they used to follow him around in high school? When he smiled at one of them their faces lit up. When he walked down the street . . . *He loses himself in reminiscences.*

LINDA, *trying to bring him out of it:* Willy, dear, I got a new kind of American-type cheese today. It's whipped.

WILLY: Why do you get American when I like Swiss?

LINDA: I just thought you'd like a change—

WILLY: I don't want a change! I want Swiss cheese. Why am I always being contradicted?

LINDA, *with a covering laugh:* I thought it would be a surprise.

WILLY: Why don't you open a window in here, for God's sake?

LINDA, *with infinite patience:* They're all open, dear.

WILLY: The way they boxed us in here. Bricks and windows, windows and bricks.

LINDA: We should've bought the land next door.

WILLY: The street is lined with cars. There's not a breath of fresh air in the neighborhood. The grass don't grow any more, you can't raise a carrot in the back yard. They should've had a law against apartment houses. Remember those two beautiful elm trees out there? When I and Biff hung the swing between them?

LINDA: Yeah, like being a million miles from the city.

WILLY: They should've arrested the builder for cutting those down. They massacred the neighborhood. *Lost:* More and more I think of those days, Linda. This time of year it was lilac and wisteria. And then the peonies would come out, and the daffodils. What fragrance in this room!

LINDA: Well, after all, people had to move somewhere.

WILLY: No, there's more people now.

LINDA: I don't think there's more people. I think—

WILLY: There's more people! That's what's ruining this country! Population is getting out of control. The competition is maddening! Smell the stink from that apartment house! And another one on the other side . . . How can they whip cheese?

On Willy's last line, Biff and Happy raise themselves up in their beds, listening.

LINDA: Go down, try it. And be quiet.

WILLY, *turning to Linda, guiltily:* You're not worried about me, are you, sweetheart?

BIFF: What's the matter?

HAPPY: Listen!

LINDA: You've got too much on the ball to worry about.

WILLY: You're my foundation and my support, Linda.

LINDA: Just try to relax, dear. You make mountains out of molehills.

WILLY: I won't fight with him any more. If he wants to go back to Texas, let him go.

LINDA: He'll find his way.

WILLY: Sure. Certain men just don't get started till later in life. Like Thomas Edison, I think. Or B. F. Goodrich. One of them was deaf. *He starts for the bedroom doorway.* I'll put my money on Biff.

LINDA: And Willy—if it's warm Sunday we'll drive in the country. And we'll open the windshield, and take lunch.

WILLY: No, the windshields don't open on the new cars.

LINDA: But you opened it today.

WILLY: Me? I didn't. *He stops.* Now isn't that peculiar! Isn't that a remarkable— *He breaks off in amazement and fright as the flute is heard distantly.*

LINDA: What, darling?

WILLY: That is the most remarkable thing.

LINDA: What, dear?

WILLY: I was thinking of the Chevy. *Slight pause.* Nineteen twenty-eight . . . when I had that red Chevy— *Breaks off.* That funny? I coulda sworn I was driving that Chevy today.

LINDA: Well, that's nothing. Something must've reminded you.

WILLY: Remarkable. Ts. Remember those days? The way Biff used to simonize that car? The dealer refused to believe there was eighty thousand miles on it. *He shakes his head.* Heh! *To Linda:* Close your eyes, I'll be right up. *He walks out of the bedroom.*

HAPPY, *to Biff:* Jesus, maybe he smashed up the car again!

LINDA, *calling after Willy:* Be careful on the stairs, dear! The cheese is on the middle shelf! *She turns, goes over to the bed, takes his jacket, and goes out of the bedroom.*

Light has risen on the boys' room. Unseen, Willy is heard talking to himself, "Eighty thousand miles," and a little laugh. Biff gets out of bed, comes downstage a bit, and stands attentively. Biff is two years older than his brother Happy, well built, but in these days bears a worn air and seems less self-assured. He has succeeded less, and his dreams are stronger and less acceptable than Happy's. Happy is tall, powerfully made. Sexuality is like a visible color on him, or a scent that many women have discovered. He, like his brother, is lost, but in a different way, for he has never allowed himself to turn his face toward defeat and is thus more confused and hard-skinned, although seemingly more content.

HAPPY, *getting out of bed:* He's going to get his license taken away if he keeps that up. I'm getting nervous about him, y'know, Biff?

BIFF: His eyes are going.

HAPPY: No, I've driven with him. He sees all right. He just doesn't keep his mind on it. I drove into the city with him last week. He stops at a green light and then it turns red and he goes. *He laughs.*

BIFF: Maybe he's color-blind.

HAPPY: Pop? Why he's got the finest eye for color in the business. You know that.

BIFF, *sitting down on his bed:* I'm going to sleep.

HAPPY: You're not still sour on Dad, are you, Biff?

BIFF: He's all right, I guess.

WILLY, *underneath them, in the living room:* Yes, sir, eighty thousand miles—eighty-two thousand!

BIFF: You smoking?

HAPPY, *holding out a pack of cigarettes:* Want one?

BIFF, *taking a cigarette:* I can never sleep when I smell it.

WILLY: What a simonizing job, heh!

HAPPY, *with deep sentiment:* Funny, Biff, y'know? Us sleeping in here again? The old beds. *He pats his bed affectionately.* All the talk that went across those two beds, huh? Our whole lives.

BIFF: Yeah. Lotta dreams and plans.

HAPPY, *with a deep and masculine laugh:* About five hundred women would like to know what was said in this room.

They share a soft laugh.

BIFF: Remember that big Betsy something—what the hell was her name—over on Bushwick Avenue?

HAPPY, *combing his hair:* With the collie dog!

BIFF: That's the one. I got you in there, remember?

HAPPY: Yeah, that was my first time—I think. Boy, there was a pig! *They laugh, almost crudely.* You taught me everything I know about women. Don't forget that.

BIFF: I bet you forgot how bashful you used to be. Especially with girls.

HAPPY: Oh, I still am, Biff.

BIFF: Oh, go on.

HAPPY: I just control it, that's all. I think I got less bashful and you got more so. What happened, Biff? Where's the old humor, the old confidence? *He shakes Biff's knee. Biff gets up and moves restlessly about the room.* What's the matter?

BIFF: Why does Dad mock me all the time?

HAPPY: He's not mocking you, he—

BIFF: Everything I say there's a twist of mockery on his face. I can't get near him.

HAPPY: He just wants you to make good, that's all. I wanted to talk to you about Dad for a long time, Biff. Something's—happening to him. He—talks to himself.

BIFF: I noticed that this morning. But he always mumbled.

HAPPY: But not so noticeable. It got so embarrassing I sent him to Florida. And you know something? Most of the time he's talking to you.

BIFF: What's he say about me?

HAPPY: I can't make it out.

BIFF: What's he say about me?

HAPPY: I think the fact that you're not settled, that you're still kind of up in the air . . .

BIFF: There's one or two other things depressing him, Happy.

HAPPY: What do you mean?

BIFF: Never mind. Just don't lay it all to me.

HAPPY: But I think if you just got started—I mean—is there any future for you out there?

BIFF: I tell ya, Hap, I don't know what the future is. I don't know—what I'm supposed to want.

HAPPY: What do you mean?

BIFF: Well, I spent six or seven years after high school trying to work myself up. Shipping clerk, salesman, business of one kind or another. And it's a measly manner of existence. To get on that subway on the hot mornings in summer. To devote your whole life to keeping stock, or making phone calls, or selling or buying. To suffer fifty weeks of the year for the sake of a two-week vacation, when all you really desire is to be outdoors, with your shirt off. And always to have to get ahead of the next fella. And still—that's how you build a future.

HAPPY: Well, you really enjoy it on a farm? Are you content out there?

BIFF, *with rising agitation:* Hap, I've had twenty or thirty different kinds of jobs since I left home before the war, and it always turns out the same. I just realized it lately. In Nebraska when I herded cattle, and the Dakotas, and Arizona, and now in Texas. It's why I came home now, I guess, because I realized it. This farm I work on, it's spring there now, see? And they've got about fifteen new colts. There's nothing more inspiring or—beautiful than the sight of a mare and a new colt. And it's cool there now, see? Texas is cool now, and it's spring. And whenever spring comes to where I am, I suddenly get the feeling, my God, I'm not gettin' anywhere! What the hell am I doing, playing around with horses, twenty-eight dollars a week! I'm thirty-four years old, I oughta be makin' my future. That's when I come running home. And now, I get here, and I don't know what to do with myself. *After a pause:* I've always made a point of not wasting my life, and every time I come back here I know that all I've done is to waste my life.

HAPPY: You're a poet, you know that, Biff? You're a—you're an idealist!

BIFF: No, I'm mixed up very bad. Maybe I oughta get married. Maybe I oughta get stuck into something. Maybe that's my trouble. I'm like a boy. I'm not married, I'm not in business, I just—I'm like a boy. Are you content, Hap? You're a success, aren't you? Are you content?

HAPPY: Hell, no!

BIFF: Why? You're making money, aren't you?

HAPPY, *moving about with energy, expressiveness:* All I can do now is wait for the merchandise manager to die. And suppose I get to be merchandise manager? He's a good friend of mine, and he just built a terrific estate on Long Island. And he lived there about two months and sold it, and now he's building another one. He can't enjoy it once it's finished. And I know that's just what I would do. I don't know what the hell I'm workin' for. Sometimes I sit in my apartment—all alone. And I think of the rent I'm paying. And it's crazy. But then, it's what I always wanted. My own apartment, a car, and plenty of women. And still, goddammit, I'm lonely.

BIFF, *with enthusiasm:* Listen, why don't you come out West with me?

HAPPY: You and I, heh?

BIFF: Sure, maybe we could buy a ranch. Raise cattle, use our muscles. Men built like we are should be working out in the open.

HAPPY, *avidly:* The Loman Brothers, heh?

BIFF, *with vast affection:* Sure, we'd be known all over the counties!

HAPPY, *enthralled:* That's what I dream about, Biff. Sometimes I want to just rip my clothes off in the middle of the store and outbox that goddam merchandise manager. I mean I can outbox, outrun, and outlift anybody in that store, and I have to take orders from those common, petty sons-of-bitches till I can't stand it any more.

BIFF: I'm tellin' you, kid, if you were with me I'd be happy out there.

HAPPY, *enthused:* See, Biff, everybody around me is so false that I'm constantly lowering my ideals . . .

BIFF: Baby, together we'd stand up for one another, we'd have someone to trust.

HAPPY: If I were around you—

BIFF: Hap, the trouble is we weren't brought up to grub for money. I don't know how to do it.

HAPPY: Neither can I!

BIFF: Then let's go!

HAPPY: The only thing is—what can you make out there?

BIFF: But look at your friend. Builds an estate and then hasn't the peace of mind to live in it.

HAPPY: Yeah, but when he walks into the store the waves part in front of him. That's fifty-two thousand dollars a year coming through the revolving door, and I got more in my pinky finger than he's got in his head.

BIFF: Yeah, but you just said—

HAPPY: I gotta show some of those pompous, self-important executives over there that Hap Loman can make the grade. I want to walk into the store the way he walks in. Then I'll go with you, Biff. We'll be together yet, I swear. But take those two we had tonight. Now weren't they gorgeous creatures?

BIFF: Yeah, yeah, most gorgeous I've had in years.

HAPPY: I get that any time I want, Biff. Whenever I feel disgusted. The only trouble is, it gets like bowling or something. I just keep knockin' them over and it doesn't mean anything. You still run around a lot?

BIFF: Naa. I'd like to find a girl—steady, somebody with substance.

HAPPY: That's what I long for.

BIFF: Go on! You'd never come home.

HAPPY: I would! Somebody with character, with resistance! Like Mom, y'know? You're gonna call me a bastard when I tell you this. That girl Charlotte I was with tonight is engaged to be married in five weeks. *He tries on his new hat.*

BIFF: No kiddin'!

HAPPY: Sure, the guy's in line for the vice-presidency of the store. I don't know what gets into me, maybe I just have an overdeveloped sense of competition or something, but I went and ruined her, and furthermore I can't get rid of her. And he's the third executive I've done that to. Isn't that a crummy characteristic? And to top it all, I go to their weddings! *Indignantly, but laughing:* Like I'm not supposed to take bribes. Manufacturers offer me a hundred-dollar bill now and then to throw an order their way. You know how honest I am, but it's like this girl, see. I hate myself for it. Because I don't want the girl, and, still, I take it and—I love it!

BIFF: Let's go to sleep.

HAPPY: I guess we didn't settle anything, heh?

BIFF: I just got one idea that I think I'm going to try.

HAPPY: What's that?

BIFF: Remember Bill Oliver?

HAPPY: Sure, Oliver is very big now. You want to work for him again?

BIFF: No, but when I quit he said something to me. He put his arm on my shoulder, and he said, "Biff, if you ever need anything, come to me."

HAPPY: I remember that. That sounds good.

BIFF: I think I'll go to see him. If I could get ten thousand or even seven or eight thousand dollars I could buy a beautiful ranch.

HAPPY: I bet he'd back you. 'Cause he thought highly of you, Biff. I mean, they all do. You're well liked, Biff. That's why I say to come back here, and we both have the apartment. And I'm tellin' you, Biff, any babe you want . . .

BIFF: No, with a ranch I could do the work I like and still be something. I just wonder though. I wonder if Oliver still thinks I stole that carton of basketballs.

HAPPY: Oh, he probably forgot that long ago. It's almost ten years. You're too sensitive. Anyway, he didn't really fire you.

BIFF: Well, I think he was going to. I think that's why I quit. I was never sure whether he knew or not. I know he thought the world of me, though. I was the only one he'd let lock up the place.

WILLY, *below:* You gonna wash the engine, Biff?

HAPPY: Shh!

Biff looks at Happy, who is gazing down, listening. Willy is mumbling in the parlor.

HAPPY: You hear that?

They listen. Willy laughs warmly.

BIFF, *growing angry:* Doesn't he know Mom can hear that?

WILLY: Don't get your sweater dirty, Biff!

A look of pain crosses Biff's face.

HAPPY: Isn't that terrible? Don't leave again, will you? You'll find a job here. You gotta stick around. I don't know what to do about him, it's getting embarrassing.

WILLY: What a simonizing job!

BIFF: Mom's hearing that!

WILLY: No kiddin', Biff, you got a date? Wonderful!

HAPPY: Go on to sleep. But talk to him in the morning, will you?

BIFF, *reluctantly getting into bed:* With her in the house. Brother!

HAPPY, *getting into bed:* I wish you'd have a good talk with him.

The light on their room begins to fade.

BIFF, *to himself in bed:* That selfish, stupid . . .

HAPPY: Sh . . . Sleep, Biff.

Their light is out. Well before they have finished speaking, Willy's form is dimly seen below in the darkened kitchen. He opens the refrigerator, searches in there, and takes out a bottle of milk. The apartment houses are fading out, and the entire house and surroundings become covered with leaves. Music insinuates itself as the leaves appear.

WILLY: Just wanna be careful with those girls, Biff, that's all. Don't make any promises. No promises of any kind. Because a girl, y'know, they always believe what you tell 'em, and you're very young, Biff, you're too young to be talking seriously to girls.

Light rises on the kitchen. Willy, talking, shuts the refrigerator door and comes downstage to the kitchen table. He pours milk into a glass. He is totally immersed in himself, smiling faintly.

WILLY: Too young entirely, Biff. You want to watch your schooling first. Then when you're all set, there'll be plenty of girls for a boy like you. *He smiles broadly at a kitchen chair.* That so? The girls pay for you? *He laughs.* Boy, you must really be makin' a hit.

Willy is gradually addressing—physically—a point offstage, speaking through the wall of the kitchen, and his voice has been rising in volume to that of a normal conversation.

WILLY: I been wondering why you polish the car so careful. Ha! Don't leave the hubcaps, boys. Get the chamois to the hubcaps. Happy, use newspaper on the windows, it's the easiest thing. Show him how to do it, Biff! You see, Happy? Pad it up, use it like a pad. That's it, that's it, good work. You're doin' all right, Hap. *He pauses, then nods in approbation for a few seconds, then looks upward.* Biff, first thing we gotta do when we get time is clip that big branch over the house. Afraid it's gonna fall in a storm and hit the roof. Tell you what. We get a rope and sling her around, and then we climb up there with a couple of saws and take her down. Soon as you finish the car, boys, I wanna see ya. I got a surprise for you, boys.

BIFF, *offstage:* Whatta ya got, Dad?

WILLY: No, you finish first. Never leave a job till you're finished—remember that. *Looking toward the "big trees":* Biff, up in Albany I saw a beautiful hammock. I think I'll buy it next trip, and we'll hang it right between those two elms. Wouldn't that be something? Just swingin' there under those branches. Boy, that would be . . .

Young Biff and Young Happy appear from the direction Willy was addressing. Happy carries rags and a pail of water. Biff, wearing a sweater with a block "S," carries a football.

BIFF, *pointing in the direction of the car offstage:* How's that, Pop, professional?

WILLY: Terrific. Terrific job, boys. Good work, Biff.

HAPPY: Where's the surprise, Pop?

WILLY: In the back seat of the car.

HAPPY: Boy! *He runs off.*

BIFF: What is it, Dad? Tell me, what'd you buy?

WILLY, *laughing, cuffs him:* Never mind, something I want you to have.

BIFF, *turns and starts off:* What is it, Hap?

HAPPY, *offstage:* It's a punching bag!

BIFF: Oh, Pop!

WILLY: It's got Gene Tunney's signature on it!

Happy runs onstage with a punching bag.

BIFF: Gee, how'd you know we wanted a punching bag?

WILLY: Well, it's the finest thing for the timing.

HAPPY, *lying down on his back and pedaling with his feet:* I'm losing weight, you notice, Pop?

WILLY, *to Happy:* Jumping rope is good too.

BIFF: Did you see the new football I got?

WILLY, *examining the ball:* Where'd you get a new ball?

BIFF: The coach told me to practice my passing.

WILLY: That so? And he gave you the ball, heh?

BIFF: Well, I borrowed it from the locker room. *He laughs confidentially.*

WILLY, *laughing with him at the theft:* I want you to return that.

HAPPY: I told you he wouldn't like it!

BIFF, *angrily:* Well, I'm bringing it back!

WILLY, *stopping the incipient argument, to Happy:* Sure, he's gotta practice with a regulation ball, doesn't he? *To Biff:* Coach'll probably congratulate you on your initiative!

BIFF: Oh, he keeps congratulating my initiative all the time, Pop.

WILLY: That's because he likes you. If somebody else took that ball there'd be an uproar. So what's the report, boys, what's the report?

BIFF: Where'd you go this time, Dad? Gee we were lonesome for you.

WILLY, *pleased, puts an arm around each boy and they come down to the apron:* Lonesome, heh?

BIFF: Missed you every minute.

WILLY: Don't say? Tell you a secret, boys. Don't breathe it to a soul. Someday I'll have my own business, and I'll never have to leave home any more.

HAPPY: Like Uncle Charley, heh?

WILLY: Bigger than Uncle Charley! Because Charley is not—liked. He's liked, but he's not—well liked.

BIFF: Where'd you go this time, Dad?

WILLY: Well, I got on the road, and I went north to Providence. Met the Mayor.

BIFF: The Mayor of Providence!

WILLY: He was sitting in the hotel lobby.

BIFF: What'd he say?

WILLY: He said, "Morning!" And I said, "You got a fine city here, Mayor." And then he had coffee with me. And then I went to Waterbury. Waterbury is a fine city. Big clock city, the famous Waterbury clock. Sold a nice bill there. And then Boston—Boston is the cradle of the Revolution. A fine city. And a couple of other towns in Mass., and on to Portland and Bangor and straight home!

BIFF: Gee, I'd love to go with you sometime, Dad.

WILLY: Soon as summer comes.

HAPPY: Promise?

WILLY: You and Hap and I, and I'll show you all the towns. America is full of beautiful towns and fine, upstanding people. And they know me, boys, they know me up and down New England. The finest people. And when I bring you fellas up, there'll be open sesame for all of us, 'cause one thing, boys: I have friends. I can park my car in any street in New England, and the cops protect it like their own. This summer, heh?

BIFF and HAPPY, *together:* Yeah! You bet!

WILLY: We'll take our bathing suits.

HAPPY: We'll carry your bags, Pop!

WILLY: Oh, won't that be something! Me comin' into the Boston stores with you boys carryin' my bags. What a sensation!

Biff is prancing around, practicing passing the ball.

WILLY: You nervous, Biff, about the game?

BIFF: Not if you're gonna be there.

WILLY: What do they say about you in school, now that they made you captain?

HAPPY: There's a crowd of girls behind him every time the classes change.

BIFF, *taking Willy's hand:* This Saturday, Pop, this Saturday—just for you, I'm going to break through for a touchdown.

HAPPY: You're supposed to pass.

BIFF: I'm takin' one play for Pop. You watch me, Pop, and when I take off my helmet, that means I'm breakin' out. Then you watch me crash through that line!

WILLY, *kissing Biff:* Oh, wait'll I tell this in Boston!

Bernard enters in knickers. He is younger than Biff, earnest and loyal, a worried boy.

BERNARD: Biff, where are you? You're supposed to study with me today.

WILLY: Hey, looka Bernard. What're you lookin' so anemic about, Bernard?

BERNARD: He's gotta study, Uncle Willy. He's got Regents next week.

HAPPY, *tauntingly, spinning Bernard around:* Let's box, Bernard!

BERNARD: Biff! *He gets away from Happy.* Listen, Biff, I heard Mr. Birnbaum say that if you don't start studyin' math he's gonna flunk you, and you won't graduate. I heard him!

WILLY: You better study with him, Biff. Go ahead now.

BERNARD: I heard him!

BIFF: Oh, Pop, you didn't see my sneakers! *He holds up a foot for Willy to look at.*

WILLY: Hey, that's a beautiful job of printing!

BERNARD, *wiping his glasses:* Just because he printed University of Virginia on his sneakers doesn't mean they've got to graduate him, Uncle Willy!

WILLY, *angrily:* What're you talking about? With scholarships to three universities they're gonna flunk him?

BERNARD: But I heard Mr. Birnbaum say—

WILLY: Don't be a pest, Bernard! *To his boys:* What an anemic!

BERNARD: Okay, I'm waiting for you in my house, Biff.

Bernard goes off. The Lomans laugh.

WILLY: Bernard is not well liked, is he?

BIFF: He's liked, but he's not well liked.

HAPPY: That's right, Pop.

WILLY: That's just what I mean. Bernard can get the best marks in school, y'understand, but when he gets out in the business world, y'understand, you are going to be five times ahead of him. That's why I thank Almighty God you're both built like Adonises. Because the man who makes an appearance in the business world, the man who creates personal interest, is the man who gets ahead. Be liked and you will never want. You take me, for instance. I never have to wait in line to see a buyer. "Willy Loman is here!" That's all they have to know, and I go right through.

BIFF: Did you knock them dead, Pop?

WILLY: Knocked 'em cold in Providence, slaughtered 'em in Boston.

HAPPY, *on his back, pedaling again:* I'm losing weight, you notice, Pop?

Linda enters, as of old, a ribbon in her hair, carrying a basket of washing.

LINDA, *with youthful energy:* Hello, dear!

WILLY: Sweetheart!

LINDA: How'd the Chevy run?

WILLY: Chevrolet, Linda, is the greatest car ever built. *To the boys:* Since when do you let your mother carry wash up the stairs?

BIFF: Grab hold there, boy!

HAPPY: Where to, Mom?

LINDA: Hang them up on the line. And you better go down to your friends, Biff. The cellar is full of boys. They don't know what to do with themselves.

BIFF: Ah, when Pop comes home they can wait!

WILLY, *laughing appreciatively:* You better go down and tell them what to do, Biff.

BIFF: I think I'll have them sweep out the furnace room.

WILLY: Good work, Biff.

BIFF—*he goes through wall-line of kitchen to doorway at back and calls down:* Fellas! Everybody sweep out the furnace room! I'll be right down!

VOICES: All right! Okay, Biff.

BIFF: George and Sam and Frank, come out back! We're hangin' up the wash! Come on, Hap, on the double! *He and Happy carry out the basket.*

LINDA: The way they obey him!

WILLY: Well, that's training, the training. I'm tellin' you, I was sellin' thousands and thousands, but I had to come home.

LINDA: Oh, the whole block'll be at that game. Did you sell anything?

WILLY: I did five hundred gross in Providence and seven hundred gross in Boston.

LINDA: No! Wait a minute, I've got a pencil. *She pulls pencil and paper out of her apron pocket.* That makes your commission . . . Two hundred—my God! Two hundred and twelve dollars!

WILLY: Well, I didn't figure it yet, but . . .

LINDA: How much did you do?

WILLY: Well, I—I did—about a hundred and eighty gross in Providence. Well, no—it came to—roughly two hundred gross on the whole trip.

LINDA, *without hesitation:* Two hundred gross. That's . . . *She figures.*

WILLY: The trouble was that three of the stores were half closed for inventory in Boston. Otherwise I woulda broke records.

LINDA: Well, it makes seventy dollars and some pennies. That's very good.

WILLY: What do we owe?

LINDA: Well, on the first there's sixteen dollars on the refrigerator—

WILLY: Why sixteen?

LINDA: Well, the fan belt broke, so it was a dollar eighty.

WILLY: But it's brand new.

LINDA: Well, the man said that's the way it is. Till they work themselves in, y'know.

They move through the wall-line into the kitchen.

WILLY: I hope we didn't get stuck on that machine.

LINDA: They got the biggest ads of any of them!

WILLY: I know, it's a fine machine. What else?

LINDA: Well, there's nine-sixty for the washing machine. And for the vacuum cleaner there's three and a half due on the fifteenth. Then the roof, you got twenty-one dollars remaining.

WILLY: It don't leak, does it?

LINDA: No, they did a wonderful job. Then you owe Frank for the carburetor.

WILLY: I'm not going to pay that man! That goddam Chevrolet, they ought to prohibit the manufacture of that car!

LINDA: Well, you owe him three and a half. And odds and ends, comes to around a hundred and twenty dollars by the fifteenth.

WILLY: A hundred and twenty dollars! My God, if business don't pick up I don't know what I'm gonna do!

LINDA: Well, next week you'll do better.

WILLY: Oh, I'll knock 'em dead next week. I'll go to Hartford. I'm very well liked in Hartford. You know, the trouble is, Linda, people don't seem to take to me.

They move onto the forestage.

LINDA: Oh, don't be foolish.

WILLY: I know it when I walk in. They seem to laugh at me.

LINDA: Why? Why would they laugh at you? Don't talk that way, Willy.

Willy moves to the edge of the stage. Linda goes into the kitchen and starts to darn stockings.

WILLY: I don't know the reason for it, but they just pass me by. I'm not noticed.

LINDA: But you're doing wonderful, dear. You're making seventy to a hundred dollars a week.

WILLY: But I gotta be at it ten, twelve hours a day. Other men—I don't know—they do it easier. I don't know why—I can't stop myself—I talk too much. A man oughta come in with a few words. One thing about Charley. He's a man of few words, and they respect him.

LINDA: You don't talk too much, you're just lively.

WILLY, *smiling:* Well, I figure, what the hell, life is short, a couple of jokes. *To himself:* I joke too much! *The smile goes.*

LINDA: Why? You're—

WILLY: I'm fat. I'm very—foolish to look at, Linda. I didn't tell you, but Christmas time I happened to be calling on F. H. Stewarts, and a salesman I know, as I was going in to see the buyer I heard him say something about—walrus. And I—I cracked him right across the face. I won't take that. I simply will not take that. But they do laugh at me. I know that.

LINDA: Darling . . .

WILLY: I gotta overcome it. I know I gotta overcome it. I'm not dressing to advantage, maybe.

LINDA: Willy, darling, you're the handsomest man in the world—

WILLY: Oh, no, Linda.

LINDA: To me you are. *Slight pause.* The handsomest.

From the darkness is heard the laughter of a woman. Willy doesn't turn to it, but it continues through Linda's lines.

LINDA: And the boys, Willy. Few men are idolized by their children the way you are.

Music is heard as behind a scrim, to the left of the house, The Woman, dimly seen, is dressing.

WILLY, *with great feeling:* You're the best there is, Linda, you're a pal, you know that? On the road—on the road I want to grab you sometimes and just kiss the life outa you.

The laughter is loud now, and he moves into a brightening area at the left, where The Woman has come from behind the scrim and is standing, putting on her hat, looking into a "mirror" and laughing.

WILLY: 'Cause I get so lonely—especially when business is bad and there's nobody to talk to. I get the feeling that I'll never sell anything again, that I won't make a living for you, or a business, a business for the boys. *He talks through The Woman's subsiding laughter; The Woman primps at the "mirror."* There's so much I want to make for—

THE WOMAN: Me? You didn't make me, Willy. I picked you.

WILLY, *pleased:* You picked me?

THE WOMAN, *who is quite proper-looking, Willy's age:* I did. I've been sitting at that desk watching all the salesmen go by, day in, day out. But you've got such a sense of humor, and we do have such a good time together, don't we?

WILLY: Sure, sure. *He takes her in his arms.* Why do you have to go now?

THE WOMAN: It's two o'clock . . .

WILLY: No, come on in! *He pulls her.*

THE WOMAN: . . . my sisters'll be scandalized. When'll you be back?

WILLY: Oh, two weeks about. Will you come up again?

THE WOMAN: Sure thing. You do make me laugh. It's good for me. *She squeezes his arm, kisses him.* And I think you're a wonderful man.

WILLY: You picked me, heh?

THE WOMAN: Sure. Because you're so sweet. And such a kidder.

WILLY: Well, I'll see you next time I'm in Boston.

THE WOMAN: I'll put you right through to the buyers.

WILLY, *slapping her bottom:* Right. Well, bottoms up!

THE WOMAN—*she slaps him gently and laughs:* You just kill me, Willy. *He suddenly grabs her and kisses her roughly.* You kill me. And thanks for the stockings. I love a lot of stockings. Well, good night.

WILLY: Good night. And keep your pores open!

THE WOMAN: Oh, Willy!

The Woman bursts out laughing, and Linda's laughter blends in. The Woman disappears into the dark. Now the area at the kitchen table brightens. Linda is sitting where she was at the kitchen table, but now is mending a pair of her silk stockings.

LINDA: You are, Willy. The handsomest man. You've got no reason to feel that—

WILLY, *coming out of The Woman's dimming area and going over to Linda:* I'll make it all up to you, Linda, I'll—

LINDA: There's nothing to make up, dear. You're doing fine, better than—

WILLY, *noticing her mending:* What's that?

LINDA: Just mending my stockings. They're so expensive—

WILLY, *angrily, taking them from her:* I won't have you mending stockings in this house! Now throw them out!

Linda puts the stockings in her pocket.

BERNARD, *entering on the run:* Where is he? If he doesn't study!

WILLY, *moving to the forestage, with great agitation:* You'll give him the answers!

BERNARD: I do, but I can't on a Regents! That's a state exam! They're liable to arrest me!

WILLY: Where is he? I'll whip him, I'll whip him!

LINDA: And he'd better give back that football, Willy, it's not nice.

WILLY: Biff! Where is he? Why is he taking everything?

LINDA: He's too rough with the girls, Willy. All the mothers are afraid of him!

WILLY: I'll whip him!

BERNARD: He's driving the car without a license!

The Woman's laugh is heard.

WILLY: Shut up!

LINDA: All the mothers—

WILLY: Shut up!

BERNARD, *backing quietly away and out:* Mr. Birnbaum says he's stuck up.

WILLY: Get outa here!

BERNARD: If he doesn't buckle down he'll flunk math! *He goes off.*

LINDA: He's right, Willy, you've gotta—

WILLY, *exploding at her:* There's nothing the matter with him! You want him to be a worm like Bernard? He's got spirit, personality . . .

As he speaks, Linda, almost in tears, exits into the living room. Willy is alone in the kitchen, wilting and staring. The leaves are gone. It is night again, and the apartment houses look down from behind.

WILLY: Loaded with it. Loaded! What is he stealing? He's giving it back, isn't he? Why is he stealing? What did I tell him? I never in my life told him anything but decent things.

Happy in pajamas has come down the stairs; Willy suddenly becomes aware of Happy's presence.

HAPPY: Let's go now, come on.

WILLY, *sitting down at the kitchen table:* Huh! Why did she have to wax the floors herself? Everytime she waxes the floors she keels over. She knows that!

HAPPY: Shh! Take it easy. What brought you back tonight?

WILLY: I got an awful scare. Nearly hit a kid in Yonkers. God! Why didn't I go to Alaska with my brother Ben that time! Ben! That man was a genius, that man was success incarnate! What a mistake! He begged me to go.

HAPPY: Well, there's no use in—

WILLY: You guys! There was a man started with the clothes on his back and ended up with diamond mines!

HAPPY: Boy, someday I'd like to know how he did it.

WILLY: What's the mystery? The man knew what he wanted and went out and got it! Walked into a jungle, and comes out, the age of twenty-one, and he's rich! The world is an oyster, but you don't crack it open on a mattress!

HAPPY: Pop, I told you I'm gonna retire you for life.

WILLY: You'll retire me for life on seventy goddam dollars a week? And your women and your car and your apartment, and you'll retire me for life! Christ's sake, I couldn't get past Yonkers today! Where are you guys, where are you? The woods are burning! I can't drive a car!

Charley has appeared in the doorway. He is a large man, slow of speech, laconic, immovable. In all he says, despite what he says, there is pity, and, now, trepidation. He has a robe over pajamas, slippers on his feet. He enters the kitchen.

CHARLEY: Everything all right?

HAPPY: Yeah, Charley, everything's . . .

WILLY: What's the matter?

CHARLEY: I heard some noise. I thought something happened. Can't we do something about the walls? You sneeze in here, and in my house hats blow off.

HAPPY: Let's go to bed, Dad. Come on.

Charley signals to Happy to go.

WILLY: You go ahead, I'm not tired at the moment.

HAPPY, *to Willy:* Take it easy, huh? *He exits.*

WILLY: What're you doin' up?

CHARLEY, *sitting down at the kitchen table opposite Willy:* Couldn't sleep good. I had a heartburn.

WILLY: Well, you don't know how to eat.

CHARLEY: I eat with my mouth.

WILLY: No, you're ignorant. You gotta know about vitamins and things like that.

CHARLEY: Come on, let's shoot. Tire you out a little.

WILLY, *hesitantly:* All right. You got cards?

CHARLEY, *taking a deck from his pocket:* Yeah, I got them. Some place. What is it with those vitamins?

WILLY, *dealing:* They build up your bones. Chemistry.

CHARLEY: Yeah, but there's no bones in a heartburn.

WILLY: What are you talkin' about? Do you know the first thing about it?

CHARLEY: Don't get insulted.

WILLY: Don't talk about something you don't know anything about.

They are playing. Pause.

CHARLEY: What're you doin' home?

WILLY: A little trouble with the car.

CHARLEY: Oh. *Pause.* I'd like to take a trip to California.

WILLY: Don't say.

CHARLEY: You want a job?

WILLY: I got a job, I told you that. *After a slight pause:* What the hell are you offering me a job for?

CHARLEY: Don't get insulted.

WILLY: Don't insult me.

CHARLEY: I don't see no sense in it. You don't have to go on this way.

WILLY: I got a good job. *Slight pause.* What do you keep comin' in here for?

CHARLEY: You want me to go?

WILLY, *after a pause, withering:* I can't understand it. He's going back to Texas again. What the hell is that?

CHARLEY: Let him go.

WILLY: I got nothin' to give him, Charley, I'm clean, I'm clean.

CHARLEY: He won't starve. None a them starve. Forget about him.

WILLY: Then what have I got to remember?

CHARLEY: You take it too hard. To hell with it. When a deposit bottle is broken you don't get your nickel back.

WILLY: That's easy enough for you to say.

CHARLEY: That ain't easy for me to say.

WILLY: Did you see the ceiling I put up in the living room?

CHARLEY: Yeah, that's a piece of work. To put up a ceiling is a mystery to me. How do you do it?

WILLY: What's the difference?

CHARLEY: Well, talk about it.

WILLY: You gonna put up a ceiling?

CHARLEY: How could I put up a ceiling?

WILLY: Then what the hell are you bothering me for?

CHARLEY: You're insulted again.

WILLY: A man who can't handle tools is not a man. You're disgusting.

CHARLEY: Don't call me disgusting, Willy.

Uncle Ben, carrying a valise and an umbrella, enters the forestage from around the right corner of the house. He is a stolid man, in his sixties, with a mustache and an authoritative air. He is utterly certain of his destiny, and there is an aura of far places about him. He enters exactly as Willy speaks.

WILLY: I'm getting awfully tired, Ben.

Ben's music is heard. Ben looks around at everything.

CHARLEY: Good, keep playing; you'll sleep better. Did you call me Ben?

Ben looks at his watch.

WILLY: That's funny. For a second there you reminded me of my brother Ben.

BEN: I only have a few minutes. *He strolls, inspecting the place. Willy and Charley continue playing.*

CHARLEY: You never heard from him again, heh? Since that time?

WILLY: Didn't Linda tell you? Couple of weeks ago we got a letter from his wife in Africa. He died.

CHARLEY: That so.

BEN, *chuckling:* So this is Brooklyn, eh?

CHARLEY: Maybe you're in for some of his money.

WILLY: Naa, he had seven sons. There's just one opportunity I had with that man . . .

BEN: I must make a train, William. There are several properties I'm looking at in Alaska.

WILLY: Sure, sure! If I'd gone with him to Alaska that time, everything would've been totally different.

CHARLEY: Go on, you'd froze to death up there.

WILLY: What're you talking about?

BEN: Opportunity is tremendous in Alaska, William. Surprised you're not up there.

WILLY: Sure, tremendous.

CHARLEY: Heh?

WILLY: There was the only man I ever met who knew the answers.

CHARLEY: Who?

BEN: How are you all?

WILLY, *taking a pot, smiling:* Fine, fine.

CHARLEY: Pretty sharp tonight.

BEN: Is Mother living with you?

WILLY: No, she died a long time ago.

CHARLEY: Who?

BEN: That's too bad. Fine specimen of a lady, Mother.

WILLY, *to Charley:* Heh?

BEN: I'd hoped to see the old girl.

CHARLEY: Who died?

BEN: Heard anything from Father, have you?

WILLY, *unnerved:* What do you mean, who died?

CHARLEY, *taking a pot:* What're you talkin' about?

BEN, *looking at his watch:* William, it's half-past eight!

WILLY—*as though to dispel his confusion he angrily stops Charley's hand:* That's my build!

CHARLEY: I put the ace—

WILLY: If you don't know how to play the game I'm not gonna throw my money away on you!

CHARLEY, *rising:* It was my ace, for God's sake!

WILLY: I'm through, I'm through!

BEN: When did Mother die?

WILLY: Long ago. Since the beginning you never knew how to play cards.

CHARLEY, *picks up the cards and goes to the door:* All right! Next time I'll bring a deck with five aces.

WILLY: I don't play that kind of game!

CHARLEY, *turning to him:* You ought to be ashamed of yourself!

WILLY: Yeah?

CHARLEY: Yeah! *He goes out.*

WILLY, *slamming the door after him:* Ignoramus!

BEN, *as Willy comes toward him through the wall-line of the kitchen:* So you're William.

WILLY, *shaking Ben's hand:* Ben! I've been waiting for you so long! What's the answer? How did you do it?

BEN: Oh, there's a story in that.

Linda enters the forestage, as of old, carrying the wash basket.

LINDA: Is this Ben?

BEN, *gallantly:* How do you do, my dear.

LINDA: Where've you been all these years? Willy's always wondered why you—

WILLY, *pulling Ben away from her impatiently:* Where is Dad? Didn't you follow him? How did you get started?

BEN: Well, I don't know how much you remember.

WILLY: Well, I was just a baby, of course, only three or four years old—

BEN: Three years and eleven months.

WILLY: What a memory, Ben!

BEN: I have many enterprises, William, and I have never kept books.

WILLY: I remember I was sitting under the wagon in—was it Nebraska?

BEN: It was South Dakota, and I gave you a bunch of wild flowers.

WILLY: I remember you walking away down some open road.

BEN, *laughing:* I was going to find Father in Alaska.

WILLY: Where is he?

BEN: At that age I had a very faulty view of geography, William. I discovered after a few days that I was heading due south, so instead of Alaska, I ended up in Africa.

LINDA: Africa!

WILLY: The Gold Coast!

BEN: Principally diamond mines.

LINDA: Diamond mines!

BEN: Yes, my dear. But I've only a few minutes—

WILLY: No! Boys! Boys! *Young Biff and Happy appear.* Listen to this. This is your Uncle Ben, a great man! Tell my boys, Ben!

BEN: Why, boys, when I was seventeen I walked into the jungle, and when I was twenty-one I walked out. *He laughs.* And by God I was rich.

WILLY, *to the boys:* You see what I been talking about? The greatest things can happen!

BEN, *glancing at his watch:* I have an appointment in Ketchikan Tuesday week.

WILLY: No, Ben! Please tell about Dad. I want my boys to hear. I want them to know the kind of stock they spring from. All I remember is a man with a big beard, and I was in Mamma's lap, sitting around a fire, and some kind of high music.

BEN: His flute. He played the flute.

WILLY: Sure, the flute, that's right!

New music is heard, a high, rollicking tune.

BEN: Father was a very great and a very wild-hearted man. We would start in Boston, and he'd toss the whole family into the wagon, and then he'd drive the team right across the country; through Ohio, and Indiana, Michigan, Illinois, and all the Western states. And we'd stop in the towns and sell the flutes that he'd made on the way. Great inventor, Father. With one gadget he made more in a week than a man like you could make in a lifetime.

WILLY: That's just the way I'm bringing them up, Ben—rugged, well liked, all-around.

BEN: Yeah? *To Biff:* Hit that, boy—hard as you can. *He pounds his stomach.*

BIFF: Oh, no, sir!

BEN, *taking boxing stance:* Come on, get to me! *He laughs.*

WILLY: Go to it, Biff! Go ahead, show him!

BIFF: Okay! *He cocks his fists and starts in.*

LINDA, *to Willy:* Why must he fight, dear?

BEN, *sparing with Biff:* Good boy! Good boy!

WILLY: How's that, Ben, heh?

HAPPY: Give him the left, Biff!

LINDA: Why are you fighting?

BEN: Good boy! *Suddenly he comes in, trips Biff, and stands over him, the point of his umbrella poised over Biff's eye.*

LINDA: Look out, Biff!

BIFF: Gee!

BEN, *patting Biff's knee:* Never fight fair with a stranger, boy. You'll never get out of the jungle that way. *Taking Linda's hand and bowing:* It was an honor and a pleasure to meet you, Linda.

LINDA, *withdrawing her hand coldly, frightened:* Have a nice—trip.

BEN, *to Willy:* And good luck with your—what do you do?

WILLY: Selling.

BEN: Yes. Well . . . *He raises his hand in farewell to all.*

WILLY: No, Ben, I don't want you to think . . . *He takes Ben's arm to show him.* It's Brooklyn, I know, but we hunt too.

BEN: Really, now.

WILLY: Oh, sure, there's snakes and rabbits and—that's why I moved out here. Why, Biff can fell any one of these trees in no time! Boys! Go right over to where they're building the apartment house and get some sand. We're gonna rebuild the entire front stoop right now! Watch this, Ben!

BIFF: Yes, sir! On the double, Hap!

HAPPY, *as he and Biff run off:* I lost weight, Pop, you notice?

Charley enters in knickers, even before the boys are gone.

CHARLEY: Listen, if they steal any more from that building the watchman'll put the cops on them!

LINDA, *to Willy:* Don't let Biff . . .

Ben laughs lustily.

WILLY: You shoulda seen the lumber they brought home last week. At least a dozen six-by-tens worth all kinds of money.

CHARLEY: Listen, if that watchman—

WILLY: I gave them hell, understand. But I got a couple of fearless characters there.

CHARLEY: Willy, the jails are full of fearless characters.

BEN, *clapping Willy on the back, with a laugh at Charley:* And the stock exchange, friend!

WILLY, *joining in Ben's laughter:* Where are the rest of your pants?

CHARLEY: My wife bought them.

WILLY: Now all you need is a golf club and you can go upstairs and go to sleep. *To Ben:* Great athlete! Between him and his son Bernard they can't hammer a nail!

BERNARD, *rushing in:* The watchman's chasing Biff!

WILLY, *angrily:* Shut up! He's not stealing anything!

LINDA, *alarmed, hurrying off left:* Where is he? Biff, dear! *She exits.*

WILLY, *moving toward the left, away from Ben:* There's nothing wrong. What's the matter with you?

BEN: Nervy boy. Good!

WILLY, *laughing:* Oh, nerves of iron, that Biff!

CHARLEY: Don't know what it is. My New England man comes back and he's bleedin', they murdered him up there.

WILLY: It's contacts, Charley, I got important contacts!

CHARLEY, *sarcastically:* Glad to hear it, Willy. Come in later, we'll shoot a little casino. I'll take some of your Portland money. *He laughs at Willy and exits.*

WILLY, *turning to Ben:* Business is bad, it's murderous. But not for me, of course.

BEN: I'll stop by on my way back to Africa.

WILLY, *longingly:* Can't you stay a few days? You're just what I need, Ben, because I—I have a fine position here, but I—well, Dad left when I was such a baby and I never had a chance to talk to him and I still feel—kind of temporary about myself.

BEN: I'll be late for my train.

They are at opposite ends of the stage.

WILLY: Ben, my boys—can't we talk? They'd go into the jaws of hell for me, see, but I—

BEN: William, you're being first-rate with your boys. Outstanding, manly chaps!

WILLY, *hanging on to his words:* Oh, Ben, that's good to hear! Because sometimes I'm afraid that I'm not teaching them the right kind of— Ben, how should I teach them?

BEN, *giving great weight to each word, and with a certain vicious audacity:* William, when I walked into the jungle, I was seventeen. When I walked out I was twenty-one. And, by God, I was rich! *He goes off into darkness around the right corner of the house.*

WILLY: . . . was rich! That's just the spirit I want to imbue them with! To walk into a jungle! I was right! I was right! I was right!

Ben is gone, but Willy is still speaking to him as Linda, in nightgown and robe, enters the kitchen, glances around for Willy, then goes to the door of the house, looks out and sees him. Comes down to his left. He looks at her.

LINDA: Willy, dear? Willy?

WILLY: I was right!

LINDA: Did you have some cheese? *He can't answer.* It's very late, darling. Come to bed, heh?

WILLY, *looking straight up:* Gotta break your neck to see a star in this yard.

LINDA: You coming in?

WILLY: Whatever happened to that diamond watch fob? Remember? When Ben came from Africa that time? Didn't he give me a watch fob with a diamond in it?

LINDA: You pawned it, dear. Twelve, thirteen years ago. For Biff's radio correspondence course.

WILLY: Gee, that was a beautiful thing. I'll take a walk.

LINDA: But you're in your slippers.

WILLY, *starting to go around the house at the left:* I was right! I was! *Half to Linda, as he goes, shaking his head:* What a man! There was a man worth talking to. I was right!

LINDA, *calling after Willy:* But in your slippers, Willy!

Willy is almost gone when Biff, in his pajamas, comes down the stairs and enters the kitchen.

BIFF: What is he doing out there?

LINDA: Sh!

BIFF: God Almighty, Mom, how long has he been doing this?

LINDA: Don't, he'll hear you.

BIFF: What the hell is the matter with him?

LINDA: It'll pass by morning.

BIFF: Shouldn't we do anything?

LINDA: Oh, my dear, you should do a lot of things, but there's nothing to do, so go to sleep.

Happy comes down the stairs and sits on the steps.

HAPPY: I never heard him so loud, Mom.

LINDA: Well, come around more often; you'll hear him. *She sits down at the table and mends the lining of Willy's jacket.*

BIFF: Why didn't you ever write me about this, Mom?

LINDA: How would I write to you? For over three months you had no address.

BIFF: I was on the move. But you know I thought of you all the time. You know that, don't you, pal?

LINDA: I know, dear, I know. But he likes to have a letter. Just to know that there's still a possibility for better things.

BIFF: He's not like this all the time, is he?

LINDA: It's when you come home he's always the worst.

BIFF: When I come home?

LINDA: When you write you're coming, he's all smiles, and talks about the future, and—he's just wonderful. And then the closer you seem to come, the more shaky he gets, and then, by the time you get here, he's arguing, and he seems angry at you. I think it's just that maybe he can't bring himself to—to open up to you. Why are you so hateful to each other? Why is that?

BIFF, *evasively:* I'm not hateful, Mom.

LINDA: But you no sooner come in the door than you're fighting!

BIFF: I don't know why. I mean to change. I'm tryin', Mom, you understand?

LINDA: Are you home to stay now?

BIFF: I don't know. I want to look around, see what's doin'.

LINDA: Biff, you can't look around all your life, can you?

BIFF: I just can't take hold, Mom. I can't take hold of some kind of a life.

LINDA: Biff, a man is not a bird, to come and go with the springtime.

BIFF: Your hair . . . *He touches her hair.* Your hair got so gray.

LINDA: Oh, it's been gray since you were in high school. I just stopped dyeing it, that's all.

BIFF: Dye it again, will ya? I don't want my pal looking old. *He smiles.*

LINDA: You're such a boy! You think you can go away for a year and . . . You've got to get it into your head now that one day you'll knock on this door and there'll be strange people here—

BIFF: What are you talking about? You're not even sixty, Mom.

LINDA: But what about your father?

BIFF, *lamely:* Well, I meant him too.

HAPPY: He admires Pop.

LINDA: Biff, dear, if you don't have any feeling for him, then you can't have any feeling for me.

BIFF: Sure I can, Mom.

LINDA: No. You can't just come to see me, because I love him. *With a threat, but only a threat, of tears:* He's the dearest man in the world to me, and I won't have anyone making him feel unwanted and low and blue. You've got to make up your mind now, darling, there's no leeway any more. Either he's your father and you pay him that respect, or else you're not to come here. I know he's not easy to get along with— nobody knows that better than me—but . . .

WILLY, *from the left, with a laugh:* Hey, hey, Biffo!

BIFF, *starting to go out after Willy:* What the hell is the matter with him? *Happy stops him.*

LINDA: Don't—don't go near him!

BIFF: Stop making excuses for him! He always, always wiped the floor with you. Never had an ounce of respect for you.

HAPPY: He's always had respect for—

BIFF: What the hell do you know about it?

HAPPY, *surlily:* Just don't call him crazy!

BIFF: He's got no character—Charley wouldn't do this. Not in his own house—spewing out that vomit from his mind.

HAPPY: Charley never had to cope with what he's got to.

BIFF: People are worse off than Willy Loman. Believe me, I've seen them!

LINDA: Then make Charley your father, Biff. You can't do that, can you? I don't say he's a great man. Willy Loman never made a lot of money. His name was never in the paper. He's not the finest character that ever lived. But he's a human being, and a terrible thing is happening to him. So attention must be paid. He's not to be allowed to fall into his grave like an old dog. Attention, attention must be finally paid to such a person. You called him crazy—

BIFF: I didn't mean—

LINDA: No, a lot of people think he's lost his—balance. But you don't have to be very smart to know what his trouble is. The man is exhausted.

HAPPY: Sure!

LINDA: A small man can be just as exhausted as a great man. He works for a company thirty-six years this March, opens up unheard-of territories to their trademark, and now in his old age they take his salary away.

HAPPY, *indignantly:* I didn't know that, Mom.

LINDA: You never asked, my dear! Now that you get your spending money someplace else you don't trouble your mind with him.

HAPPY: But I gave you money last—

LINDA: Christmas time, fifty dollars! To fix the hot water it cost ninety-seven fifty! For five weeks he's been on straight commission, like a beginner, an unknown!

BIFF: Those ungrateful bastards!

LINDA: Are they any worse than his sons? When he brought them business, when he was young, they were glad to see him. But now his old friends, the old buyers that loved him so and always found some order to hand him in a pinch—they're all dead, retired. He used to be able to make six, seven calls a day in Boston. Now he takes his valises out of the car and puts them back and takes them out again and he's exhausted. Instead of walking he talks now. He drives seven hundred miles, and when he gets there no one knows him any more, no one welcomes him. And what goes through a man's mind, driving seven hundred miles home without having earned a cent? Why shouldn't he talk to himself? Why? When he has to go to Charley and borrow fifty dollars a week and pretend to me that it's his pay? How long can that go on? How long? You see what I'm sitting here and waiting for? And you tell me he has no character? The man who never worked a day but for your benefit? When does he get the medal for that? Is this his reward—to turn around at the age of sixty-three and find his sons, who he loved better than his life, one a philandering bum—

HAPPY: Mom!

LINDA: That's all you are, my baby! *To Biff:* And you! What happened to the love you had for him? You were such pals! How you used to talk to him on the phone every night! How lonely he was till he could come home to you!

BIFF: All right, Mom. I'll live here in my room, and I'll get a job. I'll keep away from him, that's all.

LINDA: No, Biff. You can't stay here and fight all the time.

BIFF: He threw me out of this house, remember that.

LINDA: Why did he do that? I never knew why.

BIFF: Because I know he's a fake and he doesn't like anybody around who knows!

LINDA: Why a fake? In what way? What do you mean?

BIFF: Just don't lay it all at my feet. It's between me and him—that's all I have to say. I'll chip in from now on. He'll settle for half my pay check. He'll be all right. I'm going to bed. *He starts for the stairs.*

LINDA: He won't be all right.

BIFF, *turning on the stairs, furiously:* I hate this city and I'll stay here. Now what do you want?

LINDA: He's dying, Biff.

Happy turns quickly to her, shocked.

BIFF, *after a pause:* Why is he dying?

LINDA: He's been trying to kill himself.

BIFF, *with great horror:* How?

LINDA: I live from day to day.

BIFF: What're you talking about?

LINDA: Remember I wrote you that he smashed up the car again? In February?

BIFF: Well?

LINDA: The insurance inspector came. He said that they have evidence. That all these accidents in the last year—weren't—weren't—accidents.

HAPPY: How can they tell that? That's a lie.

LINDA: It seems there's a woman . . . *She takes a breath as*

{
   BIFF, *sharply but contained:* What woman?

   LINDA, *simultaneously:* . . . and this woman . . .
}

LINDA: What?

BIFF: Nothing. Go ahead.

LINDA: What did you say?

BIFF: Nothing. I just said what woman?

HAPPY: What about her?

LINDA: Well, it seems she was walking down the road and saw his car. She says that he wasn't driving fast at all, and that he didn't skid. She says he came to that little bridge, and then deliberately smashed into the railing, and it was only the shallowness of the water that saved him.

BIFF: Oh, no, he probably just fell asleep again.

LINDA: I don't think he fell asleep.

BIFF: Why not?

LINDA: Last month . . . *With great difficulty:* Oh, boys, it's so hard to say a thing like this! He's just a big stupid man to you, but I tell you there's more good in him than in many other people. *She chokes, wipes her eyes.*

I was looking for a fuse. The lights blew out, and I went down the cellar. And behind the fuse box—it happened to fall out—was a length of rubber pipe—just short.

HAPPY: No kidding?

LINDA: There's a little attachment on the end of it. I knew right away. And sure enough, on the bottom of the water heater there's a new little nipple on the gas pipe.

HAPPY, *angrily:* That—jerk.

BIFF: Did you have it taken off?

LINDA: I'm—I'm ashamed to. How can I mention it to him? Every day I go down and take away that little rubber pipe. But, when he comes home, I put it back where it was. How can I insult him that way? I don't know what to do. I live from day to day, boys. I tell you, I know every thought in his mind. It sounds so old-fashioned and silly, but I tell you he put his whole life into you and you've turned your backs on him. *She is bent over in the chair, weeping, her face in her hands.* Biff, I swear to God! Biff, his life is in your hands!

HAPPY, *to Biff:* How do you like that damned fool!

BIFF, *kissing her:* All right, pal, all right. It's all settled now. I've been remiss. I know that, Mom. But now I'll stay, and I swear to you, I'll apply myself. *Kneeling in front of her, in a fever of self-reproach:* It's just—you see, Mom, I don't fit in business. Not that I won't try. I'll try, and I'll make good.

HAPPY: Sure you will. The trouble with you in business was you never tried to please people.

BIFF: I know, I—

HAPPY: Like when you worked for Harrison's. Bob Harrison said you were tops, and then you go and do some damn fool thing like whistling whole songs in the elevator like a comedian.

BIFF, *against Happy:* So what? I like to whistle sometimes.

HAPPY: You don't raise a guy to a responsible job who whistles in the elevator!

LINDA: Well, don't argue about it now.

HAPPY: Like when you'd go off and swim in the middle of the day instead of taking the line around.

BIFF, *his resentment rising:* Well, don't you run off? You take off sometimes, don't you? On a nice summer day?

HAPPY: Yeah, but I cover myself!

LINDA: Boys!

HAPPY: If I'm going to take a fade the boss can call any number where I'm supposed to be and they'll swear to him that I just left. I'll tell you something that I hate to say, Biff, but in the business world some of them think you're crazy.

BIFF, *angered:* Screw the business world!

HAPPY: All right, screw it! Great, but cover yourself!

LINDA: Hap, Hap!

BIFF: I don't care what they think! They've laughed at Dad for years, and you know why? Because we don't belong in this nuthouse of a city! We should be mixing cement on some open plain, or—or carpenters. A carpenter is allowed to whistle!

Willy walks in from the entrance of the house, at left.

WILLY: Even your grandfather was better than a carpenter. *Pause. They watch him.* You never grew up. Bernard does not whistle in the elevator, I assure you.

BIFF, *as though to laugh Willy out of it:* Yeah, but you do, Pop.

WILLY: I never in my life whistled in an elevator! And who in the business world thinks I'm crazy?

BIFF: I didn't mean it like that, Pop. Now don't make a whole thing out of it, will ya?

WILLY: Go back to the West! Be a carpenter, a cowboy, enjoy yourself!

LINDA: Willy, he was just saying—

WILLY: I heard what he said!

HAPPY, *trying to quiet Willy:* Hey, Pop, come on now . . .

WILLY, *continuing over Happy's line:* They laugh at me, heh? Go to Filene's, go to the Hub, go to Slattery's, Boston. Call out the name Willy Loman and see what happens! Big shot!

BIFF: All right, Pop.

WILLY: Big!

BIFF: All right!

WILLY: Why do you always insult me?

BIFF: I didn't say a word. *To Linda:* Did I say a word?

LINDA: He didn't say anything, Willy.

WILLY, *going to the doorway of the living room:* All right, good night, good night.

LINDA: Willy, dear, he just decided . . .

WILLY, *to Biff:* If you get tired hanging around tomorrow, paint the ceiling I put up in the living room.

BIFF: I'm leaving early tomorrow.

HAPPY: He's going to see Bill Oliver, Pop.

WILLY, *interestedly:* Oliver? For what?

BIFF, *with reserve, but trying, trying:* He always said he'd stake me. I'd like to go into business, so maybe I can take him up on it.

LINDA: Isn't that wonderful?

WILLY: Don't interrupt. What's wonderful about it? There's fifty men in the City of New York who'd stake him. *To Biff:* Sporting goods?

BIFF: I guess so. I know something about it and—

WILLY: He knows something about it! You know sporting goods better than Spalding, for God's sake! How much is he giving you?

BIFF: I don't know, I didn't even see him yet, but—

WILLY: Then what're you talkin' about?

BIFF, *getting angry:* Well, all I said was I'm gonna see him, that's all!

WILLY, *turning away:* Ah, you're counting your chickens again.

BIFF, *starting left for the stairs:* Oh, Jesus, I'm going to sleep!

WILLY, *calling after him:* Don't curse in this house!

BIFF, *turning:* Since when did you get so clean?

HAPPY, *trying to stop them:* Wait a . . .

WILLY: Don't use that language to me! I won't have it!

HAPPY, *grabbing Biff, shouts:* Wait a minute! I got an idea. I got a feasible idea. Come here, Biff, let's talk this over now, let's talk some sense here. When I was down in Florida last time, I thought of a great idea to sell sporting goods. It just came back to me. You and I, Biff—we have a line, the Loman Line. We train a couple of weeks, and put on a couple of exhibitions, see?

WILLY: That's an idea!

HAPPY: Wait! We form two basketball teams, see? Two water-polo teams. We play each other. It's a million dollars' worth of publicity. Two brothers, see? The Loman Brothers. Displays in the Royal Palms—all the hotels. And banners over the ring and the basketball court: "Loman Brothers." Baby, we could sell sporting goods!

WILLY: That is a one-million-dollar idea!

LINDA: Marvelous!

BIFF: I'm in great shape as far as that's concerned.

HAPPY: And the beauty of it is, Biff, it wouldn't be like a business. We'd be out playin' ball again . . .

BIFF, *enthused:* Yeah, that's . . .

WILLY: Million-dollar . . .

HAPPY: And you wouldn't get fed up with it, Biff. It'd be the family again. There'd be the old honor, and comradeship, and if you wanted to go off for a swim or somethin'—well, you'd do it! Without some smart cooky gettin' up ahead of you!

WILLY: Lick the world! You guys together could absolutely lick the civilized world.

BIFF: I'll see Oliver tomorrow. Hap, if we could work that out . . .

LINDA: Maybe things are beginning to—

WILLY, *wildly enthused, to Linda:* Stop interrupting! *To Biff:* But don't wear sport jacket and slacks when you see Oliver.

BIFF: No, I'll—

WILLY: A business suit, and talk as little as possible, and don't crack any jokes.

BIFF: He did like me. Always liked me.

LINDA: He loved you!

WILLY, *to Linda:* Will you stop! *To Biff:* Walk in very serious. You are not applying for a boy's job. Money is to pass. Be quiet, fine, and serious. Everybody likes a kidder, but nobody lends him money.

HAPPY: I'll try to get some myself, Biff. I'm sure I can.

WILLY: I see great things for you kids, I think your troubles are over. But remember, start big and you'll end big. Ask for fifteen. How much you gonna ask for?

BIFF: Gee, I don't know—

WILLY: And don't say "Gee." "Gee" is a boy's word. A man walking in for fifteen thousand dollars does not say "Gee!"

BIFF: Ten, I think, would be top though.

WILLY: Don't be so modest. You always started too low. Walk in with a big laugh. Don't look worried. Start off with a couple of your good stories to lighten things up. It's not what you say, it's how you say it— because personality always wins the day.

LINDA: Oliver always thought the highest of him—

WILLY: Will you let me talk?

BIFF: Don't yell at her, Pop, will ya?

WILLY, *angrily:* I was talking, wasn't I?

BIFF: I don't like you yelling at her all the time, and I'm tellin' you, that's all.

WILLY: What're you, takin' over this house?

LINDA: Willy—

WILLY, *turning on her:* Don't take his side all the time, goddammit!

BIFF, *furiously:* Stop yelling at her!

WILLY, *suddenly pulling on his cheek, beaten down, guilt-ridden:* Give my best to Bill Oliver—he may remember me. *He exits through the living-room doorway.*

LINDA, *her voice subdued:* What'd you have to start that for? *Biff turns away.* You see how sweet he was as soon as you talked hopefully? *She goes over to Biff.* Come up and say good night to him. Don't let him go to bed that way.

HAPPY: Come on, Biff, let's buck him up.

LINDA: Please, dear. Just say good night. It takes so little to make him happy. Come. *She goes through the living-room doorway, calling upstairs from within the living room:* Your pajamas are hanging in the bathroom, Willy!

HAPPY, *looking toward where Linda went out:* What a woman! They broke the mold when they made her. You know that, Biff?

BIFF: He's off salary. My God, working on commission!

HAPPY: Well, let's face it: he's no hot-shot selling man. Except that sometimes, you have to admit, he's a sweet personality.

BIFF, *deciding:* Lend me ten bucks, will ya? I want to buy some new ties.

HAPPY: I'll take you to a place I know. Beautiful stuff. Wear one of my striped shirts tomorrow.

BIFF: She got gray. Mom got awful old. Gee, I'm gonna go in to Oliver tomorrow and knock him for a—

HAPPY: Come on up. Tell that to Dad. Let's give him a whirl. Come on.

BIFF, *steamed up:* You know, with ten thousand bucks, boy!

HAPPY, *as they go into the living room:* That's the talk, Biff, that's the first time I've heard the old confidence out of you! *From within the living room, fading off:* You're gonna live with me, kid, and any babe you want just say the word . . . *The last lines are hardly heard. They are mounting the stairs to their parents' bedroom.*

LINDA, *entering her bedroom and addressing Willy, who is in the bathroom. She is straightening the bed for him:* Can you do anything about the shower? It drips.

WILLY, *from the bathroom:* All of a sudden everything falls to pieces! Goddam plumbing, oughta be sued, those people. I hardly finished putting it in and the thing . . . *His words rumble off.*

LINDA: I'm just wondering if Oliver will remember him. You think he might?

WILLY, *coming out of the bathroom in his pajamas:* Remember him? What's the matter with you, you crazy? If he'd've stayed with Oliver he'd be on top by now! Wait'll Oliver gets a look at him. You don't know the average caliber any more. The average young man today—*he is getting into bed*—is got a caliber of zero. Greatest thing in the world for him was to bum around.

Biff and Happy enter the bedroom. Slight pause.

WILLY, *stops short, looking at Biff:* Glad to hear it, boy.

HAPPY: He wanted to say good night to you, sport.

WILLY, *to Biff:* Yeah. Knock him dead, boy. What'd you want to tell me?

BIFF: Just take it easy, Pop. Good night. *He turns to go.*

WILLY, *unable to resist:* And if anything falls off the desk while you're talking to him—like a package or something—don't you pick it up. They have office boys for that.

LINDA: I'll make a big breakfast—

WILLY: Will you let me finish? *To Biff:* Tell him you were in the business in the West. Not farm work.

BIFF: All right, Dad.

LINDA: I think everything—

WILLY, *going right through her speech:* And don't undersell yourself. No less than fifteen thousand dollars.

BIFF, *unable to bear him:* Okay. Good night, Mom. *He starts moving.*

WILLY: Because you got a greatness in you, Biff, remember that. You got all kinds a greatness . . . *He lies back, exhausted. Biff walks out.*

LINDA, *calling after Biff:* Sleep well, darling!

HAPPY: I'm gonna get married, Mom. I wanted to tell you.

LINDA: Go to sleep, dear.

HAPPY, *going:* I just wanted to tell you.

WILLY: Keep up the good work. *Happy exits.* God . . . remember that Ebbets Field game? The championship of the city?

LINDA: Just rest. Should I sing to you?

WILLY: Yeah. Sing to me. *Linda hums a soft lullaby.* When that team came out—he was the tallest, remember?

LINDA: Oh, yes. And in gold.

Biff enters the darkened kitchen, takes a cigarette, and leaves the house. He comes downstage into a golden pool of light. He smokes, staring at the night.

WILLY: Like a young god. Hercules—something like that. And the sun, the sun all around him. Remember how he waved to me? Right up from the field, with the representatives of three colleges standing by? And the buyers I brought, and the cheers when he came out—Loman, Loman, Loman! God Almighty, he'll be great yet. A star like that, magnificent, can never really fade away!

The light on Willy is fading. The gas heater begins to glow through the kitchen wall, near the stairs, a blue flame beneath red coils.

LINDA, *timidly:* Willy dear, what has he got against you?

WILLY: I'm so tired. Don't talk any more.

Biff slowly returns to the kitchen. He stops, stares toward the heater.

LINDA: Will you ask Howard to let you work in New York?

WILLY: First thing in the morning. Everything'll be all right.

Biff reaches behind the heater and draws out a length of rubber tubing. He is horrified and turns his head toward Willy's room, still dimly lit, from which the strains of Linda's desperate but monotonous humming rise.

WILLY, *staring through the window into the moonlight:* Gee, look at the moon moving between the buildings!

Biff wraps the tubing around his hand and quickly goes up the stairs.

Curtain

ACT TWO

Music is heard, gay and bright. The curtain rises as the music fades away. Willy, in shirt sleeves, is sitting at the kitchen table, sipping coffee, his hat in his lap. Linda is filling his cup when she can.

WILLY: Wonderful coffee. Meal in itself.

LINDA: Can I make you some eggs?

WILLY: No. Take a breath.

LINDA: You look so rested, dear.

WILLY: I slept like a dead one. First time in months. Imagine, sleeping till ten on a Tuesday morning. Boys left nice and early, heh?

LINDA: They were out of here by eight o'clock.

WILLY: Good work!

LINDA: It was so thrilling to see them leaving together. I can't get over the shaving lotion in this house!

WILLY, *smiling:* Mmm—

LINDA: Biff was very changed this morning. His whole attitude seemed to be hopeful. He couldn't wait to get downtown to see Oliver.

WILLY: He's heading for a change. There's no question, there simply are certain men that take longer to get—solidified. How did he dress?

LINDA: His blue suit. He's so handsome in that suit. He could be a—anything in that suit!

Willy gets up from the table. Linda holds his jacket for him.

WILLY: There's no question, no question at all. Gee, on the way home tonight I'd like to buy some seeds.

LINDA, *laughing:* That'd be wonderful. But not enough sun gets back there. Nothing'll grow any more.

WILLY: You wait, kid, before it's all over we're gonna get a little place out in the country, and I'll raise some vegetables, a couple of chickens . . .

LINDA: You'll do it yet, dear.

Willy walks out of his jacket. Linda follows him.

WILLY: And they'll get married, and come for a weekend. I'd build a little guest house. 'Cause I got so many fine tools, all I'd need would be a little lumber and some peace of mind.

LINDA, *joyfully:* I sewed the lining . . .

WILLY: I could build two guest houses, so they'd both come. Did he decide how much he's going to ask Oliver for?

LINDA, *getting him into the jacket:* He didn't mention it, but I imagine ten or fifteen thousand. You going to talk to Howard today?

WILLY: Yeah. I'll put it to him straight and simple. He'll just have to take me off the road.

LINDA: And Willy, don't forget to ask for a little advance, because we've got the insurance premium. It's the grace period now.

WILLY: That's a hundred . . . ?

LINDA: A hundred and eight, sixty-eight. Because we're a little short again.

WILLY: Why are we short?

LINDA: Well, you had the motor job on the car . . .

WILLY: That goddam Studebaker!

LINDA: And you got one more payment on the refrigerator . . .

WILLY: But it just broke again!

LINDA: Well, it's old, dear.

WILLY: I told you we should've bought a well-advertised machine. Charley bought a General Electric and it's twenty years old and it's still good, that son-of-a-bitch.

LINDA: But, Willy—

WILLY: Whoever heard of a Hastings refrigerator? Once in my life I would like to own something outright before it's broken! I'm always in a race with the junkyard! I just finished paying for the car and it's on its last legs. The refrigerator consumes belts like a goddam maniac. They time those things. They time them so when you finally paid for them, they're used up.

LINDA, *buttoning up his jacket as he unbuttons it:* All told, about two hundred dollars would carry us, dear. But that includes the last payment on the mortgage. After this payment, Willy, the house belongs to us.

WILLY: It's twenty-five years!

LINDA: Biff was nine years old when we bought it.

WILLY: Well, that's a great thing. To weather a twenty-five-year mortgage is—

LINDA: It's an accomplishment.

WILLY: All the cement, the lumber, the reconstruction I put in this house! There ain't a crack to be found in it any more.

LINDA: Well, it served its purpose.

WILLY: What purpose? Some stranger'll come along, move in, and that's that. If only Biff would take this house, and raise a family . . . *He starts to go.* Good-by, I'm late.

LINDA, *suddenly remembering:* Oh, I forgot! You're supposed to meet them for dinner.

WILLY: Me?

LINDA: At Frank's Chop House on Forty-eighth near Sixth Avenue.

WILLY: Is that so! How about you?

LINDA: No, just the three of you. They're gonna blow you to a big meal!

WILLY: Don't say! Who thought of that?

LINDA: Biff came to me this morning, Willy, and he said, "Tell Dad, we want to blow him to a big meal." Be there six o'clock. You and your two boys are going to have dinner.

WILLY: Gee whiz! That's really somethin'. I'm gonna knock Howard for a loop, kid. I'll get an advance, and I'll come home with a New York job. Goddammit, now I'm gonna do it!

LINDA: Oh, that's the spirit, Willy!

WILLY: I will never get behind a wheel the rest of my life!

LINDA: It's changing, Willy, I can feel it changing!

WILLY: Beyond a question. G'by, I'm late. *He starts to go again.*

LINDA, *calling after him as she runs to the kitchen table for a handkerchief:* You got your glasses?

WILLY—*he feels for them, then comes back in:* Yeah, yeah, got my glasses.

LINDA, *giving him the handkerchief:* And a handkerchief.

WILLY: Yeah, handkerchief.

LINDA: And your saccharine?

WILLY: Yeah, my saccharine.

LINDA: Be careful on the subway stairs.

She kisses him, and a silk stocking is seen hanging from her hand. Willy notices it.

WILLY: Will you stop mending stockings? At least while I'm in the house. It gets me nervous. I can't tell you. Please.

Linda hides the stocking in her hand as she follows Willy across the forestage in front of the house.

LINDA: Remember, Frank's Chop House.

WILLY, *passing the apron:* Maybe beets would grow out there.

LINDA, *laughing:* But you tried so many times.

WILLY: Yeah. Well, don't work hard today. *He disappears around the right corner of the house.*

LINDA: Be careful!

As Willy vanishes, Linda waves to him. Suddenly the phone rings. She runs across the stage and into the kitchen and lifts it.

LINDA: Hello? Oh, Biff! I'm so glad you called, I just . . . Yes, sure, I just told him. Yes, he'll be there for dinner at six o'clock, I didn't forget. Listen, I was just dying to tell you. You know that little rubber pipe I told you about? That he connected to the gas heater? I finally decided to go down the cellar this morning and take it away and destroy it. But it's gone! Imagine? He took it away himself, it isn't there! *She listens.* When? Oh, then you took it. Oh—nothing, it's just that I'd hoped he'd taken it away himself. Oh, I'm not worried, darling, because this morning he left in such high spirits, it was like the old days! I'm not afraid any more. Did Mr. Oliver see you? . . . Well, you wait there then. And make a nice impression on him, darling. Just don't perspire too much before you see him. And have a nice time with Dad. He may have big news too! . . . That's right, a New York job. And be sweet to him tonight, dear. Be loving to him. Because he's only a little boat looking for a harbor. *She is trembling with sorrow and joy.* Oh, that's wonderful, Biff, you'll save his life. Thanks, darling. Just put your arm around him when he comes into the restaurant. Give him a smile. That's the boy . . . Good-by, dear. . . . You got your comb? . . . That's fine. Good-by, Biff dear.

In the middle of her speech, Howard Wagner, thirty-six, wheels on a small typewriter table on which is a wire-recording machine and proceeds to plug it in. This is on the left forestage. Light slowly fades on Linda as it rises on Howard. Howard is intent on threading the machine and only glances over his shoulder as Willy appears.

WILLY: Pst! Pst!

HOWARD: Hello, Willy, come in.

WILLY: Like to have a little talk with you, Howard.

HOWARD: Sorry to keep you waiting. I'll be with you in a minute.

WILLY: What's that, Howard?

HOWARD: Didn't you ever see one of these? Wire recorder.

WILLY: Oh. Can we talk a minute?

HOWARD: Records things. Just got delivery yesterday. Been driving me crazy, the most terrific machine I ever saw in my life. I was up all night with it.

WILLY: What do you do with it?

HOWARD: I bought it for dictation, but you can do anything with it. Listen to this. I had it home last night. Listen to what I picked up. The first one is my daughter. Get this. *He flicks the switch and "Roll out the Barrel" is heard being whistled.* Listen to that kid whistle.

WILLY: That is lifelike, isn't it?

HOWARD: Seven years old. Get that tone.

WILLY: Ts, ts. Like to ask a little favor if you . . .

The whistling breaks off, and the voice of Howard's daughter is heard.

HIS DAUGHTER: "Now you, Daddy."

HOWARD: She's crazy for me! *Again the same song is whistled.* That's me! Ha! *He winks.*

WILLY: You're very good!

The whistling breaks off again. The machine runs silent for a moment.

HOWARD: Sh! Get this now, this is my son.

HIS SON: "The capital of Alabama is Montgomery; the capital of Arizona is Phoenix; the capital of Arkansas is Little Rock; the capital of California is Sacramento . . ." *and on, and on.*

HOWARD, *holding up five fingers:* Five years old, Willy!

WILLY: He'll make an announcer some day!

HIS SON, *continuing:* "The capital . . ."

HOWARD: Get that—alphabetical order! *The machine breaks off suddenly.* Wait a minute. The maid kicked the plug out.

WILLY: It certainly is a—

HOWARD: Sh, for God's sake!

HIS SON: "It's nine o'clock, Bulova watch time. So I have to go to sleep."

WILLY: That really is—

HOWARD: Wait a minute! The next is my wife.

They wait.

HOWARD'S VOICE: "Go on, say something." *Pause.* "Well, you gonna talk?"

HIS WIFE: "I can't think of anything."

HOWARD'S VOICE: "Well, talk—it's turning."

HIS WIFE, *shyly, beaten:* "Hello." *Silence.* "Oh, Howard, I can't talk into this . . ."

HOWARD, *snapping the machine off:* That was my wife.

WILLY: That is a wonderful machine. Can we—

HOWARD: I tell you, Willy, I'm gonna take my camera, and my band-saw, and all my hobbies, and out they go. This is the most fascinating relaxation I ever found.

WILLY: I think I'll get one myself.

HOWARD: Sure, they're only a hundred and a half. You can't do without it. Supposing you wanna hear Jack Benny, see? But you can't be at home at that hour. So you tell the maid to turn the radio on when Jack Benny comes on, and this automatically goes on with the radio . . .

WILLY: And when you come home you . . .

HOWARD: You can come home twelve o'clock, one o'clock, any time you like, and you get yourself a Coke and sit yourself down, throw the switch, and there's Jack Benny's program in the middle of the night!

WILLY: I'm definitely going to get one. Because lots of time I'm on the road, and I think to myself, what I must be missing on the radio!

HOWARD: Don't you have a radio in the car?

WILLY: Well, yeah, but who ever thinks of turning it on?

HOWARD: Say, aren't you supposed to be in Boston?

WILLY: That's what I want to talk to you about, Howard. You got a minute? *He draws a chair in from the wing.*

HOWARD: What happened? What're you doing here?

WILLY: Well . . .

HOWARD: You didn't crack up again, did you?

WILLY: Oh, no. No . . .

HOWARD: Geez, you had me worried there for a minute. What's the trouble?

WILLY: Well, tell you the truth, Howard. I've come to the decision that I'd rather not travel any more.

HOWARD: Not travel! Well, what'll you do?

WILLY: Remember, Christmas time, when you had the party here? You said you'd try to think of some spot for me here in town.

HOWARD: With us?

WILLY: Well, sure.

HOWARD: Oh, yeah, yeah. I remember. Well, I couldn't think of anything for you, Willy.

WILLY: I tell ya, Howard. The kids are all grown up, y'know. I don't need much any more. If I could take home—well, sixty-five dollars a week, I could swing it.

HOWARD: Yeah, but Willy, see I—

WILLY: I tell ya why, Howard. Speaking frankly and between the two of us, y'know—I'm just a little tired.

HOWARD: Oh, I could understand that, Willy. But you're a road man, Willy, and we do a road business. We've only got a half-dozen salesmen on the floor here.

WILLY: God knows, Howard, I never asked a favor of any man. But I was with the firm when your father used to carry you in here in his arms.

HOWARD: I know that, Willy, but—

WILLY: Your father came to me the day you were born and asked me what I thought of the name of Howard, may he rest in peace.

HOWARD: I appreciate that, Willy, but there just is no spot here for you. If I had a spot I'd slam you right in, but I just don't have a single solitary spot.

He looks for his lighter. Willy has picked it up and gives it to him. Pause.

WILLY, *with increasing anger:* Howard, all I need to set my table is fifty dollars a week.

HOWARD: But where am I going to put you, kid?

WILLY: Look, it isn't a question of whether I can sell merchandise, is it?

HOWARD: No, but it's a business, kid, and everybody's gotta pull his own weight.

WILLY, *desperately:* Just let me tell you a story, Howard—

HOWARD: 'Cause you gotta admit, business is business.

WILLY, *angrily:* Business is definitely business, but just listen for a minute. You don't understand this. When I was a boy—eighteen, nineteen—I was already on the road. And there was a question in my mind as to whether selling had a future for me. Because in those days I had a yearning to go to Alaska. See, there were three gold strikes in one month in Alaska, and I felt like going out. Just for the ride, you might say.

HOWARD, *barely interested:* Don't say.

WILLY: Oh, yeah, my father lived many years in Alaska. He was an adventurous man. We've got quite a little streak of self-reliance in our family. I thought I'd go out with my older brother and try to locate him, and maybe settle in the North with the old man. And I was almost decided to go, when I met a salesman in the Parker House. His name was Dave Singleman. And he was eighty-four years old, and he'd drummed merchandise in thirty-one states. And old Dave, he'd go up to his room, y'understand, put on his green velvet slippers—I'll never forget—and pick up his phone and call the buyers, and without ever leaving his room, at the age of eighty-four, he made his living. And when I saw that, I realized that selling was the greatest career a man could want. 'Cause what could be more satisfying than to be able to go, at the age of eighty-four, into twenty or thirty different cities, and pick up a phone, and be remembered and loved and helped by so many different people? Do you know? when he died—and by the way he died the death of a salesman, in his green velvet slippers in the smoker of the New York, New Haven and Hartford, going into Boston—when he died, hundreds of salesmen and buyers were at his funeral. Things were sad on a lotta trains for months after that. *He stands up. Howard has not looked at him.* In those days there was personality in it, Howard. There was respect, and comradeship, and gratitude in it. Today, it's all cut and dried, and there's no chance for bringing friendship to bear—or personality. You see what I mean? They don't know me any more.

HOWARD, *moving away, to the right:* That's just the thing, Willy.

WILLY: If I had forty dollars a week—that's all I'd need. Forty dollars, Howard.

HOWARD: Kid, I can't take blood from a stone, I—

WILLY, *desperation is on him now:* Howard, the year Al Smith was nominated, your father came to me and—

HOWARD, *starting to go off:* I've got to see some people, kid.

WILLY, *stopping him:* I'm talking about your father! There were promises made across this desk! You mustn't tell me you've got people to see— I put thirty-six years into this firm, Howard, and now I can't pay my insurance! You can't eat the orange and throw the peel away—a man is not a piece of fruit! *After a pause:* Now pay attention. Your father— in 1928 I had a big year. I averaged a hundred and seventy dollars a week in commissions.

HOWARD, *impatiently:* Now, Willy, you never averaged—

WILLY, *banging his hand on the desk:* I averaged a hundred and seventy dollars a week in the year of 1928! And your father came to me—or rather, I was in the office here—it was right over this desk—and he put his hand on my shoulder—

HOWARD, *getting up:* You'll have to excuse me, Willy, I gotta see some people. Pull yourself together. *Going out:* I'll be back in a little while.

On Howard's exit, the light on his chair grows very bright and strange.

WILLY: Pull myself together! What the hell did I say to him? My God, I was yelling at him! How could I! *Willy breaks off, staring at the light, which occupies the chair, animating it. He approaches this chair, standing across the desk from it.* Frank, Frank, don't you remember what you told me that time? How you put your hand on my shoulder, and Frank . . . *He leans on the desk and as he speaks the dead man's name he accidentally switches on the recorder, and instantly*

HOWARD'S SON: ". . . of New York is Albany. The capital of Ohio is Cincinnati, the capital of Rhode Island is . . ." *The recitation continues.*

WILLY, *leaping away with fright, shouting:* Ha! Howard! Howard! Howard!

HOWARD, *rushing in:* What happened?

WILLY, *pointing at the machine, which continues nasally, childishly, with the capital cities:* Shut it off! Shut it off!

HOWARD, *pulling the plug out:* Look, Willy . . .

WILLY, *pressing his hands to his eyes:* I gotta get myself some coffee. I'll get some coffee . . .

Willy starts to walk out. Howard stops him.

HOWARD, *rolling up the cord:* Willy, look . . .

WILLY: I'll go to Boston.

HOWARD: Willy, you can't go to Boston for us.

WILLY: Why can't I go?

HOWARD: I don't want you to represent us. I've been meaning to tell you for a long time now.

WILLY: Howard, are you firing me?

HOWARD: I think you need a good long rest, Willy.

WILLY: Howard—

HOWARD: And when you feel better, come back, and we'll see if we can work something out.

WILLY: But I gotta earn money, Howard. I'm in no position to—

HOWARD: Where are your sons? Why don't your sons give you a hand?

WILLY: They're working on a very big deal.

HOWARD: This is no time for false pride, Willy. You go to your sons and you tell them that you're tired. You've got two great boys, haven't you?

WILLY: Oh, no question, no question, but in the meantime . . .

HOWARD: Then that's that, heh?

WILLY: All right, I'll go to Boston tomorrow.

HOWARD: No, no.

WILLY: I can't throw myself on my sons. I'm not a cripple!

HOWARD: Look, kid, I'm busy this morning.

WILLY, *grasping Howard's arm:* Howard, you've got to let me go to Boston!

HOWARD, *hard, keeping himself under control:* I've got a line of people to see this morning. Sit down, take five minutes, and pull yourself together, and then go home, will ya? I need the office, Willy. *He starts to go; turns, remembering the recorder, starts to push off the table holding the recorder.* Oh, yeah. Whenever you can this week, stop by and drop off the samples. You'll feel better, Willy, and then come back and we'll talk. Pull yourself together, kid, there's people outside.

Howard exits, pushing the table off left. Willy stares into space, exhausted. Now the music is heard—Ben's music—first distantly, then closer, closer. As Willy speaks, Ben enters from the right. He carries valise and umbrella.

WILLY: Oh, Ben, how did you do it? What is the answer? Did you wind up the Alaska deal already?

BEN: Doesn't take much time if you know what you're doing. Just a short business trip. Boarding ship in an hour. Wanted to say good-by.

WILLY: Ben, I've got to talk to you.

BEN, *glancing at his watch:* Haven't the time, William.

WILLY, *crossing the apron to Ben:* Ben, nothing's working out. I don't know what to do.

BEN: Now, look here, William. I've bought timberland in Alaska and I need a man to look after things for me.

WILLY: God, timberland! Me and my boys in those grand outdoors!

BEN: You've a new continent at your doorstep, William. Get out of these cities, they're full of talk and time payments and courts of law. Screw on your fists and you can fight for a fortune up there.

WILLY: Yes, yes! Linda, Linda!

Linda enters as of old, with the wash.

LINDA: Oh, you're back?

BEN: I haven't much time.

WILLY: No, wait! Linda, he's got a proposition for me in Alaska.

LINDA: But you've got— *To Ben:* He's got a beautiful job here.

WILLY: But in Alaska, kid, I could—

LINDA: You're doing well enough, Willy!

BEN, *to Linda:* Enough for what, my dear?

LINDA, *frightened of Ben and angry at him:* Don't say those things to him! Enough to be happy right here, right now. *To Willy, while Ben laughs:* Why must everybody conquer the world? You're well liked, and the boys love you, and someday—*to Ben*—why, old man Wagner told him just the other day that if he keeps it up he'll be a member of the firm, didn't he, Willy?

WILLY: Sure, sure. I am building something with this firm, Ben, and if a man is building something he must be on the right track, mustn't he?

BEN: What are you building? Lay your hand on it. Where is it?

WILLY, *hesitantly:* That's true, Linda, there's nothing.

LINDA: Why? *To Ben:* There's a man eighty-four years old—

WILLY: That's right, Ben, that's right. When I look at that man I say, what is there to worry about?

BEN: Bah!

WILLY: It's true, Ben. All he has to do is go into any city, pick up the phone, and he's making his living and you know why?

BEN, *picking up his valise:* I've got to go.

WILLY, *holding Ben back:* Look at this boy!

Biff, in his high school sweater, enters carrying suitcase. Happy carries Biff's shoulder guards, gold helmet, and football pants.

WILLY: Without a penny to his name, three great universities are begging for him, and from there the sky's the limit, because it's not what you do, Ben. It's who you know and the smile on your face! It's contacts, Ben, contacts! The whole wealth of Alaska passes over the lunch table at the Commodore Hotel, and that's the wonder, the wonder of this country, that a man can end with diamonds here on the basis of being liked! *He turns to Biff.* And that's why when you get out on that field today it's important. Because thousands of people will be rooting for you and loving you. *To Ben, who has again begun to leave:* And Ben! when he walks into a business office his name will sound out like a bell and all the doors will open to him! I've seen it, Ben, I've seen it a thousand times! You can't feel it with your hand like timber, but it's there!

BEN: Good-by, William.

WILLY: Ben, am I right? Don't you think I'm right? I value your advice.

BEN: There's a new continent at your doorstep, William. You could walk out rich. Rich! *He is gone.*

WILLY: We'll do it here, Ben! You hear me? We're gonna do it here!

Young Bernard rushes in. The gay music of the Boys is heard.

BERNARD: Oh, gee, I was afraid you left already!

WILLY: Why? What time is it?

BERNARD: It's half-past one!

WILLY: Well, come on, everybody! Ebbets Field next stop! Where's the pennants? *He rushes through the wall-line of the kitchen and out into the living room.*

LINDA, *to Biff:* Did you pack fresh underwear?

BIFF, *who has been limbering up:* I want to go!

BERNARD: Biff, I'm carrying your helmet, ain't I?

HAPPY: No, I'm carrying the helmet.

BERNARD: Oh, Biff, you promised me.

HAPPY: I'm carrying the helmet.

BERNARD: How am I going to get in the locker room?

LINDA: Let him carry the shoulder guards. *She puts her coat and hat on in the kitchen.*

BERNARD: Can I, Biff? 'Cause I told everybody I'm going to be in the locker room.

HAPPY: In Ebbets Field it's the clubhouse.

BERNARD: I meant the clubhouse. Biff!

HAPPY: Biff!

BIFF, *grandly, after a slight pause:* Let him carry the shoulder guards.

HAPPY, *as he gives Bernard the shoulder guards:* Stay close to us now.

Willy rushes in with the pennants.

WILLY, *handing them out:* Everybody wave when Biff comes out on the field. *Happy and Bernard run off.* You set now, boy?

The music has died away.

BIFF: Ready to go, Pop. Every muscle is ready.

WILLY, *at the edge of the apron:* You realize what this means?

BIFF: That's right, Pop.

WILLY, *feeling Biff's muscles:* You're comin' home this afternoon captain of the All-Scholastic Championship Team of the City of New York.

BIFF: I got it, Pop. And remember, pal, when I take off my helmet, that touchdown is for you.

WILLY: Let's go! *He is starting out, with his arms around Biff, when Charley enters, as of old, in knickers.* I got no room for you, Charley.

CHARLEY: Room? For what?

WILLY: In the car.

CHARLEY: You goin' for a ride? I wanted to shoot some casino.

WILLY, *furiously:* Casino! *Incredulously:* Don't you realize what today is?

LINDA: Oh, he knows, Willy. He's just kidding you.

WILLY: That's nothing to kid about!

CHARLEY: No, Linda, what's goin' on?

LINDA: He's playing in Ebbets Field.

CHARLEY: Baseball in this weather?

WILLY: Don't talk to him. Come on, come on! *He is pushing them out.*

CHARLEY: Wait a minute, didn't you hear the news?

WILLY: What?

CHARLEY: Don't you listen to the radio? Ebbets Field just blew up.

WILLY: You go to hell! *Charley laughs. Pushing them out:* Come on, come on! We're late.

CHARLEY, *as they go:* Knock a homer, Biff, knock a homer!

WILLY, *the last to leave, turning to Charley:* I don't think that was funny, Charley. This is the greatest day of his life.

CHARLEY: Willy, when are you going to grow up?

WILLY: Yeah, heh? When this game is over, Charley, you'll be laughing out of the other side of your face. They'll be calling him another Red Grange. Twenty-five thousand a year.

CHARLEY, *kidding:* Is that so?

WILLY: Yeah, that's so.

CHARLEY: Well, then, I'm sorry, Willy. But tell me something.

WILLY: What?

CHARLEY: Who is Red Grange?

WILLY: Put up your hands. Goddam you, put up your hands!

Charley, chuckling, shakes his head and walks away, around the left corner of the stage. Willy follows him. The music rises to a mocking frenzy.

WILLY: Who the hell do you think you are, better than everybody else? You don't know everything, you big, ignorant, stupid . . . Put up your hands!

Light rises, on the right side of the forestage, on a small table in the reception room of Charley's office. Traffic sounds are heard. Bernard, now mature, sits whistling to himself. A pair of tennis rackets and an overnight bag are on the floor beside him.

WILLY, *offstage:* What are you walking away for? Don't walk away! If you're going to say something say it to my face! I know you laugh at me behind my back. You'll laugh out of the other side of your goddam face after this game. Touchdown! Touchdown! Eighty thousand people! Touchdown! Right between the goal posts.

Bernard is a quiet, earnest, but self-assured young man. Willy's voice is coming from right upstage now. Bernard lowers his feet off the table and listens. Jenny, his father's secretary, enters.

JENNY, *distressed:* Say, Bernard, will you go out in the hall?

BERNARD: What is that noise? Who is it?

JENNY: Mr. Loman. He just got off the elevator.

BERNARD, *getting up:* Who's he arguing with?

JENNY: Nobody. There's nobody with him. I can't deal with him any more, and your father gets all upset everytime he comes. I've got a lot of typing to do, and your father's waiting to sign it. Will you see him?

WILLY, *entering:* Touchdown! Touch— *He sees Jenny.* Jenny, Jenny, good to see you. How're ya? Workin'? Or still honest?

JENNY: Fine. How've you been feeling?

WILLY: Not much any more, Jenny. Ha, ha! *He is surprised to see the rackets.*

BERNARD: Hello, Uncle Willy.

WILLY, *almost shocked:* Bernard! Well, look who's here! *He comes quickly, guiltily, to Bernard and warmly shakes his hand.*

BERNARD: How are you? Good to see you.

WILLY: What are you doing here?

BERNARD: Oh, just stopped by to see Pop. Get off my feet till my train leaves. I'm going to Washington in a few minutes.

WILLY: Is he in?

BERNARD: Yes, he's in his office with the accountant. Sit down.

WILLY, *sitting down:* What're you going to do in Washington?

BERNARD: Oh, just a case I've got there, Willy.

WILLY: That so? *Indicating the rackets:* You going to play tennis there?

BERNARD: I'm staying with a friend who's got a court.

WILLY: Don't say. His own tennis court. Must be fine people, I bet.

BERNARD: They are, very nice. Dad tells me Biff's in town.

WILLY, *with a big smile:* Yeah, Biff's in. Working on a very big deal, Bernard.

BERNARD: What's Biff doing?

WILLY: Well, he's been doing very big things in the West. But he decided to establish himself here. Very big. We're having dinner. Did I hear your wife had a boy?

BERNARD: That's right. Our second.

WILLY: Two boys! What do you know!

BERNARD: What kind of a deal has Biff got?

WILLY: Well, Bill Oliver—very big sporting-goods man—he wants Biff very badly. Called him in from the West. Long distance, carte blanche, special deliveries. Your friends have their own private tennis court?

BERNARD: You still with the old firm, Willy?

WILLY, *after a pause:* I'm—I'm overjoyed to see how you made the grade, Bernard, overjoyed. It's an encouraging thing to see a young man really—really— Looks very good for Biff—very— *He breaks off, then:* Bernard— *He is so full of emotion, he breaks off again.*

BERNARD: What is it, Willy?

WILLY, *small and alone:* What—what's the secret?

BERNARD: What secret?

WILLY: How—how did you? Why didn't he ever catch on?

BERNARD: I wouldn't know that, Willy.

WILLY, *confidentially, desperately:* You were his friend, his boyhood friend. There's something I don't understand about it. His life ended after that Ebbets Field game. From the age of seventeen nothing good ever happened to him.

BERNARD: He never trained himself for anything.

WILLY: But he did, he did. After high school he took so many correspondence courses. Radio mechanics; television; God knows what, and never made the slightest mark.

BERNARD, *taking off his glasses:* Willy, do you want to talk candidly?

WILLY, *rising, faces Bernard:* I regard you as a very brilliant man, Bernard. I value your advice.

BERNARD: Oh, the hell with the advice, Willy. I couldn't advise you. There's just one thing I've always wanted to ask you. When he was supposed to graduate, and the math teacher flunked him—

WILLY: Oh, that son-of-a-bitch ruined his life.

BERNARD: Yeah, but, Willy, all he had to do was go to summer school and make up that subject.

WILLY: That's right, that's right.

BERNARD: Did you tell him not to go to summer school?

WILLY: Me? I begged him to go. I ordered him to go!

BERNARD: Then why wouldn't he go?

WILLY: Why? Why! Bernard, that question has been trailing me like a ghost for the last fifteen years. He flunked the subject, and laid down and died like a hammer hit him!

BERNARD: Take it easy, kid.

WILLY: Let me talk to you—I got nobody to talk to. Bernard, Bernard, was it my fault? Y'see? It keeps going around in my mind, maybe I did something to him. I got nothing to give him.

BERNARD: Don't take it so hard.

WILLY: Why did he lay down? What is the story there? You were his friend!

BERNARD: Willy, I remember, it was June, and our grades came out. And he'd flunked math.

WILLY: That son-of-a-bitch!

BERNARD: No, it wasn't right then. Biff just got very angry, I remember, and he was ready to enroll in summer school.

WILLY, *surprised:* He was?

BERNARD: He wasn't beaten by it at all. But then, Willy, he disappeared from the block for almost a month. And I got the idea that he'd gone up to New England to see you. Did he have a talk with you then?

Willy stares in silence.

BERNARD: Willy?

WILLY, *with a strong edge of resentment in his voice:* Yeah, he came to Boston. What about it?

BERNARD: Well, just that when he came back—I'll never forget this, it always mystifies me. Because I'd thought so well of Biff, even though he'd always taken advantage of me. I loved him, Willy, y'know? And he came back after that month and took his sneakers—remember those sneakers with "University of Virginia" printed on them? He was so proud of those, wore them every day. And he took them down in the cellar, and burned them up in the furnace. We had a fist fight. It lasted at least half an hour. Just the two of us, punching each other down the cellar, and crying right through it. I've often thought of how strange it was that I knew he'd given up his life. What happened in Boston, Willy?

Willy looks at him as at an intruder.

BERNARD: I just bring it up because you asked me.

WILLY, *angrily:* Nothing. What do you mean, "What happened?" What's that got to do with anything?

BERNARD: Well, don't get sore.

WILLY: What are you trying to do, blame it on me? If a boy lays down is that my fault?

BERNARD: Now, Willy, don't get—

WILLY: Well, don't—don't talk to me that way! What does that mean, "What happened?"

Charley enters. He is in his vest, and he carries a bottle of bourbon.

CHARLEY: Hey, you're going to miss that train. *He waves the bottle.*

BERNARD: Yeah, I'm going. *He takes the bottle.* Thanks, Pop. *He picks up his rackets and bag.* Good-by, Willy, and don't worry about it. You know, "If at first you don't succeed . . ."

WILLY: Yes, I believe in that.

BERNARD: But sometimes, Willy, it's better for a man just to walk away.

WILLY: Walk away?

BERNARD: That's right.

WILLY: But if you can't walk away?

BERNARD, *after a slight pause:* I guess that's when it's tough. *Extending his hand:* Good-by, Willy.

WILLY, *shaking Bernard's hand:* Good-by, boy.

CHARLEY, *an arm on Bernard's shoulder:* How do you like this kid? Gonna argue a case in front of the Supreme Court.

BERNARD, *protesting:* Pop!

WILLY, *genuinely shocked, pained, and happy:* No! The Supreme Court!

BERNARD: I gotta run. 'By, Dad!

CHARLEY: Knock 'em dead, Bernard!

Bernard goes off.

WILLY, *as Charley takes out his wallet:* The Supreme Court! And he didn't even mention it!

CHARLEY, *counting out money on the desk:* He don't have to—he's gonna do it.

WILLY: And you never told him what to do, did you? You never took any interest in him.

CHARLEY: My salvation is that I never took any interest in anything. There's some money—fifty dollars. I got an accountant inside.

WILLY: Charley, look . . . *With difficulty:* I got my insurance to pay. If you can manage it—I need a hundred and ten dollars.

Charley doesn't reply for a moment; merely stops moving.

WILLY: I'd draw it from my bank but Linda would know, and I . . .

CHARLEY: Sit down, Willy.

WILLY, *moving toward the chair:* I'm keeping an account of everything, remember. I'll pay every penny back. *He sits.*

CHARLEY: Now listen to me, Willy.

WILLY: I want you to know I appreciate . . .

CHARLEY, *sitting down on the table:* Willy, what're you doin'? What the hell is goin' on in your head?

WILLY: Why? I'm simply . . .

CHARLEY: I offered you a job. You can make fifty dollars a week. And I won't send you on the road.

WILLY: I've got a job.

CHARLEY: Without pay? What kind of a job is a job without pay? *He rises.* Now, look, kid, enough is enough. I'm no genius but I know when I'm being insulted.

WILLY: Insulted!

CHARLEY: Why don't you want to work for me?

WILLY: What's the matter with you? I've got a job.

CHARLEY: Then what're you walkin' in here every week for?

WILLY, *getting up:* Well, if you don't want me to walk in here—

CHARLEY: I am offering you a job.

WILLY: I don't want your goddam job!

CHARLEY: When the hell are you going to grow up?

WILLY, *furiously:* You big ignoramus, if you say that to me again I'll rap you one! I don't care how big you are! *He's ready to fight.*

Pause.

CHARLEY, *kindly, going to him:* How much do you need, Willy?

WILLY: Charley, I'm strapped, I'm strapped. I don't know what to do. I was just fired.

CHARLEY: Howard fired you?

WILLY: That snotnose. Imagine that? I named him. I named him Howard.

CHARLEY: Willy, when're you gonna realize that them things don't mean anything? You named him Howard, but you can't sell that. The only thing you got in this world is what you can sell. And the funny thing is that you're a salesman, and you don't know that.

WILLY: I've always tried to think otherwise, I guess. I always felt that if a man was impressive, and well liked, that nothing—

CHARLEY: Why must everybody like you? Who liked J. P. Morgan? Was he impressive? In a Turkish bath he'd look like a butcher. But with his pockets on he was very well liked. Now listen, Willy, I know you don't like me, and nobody can say I'm in love with you, but I'll give you a job because—just for the hell of it, put it that way. Now what do you say?

WILLY: I—I just can't work for you, Charley.

CHARLEY: What're you, jealous of me?

WILLY: I can't work for you, that's all, don't ask me why.

CHARLEY, *angered, taking out more bills:* You been jealous of me all your life, you damned fool! Here, pay your insurance. *He puts the money in Willy's hand.*

WILLY: I'm keeping strict accounts.

CHARLEY: I've got some work to do. Take care of yourself. And pay your insurance.

WILLY, *moving to the right:* Funny, y'know? After all the highways, and the trains, and the appointments, and the years, you end up worth more dead than alive.

CHARLEY: Willy, nobody's worth nothin' dead. *After a slight pause:* Did you hear what I said?

Willy stands still, dreaming.

CHARLEY: Willy!

WILLY: Apologize to Bernard for me when you see him. I didn't mean to argue with him. He's a fine boy. They're all fine boys, and they'll end up big—all of them. Someday they'll all play tennis together. Wish me luck, Charley. He saw Bill Oliver today.

CHARLEY: Good luck.

WILLY, *on the verge of tears:* Charley, you're the only friend I got. Isn't that a remarkable thing? *He goes out.*

CHARLEY: Jesus!

Charley stares after him a moment and follows. All light blacks out. Suddenly raucous music is heard, and a red glow rises behind the screen at right. Stanley, a young waiter, appears, carrying a table, followed by Happy, who is carrying two chairs.

STANLEY, *putting the table down:* That's all right, Mr. Loman, I can handle it myself. *He turns and takes the chairs from Happy and places them at the table.*

HAPPY, *glancing around:* Oh, this is better.

STANLEY: Sure, in the front there you're in the middle of all kinds a noise. Whenever you got a party, Mr. Loman, you just tell me and I'll put you back here. Y'know, there's a lotta people they don't like it private, because when they go out they like to see a lotta action around them because they're sick and tired to stay in the house by theirself. But I know you, you ain't from Hackensack. You know what I mean?

HAPPY, *sitting down:* So how's it coming, Stanley?

STANLEY: Ah, it's a dog's life. I only wish during the war they'd a took me in the Army. I coulda been dead by now.

HAPPY: My brother's back, Stanley.

STANLEY: Oh, he come back, heh? From the Far West.

HAPPY: Yeah, big cattle man, my brother, so treat him right. And my father's coming too.

STANLEY: Oh, your father too!

HAPPY: You got a couple of nice lobsters?

STANLEY: Hundred per cent, big.

HAPPY: I want them with the claws.

STANLEY: Don't worry, I don't give you no mice. *Happy laughs.* How about some wine? It'll put a head on the meal.

HAPPY: No. You remember, Stanley, that recipe I brought you from overseas? With the champagne in it?

STANLEY: Oh, yeah, sure. I still got it tacked up yet in the kitchen. But that'll have to cost a buck apiece anyways.

HAPPY: That's all right.

STANLEY: What'd you, hit a number or somethin'?

HAPPY: No, it's a little celebration. My brother is—I think he pulled off a big deal today. I think we're going into business together.

STANLEY: Great! That's the best for you. Because a family business, you know what I mean?—that's the best.

HAPPY: That's what I think.

STANLEY: 'Cause what's the difference? Somebody steals? It's in the family. Know what I mean? *Sotto voce:* Like this bartender here. The boss is goin' crazy what kinda leak he's got in the cash register. You put it in but it don't come out.

HAPPY, *raising his head:* Sh!

STANLEY: What?

HAPPY: You notice I wasn't lookin' right or left, was I?

STANLEY: No.

HAPPY: And my eyes are closed.

STANLEY: So what's the—?

HAPPY: Strudel's comin'.

STANLEY, *catching on, looks around:* Ah, no, there's no—

He breaks off as a furred, lavishly dressed girl enters and sits at the next table. Both follow her with their eyes.

STANLEY: Geez, how'd ya know?

HAPPY: I got radar or something. *Staring directly at her profile:* Oooooooo . . . Stanley.

STANLEY: I think that's for you, Mr. Loman.

HAPPY: Look at that mouth. Oh, God. And the binoculars.

STANLEY: Geez, you got a life, Mr. Loman.

HAPPY: Wait on her.

STANLEY, *going to the girl's table:* Would you like a menu, ma'am?

GIRL: I'm expecting someone, but I'd like a—

HAPPY: Why don't you bring her—excuse me, miss, do you mind? I sell champagne, and I'd like you to try my brand. Bring her a champagne, Stanley.

GIRL: That's awfully nice of you.

HAPPY: Don't mention it. It's all company money. *He laughs.*

GIRL: That's a charming product to be selling, isn't it?

HAPPY: Oh, gets to be like everything else. Selling is selling, y'know.

GIRL: I suppose.

HAPPY: You don't happen to sell, do you?

GIRL: No, I don't sell.

HAPPY: Would you object to a compliment from a stranger? You ought to be on a magazine cover.

GIRL, *looking at him a little archly:* I have been.

Stanley comes in with a glass of champagne.

HAPPY: What'd I say before, Stanley? You see? She's a cover girl.

STANLEY: Oh, I could see, I could see.

HAPPY, *to the Girl:* What magazine?

GIRL: Oh, a lot of them. *She takes the drink.* Thank you.

HAPPY: You know what they say in France, don't you? "Champagne is the drink of the complexion"—Hiya, Biff!

Biff has entered and sits with Happy.

BIFF: Hello, kid. Sorry I'm late.

HAPPY: I just got here. Uh, Miss—?

GIRL: Forsythe.

HAPPY: Miss Forsythe, this is my brother.

BIFF: Is Dad here?

HAPPY: His name is Biff. You might've heard of him. Great football player.

GIRL: Really? What team?

HAPPY: Are you familiar with football?

GIRL: No, I'm afraid I'm not.

HAPPY: Biff is quarterback with the New York Giants.

GIRL: Well, that is nice, isn't it? *She drinks.*

HAPPY: Good health.

GIRL: I'm happy to meet you.

HAPPY: That's my name. Hap. It's really Harold, but at West Point they called me Happy.

GIRL, *now really impressed:* Oh, I see. How do you do? *She turns her profile.*

BIFF: Isn't Dad coming?

HAPPY: You want her?

BIFF: Oh, I could never make that.

HAPPY: I remember the time that idea would never come into your head. Where's the old confidence, Biff?

BIFF: I just saw Oliver—

HAPPY: Wait a minute. I've got to see that old confidence again. Do you want her? She's on call.

BIFF: Oh, no. *He turns to look at the Girl.*

HAPPY: I'm telling you. Watch this. *Turning to the Girl:* Honey? *She turns to him.* Are you busy?

GIRL: Well, I am . . . but I could make a phone call.

HAPPY: Do that, will you, honey? And see if you can get a friend. We'll be here for a while. Biff is one of the greatest football players in the country.

GIRL, *standing up:* Well, I'm certainly happy to meet you.

HAPPY: Come back soon.

GIRL: I'll try.

HAPPY: Don't try, honey, try hard.

The Girl exits. Stanley follows, shaking his head in bewildered admiration.

HAPPY: Isn't that a shame now? A beautiful girl like that? That's why I can't get married. There's not a good woman in a thousand. New York is loaded with them, kid!

BIFF: Hap, look—

HAPPY: I told you she was on call!

BIFF, *strangely unnerved:* Cut it out, will ya? I want to say something to you.

HAPPY: Did you see Oliver?

BIFF: I saw him all right. Now look, I want to tell Dad a couple of things and I want you to help me.

HAPPY: What? Is he going to back you?

BIFF: Are you crazy? You're out of your goddam head, you know that?

HAPPY: Why? What happened?

BIFF, *breathlessly:* I did a terrible thing today, Hap. It's been the strangest day I ever went through. I'm all numb, I swear.

HAPPY: You mean he wouldn't see you?

BIFF: Well, I waited six hours for him, see? All day. Kept sending my name in. Even tried to date his secretary so she'd get me to him, but no soap.

HAPPY: Because you're not showin' the old confidence, Biff. He remembered you, didn't he?

BIFF, *stopping Happy with a gesture:* Finally, about five o'clock, he comes out. Didn't remember who I was or anything. I felt like such an idiot, Hap.

HAPPY: Did you tell him my Florida idea?

BIFF: He walked away. I saw him for one minute. I got so mad I could've torn the walls down! How the hell did I ever get the idea I was a salesman there? I even believed myself that I'd been a salesman for him! And then he gave me one look and—I realized what a ridiculous lie my whole life has been! We've been talking in a dream for fifteen years. I was a shipping clerk.

HAPPY: What'd you do?

BIFF, *with great tension and wonder:* Well, he left, see. And the secretary went out. I was all alone in the waiting room. I don't know what came over me, Hap. The next thing I know I'm in his office—paneled walls, everything. I can't explain it. I—Hap, I took his fountain pen.

HAPPY: Geez, did he catch you?

BIFF: I ran out. I ran down all eleven flights. I ran and ran and ran.

HAPPY: That was an awful dumb—what'd you do that for?

BIFF, *agonized:* I don't know, I just—wanted to take something, I don't know. You gotta help me, Hap, I'm gonna tell Pop.

HAPPY: You crazy? What for?

BIFF: Hap, he's got to understand that I'm not the man somebody lends that kind of money to. He thinks I've been spiting him all these years and it's eating him up.

HAPPY: That's just it. You tell him something nice.

BIFF: I can't.

HAPPY: Say you got a lunch date with Oliver tomorrow.

BIFF: So what do I do tomorrow?

HAPPY: You leave the house tomorrow and come back at night and say Oliver is thinking it over. And he thinks it over for a couple of weeks, and gradually it fades away and nobody's the worse.

BIFF: But it'll go on forever!

HAPPY: Dad is never so happy as when he's looking forward to something!

Willy enters.

HAPPY: Hello, scout!

WILLY: Gee, I haven't been here in years!

Stanley has followed Willy in and sets a chair for him. Stanley starts off but Happy stops him.

HAPPY: Stanley!

Stanley stands by, waiting for an order.

BIFF, *going to Willy with guilt, as to an invalid:* Sit down, Pop. You want a drink?

WILLY: Sure, I don't mind.

BIFF: Let's get a load on.

WILLY: You look worried.

BIFF: N-no. *To Stanley:* Scotch all around. Make it doubles.

STANLEY: Doubles, right. *He goes.*

WILLY: You had a couple already, didn't you?

BIFF: Just a couple, yeah.

WILLY: Well, what happened, boy? *Nodding affirmatively, with a smile:* Everything go all right?

BIFF, *takes a breath, then reaches out and grasps Willy's hand:* Pal . . . *He is smiling bravely, and Willy is smiling too.* I had an experience today.

HAPPY: Terrific, Pop.

WILLY: That so? What happened?

BIFF, *high, slightly alcoholic, above the earth:* I'm going to tell you every-thing from first to last. It's been a strange day. *Silence. He looks around, composes himself as best he can, but his breath keeps breaking the rhythm of his voice.* I had to wait quite a while for him, and—

WILLY: Oliver?

BIFF: Yeah, Oliver. All day, as a matter of cold fact. And a lot of—instances—facts, Pop, facts about my life came back to me. Who was it, Pop? Who ever said I was a salesman with Oliver?

WILLY: Well, you were.

BIFF: No, Dad, I was a shipping clerk.

WILLY: But you were practically—

BIFF, *with determination:* Dad, I don't know who said it first, but I was never a salesman for Bill Oliver.

WILLY: What're you talking about?

BIFF: Let's hold on to the facts tonight, Pop. We're not going to get anywhere bullin' around. I was a shipping clerk.

WILLY, *angrily:* All right, now listen to me—

BIFF: Why don't you let me finish?

WILLY: I'm not interested in stories about the past or any crap of that kind because the woods are burning, boys, you understand? There's a big blaze going on all around. I was fired today.

BIFF, *shocked:* How could you be?

WILLY: I was fired, and I'm looking for a little good news to tell your mother, because the woman has waited and the woman has suffered. The gist of it is that I haven't got a story left in my head, Biff. So don't give me a lecture about facts and aspects. I am not interested. Now what've you got to say to me?

Stanley enters with three drinks. They wait until he leaves.

WILLY: Did you see Oliver?

BIFF: Jesus, Dad!

WILLY: You mean you didn't go up there?

HAPPY: Sure he went up there.

BIFF: I did. I—saw him. How could they fire you?

WILLY, *on the edge of his chair:* What kind of a welcome did he give you?

BIFF: He won't even let you work on commission?

WILLY: I'm out! *Driving:* So tell me, he gave you a warm welcome?

HAPPY: Sure, Pop, sure!

BIFF, *driven:* Well, it was kind of—

WILLY: I was wondering if he'd remember you. *To Happy:* Imagine, man doesn't see him for ten, twelve years and gives him that kind of a welcome!

HAPPY: Damn right!

BIFF, *trying to return to the offensive:* Pop, look—

WILLY: You know why he remembered you, don't you? Because you impressed him in those days.

BIFF: Let's talk quietly and get this down to the facts, huh?

WILLY, *as though Biff had been interrupting:* Well, what happened? It's great news, Biff. Did he take you into his office or'd you talk in the waiting room?

BIFF: Well, he came in, see, and—

WILLY, *with a big smile:* What'd he say? Betcha he threw his arm around you.

BIFF: Well, he kinda—

WILLY: He's a fine man. *To Happy:* Very hard man to see, y'know.

HAPPY, *agreeing:* Oh, I know.

WILLY, *to Biff:* Is that where you had the drinks?

BIFF: Yeah, he gave me a couple of—no, no!

HAPPY, *cutting in:* He told him my Florida idea.

WILLY: Don't interrupt. *To Biff:* How'd he react to the Florida idea?

BIFF: Dad, will you give me a minute to explain?

WILLY: I've been waiting for you to explain since I sat down here! What happened? He took you into his office and what?

BIFF: Well—I talked. And—and he listened, see.

WILLY: Famous for the way he listens, y'know. What was his answer?

BIFF: His answer was— *He breaks off, suddenly angry.* Dad, you're not letting me tell you what I want to tell you!

WILLY, *accusing, angered:* You didn't see him, did you?

BIFF: I did see him!

WILLY: What'd you insult him or something? You insulted him, didn't you?

BIFF: Listen, will you let me out of it, will you just let me out of it!

HAPPY: What the hell!

WILLY: Tell me what happened!

BIFF, *to Happy:* I can't talk to him!

A single trumpet note jars the ear. The light of green leaves stains the house, which holds the air of night and a dream. Young Bernard enters and knocks on the door of the house.

YOUNG BERNARD, *frantically:* Mrs. Loman, Mrs. Loman!

HAPPY: Tell him what happened!

BIFF, *to Happy:* Shut up and leave me alone!

WILLY: No, no! You had to go and flunk math!

BIFF: What math? What're you talking about?

YOUNG BERNARD: Mrs. Loman, Mrs. Loman!

Linda appears in the house, as of old.

WILLY, *wildly:* Math, math, math!

BIFF: Take it easy, Pop!

YOUNG BERNARD: Mrs. Loman!

WILLY, *furiously:* If you hadn't flunked you'd've been set by now!

BIFF: Now, look, I'm gonna tell you what happened, and you're going to listen to me.

YOUNG BERNARD: Mrs. Loman!

BIFF: I waited six hours—

HAPPY: What the hell are you saying?

BIFF: I kept sending in my name but he wouldn't see me. So finally he . . . *He continues unheard as light fades low on the restaurant.*

YOUNG BERNARD: Biff flunked math!

LINDA: No!

YOUNG BERNARD: Birnbaum flunked him! They won't graduate him!

LINDA: But they have to. He's gotta go to the university. Where is he? Biff! Biff!

YOUNG BERNARD: No, he left. He went to Grand Central.

LINDA: Grand— You mean he went to Boston!

YOUNG BERNARD: Is Uncle Willy in Boston?

LINDA: Oh, maybe Willy can talk to the teacher. Oh, the poor, poor boy!

Light on house area snaps out.

BIFF, *at the table, now audible, holding up a gold fountain pen:* . . . so I'm washed up with Oliver, you understand? Are you listening to me?

WILLY, *at a loss:* Yeah, sure. If you hadn't flunked—

BIFF: Flunked what? What're you talking about?

WILLY: Don't blame everything on me! I didn't flunk math—you did! What pen?

HAPPY: That was awful dumb, Biff, a pen like that is worth—

WILLY, *seeing the pen for the first time:* You took Oliver's pen?

BIFF, *weakening:* Dad, I just explained it to you.

WILLY: You stole Bill Oliver's fountain pen!

BIFF: I didn't exactly steal it! That's just what I've been explaining to you!

HAPPY: He had it in his hand and just then Oliver walked in, so he got nervous and stuck it in his pocket!

WILLY: My God, Biff!

BIFF: I never intended to do it, Dad!

OPERATOR'S VOICE: Standish Arms, good evening!

WILLY, *shouting:* I'm not in my room!

BIFF, *frightened:* Dad, what's the matter? *He and Happy stand up.*

OPERATOR: Ringing Mr. Loman for you!

WILLY: I'm not there, stop it!

BIFF, *horrified, gets down on one knee before Willy:* Dad, I'll make good, I'll make good. *Willy tries to get to his feet. Biff holds him down.* Sit down now.

WILLY: No, you're no good, you're no good for anything.

BIFF: I am, Dad, I'll find something else, you understand? Now don't worry about anything. *He holds up Willy's face:* Talk to me, Dad.

OPERATOR: Mr. Loman does not answer. Shall I page him?

WILLY, *attempting to stand, as though to rush and silence the Operator:* No, no, no!

HAPPY: He'll strike something, Pop.

WILLY: No, no . . .

BIFF, *desperately, standing over Willy:* Pop, listen! Listen to me! I'm telling you something good. Oliver talked to his partner about the Florida idea. You listening? He—he talked to his partner, and he came to me . . . I'm going to be all right, you hear? Dad, listen to me, he said it was just a question of the amount!

WILLY: Then you . . . got it?

HAPPY: He's gonna be terrific, Pop!

WILLY, *trying to stand:* Then you got it, haven't you? You got it! You got it!

BIFF, *agonized, holds Willy down:* No, no. Look, Pop. I'm supposed to have lunch with them tomorrow. I'm just telling you this so you'll know that I can still make an impression, Pop. And I'll make good somewhere, but I can't go tomorrow, see?

WILLY: Why not? You simply—

BIFF: But the pen, Pop!

WILLY: You give it to him and tell him it was an oversight!

HAPPY: Sure, have lunch tomorrow!

BIFF: I can't say that—

WILLY: You were doing a crossword puzzle and accidentally used his pen!

BIFF: Listen, kid, I took those balls years ago, now I walk in with his fountain pen? That clinches it, don't you see? I can't face him like that! I'll try elsewhere.

PAGE'S VOICE: Paging Mr. Loman!

WILLY: Don't you want to be anything?

BIFF: Pop, how can I go back?

WILLY: You don't want to be anything, is that what's behind it?

BIFF, *now angry at Willy for not crediting his sympathy:* Don't take it that way! You think it was easy walking into that office after what I'd done to him? A team of horses couldn't have dragged me back to Bill Oliver!

WILLY: Then why'd you go?

BIFF: Why did I go? Why did I go! Look at you! Look at what's become of you!

Off left, The Woman laughs.

WILLY: Biff, you're going to go to that lunch tomorrow, or—

BIFF: I can't go. I've got no appointment!

HAPPY: Biff, for . . . !

WILLY: Are you spiting me?

BIFF: Don't take it that way! Goddammit!

WILLY—*he strikes Biff and falters away from the table:* You rotten little louse! Are you spiting me?

THE WOMAN: Someone's at the door, Willy!

BIFF: I'm no good, can't you see what I am?

HAPPY, *separating them:* Hey, you're in a restaurant! Now cut it out, both of you! *The girls enter.* Hello, girls, sit down.

The Woman laughs, off left.

MISS FORSYTHE: I guess we might as well. This is Letta.

THE WOMAN: Willy, are you going to wake up?

BIFF, *ignoring Willy:* How're ya, miss, sit down. What do you drink?

MISS FORSYTHE: Letta might not be able to stay long.

LETTA: I gotta get up very early tomorrow. I got jury duty. I'm so excited! Were you fellows ever on a jury?

BIFF: No, but I been in front of them! *The girls laugh.* This is my father.

LETTA: Isn't he cute? Sit down with us, Pop.

HAPPY: Sit him down, Biff!

BIFF, *going to him:* Come on, slugger, drink us under the table. To hell with it! Come on, sit down, pal.

On Biff's last insistence, Willy is about to sit.

THE WOMAN, *now urgently:* Willy, are you going to answer the door!

The Woman's call pulls Willy back. He starts right, befuddled.

BIFF: Hey, where are you going?

WILLY: Open the door.

BIFF: The door?

WILLY: The washroom . . . the door . . . where's the door?

BIFF, *leading Willy to the left:* Just go straight down.

Willy moves left.

THE WOMAN: Willy, Willy, are you going to get up, get up, get up, get up?

Willy exits left.

LETTA: I think it's sweet you bring your daddy along.

MISS FORSYTHE: Oh, he isn't really your father!

BIFF, *at left, turning to her resentfully:* Miss Forsythe, you've just seen a prince walk by. A fine, troubled prince. A hard-working, unappreciated prince. A pal, you understand? A good companion. Always for his boys.

LETTA: That's so sweet.

HAPPY: Well, girls, what's the program? We're wasting time. Come on, Biff. Gather round. Where would you like to go?

BIFF: Why don't you do something for him?

HAPPY: Me!

BIFF: Don't you give a damn for him, Hap?

HAPPY: What're you talking about? I'm the one who—

BIFF: I sense it, you don't give a good goddam about him. *He takes the rolled-up hose from his pocket and puts it on the table in front of Happy.* Look what I found in the cellar, for Christ's sake. How can you bear to let it go on?

HAPPY: Me? Who goes away? Who runs off and—

BIFF: Yeah, but he doesn't mean anything to you. You could help him—I can't! Don't you understand what I'm talking about? He's going to kill himself, don't you know that?

HAPPY: Don't I know it! Me!

BIFF: Hap, help him! Jesus . . . help him . . . Help me, help me, I can't bear to look at his face! *Ready to weep, he hurries out, up right.*

HAPPY, *starting after him:* Where are you going?

MISS FORSYTHE: What's he so mad about?

HAPPY: Come on, girls, we'll catch up with him.

MISS FORSYTHE, *as Happy pushes her out:* Say, I don't like that temper of his!

HAPPY: He's just a little overstrung, he'll be all right!

WILLY, *off left, as The Woman laughs:* Don't answer! Don't answer!

LETTA: Don't you want to tell your father—

HAPPY: No, that's not my father. He's just a guy. Come on, we'll catch Biff, and, honey, we're going to paint this town! Stanley, where's the check! Hey, Stanley!

They exit. Stanley looks toward left.

STANLEY, *calling to Happy indignantly:* Mr. Loman! Mr. Loman!

Stanley picks up a chair and follows them off. Knocking is heard off left. The Woman enters, laughing. Willy follows her. She is in a black slip; he is buttoning his shirt. Raw, sensuous music accompanies their speech.

WILLY: Will you stop laughing? Will you stop?

THE WOMAN: Aren't you going to answer the door? He'll wake the whole hotel.

WILLY: I'm not expecting anybody.

THE WOMAN: Whyn't you have another drink, honey, and stop being so damn self-centered?

WILLY: I'm so lonely.

THE WOMAN: You know you ruined me, Willy? From now on, whenever you come to the office, I'll see that you go right through to the buyers. No waiting at my desk any more, Willy. You ruined me.

WILLY: That's nice of you to say that.

THE WOMAN: Gee, you are self-centered! Why so sad? You are the saddest, self-centeredest soul I ever did see-saw. *She laughs. He kisses her.* Come on inside, drummer boy. It's silly to be dressing in the middle of the night. *As knocking is heard:* Aren't you going to answer the door?

WILLY: They're knocking on the wrong door.

THE WOMAN: But I felt the knocking. And he heard us talking in here. Maybe the hotel's on fire!

WILLY, *his terror rising:* It's a mistake.

THE WOMAN: Then tell him to go away!

WILLY: There's nobody there.

THE WOMAN: It's getting on my nerves, Willy. There's somebody standing out there and it's getting on my nerves!

WILLY, *pushing her away from him:* All right, stay in the bathroom here, and don't come out. I think there's a law in Massachusetts about it, so don't come out. It may be that new room clerk. He looked very mean. So don't come out. It's a mistake, there's no fire.

The knocking is heard again. He takes a few steps away from her, and she vanishes into the wing. The light follows him, and now he is facing Young Biff, who carries a suitcase. Biff steps toward him. The music is gone.

BIFF: Why didn't you answer?

WILLY: Biff! What are you doing in Boston?

BIFF: Why didn't you answer? I've been knocking for five minutes, I called you on the phone—

WILLY: I just heard you. I was in the bathroom and had the door shut. Did anything happen home?

BIFF: Dad—I let you down.

WILLY: What do you mean?

BIFF: Dad . . .

WILLY: Biffo, what's this about? *Putting his arm around Biff:* Come on, let's go downstairs and get you a malted.

BIFF: Dad, I flunked math.

WILLY: Not for the term?

BIFF: The term. I haven't got enough credits to graduate.

WILLY: You mean to say Bernard wouldn't give you the answers?

BIFF: He did, he tried, but I only got a sixty-one.

WILLY: And they wouldn't give you four points?

BIFF: Birnbaum refused absolutely. I begged him, Pop, but he won't give me those points. You gotta talk to him before they close the school. Because if he saw the kind of man you are, and you just talked to him in your way, I'm sure he'd come through for me. The class came right before practice, see, and I didn't go enough. Would you talk to him? He'd like you, Pop. You know the way you could talk.

WILLY: You're on. We'll drive right back.

BIFF: Oh, Dad, good work! I'm sure he'll change it for you!

WILLY: Go downstairs and tell the clerk I'm checkin' out. Go right down.

BIFF: Yes, sir! See, the reason he hates me, Pop—one day he was late for class so I got up at the blackboard and imitated him. I crossed my eyes and talked with a lithp.

WILLY, *laughing:* You did? The kids like it?

BIFF: They nearly died laughing!

WILLY: Yeah? What'd you do?

BIFF: The thquare root of thixthy twee is . . . *Willy bursts out laughing; Biff joins him.* And in the middle of it he walked in!

Willy laughs, and The Woman joins in offstage.

WILLY, *without hesitation:* Hurry downstairs and—

BIFF: Somebody in there?

WILLY: No, that was next door.

The Woman laughs offstage.

BIFF: Somebody got in your bathroom!

WILLY: No, it's the next room, there's a party—

THE WOMAN, *enters, laughing. She lisps this:* Can I come in? There's something in the bathtub, Willy, and it's moving!

Willy looks at Biff, who is staring open-mouthed and horrified at The Woman.

WILLY: Ah—you better go back to your room. They must be finished painting by now. They're painting her room so I let her take a shower here. Go back, go back . . . *He pushes her.*

THE WOMAN, *resisting:* But I've got to get dressed, Willy, I can't—

WILLY: Get out of here! Go back, go back . . . *Suddenly striving for the ordinary:* This is Miss Francis, Biff, she's a buyer. They're painting her room. Go back, Miss Francis, go back . . .

THE WOMAN: But my clothes, I can't go out naked in the hall!

WILLY, *pushing her offstage:* Get outa here! Go back, go back!

Biff slowly sits down on his suitcase as the argument continues offstage.

THE WOMAN: Where's my stockings? You promised me stockings, Willy!

WILLY: I have no stockings here!

THE WOMAN: You had two boxes of size nine sheers for me, and I want them!

WILLY: Here, for God's sake, will you get outa here!

THE WOMAN, *entering, holding a box of stockings:* I just hope there's nobody in the hall. That's all I hope. *To Biff:* Are you football or baseball?

BIFF: Football.

THE WOMAN, *angry, humiliated:* That's me too. G'night. *She snatches her clothes from Willy, and walks out.*

WILLY, *after a pause:* Well, better get going. I want to get to the school first thing in the morning. Get my suits out of the closet. I'll get my valise. *Biff doesn't move.* What's the matter? *Biff remains motionless, tears falling.* She's a buyer. Buys for J. H. Simmons. She lives down the hall—they're painting. You don't imagine— *He breaks off. After a pause:* Now listen, pal, she's just a buyer. She sees merchandise in her room and they have to keep it looking just so . . . *Pause. Assuming command:* All right, get my suits. *Biff doesn't move.* Now stop crying and do as I say. I gave you an order. Biff, I gave you an order! Is that what you do when I give you an order? How dare you cry! *Putting his arm around Biff:* Now look, Biff, when you grow up you'll understand about these things. You mustn't—you mustn't overemphasize a thing like this. I'll see Birnbaum first thing in the morning.

BIFF: Never mind.

WILLY, *getting down beside Biff:* Never mind! He's going to give you those points. I'll see to it.

BIFF: He wouldn't listen to you.

WILLY: He certainly will listen to me. You need those points for the U. of Virginia.

BIFF: I'm not going there.

WILLY: Heh? If I can't get him to change that mark you'll make it up in summer school. You've got all summer to—

BIFF, *his weeping breaking from him:* Dad . . .

WILLY, *infected by it:* Oh, my boy . . .

BIFF: Dad . . .

WILLY: She's nothing to me, Biff. I was lonely, I was terribly lonely.

BIFF: You—you gave her Mama's stockings! *His tears break through and he rises to go.*

WILLY, *grabbing for Biff:* I gave you an order!

BIFF: Don't touch me, you—liar!

WILLY: Apologize for that!

BIFF: You fake! You phony little fake! You fake! *Overcome, he turns quickly and weeping fully goes out with his suitcase. Willy is left on the floor on his knees.*

WILLY: I gave you an order! Biff, come back here or I'll beat you! Come back here! I'll whip you!

Stanley comes quickly in from the right and stands in front of Willy.

WILLY, *shouting at Stanley:* I gave you an order . . .

STANLEY: Hey, let's pick it up, pick it up, Mr. Loman. *He helps Willy to his feet.* Your boys left with the chippies. They said they'll see you home.

A second waiter watches some distance away.

WILLY: But we were supposed to have dinner together.

Music is heard, Willy's theme.

STANLEY: Can you make it?

WILLY: I'll—sure, I can make it. *Suddenly concerned about his clothes:* Do I—I look all right?

STANLEY: Sure, you look all right. *He flicks a speck off Willy's lapel.*

WILLY: Here—here's a dollar.

STANLEY: Oh, your son paid me. It's all right.

WILLY, *putting it in Stanley's hand:* No, take it. You're a good boy.

STANLEY: Oh, no, you don't have to . . .

WILLY: Here—here's some more, I don't need it any more. *After a slight pause:* Tell me—is there a seed store in the neighborhood?

STANLEY: Seeds? You mean like to plant?

As Willy turns, Stanley slips the money back into his jacket pocket.

WILLY: Yes. Carrots, peas . . .

STANLEY: Well, there's hardware stores on Sixth Avenue, but it may be too late now.

WILLY, *anxiously:* Oh, I'd better hurry. I've got to get some seeds. *He starts off to the right.* I've got to get some seeds, right away. Nothing's planted. I don't have a thing in the ground.

Willy hurries out as the light goes down. Stanley moves over to the right after him, watches him off. The other waiter has been staring at Willy.

STANLEY, *to the waiter:* Well, whatta you looking at?

The waiter picks up the chairs and moves off right. Stanley takes the table and follows him. The light fades on this area. There is a long pause, the sound of the flute coming over. The light gradually rises on the kitchen, which is empty. Happy appears at the door of the house, followed by Biff. Happy is carrying a large bunch of long-stemmed roses. He enters the kitchen, looks around for Linda. Not seeing her, he turns to Biff, who is just outside the house door, and makes a gesture with his hands, indicating "Not here, I guess." He looks into the living room and freezes. Inside, Linda, unseen, is seated, Willy's coat on her lap. She rises ominously and quietly and moves toward Happy, who backs up into the kitchen, afraid.

HAPPY: Hey, what're you doing up? *Linda says nothing but moves toward him implacably.* Where's Pop? *He keeps backing to the right, and now Linda is in full view in the doorway to the living room.* Is he sleeping?

LINDA: Where were you?

HAPPY, *trying to laugh it off:* We met two girls, Mom, very fine types. Here, we brought you some flowers. *Offering them to her:* Put them in your room, Ma.

She knocks them to the floor at Biff's feet. He has now come inside and closed the door behind him. She stares at Biff, silent.

HAPPY: Now what'd you do that for? Mom, I want you to have some flowers—

LINDA, *cutting Happy off, violently to Biff:* Don't you care whether he lives or dies?

HAPPY, *going to the stairs:* Come upstairs, Biff.

BIFF, *with a flare of disgust, to Happy:* Go away from me! *To Linda:* What do you mean, lives or dies? Nobody's dying around here, pal.

LINDA: Get out of my sight! Get out of here!

BIFF: I wanna see the boss.

LINDA: You're not going near him!

BIFF: Where is he? *He moves into the living room and Linda follows.*

LINDA, *shouting after Biff:* You invite him for dinner. He looks forward to it all day—*Biff appears in his parents' bedroom, looks around, and exits—* and then you desert him there. There's no stranger you'd do that to!

HAPPY: Why? He had a swell time with us. Listen, when I—*Linda comes back into the kitchen*—desert him I hope I don't outlive the day!

LINDA: Get out of here!

HAPPY: Now look, Mom . . .

LINDA: Did you have to go to women tonight? You and your lousy rotten whores!

Biff re-enters the kitchen.

HAPPY: Mom, all we did was follow Biff around trying to cheer him up! *To Biff:* Boy, what a night you gave me!

LINDA: Get out of here, both of you, and don't come back! I don't want you tormenting him any more. Go on now, get your things together! *To Biff:* You can sleep in his apartment. *She starts to pick up the flowers and stops herself.* Pick up this stuff, I'm not your maid any more. Pick it up, you bum, you!

Happy turns his back to her in refusal. Biff slowly moves over and gets down on his knees, picking up the flowers.

LINDA: You're a pair of animals! Not one, not another living soul would have had the cruelty to walk out on that man in a restaurant!

BIFF, *not looking at her:* Is that what he said?

LINDA: He didn't have to say anything. He was so humiliated he nearly limped when he came in.

HAPPY: But, Mom, he had a great time with us—

BIFF, *cutting him off violently:* Shut up!

Without another word, Happy goes upstairs.

LINDA: You! You didn't even go in to see if he was all right!

BIFF, *still on the floor in front of Linda, the flowers in his hand; with self-loathing:* No. Didn't. Didn't do a damned thing. How do you like that, heh? Left him babbling in a toilet.

LINDA: You louse. You . . .

BIFF: Now you hit it on the nose! *He gets up, throws the flowers in the wastebasket.* The scum of the earth, and you're looking at him!

LINDA: Get out of here!

BIFF: I gotta talk to the boss, Mom. Where is he?

LINDA: You're not going near him. Get out of this house!

BIFF, *with absolute assurance, determination:* No. We're gonna have an abrupt conversation, him and me.

LINDA: You're not talking to him!

Hammering is heard from outside the house, off right. Biff turns toward the noise.

LINDA, *suddenly pleading:* Will you please leave him alone?

BIFF: What's he doing out there?

LINDA: He's planting the garden!

BIFF, *quietly:* Now? Oh, my God!

Biff moves outside, Linda following. The light dies down on them and comes up on the center of the apron as Willy walks into it. He is carrying a flashlight, a hoe, and a handful of seed packets. He raps the top of the hoe sharply to fix it firmly, and then moves to the left, measuring off the distance with his foot. He holds the flashlight to look at the seed packets, reading off the instructions. He is in the blue of night.

WILLY: Carrots . . . quarter-inch apart. Rows . . . one-foot rows. *He measures it off.* One foot. *He puts down a package and measures off.* Beets. *He puts down another package and measures again.* Lettuce. *He reads the package, puts it down.* One foot— *He breaks off as Ben appears at the right and moves slowly down to him.* What a proposition, ts, ts. Terrific, terrific. 'Cause she's suffered, Ben, the woman has suffered. You understand me? A man can't go out the way he came in, Ben, a man has got to add up to something. You can't, you can't— *Ben moves toward him as though to interrupt.* You gotta consider, now. Don't answer so quick. Remember, it's a guaranteed twenty-thousand-dollar proposition. Now look, Ben, I want you to go through the ins and outs of this thing with me. I've got nobody to talk to, Ben, and the woman has suffered, you hear me?

BEN, *standing still, considering:* What's the proposition?

WILLY: It's twenty thousand dollars on the barrelhead. Guaranteed, gilt-edged, you understand?

BEN: You don't want to make a fool of yourself. They might not honor the policy.

WILLY: How can they dare refuse? Didn't I work like a coolie to meet every premium on the nose? And now they don't pay off? Impossible!

BEN: It's called a cowardly thing, William.

WILLY: Why? Does it take more guts to stand here the rest of my life ringing up a zero?

BEN, *yielding:* That's a point, William. *He moves, thinking, turns.* And twenty thousand—that *is* something one can feel with the hand, it is there.

WILLY, *now assured, with rising power:* Oh, Ben, that's the whole beauty of it! I see it like a diamond, shining in the dark, hard and rough, that I can pick up and touch in my hand. Not like—like an appointment! This would not be another damned-fool appointment, Ben, and it changes all the aspects. Because he thinks I'm nothing, see, and so he spites me. But the funeral— *Straightening up:* Ben, that funeral will be massive! They'll come from Maine, Massachusetts, Vermont, New Hampshire! All the old-timers with the strange license plates—that boy will be thunder-struck, Ben, because he never realized—I am known! Rhode Island, New York, New Jersey—I am known, Ben, and he'll see it with his eyes once and for all. He'll see what I am, Ben! He's in for a shock, that boy!

BEN, *coming down to the edge of the garden:* He'll call you a coward.

WILLY, *suddenly fearful:* No, that would be terrible.

BEN: Yes. And a damned fool.

WILLY: No, no, he mustn't, I won't have that! *He is broken and desperate.*

BEN: He'll hate you, William.

The gay music of the Boys is heard.

WILLY: Oh, Ben, how do we get back to all the great times? Used to be so full of light, and comradeship, the sleigh-riding in winter, and the ruddiness on his cheeks. And always some kind of good news coming up, always something nice coming up ahead. And never even let me carry the valises in the house, and simonizing, simonizing that little red car! Why, why can't I give him something and not have him hate me?

BEN: Let me think about it. *He glances at his watch.* I still have a little time. Remarkable proposition, but you've got to be sure you're not making a fool of yourself.

Ben drifts off upstage and goes out of sight. Biff comes down from the left.

WILLY, *suddenly conscious of Biff, turns and looks up at him, then begins picking up the packages of seeds in confusion:* Where the hell is that seed? *Indignantly:* You can't see nothing out here! They boxed in the whole goddam neighborhood!

BIFF: There are people all around here. Don't you realize that?

WILLY: I'm busy. Don't bother me.

BIFF, *taking the hoe from Willy:* I'm saying good-by to you, Pop. *Willy looks at him, silent, unable to move.* I'm not coming back any more.

WILLY: You're not going to see Oliver tomorrow?

BIFF: I've got no appointment, Dad.

WILLY: He put his arm around you, and you've got no appointment?

BIFF: Pop, get this now, will you? Every time I've left it's been a fight that sent me out of here. Today I realized something about myself and I tried to explain it to you and I—I think I'm just not smart enough to make any sense out of it for you. To hell with whose fault it is or anything like that. *He takes Willy's arm.* Let's just wrap it up, heh? Come on in, we'll tell Mom. *He gently tries to pull Willy to left.*

WILLY, *frozen, immobile, with guilt in his voice:* No, I don't want to see her.

BIFF: Come on! *He pulls again, and Willy tries to pull away.*

WILLY, *highly nervous:* No, no, I don't want to see her.

BIFF, *trying to look into Willy's face, as if to find the answer there:* Why don't you want to see her?

WILLY, *more harshly now:* Don't bother me, will you?

BIFF: What do you mean, you don't want to see her? You don't want them calling you yellow, do you? This isn't your fault; it's me, I'm a bum. Now come inside! *Willy strains to get away.* Did you hear what I said to you?

Willy pulls away and quickly goes by himself into the house. Biff follows.

LINDA, *to Willy:* Did you plant, dear?

BIFF, *at the door, to Linda:* All right, we had it out. I'm going and I'm not writing any more.

LINDA, *going to Willy in the kitchen:* I think that's the best way, dear. 'Cause there's no use drawing it out, you'll just never get along.

Willy doesn't respond.

BIFF: People ask where I am and what I'm doing, you don't know, and you don't care. That way it'll be off your mind and you can start brightening up again. All right? That clears it, doesn't it? *Willy is silent, and Biff goes to him.* You gonna wish me luck, scout? *He extends his hand.* What do you say?

LINDA: Shake his hand, Willy.

WILLY, *turning to her, seething with hurt:* There's no necessity to mention the pen at all, y'know.

BIFF, *gently:* I've got no appointment, Dad.

WILLY, *erupting fiercely:* He put his arm around . . . ?

BIFF: Dad, you're never going to see what I am, so what's the use of arguing? If I strike oil I'll send you a check. Meantime forget I'm alive.

WILLY, *to Linda:* Spite, see?

BIFF: Shake hands, Dad.

WILLY: Not my hand.

BIFF: I was hoping not to go this way.

WILLY: Well, this is the way you're going. Good-by.

Biff looks at him a moment, then turns sharply and goes to the stairs.

WILLY, *stops him with:* May you rot in hell if you leave this house!

BIFF, *turning:* Exactly what is it that you want from me?

WILLY: I want you to know, on the train, in the mountains, in the valleys, wherever you go, that you cut down your life for spite!

BIFF: No, no.

WILLY: Spite, spite, is the word of your undoing! And when you're down and out, remember what did it. When you're rotting somewhere beside the railroad tracks, remember, and don't you dare blame it on me!

BIFF: I'm not blaming it on you!

WILLY: I won't take the rap for this, you hear?

Happy comes down the stairs and stands on the bottom step, watching.

BIFF: That's just what I'm telling you!

WILLY, *sinking into a chair at the table, with full accusation:* You're trying to put a knife in me—don't think I don't know what you're doing!

BIFF: All right, phony! Then let's lay it on the line. *He whips the rubber tube out of his pocket and puts it on the table.*

HAPPY: You crazy—

LINDA: Biff! *She moves to grab the hose, but Biff holds it down with his hand.*

BIFF: Leave it there! Don't move it!

WILLY, *not looking at it:* What is that?

BIFF: You know goddam well what that is.

WILLY, *caged, wanting to escape:* I never saw that.

BIFF: You saw it. The mice didn't bring it into the cellar! What is this supposed to do, make a hero out of you? This supposed to make me sorry for you?

WILLY: Never heard of it.

BIFF: There'll be no pity for you, you hear it? No pity!

WILLY, *to Linda:* You hear the spite!

BIFF: No, you're going to hear the truth—what you are and what I am!

LINDA: Stop it!

WILLY: Spite!

HAPPY, *coming down toward Biff:* You cut it now!

BIFF, *to Happy:* The man don't know who we are! The man is gonna know! *To Willy:* We never told the truth for ten minutes in this house!

HAPPY: We always told the truth!

BIFF, *turning on him:* You big blow, are you the assistant buyer? You're one of the two assistants to the assistant, aren't you?

HAPPY: Well, I'm practically—

BIFF: You're practically full of it! We all are! And I'm through with it. *To Willy:* Now hear this, Willy, this is me.

WILLY: I know you!

BIFF: You know why I had no address for three months? I stole a suit in Kansas City and I was in jail. *To Linda, who is sobbing:* Stop crying. I'm through with it.

Linda turns away from them, her hands covering her face.

WILLY: I suppose that's my fault!

BIFF: I stole myself out of every good job since high school!

WILLY: And whose fault is that?

BIFF: And I never got anywhere because you blew me so full of hot air I could never stand taking orders from anybody! That's whose fault it is!

WILLY: I hear that!

LINDA: Don't, Biff!

BIFF: It's goddam time you heard that! I had to be boss big shot in two weeks, and I'm through with it!

WILLY: Then hang yourself! For spite, hang yourself!

BIFF: No! Nobody's hanging himself, Willy! I ran down eleven flights with a pen in my hand today. And suddenly I stopped, you hear me? And in the middle of that office building, do you hear this? I stopped in the middle of that building and I saw—the sky. I saw the things that I love in this world. The work and the food and time to sit and smoke. And I looked at the pen and said to myself, what the hell am I grabbing this for? Why am I trying to become what I don't want to be? What am I doing in an office, making a contemptuous, begging fool of myself, when all I want is out there, waiting for me the minute I say I know who I am! Why can't I say that, Willy? *He tries to make Willy face him, but Willy pulls away and moves to the left.*

WILLY, *with hatred, threateningly:* The door of your life is wide open!

BIFF: Pop! I'm a dime a dozen, and so are you!

WILLY, *turning on him now in an uncontrolled outburst:* I am not a dime a dozen! I am Willy Loman, and you are Biff Loman!

Biff starts for Willy, but is blocked by Happy. In his fury, Biff seems on the verge of attacking his father.

BIFF: I am not a leader of men, Willy, and neither are you. You were never anything but a hard-working drummer who landed in the ash can like all the rest of them! I'm one dollar an hour, Willy! I tried seven states and couldn't raise it. A buck an hour! Do you gather my meaning? I'm not bringing home any prizes any more, and you're going to stop waiting for me to bring them home!

WILLY, *directly to Biff:* You vengeful, spiteful mutt!

Biff breaks from Happy. Willy, in fright, starts up the stairs. Biff grabs him.

BIFF, *at the peak of his fury:* Pop, I'm nothing! I'm nothing, Pop. Can't you understand that? There's no spite in it any more. I'm just what I am, that's all.

Biff's fury has spent itself, and he breaks down, sobbing, holding on to Willy, who dumbly fumbles for Biff's face.

WILLY, *astonished:* What're you doing? What're you doing? *To Linda:* Why is he crying?

BIFF, *crying, broken:* Will you let me go, for Christ's sake? Will you take that phony dream and burn it before something happens? *Struggling to contain himself, he pulls away and moves to the stairs.* I'll go in the morning. Put him—put him to bed. *Exhausted, Biff moves up the stairs to his room.*

WILLY, *after a long pause, astonished, elevated:* Isn't that—isn't that re-markable? Biff—he likes me!

LINDA: He loves you, Willy!

HAPPY, *deeply moved:* Always did, Pop.

WILLY: Oh, Biff! *Staring wildly:* He cried! Cried to me. *He is choking with his love, and now cries out his promise:* That boy—that boy is going to be magnificent!

Ben appears in the light just outside the kitchen.

BEN: Yes, outstanding, with twenty thousand behind him.

LINDA, *sensing the racing of his mind, fearfully, carefully:* Now come to bed, Willy. It's all settled now.

WILLY, *finding it difficult not to rush out of the house:* Yes, we'll sleep. Come on. Go to sleep, Hap.

BEN: And it does take a great kind of a man to crack the jungle.

In accents of dread, Ben's idyllic music starts up.

HAPPY, *his arm around Linda:* I'm getting married, Pop, don't forget it. I'm changing everything. I'm gonna run that department before the year is up. You'll see, Mom. *He kisses her.*

BEN: The jungle is dark but full of diamonds, Willy.

Willy turns, moves, listening to Ben.

LINDA: Be good. You're both good boys, just act that way, that's all.

HAPPY: 'Night, Pop. *He goes upstairs.*

LINDA, *to Willy:* Come, dear.

BEN, *with greater force:* One must go in to fetch a diamond out.

WILLY, *to Linda, as he moves slowly along the edge of the kitchen, toward the door:* I just want to get settled down, Linda. Let me sit alone for a little.

LINDA, *almost uttering her fear:* I want you upstairs.

WILLY, *taking her in his arms:* In a few minutes, Linda. I couldn't sleep right now. Go on, you look awful tired. *He kisses her.*

BEN: Not like an appointment at all. A diamond is rough and hard to the touch.

WILLY: Go on now. I'll be right up.

LINDA: I think this is the only way, Willy.

WILLY: Sure, it's the best thing.

BEN: Best thing!

WILLY: The only way. Everything is gonna be—go on, kid, get to bed. You look so tired.

LINDA: Come right up.

WILLY: Two minutes.

Linda goes into the living room, then reappears in her bedroom. Willy moves just outside the kitchen door.

WILLY: Loves me. *Wonderingly:* Always loved me. Isn't that a remarkable thing? Ben, he'll worship me for it!

BEN, *with promise:* It's dark there, but full of diamonds.

WILLY: Can you imagine that magnificence with twenty thousand dollars in his pocket?

LINDA, *calling from her room:* Willy! Come up!

WILLY, *calling into the kitchen:* Yes! Yes. Coming! It's very smart, you realize that, don't you, sweetheart? Even Ben sees it. I gotta go, baby. 'By! 'By! *Going over to Ben, almost dancing:* Imagine? When the mail comes he'll be ahead of Bernard again!

BEN: A perfect proposition all around.

WILLY: Did you see how he cried to me? Oh, if I could kiss him, Ben!

BEN: Time, William, time!

WILLY: Oh, Ben, I always knew one way or another we were gonna make it, Biff and I!

BEN, *looking at his watch:* The boat. We'll be late. *He moves slowly off into the darkness.*

WILLY, *elegiacally, turning to the house:* Now when you kick off, boy, I want a seventy-yard boot, and get right down the field under the ball, and when you hit, hit low and hit hard, because it's important, boy. *He swings around and faces the audience.* There's all kinds of important people in the stands, and the first thing you know . . . *Suddenly realizing he is alone:* Ben! Ben, where do I . . . ? *He makes a sudden movement of search.* Ben, how do I . . . ?

LINDA, *calling:* Willy, you coming up?

WILLY, *uttering a gasp of fear, whirling about as if to quiet her:* Sh! *He turns around as if to find his way; sounds, faces, voices, seem to be swarming in upon him and he flicks at them, crying,* Sh! Sh! *Suddenly music, faint and high, stops him. It rises in intensity, almost to an unbearable scream. He goes up and down on his toes, and rushes off around the house.* Shhh!

LINDA: Willy?

There is no answer. Linda waits. Biff gets up off his bed. He is still in his clothes. Happy sits up. Biff stands listening.

LINDA, *with real fear:* Willy, answer me! Willy!

There is the sound of a car starting and moving away at full speed.

LINDA: No!

BIFF, *rushing down the stairs:* Pop!

As the car speeds off, the music crashes down in a frenzy of sound, which becomes the soft pulsation of a single cello string. Biff slowly returns to his bedroom. He and Happy gravely don their jackets. Linda slowly walks out of her room. The music has developed into a dead march. The leaves of day are appearing over everything. Charley and Bernard, somberly dressed, appear and knock on the kitchen door. Biff and Happy slowly descend the stairs to the kitchen as Charley and Bernard enter. All stop a moment when Linda, in clothes of mourning, bearing a little bunch of roses, comes through the draped doorway into the kitchen. She goes to Charley and takes his arm. Now all move toward the audience, through the wall-line of the kitchen. At the limit of the apron, Linda lays down the flowers, kneels, and sits back on her heels. All stare down at the grave.

REQUIEM

CHARLEY: It's getting dark, Linda.

Linda doesn't react. She stares at the grave.

BIFF: How about it, Mom? Better get some rest, heh? They'll be closing the gate soon.

Linda makes no move. Pause.

HAPPY, *deeply angered:* He had no right to do that. There was no necessity for it. We would've helped him.

CHARLEY, *grunting:* Hmmm.

BIFF: Come along, Mom.

LINDA: Why didn't anybody come?

CHARLEY: It was a very nice funeral.

LINDA: But where are all the people he knew? Maybe they blame him.

CHARLEY: Naa. It's a rough world, Linda. They wouldn't blame him.

LINDA: I can't understand it. At this time especially. First time in thirty-five years we were just about free and clear. He only needed a little salary. He was even finished with the dentist.

CHARLEY: No man only needs a little salary.

LINDA: I can't understand it.

BIFF: There were a lot of nice days. When he'd come home from a trip; or on Sundays, making the stoop; finishing the cellar; putting on the new porch; when he built the extra bathroom; and put up the garage. You know something, Charley, there's more of him in that front stoop than in all the sales he ever made.

CHARLEY: Yeah. He was a happy man with a batch of cement.

LINDA: He was so wonderful with his hands.

BIFF: He had the wrong dreams. All, all, wrong.

HAPPY, *almost ready to fight Biff:* Don't say that!

BIFF: He never knew who he was.

CHARLEY, *stopping Happy's movement and reply. To Biff:* Nobody dast blame this man. You don't understand: Willy was a salesman. And for a salesman, there is no rock bottom to the life. He don't put a bolt to a nut, he don't tell you the law or give you medicine. He's a man way out there in the blue, riding on a smile and a shoeshine. And when they start not smiling back—that's an earthquake. And then you get yourself a couple of spots on your hat, and you're finished. Nobody dast blame this man. A salesman is got to dream, boy. It comes with the territory.

BIFF: Charley, the man didn't know who he was.

HAPPY, *infuriated:* Don't say that!

BIFF: Why don't you come with me, Happy?

HAPPY: I'm not licked that easily. I'm staying right in this city, and I'm gonna beat this racket! *He looks at Biff, his chin set.* The Loman Brothers!

BIFF: I know who I am, kid.

HAPPY: All right, boy. I'm gonna show you and everybody else that Willy Loman did not die in vain. He had a good dream. It's the only dream you can have—to come out number-one man. He fought it out here, and this is where I'm gonna win it for him.

BIFF—*with a hopeless glance at Happy, he bends toward his mother:* Let's go, Mom.

LINDA: I'll be with you in a minute. Go on, Charley. *He hesitates.* I want to, just for a minute. I never had a chance to say good-by.

Charley moves away, followed by Happy. Biff remains a slight distance up and left of Linda. She sits there, summoning herself. The flute begins, not far away, playing behind her speech.

LINDA: Forgive me, dear. I can't cry. I don't know what it is, but I can't cry. I don't understand it. Why did you ever do that? Help me, Willy, I can't cry. It seems to me that you're just on another trip. I keep expecting you. Willy, dear, I can't cry. Why did you do it? I search and search and I search, and I can't understand it, Willy. I made the last payment on the house today. Today, dear. And there'll be nobody home. *A sob rises in her throat.* We're free and clear. *Sobbing more fully, released:* We're free. *Biff comes slowly toward her.* We're free . . . We're free . . .

Biff lifts her to her feet and moves out up right with her in his arms. Linda sobs quietly. Bernard and Charley come together and follow them, followed by Happy. Only the music of the flute is left on the darkening stage as over the house the hard towers of the apartment buildings rise into sharp focus, and

The Curtain Falls

THE CRUCIBLE

THE CAST
(in order of appearance)

REVEREND PARRIS	Fred Stewart
BETTY PARRIS	Janet Alexander
TITUBA	Jacqueline Andre
ABIGAIL WILLIAMS	Madeleine Sherwood
SUSANNA WALCOTT	Barbara Stanton
MRS. ANN PUTNAM	Jane Hoffman
THOMAS PUTNAM	Raymond Bramley
MERCY LEWIS	Dorothy Joliffe
MARY WARREN	Jennie Egan
JOHN PROCTOR	Arthur Kennedy
REBECCA NURSE	Jean Adair
GILES COREY	Joseph Sweeney
REVEREND JOHN HALE	E. G. Marshall
ELIZABETH PROCTOR	Beatrice Straight
FRANCIS NURSE	Graham Velsey
EZEKIEL CHEEVER	Don McHenry
MARSHAL HERRICK	George Mitchell
JUDGE HATHORNE	Philip Coolidge
DEPUTY GOVERNOR DANFORTH	Walter Hampden
SARAH GOOD	Adele Fortin
HOPKINS	Donald Marye

Directed by Jed Harris; produced by Kermit Bloomgarden. Opened January 22, 1953, Martin Beck Theatre, New York City.

A NOTE ON
THE HISTORICAL ACCURACY
OF THIS PLAY

This play is not history in the sense in which the word is used by the academic historian. Dramatic purposes have sometimes required many characters to be fused into one; the number of girls involved in the "crying-out" has been reduced; Abigail's age has been raised; while there were several judges of almost equal authority, I have symbolized them all in Hathorne and Danforth. However, I believe that the reader will discover here the essential nature of one of the strangest and most awful chapters in human history. The fate of each character is exactly that of his historical model, and there is no one in the drama who did not play a similar—and in some cases exactly the same—role in history.

As for the characters of the persons, little is known about most of them excepting what may be surmised from a few letters, the trial record, certain broadsides written at the time, and references to their conduct in sources of varying reliability. They may therefore be taken as creations of my own, drawn to the best of my ability in conformity with their known behavior, except as indicated in the commentary I have written for this text.

ACT ONE

(An Overture)

A small upper bedroom in the home of Reverend Samuel Parris, Salem, Massachusetts, in the spring of the year 1692.

There is a narrow window at the left. Through its leaded panes the morning sunlight streams. A candle still burns near the bed, which is at the right. A chest, a chair, and a small table are the other furnishings. At the back a door opens on the landing of the stairway to the ground floor. The room gives off an air of clean spareness. The roof rafters are exposed, and the wood colors are raw and unmellowed.

As the curtain rises, Reverend Parris is discovered kneeling beside the bed, evidently in prayer. His daughter, Betty Parris, aged ten, is lying on the bed, inert.

At the time of these events Parris was in his middle forties. In history he cut a villainous path, and there is very little good to be said for him. He believed he was being persecuted wherever he went, despite his best efforts to win people and God to his side. In meeting, he felt insulted if someone rose to shut the door without first asking his permission. He was a widower with no interest in children, or talent with them. He regarded them as young adults, and until this strange crisis he, like the rest of Salem, never conceived that the children were anything but thankful for being permitted to walk straight, eyes slightly lowered, arms at the sides, and mouths shut until bidden to speak.

His house stood in the "town"—but we today would hardly call it a village. The meeting house was nearby, and from this point outward—toward the bay or inland—there were a few small-windowed, dark houses snuggling against the raw Massachusetts winter. Salem had been established hardly forty years before. To the European world the whole province was a barbaric frontier inhabited by a sect of fanatics who, nevertheless, were shipping out products of slowly increasing quantity and value.

No one can really know what their lives were like. They had no novelists—and would not have permitted anyone to read a novel if one were handy. Their creed forbade anything resembling a theater or "vain enjoyment." They did not celebrate Christmas, and a holiday from work meant only that they must concentrate even more upon prayer.

Which is not to say that nothing broke into this strict and somber way of life. When a new farmhouse was built, friends assembled to "raise the roof," and there would be special foods cooked and probably some potent cider passed around. There was a good supply of ne'er-do-wells in Salem, who dallied at the shovelboard in Bridget Bishop's tavern. Probably more than the creed, hard work kept the morals of the place from spoiling, for the people were forced to fight the land like heroes for every grain of corn, and no man had very much time for fooling around.

That there were some jokers, however, is indicated by the practice of appointing a two-man patrol whose duty was to "walk forth in the time of God's worship to take notice of such as either lye about the meeting house, without attending to the word and ordinances, or that lye at home or in the fields without giving good account thereof, and to take the names of such persons, and to present them to the magistrates, whereby they may be accordingly proceeded against." This predilection for minding other people's business was time-honored among the people of Salem, and it undoubtedly created many of the suspicions which were to feed the coming madness. It was also, in my opinion, one of the things that a John Proctor would rebel against, for the time of the armed camp had almost passed, and since the country was reasonably—although not wholly—safe, the old disciplines were beginning to rankle. But, as in all such matters, the issue was not clear-cut, for danger was still a possibility, and in unity still lay the best promise of safety.

The edge of the wilderness was close by. The American continent stretched endlessly west, and it was full of mystery for them. It stood, dark and threatening, over their shoulders night and day, for out of it Indian tribes marauded from time to time, and Reverend Parris had parishioners who had lost relatives to these heathen.

The parochial snobbery of these people was partly responsible for their failure to convert the Indians. Probably they also preferred to take land from heathens rather than from fellow Christians. At any rate, very few Indians were converted, and the Salem folk believed that the virgin forest was the Devil's last preserve, his home base and the citadel of his final stand. To the best of their knowledge the American forest was the last place on earth that was not paying homage to God.

For these reasons, among others, they carried about an air of innate resistance, even of persecution. Their fathers had, of course, been persecuted in England. So now they and their church found it necessary to deny any other sect its freedom, lest their New Jerusalem be defiled and corrupted by wrong ways and deceitful ideas.

They believed, in short, that they held in their steady hands the candle that would light the world. We have inherited this belief, and it has helped and hurt us. It helped them with the discipline it gave them. They were a dedicated folk, by and large, and they had to be to survive the life they had chosen or been born into in this country.

The proof of their belief's value to them may be taken from the opposite character of the first Jamestown settlement, farther south, in Virginia. The Englishmen who landed there were motivated mainly by a hunt for profit. They had thought to pick off the wealth of the new country and then return rich to England. They were a band of individualists, and a much more ingratiating group than the Massachusetts men. But Virginia destroyed them. Massachusetts tried to kill off the Puritans, but they combined; they set up a communal society which, in the beginning, was little more than an armed camp with an autocratic and very devoted leadership. It was, however, an autocracy by consent, for they were united from top to bottom by a commonly held ideology whose perpetuation was the reason and justification for all their sufferings. So their self-denial, their purposefulness, their suspicion of all vain pursuits, their hard-handed justice, were altogether perfect instruments for the conquest of this space so antagonistic to man.

But the people of Salem in 1692 were not quite the dedicated folk that arrived on the *Mayflower*. A vast differentiation had taken place, and in their own time a revolution had unseated the royal government and substituted a junta which was at this moment in power. The times, to their eyes, must have been out of joint, and to the common folk must have seemed as insoluble and complicated as do ours today. It is not hard to see how easily many could have been led to believe that the time of confusion had been brought upon them by deep and darkling forces. No hint of such speculation appears on the court record, but social disorder in any age breeds such mystical suspicions, and when, as in Salem, wonders are brought forth from below the social surface, it is too much to expect people to hold back very long from laying on the victims with all the force of their frustrations.

The Salem tragedy, which is about to begin in these pages, developed from a paradox. It is a paradox in whose grip we still live, and there is no prospect yet that we will discover its resolution. Simply, it was this: for good purposes, even high purposes, the people of Salem developed a theocracy, a combine of state and religious power whose function was to keep the community together, and to prevent any kind of disunity that might open it to destruction by material or ideological enemies. It was forged for a necessary purpose and accomplished that purpose. But all organization is and must be grounded on the idea of exclusion and prohibition, just as two objects cannot occupy the same space. Evidently the time came in New England when the repressions of order were heavier than seemed warranted by the dangers against which the order was organized. The witch-hunt was a perverse manifestation of the panic which set in among all classes when the balance began to turn toward greater individual freedom.

When one rises above the individual villainy displayed, one can only pity them all, just as we shall be pitied someday. It is still impossible for man to organize his social life without repressions, and the balance has yet to be struck between order and freedom.

The witch-hunt was not, however, a mere repression. It was also, and as importantly, a long overdue opportunity for everyone so inclined to express publicly his guilt and sins, under the cover of accusations against the victims. It suddenly became possible—and patriotic and holy—for a man to say that Martha Corey had come into his bedroom at night, and that, while his wife was sleeping at his side, Martha laid herself down on his chest and "nearly suffocated him." Of course it was her spirit only, but his satisfaction at confessing himself was no lighter than if it had been Martha herself. One could not ordinarily speak such things in public.

Long-held hatreds of neighbors could now be openly expressed, and vengeance taken, despite the Bible's charitable injunctions. Land-lust which had been expressed by constant bickering over bounderies and deeds, could now be elevated to the arena of morality; one could cry witch against one's neighbor and feel perfectly justified in the bargain. Old scores could be settled on a plane of heavenly combat between Lucifer and the Lord; suspicions and the envy of the miserable toward the happy could and did burst out in the general revenge.

Reverend Parris is praying now, and, though we cannot hear his words, a sense of his confusion hangs about him. He mumbles, then seems about to weep; then he weeps, then prays again; but his daughter does not stir on the bed.

The door opens, and his Negro slave enters. Tituba is in her forties. Parris brought her with him from Barbados, where he spent some years as a merchant before entering the ministry. She enters as one does who can no longer bear to be barred from the sight of her beloved, but she is also very frightened because her slave sense has warned her that, as always, trouble in this house eventually lands on her back.

TITUBA, *already taking a step backward:* My Betty be hearty soon?

PARRIS: Out of here!

TITUBA, *backing to the door:* My Betty not goin' die . . .

PARRIS, *scrambling to his feet in a fury:* Out of my sight! *She is gone.* Out of my— *He is overcome with sobs. He clamps his teeth against them and closes the door and leans against it, exhausted.* Oh, my God! God help me! *Quaking with fear, mumbling to himself through his sobs, he goes to the bed and gently takes Betty's hand.* Betty. Child. Dear child. Will you wake, will you open up your eyes! Betty, little one . . .

He is bending to kneel again when his niece, Abigail Williams, seventeen, enters—a strikingly beautiful girl, an orphan, with an endless capacity for dissembling. Now she is all worry and apprehension and propriety.

ABIGAIL: Uncle? *He looks to her.* Susanna Walcott's here from Doctor Griggs.

PARRIS: Oh? Let her come, let her come.

ABIGAIL, *leaning out the door to call to Susanna, who is down the hall a few steps:* Come in, Susanna.

Susanna Walcott, a little younger than Abigail, a nervous, hurried girl, enters.

PARRIS, *eagerly:* What does the doctor say, child?

SUSANNA, *craning around Parris to get a look at Betty:* He bid me come and tell you, reverend sir, that he cannot discover no medicine for it in his books.

PARRIS: Then he must search on.

SUSANNA: Aye, sir, he have been searchin' his books since he left you, sir. But he bid me tell you, that you might look to unnatural things for the cause of it.

PARRIS, *his eyes going wide:* No—no. There be no unnatural cause here. Tell him I have sent for Reverend Hale of Beverly, and Mr. Hale will surely confirm that. Let him look to medicine and put out all thought of unnatural causes here. There be none.

SUSANNA: Aye, sir. He bid me tell you. *She turns to go.*

ABIGAIL: Speak nothin' of it in the village, Susanna.

PARRIS: Go directly home and speak nothing of unnatural causes.

SUSANNA: Aye, sir. I pray for her. *She goes out.*

ABIGAIL: Uncle, the rumor of witchcraft is all about; I think you'd best go down and deny it yourself. The parlor's packed with people, sir. I'll sit with her.

PARRIS, *pressed, turns on her:* And what shall I say to them? That my daughter and my niece I discovered dancing like heathen in the forest?

ABIGAIL: Uncle, we did dance; let you tell them I confessed it—and I'll be whipped if I must be. But they're speakin' of witchcraft. Betty's not witched.

PARRIS: Abigail, I cannot go before the congregation when I know you have not opened with me. What did you do with her in the forest?

ABIGAIL: We did dance, uncle, and when you leaped out of the bush so suddenly, Betty was frightened and then she fainted. And there's the whole of it.

PARRIS: Child. Sit you down.

ABIGAIL, *quavering, as she sits:* I would never hurt Betty. I love her dearly.

PARRIS: Now look you, child, your punishment will come in its time. But if you trafficked with spirits in the forest I must know it now, for surely my enemies will, and they will ruin me with it.

ABIGAIL: But we never conjured spirits.

PARRIS: Then why can she not move herself since midnight? This child is desperate! *Abigail lowers her eyes.* It must come out—my enemies will bring it out. Let me know what you done there. Abigail, do you understand that I have many enemies?

ABIGAIL: I have heard of it, uncle.

PARRIS: There is a faction that is sworn to drive me from my pulpit. Do you understand that?

ABIGAIL: I think so, sir.

PARRIS: Now then, in the midst of such disruption, my own household is discovered to be the very center of some obscene practice. Abominations are done in the forest—

ABIGAIL: It were sport, uncle!

PARRIS, *pointing at Betty:* You call this sport? *She lowers her eyes. He pleads:* Abigail, if you know something that may help the doctor, for God's sake tell it to me. *She is silent.* I saw Tituba waving her arms over the fire when I came on you. Why was she doing that? And I heard a screeching and gibberish coming from her mouth. She were swaying like a dumb beast over that fire!

ABIGAIL: She always sings her Barbados songs, and we dance.

PARRIS: I cannot blink what I saw, Abigail, for my enemies will not blink it. I saw a dress lying on the grass.

ABIGAIL, *innocently:* A dress?

PARRIS—*it is very hard to say:* Aye, a dress. And I thought I saw—someone naked running through the trees!

ABIGAIL, *in terror:* No one was naked! You mistake yourself, uncle!

PARRIS, *with anger:* I saw it! *He moves from her. Then, resolved:* Now tell me true, Abigail. And I pray you feel the weight of truth upon you, for now my ministry's at stake, my ministry and perhaps your cousin's life.

Whatever abomination you have done, give me all of it now, for I dare not be taken unaware when I go before them down there.

ABIGAIL: There is nothin' more. I swear it, uncle.

PARRIS—*he studies her, then nods, half convinced:* Abigail, I have fought here three long years to bend these stiff-necked people to me, and now, just now when some good respect is rising for me in the parish, you compromise my very character. I have given you a home, child, I have put clothes upon your back—now give me upright answer. Your name in the town—it is entirely white, is it not?

ABIGAIL, *with an edge of resentment:* Why, I am sure it is, sir. There be no blush about my name.

PARRIS, *to the point:* Abigail, is there any other cause than you have told me, for your being discharged from Goody Proctor's service? I have heard it said, and I tell you as I heard it, that she comes so rarely to the church this year for she will not sit so close to something soiled. What signified that remark?

ABIGAIL: She hates me, uncle, she must, for I would not be her slave. It's a bitter woman, a lying, cold, sniveling woman, and I will not work for such a woman!

PARRIS: She may be. And yet it has troubled me that you are now seven month out of their house, and in all this time no other family has ever called for your service.

ABIGAIL: They want slaves, not such as I. Let them send to Barbados for that. I will not black my face for any of them! *With ill-concealed resentment at him:* Do you begrudge my bed, uncle?

PARRIS: No—no.

ABIGAIL, *in a temper:* My name is good in the village! I will not have it said my name is soiled! Goody Proctor is a gossiping liar!

Enter Mrs. Ann Putnam. She is a twisted soul of forty-five, a death-ridden woman, haunted by dreams.

PARRIS, *as soon as the door begins to open:* No—no, I cannot have anyone. *He sees her, and a certain deference springs into him, although his worry remains.* Why, Goody Putnam, come in.

MRS. PUTNAM, *full of breath, shiny-eyed:* It is a marvel. It is surely a stroke of hell upon you.

PARRIS: No, Goody Putnam, it is—

MRS. PUTNAM, *glancing at Betty:* How high did she fly, how high?

PARRIS: No, no, she never flew—

MRS. PUTNAM, *very pleased with it:* Why, it's sure she did. Mr. Collins saw her goin' over Ingersoll's barn, and come down light as bird, he says!

PARRIS: Now, look you, Goody Putnam, she never— *Enter Thomas Putnam, a well-to-do, hard-handed landowner, near fifty.* Oh, good morning, Mr. Putnam.

PUTNAM: It is a providence the thing is out now! It is a providence. *He goes directly to the bed.*

PARRIS: What's out, sir, what's—?

Mrs. Putnam goes to the bed.

PUTNAM, *looking down at Betty:* Why, *her* eyes is closed! Look you, Ann.

MRS. PUTNAM: Why, that's strange. *To Parris:* Ours is open.

PARRIS, *shocked:* Your Ruth is sick?

MRS. PUTNAM, *with vicious certainty:* I'd not call it sick; the Devil's touch is heavier than sick. It's death, y'know, it's death drivin' into them, forked and hoofed.

PARRIS: Oh, pray not! Why, how does Ruth ail?

MRS. PUTNAM: She ails as she must—she never waked this morning, but her eyes open and she walks, and hears naught, sees naught, and cannot eat. Her soul is taken, surely.

Parris is struck.

PUTNAM, *as though for further details:* They say you've sent for Reverend Hale of Beverly?

PARRIS, *with dwindling conviction now:* A precaution only. He has much experience in all demonic arts, and I—

MRS. PUTNAM: He has indeed; and found a witch in Beverly last year, and let you remember that.

PARRIS: Now, Goody Ann, they only thought that were a witch, and I am certain there be no element of witchcraft here.

PUTNAM: No witchcraft! Now look you, Mr. Parris—

PARRIS: Thomas, Thomas, I pray you, leap not to witchcraft. I know that you—you least of all, Thomas, would ever wish so disastrous a charge laid upon me. We cannot leap to witchcraft. They will howl me out of Salem for such corruption in my house.

A word about Thomas Putnam. He was a man with many grievances, at least one of which appears justified. Some time before, his wife's brother-in-law, James Bayley, had been turned down as minister of Salem. Bayley had all the qualifications, and a two-thirds vote into the bargain, but a faction stopped his acceptance, for reasons that are not clear.

Thomas Putnam was the eldest son of the richest man in the village. He had fought the Indians at Narragansett, and was deeply interested in parish affairs. He undoubtedly felt it poor payment that the village should so blatantly disregard his candidate for one of its more important offices, especially since he regarded himself as the intellectual superior of most of the people around him.

His vindictive nature was demonstrated long before the witchcraft began. A former Salem minister, George Burroughs, had had to borrow money to pay for his wife's funeral, and, since the parish was remiss in his salary, he was soon bankrupt. Thomas and his brother John had Burroughs jailed for debts the man did not owe. The incident is important only in that Burroughs succeeded in becoming minister where Bayley, Thomas Putnam's brother-in-law, had been rejected; the motif of resentment is clear here. Thomas Putnam felt that his own name and the honor of his family had been smirched by the village, and he meant to right matters however he could.

Another reason to believe him a deeply embittered man was his attempt to break his father's will, which left a disproportionate amount to a stepbrother. As with every other public cause in which he tried to force his way, he failed in this.

So it is not surprising to find that so many accusations against people are in the handwriting of Thomas Putnam, or that his name is so often found as a witness corroborating the supernatural testimony, or that his daughter led the crying-out at the most opportune junctures of the trials, especially when— But we'll speak of that when we come to it.

PUTNAM—*at the moment he is intent upon getting Parris, for whom he has only contempt, to move toward the abyss:* Mr. Parris, I have taken your part in all contention here, and I would continue; but I cannot if you hold back in this. There are hurtful, vengeful spirits layin' hands on these children.

PARRIS: But, Thomas, you cannot—

PUTNAM: Ann! Tell Mr. Parris what you have done.

MRS. PUTNAM: Reverend Parris, I have laid seven babies unbaptized in the earth. Believe me, sir, you never saw more hearty babies born. And yet, each would wither in my arms the very night of their birth. I have spoke nothin', but my heart has clamored intimations. And now, this year, my Ruth, my only— I see her turning strange. A secret child she has become this year, and shrivels like a sucking mouth were pullin' on her life too. And so I thought to send her to your Tituba—

PARRIS: To Tituba! What may Tituba—?

MRS. PUTNAM: Tituba knows how to speak to the dead, Mr. Parris.

PARRIS: Goody Ann, it is a formidable sin to conjure up the dead!

MRS. PUTNAM: I take it on my soul, but who else may surely tell us what person murdered my babies?

PARRIS, *horrified:* Woman!

MRS. PUTNAM: They were murdered, Mr. Parris! And mark this proof! Mark it! Last night my Ruth were ever so close to their little spirits; I know it, sir. For how else is she struck dumb now except some power of darkness would stop her mouth? It is a marvelous sign, Mr. Parris!

PUTNAM: Don't you understand it, sir? There is a murdering witch among us, bound to keep herself in the dark. *Parris turns to Betty, a frantic terror rising in him.* Let your enemies make of it what they will, you cannot blink it more.

PARRIS, *to Abigail:* Then you were conjuring spirits last night.

ABIGAIL, *whispering:* Not I, sir—Tituba and Ruth.

PARRIS *turns now, with new fear, and goes to Betty, looks down at her, and then, gazing off:* Oh, Abigail, what proper payment for my charity! Now I am undone.

PUTNAM: You are not undone! Let you take hold here. Wait for no one to charge you—declare it yourself. You have discovered witch-craft—

PARRIS: In my house? In my house, Thomas? They will topple me with this! They will make of it a—

Enter Mercy Lewis, the Putnams' servant, a fat, sly, merciless girl of eighteen.

MERCY: Your pardons. I only thought to see how Betty is.

PUTNAM: Why aren't you home? Who's with Ruth?

MERCY: Her grandma come. She's improved a little, I think—she give a powerful sneeze before.

MRS. PUTNAM: Ah, there's a sign of life!

MERCY: I'd fear no more, Goody Putnam. It were a grand sneeze; another like it will shake her wits together, I'm sure. *She goes to the bed to look.*

PARRIS: Will you leave me now, Thomas? I would pray a while alone.

ABIGAIL: Uncle, you've prayed since midnight. Why do you not go down and—

PARRIS: No—no. *To Putnam:* I have no answer for that crowd. I'll wait till Mr. Hale arrives. *To get Mrs. Putnam to leave:* If you will, Goody Ann . . .

PUTNAM: Now look you, sir. Let you strike out against the Devil, and the village will bless you for it! Come down, speak to them—pray with them. They're thirsting for your word, Mister! Surely you'll pray with them.

PARRIS, *swayed:* I'll lead them in a psalm, but let you say nothing of witchcraft yet. I will not discuss it. The cause is yet unknown. I have had enough contention since I came; I want no more.

MRS. PUTNAM: Mercy, you go home to Ruth, d'y'hear?

MERCY: Aye, mum.

Mrs. Putnam goes out.

PARRIS, *to Abigail:* If she starts for the window, cry for me at once.

ABIGAIL: I will, uncle.

PARRIS, *to Putnam:* There is a terrible power in her arms today. *He goes out with Putnam.*

ABIGAIL, *with hushed trepidation:* How is Ruth sick?

MERCY: It's weirdish, I know not—she seems to walk like a dead one since last night.

ABIGAIL—*she turns at once and goes to Betty, and now, with fear in her voice:* Betty? *Betty doesn't move. She shakes her.* Now stop this! Betty! Sit up now! *Betty doesn't stir. Mercy comes over.*

MERCY: Have you tried beatin' her? I gave Ruth a good one and it waked her for a minute. Here, let me have her.

ABIGAIL, *holding Mercy back:* No, he'll be comin' up. Listen, now; if they be questioning us, tell them we danced—I told him as much already.

MERCY: Aye. And what more?

ABIGAIL: He knows Tituba conjured Ruth's sisters to come out of the grave.

MERCY: And what more?

ABIGAIL: He saw you naked.

MERCY, *clapping her hands together with a frightened laugh:* Oh, Jesus!

Enter Mary Warren, breathless. She is seventeen, a subservient, naïve, lonely girl.

MARY WARREN: What'll we do? The village is out! I just come from the farm; the whole country's talkin' witchcraft! They'll be callin' us witches, Abby!

MERCY, *pointing and looking at Mary Warren:* She means to tell, I know it.

MARY WARREN: Abby, we've got to tell. Witchery's a hangin' error, a hangin' like they done in Boston two year ago! We must tell the truth, Abby! You'll only be whipped for dancin', and the other things!

ABIGAIL: Oh, *we'll* be whipped!

MARY WARREN: I never done none of it, Abby. I only looked!

MERCY, *moving menacingly toward Mary:* Oh, you're a great one for lookin', aren't you, Mary Warren? What a grand peeping courage you have!

Betty, on the bed, whimpers. Abigail turns to her at once.

ABIGAIL: Betty? *She goes to Betty.* Now, Betty, dear, wake up now. It's Abigail. *She sits Betty up and furiously shakes her.* I'll beat you, Betty! *Betty whimpers.* My, you seem improving. I talked to your papa and I told him everything. So there's nothing to—

BETTY—*she darts off the bed, frightened of Abigail, and flattens herself against the wall:* I want my mama!

ABIGAIL, *with alarm, as she cautiously approaches Betty:* What ails you, Betty? Your mama's dead and buried.

BETTY: I'll fly to Mama. Let me fly! *She raises her arms as though to fly, and streaks for the window, gets one leg out.*

ABIGAIL, *pulling her away from the window:* I told him everything; he knows now, he knows everything we—

BETTY: You drank blood, Abby! You didn't tell him that!

ABIGAIL: Betty, you never say that again! You will never—

BETTY: You did, you did! You drank a charm to kill John Proctor's wife! You drank a charm to kill Goody Proctor!

ABIGAIL, *smashing her across the face:* Shut it! Now shut it!

BETTY, *collapsing on the bed:* Mama, Mama! *She dissolves into sobs.*

ABIGAIL: Now look you. All of you. We danced. And Tituba conjured Ruth Putnam's dead sisters. And that is all. And mark this. Let either of you breathe a word, or the edge of a word, about the other things, and I will come to you in the black of some terrible night and I will bring a pointy reckoning that will shudder you. And you know I can do it; I saw Indians smash my dear parents' heads on the pillow next to mine, and I have seen some reddish work done at night, and I can make you wish you had never seen the sun go down! *She goes to Betty and roughly sits her up.* Now, you—sit up and stop this! *But Betty collapses in her hands and lies inert on the bed.*

MARY WARREN, *with hysterical fright:* What's got her? *Abigail stares in fright at Betty.* Abby, she's going to die! It's a sin to conjure, and we—

ABIGAIL, *starting for Mary:* I say shut it, Mary Warren!

Enter John Proctor. On seeing him, Mary Warren leaps in fright.

Proctor was a farmer in his middle thirties. He need not have been a partisan of any faction in the town, but there is evidence to suggest that he had a sharp and biting way with hypocrites. He was the kind of man—powerful of body, even-tempered, and not easily led—who cannot refuse support to partisans without drawing their deepest resentment. In Proctor's presence a fool felt his foolishness instantly—and a Proctor is always marked for calumny therefore.

But as we shall see, the steady manner he displays does not spring from an untroubled soul. He is a sinner, a sinner not only against the moral fashion of the time, but against his own vision of decent conduct. These people had no ritual for the washing away of sins. It is another trait we inherited from them, and it has helped to discipline us as well as to breed hypocrisy among us. Proctor, respected and even feared in Salem, has come to regard himself as a kind of fraud. But no hint of this has yet appeared on the surface, and as he enters from the crowded parlor below it is a man in his prime we see, with a quiet confidence and an unexpressed, hidden force. Mary Warren, his servant, can barely speak for embarrassment and fear.

MARY WARREN: Oh! I'm just going home, Mr. Proctor.

PROCTOR: Be you foolish, Mary Warren? Be you deaf? I forbid you leave the house, did I not? Why shall I pay you? I am looking for you more often than my cows!

MARY WARREN: I only come to see the great doings in the world.

PROCTOR: I'll show you a great doin' on your arse one of these days. Now get you home; my wife is waitin' with your work! *Trying to retain a shred of dignity, she goes slowly out.*

MERCY LEWIS, *both afraid of him and strangely tititlated:* I'd best be off. I have my Ruth to watch. Good morning, Mr. Proctor.

Mercy sidles out. Since Proctor's entrance, Abigail has stood as though on tiptoe, absorbing his presence, wide-eyed. He glances at her, then goes to Betty on the bed.

ABIGAIL: Gah! I'd almost forgot how strong you are, John Proctor!

PROCTOR, *looking at Abigail now, the faintest suggestion of a knowing smile on his face:* What's this mischief here?

ABIGAIL, *with a nervous laugh:* Oh, she's only gone silly somehow.

PROCTOR: The road past my house is a pilgrimage to Salem all morning. The town's mumbling witchcraft.

ABIGAIL: Oh, posh! *Winningly she comes a little closer, with a confidential, wicked air.* We were dancin' in the woods last night, and my uncle leaped in on us. She took fright, is all.

PROCTOR, *his smile widening:* Ah, you're wicked yet, aren't y'! *A trill of expectant laughter escapes her, and she dares come closer, feverishly looking into his eyes.* You'll be clapped in the stocks before you're twenty.

He takes a step to go, and she springs into his path.

ABIGAIL: Give me a word, John. A soft word. *Her concentrated desire destroys his smile.*

PROCTOR: No, no, Abby. That's done with.

ABIGAIL, *tauntingly:* You come five mile to see a silly girl fly? I know you better.

PROCTOR, *setting her firmly out of his path:* I come to see what mischief your uncle's brewin' now. *With final emphasis:* Put it out of mind, Abby.

ABIGAIL, *grasping his hand before he can release her:* John—I am waitin' for you every night.

PROCTOR: Abby, I never give you hope to wait for me.

ABIGAIL, *now beginning to anger—she can't believe it:* I have something better than hope, I think!

PROCTOR: Abby, you'll put it out of mind. I'll not be comin' for you more.

ABIGAIL: You're surely sportin' with me.

PROCTOR: You know me better.

ABIGAIL: I know how you clutched my back behind your house and sweated like a stallion whenever I come near! Or did I dream that? It's she put me out, you cannot pretend it were you. I saw your face when she put me out, and you loved me then and you do now!

PROCTOR: Abby, that's a wild thing to say—

ABIGAIL: A wild thing may say wild things. But not so wild, I think. I have seen you since she put me out; I have seen you nights.

PROCTOR: I have hardly stepped off my farm this seven month.

ABIGAIL: I have a sense for heat, John, and yours has drawn me to my window, and I have seen you looking up, burning in your loneliness. Do you tell me you've never looked up at my window?

PROCTOR: I may have looked up.

ABIGAIL, *now softening:* And you must. You are no wintry man. I know you, John. I *know* you. *She is weeping.* I cannot sleep for dreamin'; I cannot dream but I wake and walk about the house as though I'd find you comin' through some door. *She clutches him desperately.*

PROCTOR, *gently pressing her from him, with great sympathy but firmly:* Child—

ABIGAIL, *with a flash of anger:* How do you call me child!

PROCTOR: Abby, I may think of you softly from time to time. But I will cut off my hand before I'll ever reach for you again. Wipe it out of mind. We never touched, Abby.

ABIGAIL: Aye, but we did.

PROCTOR: Aye, but we did not.

ABIGAIL, *with a bitter anger:* Oh, I marvel how such a strong man may let such a sickly wife be—

PROCTOR, *angered—at himself as well:* You'll speak nothin' of Elizabeth!

ABIGAIL: She is blackening my name in the village! She is telling lies about me! She is a cold, sniveling woman, and you bend to her! Let her turn you like a—

PROCTOR, *shaking her:* Do you look for whippin'?

A psalm is heard being sung below.

ABIGAIL, *in tears:* I look for John Proctor that took me from my sleep and put knowledge in my heart! I never knew what pretense Salem was, I never knew the lying lessons I was taught by all these Christian women and their covenanted men! And now you bid me tear the light out of my eyes? I will not, I cannot! You loved me, John Proctor, and whatever sin it is, you love me yet! *He turns abruptly to go out. She rushes to him.* John, pity me, pity me!

The words "going up to Jesus" are heard in the psalm, and Betty claps her ears suddenly and whines loudly.

ABIGAIL: Betty? *She hurries to Betty, who is now sitting up and screaming. Proctor goes to Betty as Abigail is trying to pull her hands down, calling "Betty!"*

PROCTOR, *growing unnerved:* What's she doing? Girl, what ails you? Stop that wailing!

The singing has stopped in the midst of this, and now Parris rushes in.

PARRIS: What happened? What are you doing to her? Betty! *He rushes to the bed, crying, "Betty, Betty!" Mrs. Putnam enters, feverish with curiosity, and with her Thomas Putnam and Mercy Lewis. Parris, at the bed, keeps lightly slapping Betty's face, while she moans and tries to get up.*

ABIGAIL: She heard you singin' and suddenly she's up and screamin'.

MRS. PUTNAM: The psalm! The psalm! She cannot bear to hear the Lord's name!

PARRIS: No, God forbid. Mercy, run to the doctor! Tell him what's happened here! *Mercy Lewis rushes out.*

MRS. PUTNAM: Mark it for a sign, mark it!

Rebecca Nurse, seventy-two, enters. She is white-haired, leaning upon her walking-stick.

PUTNAM, *pointing at the whimpering Betty:* That is a notorious sign of witchcraft afoot, Goody Nurse, a prodigious sign!

MRS. PUTNAM: My mother told me that! When they cannot bear to hear the name of—

PARRIS, *trembling:* Rebecca, Rebecca, go to her, we're lost. She suddenly cannot bear to hear the Lord's—

Giles Corey, eighty-three, enters. He is knotted with muscle, canny, inquisitive, and still powerful.

REBECCA: There is hard sickness here, Giles Corey, so please to keep the quiet.

GILES: I've not said a word. No one here can testify I've said a word. Is she going to fly again? I hear she flies.

PUTNAM: Man, be quiet now!

Everything is quiet. Rebecca walks across the room to the bed. Gentleness exudes from her. Betty is quietly whimpering, eyes shut. Rebecca simply stands over the child, who gradually quiets.

And while they are so absorbed, we may put a word in for Rebecca. Rebecca was the wife of Francis Nurse, who, from all accounts, was one of those men for whom both sides of the argument had to have respect. He was called upon to arbitrate disputes as though he were an unofficial judge, and Rebecca also enjoyed the high opinion most people had for him. By the time of the delusion, they had three hundred acres, and their children were settled in separate homesteads within the same estate. However, Francis had originally rented the land, and one theory has it that, as he gradually paid for it and raised his social status, there were those who resented his rise.

Another suggestion to explain the systematic campaign against Rebecca, and inferentially against Francis, is the land war he fought with his neighbors, one of whom was a Putnam. This squabble grew to the proportions of a battle in the woods between partisans of both sides, and it is said to have lasted for two days. As for Rebecca herself, the general opinion of her character was so high that to explain how anyone dared cry her out for a witch—and more, how adults could bring themselves to lay hands on her—we must look to the fields and boundaries of that time.

As we have seen, Thomas Putnam's man for the Salem ministry was Bayley. The Nurse clan had been in the faction that prevented Bayley's taking office. In addition, certain families allied to the Nurses by blood or friendship, and whose farms were contiguous with the Nurse farm or close to it, combined to break away from the Salem town authority and set up Topsfield, a new and independent entity whose existence was resented by old Salemites.

That the guiding hand behind the outcry was Putnam's is indicated by the fact that, as soon as it began, this Topsfield-Nurse faction absented themselves from church in protest and disbelief. It was Edward and Jonathan Putnam who signed the first complaint against Rebecca; and Thomas Putnam's little daughter was the one who fell into a fit at the hearing and pointed to Rebecca as her attacker. To top it all, Mrs. Putnam—who is now staring at the bewitched child on the bed—soon accused Rebecca's spirit of "tempting her to iniquity," a charge that had more truth in it than Mrs. Putnam could know.

MRS. PUTNAM, *astonished:* What have you done?

Rebecca, in thought, now leaves the bedside and sits.

PARRIS, *wondrous and relieved:* What do you make of it, Rebecca?

PUTNAM, *eagerly:* Goody Nurse, will you go to my Ruth and see if you can wake her?

REBECCA, *sitting:* I think she'll wake in time. Pray calm yourselves. I have eleven children, and I am twenty-six times a grandma, and I have seen them all through their silly seasons, and when it come on them they will run the Devil bowlegged keeping up with their mischief. I think she'll wake when she tires of it. A child's spirit is like a child, you can never catch it by running after it; you must stand still, and, for love, it will soon itself come back.

PROCTOR: Aye, that's the truth of it, Rebecca.

MRS. PUTNAM: This is no silly season, Rebecca. My Ruth is bewildered, Rebecca; she cannot eat.

REBECCA: Perhaps she is not hungered yet. *To Parris:* I hope you are not decided to go in search of loose spirits, Mr. Parris. I've heard promise of that outside.

PARRIS: A wide opinion's running in the parish that the Devil may be among us, and I would satisfy them that they are wrong.

PROCTOR: Then let you come out and call them wrong. Did you consult the wardens before you called this minister to look for devils?

PARRIS: He is not coming to look for devils!

PROCTOR: Then what's he coming for?

PUTNAM: There be children dyin' in the village, Mister!

PROCTOR: I seen none dyin'. This society will not be a bag to swing around your head, Mr. Putnam. *To Parris:* Did you call a meeting before you—?

PUTNAM: I am sick of meetings; cannot the man turn his head without he have a meeting?

PROCTOR: He may turn his head, but not to Hell!

REBECCA: Pray, John, be calm. *Pause. He defers to her.* Mr. Parris, I think you'd best send Reverend Hale back as soon as he come. This will set us all to arguin' again in the society, and we thought to have peace this year. I think we ought rely on the doctor now, and good prayer.

MRS. PUTNAM: Rebecca, the doctor's baffled!

REBECCA: If so he is, then let us go to God for the cause of it. There is prodigious danger in the seeking of loose spirits. I fear it, I fear it. Let us rather blame ourselves and—

PUTNAM: How may we blame ourselves? I am one of nine sons; the Putnam seed have peopled this province. And yet I have but one child left of eight—and now she shrivels!

REBECCA: I cannot fathom that.

MRS. PUTNAM, *with a growing edge of sarcasm:* But I must! You think it God's work you should never lose a child, nor grandchild either, and I bury all but one? There are wheels within wheels in this village, and fires within fires!

PUTNAM, *to Parris:* When Reverend Hale comes, you will proceed to look for signs of witchcraft here.

PROCTOR, *to Putnam:* You cannot command Mr. Parris. We vote by name in this society, not by acreage.

PUTNAM: I never heard you worried so on this society, Mr. Proctor. I do not think I saw you at Sabbath meeting since snow flew.

PROCTOR: I have trouble enough without I come five mile to hear him preach only hellfire and bloody damnation. Take it to heart, Mr. Parris. There are many others who stay away from church these days because you hardly ever mention God any more.

PARRIS, *now aroused:* Why, that's a drastic charge!

REBECCA: It's somewhat true; there are many that quail to bring their children—

PARRIS: I do not preach for children, Rebecca. It is not the children who are unmindful of their obligations toward this ministry.

REBECCA: Are there really those unmindful?

PARRIS: I should say the better half of Salem village—

PUTNAM: And more than that!

PARRIS: Where is my wood? My contract provides I be supplied with all my firewood. I am waiting since November for a stick, and even in November I had to show my frostbitten hands like some London beggar!

GILES: You are allowed six pound a year to buy your wood, Mr. Parris.

PARRIS: I regard that six pound as part of my salary. I am paid little enough without I spend six pound on firewood.

PROCTOR: Sixty, plus six for firewood—

PARRIS: The salary is sixty-six pound, Mr. Proctor! I am not some preaching farmer with a book under my arm; I am a graduate of Harvard College.

GILES: Aye, and well instructed in arithmetic!

PARRIS: Mr. Corey, you will look far for a man of my kind at sixty pound a year! I am not used to this poverty; I left a thrifty business in the Barbados to serve the Lord. I do not fathom it, why am I persecuted here? I cannot offer one proposition but there be a howling riot of argument. I have often wondered if the Devil be in it somewhere; I cannot understand you people otherwise.

PROCTOR: Mr. Parris, you are the first minister ever did demand the deed to this house—

PARRIS: Man! Don't a minister deserve a house to live in?

PROCTOR: To live in, yes. But to ask ownership is like you shall own the meeting house itself; the last meeting I were at you spoke so long on deeds and mortgages I thought it were an auction.

PARRIS: I want a mark of confidence, is all! I am your third preacher in seven years. I do not wish to be put out like the cat whenever some majority feels the whim. You people seem not to comprehend that a minister is the Lord's man in the parish; a minister is not to be so lightly crossed and contradicted—

PUTNAM: Aye!

PARRIS: There is either obedience or the church will burn like Hell is burning!

PROCTOR: Can you speak one minute without we land in Hell again? I am sick of Hell!

PARRIS: It is not for you to say what is good for you to hear!

PROCTOR: I may speak my heart, I think!

PARRIS, *in a fury:* What, are we Quakers? We are not Quakers here yet, Mr. Proctor. And you may tell that to your followers!

PROCTOR: My followers!

PARRIS—*now he's out with it:* There is a party in this church. I am not blind; there is a faction and a party.

PROCTOR: Against you?

PUTNAM: Against him and all authority!

PROCTOR: Why, then I must find it and join it.

There is shock among the others.

REBECCA: He does not mean that.

PUTNAM: He confessed it now!

PROCTOR: I mean it solemnly, Rebecca; I like not the smell of this "authority."

REBECCA: No, you cannot break charity with your minister. You are another kind, John. Clasp his hand, make your peace.

PROCTOR: I have a crop to sow and lumber to drag home. *He goes angrily to the door and turns to Corey with a smile.* What say you, Giles, let's find the party. He says there's a party.

GILES: I've changed my opinion of this man, John. Mr. Parris, I beg your pardon. I never thought you had so much iron in you.

PARRIS, *surprised:* Why, thank you, Giles!

GILES: It suggests to the mind what the trouble be among us all these years. *To all:* Think on it. Wherefore is everybody suing everybody else? Think on it now, it's a deep thing, and dark as a pit. I have been six time in court this year—

PROCTOR, *familiarly, with warmth, although he knows he is approaching the edge of Giles' tolerance with this:* Is it the Devil's fault that a man cannot say you good morning without you clap him for defamation? You're old, Giles, and you're not hearin' so well as you did.

GILES—*he cannot be crossed:* John Proctor, I have only last month collected four pound damages for you publicly sayin' I burned the roof off your house, and I—

PROCTOR, *laughing:* I never said no such thing, but I've paid you for it, so I hope I can call you deaf without charge. Now come along, Giles, and help me drag my lumber home.

PUTNAM: A moment, Mr. Proctor. What lumber is that you're draggin', if I may ask you?

PROCTOR: My lumber. From out my forest by the riverside.

PUTNAM: Why, we are surely gone wild this year. What anarchy is this? That tract is in my bounds, it's in my bounds, Mr. Proctor.

PROCTOR: In your bounds! *Indicating Rebecca:* I bought that tract from Goody Nurse's husband five months ago.

PUTNAM: He had no right to sell it. It stands clear in my grandfather's will that all the land between the river and—

PROCTOR: Your grandfather had a habit of willing land that never belonged to him, if I may say it plain.

GILES: That's God's truth; he nearly willed away my north pasture but he knew I'd break his fingers before he'd set his name to it. Let's get your lumber home, John. I feel a sudden will to work coming on.

PUTNAM: You load one oak of mine and you'll fight to drag it home!

GILES: Aye, and we'll win too, Putnam—this fool and I. Come on! *He turns to Proctor and starts out.*

PUTNAM: I'll have my men on you, Corey! I'll clap a writ on you!

Enter Reverend John Hale of Beverly.

Mr. Hale is nearing forty, a tight-skinned, eager-eyed intellectual. This is a beloved errand for him; on being called here to ascertain witchcraft he felt the pride of the specialist whose unique knowledge has at last been publicly called for. Like almost all men of learning, he spent a good deal of his time pondering the invisible world, especially since he had himself encountered a witch in his parish not long before. That woman, however, turned into a mere pest under his searching scrutiny, and the child she had allegedly been afflicting recovered her normal behavior after Hale had given her his kindness and a few days of rest in his own house. However, that experience never raised a doubt in his mind as to the reality of the underworld or the existence of Lucifer's many-faced lieutenants. And his belief is not to his discredit. Better minds than Hale's were—and still are—convinced that there is a society of spirits beyond our ken. One cannot help noting that one of his lines has never yet raised a laugh in any audience that has seen this play; it is his assurance that "We cannot look to superstition in this. The Devil is precise." Evidently we are not quite certain even now whether diabolism is holy and not to be scoffed at. And it is no accident that we should be so bemused.

Like Reverend Hale and the others on this stage, we conceive the Devil as a necessary part of a respectable view of cosmology. Ours is a divided empire in which certain ideas and emotions and actions are of God, and their opposites are of Lucifer. It is as impossible for most men to conceive of a morality without sin as of an earth without "sky." Since 1692 a great but superficial change has wiped out God's beard and the Devil's horns, but the world is still gripped between two diametrically opposed absolutes. The concept of unity, in which positive and negative are attributes of the same force, in which good and evil are relative, ever-changing, and always joined to the same phenomenon—such a concept is still reserved to the physical sciences and to the few who have grasped the history of ideas. When it is recalled that until the Christian era the underworld was never regarded as a hostile area, that all gods were useful and essentially friendly to man despite occasional lapses; when we see the steady and methodical inculcation into humanity of the idea of man's worthlessness—until redeemed—the necessity of the Devil may become evident as a weapon, a weapon designed and used time and time again in every age to whip men into a surrender to a particular church or church-state.

Our difficulty in believing the—for want of a better word—political inspiration of the Devil is due in great part to the fact that he is called up and damned not only by our social antagonists but by our own side, whatever it may be. The Catholic Church, through its Inquisition, is famous for cultivating Lucifer as the arch-fiend, but the Church's enemies relied no less upon the Old Boy to keep the human mind enthralled. Luther was himself accused of alliance with Hell, and he in turn accused his enemies. To complicate matters further, he believed that he had had contact with the Devil and had argued theology with him. I am not surprised at this, for at my own university a professor of history—a Lutheran, by the way—used to assemble his graduate students, draw the shades, and commune in the classroom with Erasmus. He was never, to my knowledge, officially scoffed at for this, the reason being that the university officials, like most of us, are the children of a history which still sucks at the Devil's teats. At this writing, only England has held back before the temptations of contemporary diabolism. In the countries of the Communist ideology, all resistance of any import is linked to the totally malign capitalist succubi, and in America any man who is not reactionary in his views is open to the charge of alliance with the Red hell. Political opposition, thereby, is given an inhumane overlay which then justifies the abrogation of all normally applied customs of civilized intercourse. A political policy is equated with moral right, and opposition to it with diabolical malevolence. Once such an equation is effectively made, society becomes a congeries of plots and counterplots, and the main role of government changes from that of the arbiter to that of the scourge of God.

The results of this process are no different now from what they ever were, except sometimes in the degree of cruelty inflicted, and not always even in that department. Normally the actions and deeds of a man were all that society felt comfortable in judging. The secret intent of an action was left to the ministers, priests, and rabbis to deal with. When diabolism rises, however, actions are the least important manifests of the true nature of a man. The Devil, as Reverend Hale said, is a wily one, and, until an hour before he fell, even God thought him beautiful in Heaven.

The analogy, however, seems to falter when one considers that, while there were no witches then, there are Communists and capitalists now, and in each camp there is certain proof that spies of each side are at work undermining the other. But this is a snobbish objection and not at all warranted by the facts. I have no doubt that people *were* communing with, and even worshiping, the Devil in Salem, and if the whole truth could be known in this case, as it is in others, we should discover a regular and conventionalized propitiation of the dark spirit. One certain evidence of this is the confession of Tituba, the slave of Reverend Parris, and another is the behavior of the children who were known to have indulged in sorceries with her.

There are accounts of similar *klatches* in Europe, where the daughters of the towns would assemble at night and, sometimes with fetishes, sometimes with a selected young man, give themselves to love, with some bastardly results. The Church, sharp-eyed as it must be when gods long dead are brought to life, condemned these orgies as witchcraft and interpreted them rightly, as a resurgence of the Dionysiac forces it had crushed long before. Sex, sin, and the Devil were early linked, and so they continued to be in Salem, and are today. From all accounts there are no more puritanical mores in the world than those enforced by the Communists in Russia, where women's fashions, for instance, are as prudent and all-covering as any American Baptist would desire. The divorce laws lay a tremendous responsibility on the father for the care of his children. Even the laxity of divorce regulations in the early years of the revolution was undoubtedly a revulsion from the nineteenth-century Victorian immobility of marriage and the consequent hypocrisy that developed from it. If for no other reasons, a state so powerful, so jealous of the uniformity of its citizens, cannot long tolerate the atomization of the family. And yet, in American eyes at least, there remains the conviction that the Russian attitude toward women is lascivious. It is the Devil working again, just as he is working within the Slav who is shocked at the very idea of a woman's disrobing herself in a burlesque show. Our opposites are always robed in sexual sin, and it is from this unconscious conviction that demonology gains both its attractive sensuality and its capacity to infuriate and frighten.

Coming into Salem now, Reverend Hale conceives of himself much as a young doctor on his first call. His painfully acquired armory of symptoms, catchwords, and diagnostic procedures is now to be put to use at last. The road from Beverly is unusually busy this morning, and he has passed a hundred rumors that make him smile at the ignorance of the yeomanry in this most precise science. He feels himself allied with the best minds of Europe—kings, philosophers, scientists, and ecclesiasts of all churches. His goal is light, goodness and its preservation, and he knows the exaltation of the blessed whose intelligence, sharpened by minute examinations of enormous tracts, is finally called upon to face what may be a bloody fight with the Fiend himself.

He appears loaded down with half a dozen heavy books.

HALE: Pray you, someone take these!

PARRIS, *delighted:* Mr. Hale! Oh! it's good to see you again! *Taking some books:* My, they're heavy!

HALE, *setting down his books:* They must be; they are weighted with authority.

PARRIS, *a little scared:* Well, you do come prepared!

HALE: We shall need hard study if it comes to tracking down the Old Boy. *Noticing Rebecca:* You cannot be Rebecca Nurse?

REBECCA: I am, sir. Do you know me?

HALE: It's strange how I knew you, but I suppose you look as such a good soul should. We have all heard of your great charities in Beverly.

PARRIS: Do you know this gentleman? Mr. Thomas Putnam. And his good wife Ann.

HALE: Putnam! I had not expected such distinguished company, sir.

PUTNAM, *pleased:* It does not seem to help us today, Mr. Hale. We look to you to come to our house and save our child.

HALE: Your child ails too?

MRS. PUTNAM: Her soul, her soul seems flown away. She sleeps and yet she walks . . .

PUTNAM: She cannot eat.

HALE: Cannot eat! *Thinks on it. Then, to Proctor and Giles Corey:* Do you men have afflicted children?

PARRIS: No, no, these are farmers. John Proctor—

GILES COREY: He don't believe in witches.

PROCTOR, *to Hale:* I never spoke on witches one way or the other. Will you come, Giles?

GILES: No—no, John, I think not. I have some few queer questions of my own to ask this fellow.

PROCTOR: I've heard you to be a sensible man, Mr. Hale. I hope you'll leave some of it in Salem.

Proctor goes. Hale stands embarrassed for an instant.

PARRIS, *quickly:* Will you look at my daughter, sir? *Leads Hale to the bed.* She has tried to leap out the window; we discovered her this morning on the highroad, waving her arms as though she'd fly.

HALE, *narrowing his eyes:* Tries to fly.

PUTNAM: She cannot bear to hear the Lord's name, Mr. Hale; that's a sure sign of witchcraft afloat.

HALE, *holding up his hands:* No, no. Now let me instruct you. We cannot look to superstition in this. The Devil is precise; the marks of his presence are definite as stone, and I must tell you all that I shall not proceed unless you are prepared to believe me if I should find no bruise of Hell upon her.

PARRIS: It is agreed, sir—it is agreed—we will abide by your judgment.

HALE: Good then, *He goes to the bed, looks down at Betty. To Parris:* Now, sir, what were your first warning of this strangeness?

PARRIS: Why, sir—I discovered her—*indicating Abigail*—and my niece and ten or twelve of the other girls, dancing in the forest last night.

HALE, *surprised:* You permit dancing?

PARRIS: No, no, it were secret—

MRS. PUTNAM, *unable to wait:* Mr. Parris's slave has knowledge of conjurin', sir.

PARRIS, *to Mrs. Putnam:* We cannot be sure of that, Goody Ann—

MRS. PUTNAM, *frightened, very softly:* I know it, sir. I sent my child—she should learn from Tituba who murdered her sisters.

REBECCA, *horrified:* Goody Ann! You sent a child to conjure up the dead?

MRS. PUTNAM: Let God blame me, not you, not you, Rebecca! I'll not have you judging me any more! *To Hale:* Is it a natural work to lose seven children before they live a day?

PARRIS: Sssh!

Rebecca, with great pain, turns her face away. There is a pause.

HALE: Seven dead in childbirth.

MRS. PUTNAM, *softly:* Aye. *Her voice breaks; she looks up at him. Silence. Hale is impressed. Parris looks to him. He goes to his books, opens one, turns pages, then reads. All wait, avidly.*

PARRIS, *hushed:* What book is that?

MRS. PUTNAM: What's there, sir?

HALE, *with a tasty love of intellectual pursuit:* Here is all the invisible world, caught, defined, and calculated. In these books the Devil stands stripped of all his brute disguises. Here are all your familiar spirits—your incubi and succubi; your witches that go by land, by air, and by sea; your wizards of the night and of the day. Have no fear now—we shall find him out if he has come among us, and I mean to crush him utterly if he has shown his face! *He starts for the bed.*

REBECCA: Will it hurt the child, sir?

HALE: I cannot tell. If she is truly in the Devil's grip we may have to rip and tear to get her free.

REBECCA: I think I'll go, then. I am too old for this. *She rises.*

PARRIS, *striving for conviction:* Why, Rebecca, we may open up the boil of all our troubles today!

REBECCA: Let us hope for that. I go to God for you, sir.

PARRIS, *with trepidation—and resentment:* I hope you do not mean we go to Satan here! *Slight pause.*

REBECCA: I wish I knew. *She goes out; they feel resentful of her note of moral superiority.*

PUTNAM, *abruptly:* Come, Mr. Hale, let's get on. Sit you here.

GILES: Mr. Hale, I have always wanted to ask a learned man—what signifies the readin' of strange books?

HALE: What books?

GILES: I cannot tell; she hides them.

HALE: Who does this?

GILES: Martha, my wife. I have waked at night many a time and found her in a corner, readin' of a book. Now what do you make of that?

HALE: Why, that's not necessarily—

GILES: It discomfits me! Last night—mark this—I tried and tried and could not say my prayers. And then she close her book and walks out of the house, and suddenly—mark this—I could pray again!

Old Giles must be spoken for, if only because his fate was to be so remarkable and so different from that of all the others. He was in his early eighties at this time, and was the most comical hero in the history. No man has ever been blamed for so much. If a cow was missed, the first thought was to look for her around Corey's house; a fire blazing up at night brought suspicion of arson to his door. He didn't give a hoot for public opinion, and only in his last years—after he had married Martha—did he bother much with the church. That she stopped his prayer is very probable, but he forgot to say that he'd only recently learned any prayers and it didn't take much to make him stumble over them. He was a crank and a nuisance, but withal a deeply innocent and brave man. In court, once, he was asked if it were true that he had been frightened by the strange behavior of a hog and had then said he knew it to be the Devil in an animal's shape. "What frighted you?" he was asked. He forgot everything but the word "frighted," and instantly replied, "I do not know that I ever spoke that word in my life."

HALE: Ah! The stoppage of prayer—that is strange. I'll speak further on that with you.

GILES: I'm not sayin' she's touched the Devil, now, but I'd admire to know what books she reads and why she hides them. She'll not answer me, y' see.

HALE: Aye, we'll discuss it. *To all:* Now mark me, if the Devil is in her you will witness some frightful wonders in this room, so please to keep your wits about you. Mr. Putnam, stand close in case she flies. Now, Betty, dear, will you sit up? *Putnam comes in closer, ready-handed. Hale sits Betty up, but she hangs limp in his hands.* Hmmm. *He observes her carefully. The others watch breathlessly.* Can you hear me? I am John Hale, minister of Beverly. I have come to help you, dear. Do you remember my two little girls in Beverly? *She does not stir in his hands.*

PARRIS, *in fright:* How can it be the Devil? Why would he choose my house to strike? We have all manner of licentious people in the village!

HALE: What victory would the Devil have to win a soul already bad? It is the best the Devil wants, and who is better than the minister?

GILES: That's deep, Mr. Parris, deep, deep!

PARRIS, *with resolution now:* Betty! Answer Mr. Hale! Betty!

HALE: Does someone afflict you, child? It need not be a woman, mind you, or a man. Perhaps some bird invisible to others comes to you—perhaps a pig, a mouse, or any beast at all. Is there some figure bids you fly? *The child remains limp in his hands. In silence he lays her back on the pillow. Now, holding out his hands toward her, he intones:* In nomine Domini Sabaoth sui filiique ite ad infernos. *She does not stir. He turns to Abigail, his eyes narrowing.* Abigail, what sort of dancing were you doing with her in the forest?

ABIGAIL: Why—common dancing is all.

PARRIS: I think I ought to say that I—I saw a kettle in the grass where they were dancing.

ABIGAIL: That were only soup.

HALE: What sort of soup were in this kettle, Abigail?

ABIGAIL: Why, it were beans—and lentils, I think, and—

HALE: Mr. Parris, you did not notice, did you, any living thing in the kettle? A mouse, perhaps, a spider, a frog—?

PARRIS, *fearfully:* I—do believe there were some movement—in the soup.

ABIGAIL: That jumped in, we never put it in!

HALE, *quickly:* What jumped in?

ABIGAIL: Why, a very little frog jumped—

PARRIS: A frog, Abby!

HALE, *grasping Abigail:* Abigail, it may be your cousin is dying. Did you call the Devil last night?

ABIGAIL: I never called him! Tituba, Tituba . . .

PARRIS, *blanched:* She called the Devil?

HALE: I should like to speak with Tituba.

PARRIS: Goody Ann, will you bring her up? *Mrs. Putnam exits.*

HALE: How did she call him?

ABIGAIL: I know not—she spoke Barbados.

HALE: Did you feel any strangeness when she called him? A sudden cold wind, perhaps? A trembling below the ground?

ABIGAIL: I didn't see no Devil! *Shaking Betty:* Betty, wake up. Betty! Betty!

HALE: You cannot evade me, Abigail. Did your cousin drink any of the brew in that kettle?

ABIGAIL: She never drank it!

HALE: Did you drink it?

ABIGAIL: No, sir!

HALE: Did Tituba ask you to drink it?

ABIGAIL: She tried, but I refused.

HALE: Why are you concealing? Have you sold yourself to Lucifer?

ABIGAIL: I never sold myself! I'm a good girl! I'm a proper girl!

Mrs. Putnam enters with Tituba, and instantly Abigail points at Tituba.

ABIGAIL: She made me do it! She made Betty do it!

TITUBA, *shocked and angry:* Abby!

ABIGAIL: She makes me drink blood!

PARRIS: Blood!!

MRS. PUTNAM: My baby's blood?

TITUBA: No, no, chicken blood. I give she chicken blood!

HALE: Woman, have you enlisted these children for the Devil?

TITUBA: No, no, sir, I don't truck with no Devil!

HALE: Why can she not wake? Are you silencing this child?

TITUBA: I love me Betty!

HALE: You have sent your spirit out upon this child, have you not? Are you gathering souls for the Devil?

ABIGAIL: She sends her spirit on me in church; she makes me laugh at prayer!

PARRIS: She have often laughed at prayer!

ABIGAIL: She comes to me every night to go and drink blood!

TITUBA: You beg *me* to conjure! She beg *me* make charm—

ABIGAIL: Don't lie! *To Hale:* She comes to me while I sleep; she's always making me dream corruptions!

TITUBA: Why you say that, Abby?

ABIGAIL: Sometimes I wake and find myself standing in the open door-way and not a stitch on my body! I always hear her laughing in my sleep. I hear her singing her Barbados songs and tempting me with—

TITUBA: Mister Reverend, I never—

HALE, *resolved now:* Tituba, I want you to wake this child.

TITUBA: I have no power on this child, sir.

HALE: You most certainly do, and you will free her from it now! When did you compact with the Devil?

TITUBA: I don't compact with no Devil!

PARRIS: You will confess yourself or I will take you out and whip you to your death, Tituba!

PUTNAM: This woman must be hanged! She must be taken and hanged!

TITUBA, *terrified, falls to her knees:* No, no, don't hang Tituba! I tell him I don't desire to work for him, sir.

PARRIS: The Devil?

HALE: Then you saw him! *Tituba weeps.* Now Tituba, I know that when we bind ourselves to Hell it is very hard to break with it. We are going to help you tear yourself free—

TITUBA, *frightened by the coming process:* Mister Reverend, I do believe somebody else be witchin' these children.

HALE: Who?

TITUBA: I don't know, sir, but the Devil got him numerous witches.

HALE: Does he! *It is a clue.* Tituba, look into my eyes. Come, look into me. *She raises her eyes to his fearfully.* You would be a good Christian woman, would you not, Tituba?

TITUBA: Aye, sir, a good Christian woman.

HALE: And you love these little children?

TITUBA: Oh, yes, sir, I don't desire to hurt little children.

HALE: And you love God, Tituba?

TITUBA: I love God with all my bein'.

HALE: Now, in God's holy name—

TITUBA: Bless Him. Bless Him. *She is rocking on her knees, sobbing in terror.*

HALE: And to His glory—

TITUBA: Eternal glory. Bless Him—bless God . . .

HALE: Open yourself, Tituba—open yourself and let God's holy light shine on you.

TITUBA: Oh, bless the Lord.

HALE: When the Devil comes to you does he ever come—with another person? *She stares up into his face.* Perhaps another person in the village? Someone you know.

PARRIS: Who came with him?

PUTNAM: Sarah Good? Did you ever see Sarah Good with him? Or Osburn?

PARRIS: Was it man or woman came with him?

TITUBA: Man or woman. Was—was woman.

PARRIS: What woman? A woman, you said. What woman?

TITUBA: It was black dark, and I—

PARRIS: You could see him, why could you not see her?

TITUBA: Well, they was always talking; they was always runnin' round and carryin' on—

PARRIS: You mean out of Salem? Salem witches?

TITUBA: I believe so, yes, sir.

Now Hale takes her hand. She is surprised.

HALE: Tituba. You must have no fear to tell us who they are, do you understand? We will protect you. The Devil can never overcome a minister. You know that, do you not?

TITUBA—*she kisses Hale's hand:* Aye, sir, oh, I do.

HALE: You have confessed yourself to witchcraft, and that speaks a wish to come to Heaven's side. And we will bless you, Tituba.

TITUBA, *deeply relieved:* Oh, God bless you, Mr. Hale!

HALE, *with rising exaltation:* You are God's instrument put in our hands to discover the Devil's agents among us. You are selected, Tituba, you are chosen to help us cleanse our village. So speak utterly, Tituba, turn your back on him and face God—face God, Tituba, and God will protect you.

TITUBA, *joining with him:* Oh, God, protect Tituba!

HALE, *kindly:* Who came to you with the Devil? Two? Three? Four? How many?

Tituba pants and begins rocking back and forth again, staring ahead.

TITUBA: There was four. There was four.

PARRIS, *pressing in on her:* Who? Who? Their names, their names!

TITUBA, *suddenly bursting out:* Oh, how many times he bid me kill you, Mr. Parris!

PARRIS: Kill me!

TITUBA, *in a fury:* He say Mr. Parris must be kill! Mr. Parris no goodly man, Mr. Parris mean man and no gentle man, and he bid me rise out of my bed and cut your throat! *They gasp.* But I tell him "No! I don't hate that man. I don't want kill that man." But he say, "You work for me, Tituba, and I make you free! I give you pretty dress to wear, and put you way high up in the air, and you gone fly back to Barbados!" And I say, "You lie, Devil, you lie!" And then he come one stormy night to me, and he say, "Look! I have *white* people belong to me." And I look—and there was Goody Good.

PARRIS: Sarah Good!

TITUBA, *rocking and weeping:* Aye, sir, and Goody Osburn.

MRS. PUTNAM: I knew it! Goody Osburn were midwife to me three times. I begged you, Thomas, did I not? I begged him not to call Osburn because I feared her. My babies always shriveled in her hands!

HALE: Take courage, you must give us all their names. How can you bear to see this child suffering? Look at her, Tituba. *He is indicating Betty on the bed.* Look at her God-given innocence; her soul is so tender; we must protect her, Tituba; the Devil is out and preying on her like a beast upon the flesh of the pure lamb. God will bless you for your help.

Abigail rises, staring as though inspired, and cries out.

ABIGAIL: I want to open myself! *They turn to her, startled. She is enraptured, as though in a pearly light.* I want the light of God, I want the sweet love of Jesus! I danced for the Devil; I saw him; I wrote in his book; I go back to Jesus; I kiss His hand. I saw Sarah Good with the Devil! I saw Goody Osburn with the Devil! I saw Bridget Bishop with the Devil!

As she is speaking, Betty is rising from the bed, a fever in her eyes, and picks up the chant.

BETTY, *staring too:* I saw George Jacobs with the Devil! I saw Goody Howe with the Devil!

PARRIS: She speaks! *He rushes to embrace Betty.* She speaks!

HALE: Glory to God! It is broken, they are free!

BETTY, *calling out hysterically and with great relief:* I saw Martha Bellows with the Devil!

ABIGAIL: I saw Goody Sibber with the Devil! *It is rising to a great glee.*

PUTNAM: The marshal, I'll call the marshal!

Parris is shouting a prayer of thanksgiving.

BETTY: I saw Alice Barrow with the Devil!

The curtain begins to fall.

HALE, *as Putnam goes out:* Let the marshal bring irons!

ABIGAIL: I saw Goody Hawkins with the Devil!

BETTY: I saw Goody Bibber with the Devil!

ABIGAIL: I saw Goody Booth with the Devil!

On their ecstatic cries

The Curtain Falls

ACT TWO

The common room of Proctor's house, eight days later.

At the right is a door opening on the fields outside. A fireplace is at the left, and behind it a stairway leading upstairs. It is the low, dark, and rather long living room of the time. As the curtain rises, the room is empty. From above, Elizabeth is heard softly singing to the children. Presently the door opens and John Proctor enters, carrying his gun. He glances about the room as he comes toward the fireplace, then halts for an instant as he hears her singing. He continues on to the fireplace, leans the gun against the wall as he swings a pot out of the fire and smells it. Then he lifts out the ladle and tastes. He is not quite pleased. He reaches to a cupboard, takes a pinch of salt, and drops it into the pot. As he is tasting again, her footsteps are heard on the stair. He swings the pot into the fireplace and goes to a basin and washes his hands and face. Elizabeth enters.

ELIZABETH: What keeps you so late? It's almost dark.

PROCTOR: I were planting far out to the forest edge.

ELIZABETH: Oh, you're done then.

PROCTOR: Aye, the farm is seeded. The boys asleep?

ELIZABETH: They will be soon. *And she goes to the fireplace, proceeds to ladle up stew in a dish.*

PROCTOR: Pray now for a fair summer.

ELIZABETH: Aye.

PROCTOR: Are you well today?

ELIZABETH: I am. *She brings the plate to the table, and, indicating the food:* It is a rabbit.

PROCTOR, *going to the table:* Oh, is it! In Jonathan's trap?

ELIZABETH: No, she walked into the house this afternoon; I found her sittin' in the corner like she come to visit.

PROCTOR: Oh, that's a good sign walkin' in.

ELIZABETH: Pray God. It hurt my heart to strip her, poor rabbit. *She sits and watches him taste it.*

PROCTOR: It's well seasoned.

ELIZABETH, *blushing with pleasure:* I took great care. She's tender?

PROCTOR: Aye. *He eats. She watches him.* I think we'll see green fields soon. It's warm as blood beneath the clods.

ELIZABETH: That's well.

Proctor eats, then looks up.

PROCTOR: If the crop is good I'll buy George Jacobs' heifer. How would that please you?

ELIZABETH: Aye, it would.

PROCTOR, *with a grin:* I mean to please you, Elizabeth.

ELIZABETH—*it is hard to say:* I know it, John.

He gets up, goes to her, kisses her. She receives it. With a certain disappointment, he returns to the table.

PROCTOR, *as gently as he can:* Cider?

ELIZABETH, *with a sense of reprimanding herself for having forgot:* Aye! *She gets up and goes and pours a glass for him. He now arches his back.*

PROCTOR: This farm's a continent when you go foot by foot droppin' seeds in it.

ELIZABETH, *coming with the cider:* It must be.

PROCTOR—*he drinks a long draught, then, putting the glass down:* You ought to bring some flowers in the house.

ELIZABETH: Oh! I forgot! I will tomorrow.

PROCTOR: It's winter in here yet. On Sunday let you come with me, and we'll walk the farm together; I never see such a load of flowers on the earth. *With good feeling he goes and looks up at the sky through the open doorway.* Lilacs have a purple smell. Lilac is the smell of nightfall, I think. Massachusetts is a beauty in the spring!

ELIZABETH: Aye, it is.

There is a pause. She is watching him from the table as he stands there absorbing the night. It is as though she would speak but cannot. Instead, now, she takes up his plate and glass and fork and goes with them to the basin. Her back is turned to him. He turns to her and watches her. A sense of their separation rises.

PROCTOR: I think you're sad again. Are you?

ELIZABETH—*she doesn't want friction, and yet she must:* You come so late I thought you'd gone to Salem this afternoon.

PROCTOR: Why? I have no business in Salem.

ELIZABETH: You did speak of going, earlier this week.

PROCTOR—*he knows what she means:* I thought better of it since.

ELIZABETH: Mary Warren's there today.

PROCTOR: Why'd you let her? You heard me forbid her to go to Salem any more!

ELIZABETH: I couldn't stop her.

PROCTOR, *holding back a full condemnation of her:* It is a fault, it is a fault, Elizabeth—you're the mistress here, not Mary Warren.

ELIZABETH: She frightened all my strength away.

PROCTOR: How may that mouse frighten you, Elizabeth? You—

ELIZABETH: It is a mouse no more. I forbid her go, and she raises up her chin like the daughter of a prince and says to me, "I must go to Salem, Goody Proctor; I am an official of the court!"

PROCTOR: Court! What court?

ELIZABETH: Aye, it is a proper court they have now. They've sent four judges out of Boston, she says, weighty magistrates of the General Court, and at the head sits the Deputy Governor of the Province.

PROCTOR, *astonished:* Why, she's mad.

ELIZABETH: I would to God she were. There be fourteen people in the jail now, she says. *Proctor simply looks at her, unable to grasp it.* And they'll be tried, and the court have power to hang them too, she says.

PROCTOR, *scoffing, but without conviction:* Ah, they'd never hang—

ELIZABETH: The Deputy Governor promise hangin' if they'll not confess, John. The town's gone wild, I think. She speak of Abigail, and I thought she were a saint, to hear her. Abigail brings the other girls into the court, and where she walks the crowd will part like the sea for Israel. And folks are brought before them, and if they scream and howl and fall to the floor—the person's clapped in the jail for bewitchin' them.

PROCTOR, *wide-eyed:* Oh, it is a black mischief.

ELIZABETH: I think you must go to Salem, John. *He turns to her.* I think so. You must tell them it is a fraud.

PROCTOR, *thinking beyond this:* Aye, it is, it is surely.

ELIZABETH: Let you go to Ezekiel Cheever—he knows you well. And tell him what she said to you last week in her uncle's house. She said it had naught to do with witchcraft, did she not?

PROCTOR, *in thought:* Aye, she did, she did. *Now a pause.*

ELIZABETH, *quietly, fearing to anger him by prodding:* God forbid you keep that from the court, John. I think they must be told.

PROCTOR, *quietly, struggling with his thought:* Aye, they must, they must. It is a wonder they do believe her.

ELIZABETH: I would go to Salem now, John—let you go tonight.

PROCTOR: I'll think on it.

ELIZABETH, *with her courage now:* You cannot keep it, John.

PROCTOR, *angering:* I know I cannot keep it. I say I will think on it!

ELIZABETH, *hurt, and very coldly:* Good, then, let you think on it. *She stands and starts to walk out of the room.*

PROCTOR: I am only wondering how I may prove what she told me, Elizabeth. If the girl's a saint now, I think it is not easy to prove she's fraud, and the town gone so silly. She told it to me in a room alone— I have no proof for it.

ELIZABETH: You were alone with her?

PROCTOR, *stubbornly:* For a moment alone, aye.

ELIZABETH: Why, then, it is not as you told me.

PROCTOR, *his anger rising:* For a moment, I say. The others come in soon after.

ELIZABETH, *quietly—she has suddenly lost all faith in him:* Do as you wish, then. *She starts to turn.*

PROCTOR: Woman. *She turns to him.* I'll not have your suspicion any more.

ELIZABETH, *a little loftily:* I have no—

PROCTOR: I'll not have it!

ELIZABETH: Then let you not earn it.

PROCTOR, *with a violent undertone:* You doubt me yet?

ELIZABETH, *with a smile, to keep her dignity:* John, if it were not Abigail that you must go to hurt, would you falter now? I think not.

PROCTOR: Now look you—

ELIZABETH: I see what I see, John.

PROCTOR, *with solemn warning:* You will not judge me more, Elizabeth. I have good reason to think before I charge fraud on Abigail, and I will think on it. Let you look to your own improvement before you go to judge your husband any more. I have forgot Abigail, and—

ELIZABETH: And I.

PROCTOR: Spare me! You forget nothin' and forgive nothin'. Learn charity, woman. I have gone tiptoe in this house all seven month since she is gone. I have not moved from there to there without I think to please you, and still an everlasting funeral marches round your heart. I cannot speak but I am doubted, every moment judged for lies, as though I come into a court when I come into this house!

ELIZABETH: John, you are not open with me. You saw her with a crowd, you said. Now you—

PROCTOR: I'll plead my honesty no more, Elizabeth.

ELIZABETH—*now she would justify herself:* John, I am only—

PROCTOR: No more! I should have roared you down when first you told me your suspicion. But I wilted, and, like a Christian, I confessed. Confessed! Some dream I had must have mistaken you for God that day. But you're not, you're not, and let you remember it! Let you look sometimes for the goodness in me, and judge me not.

ELIZABETH: I do not judge you. The magistrate sits in your heart that judges you. I never thought you but a good man, John—*with a smile*—only somewhat bewildered.

PROCTOR, *laughing bitterly:* Oh, Elizabeth, your justice would freeze beer! *He turns suddenly toward a sound outside. He starts for the door as Mary Warren enters. As soon as he sees her, he goes directly to her and grabs her by her cloak, furious.* How do you go to Salem when I forbid it? Do you mock me? *Shaking her:* I'll whip you if you dare leave this house again! *Strangely, she doesn't resist him but hangs limply by his grip.*

MARY WARREN: I am sick, I am sick, Mr. Proctor. Pray, pray, hurt me not. *Her strangeness throws him off, and her evident pallor and weakness. He frees her.* My insides are all shuddery; I am in the proceedings all day, sir.

PROCTOR, *with draining anger—his curiosity is draining it:* And what of these proceedings here? When will you proceed to keep this house, as you are paid nine pound a year to do—and my wife not wholly well? *As though to compensate, Mary Warren goes to Elizabeth with a small rag doll.*

MARY WARREN: I made a gift for you today, Goody Proctor. I had to sit long hours in a chair, and passed the time with sewing.

ELIZABETH, *perplexed, looking at the doll:* Why, thank you, it's a fair poppet.

MARY WARREN, *with a trembling, decayed voice:* We must all love each other now, Goody Proctor.

ELIZABETH, *amazed at her strangeness:* Aye, indeed, we must.

MARY WARREN, *glancing at the room:* I'll get up early in the morning and clean the house. I must sleep now. *She turns and starts off.*

PROCTOR: Mary. *She halts.* Is it true? There be fourteen women arrested?

MARY WARREN: No, sir. There be thirty-nine now— *She suddenly breaks off and sobs and sits down, exhausted.*

ELIZABETH: Why, she's weepin'! What ails you, child?

MARY WARREN: Goody Osburn—will hang! *There is a shocked pause, while she sobs.*

PROCTOR: Hang! *He calls into her face.* Hang, y'say?

MARY WARREN, *through her weeping:* Aye.

PROCTOR: The Deputy Governor will permit it?

MARY WARREN: He sentenced her. He must. *To ameliorate it:* But not Sarah Good. For Sarah Good confessed, y'see.

PROCTOR: Confessed! To what?

MARY WARREN: That she—*in horror at the memory*—she sometimes made a compact with Lucifer, and wrote her name in his black book— with her blood—and bound herself to torment Christians till God's thrown down—and we all must worship Hell forevermore.

Pause.

PROCTOR: But—surely you know what a jabberer she is. Did you tell them that?

MARY WARREN: Mr. Proctor, in open court she near to choked us all to death.

PROCTOR: How, choked you?

MARY WARREN: She sent her spirit out.

ELIZABETH: Oh, Mary, Mary, surely you—

MARY WARREN, *with an indignant edge:* She tried to kill me many times, Goody Proctor!

ELIZABETH: Why, I never heard you mention that before.

MARY WARREN: I never knew it before. I never knew anything before. When she come into the court I say to myself, I must not accuse this woman, for she sleep in ditches, and so very old and poor. But then—then she sit there, denying and denying, and I feel a misty coldness climbin' up my back, and the skin on my skull begin to creep, and I feel a clamp around my neck and I cannot breathe air; and then—*entranced*—I hear a voice, a screamin' voice, and it were my voice—and all at once I remember everything she done to me!

PROCTOR: Why? What did she do to you?

MARY WARREN, *like one awakened to a marvelous secret insight:* So many time, Mr. Proctor, she come to this very door, beggin' bread and a cup of cider—and mark this: whenever I turned her away empty, she *mumbled.*

ELIZABETH: Mumbled! She may mumble if she's hungry.

MARY WARREN: But *what* does she mumble? You must remember, Goody Proctor. Last month—a Monday, I think—she walked away, and I thought my guts would burst for two days after. Do you remember it?

ELIZABETH: Why—I do, I think, but—

MARY WARREN: And so I told that to Judge Hathorne, and he asks her so. "Goody Osburn," says he, "what curse do you mumble that this girl must fall sick after turning you away?" And then she replies—*mimicking an old crone*—"Why, your excellence, no curse at all. I only say my commandments; I hope I may say my commandments," says she!

ELIZABETH: And that's an upright answer.

MARY WARREN: Aye, but then Judge Hathorne say, "Recite for us your commandments!"—*leaning avidly toward them*—and of all the ten she could not say a single one. She never knew no commandments, and they had her in a flat lie!

PROCTOR: And so condemned her?

MARY WARREN, *now a little strained, seeing his stubborn doubt:* Why, they must when she condemned herself.

PROCTOR: But the proof, the proof!

MARY WARREN, *with greater impatience with him:* I told you the proof. It's hard proof, hard as rock, the judges said.

PROCTOR—*he pauses an instant, then:* You will not go to court again, Mary Warren.

MARY WARREN: I must tell you, sir, I will be gone every day now. I am amazed you do not see what weighty work we do.

PROCTOR: What work you do! It's strange work for a Christian girl to hang old women!

MARY WARREN: But, Mr. Proctor, they will not hang them if they confess. Sarah Good will only sit in jail some time—*recalling*—and here's a wonder for you; think on this. Goody Good is pregnant!

ELIZABETH: Pregnant! Are they mad? The woman's near to sixty!

MARY WARREN: They had Doctor Griggs examine her, and she's full to the brim. And smokin' a pipe all these years, and no husband either! But she's safe, thank God, for they'll not hurt the innocent child. But be that not a marvel? You must see it, sir, it's God's work we do. So I'll be gone every day for some time. I'm—I am an official of the court, they say, and I— *She has been edging toward offstage.*

PROCTOR: I'll official you! *He strides to the mantel, takes down the whip hanging there.*

MARY WARREN, *terrified, but coming erect, striving for her authority:* I'll not stand whipping any more!

ELIZABETH, *hurriedly, as Proctor approaches:* Mary, promise now you'll stay at home—

MARY WARREN, *backing from him, but keeping her erect posture, striving, striving for her way:* The Devil's loose in Salem, Mr. Proctor; we must discover where he's hiding!

PROCTOR: I'll whip the Devil out of you! *With whip raised he reaches out for her, and she streaks away and yells.*

MARY WARREN, *pointing at Elizabeth:* I saved her life today!

Silence. His whip comes down.

ELIZABETH, *softly:* I am accused?

MARY WARREN, *quaking:* Somewhat mentioned. But I said I never see no sign you ever sent your spirit out to hurt no one, and seeing I do live so closely with you, they dismissed it.

ELIZABETH: Who accused me?

MARY WARREN: I am bound by law, I cannot tell it. *To Proctor:* I only hope you'll not be so sarcastical no more. Four judges and the King's deputy sat to dinner with us but an hour ago. I—I would have you speak civilly to me, from this out.

PROCTOR, *in horror, muttering in disgust at her:* Go to bed.

MARY WARREN, *with a stamp of her foot:* I'll not be ordered to bed no more, Mr. Proctor! I am eighteen and a woman, however single!

PROCTOR: Do you wish to sit up? Then sit up.

MARY WARREN: I wish to go to bed!

PROCTOR, *in anger:* Good night, then!

MARY WARREN: Good night. *Dissatisfied, uncertain of herself, she goes out. Wide-eyed, both Proctor and Elizabeth stand staring.*

ELIZABETH, *quietly:* Oh, the noose, the noose is up!

PROCTOR: There'll be no noose.

ELIZABETH: She wants me dead. I knew all week it would come to this!

PROCTOR, *without conviction:* They dismissed it. You heard her say—

ELIZABETH: And what of tomorrow? She will cry me out until they take me!

PROCTOR: Sit you down.

ELIZABETH: She wants me dead, John, you know it!

PROCTOR: I say sit down! *She sits, trembling. He speaks quietly, trying to keep his wits.* Now we must be wise, Elizabeth.

ELIZABETH, *with sarcasm, and a sense of being lost:* Oh, indeed, indeed!

PROCTOR: Fear nothing. I'll find Ezekiel Cheever. I'll tell him she said it were all sport.

ELIZABETH: John, with so many in the jail, more than Cheever's help is needed now, I think. Would you favor me with this? Go to Abigail.

PROCTOR, *his soul hardening as he senses:* . . . . What have I to say to Abigail?

ELIZABETH, *delicately:* John—grant me this. You have a faulty understanding of young girls. There is a promise made in any bed—

PROCTOR, *striving against his anger:* What promise!

ELIZABETH: Spoke or silent, a promise is surely made. And she may dote on it now—I am sure she does—and thinks to kill me, then to take my place.

Proctor's anger is rising; he cannot speak.

ELIZABETH: It is her dearest hope, John, I know it. There be a thousand names; why does she call mine? There be a certain danger in calling such a name—I am no Goody Good that sleeps in ditches, nor Osburn, drunk and half-witted. She'd dare not call out such a farmer's wife but there be monstrous profit in it. She thinks to take my place, John.

PROCTOR: She cannot think it! *He knows it is true.*

ELIZABETH, *"reasonably":* John, have you ever shown her somewhat of contempt? She cannot pass you in the church but you will blush—

PROCTOR: I may blush for my sin.

ELIZABETH: I think she sees another meaning in that blush.

PROCTOR: And what see you? What see you, Elizabeth?

ELIZABETH, *"conceding":* I think you be somewhat ashamed, for I am there, and she so close.

PROCTOR: When will you know me, woman? Were I stone I would have cracked for shame this seven month!

ELIZABETH: Then go and tell her she's a whore. Whatever promise she may sense—break it, John, break it.

PROCTOR, *between his teeth:* Good, then. I'll go. *He starts for his rifle.*

ELIZABETH, *trembling, fearfully:* Oh, how unwillingly!

PROCTOR, *turning on her, rifle in hand:* I will curse her hotter than the oldest cinder in hell. But pray, begrudge me not my anger!

ELIZABETH: Your anger! I only ask you—

PROCTOR: Woman, am I so base? Do you truly think me base?

ELIZABETH: I never called you base.

PROCTOR: Then how do you charge me with such a promise? The promise that a stallion gives a mare I gave that girl!

ELIZABETH: Then why do you anger with me when I bid you break it?

PROCTOR: Because it speaks deceit, and I am honest! But I'll plead no more! I see now your spirit twists around the single error of my life, and I will never tear it free!

ELIZABETH, *crying out:* You'll tear it free—when you come to know that I will be your only wife, or no wife at all! She has an arrow in you yet, John Proctor, and you know it well!

Quite suddenly, as though from the air, a figure appears in the doorway. They start slightly. It is Mr. Hale. He is different now—drawn a little, and there is a quality of deference, even of guilt, about his manner now.

HALE: Good evening.

PROCTOR, *still in his shock:* Why, Mr. Hale! Good evening to you, sir. Come in, come in.

HALE, *to Elizabeth:* I hope I do not startle you.

ELIZABETH: No, no, it's only that I heard no horse—

HALE: You are Goodwife Proctor.

PROCTOR: Aye; Elizabeth.

HALE—*he nods, then:* I hope you're not off to bed yet.

PROCTOR, *setting down his gun:* No, no. *Hale comes further into the room. And Proctor, to explain his nervousness:* We are not used to visitors after dark, but you're welcome here. Will you sit you down, sir?

HALE: I will. *He sits.* Let you sit, Goodwife Proctor. *She does, never letting him out of her sight. There is a pause as Hale looks about the room.*

PROCTOR, *to break the silence:* Will you drink cider, Mr. Hale?

HALE: No, it rebels my stomach; I have some further traveling yet tonight. Sit you down, sir. *Proctor sits.* I will not keep you long, but I have some business with you.

PROCTOR: Business of the court?

HALE: No—no, I come of my own, without the court's authority. Hear me. *He wets his lips.* I know not if you are aware, but your wife's name is—mentioned in the court.

PROCTOR: We know it, sir. Our Mary Warren told us. We are entirely amazed.

HALE: I am a stranger here, as you know. And in my ignorance I find it hard to draw a clear opinion of them that come accused before the court. And so this afternoon, and now tonight, I go from house to house—I come now from Rebecca Nurse's house and—

ELIZABETH, *shocked:* Rebecca's charged!

HALE: God forbid such a one be charged. She is, however—mentioned somewhat.

ELIZABETH, *with an attempt at a laugh:* You will never believe, I hope, that Rebecca trafficked with the Devil.

HALE: Woman, it is possible.

PROCTOR, *taken aback:* Surely you cannot think so.

HALE: This is a strange time, Mister. No man may longer doubt the powers of the dark are gathered in monstrous attack upon this village. There is too much evidence now to deny it. You will agree, sir?

PROCTOR, *evading:* I—have no knowledge in that line. But it's hard to think so pious a woman be secretly a Devil's bitch after seventy year of such good prayer.

HALE: Aye. But the Devil is a wily one, you cannot deny it. However, she is far from accused, and I know she will not be. *Pause.* I thought, sir, to put some questions as to the Christian character of this house, if you'll permit me.

PROCTOR, *coldly, resentful:* Why, we—have no fear of questions, sir.

HALE: Good, then. *He makes himself more comfortable.* In the book of record that Mr. Parris keeps, I note that you are rarely in the church on Sabbath Day.

PROCTOR: No, sir, you are mistaken.

HALE: Twenty-six time in seventeen month, sir. I must call that rare. Will you tell me why you are so absent?

PROCTOR: Mr. Hale, I never knew I must account to that man for I come to church or stay at home. My wife were sick this winter.

HALE: So I am told. But you, Mister, why could you not come alone?

PROCTOR: I surely did come when I could, and when I could not I prayed in this house.

HALE: Mr. Proctor, your house is not a church; your theology must tell you that.

PROCTOR: It does, sir, it does; and it tells me that a minister may pray to God without he have golden candlesticks upon the altar.

HALE: What golden candlesticks?

PROCTOR: Since we built the church there were pewter candlesticks upon the altar; Francis Nurse made them, y'know, and a sweeter hand never touched the metal. But Parris came, and for twenty week he preach nothin' but golden candlesticks until he had them. I labor the earth from dawn of day to blink of night, and I tell you true, when I look to heaven and see my money glaring at his elbows—it hurt my prayer, sir, it hurt my prayer. I think, sometimes, the man dreams cathedrals, not clapboard meetin' houses.

HALE—*he thinks, then:* And yet, Mister, a Christian on Sabbath Day must be in church. *Pause.* Tell me—you have three children?

PROCTOR: Aye. Boys.

HALE: How comes it that only two are baptized?

PROCTOR—*he starts to speak, then stops, then, as though unable to restrain this:* I like it not that Mr. Parris should lay his hand upon my baby. I see no light of God in that man. I'll not conceal it.

HALE: I must say it, Mr. Proctor; that is not for you to decide. The man's ordained, therefore the light of God is in him.

PROCTOR, *flushed with resentment but trying to smile:* What's your suspicion, Mr. Hale?

HALE: No, no, I have no—

PROCTOR: I nailed the roof upon the church, I hung the door—

HALE: Oh, did you! That's a good sign, then.

PROCTOR: It may be I have been too quick to bring the man to book, but you cannot think we ever desired the destruction of religion. I think that's in your mind, is it not?

HALE, *not altogether giving way:* I—have—there is a softness in your record, sir, a softness.

ELIZABETH: I think, maybe, we have been too hard with Mr. Parris, I think so. But sure we never loved the Devil here.

HALE—*he nods, deliberating this. Then, with the voice of one administering a secret test:* Do you know your Commandments, Elizabeth?

ELIZABETH, *without hesitation, even eagerly:* I surely do. There be no mark of blame upon my life, Mr. Hale. I am a convenanted Christian woman.

HALE: And you, Mister?

PROCTOR, *a trifle unsteadily:* I—am sure I do, sir.

HALE—*he glances at her open face, then at John, then:* Let you repeat them, if you will.

PROCTOR: The Commandments.

HALE: Aye.

PROCTOR, *looking off, beginning to sweat:* Thou shalt not kill.

HALE: Aye.

PROCTOR, *counting on his fingers:* Thou shalt not steal. Thou shalt not covet thy neighbor's goods, nor make unto thee any graven image. Thou shalt not take the name of the Lord in vain; thou shalt have no other gods before me. *With some hesitation:* Thou shalt remember the Sabbath Day and keep it holy. *Pause. Then:* Thou shalt honor thy father and mother. Thou shalt not bear false witness. *He is stuck. He counts back on his fingers, knowing one is missing.* Thou shalt not make unto thee any graven image.

HALE: You have said that twice, sir.

PROCTOR, *lost:* Aye. *He is flailing for it.*

ELIZABETH, *delicately:* Adultery, John.

PROCTOR, *as though a secret arrow had pained his heart:* Aye. *Trying to grin it away—to Hale:* You see, sir, between the two of us we do know them all. *Hale only looks at Proctor, deep in his attempt to define this man. Proctor grows more uneasy.* I think it be a small fault.

HALE: Theology, sir, is a fortress; no crack in a fortress may be accounted small. *He rises; he seems worried now. He paces a little, in deep thought.*

PROCTOR: There be no love for Satan in this house, Mister.

HALE: I pray it, I pray it dearly. *He looks to both of them, an attempt at a smile on his face, but his misgivings are clear.* Well, then—I'll bid you good night.

ELIZABETH, *unable to restrain herself:* Mr. Hale. *He turns.* I do think you are suspecting me somewhat? Are you not?

HALE, *obviously disturbed—and evasive:* Goody Proctor, I do not judge you. My duty is to add what I may to the godly wisdom of the court. I pray you both good health and good fortune. *To John:* Good night, sir. *He starts out.*

ELIZABETH, *with a note of desperation:* I think you must tell him, John.

HALE: What's that?

ELIZABETH, *restraining a call:* Will you tell him?

Slight pause. Hale looks questioningly at John.

PROCTOR, *with difficulty:* I—I have no witness and cannot prove it, except my word be taken. But I know the children's sickness had naught to do with witchcraft.

HALE, *stopped, struck:* Naught to do—?

PROCTOR: Mr. Parris discovered them sportin' in the woods. They were startled and took sick.

Pause.

HALE: Who told you this?

PROCTOR—*he hesitates, then:* Abigail Williams.

HALE: Abigail!

PROCTOR: Aye.

HALE, *his eyes wide:* Abigail Williams told you it had naught to do with witchcraft!

PROCTOR: She told me the day you came, sir.

HALE, *suspiciously:* Why—why did you keep this?

PROCTOR: I never knew until tonight that the world is gone daft with this nonsense.

HALE: Nonsense! Mister, I have myself examined Tituba, Sarah Good, and numerous others that have confessed to dealing with the Devil. They have *confessed* it.

PROCTOR: And why not, if they must hang for denyin' it? There are them that will swear to anything before they'll hang; have you never thought of that?

HALE: I have. I—I have indeed. *It is his own suspicion, but he resists it. He glances at Elizabeth, then at John.* And you—would you testify to this in court?

PROCTOR: I—had not reckoned with goin' into court. But if I must I will.

HALE: Do you falter here?

PROCTOR: I falter nothing, but I may wonder if my story will be credited in such a court. I do wonder on it, when such a steady-minded minister as you will suspicion such a woman that never lied, and cannot, and the world knows she cannot! I may falter somewhat, Mister; I am no fool.

HALE, *quietly—it has impressed him:* Proctor, let you open with me now, for I have a rumor that troubles me. It's said you hold no belief that there may even be witches in the world. Is that true, sir?

PROCTOR—*he knows this is critical, and is striving against his disgust with Hale and with himself for even answering:* I know not what I have said, I may have said it. I have wondered if there be witches in the world—although I cannot believe they come among us now.

HALE: Then you do not believe—

PROCTOR: I have no knowledge of it; the Bible speaks of witches, and I will not deny them.

HALE: And you, woman?

ELIZABETH: I—I cannot believe it.

HALE, *shocked:* You cannot!

PROCTOR: Elizabeth, you bewilder him!

ELIZABETH, *to Hale:* I cannot think the Devil may own a woman's soul, Mr. Hale, when she keeps an upright way, as I have. I am a good woman, I know it; and if you believe I may do only good work in the world, and yet be secretly bound to Satan, then I must tell you, sir, I do not believe it.

HALE: But, woman, you do believe there are witches in—

ELIZABETH: If you think that I am one, then I say there are none.

HALE: You surely do not fly against the Gospel, the Gospel—

PROCTOR: She believe in the Gospel, every word!

ELIZABETH: Question Abigail Williams about the Gospel, not myself!

Hale stares at her.

PROCTOR: She do not mean to doubt the Gospel, sir, you cannot think it. This be a Christian house, sir, a Christian house.

HALE: God keep you both; let the third child be quickly baptized, and go you without fail each Sunday in to Sabbath prayer; and keep a solemn, quiet way among you. I think—

Giles Corey appears in doorway.

GILES: John!

PROCTOR: Giles! What's the matter?

GILES: They take my wife.

Francis Nurse enters.

GILES: And his Rebecca!

PROCTOR, *to Francis:* Rebecca's in the *jail*!

FRANCIS: Aye, Cheever come and take her in his wagon. We've only now come from the jail, and they'll not even let us in to see them.

ELIZABETH: They've surely gone wild now, Mr. Hale!

FRANCIS, *going to Hale:* Reverend Hale! Can you not speak to the Deputy Governor? I'm sure he mistakes these people—

HALE: Pray calm yourself, Mr. Nurse.

FRANCIS: My wife is the very brick and mortar of the church, Mr. Hale—*indicating Giles*—and Martha Corey, there cannot be a woman closer yet to God than Martha.

HALE: How is Rebecca charged, Mr. Nurse?

FRANCIS, *with a mocking, half-hearted laugh:* For murder, she's charged! *Mockingly quoting the warrant:* "For the marvelous and supernatural murder of Goody Putnam's babies." What am I to do, Mr. Hale?

HALE, *he turns from Francis, deeply troubled, then:* Believe me, Mr. Nurse, if Rebecca Nurse be tainted, then nothing's left to stop the whole green world from burning. Let you rest upon the justice of the court; the court will send her home, I know it.

FRANCIS: You cannot mean she will be tried in court!

HALE, *pleading:* Nurse, though our hearts break, we cannot flinch; these are new times, sir. There is a misty plot afoot so subtle we should be criminal to cling to old respects and ancient friendships. I have seen too many frightful proofs in court—the Devil is alive in Salem, and we dare not quail to follow wherever the accusing finger points!

PROCTOR, *angered:* How may such a woman murder children?

HALE, *in great pain:* Man, remember, until an hour before the Devil fell, God thought him beautiful in Heaven.

GILES: I never said my wife were a witch, Mr. Hale; I only said she were reading books!

HALE: Mr. Corey, exactly what complaint were made on your wife?

GILES: That bloody mongrel Walcott charge her. Y'see, he buy a pig of my wife four or five year ago, and the pig died soon after. So he come dancin' in for his money back. So my Martha, she says to him, "Walcott, if you haven't the wit to feed a pig properly, you'll not live to own many," she says. Now he goes to court and claims that from that day to this he cannot keep a pig alive for more than four weeks because my Martha bewitch them with her books!

Enter Ezekiel Cheever. A shocked silence.

CHEEVER: Good evening to you, Proctor.

PROCTOR: Why, Mr. Cheever. Good evening.

CHEEVER: Good evening, all. Good evening, Mr. Hale.

PROCTOR: I hope you come not on business of the court.

CHEEVER: I do, Proctor, aye. I am clerk of the court now, y'know.

Enter Marshal Herrick, a man in his early thirties, who is somewhat shamefaced at the moment.

GILES: It's a pity, Ezekiel, that an honest tailor might have gone to Heaven must burn in Hell. You'll burn for this, do you know it?

CHEEVER: You know yourself I must do as I'm told. You surely know that, Giles. And I'd as lief you'd not be sending me to Hell. I like not the sound of it, I tell you; I like not the sound of it. *He fears Proctor, but starts to reach inside his coat.* Now believe me, Proctor, how heavy be the law, all its tonnage I do carry on my back tonight. *He takes out a warrant.* I have a warrant for your wife.

PROCTOR, *to Hale:* You said she were not charged!

HALE: I know nothin' of it. *To Cheever:* When were she charged?

CHEEVER: I am given sixteen warrant tonight, sir, and she is one.

PROCTOR: Who charged her?

CHEEVER: Why, Abigail Williams charge her.

PROCTOR: On what proof, what proof?

CHEEVER, *looking about the room:* Mr. Proctor, I have little time. The court bid me search your house, but I like not to search a house. So will you hand me any poppets that your wife may keep here?

PROCTOR: Poppets?

ELIZABETH: I never kept no poppets, not since I were a girl.

CHEEVER, *embarrassed, glancing toward the mantel where sits Mary Warren's poppet:* I spy a poppet, Goody Proctor.

ELIZABETH: Oh! *Going for it:* Why, this is Mary's.

CHEEVER, *shyly:* Would you please to give it to me?

ELIZABETH, *handing it to him, asks Hale:* Has the court discovered a text in poppets now?

CHEEVER, *carefully holding the poppet:* Do you keep any others in this house?

PROCTOR: No, nor this one either till tonight. What signifies a poppet?

CHEEVER: Why, a poppet—*he gingerly turns the poppet over*—a poppet may signify— Now, woman, will you please to come with me?

PROCTOR: She will not! *To Elizabeth:* Fetch Mary here.

CHEEVER, *ineptly reaching toward Elizabeth:* No, no, I am forbid to leave her from my sight.

PROCTOR, *pushing his arm away:* You'll leave her out of sight and out of mind, Mister. Fetch Mary, Elizabeth. *Elizabeth goes upstairs.*

HALE: What signifies a poppet, Mr. Cheever?

CHEEVER, *turning the poppet over in his hands:* Why, they say it may signify that she— *He has lifted the poppet's skirt, and his eyes widen in astonished fear.* Why, this, this—

PROCTOR, *reaching for the poppet:* What's there?

CHEEVER: Why—*he draws out a long needle from the poppet*—it is a needle! Herrick, Herrick, it is a needle!

Herrick comes toward him.

PROCTOR, *angrily, bewildered:* And what signifies a needle!

CHEEVER, *his hands shaking:* Why, this go hard with her, Proctor, this—I had my doubts, Proctor, I had my doubts, but here's calamity. *To Hale, showing the needle:* You see it, sir, it is a needle!

HALE: Why? What meanin' has it?

CHEEVER, *wide-eyed, trembling:* The girl, the Williams girl, Abigail Williams, sir. She sat to dinner in Reverend Parris's house tonight, and without word nor warnin' she falls to the floor. Like a struck beast, he says, and screamed a scream that a bull would weep to hear. And he goes to save her, and, stuck two inches in the flesh of her belly, he draw a needle out. And demandin' of her how she come to be so stabbed, she—*to Proctor now*—testify it were your wife's familiar spirit pushed it in.

PROCTOR: Why, she done it herself! *To Hale:* I hope you're not takin' this for proof, Mister!

Hale, struck by the proof, is silent.

CHEEVER: 'Tis hard proof! *To Hale:* I find here a poppet Goody Proctor keeps. I have found it, sir. And in the belly of the poppet a needle's stuck. I tell you true, Proctor, I never warranted to see such proof of Hell, and I bid you obstruct me not, for I—

Enter Elizabeth with Mary Warren. Proctor, seeing Mary Warren, draws her by the arm to Hale.

PROCTOR: Here now! Mary, how did this poppet come into my house?

MARY WARREN, *frightened for herself, her voice very small:* What poppet's that, sir?

PROCTOR, *impatiently, pointing at the doll in Cheever's hand:* This poppet, this poppet.

MARY WARREN, *evasively, looking at it:* Why, I—I think it is mine.

PROCTOR: It is your poppet, is it not?

MARY WARREN, *not understanding the direction of this:* It—is, sir.

PROCTOR: And how did it come into this house?

MARY WARREN, *glancing about at the avid faces:* Why—I made it in the court, sir, and—give it to Goody Proctor tonight.

PROCTOR, *to Hale:* Now, sir—do you have it?

HALE: Mary Warren, a needle have been found inside this poppet.

MARY WARREN, *bewildered:* Why, I meant no harm by it, sir.

PROCTOR, *quickly:* You stuck that needle in yourself?

MARY WARREN: I—I believe I did, sir, I—

PROCTOR, *to Hale:* What say you now?

HALE, *watching Mary Warren closely:* Child, you are certain this be your natural memory? May it be, perhaps, that someone conjures you even now to say this?

MARY WARREN: Conjures me? Why, no, sir, I am entirely myself, I think. Let you ask Susanna Walcott—she saw me sewin' it in court. *Or better still:* Ask Abby, Abby sat beside me when I made it.

PROCTOR, *to Hale, of Cheever:* Bid him begone. Your mind is surely settled now. Bid him out, Mr. Hale.

ELIZABETH: What signifies a needle?

HALE: Mary—you charge a cold and cruel murder on Abigail.

MARY WARREN: Murder! I charge no—

HALE: Abigail were stabbed tonight; a needle were found stuck into her belly—

ELIZABETH: And she charges me?

HALE: Aye.

ELIZABETH, *her breath knocked out:* Why—! The girl is murder! She must be ripped out of the world!

CHEEVER, *pointing at Elizabeth:* You've heard that, sir! Ripped out of the world! Herrick, you heard it!

PROCTOR, *suddenly snatching the warrant out of Cheever's hands:* Out with you.

CHEEVER: Proctor, you dare not touch the warrant.

PROCTOR, *ripping the warrant:* Out with you!

CHEEVER: You've ripped the Deputy Governor's warrant, man!

PROCTOR: Damn the Deputy Governor! Out of my house!

HALE: Now, Proctor, Proctor!

PROCTOR: Get y'gone with them! You are a broken minister.

HALE: Proctor, if she is innocent, the court—

PROCTOR: If *she* is innocent! Why do you never wonder if Parris be innocent, or Abigail? Is the accuser always holy now? Were they born this morning as clean as God's fingers? I'll tell you what's walking Salem—vengeance is walking Salem. We are what we always were in Salem, but now the little crazy children are jangling the keys of the kingdom, and common vengeance writes the law! This warrant's vengeance! I'll not give my wife to vengeance!

ELIZABETH: I'll go, John—

PROCTOR: You will not go!

HERRICK: I have nine men outside. You cannot keep her. The law binds me, John, I cannot budge.

PROCTOR, *to Hale, ready to break him:* Will you see her taken?

HALE: Proctor, the court is just—

PROCTOR: Pontius Pilate! God will not let you wash your hands of this!

ELIZABETH: John—I think I must go with them. *He cannot bear to look at her.* Mary, there is bread enough for the morning; you will bake, in the afternoon. Help Mr. Proctor as you were his daughter—you owe me that, and much more. *She is fighting her weeping.* To Proctor: When the children wake, speak nothing of witchcraft—it will frighten them. *She cannot go on.*

PROCTOR: I will bring you home. I will bring you soon.

ELIZABETH: Oh, John, bring me soon!

PROCTOR: I will fall like an ocean on that court! Fear nothing, Elizabeth.

ELIZABETH, *with great fear:* I will fear nothing. *She looks about the room, as though to fix it in her mind.* Tell the children I have gone to visit someone sick.

She walks out the door, Herrick and Cheever behind her. For a moment, Proctor watches from the doorway. The clank of chain is heard.

PROCTOR: Herrick! Herrick, don't chain her! *He rushes out the door. From outside:* Damn you, man, you will not chain her! Off with them! I'll not have it! I will not have her chained!

There are other men's voices against his. Hale, in a fever of guilt and uncertainty, turns from the door to avoid the sight; Mary Warren bursts into tears and sits weeping. Giles Corey calls to Hale.

GILES: And yet silent, minister? It is fraud, you know it is fraud! What keeps you, man?

Proctor is half braced, half pushed into the room by two deputies and Herrick.

PROCTOR: I'll pay you, Herrick, I will surely pay you!

HERRICK, *panting:* In God's name, John, I cannot help myself. I must chain them all. Now let you keep inside this house till I am gone! *He goes out with his deputies.*

Proctor stands there, gulping air. Horses and a wagon creaking are heard.

HALE, *in great uncertainty:* Mr. Proctor—

PROCTOR: Out of my sight!

HALE: Charity, Proctor, charity. What I have heard in her favor, I will not fear to testify in court. God help me, I cannot judge her guilty or innocent—I know not. Only this consider: the world goes mad, and it profit nothing you should lay the cause to the vengeance of a little girl.

PROCTOR: You are a coward! Though you be ordained in God's own tears, you are a coward now!

HALE: Proctor, I cannot think God be provoked so grandly by such a petty cause. The jails are packed—our greatest judges sit in Salem now—and hangin's promised. Man, we must look to cause proportionate. Were there murder done, perhaps, and never brought to light? Abomination? Some secret blasphemy that stinks to Heaven? Think on cause, man, and let you help me to discover it. For there's your way, believe it, there is your only way, when such confusion strikes upon the world. *He goes to Giles and Francis.* Let you counsel among yourselves; think on your village and what may have drawn from Heaven such thundering wrath upon you all. I shall pray God open up our eyes.

Hale goes out.

FRANCIS, *struck by Hale's mood:* I never heard no murder done in Salem.

PROCTOR—*he has been reached by Hale's words:* Leave me, Francis, leave me.

GILES, *shaken:* John—tell me, are we lost?

PROCTOR: Go home now, Giles. We'll speak on it tomorrow.

GILES: Let you think on it. We'll come early, eh?

PROCTOR: Aye. Go now, Giles.

GILES: Good night, then.

Giles Corey and Francis Nurse go out. After a moment:

MARY WARREN, *in a fearful squeak of a voice:* Mr. Proctor, very likely they'll let her come home once they're given proper evidence.

PROCTOR: You're coming to the court with me, Mary. You will tell it in the court.

MARY WARREN: I cannot charge murder on Abigail.

PROCTOR, *moving menacingly toward her:* You will tell the court how that poppet come here and who stuck the needle in.

MARY WARREN: She'll kill me for sayin' that! *Proctor continues toward her.* Abby'll charge lechery on you, Mr. Proctor!

PROCTOR, *halting:* She's told you!

MARY WARREN: I have known it, sir. She'll ruin you with it, I know she will.

PROCTOR, *hesitating, and with deep hatred of himself:* Good. Then her saintliness is done with. *Mary backs from him.* We will slide together into our pit; you will tell the court what you know.

MARY WARREN, *in terror:* I cannot, they'll turn on me—

Proctor strides and catches her, and she is repeating, "I cannot, I cannot!"

PROCTOR: My wife will never die for me! I will bring your guts into your mouth but that goodness will not die for me!

MARY WARREN, *struggling to escape him:* I cannot do it, I cannot!

PROCTOR, *grasping her by the throat as though he would strangle her:* Make your peace with it! Now Hell and Heaven grapple on our backs, and all our old pretense is ripped away—make your peace! *He throws her to the floor, where she sobs, "I cannot, I cannot . . ."* And now, half to himself, staring, and turning to the open door: Peace. It is a providence, and no great change; we are only what we always were, but naked now. *He walks as though toward a great horror, facing the open sky.* Aye, naked! And the wind, God's icy wind, will blow!

And she is over and over again sobbing, "I cannot, I cannot, I cannot," as

THE CURTAIN FALLS★

★ Act II, Scene 2, which appeared in the original production, was dropped by the author from the published reading version, the *Collected Plays*, and all Compass editions prior to 1970. It has not been included in most productions subsequent to the revival at New York's Martinique Theatre in 1958 and was dropped by Sir Laurence Olivier in his London production in 1965. It is included here as an appendix on page 254.

ACT THREE

The vestry room of the Salem meeting house, now serving as the anteroom of the General Court.

As the curtain rises, the room is empty, but for sunlight pouring through two high windows in the back wall. The room is solemn, even forbidding. Heavy beams jut out, boards of random widths make up the walls. At the right are two doors leading into the meeting house proper, where the court is being held. At the left another door leads outside.

There is a plain bench at the left, and another at the right. In the center a rather long meeting table, with stools and a considerable armchair snugged up to it.

Through the partitioning wall at the right we hear a prosecutor's voice, Judge Hathorne's, asking a question; then a woman's voice, Martha Corey's, replying.

HATHORNE'S VOICE: Now, Martha Corey, there is abundant evidence in our hands to show that you have given yourself to the reading of fortunes. Do you deny it?

MARTHA COREY'S VOICE: I am innocent to a witch. I know not what a witch is.

HATHORNE'S VOICE: How do you know, then, that you are not a witch?

MARTHA COREY'S VOICE: If I were, I would know it.

HATHORNE'S VOICE: Why do you hurt these children?

MARTHA COREY'S VOICE: I do not hurt them. I scorn it!

GILES' VOICE, *roaring:* I have evidence for the court!

Voices of townspeople rise in excitement.

DANFORTH'S VOICE: You will keep your seat!

GILES' VOICE: Thomas Putnam is reaching out for land!

DANFORTH'S VOICE: Remove that man, Marshal!

GILES' VOICE: You're hearing lies, lies!

A roaring goes up from the people.

HATHORNE'S VOICE: Arrest him, excellency!

GILES' VOICE: I have evidence. Why will you not hear my evidence?

The door opens and Giles is half carried into the vestry room by Herrick. Francis Nurse enters trailing behind Giles.

GILES: Hands off, damn you, let me go!

HERRICK: Giles, Giles!

GILES: Out of my way, Herrick! I bring evidence—

HERRICK: You cannot go in there, Giles; it's a court!

Enter Hale from the court.

HALE: Pray be calm a moment.

GILES: You, Mr. Hale, go in there and demand I speak.

HALE: A moment, sir, a moment.

GILES: They'll be hangin' my wife!

Judge Hathorne enters. He is in his sixties, a bitter, remorseless Salem judge.

HATHORNE: How do you dare come roarin' into this court! Are you gone daft, Corey?

GILES: You're not a Boston judge yet, Hathorne. You'll not call me daft!

Enter Deputy Governor Danforth and, behind him, Ezekiel Cheever and Parris. On his appearance, silence falls. Danforth is a grave man in his sixties, of some humor and sophistication that do not, however, interfere with an exact loyalty to his position and his cause. He comes down to Giles, who awaits his wrath.

DANFORTH, *looking directly at Giles:* Who is this man?

PARRIS: Giles Corey, sir, and a more contentious—

GILES, *to Parris:* I am asked the question, and I am old enough to answer it! *To Danforth, who impresses him and to whom he smiles through his strain:* My name is Corey, sir, Giles Corey. I have six hundred acres, and timber in addition. It is my wife you be condemning now. *He indicates the courtroom.*

DANFORTH: And how do you imagine to help her cause with such contemptuous riot? Now be gone. Your old age alone keeps you out of jail for this.

GILES, *beginning to plead:* They be tellin' lies about my wife, sir, I—

DANFORTH: Do you take it upon yourself to determine what this court shall believe and what it shall set aside?

GILES: Your Excellency, we mean no disrespect for—

DANFORTH: Disrespect indeed! It is disruption, Mister. This is the highest court of the supreme government of this province, do you know it?

GILES, *beginning to weep:* Your Excellency, I only said she were readin' books, sir, and they come and take her out of my house for—

DANFORTH, *mystified:* Books! What books?

GILES, *through helpless sobs:* It is my third wife, sir; I never had no wife that be so taken with books, and I thought to find the cause of it, d'y'see, but it were no witch I blamed her for. *He is openly weeping.* I have broke charity with the woman, I have broke charity with her. *He covers his face, ashamed. Danforth is respectfully silent.*

HALE: Excellency, he claims hard evidence for his wife's defense. I think that in all justice you must—

DANFORTH: Then let him submit his evidence in proper affidavit. You are certainly aware of our procedure here, Mr. Hale. *To Herrick:* Clear this room.

HERRICK: Come now, Giles. *He gently pushes Corey out.*

FRANCIS: We are desperate, sir; we come here three days now and cannot be heard.

DANFORTH: Who is this man?

FRANCIS: Francis Nurse, Your Excellency.

HALE: His wife's Rebecca that were condemned this morning.

DANFORTH: Indeed! I am amazed to find you in such uproar. I have only good report of your character, Mr. Nurse.

HATHORNE: I think they must both be arrested in contempt, sir.

DANFORTH, *to Francis:* Let you write your plea, and in due time I will—

FRANCIS: Excellency, we have proof for your eyes; God forbid you shut them to it. The girls, sir, the girls are frauds.

DANFORTH: What's that?

FRANCIS: We have proof of it, sir. They are all deceiving you.

Danforth is shocked, but studying Francis.

HATHORNE: This is contempt, sir, contempt!

DANFORTH: Peace, Judge Hathorne. Do you know who I am, Mr. Nurse?

FRANCIS: I surely do, sir, and I think you must be a wise judge to be what you are.

DANFORTH: And do you know that near to four hundred are in the jails from Marblehead to Lynn, and upon my signature?

FRANCIS: I—

DANFORTH: And seventy-two condemned to hang by that signature?

FRANCIS: Excellency, I never thought to say it to such a weighty judge, but you are deceived.

Enter Giles Corey from left. All turn to see as he beckons in Mary Warren with Proctor. Mary is keeping her eyes to the ground; Proctor has her elbow as though she were near collapse.

PARRIS, *on seeing her, in shock:* Mary Warren! *He goes directly to bend close to her face.* What are you about here?

PROCTOR, *pressing Parris away from her with a gentle but firm motion of protectiveness:* She would speak with the Deputy Governor.

DANFORTH—*shocked by this, he turns to Herrick:* Did you not tell me Mary Warren were sick in bed?

HERRICK: She were, Your Honor. When I go to fetch her to the court last week, she said she were sick.

GILES: She has been strivin' with her soul all week, Your Honor; she comes now to tell the truth of this to you.

DANFORTH: Who is this?

PROCTOR: John Proctor, sir. Elizabeth Proctor is my wife.

PARRIS: Beware this man, Your Excellency, this man is mischief.

HALE, *excitedly:* I think you must hear the girl, sir, she—

DANFORTH, *who has become very interested in Mary Warren and only raises a hand toward Hale:* Peace. What would you tell us, Mary Warren?

Proctor looks at her, but she cannot speak.

PROCTOR: She never saw no spirits, sir.

DANFORTH, *with great alarm and surprise, to Mary:* Never saw no spirits!

GILES, *eagerly:* Never.

PROCTOR, *reaching into his jacket:* She has signed a deposition, sir—

DANFORTH, *instantly:* No, no, I accept no depositions. *He is rapidly calculating this; he turns from her to Proctor.* Tell me, Mr. Proctor, have you given out this story in the village?

PROCTOR: We have not.

PARRIS: They've come to overthrow the court, sir! This man is—

DANFORTH: I pray you, Mr. Parris. Do you know, Mr. Proctor, that the entire contention of the state in these trials is that the voice of Heaven is speaking through the children?

PROCTOR: I know that, sir.

DANFORTH—*he thinks, staring at Proctor, then turns to Mary Warren:* And you, Mary Warren, how came you to cry out people for sending their spirits against you?

MARY WARREN: It were pretense, sir.

DANFORTH: I cannot hear you.

PROCTOR: It were pretense, she says.

DANFORTH: Ah? And the other girls? Susanna Walcott, and—the others? They are also pretending?

MARY WARREN: Aye, sir.

DANFORTH, *wide-eyed:* Indeed. *Pause. He is baffled by this. He turns to study Proctor's face.*

PARRIS, *in a sweat:* Excellency, you surely cannot think to let so vile a lie be spread in open court!

DANFORTH: Indeed not, but it strike hard upon me that she will dare come here with such a tale. Now, Mr. Proctor, before I decide whether I shall hear you or not, it is my duty to tell you this. We burn a hot fire here; it melts down all concealment.

PROCTOR: I know that, sir.

DANFORTH: Let me continue. I understand well, a husband's tenderness may drive him to extravagance in defense of a wife. Are you certain in your conscience, Mister, that your evidence is the truth?

PROCTOR: It is. And you will surely know it.

DANFORTH: And you thought to declare this revelation in the open court before the public?

PROCTOR: I thought I would, aye—with your permission.

DANFORTH, *his eyes narrowing:* Now, sir, what is your purpose in so doing?

PROCTOR: Why, I—I would free my wife, sir.

DANFORTH: There lurks nowhere in your heart, nor hidden in your spirit, any desire to undermine this court?

PROCTOR, *with the faintest faltering:* Why, no, sir.

CHEEVER—*he clears his throat, awakening:* I— Your Excellency.

DANFORTH: Mr. Cheever.

CHEEVER: I think it be my duty, sir— *Kindly, to Proctor:* You'll not deny it, John. *To Danforth:* When we come to take his wife, he damned the court and ripped your warrant.

PARRIS: Now you have it!

DANFORTH: He did that, Mr. Hale?

HALE—*he takes a breath:* Aye, he did.

PROCTOR: It were a temper, sir. I knew not what I did.

DANFORTH, *studying him:* Mr. Proctor.

PROCTOR: Aye, sir.

DANFORTH, *straight into his eyes:* Have you ever seen the Devil?

PROCTOR: No, sir.

DANFORTH: You are in all respects a Gospel Christian?

PROCTOR: I am, sir.

PARRIS: Such a Christian that will not come to church but once in a month!

DANFORTH, *restrained—he is curious:* Not come to church?

PROCTOR: I—I have no love for Mr. Parris. It is no secret. But God I surely love.

CHEEVER: He plow on Sunday, sir.

DANFORTH: Plow on Sunday!

CHEEVER, *apologetically:* I think it be evidence, John. I am an official of the court, I cannot keep it.

PROCTOR: I—I have once or twice plowed on Sunday. I have three children, sir, and until last year my land give little.

GILES: You'll find other Christians that do plow on Sunday if the truth be known.

HALE: Your Honor, I cannot think you may judge the man on such evidence.

DANFORTH: I judge nothing. *Pause. He keeps watching Proctor, who tries to meet his gaze.* I tell you straight, Mister—I have seen marvels in this court. I have seen people choked before my eyes by spirits; I have seen them stuck by pins and slashed by daggers. I have until this moment not the slightest reason to suspect that the children may be deceiving me. Do you understand my meaning?

PROCTOR: Excellency, does it not strike upon you that so many of these women have lived so long with such upright reputation, and—

PARRIS: Do you read the Gospel, Mr. Proctor?

PROCTOR: I read the Gospel.

PARRIS: I think not, or you should surely know that Cain were an upright man, and yet he did kill Abel.

PROCTOR: Aye, God tells us that. *To Danforth:* But who tells us Rebecca Nurse murdered seven babies by sending out her spirit on them? It is the children only, and this one will swear she lied to you.

Danforth considers, then beckons Hathorne to him. Hathorne leans in, and he speaks in his ear. Hathorne nods.

HATHORNE: Aye, she's the one.

DANFORTH: Mr. Proctor, this morning, your wife send me a claim in which she states that she is pregnant now.

PROCTOR: My wife pregnant!

DANFORTH: There be no sign of it—we have examined her body.

PROCTOR: But if she say she is pregnant, then she must be! That woman will never lie, Mr. Danforth.

DANFORTH: She will not?

PROCTOR: Never, sir, never.

DANFORTH: We have thought it too convenient to be credited. However, if I should tell you now that I will let her be kept another month; and if she begin to show her natural signs, you shall have her living yet another year until she is delivered—what say you to that? *John Proctor is struck silent.* Come now. You say your only purpose is to save your wife. Good, then, she is saved at least this year, and a year is long. What say you, sir? It is done now. *In conflict, Proctor glances at Francis and Giles.* Will you drop this charge?

PROCTOR: I—I think I cannot.

DANFORTH, *now an almost imperceptible hardness in his voice:* Then your purpose is somewhat larger.

PARRIS: He's come to overthrow this court, Your Honor!

PROCTOR: These are my friends. Their wives are also accused—

DANFORTH, *with a sudden briskness of manner:* I judge you not, sir. I am ready to hear your evidence.

PROCTOR: I come not to hurt the court; I only—

DANFORTH, *cutting him off:* Marshal, go into the court and bid Judge Stoughton and Judge Sewall declare recess for one hour. And let them go to the tavern, if they will. All witnesses and prisoners are to be kept in the building.

HERRICK: Aye, sir. *Very deferentially:* If I may say it, sir, I know this man all my life. It is a good man, sir.

DANFORTH—*it is the reflection on himself he resents:* I am sure of it, Marshal. *Herrick nods, then goes out.* Now, what deposition do you have for us, Mr. Proctor? And I beg you be clear, open as the sky, and honest.

PROCTOR, *as he takes out several papers:* I am no lawyer, so I'll—

DANFORTH: The pure in heart need no lawyers. Proceed as you will.

PROCTOR, *handing Danforth a paper:* Will you read this first, sir? It's a sort of testament. The people signing it declare their good opinion of Rebecca, and my wife, and Martha Corey. *Danforth looks down at the paper.*

PARRIS, *to enlist Danforth's sarcasm:* Their good opinion! *But Danforth goes on reading, and Proctor is heartened.*

PROCTOR: These are all landholding farmers, members of the church. *Delicately, trying to point out a paragraph:* If you'll notice, sir—they've known the women many years and never saw no sign they had dealings with the Devil.

Parris nervously moves over and reads over Danforth's shoulder.

DANFORTH, *glancing down a long list:* How many names are here?

FRANCIS: Ninety-one, Your Excellency.

PARRIS, *sweating:* These people should be summoned. *Danforth looks up at him questioningly.* For questioning.

FRANCIS, *trembling with anger:* Mr. Danforth, I gave them all my word no harm would come to them for signing this.

PARRIS: This is a clear attack upon the court!

HALE, *to Parris, trying to contain himself:* Is every defense an attack upon the court? Can no one—?

PARRIS: All innocent and Christian people are happy for the courts in Salem! These people are gloomy for it. *To Danforth directly:* And I think you will want to know, from each and every one of them, what discontents them with you!

HATHORNE: I think they ought to be examined, sir.

DANFORTH: It is not necessarily an attack, I think. Yet—

FRANCIS: These are all covenanted Christians, sir.

DANFORTH: Then I am sure they may have nothing to fear. *Hands Cheever the paper.* Mr. Cheever, have warrants drawn for all of these— arrest for examination. *To Proctor:* Now, Mister, what other information do you have for us? *Francis is still standing, horrified.* You may sit, Mr. Nurse.

FRANCIS: I have brought trouble on these people; I have—

DANFORTH: No, old man, you have not hurt these people if they are of good conscience. But you must understand, sir, that a person is either with this court or he must be counted against it, there be no road between. This is a sharp time, now, a precise time—we live no longer in the dusky afternoon when evil mixed itself with good and befuddled the world. Now, by God's grace, the shining sun is up, and them that fear not light will surely praise it. I hope you will be one of those. *Mary Warren suddenly sobs.* She's not hearty, I see.

PROCTOR: No, she's not, sir. *To Mary, bending to her, holding her hand, quietly:* Now remember what the angel Raphael said to the boy Tobias. Remember it.

MARY WARREN, *hardly audible:* Aye.

PROCTOR: "Do that which is good, and no harm shall come to thee."

MARY WARREN: Aye.

DANFORTH: Come, man, we wait you.

Marshal Herrick returns, and takes his post at the door.

GILES: John, my deposition, give him mine.

PROCTOR: Aye. *He hands Danforth another paper.* This is Mr. Corey's deposition.

DANFORTH: Oh? *He looks down at it. Now Hathorne comes behind him and reads with him.*

HATHORNE, *suspiciously:* What lawyer drew this, Corey?

GILES: You know I never hired a lawyer in my life, Hathorne.

DANFORTH, *finishing the reading:* It is very well phrased. My compliments. Mr. Parris, if Mr. Putnam is in the court, will you bring him in? *Hathorne takes the deposition, and walks to the window with it. Parris goes into the court.* You have no legal training, Mr. Corey?

GILES, *very pleased:* I have the best, sir—I am thirty-three time in court in my life. And always plaintiff, too.

DANFORTH: Oh, then you're much put-upon.

GILES: I am never put-upon; I know my rights, sir, and I will have them. You know, your father tried a case of mine—might be thirty-five year ago, I think.

DANFORTH: Indeed.

GILES: He never spoke to you of it?

DANFORTH: No, I cannot recall it.

GILES: That's strange, he give me nine pound damages. He were a fair judge, your father. Y'see, I had a white mare that time, and this fellow come to borrow the mare— *Enter Parris with Thomas Putnam. When he sees Putnam, Giles' ease goes; he is hard.* Aye, there he is.

DANFORTH: Mr. Putnam, I have here an accusation by Mr. Corey against you. He states that you coldly prompted your daughter to cry witchery upon George Jacobs that is now in jail.

PUTNAM: It is a lie.

DANFORTH, *turning to Giles:* Mr. Putnam states your charge is a lie. What say you to that?

GILES, *furious, his fists clenched:* A fart on Thomas Putnam, that is what I say to that!

DANFORTH: What proof do you submit for your charge, sir?

GILES: My proof is there! *Pointing to the paper.* If Jacobs hangs for a witch he forfeit up his property—that's law! And there is none but Putnam with the coin to buy so great a piece. This man is killing his neighbors for their land!

DANFORTH: But proof, sir, proof.

GILES, *pointing at his deposition:* The proof is there! I have it from an honest man who heard Putnam say it! The day his daughter cried out on Jacobs, he said she'd given him a fair gift of land.

HATHORNE: And the name of this man?

GILES, *taken aback:* What name?

HATHORNE: The man that give you this information.

GILES—*he hesitates, then:* Why, I—I cannot give you his name.

HATHORNE: And why not?

GILES—*he hesitates, then bursts out:* You know well why not! He'll lay in jail if I give his name!

HATHORNE: This is contempt of the court, Mr. Danforth!

DANFORTH, *to avoid that:* You will surely tell us the name.

GILES: I will not give you no name. I mentioned my wife's name once and I'll burn in Hell long enough for that. I stand mute.

DANFORTH: In that case, I have no choice but to arrest you for contempt of this court, do you know that?

GILES: This is a hearing; you cannot clap me for contempt of a hearing.

DANFORTH: Oh, it is a proper lawyer! Do you wish me to declare the court in full session here? Or will you give me good reply?

GILES, *faltering:* I cannot give you no name, sir, I cannot.

DANFORTH: You are a foolish old man. Mr. Cheever, begin the record. The court is now in session. I ask you, Mr. Corey—

PROCTOR, *breaking in:* Your Honor—he has the story in confidence, sir, and he—

PARRIS: The Devil lives on such confidences! *To Danforth:* Without confidences there could be no conspiracy, Your Honor!

HATHORNE: I think it must be broken, sir.

DANFORTH, *to Giles:* Old man, if your informant tells the truth let him come here openly like a decent man. But if he hide in anonymity I must know why. Now sir, the government and central church demand of you the name of him who reported Mr. Thomas Putnam a common murderer.

HALE: Excellency—

DANFORTH: Mr. Hale.

HALE: We cannot blink it more. There is a prodigious fear of this court in the country—

DANFORTH: Then there is a prodigious guilt in the country. Are *you* afraid to be questioned here?

HALE: I may only fear the Lord, sir, but there is fear in the country nevertheless.

DANFORTH, *angered now:* Reproach me not with the fear in the country; there is fear in the country because there is a moving plot to topple Christ in the country!

HALE: But it does not follow that everyone accused is part of it.

DANFORTH: No uncorrupted man may fear this court, Mr. Hale! None! *To Giles:* You are under arrest in contempt of this court. Now sit you down and take counsel with yourself, or you will be set in the jail until you decide to answer all questions.

Giles Corey makes a rush for Putnam. Proctor lunges and holds him.

PROCTOR: No, Giles!

GILES, *over Proctor's shoulder at Putnam:* I'll cut your throat, Putnam, I'll kill you yet!

PROCTOR, *forcing him into a chair:* Peace, Giles, peace. *Releasing him.* We'll prove ourselves. Now we will. *He starts to turn to Danforth.*

GILES: Say nothin' more, John. *Pointing at Danforth:* He's only playin' you! He means to hang us all!

Mary Warren bursts into sobs.

DANFORTH: This is a court of law, Mister. I'll have no effrontery here!

PROCTOR: Forgive him, sir, for his old age. Peace, Giles, we'll prove it all now. *He lifts up Mary's chin.* You cannot weep, Mary. Remember the angel, what he say to the boy. Hold to it, now; there is your rock. *Mary quiets. He takes out a paper, and turns to Danforth.* This is Mary Warren's deposition. I—I would ask you remember, sir, while you read it, that until two week ago she were no different than the other children are today. *He is speaking reasonably, restraining all his fears, his anger, his anxiety.* You saw her scream, she howled, she swore familiar spirits choked her; she even testified that Satan, in the form of women now in jail, tried to win her soul away, and then when she refused—

DANFORTH: We know all this.

PROCTOR: Aye, sir. She swears now that she never saw Satan; nor any spirit, vague or clear, that Satan may have sent to hurt her. And she declares her friends are lying now.

Proctor starts to hand Danforth the deposition, and Hale comes up to Danforth in a trembling state.

HALE: Excellency, a moment. I think this goes to the heart of the matter.

DANFORTH, *with deep misgivings:* It surely does.

HALE: I cannot say he is an honest man; I know him little. But in all justice, sir, a claim so weighty cannot be argued by a farmer. In God's name, sir, stop here; send him home and let him come again with a lawyer—

DANFORTH, *patiently:* Now look you, Mr. Hale—

HALE: Excellency, I have signed seventy-two death warrants; I am a minister of the Lord, and I dare not take a life without there be a proof so immaculate no slightest qualm of conscience may doubt it.

DANFORTH: Mr. Hale, you surely do not doubt my justice.

HALE: I have this morning signed away the soul of Rebecca Nurse, Your Honor. I'll not conceal it, my hand shakes yet as with a wound! I pray you, sir, *this* argument let lawyers present to you.

DANFORTH: Mr. Hale, believe me; for a man of such terrible learning you are most bewildered—I hope you will forgive me. I have been thirty-two year at the bar, sir, and I should be confounded were I called upon to defend these people. Let you consider, now— *To Proctor and the others:* And I bid you all do likewise. In an ordinary crime, how does one defend the accused? One calls up witnesses to prove his innocence. But witchcraft is *ipso facto,* on its face and by its nature, an invisible crime, is it not? Therefore, who may possibly be witness to it? The witch and the victim. None other. Now we cannot hope the witch will accuse herself; granted? Therefore, we must rely upon her victims—and they do testify, the children certainly do testify. As for the witches, none will deny that we are most eager for all their confessions. Therefore, what is left for a lawyer to bring out? I think I have made my point. Have I not?

HALE: But this child claims the girls are not truthful, and if they are not—

DANFORTH: That is precisely what I am about to consider, sir. What more may you ask of me? Unless you doubt my probity?

HALE, *defeated:* I surely do not, sir. Let you consider it, then.

DANFORTH: And let you put your heart to rest. Her deposition, Mr. Proctor.

Proctor hands it to him. Hathorne rises, goes beside Danforth, and starts reading. Parris comes to his other side. Danforth looks at John Proctor, then proceeds to read. Hale gets up, finds position near the judge, reads too. Proctor glances at Giles. Francis prays silently, hands pressed together. Cheever waits placidly, the sublime official, dutiful. Mary Warren sobs once. John Proctor touches her head reassuringly. Presently Danforth lifts his eyes, stands up, takes out a kerchief and blows his nose. The others stand aside as he moves in thought toward the window.

PARRIS, *hardly able to contain his anger and fear:* I should like to question—

DANFORTH—*his first real outburst, in which his contempt for Parris is clear:* Mr. Parris, I bid you be silent! *He stands in silence, looking out the window. Now, having established that he will set the gait:* Mr. Cheever, will you go into the court and bring the children here? *Cheever gets up and goes out upstage. Danforth now turns to Mary.* Mary Warren, how came you to this turnabout? Has Mr. Proctor threatened you for this deposition?

MARY WARREN: No, sir.

DANFORTH: Has he ever threatened you?

MARY WARREN, *weaker:* No, sir.

DANFORTH, *sensing a weakening:* Has he threatened you?

MARY WARREN: No, sir.

DANFORTH: Then you tell me that you sat in my court, callously lying, when you knew that people would hang by your evidence? *She does not answer.* Answer me!

MARY WARREN, *almost inaudibly:* I did, sir.

DANFORTH: How were you instructed in your life? Do you not know that God damns all liars? *She cannot speak.* Or is it now that you lie?

MARY WARREN: No, sir—I am with God now.

DANFORTH: You are with God now.

MARY WARREN: Aye, sir.

DANFORTH, *containing himself:* I will tell you this—you are either lying now, or you were lying in the court, and in either case you have committed perjury and you will go to jail for it. You cannot lightly say you lied, Mary. Do you know that?

MARY WARREN: I cannot lie no more. I am with God, I am with God.

But she breaks into sobs at the thought of it, and the right door opens, and enter Susanna Walcott, Mercy Lewis, Betty Parris, and finally Abigail. Cheever comes to Danforth.

CHEEVER: Ruth Putnam's not in the court, sir, nor the other children.

DANFORTH: These will be sufficient. Sit you down, children. *Silently they sit.* Your friend, Mary Warren, has given us a deposition. In which she swears that she never saw familiar spirits, apparitions, nor any manifest of the Devil. She claims as well that none of you have seen these things either. *Slight pause.* Now, children, this is a court of law. The law, based upon the Bible, and the Bible, writ by Almighty God, forbid the practice of witchcraft, and describe death as the penalty thereof. But likewise, children, the law and Bible damn all bearers of false witness. *Slight pause.* Now then. It does not escape me that this deposition may be devised to blind us; it may well be that Mary Warren has been conquered by Satan, who sends her here to distract our sacred purpose. If so, her neck will break for it. But if she speak true, I bid you now drop your guile and confess your pretense, for a quick confession will go easier with you. *Pause.* Abigail Williams, rise. *Abigail slowly rises.* Is there any truth in this?

ABIGAIL: No, sir.

DANFORTH—*he thinks, glances at Mary, then back to Abigail:* Children, a very auger bit will now be turned into your souls until your honesty is proved. Will either of you change your positions now, or do you force me to hard questioning?

ABIGAIL: I have naught to change, sir. She lies.

DANFORTH, *to Mary:* You would still go on with this?

MARY WARREN, *faintly:* Aye, sir.

DANFORTH, *turning to Abigail:* A poppet were discovered in Mr. Proctor's house, stabbed by a needle. Mary Warren claims that you sat beside her in the court when she made it, and that you saw her make it and witnessed how she herself stuck her needle into it for safe-keeping. What say you to that?

ABIGAIL, *with a slight note of indignation:* It is a lie, sir.

DANFORTH, *after a slight pause:* While you worked for Mr. Proctor, did you see poppets in that house?

ABIGAIL: Goody Proctor always kept poppets.

PROCTOR: Your Honor, my wife never kept no poppets. Mary Warren confesses it was her poppet.

CHEEVER: Your Excellency.

DANFORTH: Mr. Cheever.

CHEEVER: When I spoke with Goody Proctor in that house, she said she never kept no poppets. But she said she did keep poppets when she were a girl.

PROCTOR: She has not been a girl these fifteen years, Your Honor.

HATHORNE: But a poppet will keep fifteen years, will it not?

PROCTOR: It will keep if it is kept, but Mary Warren swears she never saw no poppets in my house, nor anyone else.

PARRIS: Why could there not have been poppets hid where no one ever saw them?

PROCTOR, *furious:* There might also be a dragon with five legs in my house, but no one has ever seen it.

PARRIS: We are here, Your Honor, precisely to discover what no one has ever seen.

PROCTOR: Mr. Danforth, what profit this girl to turn herself about? What may Mary Warren gain but hard questioning and worse?

DANFORTH: You are charging Abigail Williams with a marvelous cool plot to murder, do you understand that?

PROCTOR: I do, sir. I believe she means to murder.

DANFORTH, *pointing at Abigail, incredulously:* This child would murder your wife?

PROCTOR: It is not a child. Now hear me, sir. In the sight of the congregation she were twice this year put out of this meetin' house for laughter during prayer.

DANFORTH, *shocked, turning to Abigail:* What's this? Laughter during—!

PARRIS: Excellency, she were under Tituba's power at that time, but she is solemn now.

GILES: Aye, now she is solemn and goes to hang people!

DANFORTH: Quiet, man.

HATHORNE: Surely it have no bearing on the question, sir. He charges contemplation of murder.

DANFORTH: Aye. *He studies Abigail for a moment, then:* Continue, Mr. Proctor.

PROCTOR: Mary. Now tell the Governor how you danced in the woods.

PARRIS, *instantly:* Excellency, since I come to Salem this man is blackening my name. He—

DANFORTH: In a moment, sir. *To Mary Warren, sternly, and surprised:* What is this dancing?

MARY WARREN: I— *She glances at Abigail, who is staring down at her remorselessly. Then, appealing to Proctor:* Mr. Proctor—

PROCTOR, *taking it right up:* Abigail leads the girls to the woods, Your Honor, and they have danced there naked—

PARRIS: Your Honor, this—

PROCTOR, *at once:* Mr. Parris discovered them himself in the dead of night! There's the "child" she is!

DANFORTH—*it is growing into a nightmare, and he turns, astonished, to Parris:* Mr. Parris—

PARRIS: I can only say, sir, that I never found any of them naked, and this man is—

DANFORTH: But you discovered them dancing in the woods? *Eyes on Parris, he points at Abigail.* Abigail?

HALE: Excellency, when I first arrived from Beverly, Mr. Parris told me that.

DANFORTH: Do you deny it, Mr. Parris?

PARRIS: I do not, sir, but I never saw any of them naked.

DANFORTH: But she have *danced*?

PARRIS, *unwillingly:* Aye, sir.

Danforth, as though with new eyes, looks at Abigail.

HATHORNE: Excellency, will you permit me? *He points at Mary Warren.*

DANFORTH, *with great worry:* Pray, proceed.

HATHORNE: You say you never saw no spirits, Mary, were never threatened or afflicted by any manifest of the Devil or the Devil's agents.

MARY WARREN, *very faintly:* No, sir.

HATHORNE, *with a gleam of victory:* And yet, when people accused of witchery confronted you in court, you would faint, saying their spirits came out of their bodies and choked you—

MARY WARREN: That were pretense, sir.

DANFORTH: I cannot hear you.

MARY WARREN: Pretense, sir.

PARRIS: But you did turn cold, did you not? I myself picked you up many times, and your skin were icy. Mr. Danforth, you—

DANFORTH: I saw that many times.

PROCTOR: She only pretended to faint, Your Excellency. They're all marvelous pretenders.

HATHORNE: Then can she pretend to faint now?

PROCTOR: Now?

PARRIS: Why not? Now there are no spirits attacking her, for none in this room is accused of witchcraft. So let her turn herself cold now, let her pretend she is attacked now, let her faint. *He turns to Mary Warren.* Faint!

MARY WARREN: Faint?

PARRIS: Aye, faint. Prove to us how you pretended in the court so many times.

MARY WARREN, *looking to Proctor:* I—cannot faint now, sir.

PROCTOR, *alarmed, quietly:* Can you not pretend it?

MARY WARREN: I— *She looks about as though searching for the passion to faint.* I—have no *sense* of it now, I—

DANFORTH: Why? What is lacking now?

MARY WARREN: I—cannot tell, sir, I—

DANFORTH: Might it be that here we have no afflicting spirit loose, but in the court there were some?

MARY WARREN: I never saw no spirits.

PARRIS: Then see no spirits now, and prove to us that you can faint by your own will, as you claim.

MARY WARREN—*she stares, searching for the emotion of it, and then shakes her head:* I—cannot do it.

PARRIS: Then you will confess, will you not? It were attacking spirits made you faint!

MARY WARREN: No, sir, I—

PARRIS: Your Excellency, this is a trick to blind the court!

MARY WARREN: It's not a trick! *She stands.* I—I used to faint because I—I thought I saw spirits.

DANFORTH: *Thought* you saw them!

MARY WARREN: But I did not, Your Honor.

HATHORNE: How could you think you saw them unless you saw them?

MARY WARREN: I—I cannot tell how, but I did. I—I heard the other girls screaming, and you, Your Honor, you seemed to believe them, and I— It were only sport in the beginning, sir, but then the whole world cried spirits, spirits, and I—I promise you, Mr. Danforth, I only thought I saw them but I did not.

Danforth peers at her.

PARRIS, *smiling, but nervous because Danforth seems to be struck by Mary Warren's story:* Surely Your Excellency is not taken by this simple lie.

DANFORTH, *turning worriedly to Abigail:* Abigail. I bid you now search your heart and tell me this—and beware of it, child, to God every soul is precious and His vengeance is terrible on them that take life without cause. Is it possible, child, that the spirits you have seen are illusion only, some deception that may cross your mind when—

ABIGAIL: Why, this—this—is a base question, sir.

DANFORTH: Child, I would have you consider it—

ABIGAIL: I have been hurt, Mr. Danforth; I have seen my blood runnin' out! I have been near to murdered every day because I done my duty pointing out the Devil's people—and this is my reward? To be mistrusted, denied, questioned like a—

DANFORTH, *weakening:* Child, I do not mistrust you—

ABIGAIL, *in an open threat:* Let *you* beware, Mr. Danforth. Think you to be so mighty that the power of Hell may not turn *your* wits? Beware of it! There is— *Suddenly, from an accusatory attitude, her face turns, looking into the air above—it is truly frightened.*

DANFORTH, *apprehensively:* What is it, child?

ABIGAIL, *looking about in the air, clasping her arms about her as though cold:* I—I know not. A wind, a cold wind, has come. *Her eyes fall on Mary Warren.*

MARY WARREN, *terrified, pleading:* Abby!

MERCY LEWIS, *shivering:* Your Honor, I freeze!

PROCTOR: They're pretending!

HATHORNE, *touching Abigail's hand:* She is cold, Your Honor, touch her!

MERCY LEWIS, *through chattering teeth:* Mary, do you send this shadow on me?

MARY WARREN: Lord, save me!

SUSANNA WALCOTT: I freeze, I freeze!

ABIGAIL, *shivering visibly:* It is a wind, a wind!

MARY WARREN: Abby, don't do that!

DANFORTH, *himself engaged and entered by Abigail:* Mary Warren, do you witch her? I say to you, do you send your spirit out?

With a hysterical cry Mary Warren starts to run. Proctor catches her.

MARY WARREN, *almost collapsing:* Let me go, Mr. Proctor, I cannot, I cannot—

ABIGAIL, *crying to Heaven:* Oh, Heavenly Father, take away this shadow!

Without warning or hesitation, Proctor leaps at Abigail and, grabbing her by the hair, pulls her to her feet. She screams in pain. Danforth, astonished, cries, "What are you about?" and Hathorne and Parris call, "Take your hands off her!" and out of it all comes Proctor's roaring voice.

PROCTOR: How do you call Heaven! Whore! Whore!

Herrick breaks Proctor from her.

HERRICK: John!

DANFORTH: Man! Man, what do you—

PROCTOR, *breathless and in agony:* It is a whore!

DANFORTH, *dumfounded:* You charge—?

ABIGAIL: Mr. Danforth, he is lying!

PROCTOR: Mark her! Now she'll suck a scream to stab me with, but—

DANFORTH: You will prove this! This will not pass!

PROCTOR, *trembling, his life collapsing about him:* I have known her, sir. I have known her.

DANFORTH: You—you are a lecher?

FRANCIS, *horrified:* John, you cannot say such a—

PROCTOR: Oh, Francis, I wish you had some evil in you that you might know me! *To Danforth:* A man will not cast away his good name. You surely know that.

DANFORTH, *dumfounded:* In—in what time? In what place?

PROCTOR, *his voice about to break, and his shame great:* In the proper place—where my beasts are bedded. On the last night of my joy, some eight months past. She used to serve me in my house, sir. *He has to clamp his jaw to keep from weeping.* A man may think God sleeps, but God sees everything, I know it now. I beg you, sir, I beg you—see her what she is. My wife, my dear good wife, took this girl soon after, sir, and put her out on the highroad. And being what she is, a lump of vanity, sir — *He is being overcome.* Excellency, forgive me, forgive me. *Angrily against himself, he turns away from the Governor for a moment. Then, as though to cry out is his only means of speech left:* She thinks to dance with me on my wife's grave! And well she might, for I thought of her softly. God help me, I lusted, and there *is* a promise in such sweat. But it is a whore's vengeance, and you must see it; I set myself entirely in your hands. I know you must see it now.

DANFORTH, *blanched, in horror, turning to Abigail:* You deny every scrap and tittle of this?

ABIGAIL: If I must answer that, I will leave and I will not come back again!

Danforth seems unsteady.

PROCTOR: I have made a bell of my honor! I have rung the doom of my good name—you will believe me, Mr. Danforth! My wife is in- nocent, except she knew a whore when she saw one!

ABIGAIL, *stepping up to Danforth:* What look do you give me? *Danforth cannot speak.* I'll not have such looks! *She turns and starts for the door.*

DANFORTH: You will remain where you are! *Herrick steps into her path. She comes up short, fire in her eyes.* Mr. Parris, go into the court and bring Goodwife Proctor out.

PARRIS, *objecting:* Your Honor, this is all a—

DANFORTH, *sharply to Parris:* Bring her out! And tell her not one word of what's been spoken here. And let you knock before you enter. *Parris goes out.* Now we shall touch the bottom of this swamp. *To Proctor:* Your wife, you say, is an honest woman.

PROCTOR: In her life, sir, she have never lied. There are them that cannot sing, and them that cannot weep—my wife cannot lie. I have paid much to learn it, sir.

DANFORTH: And when she put this girl out of your house, she put her out for a harlot?

PROCTOR: Aye, sir.

DANFORTH: And knew her for a harlot?

PROCTOR: Aye, sir, she knew her for a harlot.

DANFORTH: Good then. *To Abigail:* And if she tell me, child, it were for harlotry, may God spread His mercy on you! *There is a knock. He calls to the door.* Hold! *To Abigail:* Turn your back. Turn your back. *To Proctor:* Do likewise. *Both turn their backs—Abigail with indignant slowness.* Now let neither of you turn to face Goody Proctor. No one in this room is to speak one word, or raise a gesture aye or nay. *He turns toward the door, calls:* Enter! *The door opens. Elizabeth enters with Parris. Parris leaves her. She stands alone, her eyes looking for Proctor.* Mr. Cheever, report this testimony in all exactness. Are you ready?

CHEEVER: Ready, sir.

DANFORTH: Come here, woman. *Elizabeth comes to him, glancing at Proctor's back.* Look at me only, not at your husband. In my eyes only.

ELIZABETH, *faintly:* Good, sir.

DANFORTH: We are given to understand that at one time you dismissed your servant, Abigail Williams.

ELIZABETH: That is true, sir.

DANFORTH: For what cause did you dismiss her? *Slight pause. Then Elizabeth tries to glance at Proctor.* You will look in my eyes only and not at your husband. The answer is in your memory and you need no help to give it to me. Why did you dismiss Abigail Williams?

ELIZABETH, *not knowing what to say, sensing a situation, wetting her lips to stall for time:* She—dissatisfied me. *Pause.* And my husband.

DANFORTH: In what way dissatisfied you?

ELIZABETH: She were— *She glances at Proctor for a cue.*

DANFORTH: Woman, look at me! *Elizabeth does.* Were she slovenly? Lazy? What disturbance did she cause?

ELIZABETH: Your Honor, I—in that time I were sick. And I— My husband is a good and righteous man. He is never drunk as some are, nor wastin' his time at the shovelboard, but always at his work. But in my sickness—you see, sir, I were a long time sick after my last baby, and I thought I saw my husband somewhat turning from me. And this girl— *She turns to Abigail.*

DANFORTH: Look at me.

ELIZABETH: Aye, sir. Abigail Williams— *She breaks off.*

DANFORTH: What of Abigail Williams?

ELIZABETH: I came to think he fancied her. And so one night I lost my wits, I think, and put her out on the highroad.

DANFORTH: Your husband—did he indeed turn from you?

ELIZABETH, *in agony:* My husband—is a goodly man, sir.

DANFORTH: Then he did not turn from you.

ELIZABETH, *starting to glance at Proctor:* He—

DANFORTH, *reaches out and holds her face, then:* Look at me! To your own knowledge, has John Proctor ever committed the crime of lechery? *In a crisis of indecision she cannot speak.* Answer my question! Is your husband a lecher!

ELIZABETH, *faintly:* No, sir.

DANFORTH: Remove her, Marshal.

PROCTOR: Elizabeth, tell the truth!

DANFORTH: She has spoken. Remove her!

PROCTOR, *crying out:* Elizabeth, I have confessed it!

ELIZABETH: Oh, God! *The door closes behind her.*

PROCTOR: She only thought to save my name!

HALE: Excellency, it is a natural lie to tell; I beg you, stop now before another is condemned! I may shut my conscience to it no more—private vengeance is working through this testimony! From the beginning this man has struck me true. By my oath to Heaven, I believe him now, and I pray you call back his wife before we—

DANFORTH: She spoke nothing of lechery, and this man has lied!

HALE: I believe him! *Pointing at Abigail:* This girl has always struck me false! She has—

Abigail, with a weird, wild, chilling cry, screams up to the ceiling.

ABIGAIL: You will not! Begone! Begone, I say!

DANFORTH: What is it, child? *But Abigail, pointing with fear, is now raising up her frightened eyes, her awed face, toward the ceiling—the girls are doing the same—and now Hathorne, Hale, Putnam, Cheever, Herrick, and Danforth do the same.* What's there? *He lowers his eyes from the ceiling, and now he is frightened; there is real tension in his voice.* Child! *She is transfixed—with all the girls, she is whimpering open-mouthed, agape at the ceiling.* Girls! Why do you—?

MERCY LEWIS, *pointing:* It's on the beam! Behind the rafter!

DANFORTH, *looking up:* Where!

ABIGAIL: Why—? *She gulps.* Why do you come, yellow bird?

PROCTOR: Where's a bird? I see no bird!

ABIGAIL, *to the ceiling:* My face? My face?

PROCTOR: Mr. Hale—

DANFORTH: Be quiet!

PROCTOR, *to Hale:* Do you see a bird?

DANFORTH: Be quiet!!

ABIGAIL, *to the ceiling, in a genuine conversation with the "bird," as though trying to talk it out of attacking her:* But God made my face; you cannot want to tear my face. Envy is a deadly sin, Mary.

MARY WARREN, *on her feet with a spring, and horrified, pleading:* Abby!

ABIGAIL, *unperturbed, continuing to the "bird"*: Oh, Mary, this is a black art to change your shape. No, I cannot, I cannot stop my mouth; it's God's work I do.

MARY WARREN: Abby, I'm *here*!

PROCTOR, *frantically*: They're pretending, Mr. Danforth!

ABIGAIL—*now she takes a backward step, as though in fear the bird will swoop down momentarily*: Oh, please, Mary! Don't come down.

SUSANNA WALCOTT: Her claws, she's stretching her claws!

PROCTOR: Lies, lies.

ABIGAIL, *backing further, eyes still fixed above*: Mary, please don't hurt me!

MARY WARREN, *to Danforth*: I'm not hurting her!

DANFORTH, *to Mary Warren*: Why does she see this vision?

MARY WARREN: She sees nothin'!

ABIGAIL, *now staring full front as though hypnotized, and mimicking the exact tone of Mary Warren's cry*: She sees nothin'!

MARY WARREN, *pleading*: Abby, you mustn't!

ABIGAIL and ALL THE GIRLS, *all transfixed*: Abby, you mustn't!

MARY WARREN, *to all the girls*: I'm here, I'm here!

GIRLS: I'm here, I'm here!

DANFORTH, *horrified*: Mary Warren! Draw back your spirit out of them!

MARY WARREN: Mr. Danforth!

GIRLS, *cutting her off*: Mr. Danforth!

DANFORTH: Have you compacted with the Devil? Have you?

MARY WARREN: Never, never!

GIRLS: Never, never!

DANFORTH, *growing hysterical*: Why can they only repeat you?

PROCTOR: Give me a whip—I'll stop it!

MARY WARREN: They're sporting. They—!

GIRLS: They're sporting!

MARY WARREN, *turning on them all hysterically and stamping her feet:* Abby, stop it!

GIRLS, *stamping their feet:* Abby, stop it!

MARY WARREN: Stop it!

GIRLS: Stop it!

MARY WARREN, *screaming it out at the top of her lungs, and raising her fists:* Stop it!!

GIRLS, *raising their fists:* Stop it!!

Mary Warren, utterly confounded, and becoming overwhelmed by Abigail's— and the girls'—utter conviction, starts to whimper, hands half raised, powerless, and all the girls begin whimpering exactly as she does.

DANFORTH: A little while ago you were afflicted. Now it seems you afflict others; where did you find this power?

MARY WARREN, *staring at Abigail:* I—have no power.

GIRLS: I have no power.

PROCTOR: They're gulling you, Mister!

DANFORTH: Why did you turn about this past two weeks? You have seen the Devil, have you not?

HALE, *indicating Abigail and the girls:* You cannot believe them!

MARY WARREN: I—

PROCTOR, *sensing her weakening:* Mary, God damns all liars!

DANFORTH, *pounding it into her:* You have seen the Devil, you have made compact with Lucifer, have you not?

PROCTOR: God damns liars, Mary!

Mary utters something unintelligible, staring at Abigail, who keeps watching the "bird" above.

DANFORTH: I cannot hear you. What do you say? *Mary utters again unintelligibly.* You will confess yourself or you will hang! *He turns her roughly to face him.* Do you know who I am? I say you will hang if you do not open with me!

PROCTOR: Mary, remember the angel Raphael—do that which is good and—

ABIGAIL, *pointing upward:* The wings! Her wings are spreading! Mary, please, don't, don't—!

HALE: I see nothing, Your Honor!

DANFORTH: Do you confess this power! *He is an inch from her face.* Speak!

ABIGAIL: She's going to come down! She's walking the beam!

DANFORTH: Will you speak!

MARY WARREN, *staring in horror:* I cannot!

GIRLS: I cannot!

PARRIS: Cast the Devil out! Look him in the face! Trample him! We'll save you, Mary, only stand fast against him and—

ABIGAIL, *looking up:* Look out! She's coming down!

She and all the girls run to one wall, shielding their eyes. And now, as though cornered, they let out a gigantic scream, and Mary, as though infected, opens her mouth and screams with them. Gradually Abigail and the girls leave off, until only Mary is left there, staring up at the "bird," screaming madly. All watch her, horrified by this evident fit. Proctor strides to her.

PROCTOR: Mary, tell the Governor what they— *He has hardly got a word out, when, seeing him coming for her, she rushes out of his reach, screaming in horror.*

MARY WARREN: Don't touch me—don't touch me! *At which the girls halt at the door.*

PROCTOR, *astonished:* Mary!

MARY WARREN, *pointing at Proctor:* You're the Devil's man!

He is stopped in his tracks.

PARRIS: Praise God!

GIRLS: Praise God!

PROCTOR, *numbed:* Mary, how—?

MARY WARREN: I'll not hang with you! I love God, I love God.

DANFORTH, *to Mary:* He bid you do the Devil's work?

MARY WARREN, *hysterically, indicating Proctor:* He come at me by night and every day to sign, to sign, to—

DANFORTH: Sign what?

PARRIS: The Devil's book? He come with a book?

MARY WARREN, *hysterically, pointing at Proctor, fearful of him:* My name, he want my name. "I'll murder you," he says, "if my wife hangs! We must go and overthrow the court," he says!

Danforth's head jerks toward Proctor, shock and horror in his face.

PROCTOR, *turning, appealing to Hale:* Mr. Hale!

MARY WARREN, *her sobs beginning:* He wake me every night, his eyes were like coals and his fingers claw my neck, and I sign, I sign . . .

HALE: Excellency, this child's gone wild!

PROCTOR, *as Danforth's wide eyes pour on him:* Mary, Mary!

MARY WARREN, *screaming at him:* No, I love God; I go your way no more. I love God, I bless God. *Sobbing, she rushes to Abigail.* Abby, Abby, I'll never hurt you more! *They all watch, as Abigail, out of her infinite charity, reaches out and draws the sobbing Mary to her, and then looks up to Danforth.*

DANFORTH, *to Proctor:* What are you? *Proctor is beyond speech in his anger.* You are combined with anti-Christ, are you not? I have seen your power; you will not deny it! What say you, Mister?

HALE: Excellency—

DANFORTH: I will have nothing from you, Mr. Hale! *To Proctor:* Will you confess yourself befouled with Hell, or do you keep that black allegiance yet? What say you?

PROCTOR, *his mind wild, breathless:* I say—I say—God is dead!

PARRIS: Hear it, hear it!

PROCTOR—*he laughs insanely, then:* A fire, a fire is burning! I hear the boot of Lucifer, I see his filthy face! And it is my face, and yours, Danforth! For them that quail to bring men out of ignorance, as I have quailed, and as you quail now when you know in all your black hearts that this be fraud—God damns our kind especially, and we will burn, we will burn together!

DANFORTH: Marshal! Take him and Corey with him to the jail!

HALE, *starting across to the door:* I denounce these proceedings!

PROCTOR: You are pulling Heaven down and raising up a whore!

HALE: I denounce these proceedings, I quit this court! *He slams the door to the outside behind him.*

DANFORTH, *calling to him in a fury:* Mr. Hale! Mr. Hale!

The Curtain Falls

ACT FOUR

A cell in Salem jail, that fall.

At the back is a high barred window; near it, a great, heavy door. Along the walls are two benches.

The place is in darkness but for the moonlight seeping through the bars. It appears empty. Presently footsteps are heard coming down a corridor beyond the wall, keys rattle, and the door swings open. Marshal Herrick enters with a lantern.

He is nearly drunk, and heavy-footed. He goes to a bench and nudges a bundle of rags lying on it.

HERRICK: Sarah, wake up! Sarah Good! *He then crosses to the other bench.*

SARAH GOOD, *rising in her rags:* Oh, Majesty! Comin', comin'! Tituba, he's here, His Majesty's come!

HERRICK: Go to the north cell; this place is wanted now. *He hangs his lantern on the wall. Tituba sits up.*

TITUBA: That don't look to me like His Majesty; look to me like the marshal.

HERRICK, *taking out a flask:* Get along with you now, clear this place. *He drinks, and Sarah Good comes and peers up into his face.*

SARAH GOOD: Oh, is it you, Marshal! I thought sure you be the Devil comin' for us. Could I have a sip of cider for me goin'-away?

HERRICK, *handing her the flask:* And where are you off to, Sarah?

TITUBA, *as Sarah drinks:* We goin' to Barbados, soon the Devil gits here with the feathers and the wings.

HERRICK: Oh? A happy voyage to you.

SARAH GOOD: A pair of bluebirds wingin' southerly, the two of us! Oh, it be a grand transformation, Marshal! *She raises the flask to drink again.*

HERRICK, *taking the flask from her lips:* You'd best give me that or you'll never rise off the ground. Come along now.

TITUBA: I'll speak to him for you, if you desires to come along, Marshal.

HERRICK: I'd not refuse it, Tituba; it's the proper morning to fly into Hell.

TITUBA: Oh, it be no Hell in Barbados. Devil, him be pleasure-man in Barbados, him be singin' and dancin' in Barbados. It's you folks—you riles him up 'round here; it be too cold 'round here for that Old Boy. He freeze his soul in Massachusetts, but in Barbados he just as sweet and— *A bellowing cow is heard, and Tituba leaps up and calls to the window:* Aye, sir! That's him, Sarah!

SARAH GOOD: I'm here, Majesty! *They hurriedly pick up their rags as Hopkins, a guard, enters.*

HOPKINS: The Deputy Governor's arrived.

HERRICK, *grabbing Tituba:* Come along, come along.

TITUBA, *resisting him:* No, he comin' for me. I goin' home!

HERRICK, *pulling her to the door:* That's not Satan, just a poor old cow with a hatful of milk. Come along now, out with you!

TITUBA, *calling to the window:* Take me home, Devil! Take me home!

SARAH GOOD, *following the shouting Tituba out:* Tell him I'm goin', Tituba! Now you tell him Sarah Good is goin' too!

In the corridor outside Tituba calls on— "Take me home, Devil; Devil take me home!" and Hopkins' voice orders her to move on. Herrick returns and begins to push old rags and straw into a corner. Hearing footsteps, he turns, and enter Danforth and Judge Hathorne. They are in greatcoats and wear hats against the bitter cold. They are followed in by Cheever, who carries a dispatch case and a flat wooden box containing his writing materials.

HERRICK: Good morning, Excellency.

DANFORTH: Where is Mr. Parris?

HERRICK: I'll fetch him. *He starts for the door.*

DANFORTH: Marshal. *Herrick stops.* When did Reverend Hale arrive?

HERRICK: It were toward midnight, I think.

DANFORTH, *suspiciously:* What is he about here?

HERRICK: He goes among them that will hang, sir. And he prays with them. He sits with Goody Nurse now. And Mr. Parris with him.

DANFORTH: Indeed. That man have no authority to enter here, Marshal. Why have you let him in?

HERRICK: Why, Mr. Parris command me, sir. I cannot deny him.

DANFORTH: Are you drunk, Marshal?

HERRICK: No, sir; it is a bitter night, and I have no fire here.

DANFORTH, *containing his anger:* Fetch Mr. Parris.

HERRICK: Aye, sir.

DANFORTH: There is a prodigious stench in this place.

HERRICK: I have only now cleared the people out for you.

DANFORTH: Beware hard drink, Marshal.

HERRICK: Aye, sir. *He waits an instant for further orders. But Danforth, in dissatisfaction, turns his back on him, and Herrick goes out. There is a pause. Danforth stands in thought.*

HATHORNE: Let you question Hale, Excellency; I should not be surprised he have been preaching in Andover lately.

DANFORTH: We'll come to that; speak nothing of Andover. Parris prays with him. That's strange. *He blows on his hands, moves toward the window, and looks out.*

HATHORNE: Excellency, I wonder if it be wise to let Mr. Parris so continuously with the prisoners. *Danforth turns to him, interested.* I think, sometimes, the man has a mad look these days.

DANFORTH: Mad?

HATHORNE: I met him yesterday coming out of his house, and I bid him good morning—and he wept and went his way. I think it is not well the village sees him so unsteady.

DANFORTH: Perhaps he have some sorrow.

CHEEVER, *stamping his feet against the cold:* I think it be the cows, sir.

DANFORTH: Cows?

CHEEVER: There be so many cows wanderin' the highroads, now their masters are in the jails, and much disagreement who they will belong to now. I know Mr. Parris be arguin' with farmers all yesterday—there is great contention, sir, about the cows. Contention make him weep, sir; it were always a man that weep for contention. *He turns, as do Hathorne and Danforth, hearing someone coming up the corridor. Danforth raises his head as Parris enters. He is gaunt, frightened, and sweating in his greatcoat.*

PARRIS, *to Danforth, instantly:* Oh, good morning, sir, thank you for coming, I beg your pardon wakin' you so early. Good morning, Judge Hathorne.

DANFORTH: Reverend Hale have no right to enter this—

PARRIS: Excellency, a moment. *He hurries back and shuts the door.*

HATHORNE: Do you leave him alone with the prisoners?

DANFORTH: What's his business here?

PARRIS, *prayerfully holding up his hands:* Excellency, hear me. It is a providence. Reverend Hale has returned to bring Rebecca Nurse to God.

DANFORTH, *surprised:* He bids her confess?

PARRIS, *sitting:* Hear me. Rebecca have not given me a word this three month since she came. Now she sits with him, and her sister and Martha Corey and two or three others, and he pleads with them, confess their crimes and save their lives.

DANFORTH: Why—this is indeed a providence. And they soften, they soften?

PARRIS: Not yet, not yet. But I thought to summon you, sir, that we might think on whether it be not wise, to— *He dares not say it.* I had thought to put a question, sir, and I hope you will not—

DANFORTH: Mr. Parris, be plain, what troubles you?

PARRIS: There is news, sir, that the court—the court must reckon with. My niece, sir, my niece—I believe she has vanished.

DANFORTH: Vanished!

PARRIS: I had thought to advise you of it earlier in the week, but—

DANFORTH: Why? How long is she gone?

PARRIS: This be the third night. You see, sir, she told me she would stay a night with Mercy Lewis. And next day, when she does not return, I send to Mr. Lewis to inquire. Mercy told him she would sleep in *my* house for a night.

DANFORTH: They are both gone?!

PARRIS, *in fear of him:* They are, sir.

DANFORTH, *alarmed:* I will send a party for them. Where may they be?

PARRIS: Excellency, I think they be aboard a ship. *Danforth stands agape.* My daughter tells me how she heard them speaking of ships last week, and tonight I discover my—my strongbox is broke into. *He presses his fingers against his eyes to keep back tears.*

HATHORNE, *astonished:* She have robbed you?

PARRIS: Thirty-one pound is gone. I am penniless. *He covers his face and sobs.*

DANFORTH: Mr. Parris, you are a brainless man! *He walks in thought, deeply worried.*

PARRIS: Excellency, it profit nothing you should blame me. I cannot think they would run off except they fear to keep in Salem any more. *He is pleading.* Mark it, sir, Abigail had close knowledge of the town, and since the news of Andover has broken here—

DANFORTH: Andover is remedied. The court returns there on Friday, and will resume examinations.

PARRIS: I am sure of it, sir. But the rumor here speaks rebellion in Andover, and it—

DANFORTH: There is no rebellion in Andover!

PARRIS: I tell you what is said here, sir. Andover have thrown out the court, they say, and will have no part of witchcraft. There be a faction here, feeding on that news, and I tell you true, sir, I fear there will be riot here.

HATHORNE: Riot! Why at every execution I have seen naught but high satisfaction in the town.

PARRIS: Judge Hathorne—it were another sort that hanged till now. Rebecca Nurse is no Bridget that lived three year with Bishop before she married him. John Proctor is not Isaac Ward that drank his family to ruin. *To Danforth:* I would to God it were not so, Excellency, but these people have great weight yet in the town. Let Rebecca stand upon the gibbet and send up some righteous prayer, and I fear she'll wake a vengeance on you.

HATHORNE: Excellency, she is condemned a witch. The court have—

DANFORTH, *in deep concern, raising a hand to Hathorne:* Pray you. *To Parris:* How do you propose, then?

PARRIS: Excellency, I would postpone these hangin's for a time.

DANFORTH: There will be no postponement.

PARRIS: Now Mr. Hale's returned, there is hope, I think—for if he bring even one of these to God, that confession surely damns the others in the public eye, and none may doubt more that they are all linked to Hell. This way, unconfessed and claiming innocence, doubts are multiplied, many honest people will weep for them, and our good purpose is lost in their tears.

DANFORTH, *after thinking a moment, then going to Cheever:* Give me the list.

Cheever opens the dispatch case, searches.

PARRIS: It cannot be forgot, sir, that when I summoned the congregation for John Proctor's excommunication there were hardly thirty people come to hear it. That speak a discontent, I think, and—

DANFORTH, *studying the list:* There will be no postponement.

PARRIS: Excellency—

DANFORTH: Now, sir—which of these in your opinion may be brought to God? I will myself strive with him till dawn. *He hands the list to Parris, who merely glances at it.*

PARRIS: There is not sufficient time till dawn.

DANFORTH: I shall do my utmost. Which of them do you have hope for?

PARRIS, *not even glancing at the list now, and in a quavering voice, quietly:* Excellency—a dagger— *He chokes up.*

DANFORTH: What do you say?

PARRIS: Tonight, when I open my door to leave my house—a dagger clattered to the ground. *Silence. Danforth absorbs this. Now Parris cries out:* You cannot hang this sort. There is danger for me. I dare not step outside at night!

Reverend Hale enters. They look at him for an instant in silence. He is steeped in sorrow, exhausted, and more direct than he ever was.

DANFORTH: Accept my congratulations, Reverend Hale; we are gladdened to see you returned to your good work.

HALE, *coming to Danforth now:* You must pardon them. They will not budge.

Herrick enters, waits.

DANFORTH, *conciliatory:* You misunderstand, sir; I cannot pardon these when twelve are already hanged for the same crime. It is not just.

PARRIS, *with failing heart:* Rebecca will not confess?

HALE: The sun will rise in a few minutes. Excellency, I must have more time.

DANFORTH: Now hear me, and beguile yourselves no more. I will not receive a single plea for pardon or postponement. Them that will not confess will hang. Twelve are already executed; the names of these seven are given out, and the village expects to see them die this morning.

Postponement now speaks a floundering on my part; reprieve or pardon must cast doubt upon the guilt of them that died till now. While I speak God's law, I will not crack its voice with whimpering. If retaliation is your fear, know this—I should hang ten thousand that dared to rise against the law, and an ocean of salt tears could not melt the resolution of the statutes. Now draw yourselves up like men and help me, as you are bound by Heaven to do. Have you spoken with them all, Mr. Hale?

HALE: All but Proctor. He is in the dungeon.

DANFORTH, to Herrick: What's Proctor's way now?

HERRICK: He sits like some great bird; you'd not know he lived except he will take food from time to time.

DANFORTH, after thinking a moment: His wife—his wife must be well on with child now.

HERRICK: She is, sir.

DANFORTH: What think you, Mr. Parris? You have closer knowledge of this man; might her presence soften him?

PARRIS: It is possible, sir. He have not laid eyes on her these three months. I should summon her.

DANFORTH, to Herrick: Is he yet adamant? Has he struck at you again?

HERRICK: He cannot, sir, he is chained to the wall now.

DANFORTH, after thinking on it: Fetch Goody Proctor to me. Then let you bring him up.

HERRICK: Aye, sir. Herrick goes. There is silence.

HALE: Excellency, if you postpone a week and publish to the town that you are striving for their confessions, that speak mercy on your part, not faltering.

DANFORTH: Mr. Hale, as God have not empowered me like Joshua to stop this sun from rising, so I cannot withhold from them the perfection of their punishment.

HALE, harder now: If you think God wills you to raise rebellion, Mr. Danforth, you are mistaken!

DANFORTH, *instantly:* You have heard rebellion spoken in the town?

HALE: Excellency, there are orphans wandering from house to house; abandoned cattle bellow on the highroads, the stink of rotting crops hangs everywhere, and no man knows when the harlots' cry will end his life—and you wonder yet if rebellion's spoke? Better you should marvel how they do not burn your province!

DANFORTH: Mr. Hale, have you preached in Andover this month?

HALE: Thank God they have no need of me in Andover.

DANFORTH: You baffle me, sir. Why have you returned here?

HALE: Why, it is all simple. I come to do the Devil's work. I come to counsel Christians they should belie themselves. *His sarcasm collapses.* There is blood on my head! Can you not see the blood on my head!!

PARRIS: Hush! *For he has heard footsteps. They all face the door. Herrick enters with Elizabeth. Her wrists are linked by heavy chain, which Herrick now removes. Her clothes are dirty; her face is pale and gaunt. Herrick goes out.*

DANFORTH, *very politely:* Goody Proctor. *She is silent.* I hope you are hearty?

ELIZABETH, *as a warning reminder:* I am yet six month before my time.

DANFORTH: Pray be at your ease, we come not for your life. We— *uncertain how to plead, for he is not accustomed to it.* Mr. Hale, will you speak with the woman?

HALE: Goody Proctor, your husband is marked to hang this morning.

Pause.

ELIZABETH, *quietly:* I have heard it.

HALE: You know, do you not, that I have no connection with the court? *She seems to doubt it.* I come of my own, Goody Proctor. I would save your husband's life, for if he is taken I count myself his murderer. Do you understand me?

ELIZABETH: What do you want of me?

HALE: Goody Proctor, I have gone this three month like our Lord into the wilderness. I have sought a Christian way, for damnation's doubled on a minister who counsels men to lie.

HATHORNE: It is no lie, you cannot speak of lies.

HALE: It is a lie! They are innocent!

DANFORTH: I'll hear no more of that!

HALE, *continuing to Elizabeth:* Let you not mistake your duty as I mistook my own. I came into this village like a bridegroom to his beloved, bearing gifts of high religion; the very crowns of holy law I brought, and what I touched with my bright confidence, it died; and where I turned the eye of my great faith, blood flowed up. Beware, Goody Proctor—cleave to no faith when faith brings blood. It is mistaken law that leads you to sacrifice. Life, woman, life is God's most precious gift; no principle, however glorious, may justify the taking of it. I beg you, woman, prevail upon your husband to confess. Let him give his lie. Quail not before God's judgment in this, for it may well be God damns a liar less than he that throws his life away for pride. Will you plead with him? I cannot think he will listen to another.

ELIZABETH, *quietly:* I think that be the Devil's argument.

HALE, *with a climactic desperation:* Woman, before the laws of God we are as swine! We cannot read His will!

ELIZABETH: I cannot dispute with you, sir; I lack learning for it.

DANFORTH, *going to her:* Goody Proctor, you are not summoned here for disputation. Be there no wifely tenderness within you? He will die with the sunrise. Your husband. Do you understand it? *She only looks at him.* What say you? Will you contend with him? *She is silent.* Are you stone? I tell you true, woman, had I no other proof of your unnatural life, your dry eyes now would be sufficient evidence that you delivered up your soul to Hell! A very ape would weep at such calamity! Have the Devil dried up any tear of pity in you? *She is silent.* Take her out. It profit nothing she should speak to him!

ELIZABETH, *quietly:* Let me speak with him, Excellency.

PARRIS, *with hope:* You'll strive with him? *She hesitates.*

DANFORTH: Will you plead for his confession or will you not?

ELIZABETH: I promise nothing. Let me speak with him.

A sound—the sibilance of dragging feet on stone. They turn. A pause. Herrick enters with John Proctor. His wrists are chained. He is another man, bearded, filthy, his eyes misty as though webs had overgrown them. He halts inside the doorway, his eye caught by the sight of Elizabeth. The emotion flowing between them prevents anyone from speaking for an instant. Now Hale, visibly affected, goes to Danforth and speaks quietly.

HALE: Pray, leave them, Excellency.

DANFORTH, *pressing Hale impatiently aside:* Mr. Proctor, you have been notified, have you not? *Proctor is silent, staring at Elizabeth.* I see light in the sky, Mister; let you counsel with your wife, and may God help you turn your back on Hell. *Proctor is silent, staring at Elizabeth.*

HALE, *quietly:* Excellency, let—

Danforth brushes past Hale and walks out. Hale follows. Cheever stands and follows, Hathorne behind. Herrick goes. Parris, from a safe distance, offers:

PARRIS: If you desire a cup of cider, Mr. Proctor, I am sure I— *Proctor turns an icy stare at him, and he breaks off. Parris raises his palms toward Proctor.* God lead you now. *Parris goes out.*

Alone. Proctor walks to her, halts. It is as though they stood in a spinning world. It is beyond sorrow, above it. He reaches out his hand as though toward an embodiment not quite real, and as he touches her, a strange soft sound, half laughter, half amazement, comes from his throat. He pats her hand. She covers his hand with hers. And then, weak, he sits. Then she sits, facing him.

PROCTOR: The child?

ELIZABETH: It grows.

PROCTOR: There is no word of the boys?

ELIZABETH: They're well. Rebecca's Samuel keeps them.

PROCTOR: You have not seen them?

ELIZABETH: I have not. *She catches a weakening in herself and downs it.*

PROCTOR: You are a—marvel, Elizabeth.

ELIZABETH: You—have been tortured?

PROCTOR: Aye. *Pause. She will not let herself be drowned in the sea that threatens her.* They come for my life now.

ELIZABETH: I know it.

Pause.

PROCTOR: None—have yet confessed?

ELIZABETH: There be many confessed.

PROCTOR: Who are they?

ELIZABETH: There be a hundred or more, they say. Goody Ballard is one; Isaiah Goodkind is one. There be many.

PROCTOR: Rebecca?

ELIZABETH: Not Rebecca. She is one foot in Heaven now; naught may hurt her more.

PROCTOR: And Giles?

ELIZABETH: You have not heard of it?

PROCTOR: I hear nothin', where I am kept.

ELIZABETH: Giles is dead.

He looks at her incredulously.

PROCTOR: When were he hanged?

ELIZABETH, *quietly, factually:* He were not hanged. He would not answer aye or nay to his indictment; for if he denied the charge they'd hang him surely, and auction out his property. So he stand mute, and died Christian under the law. And so his sons will have his farm. It is the law, for he could not be condemned a wizard without he answer the indictment, aye or nay.

PROCTOR: Then how does he die?

ELIZABETH, *gently:* They press him, John.

PROCTOR: Press?

ELIZABETH: Great stones they lay upon his chest until he plead aye or nay. *With a tender smile for the old man:* They say he give them but two words. "More weight," he says. And died.

PROCTOR, *numbed—a thread to weave into his agony:* "More weight."

ELIZABETH: Aye. It were a fearsome man, Giles Corey.

Pause.

PROCTOR, *with great force of will, but not quite looking at her:* I have been thinking I would confess to them, Elizabeth. *She shows nothing.* What say you? If I give them that?

ELIZABETH: I cannot judge you, John.

Pause.

PROCTOR, *simply—a pure question:* What would you have me do?

ELIZABETH: As you will, I would have it. *Slight pause.* I want you living, John. That's sure.

PROCTOR—*he pauses, then with a flailing of hope:* Giles' wife? Have she confessed?

ELIZABETH: She will not.

Pause.

PROCTOR: It is a pretense, Elizabeth.

ELIZABETH: What is?

PROCTOR: I cannot mount the gibbet like a saint. It is a fraud. I am not that man. *She is silent.* My honesty is broke, Elizabeth; I am no good man. Nothing's spoiled by giving them this lie that were not rotten long before.

ELIZABETH: And yet you've not confessed till now. That speak goodness in you.

PROCTOR: Spite only keeps me silent. It is hard to give a lie to dogs. *Pause, for the first time he turns directly to her.* I would have your forgiveness, Elizabeth.

ELIZABETH: It is not for me to give, John, I am—

PROCTOR: I'd have you see some honesty in it. Let them that never lied die now to keep their souls. It is pretense for me, a vanity that will not blind God nor keep my children out of the wind. *Pause.* What say you?

ELIZABETH, *upon a heaving sob that always threatens:* John, it come to naught that I should forgive you, if you'll not forgive yourself. *Now he turns away a little, in great agony.* It is not my soul, John, it is yours. *He stands, as though in physical pain, slowly rising to his feet with a great immortal longing to find his answer. It is difficult to say, and she is on the verge of tears.* Only be sure of this, for I know it now: Whatever you will do, it is a good man does it. *He turns his doubting, searching gaze upon her.* I have read my heart this three month, John. *Pause.* I have sins of my own to count. It needs a cold wife to prompt lechery.

PROCTOR, *in great pain:* Enough, enough—

ELIZABETH, *now pouring out her heart:* Better you should know me!

PROCTOR: I will not hear it! I know you!

ELIZABETH: You take my sins upon you, John—

PROCTOR, *in agony:* No, I take my own, my own!

ELIZABETH: John, I counted myself so plain, so poorly made, no honest love could come to me! Suspicion kissed you when I did; I never knew how I should say my love. It were a cold house I kept! *In fright, she swerves, as Hathorne enters.*

HATHORNE: What say you, Proctor? The sun is soon up.

Proctor, his chest heaving, stares, turns to Elizabeth. She comes to him as though to plead, her voice quaking.

ELIZABETH: Do what you will. But let none be your judge. There be no higher judge under Heaven than Proctor is! Forgive me, forgive me, John—I never knew such goodness in the world! *She covers her face, weeping.*

Proctor turns from her to Hathorne; he is off the earth, his voice hollow.

PROCTOR: I want my life.

HATHORNE, *electrified, surprised:* You'll confess yourself?

PROCTOR: I will have my life.

HATHORNE, *with a mystical tone:* God be praised! It is a providence! *He rushes out the door, and his voice is heard calling down the corridor:* He will confess! Proctor will confess!

PROCTOR, *with a cry, as he strides to the door:* Why do you cry it? *In great pain he turns back to her.* It is evil, is it not? It is evil.

ELIZABETH, *in terror, weeping:* I cannot judge you, John, I cannot!

PROCTOR: Then who will judge me? *Suddenly clasping his hands:* God in Heaven, what is John Proctor, what is John Proctor? *He moves as an animal, and a fury is riding in him, a tantalized search.* I think it is honest, I think so; I am no saint. *As though she had denied this he calls angrily at her:* Let Rebecca go like a saint; for me it is fraud!

Voices are heard in the hall, speaking together in suppressed excitement.

ELIZABETH: I am not your judge, I cannot be. *As though giving him release:* Do as you will, do as you will!

PROCTOR: Would you give them such a lie? Say it. Would you ever give them this? *She cannot answer.* You would not; if tongs of fire were singeing you you would not! It is evil. Good, then—it is evil, and I do it!

Hathorne enters with Danforth, and, with them, Cheever, Parris, and Hale. It is a businesslike, rapid entrance, as though the ice had been broken.

DANFORTH, *with great relief and gratitude:* Praise to God, man, praise to God; you shall be blessed in Heaven for this. *Cheever has hurried to the bench with pen, ink, and paper. Proctor watches him.* Now then, let us have it. Are you ready, Mr. Cheever?

PROCTOR, *with a cold, cold horror at their efficiency:* Why must it be written?

DANFORTH: Why, for the good instruction of the village, Mister; this we shall post upon the church door! *To Parris, urgently:* Where is the marshal?

PARRIS—*he runs to the door and calls down the corridor:* Marshal! Hurry!

DANFORTH: Now, then, Mister, will you speak slowly, and directly to the point, for Mr. Cheever's sake. *He is on record now, and is really dictating to Cheever, who writes.* Mr. Proctor, have you seen the Devil in your life? *Proctor's jaws lock.* Come, man, there is light in the sky; the town waits at the scaffold; I would give out this news. Did you see the Devil?

PROCTOR: I did.

PARRIS: Praise God!

DANFORTH: And when he come to you, what were his demand? *Proctor is silent. Danforth helps.* Did he bid you to do his work upon the earth?

PROCTOR: He did.

DANFORTH: And you bound yourself to his service? *Danforth turns, as Rebecca Nurse enters, with Herrick helping to support her. She is barely able to walk.* Come in, come in, woman!

REBECCA, *brightening as she sees Proctor:* Ah, John! You are well, then, eh?

Proctor turns his face to the wall.

DANFORTH: Courage, man, courage—let her witness your good example that she may come to God herself. Now hear it, Goody Nurse! Say on, Mr. Proctor. Did you bind yourself to the Devil's service?

REBECCA, *astonished:* Why, John!

PROCTOR, *through his teeth, his face turned from Rebecca:* I did.

DANFORTH: Now, woman, you surely see it profit nothin' to keep this conspiracy any further. Will you confess yourself with him?

REBECCA: Oh, John—God send his mercy on you!

DANFORTH: I say, will you confess yourself, Goody Nurse?

REBECCA: Why, it is a lie, it is a lie; how may I damn myself? I cannot, I cannot.

DANFORTH: Mr. Proctor. When the Devil came to you did you see Rebecca Nurse in his company? *Proctor is silent.* Come, man, take courage—did you ever see her with the Devil?

PROCTOR, *almost inaudibly:* No.

Danforth, now sensing trouble, glances at John and goes to the table, and picks up a sheet—the list of condemned.

DANFORTH: Did you ever see her sister, Mary Easty, with the Devil?

PROCTOR: No, I did not.

DANFORTH, *his eyes narrow on Proctor:* Did you ever see Martha Corey with the Devil?

PROCTOR: I did not.

DANFORTH, *realizing, slowly putting the sheet down:* Did you ever see anyone with the Devil?

PROCTOR: I did not.

DANFORTH: Proctor, you mistake me. I am not empowered to trade your life for a lie. You have most certainly seen some person with the Devil. *Proctor is silent.* Mr. Proctor, a score of people have already testified they saw this woman with the Devil.

PROCTOR: Then it is proved. Why must I say it?

DANFORTH: Why "must" you say it! Why, you should rejoice to say it if your soul is truly purged of any love for Hell!

PROCTOR: They think to go like saints. I like not to spoil their names.

DANFORTH, *inquiring, incredulous:* Mr. Proctor, do you think they go like saints?

PROCTOR, *evading:* This woman never thought she done the Devil's work.

DANFORTH: Look you, sir. I think you mistake your duty here. It matters nothing what she thought—she is convicted of the unnatural murder of children, and you for sending your spirit out upon Mary Warren. Your soul alone is the issue here, Mister, and you will prove its whiteness or you cannot live in a Christian country. Will you tell me now what persons conspired with you in the Devil's company? *Proctor is silent.* To your knowledge was Rebecca Nurse ever—

PROCTOR: I speak my own sins; I cannot judge another. *Crying out, with hatred:* I have no tongue for it.

HALE, *quickly to Danforth:* Excellency, it is enough he confess himself. Let him sign it, let him sign it.

PARRIS, *feverishly:* It is a great service, sir. It is a weighty name; it will strike the village that Proctor confess. I beg you, let him sign it. The sun is up, Excellency!

DANFORTH—*he considers; then with dissatisfaction:* Come, then, sign your testimony. *To Cheever:* Give it to him. *Cheever goes to Proctor, the confession and a pen in hand. Proctor does not look at it.* Come, man, sign it.

PROCTOR, *after glancing at the confession:* You have all witnessed it—it is enough.

DANFORTH: You will not sign it?

PROCTOR: You have all witnessed it; what more is needed?

DANFORTH: Do you sport with me? You will sign your name or it is no confession, Mister! *His breast heaving with agonized breathing, Proctor now lays the paper down and signs his name.*

PARRIS: Praise be to the Lord!

Proctor has just finished signing when Danforth reaches for the paper. But Proctor snatches it up, and now a wild terror is rising in him, and a boundless anger.

DANFORTH, *perplexed, but politely extending his hand:* If you please, sir.

PROCTOR: No.

DANFORTH, *as though Proctor did not understand:* Mr. Proctor, I must have—

PROCTOR: No, no. I have signed it. You have seen me. It is done! You have no need for this.

PARRIS: Proctor, the village must have proof that—

PROCTOR: Damn the village! I confess to God, and God has seen my name on this! It is enough!

DANFORTH: No, sir, it is—

PROCTOR: You came to save my soul, did you not? Here! I have confessed myself; it is enough!

DANFORTH: You have not con—

PROCTOR: I have confessed myself! Is there no good penitence but it be public? God does not need my name nailed upon the church! God sees my name; God knows how black my sins are! It is enough!

DANFORTH: Mr. Proctor—

PROCTOR: You will not use me! I am no Sarah Good or Tituba, I am John Proctor! You will not use me! It is no part of salvation that you should use me!

DANFORTH: I do not wish to—

PROCTOR: I have three children—how may I teach them to walk like men in the world, and I sold my friends?

DANFORTH: You have not sold your friends—

PROCTOR: Beguile me not! I blacken all of them when this is nailed to the church the very day they hang for silence!

DANFORTH: Mr. Proctor, I must have good and legal proof that you—

PROCTOR: You are the high court, your word is good enough! Tell them I confessed myself; say Proctor broke his knees and wept like a woman; say what you will, but my name cannot—

DANFORTH, *with suspicion:* It is the same, is it not? If I report it or you sign to it?

PROCTOR—*he knows it is insane:* No, it is not the same! What others say and what I sign to is not the same!

DANFORTH: Why? Do you mean to deny this confession when you are free?

PROCTOR: I mean to deny nothing!

DANFORTH: Then explain to me, Mr. Proctor, why you will not let—

PROCTOR, *with a cry of his whole soul:* Because it is my name! Because I cannot have another in my life! Because I lie and sign myself to lies! Because I am not worth the dust on the feet of them that hang! How may I live without my name? I have given you my soul; leave me my name!

DANFORTH, *pointing at the confession in Proctor's hand:* Is that document a lie? If it is a lie I will not accept it! What say you? I will not deal in lies, Mister! *Proctor is motionless.* You will give me your honest confession in my hand, or I cannot keep you from the rope. *Proctor does not reply.* Which way do you go, Mister?

His breast heaving, his eyes staring, Proctor tears the paper and crumples it, and he is weeping in fury, but erect.

DANFORTH: Marshal!

PARRIS, *hysterically, as though the tearing paper were his life:* Proctor, Proctor!

HALE: Man, you will hang! You cannot!

PROCTOR, *his eyes full of tears:* I can. And there's your first marvel, that I can. You have made your magic now, for now I do think I see some shred of goodness in John Proctor. Not enough to weave a banner with, but white enough to keep it from such dogs. *Elizabeth, in a burst of terror, rushes to him and weeps against his hand.* Give them no tear! Tears pleasure them! Show honor now, show a stony heart and sink them with it! *He has lifted her, and kisses her now with great passion.*

REBECCA: Let you fear nothing! Another judgment waits us all!

DANFORTH: Hang them high over the town! Who weeps for these, weeps for corruption! *He sweeps out past them. Herrick starts to lead Rebecca, who almost collapses, but Proctor catches her, and she glances up at him apologetically.*

REBECCA: I've had no breakfast.

HERRICK: Come, man. *Herrick escorts them out, Hathorne and Cheever behind them. Elizabeth stands staring at the empty doorway.*

PARRIS, *in deadly fear, to Elizabeth:* Go to him, Goody Proctor! There is yet time!

From outside a drumroll strikes the air. Parris is startled. Elizabeth jerks about toward the window.

PARRIS: Go to him! *He rushes out the door, as though to hold back his fate.* Proctor! Proctor!

Again, a short burst of drums.

HALE: Woman, plead with him! *He starts to rush out the door, and then goes back to her.* Woman! It is pride, it is vanity. *She avoids his eyes, and moves to the window. He drops to his knees.* Be his helper! What profit him to bleed? Shall the dust praise him? Shall the worms declare his truth? Go to him, take his shame away!

ELIZABETH, *supporting herself against collapse, grips the bars of the window, and with a cry:* He have his goodness now. God forbid I take it from him!

The final drumroll crashes, then heightens violently. Hale weeps in frantic prayer, and the new sun is pouring in upon her face, and the drums rattle like bones in the morning air.

The Curtain Falls

ECHOES DOWN THE CORRIDOR

Not long after the fever died, Parris was voted from office, walked out on the highroad, and was never heard of again.

The legend has it that Abigail turned up later as a prostitute in Boston.

Twenty years after the last execution, the government awarded compensation to the victims still living, and to the families of the dead. However, it is evident that some people still were unwilling to admit their total guilt, and also that the factionalism was still alive, for some beneficiaries were actually not victims at all, but informers.

Elizabeth Proctor married again, four years after Proctor's death.

In solemn meeting, the congregation rescinded the excommunications—this in March 1712. But they did so upon orders of the government. The jury, however, wrote a statement praying forgiveness of all who had suffered.

Certain farms which had belonged to the victims were left to ruin, and for more than a century no one would buy them or live on them.

To all intents and purposes, the power of theocracy in Massachusetts was broken.

Appendix: ACT TWO,

Scene Two*

A wood. Night.
    Proctor enters with lantern, glowing behind him, then halts, holding lantern raised. Abigail appears with a wrap over her nightgown, her hair down. A moment of questioning silence.

PROCTOR, *searching:* I must speak with you, Abigail. *She does not move, staring at him.* Will you sit?

ABIGAIL: How do you come?

PROCTOR: Friendly.

ABIGAIL, *glancing about:* I don't like the woods at night. Pray you, stand closer. *He comes closer to her.* I knew it must be you. When I heard the pebbles on the window, before I opened up my eyes I knew. *Sits on log.* I thought you would come a good time sooner.

PROCTOR: I had thought to come many times.

ABIGAIL: Why didn't you? I am so alone in the world now.

PROCTOR, *as a fact, not bitterly:* Are you! I've heard that people ride a hundred mile to see your face these days.

ABIGAIL: Aye, my face. Can you see my face?

PROCTOR—*he holds the lantern to her face:* Then you're troubled?

ABIGAIL: Have you come to mock me?

* See note on page 199.

254

PROCTOR—*he sets lantern on ground and sits next to her:* No, no, but I hear only that you go to the tavern every night, and play shovelboard with the Deputy Governor, and they give you cider.

ABIGAIL: I have once or twice played the shovelboard. But I have no joy in it.

PROCTOR: This is a surprise, Abby. I'd thought to find you gayer than this. I'm told a troop of boys go step for step with you wherever you walk these days.

ABIGAIL: Aye, they do. But I have only lewd looks from the boys.

PROCTOR: And you like that not?

ABIGAIL: I cannot bear lewd looks no more, John. My spirit's changed entirely. I ought be given Godly looks when I suffer for them as I do.

PROCTOR: Oh? How do you suffer, Abby?

ABIGAIL, *pulling up her dress:* Why, look at my leg. I'm holes all over from their damned needles and pins. *Touching her stomach:* The jab your wife gave me's not healed yet, y'know.

PROCTOR, *seeing her madness now:* Oh, it isn't?

ABIGAIL: I think sometimes she pricks it open again while I sleep.

PROCTOR: Ah?

ABIGAIL: And George Jacobs—*sliding up her sleeve*—he comes again and again and raps me with his stick—the same spot every night all this week. Look at the lump I have.

PROCTOR: Abby, George Jacobs is in the jail all this month.

ABIGAIL: Thank God he is, and bless the day he hangs and lets me sleep in peace again! Oh, John, the world's so full of hypocrites! *Astonished, outraged:* They pray in jail! I'm told they all pray in jail!

PROCTOR: They may not pray?

ABIGAIL: And torture me in my bed while sacred words are comin' from their mouths? Oh, it will need God Himself to cleanse this town properly!

PROCTOR: Abby—you mean to cry out still others?

ABIGAIL: If I live, if I am not murdered, I surely will, until the last hypocrite is dead.

PROCTOR: Then there is no good?

ABIGAIL: Aye, there is one. *You* are good.

PROCTOR: Am I! How am I good?

ABIGAIL: Why, you taught me goodness, therefore you are good. It were a fire you walked me through, and all my ignorance was burned away. It were a fire, John, we lay in fire. And from that night no woman dare call me wicked any more but I knew my answer. I used to weep for my sins when the wind lifted up my skirts; and blushed for shame because some old Rebecca called me loose. And then you burned my ignorance away. As bare as some December tree I saw them all—walking like saints to church, running to feed the sick, and hypocrites in their hearts! And God gave me strength to call them liars, and God made men to listen to me, and by God I will scrub the world clean for the love of Him! Oh, John, I will make you such a wife when the world is white again! *She kisses his hand.* You will be amazed to see me every day, a light of heaven in your house, a— *He rises, backs away, amazed.* Why are you cold?

PROCTOR: My wife goes to trial in the morning, Abigail.

ABIGAIL, *distantly:* Your wife?

PROCTOR: Surely you knew of it?

ABIGAIL: I do remember it now. How—how— Is she well?

PROCTOR: As well as she may be, thirty-six days in that place.

ABIGAIL: You said you came friendly.

PROCTOR: She will not be condemned, Abby.

ABIGAIL: You brought me from my bed to speak of her?

PROCTOR: I come to tell you, Abby, what I will do tomorrow in the court. I would not take you by surprise, but give you all good time to think on what to do to save yourself.

ABIGAIL: Save myself!

PROCTOR: If you do not free my wife tomorrow, I am set and bound to ruin you, Abby.

ABIGAIL, *her voice small—astonished:* How—ruin me?

PROCTOR: I have rocky proof in documents that you knew that poppet were none of my wife's; and that you yourself bade Mary Warren stab that needle into it.

ABIGAIL—*wildness stirs in her, a child is standing here who is unutterably frustrated, denied her wish, but she is still grasping for her wits:* I bade Mary Warren—?

PROCTOR: You know what you do, you are not so mad!

ABIGAIL: Oh, hypocrites! Have you won him, too? John, why do you let them send you?

PROCTOR: I warn you, Abby!

ABIGAIL: They send you! They steal your honesty and—

PROCTOR: I have found my honesty!

ABIGAIL: No, this is your wife pleading, your sniveling, envious wife! This is Rebecca's voice, Martha Corey's voice. You were no hypocrite!

PROCTOR: I will prove you for the fraud you are!

ABIGAIL: And if they ask you why Abigail would ever do so murderous a deed, what will you tell them?

PROCTOR: I will tell them why.

ABIGAIL: What will you tell? You will confess to fornication? In the court?

PROCTOR: If you will have it so, so I will tell it! *She utters a disbelieving laugh.* I say I will! *She laughs louder, now with more assurance he will never do it. He shakes her roughly.* If you can still hear, hear this! Can you hear! *She is trembling, staring up at him as though he were out of his mind.* You will tell the court you are blind to spirits; you cannot see them any more, and you will never cry witchery again, or I will make you famous for the whore you are!

ABIGAIL, *grabbing him:* Never in this world! I know you, John. You are this moment singing secret hallelujahs that your wife will hang!

PROCTOR, *throwing her down:* You mad, you murderous bitch!

ABIGAIL: Oh, how hard it is when pretense falls! But it falls, it falls! *She wraps herself up as though to go.* You have done your duty by her. I hope it is your last hypocrisy. I pray you will come again with sweeter news for me. I know you will—now that your duty's done. Good night, John. *She is backing away, raising her hand in farewell.* Fear naught. I will save you tomorrow. *As she turns and goes:* From yourself I will save you. *She is gone.*

Proctor is left alone, amazed, in terror. He takes up his lantern and slowly exits.

The Curtain Falls

AFTER THE FALL

A Play in Two Acts

THE CAST
(In order of appearance)

QUENTIN	Jason Robards, Jr.
FELICE	Zohra Lampert
MAGGIE	Barbara Loden
HOLGA	Salome Jens
DAN	Michael Strong
FATHER	Paul Mann
MOTHER	Virginia Kaye
NURSES	Faye Dunaway, Diane Shalet
ELSIE	Patricia Roe
LOUISE	Mariclare Costello
LOU	David J. Stewart
MICKEY	Ralph Meeker
MAN IN PARK	Stanley Beck
CARRIE	Ruth Attaway
LUCAS	Harold Scott
CHAIRMAN	David Wayne
HARLEY BARNES	Hal Holbrook
PORTER	Jack Waltzer
MAGGIE'S SECRETARY	Crystal Field
PIANIST	Scott Cunningham
OTHERS	Clint Kimbrough, John Phillip Law, Barry Primus, James Greene

Directed by Elia Kazan; produced by Robert Whitehead for the Lincoln Center Repertory Company. First performed on January 23, 1964, at the ANTA–Washington Square Theatre, New York City.

ACT ONE

The action takes place in the mind, thought, and memory of Quentin. Except for one chair there is no furniture in the conventional sense; there are no walls or substantial boundaries.

The setting consists of three levels rising to the highest at the back, crossing in a curve from one side of the stage to the other. Rising above it, and dominating the stage, is the blasted stone tower of a German concentration camp. Its wide lookout windows are like eyes which at the moment seem blind and dark; bent reinforcing rods stick out of it like broken tentacles.

On the two lower levels are sculpted areas; indeed, the whole effect is neolithic, a lava-like, supple geography in which, like pits and hollows found in lava, the scenes take place. The mind has no color but its memories are brilliant against the grayness of its landscape. When people sit they do so on any of the abutments, ledges, or crevices. A scene may start in a confined area, but spread or burst out onto the entire stage, overrunning any other area.

People appear and disappear instantaneously, as in the mind; but it is not necessary that they walk off the stage. The dialogue will make clear who is "alive" at any moment and who is in abeyance.

The effect, therefore, will be the surging, flitting, instantaneousness of a mind questing over its own surfaces and into its depths.

The stage is dark. Now there is a sense that some figure has moved in the farthest distance; a footstep is heard, then others. As light dimly rises, the persons in the play move in a random way up from beneath the high back platform. Some sit at once, others come farther downstage, seem to recognize each other, still others move alone and in total separateness. They are speaking toward Quentin in sibilant whispers, some angrily, some in appeal to him. Now Quentin, a man in his forties, moves out of this mass and continues down to the front of the stage. All movement ceases. Quentin addresses the Listener, who, if he could be seen, would be sitting just beyond the edge of the stage itself.

QUENTIN: Hello! God, it's good to see you again! I'm very well. I hope it wasn't too inconvenient on such short notice. Fine, I just wanted to say hello, really. Thanks. *He sits on invitation. Slight pause.* Actually, I called you on the spur of the moment this morning; I have a bit of a decision to make. You know—you mull around about something for months and all of a sudden there it is and you don't know what to do.

He sets himself to begin, looks off.

Ah . . .

Interrupted, he turns back to Listener, surprised.

I've quit the firm, didn't I write you about that? Really! I was sure I'd written. Oh, about fourteen months ago; a few weeks after Maggie died. *Maggie stirs on the second platform.* It just got to where I couldn't concentrate on a case any more; not the way I used to. I felt I was merely in the service of my own success. It all lost any point. Although I do wonder sometimes if I am simply trying to destroy myself. . . . Well, I have walked away from what passes for an important career. . . . Not very much, I'm afraid; I still live in the hotel, see a few people, read a good deal—*Smiles*—stare out the window. I don't know why I'm smiling; maybe I feel that's all over now, and I'll harness myself to something again. Although I've had that feeling before and done nothing about it, I—

Again, interrupted, he looks surprised.

God, I wrote you about *that*, didn't I? Maybe I dream these letters. Mother died. Oh, it's four—*Airplane sound is heard behind him*—five months ago now. Yes, quite suddenly; I was in Germany at the time and—it's one of the things I wanted—*Holga appears on upper platform, looking about for him*—to talk to you about. I . . . met a woman there. *He grins.* I never thought it could happen again, but we became quite close. In fact, she's arriving tonight, for some conference at Columbia—she's an archaeologist. I'm not sure, you see, if I want to lose her, and yet it's outrageous to think of committing myself again.

. . . Well, yes, but look at my life. A life, after all, is evidence, and I have two divorces in my safe-deposit box. *Turning to glance up at Holga:* I tell you frankly, I'm a little afraid. . . . Well, of who and what I'm bringing to her. *He sits again, leans forward.* You know, more and more I think that for many years I looked at life like a case at law, a series of proofs. When you're young you prove how brave you are, or smart; then, what a good lover; then, a good father; finally, how wise, or powerful or what-the-hell-ever. But underlying it all, I see now, there was a presumption. That I was moving on an upward path toward some elevation, where—God knows what—I would be justified, or even condemned—a verdict anyway. I think now that my disaster really began when I looked up one day—and the bench was empty. No judge in sight. And all that remained was the endless argument with oneself— this pointless litigation of existence before an empty bench. Which, of course, is another way of saying—despair. And, of course, despair can be a way of life; but you have to believe in it, pick it up, take it to heart, and move on again. Instead, I seem to be hung up. *Slight pause.* And the days and the months and now the years are draining away. A couple of weeks ago I suddenly became aware of a strange fact. With all this darkness, the truth is that every morning when I awake, I'm full of hope! With everything I know—I open my eyes, I'm like a boy! For an instant there's some—unformed promise in the air. I jump out of bed, I shave, I can't wait to finish breakfast—and then, it seeps in my room, my life and its pointlessness. And I thought—if I could corner that hope, find what it consists of and either kill it for a lie, or really make it mine . . .

FELICE, *having entered:* You do remember me, don't you? Two years ago in your office, when you got my husband to sign the divorce papers?

QUENTIN, *to Listener:* I'm not sure why I bring her up. I ran into her on the street last month . . .

FELICE: I always wanted to tell you this—you changed my life!

QUENTIN, *to Listener:* There's something about that girl unnerves me.

FELICE, *facing front, standing beside him:* You see, my husband was always so childish, alone with me. But the way you talked to him; it made him act so dignified I almost began to love him! And when we got out in the street he asked me something. Should I tell you, or do you know already?

QUENTIN, *now turning to her:* He asked to go to bed with you one last time?

FELICE: How did you know that?

QUENTIN: Well, what harm would it have done?

FELICE: But wouldn't it be funny the same day we agreed to divorce?

QUENTIN: Honey, you never stop loving whoever you loved. Why must you try?

Louise starts down toward him, and Maggie appears far upstage in gold dress among anonymous men. Quentin turns back to Listener.

Why do I make such stupid statements!

MAGGIE, *from among the men, laughing as though with joy at seeing him:* Quentin! *She is gone.*

QUENTIN: These goddamned women have injured me! Have I learned nothing?

HOLGA, *appearing under the tower with flowers as Maggie and men go dark:* Would you like to see Salzburg? I think they play *The Magic Flute* tonight.

QUENTIN, *of Holga:* I don't know what I'd be bringing to that girl.

Holga exits. Louise has moved down in front of him, and he glances at her.

I don't know how to blame with confidence.

FELICE, *as Louise moves thoughtfully upstage and exits:* But I finally got your point! It's that there is no point, right? No one has to be to blame! And as soon as I realized that, I started to dance better!

QUENTIN, *to Listener:* God, what excellent advice I give!

FELICE: I almost feel free when I dance now! Sometimes I only have to think high and I go high! I get a long thought and I fly across the floor. *She flies out into darkness.*

QUENTIN: And on top of that she came back again the other night, flew into my room—reborn! She made me wonder how much I believe in life.

FELICE, *rushing on:* I had my nose fixed! Could I show it to you? The doctor took the bandage off, but I put it back because I wanted you to be the first! Do you mind?

QUENTIN, *turning to her:* No. But why me?

FELICE: Because—remember that night I came up here? I was trying to decide if I should have it done. 'Cause there could be something insincere about changing your nose; I wouldn't want to build everything on the shape of a piece of cartilage. You don't absolutely have to answer me, but—I think you wanted to make love to me that night. Didn't you?

QUENTIN: I did, yes.

FELICE: I knew it! And I felt it didn't matter what kind of nose I had! So I might as well have a short one! Could I show it to you?

QUENTIN: I'd like very much to see it.

FELICE: Close your eyes. *He does. She lifts the bandage.* Okay. *He looks. She raises her arm in blessing.* I'll always bless you. Always!

He slowly turns to the Listener as she walks into darkness.

QUENTIN: And I even liked her first nose better. And yet I may stand in her mind like some important corner she turned in life. And she meant so little to me. I feel like a mirror in which she somehow saw herself as glorious.

Two pallbearers in the distance carry an invisible coffin.

It's like my mother's funeral;

Mother appears on upper platform, arms crossed as in death.

I still hear her voice in the street sometimes, loud and real, calling me. And yet she's under the ground. That whole cemetery—I saw it like a field of buried mirrors in which the living merely saw themselves. I don't seem to know how to grieve for her.

Father appears, a blanket over him; two nurses tend him.

Or maybe I don't believe that grief is grief unless it kills you.

Dan appears, talking to a nurse.

Like when I flew back and met my brother in the hospital.

The nurse hurries out, and Quentin has gotten up and moved to Dan.

DAN: I'm so glad you got here, kid; I wouldn't have wired you, but I don't know what to do. You have a good flight?

QUENTIN, *to Dan:* But what's the alternative? She's dead, he has to know.

DAN, *to Quentin:* But he was only operated on this morning. How can we walk in and say, "Your wife is dead"? It's like sawing off his arm. Suppose we tell him she's on her way, then give him a sedative?

QUENTIN: But Dan, don't you think it belongs to him? After fifty years you owe one another a death.

DAN: Kid, the woman was his right hand; without her he was never very much, you know—he'll fall apart.

QUENTIN: I can't agree; I think he's got a lot of stuff—*Without halt, to the Listener:* Which is hilarious! . . . Because! He was always the one who idolized the old man, and I saw through him from the beginning! Suddenly we're changing places, like children in a game! I don't know any more what people *are* to one another!

DAN, *as though he had come to a decision:* All right; let's go in, then.

QUENTIN: You want me to tell him?

DAN, *unwillingly, afraid but challenged:* I'll do it.

QUENTIN: I could do it, Dan. It belongs to him, as much as his wedding.

DAN, *relieved:* All right, if you don't mind.

They turn together toward Father in the bed. He does not see them yet. They move with the weight of their news. Quentin turns toward Listener as he walks.

QUENTIN: Or is it simply that I am crueler than he?

Now Father sees them and raises up his arm.

DAN, *indicating Quentin:* Dad, look . . .

FATHER: For cryin' out loud! Look who's here! I thought you were in Europe!

QUENTIN: Just got back. How are you?

DAN: You look wonderful, Dad.

FATHER: What do you mean, "look"? I *am* wonderful! I tell you, I'm ready to go through it again! *They laugh proudly with him.* I mean it— the way that doctor worries, I finally told him, "Look, if it makes you feel so bad you lay down and I'll operate!" Very fine man. I thought you'd be away couple months more.

QUENTIN, *hesitantly:* I decided to come back and—

DAN, *breaking in, his voice turning strange:* Sylvia'll be right in. She's downstairs buying you something.

FATHER: Oh, that's nice! I tell you something, fellas—that kid is more and more like Mother. Been here every day . . . Where is Mother? I been calling the house.

The slightest empty, empty pause.

DAN: One second, Dad, I just want to—

Crazily, without evident point, he starts calling, and moving upstage toward the nurse. Quentin is staring at his father.

Nurse! Ah . . . could you call down to the gift shop and see if my sister . . .

FATHER: Dan! Tell her to get some ice. When Mother comes you'll all have a drink! I got a bottle of rye in the closet. *To Quentin:* I tell you, kid, I'm going to be young. Mother's right; just because I got old I don't have to act old. I mean we could go to Florida, we could—

QUENTIN: Dad.

FATHER: What? Is that a new suit?

QUENTIN: No, I've had it.

FATHER, *remembering—to Dan, of the nurse:* Oh, tell her glasses, we'll need more glasses.

QUENTIN: Listen, Dad.

Dan halts and turns back.

FATHER, *totally unaware, smiling at his returned son:* Yeah?

QUENTIN: Mother died. She had a heart attack last night on her way home.

FATHER: Oh, no, no, no, no.

QUENTIN: We didn't want to tell you but—

FATHER: Ahhh! Ahhh, no, no, no.

DAN: There's nothing anybody could have done, Dad.

FATHER: Oh. Oh. Oh!

QUENTIN, *grasping his hand:* Now look, Dad, you're going to be all right, you'll—

FATHER—*it is all turning into a deep gasping for breath:* Oh boy. Oh boy! No, no.

DAN: Now look, Dad, you're a hell of a fella. Dad, listen—

FATHER: Goddammit! I couldn't take care of myself, I knew she was working too hard!

QUENTIN: Dad, it's not your fault, that can happen to anyone—

FATHER: But she was sitting right here. She was—she was right here!

QUENTIN: Pa . . . Pa . . .

Dan moves in close, as though to share him.

FATHER: Oh, boys—she was my right hand! *He raises his fist and seems about to lose his control again.*

DAN: We'll take care of you, Dad. I don't want you to worry about—

FATHER: No-no. I'll be all right. God! Now I'm better! Now, *now* I'm better!

They are silent.

So where is she?

QUENTIN: In the funeral parlor.

FATHER, *shaking his head—an explosive blow of air:* Paaaaaah!

QUENTIN: We didn't want to tell you but we figured you'd rather know.

FATHER: Ya. Thanks. Thanks. I'll . . . *He looks up at Quentin.* I'll just have to be stronger.

QUENTIN: That's right, Dad.

FATHER, *to no one, as Mother disappears above:* This . . . will make me stronger. *But the weeping threatens; he clenches his jaw, shakes his head, and indicates a point.* She was right here!

He is taken away by the nurses and Dan. Quentin comes slowly to the Listener.

QUENTIN: Still and all, a couple months later he bothered to register and vote. . . . Well, I mean . . . it didn't kill him either, with all his tears. I don't know what the hell I'm driving at. It's connected to . . .

The tower gradually begins to light. He is caught by it.

I visited a concentration camp in Germany.

He has started toward the tower when Felice appears, raising her arm in blessing.

FELICE: Close your eyes, okay?

QUENTIN, *turned by her force:* I don't understand why that girl sticks in my mind. *He moves toward her now.* She did, she offered me some . . . love, I guess. And if I don't return it—it's like owing for a gift that you didn't ask for.

Mother has appeared again; she raises her hand in blessing as Felice does.

FELICE: I'll always bless you!

She exits and Mother is gone.

QUENTIN: When she left . . . I did a stupid thing. I don't understand it. There are two light fixtures on the wall of my hotel room . . .

As he speaks Maggie enters onto second platform, dressed in negligee, hair disheveled. Quentin struggles against his own disgust.

I noticed for the first time that they're . . . a curious distance apart. And I suddenly saw that if you stood between them—*He spreads out his arms*—you could reach out and rest your arms.

Just before he completely spreads his arms, Maggie sits up, her breathing sounds.

MAGGIE: Liar! Judge!

He drops his arms, aborting the image; Maggie exits.

Now Holga appears and is bending to read a legend fixed to the wall of a torture chamber.

QUENTIN: Oh. The concentration camp . . . this woman . . . Holga took me there.

HOLGA, *turning to "him," as though he stood beside her:* This is the room where they tortured them. No, I don't mind, I'll translate it.

She returns to the legend; he slowly approaches behind her.

"The door to the left leads into the chamber where their teeth were extracted for gold; the drain in the floor carried off the blood. At times, instead of shooting, they were individually strangled to death. The barracks on the right were the bordello where women—"

QUENTIN: I think you've had enough, Holga.

HOLGA: No, if you want to see the rest—

QUENTIN, *taking her arm:* Let's walk, dear. Country looks lovely out there.

They walk. The light changes to day.

They sure built solid watchtowers, didn't they! Here, this grass looks dry; let's sit down.

They sit. Pause.

I always thought the Danube was blue.

HOLGA: Only the waltz; although it does change near Vienna, out of some lingering respect for Strauss, I suppose.

QUENTIN: I don't know why this hit me so.

HOLGA: I'm sorry! *Starting to rise as she senses an estrangement—to raise his spirits:* You still want to see Salzburg? I'd love to show you Mozart's house. And the cafés are excellent there.

QUENTIN, *turning to her now:* Was there somebody you knew died here?

HOLGA: Oh no. I feel people ought to see it, that's all. And you seemed so interested.

QUENTIN: Yes, but I'm an American. I can afford to be interested.

HOLGA: Don't be too sure. When I first visited America after the war I was three days under questioning before they let me in. How could one be in forced labor for two years if one were not a Communist or a Jew? In fact, it was only when I told them I had blood relatives in several Nazi ministries that they were reassured. It's as though fifteen years of one's life had simply vanished in some insane confusion. So I was very glad you were so interested.

QUENTIN, *glancing up at the tower:* I guess I thought I'd be indignant, or angry. But it's like swallowing a lump of earth. It's strange.

HOLGA, *pressing him to lie down, cheerfully:* Come, lie down here for a while and perhaps—

QUENTIN: No, I'm—*He has fended off her hand.* I'm sorry, dear, I didn't mean to push you away.

HOLGA, *rebuffed and embarrassed:* I see wildflowers on that hill; I'll pick some for the car! *She gets up quickly.*

QUENTIN: Holga? *She continues off. He jumps up and hurries to her, turning her.* Holga. *He does not know what to say.*

HOLGA: Perhaps we've been together too much. I could rent another car at Linz; we could meet in Vienna sometime.

QUENTIN: I don't want to lose you, Holga.

HOLGA: I hear your wings opening, Quentin. I am not helpless alone. I love my work. It's simply that from the moment you spoke to me I felt somehow familiar, and it was never so before. . . . It isn't a question of getting married; I am not ashamed this way. But I must have *something.*

QUENTIN: I don't give you anything?

HOLGA: You give me very much. . . . It's difficult for me to speak like this. I am not a woman who must be reassured every minute, those women are stupid to me. . . .

QUENTIN, *turning her face to him:* Holga, are you weeping—for *me?*

HOLGA: Yes.

QUENTIN: It's that I don't want to abuse your feeling for me—I swear I don't know if I have lived in good faith. And the doubt ties my tongue when I think of promising anything again.

HOLGA: But how can one ever be sure of one's good faith?

QUENTIN, *surprised:* God, it's wonderful to hear you say that. All my women have been so goddamned sure!

HOLGA: But how can one ever be?

QUENTIN—*he kisses her gratefully:* Why do you keep coming back to this place? It seems to tear you apart.

Mother is heard softly singing a musical comedy ballad of the twenties.

HOLGA, *after a pause; she is disturbed, uncertain:* I . . . don't know. Perhaps . . . because I didn't die here.

QUENTIN, *turning quickly to Listener:* What?

HOLGA: Although that would make no sense! I don't really know!

QUENTIN, *going toward the Listener at the edge of the stage:* That people . . . what? "Wish to die for the dead." No-no, I can understand it; survival can be hard to bear. But I—I don't think I feel that way. . . . Although I do think of my mother now, and she's dead. Yes! *He turns to Holga.* And maybe the dead do bother her.

HOLGA: It was the middle of the war. I had just come out of a class and there were British leaflets on the sidewalk. And photographs of a concentration camp. And emaciated people. One tended to believe the British. I'd had no idea. Truly. It isn't easy to turn against your country; not in a war. Do Americans turn against America because of Hiroshima? There are reasons always. And I took the leaflet to my godfather—he was still commanding our Intelligence. And I asked if it were true. "Of course," he said, "why does it excite you?" And I said, "You are a swine. You are all swine." I threw my briefcase at him. And he opened it and put some papers in it and asked me to deliver it to a certain address. And I became a courier for the officers who were planning to assassinate Hitler. . . . They were all hanged.

QUENTIN: Why not you?

HOLGA: They didn't betray me.

QUENTIN: Then why do you say good faith is never sure?

HOLGA, *after a pause:* It was my country—longer, perhaps, than it should have been. But I didn't know. And now I don't know how I could not have known.

QUENTIN: Holga, I bless your uncertainty. You don't seem to be look-ing for some goddamned . . . moral *victory*. Forgive me, I didn't mean to be distant with you. I—*Looks up.*

HOLGA: I'll get the flowers! *She starts away.*

QUENTIN: It's only this place!

HOLGA, *turning, and with great love:* I know! I'll be right back! *She hurries away.*

He stands in stillness a moment; the presence of the tower bores in on him; its color changes; he now looks up at it and addresses the Listener.

QUENTIN: I think I expected it to be more unfamiliar. I never thought the stones would look so ordinary. And the view from here is rather pastoral. Why do I *know* something here? Even hollow now and empty, it has a face, and asks a sort of question: "What do you believe as true as this?" Yes! Believers built this, maybe that's the fright—and I, without belief, stand here disarmed. I can see the convoys grinding up this hill, and I inside; no one knows my name and yet they'll smash my head on a concrete floor! And no appeal . . . *He turns quickly to the Listener.* Yes! It's that I no longer see some final saving grace! Socialism once, then love; some final hope is gone that always saved before the end!

Mother appears; Dan enters, kisses her, and exits.

MOTHER, *to an invisible small boy:* Not too much cake, darling, there'll be a lot of food at this wedding.

QUENTIN: Mother! That's strange. And murder?

MOTHER, *getting down on her knees to tend the little boy:* Yes, garters, Quentin, and don't argue with me. . . . Because it's my brother's wedding and your stockings are not to hang over your shoes!

QUENTIN—*he has started to laugh but it turns into:* Why can't I mourn her? And Holga wept in there, why can't I weep? Why do I feel an understanding with this slaughterhouse?

Mother laughs. He turns to her.

MOTHER, *to the little boy:* My brothers! Why must every wedding in this family be a catastrophe! . . . Because the girl is pregnant, darling, and she's got no money, she's stupid, and I tell you this one is going to end up with a mustache! That's why, darling, when you grow up, I hope you learn how to disappoint people. Especially women.

QUENTIN, *watching her, sitting nearby:* But what the hell has this got to do with a concentration camp?

MOTHER: Will you stop playing with matches? *Slaps an invisible boy's hand.* You'll pee in bed! Why don't you practice your penmanship instead? You write like a monkey, darling. And where is your father? If he went to sleep in the Turkish bath again, I'll kill him! Like he forgot my brother Herbert's wedding and goes to the Dempsey-Tunney fight. And ends up in the men's room with the door stuck, so by the time they get him out my brother's married, there's a new champion, and it cost him a hundred dollars to go to the men's room! *She is laughing.*

Father with secretary has appeared on upper platform, an invisible phone to his ear.

FATHER: Then cable Southampton.

MOTHER: But you mustn't laugh at him, he's a wonderful man.

FATHER: Sixty thousand tons. Sixty.

Father disappears.

MOTHER: To this day he walks into a room you want to bow! *Warmly:* Any restaurant—one look at him and the waiters start moving tables around. *Because,* dear, people know that this is a *man.* Even Doctor Strauss, at my wedding he came over to me, says, "Rose, I can see it looking at him, you've got a wonderful man," and he was always in love with me, Strauss. . . . Oh, sure, but he was only a penniless medical student then, my father wouldn't let him in the house. Who knew he'd end up so big in the gallstones? That poor boy! Used to bring me novels to read, poetry, philosophy, God knows what! One time we even sneaked off to hear Rachmaninoff together. *She laughs sadly; and with wonder more than bitterness.* That's why, you see, two weeks after we were married; sit down to dinner and Papa hands me a menu and asks me to read it to him. Couldn't *read*! I got so frightened I nearly ran away! . . . Why? Because your grandmother is such a fine, unselfish woman; two months in school and they put him into the shop! That's what some women are, my dear—and now he goes and buys her a new Packard every year. *With a strange and deep fear:* Please, darling, I want you to *draw* the letters, that scribbling is ugly, dear; and your posture, your speech, it can all be beautiful! Ask Miss Fisher, for years they kept my handwriting pinned up on the bulletin board; God, I'll never forget it, valedictorian of the class with a scholarship to Hunter in my hand . . . *A blackness flows into her soul.* And I came home, and Grandpa says, "You're getting married!" I was like—like with small wings, just getting ready to fly; I slept all year with the catalogue under my pillow. To learn, to learn everything! Oh, darling, the whole thing is such a mystery!

Father enters the area, talking to the young, invisible Quentin.

FATHER: Quentin, would you get the office on the phone? *To Mother:* Why would you call the Turkish bath?

MOTHER: I thought you forgot about the wedding.

FATHER: I wish I could, but I'm paying for it.

MOTHER: He'll pay you back!

FATHER: I believe it, I just wouldn't want to hang by my hair that long. *He turns, and, going to a point, he takes up an invisible phone.* Herman? Hold the wire.

MOTHER: I don't want to be late, now.

FATHER: She won't give birth if we're half-hour late.

MOTHER: Don't be so smart! He fell in love, what's so terrible about that?

FATHER: They all fall in love on my money. I married into a love nest! *He turns to Quentin, laughing.* Did they pass a law that kid can't get a haircut? *Reaching into his pocket, tossing a coin:* Here, at least get a shine. *To Mother:* I'll be right up, dear, go ahead.

MOTHER: I'll put in your studs. God, he's so beautiful in a tuxedo!

She goes a distance out of the area, but halts, turns, eavesdrops on Father.

FATHER, *into phone:* Herman? The accountant still there? Put him on.

QUENTIN, *suddenly, recalling, to the Listener:* Oh, yes!

FATHER: Billy? You finished? Well, what's the story, where am I?

QUENTIN: Yes!

FATHER: Don't you read the papers? What'll I do with Irving Trust? I can't give it away. What bank?

Mother descends a step, alarmed.

I been to every bank in New York, I can't get a bill paid, how the hell they going to lend me money? No-no, there's no money in London, there's no money in Hamburg, there ain't a cargo moving in the world, the ocean's empty, Billy—now tell me the truth, where am I?

He puts down the phone. Pause. Mother comes up behind him. He stands almost stiffly, as though to take a storm.

MOTHER: What's that about? What are you winding up?

Father stands staring; but she seems to hear additional shocking facts.

What are you talking about? When did this start? . . . Well, how much are you taking out of it? . . . You lost your mind? You've got over four hundred thousand dollars' worth of stocks, you can sell the—

Father laughs silently.

You sold those wonderful stocks? I just bought a new grand piano, why didn't you say something? And a silver service for my brother, and you don't say anything! *More subdued, she walks a few steps in thought.* Well, then—you'd better cash your insurance; you've got at least seventy-five thousand cash value—*Halts, turning in shock.* When!

Father is gradually losing his stance, his grandeur; he pulls his tie loose.

All right, then—we'll get rid of my bonds. Do it tomorrow. . . . What do you mean? Well, you get them back, I've got ninety-one thousand dollars in bonds you gave me. Those are my bonds. I've got bonds— *She breaks off, open horror on her face and now a growing contempt.* You mean you saw everything going down and you throw good money after bad? Are you some kind of a moron?

FATHER: You don't walk away from a business; I came to this country with a tag around my neck like a package in the bottom of the boat!

MOTHER: I should have run the day I met you.

FATHER, *as though stabbed:* Rose! *He sits, closing his eyes, his neck bent.*

MOTHER: I should have done what my sisters did, tell my parents to go to hell and thought of myself for once! I should have run for my life!

FATHER, *indicating a point nearby:* Sssh, I hear the kids—

MOTHER: I ought to get a divorce!

FATHER: Rose, the college men are jumping out of windows.

MOTHER: But your last dollar! *Bending over, into his face:* You are an idiot!

Her nearness forces him to stand; they look at each other, strangers.

QUENTIN, *looking up at the tower:* Yes! For no reason—they don't even ask your name!

FATHER, *looking toward the nearby point:* Somebody crying? Quentin's in there. You better talk to him.

She goes in some trepidation toward the indicated point. A foot or so from it, she halts.

MOTHER: Quentin? Darling? You better get dressed. Don't cry, dear—

She is stopped short by something "Quentin" has said.

What *I* said? Why, what did I say? . . . Well, I was a little angry, that's all, but I never said *that*. I think he's a wonderful man! *Laughs.* How could I say a thing like that? Quentin! *As though he is disappearing, she extends her arms.* I didn't say anything! *With a cry toward someone lost, rushing out after the boy:* Darling, I didn't say anything!

Father and Dan exit.

Instantly Holga appears, coming toward him.

QUENTIN, *to himself, turning up toward the tower:* They don't even ask your name.

HOLGA, *looking about for him:* Quentin? Quentin?

QUENTIN, *to Holga:* You love me, don't you?

HOLGA: Yes. *Of the wildflowers in her arms:* Look, the car will be all sweet inside!

QUENTIN, *clasping her hands:* Let's get out of this dump. Come on, I'll race you to the car!

HOLGA: Okay! On your mark!

They get set.

QUENTIN: Last one there's a rancid wurst!

HOLGA: Get ready! Set!

Quentin suddenly looks up at the tower and sits on the ground as though he had committed a sacrilege.

She has read his emotion, touches his face.

Quentin, dear—no one they didn't kill can be innocent again.

QUENTIN: But how did you solve it? How do you get so purposeful? You're so full of hope!

HOLGA: Quentin, I think it's a mistake to ever look for hope outside one's self. One day the house smells of fresh bread, the next of smoke and blood. One day you faint because the gardener cut his finger off, within a week you're climbing over the corpses of children bombed in a subway. What hope can there be if that is so? I tried to die near the end of the war. *She rises, moves up the stair toward the tower.* The same dream returned each night until I dared not go to sleep and grew quite ill. I dreamed I had a child, and even in the dream I saw it was my life, and it was an idiot, and I ran away. But it always crept onto my lap again, clutched at my clothes. Until I thought, if I could kiss it, whatever in it was my own, perhaps I could sleep. And I bent to its broken face, and it was horrible . . . but I kissed it. I think one must finally take one's life in one's arms, Quentin. Come, they play *The Magic Flute* tonight. You like *The Magic Flute*?

She exits from beneath the tower on the upper level.

QUENTIN, *alone:* I miss her . . . badly. And yet, I can't sign my letters to her "With love." I put, "Sincerely," or "As ever"—*Felice enters far away upstage*—some such brilliant evasion. I've lost the sense of some absolute necessity. Whether I open a book or think of marrying again, it's so damned clear I'm choosing what I do—and it cuts the strings between my hands and heaven. It sounds foolish, but I feel . . . unblessed.

Felice holds up her hand in blessing, then exits.

And I keep looking back to when there seemed to be some duty in the sky. I had a dinner table and a wife—*In the distance Louise appears with a dishcloth, wiping silver, wearing a kitchen apron*—a child and the world so wonderfully threatened by injustices I was born to correct! It seems so fine! Remember—when there were good people and bad people! And how easy it was to tell! The worst son of a bitch, if he loved Jews and hated Hitler, he was a buddy. Like some kind of paradise compared to this.

He is aware of Elsie appearing on second platform; a beach robe hangs from her shoulders, her arms out of the sleeves, her back to us.

Until I begin to look at it. God, when I think of what I believed I want to hide! *Glancing at Elsie:* But I wasn't all that young! A man of thirty-two sees a guest changing out of a wet bathing suit in his bedroom . . .

Elsie, as he approaches, turns to him and her robe slips off one shoulder.

. . . and she stands there with her two bare faces hanging out.

ELSIE: Oh, are you through working? Why don't you swim now? The water's just right.

QUENTIN—*a laugh of great pain, crying out:* I tell you I didn't believe she knew she was naked!

Louise enters and sits at right, as though on the ground. Elsie descends to join her and Quentin follows her with his eyes.

It's Eden! . . . Well, because she was *married*! How could a woman who can tell when the Budapest String Quartet is playing off key; who refuses to wear silk stockings—*Lou enters upstage, reading a brief*—because the Japanese are invading Manchuria; whose husband, my friend, a saintly professor of law, is editing my first appeal to the Supreme Court on the grass outside that window—I could see the top of his head past her tit, for God's sake! Of course I saw, but it's what you allow yourself to admit! To admit what you see endangers principles!

Quentin turns to Louise and Elsie seated on the ground. They are talking in an intense whisper. He now approaches them from behind. Halts, turns to the Listener.

And you know? When two women are whispering, and they stop abruptly when you appear . . .

ELSIE and LOUISE, *turning to him after an abrupt stop to their talking:* Hi.

QUENTIN: The subject must have been sex. And if one of them is your wife . . . she must have been talking about you.

ELSIE, *as though to get him to go:* Lou's behind the house, reading your brief. He says it's superb!

QUENTIN: I hope so, Elsie. I've been kind of nervous about what he'd say.

ELSIE: I wish you'd tell him that, Quentin! Will you? Just how much his opinion means to you. It's important you tell him. It's so enchanting here. *Taking in Louise, standing:* I envy you both so much!

She goes upstage, pausing beside her husband, Lou. He is a very tender, kindly man in shorts; he is absorbed in reading the brief.

I want one more walk along the beach before the train. Did you comb your hair today?

LOU: I think so. *Closing the brief, coming down to Quentin:* Quentin! This is superb! It's hardly like a brief at all; there's a majestic quality, like a classic opinion! *Elsie exits. Lou, chuckling, tugs Quentin's sleeve.* I almost feel honored to have known you!

QUENTIN: I'm so glad, Lou—

LOU, *with an arm around Louise:* Your whole career will change with this! Could I ask a favor?

QUENTIN: Oh, anything, Lou.

LOU: Would you offer it to Elsie, to read? I know it seems an extraordinary request, but—

QUENTIN: No, I'd be delighted.

LOU: It's shaken her terribly—my being subpoenaed and all those damned headlines. Despite everything, it does affect one's whole relationship. So any gesture of respect—for example I gave her the manuscript of my new textbook and I've even called off publication for a while to incorporate her criticisms. It may be her psychoanalysis, but she's become remarkably acute—

LOUISE: My roast! *She exits upstage.*

QUENTIN: But I hope you don't delay it too long, Lou; it'd be wonderful to publish something now. Just to show those bastards.

LOU, *glancing behind him:* But you see, it's a textbook for the schools, and Elsie feels that it will only start a new attack on me.

QUENTIN: But they've investigated you. What more damage could they do?

LOU: Another attack might knock me off the faculty. It's only Mickey's vote that saved me the last time. He made a marvelous speech at the dean's meeting when I refused to testify.

QUENTIN: Well, that's Mickey.

LOU: Yes, but Elsie feels—I'd just be drawing down the lightning again to publish now. And yet to put that book away is like a kind of suicide to me—everything I know is in that book.

QUENTIN: Lou, you have a right to publish; a radical past is not leprosy—we only turned left because it seemed the truth was there. You mustn't be ashamed.

LOU, *in pain:* Goddammit, yes! Except—I never told you this, Quentin. . . . *He holds his position, de-animated.*

QUENTIN, *to Listener, as he comes down to the edge of the stage:* Yes, the day the world ended and nobody was innocent again. God, how swiftly it all fell down!

LOU, *speaking straight front:* When I returned from Russia and published my study of Soviet law—I left out many things I saw. I lied. For a good cause, I thought, but all that lasts is the lie.

Elsie and Louise enter, talking together intimately and unheard.

And it's so strange to me now—I have many failings, but I have never been a liar. And I lied for the Party, over and over, year after year. And that's why now, with this book of mine, I want so much to be true to myself! You see, it's no attack I fear, but being forced to defend my own incredible lies! *He turns, surprised, to see Elsie.*

ELSIE: Lou, I'm quite surprised. I thought we'd settled this.

Father and Dan appear upstage.

LOU: Yes, dear, I only wanted Quentin's feeling—

ELSIE: Your shirt's out, dear.

He quickly tucks it into his shorts. And she turns to Quentin.

You certainly don't think he ought to publish.

QUENTIN: But the alternative seems—

ELSIE, *with a volcanic, suppressed alarm:* But, dear, that's the *situation*! Lou's not like you, Quentin; you and Mickey can function in the rough-and-tumble of private practice, but Lou's a purely academic person. He's *incapable* of going out and—

Upstage, Mother appears beside Father.

LOU, *with a difficult grin and chuckle:* Well, dear, I'm not all that delicate, I—

ELSIE, *with a sudden flash of contempt, to Lou:* This is hardly the time for illusions!

MOTHER: You *idiot*!

Quentin is shocked, turns quickly to Mother, who stands accusingly over the seated Father.

My bonds?

QUENTIN, *watching Mother go:* Why do I think of things falling apart? Were they ever whole?

Mother exits; for a moment Father and Dan stay on in darkness, frozen in their despair.

Louise now stands up.

LOUISE: Quentin?

He turns his eyes to the ground, then to the Listener. . . .

QUENTIN: Wasn't that a terrifying thing, what Holga said?

LOUISE: I've decided to go into psychoanalysis.

QUENTIN: To take up your life—like an idiot child?

LOUISE: I want to talk about some things with you.

QUENTIN: But can anybody really do that? Kiss his life?

LOUISE, *at a loss for an instant:* Sit down, will you?

She gathers her thoughts. He hesitates, as though pained at the memory, and also because at the time he lived this it was an agony. And as he approaches his chair . . .

QUENTIN, *to the Listener:* It was like—a meeting. In seven years we had never had a meeting. Never, never what you'd call—a meeting.

LOUISE: We don't seem—*A long pause while she peers at a forming thought*—married.

QUENTIN: We?

It is sincere, what she says, but she has had to learn the words, so there is the faintest air of a formula in her way of speaking.

LOUISE: You don't pay any attention to me.

QUENTIN, *to help her:* You mean like Friday night? When I didn't open the car door for you?

LOUISE: Yes, that's part of what I mean.

QUENTIN: But I told you; you always opened the car door for yourself.

LOUISE: I've always done everything for myself, but that doesn't mean it's right. Everybody notices it, Quentin.

QUENTIN: What?

LOUISE: The way you behave toward me. I don't exist. People are supposed to find out about each other. I am not all this uninteresting. Many people, men *and* women, think I *am* interesting.

QUENTIN: Well, I—*He breaks off.* I—don't know what you mean.

LOUISE: You have no conception of what a woman is.

QUENTIN: But I do pay attention—just last night I read you my whole brief.

LOUISE: Quentin, you think reading a brief to a woman is talking to her?

QUENTIN: But that's what's on my mind.

LOUISE: But if that's all on your mind, what do you need a wife for?

QUENTIN: Now what kind of a question is that?

LOUISE: Quentin, that's the question!

QUENTIN, *after a slight pause, with fear, astonishment:* What's the question?

LOUISE: What am I to you? Do you—do you ever *ask* me anything? Anything personal?

QUENTIN, *with rising alarm:* But Louise, what am I supposed to ask you? I *know* you!

LOUISE: No. *She stands with dangerous dignity.* You don't know me. *Pause. She proceeds now with caution.* I don't intend to be ashamed of myself any more. I used to think it was normal, or even that you don't see me because I'm not worth seeing. But I think now that you don't really see any woman. Except in some ways your mother. You do sense her feelings; you do know when she's unhappy or anxious, but not me. Or any other woman.

Elsie appears on second platform, about to drop her robe as before.

QUENTIN: That's not true, though. I—

LOUISE: Elsie's noticed it too.

QUENTIN, *guiltily snapping away from the vision of Elsie:* What?

LOUISE: She's amazed at you.

QUENTIN: Why, what'd she say?

LOUISE: She says you don't seem to notice when a woman is *present*.

QUENTIN: Oh. *He is disarmed, confused, and silent.*

LOUISE: And you know how she admires you. *Elsie disappears. Quentin nods seriously. Suddenly he turns to the Listener and bursts into an agonized, ironical laughter. He abruptly breaks it off and returns to silence before Louise. With uncertainty; it is her first attempt at confrontation:* Quentin?

He stands in silence.

Quentin?

He is silent.

Silence is not going to solve it any more, Quentin. I can't live this way.

Pause. Quentin gathers courage.

QUENTIN: Maybe I don't speak because the one time I did tell you my feelings you didn't get over it for six months.

LOUISE, *angered:* It wasn't six months, it was a few weeks. I did over-react, but it's understandable. You come back from a trip and tell me you'd met a woman you wanted to sleep with.

QUENTIN: That's not the way I said it.

LOUISE: It's exactly the way. And we were married a year.

QUENTIN: It is not the way I said it, Louise. It was an idiotic thing to tell you, but I still say I meant it as a compliment; that I did not touch her because I realized what you meant to me. And for damn near a year you looked at me as though I were some kind of a monster who could never be trusted again. *Immediately to the Listener:* And why do I believe she's right! That's the point! Yes—now, now! It's innocence, isn't it? The innocent are always better, aren't they? Then why can't I be innocent?

The tower appears.

Even this slaughterhouse! Why does something in me bow its head like an accomplice in this place!

Mother appears upstage.

Huh? Please, yes, if you think you know. *Turning to Mother:* In what sense treacherous?

MOTHER: What poetry he brought me! He understood me, Strauss. And two weeks after the wedding, Papa hands me the menu. To *read*!

QUENTIN: Huh! Yes! And to a little boy—who knows how to read; a powerful reader, that little boy!

MOTHER: I want your handwriting beautiful, darling; I want you to be . . .

QUENTIN, *realizing:* . . . an accomplice!

MOTHER, *turning on Father, who still sits dejectedly:* My *bonds*? And you don't even tell me anything. Are you a moron? You idiot!

QUENTIN, *watching her and Father go dark, to the Listener:* But why is the world so treacherous?

Mickey appears upstage, faces Louise in silence.

Shall we lay it all to mothers? Aren't there mothers who keep dissatisfaction hidden to the grave, and do not split the faith of sons until they go in guilt for what they did not do? And I'll go further—here's the final bafflement for me—is it altogether good to be not guilty for what another does?

Father and Dan exit in darkness. The tower goes dark.

MICKEY, *to Louise, grinning:* You proud of him?

LOUISE: Yes!

MICKEY, *coming to Quentin, who turns to him:* The brief is fine, kid; it almost began to move me.

LOUISE: Lou and Elsie are here.

MICKEY: Oh! I didn't know. You look wonderful, Louise. You look all excited.

LOUISE: Thanks! It's nice to hear! *She shyly, soundlessly laughs, glancing at Quentin, and goes.*

MICKEY: You got trouble?

QUENTIN, *embarrassed:* I don't think so, she's going into psychoanalysis.

MICKEY: You got trouble. *Shakes his head, laughing thoughtfully.* I think maybe you got married too young; I did too. Although, *you* don't fool around, do you?

QUENTIN: I don't, no.

MICKEY: Then what the hell are you so guilty about?

QUENTIN: I didn't know I was till lately.

MICKEY: You know, when it first happened to me, I set aside five minutes a day just imagining my wife as a stranger. As though I hadn't made her yet. You got to generate some respect for her mystery. Start with five minutes; I can go as long as an hour, now.

QUENTIN: Makes it seem like a game, though, doesn't it?

MICKEY: Well, it is, isn't it, in a way? As soon as there's two people, you can't be absolutely sincere, can you? I mean she's not your rib.

QUENTIN: I guess that's right, yes.

Pause. Lou and Elsie are heard offstage. Mickey walks to a point, looks down as over a cliff.

MICKEY: Dear Lou; look at him down there, he never learned how to swim, always paddled like a dog. *Comes back.* I used to love that man. I still do. Quentin, I've been subpoenaed.

QUENTIN, *shocked:* Oh, God! The Committee?

MICKEY: Yes. I wish you'd have come into town when I called you. But it doesn't matter now.

QUENTIN: I had a feeling it was something like that. I guess I—I didn't want to know any more. I'm sorry, Mick. *To Listener:* Yes, not to see! To be innocent!

A long pause. They find it hard to look directly at each other.

MICKEY: I've been going through hell, Quent. It's strange—to have to examine what you stand for; not theoretically, but on a life-and-death basis. A lot of things don't stand up.

QUENTIN: I guess the main thing is not to be afraid.

MICKEY, *after a pause:* I don't think I am now.

A pause. Both sit staring ahead. Finally Mickey turns and looks at Quentin, who now faces him. Mickey tries to smile.

You may not be my friend any more.

QUENTIN, *trying to laugh it away—a terror rising in him:* Why?

MICKEY: I'm going to tell the truth.

Pause.

QUENTIN: How do you mean?

MICKEY: I'm—going to name names.

QUENTIN, *incredulously:* Why?

MICKEY: Because—I want to. Fifteen years, wherever I go, whatever I talk about, the feeling is always there that I'm deceiving people.

QUENTIN: But why couldn't you just tell about yourself?

Maggie enters, lies down on second platform.

MICKEY: They want the names, and they mean to destroy anyone who—

QUENTIN: I think it's a mistake, Mick. All this is going to pass, and I think you'll regret it. And anyway, Max has always talked against this kind of thing!

MICKEY: I've had it out with Max. I testify or I'll be voted out of the firm.

QUENTIN: I can't believe it! What about DeVries?

MICKEY: DeVries was there, and Burton, and most of the others. I wish you'd have seen their faces when I told them. Men I've worked with for thirteen years. Played tennis; intimate friends, you know? And as soon as I said, "I had been"—stones.

The tower lights.

QUENTIN, *to the Listener:* Everything is one thing! You see—I don't know what we are to one another!

MICKEY: I only know one thing, Quent, I want to live a straight-forward, open life!

Lou enters in bathing trunks, instantly overjoyed at seeing Mickey. The tower goes dark.

LOU: Mick! I *thought* I heard your voice! *Grabs his hand.* How are you!

Lou and Mickey de-animate in an embrace. Holga appears with flowers on upper level.

QUENTIN, *glancing up at Holga:* How do you dare make promises again? I have lived through all the promises, you see?

Holga exits.

LOU, *resuming, moving downstage with Mickey:* Just the question of publishing my book, now. Elsie's afraid it will wake up all the sleeping dogs again.

MICKEY: But don't you have to take that chance? I think a man's got to take the rap, Lou, for what he's done, for what he is. After all, it's your work.

LOU: I feel exactly that way! *Grabs his arm, including Quentin in his feeling.* Golly, Mick! Why don't we get together as we used to! I miss all that wonderful talk! Of course I know how busy you are now, but—

MICKEY: Elsie coming up?

LOU: You want to see her? I could call down to the beach. *He starts off, but Mickey stops him.*

MICKEY: Lou.

LOU, *sensing something odd:* Yes, Mick.

QUENTIN, *facing the sky:* Dear God.

MICKEY: I've been subpoenaed.

LOU: No! *Mickey nods, looks at the ground. Lou grips his arm.* Oh, I'm terribly sorry, Mick. But can I say something—it might ease your mind; once you're in front of them it all gets remarkably simple!

QUENTIN: Oh dear God!

LOU: Everything kind of falls away excepting—one's self. One's truth.

MICKEY, *after a slight pause:* I've already been in front of them, Lou. Two weeks ago.

LOU: Oh! Then what do they want with you again?

MICKEY, *after a pause, with a fixed smile on his face:* I asked to be heard again.

LOU, *puzzled, open-eyed:* Why?

MICKEY—*he carefully forms his thought:* Because I want to tell the truth.

LOU, *with the first rising of incredulous fear:* In—what sense? What do you mean?

MICKEY: Lou, when I left the hearing room I didn't feel I had spoken. Something else had spoken, something automatic and inhuman. I asked myself, what am I protecting by refusing to answer? Lou, you must let me finish! You must. The Party? But I despise the Party, and have for many years. Just like you. Yet there is something, something that closes my throat when I think of telling names. What am I defending? It's a dream now, a dream of solidarity. But the fact is, I have no solidarity with the people I could name—excepting for you. And not because we were Communists together, but because we were young together. Because we—when we talked it was like some brotherhood opposed to all the world's injustice. Therefore, in the name of that love, I ought to be true to myself now. And the truth, Lou, my truth, is that I think the Party *is* a conspiracy—let me finish. I think we *were* swindled; they took our lust for the right and used it for Russian purposes. And I don't think we can go on turning our backs on the truth simply because reactionaries are saying it. What I propose—is that we try to separate our love for one another from this political morass. And I've said nothing just now that we haven't told each other for the past five years.

LOU: Then—what's your proposal?

MICKEY: That we go back together. Come with me. And answer the questions.

LOU: Name—the names?

MICKEY: Yes. I've talked to all the others in the unit. They've agreed, excepting for Ward and Harry. They cursed me out, but I expected that.

LOU, *dazed:* Let me understand—you are asking my permission to name me?

Pause.

You may not mention my name. *He begins physically shaking.* And if you do it, Mickey, you are selling me for your own prosperity. If you use my name I will be dismissed. You will ruin me. You will destroy my career.

MICKEY: Lou, I think I have a right to know exactly why you—

LOU: Because if everyone broke faith there would be no civilization! That is why that Committee is the face of the Philistine! And it astounds me that you can speak of truth and justice in relation to that gang of cheap publicity hounds! Not one syllable will they get from me! Not one word from my lips! No—your eleven-room apartment, your automobile, your money are not worth this.

MICKEY, *stiffened:* That's a lie! You can't reduce it all to money, Lou! *That* is false!

LOU, *turning on him:* There is only one truth here. You are terrified! They have bought your soul!

Elsie appears upstage, listening. Louise enters, watches.

MICKEY, *angrily, but contained:* And yours? Lou! Is it all yours, your soul?

LOU, *beginning to show tears:* How dare you speak of my—

MICKEY, *quaking with anger:* You've got to take it if you're going to dish it out, don't you? Have you really earned this high moral tone—this perfect integrity? I happen to remember when you came back from your trip to Russia; and I remember who made you throw your first version into my fireplace!

LOU, *with a glance toward Elsie:* The idea!

MICKEY: I saw you burn a true book and write another that told lies! Because she demanded it, because she terrified you, because she has taken your soul!

LOU, *shaking his fist in the air:* I condemn you!

MICKEY: But from your conscience or from hers? Who is speaking to me, Lou?

LOU: You are a monster!

Lou bursts into tears, walks off toward Elsie; he meets her in the near distance; her face shows horror. At the front of stage Mickey turns and looks across the full width toward Quentin at the farthest edge of light, and . . .

MICKEY, *reading Quentin's feelings:* I guess you'll want to get somebody else to go over your brief with you. *Pause.* Quent—

Quentin, indecisive, but not contradicting him, now turns to him.

Good-by, Quentin.

QUENTIN, *in a dead tone:* Good-by, Mickey.

Mickey goes out.

ELSIE: He's a *moral idiot!*

Holga enters above. Quentin turns to Elsie; something perhaps in his gaze or in the recesses of her mind makes her close her robe, which she holds tightly shut.

Isn't that *incredible?*

Louise exits.

QUENTIN, *quietly:* Yes.

ELSIE: After such friendship! Such love between them! And for so many years!

She goes to Lou. Lifts him and tenderly leads him off.

The camp tower comes alive, and Quentin moves out of this group, slowly toward it, looking up.

Holga descends, carrying flowers. She is a distance away from Quentin, who turns to her.

QUENTIN: You—love me, don't you?

HOLGA: Yes.

An instant's hesitation, and he turns quickly to Listener and cries out.

QUENTIN: Is it that I'm looking for some simple-minded constancy that never is and never was?

Holga exits. Now Louise approaches him. They are alone.

LOUISE: Quentin, I'm trying to understand why you got so angry with me at the party the other night.

QUENTIN: I wasn't *angry*; I simply felt that every time I began to talk you cut in to explain what I was about to say. *He goes and gets a sheaf of paper, sits.*

LOUISE: Well, I'd had a drink; I was a little high; I felt happy, I guess, that you weren't running for cover when everybody else was.

QUENTIN: Yes, but Max was there and DeVries, and they don't feel they're running for cover. I only want to win Lou's case, not some moral victory over the firm—I felt you were putting me out on a limb.

LOUISE: Quentin, I saw you getting angry when I was talking about that new anti-virus vaccine.

He tries to remember, believing she is right.

What is it? The moment I begin to assert myself it seems to threaten you. I don't think you *want* me to be happy.

QUENTIN—*there is a basic concession made by his tone of admitted bewilderment:* I tell you the truth, Louise, I don't think I feel very sure of myself any more. I'm glad I took on Lou, but it only hit me lately that no respectable lawyer would touch him. It's like some unseen web of connection between people is simply not there. And I always relied on it, somehow; I never quite believed that people could be so easily disposed of. And it's larger than the political question. I think it's got me a little scared.

LOUISE, *with a wish for his sympathy, not accusing:* Well, then, you must know how I felt when I found that letter in your suit.

QUENTIN, *turning to her, aware:* I didn't do that to dispose of you, Louise. *She does not reply.* I thought we'd settled about that girl. Is that what this is about? *She still does not reply.* You mean you think I'm still—

LOUISE, *directly at him:* I don't know what you're doing. I thought you told the truth about that other girl years ago, but after what happened again this spring—I don't know anything.

QUENTIN, *after a pause:* Tell me something; until this party the other night—in fact this whole year, I thought you seemed much happier. I swear to God, Louise, I thought we were building something till the other night!

LOUISE: But why?

QUENTIN: I've been trying like hell to show what I think of you. You've seen that, haven't you?

LOUISE: Quentin, you are full of resentment against me, you think I'm blind?

QUENTIN: What I resent is being forever on trial, Louise. Are you an innocent bystander here?

LOUISE: I said I did contribute; I demanded nothing for much too long.

QUENTIN: You mean the summer before last you didn't come to me and say that if I didn't change you would divorce me?

LOUISE: I never said I was *planning* a—

QUENTIN: You said if it came down to it you would divorce me—that's not a contribution?

LOUISE: Well, it certainly ought not send a man out to play doctor with the first girl he could lay his hands on.

QUENTIN: How much shame do you want me to feel? I hate what I did. But, I think I've explained it—I felt like nothing; I shouldn't have, but I did, and I took the only means I knew to—

LOUISE: This is exactly what I mean, Quentin—you are still defending it. Right now.

He is stopped by this truth.

QUENTIN: Look, you're—not at all to blame, hey?

LOUISE: But how?

QUENTIN: Well, for example—you never turn your back on me in bed?

LOUISE: I never turned my—

QUENTIN: You have turned you back on me in bed, Louise, I am not insane!

LOUISE: Well, what do you expect? Silent, cold, you lay your hand on me?

QUENTIN, *fallen:* Well, I—I'm not very demonstrative, I guess. *Slight pause. He throws himself on her compassion.* Louise—I worry about you all day. And all night.

LOUISE—*it is something, but not enough:* Well, you've got a child; I'm sure that worries you.

QUENTIN, *deeply hurt:* Is that all?

LOUISE, *with intense reasonableness:* Look, Quentin, you want a woman to provide an—atmosphere, in which there are never any issues, and you'll fly around in a constant bath of praise—

QUENTIN: Well, I wouldn't mind a little praise, what's wrong with praise?

LOUISE: Quentin, I am not a praise machine! I am not a blur and I am not your mother! I am a separate person!

QUENTIN, *staring at her, and what lies beyond her:* I see that now.

LOUISE: It's no crime! Not if you're adult and grown-up!

QUENTIN, *quietly:* I guess not. But it bewilders me. In fact, I got the same idea when I realized that Lou had gone from one of his former students to another and none would take him—

LOUISE: What's Lou got to do with it? I think it's admirable that you—

QUENTIN: Yes, but I am doing what you call an admirable thing because I can't bear to be—a separate person. I think so. I really don't want to be known as a Red lawyer; and I really don't want the newspapers to eat me alive; and if it came down to it Lou could defend himself. But when that decent, broken man who never wanted anything but the good of the world sits across my desk—I don't know how to say that my interests are no longer the same as his, and that if he doesn't change I consign him to hell because we are separate persons!

LOUISE: You are completely confused! Lou's case has nothing—

QUENTIN, *grasping for his thought:* I am telling you my confusion! I think Mickey also became a separate person—

LOUISE: You're incredible!

QUENTIN: I think of my mother, I think she almost became—

LOUISE: Are you identifying *me* with—

QUENTIN: Louise, I am asking you to explain this to me because this is when I go blind! When you've finally become a separate person, what the hell is there?

LOUISE, *with a certain unsteady pride:* Maturity.

QUENTIN: I don't know what that means.

LOUISE: It means that you know another person exists, Quentin. I'm not in analysis for nothing.

QUENTIN, *questing:* It's probably the symptom of a typical case of some kind, but I swear, Louise, if you would just once, of your own will, as right as you are—if you would come to me and say that something, something important was your fault and that you were sorry, it would help.

In her pride she is silent, in her refusal to be brought down again.

Louise?

LOUISE: Good God! What an idiot! *She exits.*

QUENTIN: Louise . . .

He looks at his papers, the lights change. A sprightly music is heard. Anonymous park loungers appear and sit or lie about.

How few the days are that hold the mind in place; like a tapestry hung on four or five hooks. Especially the day you stop becoming; the day you merely are. I suppose it's when the principles dissolve, and instead of the general gray of what ought to be you begin to see what is. Even the bench by the park seems alive, having held so many actual men. The word "now" is like a bomb through the window, and it ticks.

An old woman crosses with a caged parrot.

Now a woman takes a parrot for a walk. What will happen to it when she's gone? Everything suddenly has consequences.

A plain girl in tweeds passes, reading a paperback.

And how bravely a homely woman has to be! How disciplined of her, not to set fire to the Museum of Art.

A Negro appears, in pantomime asking for a light, which Quentin gives him.

And how does he keep so neat, and the bathroom on another floor? He must be furious when he shaves.

The Negro hurries off, seeing his girl.

Alone: And whatever made me think that at the end of the day I absolutely had to go home?

Maggie appears, looking about for someone, as Quentin sits on "park bench."

Now there's a truth; symmetrical, lovely skin, undeniable.

MAGGIE: 'Scuse me, did you see a man with a big dog?

QUENTIN: No. But I saw a woman with a little bird.

MAGGIE: No, that's not him. Is this the bus stop?

QUENTIN: Ya, the sign says—

MAGGIE, *sitting beside him:* I was standing over there and a man came with this big dog and just put the leash in my hand and walked away. So I started to go after him but the dog wouldn't move. And then this other man came and took the leash and went away. But I don't think it's really his dog. I think it's the first man's dog.

QUENTIN: But he obviously doesn't want it.

MAGGIE: But maybe he wanted for me to have it. I think the other man just saw it happening and figured he could get a free dog.

QUENTIN: Well, you want the dog?

MAGGIE: How could I keep a dog? I don't even think they allow dogs where I live. What bus is this?

QUENTIN: Fifth Avenue. This is the downtown side. Where do you want to go?

MAGGIE, *after thinking:* Well, I could go there.

QUENTIN: Where?

MAGGIE: Downtown.

QUENTIN: Lot of funny things go on, don't they?

MAGGIE: Well, he probably figured I would like a dog. Whereas I would if I had a way to keep it, but I don't even have a refrigerator.

QUENTIN: Yes. That must be it. I guess he thought you had a refrigerator.

She shrugs. Pause. He looks at her as she watches for the bus. He has no more to say.

LOUISE, *appearing:* You don't talk to any woman—not like a *woman!* You think reading your brief is *talking* to me?

She exits. In tension Quentin leans forward, arms resting on his knees. He looks at Maggie again.

QUENTIN, *with an effort:* What do you do?

MAGGIE, *as though he should know:* On the switchboard. *Laughs.* Don't you remember me?

QUENTIN, *surprised:* Me?

MAGGIE: I always sort of nod to you every morning through the window.

QUENTIN, *after an instant:* Oh. In the reception room!

MAGGIE: Sure! Maggie! *Points to herself.*

QUENTIN: Of course! You get my numbers sometimes.

MAGGIE: Did you think I just came up and started talking to you?

QUENTIN: I had no idea.

MAGGIE—*laughs:* Well, what must you have thought! I guess it's that you never saw me altogether. I mean just my head through that little window.

QUENTIN: Well, it's nice to meet all of you, finally.

MAGGIE—*laughs:* You go back to work again tonight?

QUENTIN: No, I'm just resting for a few minutes.

MAGGIE, *with a sense of his loneliness:* Oh. That's nice to do that. *She looks idly about. He glances down her body as she rises.* Is that my bus down there?

QUENTIN: I'm not really sure where you want to go. . . .

A man appears, eyes her, glances up toward the bus, back to her, staring.

MAGGIE: I wanted to find one of those discount stores; I just bought a phonograph but I only have one record. I'll see you! *She is half backing off toward the man.*

MAN: There's one on Twenty-seventh and Sixth Avenue.

MAGGIE, *turning, surprised:* Oh, thanks!

QUENTIN, *standing:* There's a record store around the corner, you know.

MAGGIE: But is it discount?

QUENTIN: Well, they all discount—

MAN, *slipping his hand under her arm:* What, ten per cent? Come on, honey, I'll get you an easy fifty per cent off.

MAGGIE, *to the man, starting to move off with him:* Really? But a Perry Sullivan . . . ?

MAN: Look, I'll give it to you—I'll give you two Perry Sullivans. Come on!

MAGGIE—*she halts, suddenly aware, disengages her arm, backs:* 'Scuse me, I—I—forgot something.

MAN, *reaching toward her:* Look, I'll give you ten records. *Calls off:* Hold that door! *Grabs her.* Come on!

QUENTIN, *moving toward him:* Hey!

MAN, *letting her go, to Quentin:* Ah, get lost! *He rushes off.* Hold it, hold the door!

Quentin watches the "bus" go by, then turns to her. She is absorbed in arranging her hair—but with a strangely doughy expression, removed.

QUENTIN: I'm sorry, I thought you knew him.

MAGGIE: No. I never saw him.

QUENTIN: Well—what were you going with him for?

MAGGIE: He said he knew a store. Where's the one you're talking about?

QUENTIN: I'll have to think a minute. Let's see . . .

MAGGIE: Could I sit with you? While you're thinking?

QUENTIN: Sure!

They return to the bench. He waits till she is seated; she is aware of the politeness, glances at him as he sits. Then she looks at him fully, for some reason amazed.

That happen to you very often?

MAGGIE, *factually:* Pretty often.

QUENTIN: It's because you talk to them.

MAGGIE: But they talk to me, so I have to answer.

QUENTIN: Not if they're rude. Just turn your back.

MAGGIE—*she thinks about that, and indecisively:* Oh, okay. *As though remotely aware of another world, his world:* Thanks, though—for stopping it.

QUENTIN: Well, anybody would.

MAGGIE: No, they laugh. I'm a joke to them. You—going to rest here very long?

QUENTIN: Just a few minutes. I'm on my way home—I never did this before.

MAGGIE: Oh! You look like you always did. Like you could sit for hours under these trees, just thinking.

QUENTIN: No. I usually go right home. *Grinning:* I've always gone right home.

MAGGIE: See, I'm still paying for the phonograph, whereas they don't sell records on time, you know.

QUENTIN: They're afraid they'll wear out, I guess.

MAGGIE: Oh, that must be it! I always wondered. 'Cause you *can* get phonographs. How'd you know that?

QUENTIN: I'm just guessing.

MAGGIE, *laughing:* I can never guess those things! I don't know why they do anything half the time! *She laughs more deeply. He does.* I had about ten or twenty records in Washington, but my friend got sick, and I had to leave. *Pause. Thinks.* His family lived right over there on Park Avenue.

QUENTIN: Oh. Is he better?

MAGGIE: He died. *Tears come into her eyes quite suddenly.*

QUENTIN, *entirely perplexed:* When was this?

MAGGIE: Friday. Remember they closed the office for the day?

QUENTIN: You mean—*Astounded*—Judge Cruse?

MAGGIE: Ya.

QUENTIN: Oh, I didn't know that you—

MAGGIE: Yeah.

QUENTIN: He was a great lawyer. And a great judge too.

MAGGIE, *rubbing tears away:* He was very nice to me.

QUENTIN: I was at the funeral; I didn't see you, though.

MAGGIE, *with difficulty against her tears:* His wife wouldn't let me come. I got into the hospital before he died. But the family pushed me out and—I could hear him calling, "Maggie . . . Maggie!" *Pause.* They kept trying to offer me a thousand dollars. But I didn't want anything, I just wanted to say good-by to him! *She opens her purse, takes out an office envelope, opens it.* I have a little of the dirt. See? That's from his grave. His chauffeur drove me out—Alexander.

QUENTIN: Did you love him very much?

MAGGIE: No. In fact, a couple of times I really left him.

QUENTIN: Why didn't you altogether?

MAGGIE: He didn't want me to.

QUENTIN: Oh. *Pause.* So what are you going to do now?

MAGGIE: I'd love to get that record if I knew where they had a discount—

QUENTIN: No, I mean in general.

MAGGIE: Why, they going to fire me now?

QUENTIN: Oh, I wouldn't know about that.

MAGGIE: Although I'm not worried. Whereas I can always go back to hair.

QUENTIN: To where?

MAGGIE: I used to demonstrate hair preparations. *Laughs, squirts her hair with an imaginary bottle.* You know, in department stores? I was almost on TV once. *Tilting her head under his chin:* It's because I have very thick hair, you see? I have my mother's hair. And it's not broken. You notice I have no broken hair? Most women's hair is broken. Here, feel it, feel how—*She has lifted his hand to her head and suddenly lets go of it.* Oh, 'scuse me!

QUENTIN: That's all right!

MAGGIE: I just thought you might want to feel it.

QUENTIN: Sure.

MAGGIE: Go ahead. I mean if you want to. *She leans her head to him again. He touches the top of her head.*

QUENTIN: It is, ya! Very soft.

MAGGIE, *proudly:* I once went from page boy to bouffant in less than ten minutes!

QUENTIN: What made you quit?

A student sitting nearby looks at her.

MAGGIE: They start sending me to conventions and all. You're supposed to entertain, you see.

QUENTIN: Oh yes.

MAGGIE: There were parts of it I didn't like—any more. *She looks at the student, who turns away in embarrassment.* Aren't they sweet when they look up from their books!

The student walks off, mortified. She turns with a laugh to Quentin. He looks at her warmly, smiling. A clock strikes eight in a distant tower.

QUENTIN: Well, I've got to go now.

MAGGIE: 'Scuse me I put your hand on my head.

QUENTIN: Oh, that's all right. I'm not *that* bad. *He laughs softly, embarrassed.*

MAGGIE: It's not bad to be shy.

Pause. They look at each other.

QUENTIN: You're very beautiful, Maggie.

She smiles, straightens as though his words had entered her.

And I wish you knew how to take care of yourself.

MAGGIE: Oh . . . *Holding a ripped seam in her dress:* I got this torn on the bus this morning. I'm going to sew it home.

QUENTIN: I don't mean that.

She meets his eyes again—she looks chastised.

Not that I'm criticizing you. I'm not at all. You understand?

She nods, absorbed in his face.

MAGGIE: I understand. I think I'll take a walk in the park.

QUENTIN: You shouldn't. It's getting dark.

MAGGIE: But it's beautiful at night. I slept there one night when it was hot in my room.

QUENTIN: God, you don't want to do that. *Glancing at the park loungers:* Most of the animals around here are not in the zoo.

MAGGIE: Okay. I'll get a record, then. 'Scuse me about my hair if I embarrassed you.

QUENTIN, *laughing:* You didn't.

MAGGIE, *touching the top of her head as she backs away:* It's just that it's not broken. *He nods.* I'm going to sew this home. *He nods. She indicates the park, upstage.* I didn't *mean* to sleep there. I just fell asleep.

Several young men now rise, watching her.

QUENTIN: I understand.

MAGGIE: Well . . . see you! *Laughs.* If they don't fire me!

QUENTIN: 'By.

She passes two men who walk step for step behind her, whispering in her ear together. She doesn't turn or answer. Now a group of men is beginning to surround her. Quentin, in anguish, goes and draws her away from them.

Maggie! *He takes a bill from his pocket, moving her across stage.* Here, why don't you take a cab? It's on me. Go ahead, there's one right there! *Points and whistles upstage and right.* Go on, grab it!

MAGGIE: Where—where will I tell him to go but?

QUENTIN: Just cruise in the Forties—you've got enough there.

MAGGIE: Okay, 'by! *Backing out:* You—you just going to rest more?

QUENTIN: I don't know.

MAGGIE: Golly, that's nice!

The men walk off as Louise enters between Quentin and Maggie, continuing to her seat downstage. Maggie turns and goes to the second platform and lies down as before. Quentin moves down toward Louise, stands a few yards from her, staring at her optimistically. She remains unaware of him, reading.

QUENTIN: Yes. She has legs, breasts, mouth, eyes . . . how beautiful! A woman of my own! What a miracle! In my own house! *He bends and kisses Louise who looks up at him surprised, perplexed, lighting a cigarette.* Hi. *She keeps looking up at him, aware of some sea-like opening in the world.* What's the matter? *She still doesn't speak.* Well, what's the matter?

LOUISE: Nothing.

She returns to her book. Mystified, disappointed, he stands watching, then opens his briefcase and begins taking out papers.

Close the door if you're going to type.

QUENTIN: I always do.

LOUISE: Not always.

QUENTIN: Almost always. *He almost laughs, he feels loose, but she won't be amused, and returns again to her book.* How about eating out tomorrow night? Before the parents' meeting?

LOUISE: What parents' meeting?

QUENTIN: The school.

LOUISE: That was tonight.

QUENTIN, *shocked:* Really?

LOUISE: Of course. I just got back.

QUENTIN: Why didn't you remind me when I called today? You know I often forget those things. I told you I wanted to talk to her teacher.

LOUISE, *just a little more sharply:* People do what they want to do, Quentin. *An unwilling shout:* And you said you had to work tonight! *She returns to her book.*

QUENTIN: I didn't work.

LOUISE, *keeping to her book: I* know you didn't work.

QUENTIN, *surprised, an alarm beginning:* How did you know?

LOUISE: Well, for one thing, Max called here at seven-thirty.

QUENTIN: Max? What for?

LOUISE: Apparently the whole executive committee was in his office, waiting to meet with you tonight. *His hand goes to his head; open alarm shows on his face.* He called three times, as a matter of fact.

QUENTIN: My God, I— How could I do that? What's his home number?

LOUISE: The book is in the bedroom.

QUENTIN: We were supposed to discuss my handling Lou's case. DeVries stayed in town tonight just to—settle everything. *Breaks off.* What's Max's number, Murray Hill 3 . . . what is it?

LOUISE: The book is next to the bed.

QUENTIN: You remember it, Murray Hill 3, something.

LOUISE: It's in the book.

Pause. He looks at her, puzzled.

I'm not the keeper of your phone numbers. You can remember them just as well as I. Please don't use that phone, you'll wake her up.

QUENTIN, *turning:* I had no intention of calling in there.

LOUISE: I thought you might want to be private.

QUENTIN: There's nothing "private" about this. This concerns the food in your mouth. The meeting was called to decide whether I should separate from the firm until Lou's case is over—or permanently, for all I know. *Remembering the number, he goes to the phone.* I've got it—Murray Hill 3 . . .

She watches him go to the phone. He picks it up, dials one digit. And much against her will . . .

LOUISE: That's the old number.

QUENTIN: Murray Hill 3-4598.

LOUISE: It's been changed. *A moment.* Cortland 7-7098.

QUENTIN—*she is not facing him; he senses what he thinks is victory:* Thanks. *Starts again to dial, puts down the phone.* I don't know what to say to him. *She is silent.* We arranged for everybody to come back after dinner. It'll sound idiotic that I forgot about it.

LOUISE: You were probably frightened.

QUENTIN: But I made notes all afternoon about what I would say tonight! It's incredible!

LOUISE, *with an over-meaning:* You probably don't realize how frightened you are.

QUENTIN: I guess I don't. He said a dreadful thing today—Max. He was trying to argue me into dropping Lou and I said, "We should be careful not to adopt some new behavior just because there's hysteria in the country." I thought it was a perfectly ordinary thing to say but he—he's never looked at me that way, like we were suddenly standing on two distant mountains; and he said, "I don't know of any hysteria. Not in this office."

LOUISE: But why does all that surprise you? Max is not going to endanger his whole firm to defend a Communist. You tend to make relatives out of people.

QUENTIN: You mean . . .

LOUISE: I mean you can't have everything; if you feel this strongly about Lou you probably will have to resign.

QUENTIN, *after a pause:* You think I should?

LOUISE: That depends on how deeply you feel about Lou.

QUENTIN: I'm trying to determine that; I don't know for sure. What do you think?

LOUISE, *in anguish:* It's not my decision, Quentin.

QUENTIN, *puzzled and surprised:* But aren't you involved?

LOUISE: Of course I'm involved.

QUENTIN: I'm only curious how you—

LOUISE: You? Curious about me?

QUENTIN: Oh. We're not talking about what we're talking about, are we?

LOUISE, *nodding in emphasis:* You have to decide what you feel about a certain human being. For once in your life. And then maybe you'll decide what you feel about other human beings. Clearly and decisively.

QUENTIN: In other words . . . where was I tonight.

LOUISE: I don't care where you were tonight.

QUENTIN, *after a pause:* I sat by the park for a while. And this is what I thought. *With difficulty:* I don't sleep with other women, but I think I behave as though I do. *She is listening; he sees it and is enlivened by hope.* Maybe I invite your suspicion in order to—to come down off some bench, to stop judging others so perfectly. Because I do judge, and harshly too, when the fact is I'm bewildered. I wonder if I left that letter for you to read about that girl—in order somehow to start being real. *Against his own trepidation but encouraged by her evident uncertainty:* I met a girl tonight. Just happened to come by, one of the phone operators in the office. I probably shouldn't tell you this, but I will. Quite stupid, silly kid. Sleeps in the park, her dress ripped. She said some ridiculous things. But one thing struck me; she wasn't defending anything, upholding anything, or accusing—she was just *there*, like a tree or a cat. And I felt strangely abstract beside her. And I saw that we are killing one another with abstractions. I'm defending Lou because I love him, yet the society transforms that love into a kind of treason, what they call an issue, and I end up suspect and hated. Why can't we speak with the voice that speaks below the "issues"—with our real uncertainty? I came home just now—and I had a tremendous wish to come out—to you. And you to me. It sounds absurd, but this city is full of people rushing to meet one another. This city is full of lovers.

LOUISE: And what did she say?

QUENTIN: I guess I shouldn't have told you about it.

LOUISE: Why not?

QUENTIN: Louise, I don't know what's permissible to say any more.

LOUISE, *nodding:* You don't know how much to hide.

QUENTIN, *angering:* All right, let's not hide anything; it would have been easy to make love to her. *Louise reddens, stiffens.* And I didn't because I thought of you, and in a new way—like a stranger I had never gotten to know. And by some miracle you were waiting for me, in my own home.

LOUISE: What do you want, my congratulations? You don't imagine a real woman goes to bed with any man who happens to come along? Or that a real man goes to bed with every woman who'll have him? Especially a slut, which she obviously is?

QUENTIN: How do you know she's a—

LOUISE, *laughing:* Oh, excuse me, I didn't mean to insult her! You're unbelievable! Suppose I came home and told you I'd met a man on the street I wanted to go to bed with—because he made the city seem full of lovers.

QUENTIN, *humiliated:* I understand. I'm sorry. I would get angry too but I would see that you were struggling. And I would ask myself—maybe I'd even be brave enough to ask you—how *I* had failed.

LOUISE: Well, you've given me notice; I get the message. *She starts out.*

QUENTIN: Louise, don't you ever doubt yourself? Is it enough to prove a case, to even win it—*Shouts*—when we are dying?

Mickey enters at the edge of the stage. Elsie enters on second platform, opening her robe as before.

LOUISE, *turning, in full possession:* I'm not dying. I'm not the one who wanted to break this up. And that's all it's about. It's all it's been about the last three years. You don't want me. *She goes out.*

QUENTIN, *to himself:* God! Can that be true?

MICKEY: There's only one thing I can tell you for sure, kid—don't ever be guilty.

QUENTIN: Yes! *Seeking strength, he stretches upward.* Yes! *But his conviction wavers; he turns toward the vision.* But if you had felt more guilt, maybe you wouldn't have . . .

ELSIE, *closing her robe:* He's a moral idiot!

QUENTIN: Yes! That is right. And yet . . . What the hell is moral? And what am I, to even ask that question? A man ought to know—a decent man knows that like he knows his own face!

Louise enters with a folded sheet and a pillow.

LOUISE: I don't want to sleep with you.

QUENTIN: Louise, for God's sake!

LOUISE: You are disgusting!

QUENTIN: But in the morning Betty will see . . .

LOUISE: You should have thought of that.

The phone rings. He looks at sheets, makes no move to answer.

Did you give her this number?

It rings again.

Did you give her this number? *With which she strides to the phone.* Hello! Oh, yes. He's here. Hold on, please.

QUENTIN: I can't sleep out here; I don't want her to see it. *He goes to the phone with a look of hatred.*

LOUISE: It's Max.

Surprised, he takes the phone from her.

QUENTIN, *into phone:* Max? I'm sorry, the whole thing just slipped my mind. I don't know how to explain it, I just went blank, I guess. *Pause.* The radio? No, why? . . . *What?* When? *Long pause.* Thanks . . . for letting me know. Yes, he was. Good night . . . Ya, see you in the morning. *Hangs up. Pause. He stands staring.*

LOUISE: What is it?

QUENTIN: Lou. Was killed by a subway train tonight.

LOUISE—*gasps:* How?

QUENTIN: They don't know. They say "fell or jumped."

LOUISE: He couldn't have! The crowd must have pushed him!

QUENTIN: There is no crowd at eight o'clock. It was eight o'clock.

LOUISE: But *why*? Lou *knew* himself! He knew where he *stood*! It's impossible!

QUENTIN, *staring:* Maybe it's not enough—to know yourself. Or maybe it's too much. I think he did it.

LOUISE: But *why*? It's inconceivable!

QUENTIN: When I saw him last week he said a dreadful thing. I tried not to hear it. *Pause. She waits.* That I turned out to be the only friend he had.

LOUISE, *genuinely:* Why is that dreadful?

QUENTIN, *evasively, almost slyly:* It just was. I don't know why. *Tears forming in his eyes, he comes toward Listener.* I didn't dare know why! But I dare now. It was dreadful because I was not his friend either, and he knew it. I'd have stuck it to the end but I hated the danger in it for myself, and he saw through my faithfulness; and he was not telling me what a friend I was, he was praying I would be—"Please be my friend, Quentin" is what he was saying to me, "I am drowning, throw me a rope!" Because I wanted out, to be a good American again, kosher again—and proved it in the joy . . . the joy . . . the joy I felt now that my danger had spilled out on the subway track! So it is not bizarre to me.

The tower blazes into life, and he walks with his eyes upon it.

This is not some crazy aberration of human nature to me. I can easily see the perfectly normal contractors and their cigars, the carpenters, plumbers, sitting at their ease over lunch pails; I can see them laying the pipes to run the blood out of this mansion; good fathers, devoted sons, grateful that someone else will die, not they, and how can one understand that, if one is innocent? If somewhere in one's soul there is no accomplice—of that joy, that joy, that joy when a burden dies . . . and leaves you safe?

Maggie's difficult breathing is heard. He turns in pain from it, comes to a halt on one side of the sheets and pillow lying on the floor at Louise's feet.

I've got to sleep; I'm very tired. *He bends to pick up the sheets. She makes an aborted move to pick up the pillow.*

LOUISE, *with great difficulty:* I—I've always been proud you took Lou's case. *He picks up sheets and pillow, stands waiting.* It was—courageous. *She stands there, empty-handed, not fully looking at him.*

QUENTIN: I'm glad you feel that way. *But he makes no move either. The seconds are ticking by. Neither can let down his demand for apology, or grace. With difficulty:* And that you told me. Thanks.

LOUISE: But—you are honest, that way. I've often told you.

QUENTIN: Recently?

LOUISE: Good night.

She starts away, and he feels the unwillingness with which she leaves.

QUENTIN: Louise, if there's one thing I've been trying to do it's to be honest with you.

LOUISE: No, you've been trying to keep the home fires burning and see the world at the same time.

QUENTIN: So that all I am is deceptive and cunning.

LOUISE: Not all, but mostly.

QUENTIN: And there is no struggle. There is no pain. There is no struggle to find a way back to you?

LOUISE: That isn't the struggle.

QUENTIN: Then what are you doing here?

LOUISE: I—

QUENTIN: What the hell are you compromising yourself for if you're so goddamned honest!

He starts a clench-fisted move toward her and she backs away, terrified and strangely alive. Her look takes note of the aborted violence, and she is very straight and yet ready to flee.

LOUISE: I've been waiting for the struggle to begin.

He is dumbstruck—by her sincerity, her adamance. With a straight look at him, she turns and goes out.

QUENTIN, *alone, and to himself:* Good God, can there be more? Can there be worse? *Turning to the Listener:* See, that's what's incredible to me—three years more! What did I expect to save us? Suddenly, God knows why, she'd hold out her hand and I hold out mine, and laugh, laugh it all away, laugh it all back to—her dear, honest face looking up to mine . . . *Breaks off, staring into the distance. Far upstage, Louise looks at him with pride, as of old.* Back to some everlasting smile that saves. That's maybe why I came; I think I still believe it. That underneath we're all profoundly friends! I can't believe this world; all this hatred isn't real to me! *Turns back to his "living room," the sheets. Louise is gone now.* To bed down like a dog in my living room, how can that be necessary? Then go in to her, open your heart, confess the lechery, the mystery of women, say it all. . . . *He has moved toward where she exited, now halts.* But I did that. So the truth, after all, may merely be murderous? The truth killed Lou, destroyed Mickey. Then how do you live? A workable lie? But that comes from a clear conscience! Or a dead one. Not to see one's own evil—there's power! And rightness too!—so kill conscience. Kill it. *Glancing toward her exit:* Know all, admit nothing, shave closely, remember birthdays, open car doors, pursue Louise not with truth but with attention. Be uncertain on your own time, in bed be absolute. And thus be a man—and join the world. And in the morning, a dagger in that dear little daughter's heart! *Flinging it toward Louise's exit:* Bitch! *Sits.* I'll say I have a cold. Didn't want to give it to Mommy. *With disgust:* Pah! Papapapapa. *Sniffs, tries to talk through his nose.* Got a cold in my nose, baby girl . . .

He groans. Pause. He stares; stalemate. A jet plane is heard. An airport porter appears, carrying two bags, as Holga, dressed for travel, moves onto the highest level, looking about for Quentin. A distant jet roars in take-off. Quentin glances at his watch, and, coming down to the chair . . .

Six o'clock, Idlewild. *Now he glances up at Holga, who is still looking about her as in a crowd.* It's that the evidence is bad for promises. But how else do you touch the world—except with a promise? And yet, I must not forget the way I wake; I open up my eyes each morning like a boy, even now; even now. That's as true as anything I know, but where's the evidence? Or is it simply that my heart still beats? . . . Certainly, go ahead, I'll wait.

He follows the departing Listener with his eyes; now he rises, follows "him" upstage.

You don't mind my staying? I'd like to settle this. Although actually, I—*Laughs*—only came to say hello.

He turns front. He stares ahead; a different kind of relaxation is on him now, alone. The stage is dark but for a light on him. Now the tower is seen, and Maggie on the second platform near him. Suddenly she raises herself up.

MAGGIE: Quentin? Quentin?

QUENTIN, *in agony:* I'll get to it, honey. *He closes his eyes.* I'll get to it.

He strikes sparks from a lighter held to a cigarette. All light is gone.

ACT TWO

The stage is dark. A spark is seen, a flame fires up. When the stage illuminates, Quentin is discovered lighting his cigarette—no time has passed. He continues to await the Listener's return and walks a few steps in thought, and as he does a jet plane is heard, and the airport announcer's voice: ". . . from Frankfurt is now unloading at gate nine, passengers will please . . ." It becomes a watery garble, and at the same moment Holga, as before, walks onto the upper level with the airport porter, who leaves her bags and goes. She looks about as in a crowd, then, seeing "Quentin," stands on tiptoe and waves.

HOLGA: Quentin! Here! Here! *She opens her arms as he evidently approaches.* Hello! Hello!

He turns from her to the returned Listener at front and comes to him downstage. Holga moves out.

QUENTIN: Oh, that's all right, I didn't mind waiting. How much time do I have?

He sits at the forward edge of the stage, looks at his watch. Maggie appears on the second platform, in a lace wedding dress; Lucas, a designer, is on his knees, finishing the vast hem. Carrie, a Negro maid, stands by, holding her veil. Maggie is nervous, on the edge of life, looking into a mirror.

I think I can be clearer now.

MAGGIE, *in an ecstasy of fear and hope:* All right, Carrie, tell him to come in! *As though trying the angular words:* My *husband!*

CARRIE, *walking a few steps to a point, where she halts:* You can see her now, Mr. Quentin.

314

They are gone. Quentin continues to the Listener.

QUENTIN: I am bewildered by the death of love. And my responsibility for it.

Holga moves into light again, looking about for him at the airport.

This woman's on my side; I have no doubt of it. And I wouldn't want to outlive another accusation. Not hers.

Holga exits. He stands, agitated.

I suddenly wonder why I risk it again. Except . . .

Felice and Mother appear.

You ever felt you once saw yourself—absolutely true? I may have dreamed it, but I swear that somewhere along the line—with Maggie, I think—for one split second I saw my life; what I had done, what had been done to me, and even when I ought to do. And that vision sometimes hangs behind my head, blind now, bleached out like the moon in the morning; and if I could only let in some necessary darkness it would shine again. I think it had to do with power.

Felice approaches, about to remove the bandage.

Maybe that's why she sticks in my mind. *He walks around her, peering.* Well, that's power, isn't it? To influence a girl to change her nose, her life? . . . It does, yes, it frightens me, and I wish to God—*Felice raises her arm*—she'd stop blessing me! *Mother exits on upper platform. He laughs uneasily, surprised at the force of his fear.* Well, I suppose because there is a fraud involved; I have no such power.

Maggie suddenly appears in man's pajamas, talking into a phone, coming down to the bed, center.

MAGGIE, *with timid idolatry:* Hello? Is— How'd you know it's me? *Laughs as she lies down.* You really remember me? Maggie? From that park that day? Well, 'cause it's almost four years so I . . .

He comes away from her as she continues talking, unheard.

QUENTIN, *to the Listener, glancing from Maggie to Felice:* I do, yes, I see the similarity.

Laughter is heard as Holga appears at a café table, an empty chair beside her, the music of a café fiddle in the air.

HOLGA, *to an empty seat beside her:* I love the way you eat! You eat like a Pasha, a grand duke!

QUENTIN, *to Listener, looking toward her:* Yes, adored again! But . . . there is something different here. *As he moves toward Holga, he says to Listener:* Now keep me to my theme, I spoke of power.

He sits beside her. As he speaks now, Holga's aspect changes; she becomes moody, doesn't face him, seems hurt. And, sitting beside her, he speaks to the Listener.

We were in a café one afternoon in Salzburg, and quite suddenly, I don't know why—it all seemed to be dying between us. And I saw it all happening again. You know that moment, when you begin desperately to talk about architecture?

HOLGA: Fifteen thirty-five. The Archbishop designed it himself.

QUENTIN: Beautiful.

HOLGA, *distantly:* Yes.

QUENTIN, *as though drawing on his courage, suddenly turning to her:* Holga. I thought I noticed your pillow was wet this morning.

HOLGA: It really isn't anything important.

QUENTIN: There are no unimportant tears.

HOLGA: I feel sometimes—*Breaks off, then:* —that I'm boring you.

LOUISE, *entering upstage:* I am not all this uninteresting, Quentin!

He stares at her, trying to join this with his lost vision, and in that mood he turns out to the Listener.

QUENTIN: The question is power, but I've lost the . . . Yes! *He springs up and circles Louise.* I tell you there were times when she looked into the mirror and I saw she didn't like her face, and I wanted to step between her and her suffering.

HOLGA: I may not be all that interesting.

QUENTIN, *of Louise:* I felt guilty even for her face! But . . . with her— *He returns to the café table*—there was some new permission . . . not to blind her to her own unhappiness. I saw that it belonged to her as mine belonged to me. And suddenly there was only good will and a mystery.

HOLGA: I wish you'd believe me, Quentin; you have no duty here.

QUENTIN: Holga, I would go. But I know I'd be looking for you tomorrow.

Mother enters, taking Holga's place on the seat beside him. He continues speaking without pause.

But there's truth in what you feel. The time does come when I feel I must go. Not toward anything, or away from you. . . . But there is some freedom in the going.

MOTHER: Darling, there is never a depression for great people! The first time I felt you move, I was standing on the beach at Rockaway. . . .

Quentin has gotten up.

QUENTIN, *to Listener:* But power. Where is the . . .

MOTHER: And I saw a star, and it got bright, and brighter, and brighter! And suddenly it fell, like some great man had died, and you were being pulled out of me to take his place, and be a light, a light in the world!

QUENTIN, *to Listener:* Why is there some . . . air of treachery in that?

FATHER, *suddenly appearing with Dan behind him, to Mother:* What the hell are you talking about? We're just getting started again. I need him!

Quentin avidly turns from one to the other as they argue.

MOTHER: You've got Dan, you don't need him! He wants to try to get a job, go to college maybe.

FATHER: He's got a job!

MOTHER: He means with pay! I don't want his young years going by. He wants a life!

FATHER, *indicating Dan; they have surrounded Quentin:* Why don't *he* "want a life"?

MOTHER: Because he's different!

FATHER: Because *he* knows what's right! *Indicating Mother and Quentin together:* You're two of a kind—what you "want"! Chrissake, when I was his age I was supporting six people! *He comes up to Quentin.* What are you, a stranger? What are you!

QUENTIN, *peering into the revulsion on his father's face:* Yes, I felt a power, in the going . . . and treason in it. Because there's failure, and you turn your back on failure . . .

Father exits with Mother.

FATHER: I need him!

DAN, *putting an arm around Quentin:* No, kid, don't feel that way. I just want to see him big again, but you go. I'll go back to school if things pick up.

QUENTIN, *peering at Dan, who has walked on past him and is talking to an invisible Quentin:* Yes, good men stay . . . although they die there . . .

DAN, *indicating a book in his hand, addressing an invisible Quentin:* It's my Byron, I'll put it in your valise, and I've put in my new Argyles, just don't wash them in hot water. And remember, kid, wherever you are . . . *A train whistle is heard far off. Dan rushes onto second platform, calling:* Wherever you are, this family's behind you! So buckle down, now, I'll send you a list of books to read.

Mother, Father, and Dan disappear, waving farewell. Felice is gone.

MAGGIE, *suddenly sitting up on her bed, addressing an empty space at the foot:* But could I read them?

QUENTIN, *spinning about in quick surprise:* Huh!

All the others have gone dark but him and Maggie.

MAGGIE: I mean what kind of books? 'Cause, see—I never really graduated high school. Although I always liked poetry.

QUENTIN—*breaks his stare at her and quickly comes down to the Listener:* It's that I can't find myself in this vanity any more.

MAGGIE, *enthralled, on bed:* I can't hardly believe you came! Can you stay five minutes? I'm a singer now, see? In fact—*With a laugh at herself*—I'm in the top three. And for a long time I been wanting to tell you that . . . none of it would have happened to me if I hadn't met you that day.

QUENTIN: Why do you speak of love? All I can see now is the power she offered me. All right. *Turns to her in conflict, and unwillingly.* I'll try. *He approaches her.*

MAGGIE: I'm sorry if I sounded frightened on the phone but I didn't think you'd be in the office after midnight. *Laughs at herself nervously.* See, I only pretended to call you. Can you stay like five minutes?

QUENTIN, *backing into the chair:* Sure. Don't rush.

MAGGIE: That's what I mean, you know I'm rushing! Would you like a drink? Or a steak? They have two freezers here. My agent went to Jamaica so I'm just staying here this week till I go to London Friday. It's the Palladium, like a big vaudeville house, and it's kind of an honor but I'm a little scared to go.

QUENTIN: Why? I've heard you; you're marvelous. Especially . . . *He can't remember a title.*

MAGGIE: No, I'm just flapping my wings yet. But did you read what that *News* fellow wrote? He keeps my records in the 'frigerator, case they melt!

QUENTIN—*laughs with her, then recalls:* "Little Girl Blue"! It's very moving, the way you do that.

MAGGIE: Really? 'Cause, see, it's not I say to myself, "I'm going to sound sexy," I just try to come *through*—like in love or . . . *Laughs.* I really can't believe you're here!

QUENTIN: Why? I'm glad you called; I've often thought about you the last couple of years. All the great things happening to you gave me a secret satisfaction for some reason.

MAGGIE: Maybe 'cause you did it.

QUENTIN: Why do you say that?

MAGGIE: I don't know, just the way you looked at me. I didn't even have the nerve to go see an agent before that day.

QUENTIN: *How did* I look at you?

MAGGIE, *squinching up her shoulders, a mystery:* Like . . . out of your *self*. Most people, they . . . just look *at* you. I can't explain it. And the way you talked to me . . .

LOUISE, *who has been sitting right, playing solitaire:* You think reading your brief is talking to me?

MAGGIE: What did you mean—it gave you a secret satisfaction?

QUENTIN: Just that—like in the office, I'd hear people laughing that Maggie had the world at her feet—

MAGGIE, *hurt, mystified:* They laughed!

QUENTIN: In a way.

MAGGIE, *in pain:* That's what I mean; I'm a joke to most people.

QUENTIN: No, it's that you say what you mean, Maggie. You don't seem to be upholding anything, you're not—ashamed of what you are.

MAGGIE: W—what do you mean, of what I am?

Louise looks up. She is playing solitaire.

QUENTIN, *suddenly aware he has touched a nerve:* Well . . . that you love life, and . . . It's hard to define, I . . .

LOUISE: The word is tart. But what did it matter as long as she praised you?

QUENTIN, *to Listener, standing, and moving within Maggie's area:* There's truth in it—I hadn't had a woman's praise, even a girl I'd laughed at with the others—

MAGGIE: But you didn't, did you?

He turns to her in agony.

Laugh at me?

QUENTIN: No. *He suddenly stands and cries out to Listener.* Fraud! From the first five minutes! . . . Because! I should have agreed she *was* a joke, a beautiful piece, trying to take herself seriously! Why did I lie to her, play this cheap benefactor, this—*Listens, and now unwillingly he turns back to her.*

MAGGIE: Like when you told me to fix where my dress was torn? You wanted me to be—proud of myself. Didn't you?

QUENTIN, *surprised:* I guess I did, yes. *To Listener:* By God I did!

MAGGIE, *feeling she has budged him:* Would you like a drink?

QUENTIN, *relaxing:* I wouldn't mind. *Glancing around:* What's all the flowers?

MAGGIE, *pouring:* Oh, that's that dopey prince or a king or whatever he is. He keeps sending me a contract—whereas I get a hundred thousand dollars if we ever divorce. I'd be like a queen or something, but I only met him in El Morocco *once! She laughs, handing him his drink.* I'm supposed to be his girl friend too! I don't know why they print those things.

QUENTIN: Well, I guess everybody wants to touch you now.

MAGGIE: Cheers! *They drink; she makes a face.* I hate the taste but I love the effect! Would you like to take off your shoes? I mean just to rest.

QUENTIN: I'm okay. I thought you sounded on the phone like something frightened you.

MAGGIE: Do you have to go home right away?

QUENTIN: Are you all alone here?

MAGGIE: It's okay. Oh hey! I cut your picture out of the paper last month. When you were defending that Reverend Harley Barnes in Washington? *Taking a small framed photo from under her pillow:* See? I framed it!

QUENTIN: Is something frightening you, Maggie?

MAGGIE: No, it's just you're here! It's odd how I found this—I went up to see my father—

QUENTIN: He must be very proud of you now.

MAGGIE, *laughing:* Oh, no—he left when I was eighteen months, see— 'cause he said I wasn't from him, although my mother always said I was. And they keep interviewing me now and I never know what to answer, when they ask where you were born, and all. So I thought if he would just see me, and you know, just—look at me . . . I can't explain it.

QUENTIN: Maybe so you'll know who you are.

MAGGIE: Yes! But he wouldn't even talk to me on the phone—just said, "See my lawyer," and hung up. But on the train back there was your picture, right on the seat looking up at me. And I said, "I know who I am! I'm Quentin's friend!" But don't worry about it—I mean you could just be somebody's friend, couldn't you?

QUENTIN, *after a slight pause:* Yes, Maggie, I can be somebody's friend. It's just that you're so beautiful—and I don't only mean your body and your face.

MAGGIE: You wouldn't even have to see me again. I would do anything for you, Quentin—you're like a god!

QUENTIN: But anybody would have told you to mend your dress.

MAGGIE: No, they'd have laughed or tried for a quick one. You know.

QUENTIN, *to Listener:* Yes! It's all so clear—the honor! The first honor was that I hadn't tried to go to bed with her! She took it for a tribute to her "value," and I was only afraid! God, the hypocrisy! . . . But why do you speak of love?

MAGGIE: Oh hey! You know what I did because of you? *He turns back to her.* I was christening a submarine in the Groton shipyard; 'cause I was voted the favorite of all the workers! And I made them bring about ten workers up on the platform, whereas they're the ones built it, right? And you know what the admiral said? I better watch out or I'll be a Communist. And suddenly I thought of you and I said, "I don't know what's so terrible; they're for the poor people." Isn't that what you believe?

QUENTIN: I did but it's a lot more complicated, honey.

MAGGIE: Oh! I wish I knew something.

QUENTIN: You know how to see it all with your own eyes, Maggie, that's more important than all the books.

MAGGIE: But you know if it's true. What you see.

QUENTIN, *puzzled:* You frightened *now?* . . . You are, aren't you? *Maggie stares at him in tension; a long moment passes.* What is it, dear? You afraid to be alone here? *Pause.* Why don't you call somebody to stay with you?

MAGGIE: I don't know anybody . . . like that.

QUENTIN, *after a slight pause:* Can I do anything? . . . Don't be afraid to ask me.

MAGGIE, *in a struggle, finally:* Would you . . . open that closet door?

QUENTIN—*looks off, then back to her:* Just open it?

MAGGIE: Yes.

He walks into the dark periphery; she sits up warily, watching. He opens a "door." He returns. And she lies back.

QUENTIN: Do you want to tell me something? I'm not going to laugh. *Sits.* What is it?

MAGGIE, *with great difficulty:* When I start to go to sleep before. And suddenly I saw smoke coming out of that closet under the door. Kept coming and coming. It start to fill the whole room!

She breaks off, near weeping. He reaches and takes her hand.

QUENTIN: Oh, kid—you've often dreamed such things, haven't you?

MAGGIE: But I was awake!

QUENTIN: Well it was a waking dream. It just couldn't stay down till you went to sleep. These things can be explained if you trace them back.

MAGGIE: I know. I go to an analyst.

QUENTIN: Then tell him about it, you'll figure it out.

MAGGIE: It's when I start to call you before. *She is now absorbed in her own connections.* See, my mother—she used to get dressed in the closet. She was very—like moral, you know? But sometimes she'd smoke in there. And she'd come out—you know? with a whole cloud of smoke around her.

QUENTIN: Well—possibly you felt she didn't want you to call me.

MAGGIE, *astounded:* How'd you know that?

QUENTIN: You said she was so moral. And here you're calling a married man.

MAGGIE: Yes! She tried to kill me once with a pillow on my face 'cause I would turn out bad because of—like her sin. And I have her hair, and the same back. *She turns half to him, showing a naked back.* 'Cause I have a good back, see? Every masseur says.

QUENTIN: Yes, it is. It's beautiful. But it's no sin to call me.

MAGGIE, *shaking her head like a child with a relieved laugh at herself:* Doesn't make me bad. Right?

QUENTIN: You're a very moral girl, Maggie.

MAGGIE, *delicately and afraid:* W—what's moral?

QUENTIN: You tell the truth, even against yourself. You're not pretending to be—*Turns out to the Listener, with a dread joy*—innocent! Yes, that suddenly there was someone who—could not club you to death with their innocence! And now it's all laughable!

Mother appears, raising her arm. Louise exits.

MOTHER: I saw a star . . .

MAGGIE: I bless you, Quentin! *Mother vanishes as he turns back to Maggie, who takes up his photo again.* Lots of nights, I take your picture, and I bless you. You mind? *She has pressed the picture against her cheek.*

QUENTIN: I hope you sleep.

MAGGIE: I will now! *Lies back.* Honestly! I feel . . . all clear!

QUENTIN, *with a wave of his hand:* Good luck in London.

MAGGIE: And—what's moral, again?

QUENTIN: To live the truth.

MAGGIE: That's you!

QUENTIN: Not yet, dear; but I intend to try. Don't be afraid to call me if you need any help. *She is suddenly gone. Alone, he continues the thought.* Any time—*Dan appears in crew-necked sweater with his book*—you need anything, you call, y'hear?

DAN: This family's behind you, Quentin. *Backing into darkness, with a wave of farewell as train whistle sounds:* Any time you need anything . . .

QUENTIN—*surprised, he has turned quickly to Dan, who disappears; and to the Listener, as he still stares at the empty space Dan has left:* You know? It isn't fraud, but some . . . disguise. I came to her like Dan—his goodness! No wonder I can't find myself!

Felice appears as Maggie exits. She is about to remove the bandage, and he grasps for the concept.

And that girl the other night. When she left. It's still not clear, but suddenly those two fixtures on my wall. *He walks toward a "wall," looking up.* I didn't do it, but I wanted to. Like—*He turns and spreads his arms in crucifixion*—this! *In disgust, he lowers his arms.* I don't know! Because she . . . *gave* me something! The power to change her! As though I—*Cries out*—felt something for her! *He almost laughs.* What the hell am I trying to do, love *everybody*?

The line ends in self-contempt and anger. And suddenly, extremely fast, a woman appears in World War I costume—a Gibson Girl hat and veil over her face, ankle-length cloak, and in her hand a toy sailboat. She is bent over, as though offering the boat to a little boy, and her voice is like a whisper, distant, obscure. Father enters, calling, followed by Dan.

MOTHER: Quentin? Look what we brought you from Atlantic City—from the boardwalk!

The boy evidently runs away; Mother instantly is anxious and angering and rushes to a point and halts, as though calling through a closed door.

Don't lock this door! But darling, we didn't trick you, we took Dan because he's older and I wanted a rest! But Fanny told you we were coming back, didn't she? Why are you running that water? Quentin, stop that water! Ike, come quick! Break down the door! Break down the door! *She has rushed off into darkness.*

But a strange anger is on his face, and he has started after her. And to the Listener . . .

QUENTIN: They sent me out for a walk with the maid. When I came back the house was empty. God, why is betrayal the only truth that sticks? I adored that woman. It's monstrous I can't mourn her!

The park bench lights. Maggie appears in a heavy white man's sweater, a white angora skating cap over a red wig, moccasins and sun glasses.

MAGGIE, *to the empty bench:* Hi! It's me! Maggie!

QUENTIN: Or mourn her either. . . . No, it's not that I think I killed her. It's . . .

MAGGIE, *to the empty bench:* See? I told you nobody recognizes me!

QUENTIN: . . . that I can't find myself in it. Either the guilt comes or the innocence! But where's my love or even my crime? And I tell you I saw it once! I saw *Quentin* here!

MAGGIE: Golly, I fell asleep the minute you left, the other night! You like my wig? See? And moccasins!

Slight pause. Now he smiles, comes beside her on the bench.

QUENTIN: All you need is roller skates.

MAGGIE, *clapping her hands with joy:* You're funny!

QUENTIN, *half to Listener:* I keep forgetting—*Wholly to her*—how beautiful you are. Your eyes make me shiver.

She is silent for a moment, adoring.

MAGGIE: Like to see my new apartment? There's no elevator even, or a doorman. Nobody would know. If you want to rest before you go to Washington. *He doesn't reply.* 'Cause I just found out—I go to Paris after London.

QUENTIN: So . . . how long will you be gone?

MAGGIE: It's maybe two months, I think. *They both arrive at the same awareness—the separation is pain. Tears are in her eyes.* Quentin?

QUENTIN: Honey . . . *Takes her hand.* Don't look for anything more from me.

MAGGIE: I'm not! But if I went to Washington . . . I could register in the hotel as Miss None.

QUENTIN: N-u-n?

MAGGIE: No—"n-o-n-e"—like nothing. I made it up once 'cause I can never remember a fake name, so I just have to think of nothing and that's me! *She laughs with joy.* I've done it.

QUENTIN: It *is* a marvelous thought. The whole government's hating me, and meanwhile back at the hotel . . .

MAGGIE: That's what I mean! Just when that committee is knocking on your head you could think of me like naked—

QUENTIN: What a lovely thought!

MAGGIE: And it would make you happy.

QUENTIN, *smiling warmly at her:* And nervous.

MAGGIE: Because it should all be one one thing, you know? Helping people, and sex. You might even argue better the next day!

QUENTIN, *with a new awareness, astonishment:* You know? There's one word written on your forehead.

MAGGIE: What?

QUENTIN: "Now."

MAGGIE: But what else is there?

QUENTIN: A future. And I've been carrying it around all my life, like a vase that must never be dropped. So you can't ever touch anybody, you see?

MAGGIE: But why can't you just hold it in one hand?—*He laughs*—and touch with the other! I would never bother you, Quentin. *He looks at his watch, as though beginning to calculate if there might not be time. Maggie, encouraged, glances at his watch.* Just make it like when you're thirsty. And you drink and walk away, that's all.

QUENTIN: But what about you?

MAGGIE: Well . . . I would have what I gave.

QUENTIN: You're all love, aren't you?

MAGGIE: That's all I am! A person could die any minute, you know. *Suddenly:* Oh, hey! I've got a will! *Digging into her pocket, she brings out a folded sheet of notepaper.* But is it legal if it's not typewritten?

QUENTIN, *taking it:* What do you want with a will? *He starts reading the will.*

MAGGIE: I'm supposed to be like a millionaire in about two years! And I've got to do a lot of flying now.

QUENTIN, *looking at her:* Who wrote this?

MAGGIE: Jerry Moon. He's a friend of my agent Andy in the building business, but he knows a lot about law. He signed it there for a witness. I saw him sign it. In my bedroom—

QUENTIN: It leaves everything to the agency.

MAGGIE: I know, but just for temporary, till I can think of somebody to put down.

QUENTIN: Don't you have anybody at all?

MAGGIE: No!

QUENTIN: What's all the rush?

MAGGIE: Well, in case Andy's plane goes down. He's got five children, see, and his—

QUENTIN: But do you feel responsible for his family?

MAGGIE: Well, no. But he did help me, he loaned me money when I—

QUENTIN: A million dollars?

Two boys enter upstage, carrying baseball gloves.

MAGGIE, *with a dawning awareness and fear:* Well, not a million . . .

QUENTIN: Who's your lawyer?

MAGGIE: Well, nobody.

QUENTIN, *with a certain unwillingness, even a repugnance about interfering— he sounds neutral:* Didn't anybody suggest you get your own lawyer?

MAGGIE: But if you trust somebody you trust them—don't you?

Slight pause. A decision seizes him; he takes her hand.

QUENTIN: Come on, I'll walk you home.

MAGGIE, *as she stands with him:* Okay! 'Cause what's good for Andy's good for me, right?

QUENTIN: I can't advise you, honey, maybe you get something out of this that I don't understand. Let's go.

MAGGIE: No! I'm not involved with Andy. I . . . don't really sleep around with everybody, Quentin! *He starts to take her but she continues.* I was with a lot of men but I never got anything for it. It was like charity, see. My analyst said I gave to those in need. Whereas, I'm not an institution. You believe me?

QUENTIN, *wanting her feverishly:* I believe you. Come on.

A small gang of boys with baseball equipment obstructs them; one of the first pair points at her.

BOY: It's Maggie, I told you!

MAGGIE, *pulling at Quentin's arm, defensively, but excited:* No, I just look like her, I'm Sarah None!

QUENTIN: Let's go! *He tries to draw her off, but the boys grab her, and she begins accepting pencils and pieces of paper to autograph.* Hey!

CROWD: How about an autograph, Maggie! Whyn't you come down to the club! When's your next spectacular! Hey, Mag, I got all your records! Sing something! *Handing over a paper for her to sign:* For my brother, Mag! Take off your sweater, Mag, it's hot out! How about that dance like you did on TV!—*A boy wiggles sensuously.*

QUENTIN: That's enough!

Quentin has been thrust aside; he now reaches in, grabs her, and draws her away as she walks backward, still signing, laughing with them. And into darkness, and the boys gone, and she turns to him.

MAGGIE: I'm sorry!

QUENTIN: It's like they're eating you. You like that?

MAGGIE: No, but they're just people. Could you sit down till the train? All I got so far is this French Provincial. *Taking off her sweater:* You like it? I picked it out myself. And my bed, and my record player. But it could be a nice apartment, couldn't it?

In silence Quentin takes her hand; now he draws her to him; now he kisses her.

MAGGIE: I love you, Quentin. I would do anything for you. And I would never bother you, I swear.

QUENTIN: You're so beautiful it's hard to look at you.

MAGGIE: You didn't even see me! *Backing away:* Why don't you just stand there and I'll come out naked! Or isn't there a later train?

QUENTIN, *after a pause:* Sure. There's always a later train. *He starts unbuttoning his jacket.*

MAGGIE: I'll put music!

QUENTIN—*now he laughs through his words:* Yeah, put music! *He strives for his moment; to the Listener as he opens his jacket:* Here; it was somewhere here! I don't know, a—a fraud!

A driving jazz comes on.

MAGGIE: Here, let me take off your shoes!

Father, Mother, Dan enter. Maggie drops to his feet, starting to unlace. Stiffly, with a growing horror, he looks down at her. Now shapes move in the darkness.

QUENTIN: Maggie?

MAGGIE, *looking up from the floor, leaving off unlacing:* Yes?

He looks around in the darkness; and suddenly his father charges forward.

FATHER: What you *want*! Always what you *want*! Chrissake, *what are you!*

Now Louise appears, reading a book, but Dan is standing beside her, almost touching her with his hand.

DAN: This family's behind you, kid.

And Mother, isolated, moving almost sensuously—and Quentin is pressed, as though by them, away from Maggie.

QUENTIN, *roaring out to all of them, his fists angrily in air against them:* But where is *Quentin?*

MOTHER: Oh, what poetry he brought me, Strauss, and novels to read . . .

QUENTIN, *going toward Mother in her longing:* Yes, yes! But I know that treason! And the terror of complicity in that desire; yes, and not to be unworthy of these loyal, failing men! But where is Quentin? Instead of taking off my clothes, this—posture! Maggie—

MAGGIE: Okay. Maybe when I get back . . .

QUENTIN: You . . . have to tear up that will. *To Listener:* Can't even go to bed without a principle! But how can you speak of love, she was chewed and spat out by a long line of grinning men! Her name floating in the stench of locker rooms and parlor-car cigar smoke! She had the truth that day, I brought the lie that she had to be "saved"! From what? Except my own contempt!

MAGGIE, *to the empty space where Quentin was:* But even my analyst said it was okay. 'Cause a person like me has to have somebody.

QUENTIN: Maggie—honest men don't draw wills like that.

MAGGIE: But it's just for temporary—

QUENTIN: Darling, if I went to Andy, and this adviser, and the analyst too, perhaps—I think they'd offer me a piece, to shut up. They've got you on a table, honey, and they're carving you—

MAGGIE: But . . . I can't spend all that money anyway! I can't even *think* over twenty-five dollars!

QUENTIN: It's not the money they take, it's the dignity they destroy. You're not a piece of meat; you seem to think you owe people whatever they demand!

MAGGIE: I know. *She lowers her head with a cry, trembling with hope and shame.*

QUENTIN, *tilting up her face:* But Maggie, you're somebody! You're not a kid any more, running around looking for a place to sleep! It's not only your success or that you're rich—you're straight, you're serious, you're first-class, people *mean* something to you; you don't have to go begging shady people for advice like some—some tramp! *With a sob of love and desperation she slides to the floor and grasps his thighs, kissing his trousers. He watches, then suddenly lifts her, and with immense pity and hope:* Maggie, stand up!

The music flies in now, and she smiles strangely through her tears, and with a kind of statement of her persisting nature begins unbuttoning her blouse. Maggie's body writhes to the beat within her clothing. And as soon as she starts her dance, his head shakes—and to the Listener . . .

No, not love; to stop impersonating, that's all! To live—*Groping*—to live in good faith if only with my guts! To—*To Dan and Father:* Yes! To be "good" no more! Disguised no more! *To Mother:* Afraid no more to show what Quentin, Quentin, Quentin—is!

LOUISE: You haven't even the decency to . . .

A high tribunal appears, and a flag; a chairman bangs his gavel once; he is flanked by others looking down on Quentin from on high.

QUENTIN: That decency is murderous! Speak truth, not decency. I curse the whole high administration of fake innocence! *To the chairman:* I declare it, I am not innocent!—nor good!

CHAIRMAN: But surely Reverend Barnes cannot object to answering whether he attended the Communist-run Peace Congress in Prague, Czechoslovakia. No—no, counsel will not be allowed to confer with the witness, this is not a trial! Any innocent man would be—

QUENTIN: And this question—innocent! How many Negroes you allow to vote in your patriotic district? And which of your social, political, or racial sentiments would Hitler have disapproved? And not a trial? You fraud, your "investigators" this moment are working in this man's church to hound him out of it!

HARLEY BARNES, *rising to his feet, wearing a clerical collar:* I decline on the grounds of the First and Fifth Amendments to the Constitution.

QUENTIN, *with intense sorrow:* But are we sure, Harley—I ask it, I ask it—if the tables were turned, and they were in front of you, would you permit *them* not to answer? Hateful men that they are? *Harley looks at him indignantly, suspiciously.* I am not sure what we are upholding any more—are we good by merely saying no to evil? Even in a righteous "no" there's some disguise. Isn't it necessary—to say—*Harley is gone, and the tribunal; Maggie is there, snapping her fingers, letting down her hair—* to finally say yes—to *something*? *Turning toward Maggie, who lies down on the bed:* Yes, yes, yes.

MAGGIE: Say anything to me.

QUENTIN, *looking down at her:* A fact . . . a fact . . . a fact, a thing.

MAGGIE: Sing inside me.

Quentin crosses to Listener.

QUENTIN: Even condemned, unspeakable like all truth!

MAGGIE: Become happy.

QUENTIN: Contemptible like all truth.

MAGGIE: That's all I am.

QUENTIN: Covered like truth with slime: blind, ignorant.

MAGGIE: But nobody ever said to me, stand up!

QUENTIN: The blood's fact, the world's blind gut—yes!

MAGGIE: Now.

QUENTIN, *sitting before the Listener, his back to Maggie:* To this, yes.

MAGGIE: Now . . . Now. *Pause.* Quentin? *She rises off the bed, drawing the blanket around her, and in a languid voice addresses a point upstage.* Quenny? That soap is odorless, so you don't have to worry. *Slight pause.* It's okay! Don't rush; I love to wait for you! *She glances down at the floor.* I love your shoes. You have good taste! *She moves upstage.* 'Scuse me I didn't have anything for you to eat, but I didn't know! I'll get eggs, though, case maybe in the mornings. And steaks—case at night. I mean just in case. You could have it just the way you want, just any time. *She turns, looking front.* Like me?

Holga appears above, in the airport, looking about for him.

QUENTIN, *to the Listener, his back to Maggie:* It's all true, but it isn't the truth. I know it because it all comes back so cheap; I loved that girl. My bitterness is making me lie. I'm afraid. To make a promise. *Glancing up at Holga:* Because I don't know who'll be making it. I'm a stranger to my life.

MAGGIE—*she has lifted a "tie" off the floor:* Oh, your tie got all wrinkled! I'm sorry! But hey, I have a tie! It's beautiful, a regular man's tie. *Catching herself:* I . . . just happen to have it! *She laughs it off and goes into darkness. Holga is gone.*

QUENTIN: I tell you, below this fog of tawdriness and vanity, there is a law in this disaster, and I saw it as hard and clear as a statute. But I think I saw it . . . with some love. Or can one ever remember love? It's like trying to summon up the smell of roses in a cellar. You might see a rose, but never the perfume. And that's the truth of roses, isn't it—the perfume?

On the second platform Maggie appears in light in a wedding dress; Carrie, a Negro maid, is just placing a veiled hat on her head; Lucas, a designer, is on his knees, hurriedly fixing the last hem, as before. Maggie is turning herself, wide-eyed, in an unseen mirror. Quentin begins to rise.

MAGGIE: Hurry, Lucas, the ceremony is for three! Hurry, please! *Lucas sews faster.*

QUENTIN, *to Listener:* I want to see her with . . . that love again! Why is it so hard? Standing there, that wishing girl, that victory in lace.

MAGGIE, *looking ahead on the edge of life as Lucas bites off the last threads:* You won't hardly know me any more, Lucas! He saved me, I mean it! I've got a new will and I even changed my analyst—I've got a wonderful doctor now! And we're going to do all my contracts over, which I never got properly paid. And Ludwig Reiner's taking me! And he won't take even opera singers unless they're, you know, like artists! No matter how much you want to pay him. I didn't even dare, but Quentin made me go—and now he took me, Ludwig Reiner, imagine!

Now she turns, seeing Quentin entering. An awe of the moment takes them both; Lucas goes. Carrie lightly touches Maggie's forehead and silently prays.

QUENTIN: Oh, my darling. How perfect you are.

MAGGIE, *descending toward him:* Like me?

Clergyman and woman guest enter on second platform.

QUENTIN: Good God! To come home every night—to *you!*

He starts for her, open-armed, laughing, but she touches his chest, excited and strangely fearful.

MAGGIE: You still don't have to do it, Quentin. I could just come to you whenever you want.

QUENTIN: You just can't believe in something good really happening. But it's real, darling, you're my wife!

MAGGIE, *with a hush of fear on her voice:* I want to tell you why I went into analysis.

QUENTIN: Darling, you're always making new revelations, but—

MAGGIE: But you said we have to love what happened, didn't you? Even the bad things?

QUENTIN, *seriously now, to match her intensity:* Yes, I did.

Clergyman and woman exit.

MAGGIE: I . . . was with two men . . . the same day.

She has turned her eyes from him. A group of wedding guests appears on second platform.

I mean the same day, see. *She almost weeps now, and looks at him, subservient and oddly chastened.* I'll always love you, Quentin. But we could just tell them we changed our mind—

QUENTIN: Sweetheart—an event itself is not important; it's what you took from it. Whatever happened to you, this is what you made of it, and I love this! *Quickly to Listener:* Yes!—that we conspired to violate the past, and the past is holy and its horrors are holiest of all! *Turning back to Maggie:* And . . . something . . . more . . .

MAGGIE, *with hope now:* Maybe . . . it would even make me a better wife, right?

QUENTIN: That's the way to talk!

Elsie enters above and joins group of guests.

MAGGIE, *with gladness, seeing a fruit of past pain:* 'Cause I'm not curious! You be surprised, these so-called respectable women, they smile and their husbands never know, but they're curious. But I *know* all that, so I know I have a king! But there's people who're going to laugh at you!

QUENTIN: Not any more, dear, they're going to see what I see. Come!

MAGGIE, *not moving with him:* What do you see? Tell me! *Bursting out of her:* 'Cause I think . . . you were ashamed once, weren't you?

QUENTIN: I see your suffering, Maggie; and once I saw it, all shame fell away.

MAGGIE: You . . . were ashamed!?

QUENTIN, *with difficulty:* Yes. But you're a victory, Maggie, you're like a flag to me, a kind of proof, somehow, that people can win.

Louise enters upstage, brushing her hair.

MAGGIE: And you—you won't ever look at any other woman, right?

QUENTIN: Darling, a wife can be loved!

MAGGIE, *with a new intensity of conflict:* Before, though—why did you kiss that Elsie?

QUENTIN: Just hello. She always throws her arms around people.

MAGGIE: But—why'd you let her rub her body against you?

QUENTIN, *laughing:* She wasn't rub—

MAGGIE, *downing a much greater anxiety:* I saw it. And you stood there.

QUENTIN, *trying to laugh:* Maggie, it was a meaningless gesture—

MAGGIE: You want me to be like I used to be—like it's all a fog? *Now pleadingly, and faintly wronged:* You told me yourself that I have to look for the meaning of things, didn't you? Why did you let her do that?

QUENTIN: She came up to me and threw her arms around me, what could I do?

MAGGIE, *in a flash of frightened anger:* Just tell her to knock it off!

QUENTIN, *taken aback:* I . . . don't think you want to sound like this, honey.

WOMAN GUEST: Ready! Ready!

The guests line up on the steps, forming a corridor for Maggie and Quentin.

QUENTIN: Come, they're waiting.

He puts her arm in his; they turn to go. A wedding march is heard.

MAGGIE, *almost in tears:* Teach me, Quentin! I don't know how to be! Forgive me I sounded that way.

QUENTIN, *as against the vision of Louise:* No. *Say* what you feel; the truth is on our side; always say it!

MAGGIE, *with a plea, but going on toward the guests:* You're not holding me!

QUENTIN, *half the stage away now, and turning toward the empty air, his arm still held as though he were walking beside her:* I am, darling, I'm with you!

MAGGIE, *moving along the corridor of guests:* I'm going to be a good wife. I'm going to be a good wife.

CARRIE: God bless this child.

MAGGIE, *faltering as she walks into darkness:* Quentin, I don't feel it!

The wedding march is gone. Louise exits upstage.

QUENTIN, *both frustrated and with an appeal to her, moving downstage with ''her'' on his arm:* I'm holding you! See everybody smiling, adoring you? Look at the orchestra guys making a V for victory! Everyone loves you, darling! Why are you sad?

Suddenly, from the far depths of the stage, she calls out with a laugh and hurries on in a fur coat, indicating a wall at front.

MAGGIE: Surprise! You like it? They rushed it while we were away!

QUENTIN—*they are half a stage apart:* Yes, it's beautiful!

MAGGIE: See how large it makes the living room? *Rushing toward left:* And I want to take down that wall too! Okay?

QUENTIN, *not facing in her direction; to his memory of it:* But we just finished putting those walls in.

MAGGIE: Well, it's only money; I want it big, like a castle for you!

QUENTIN: It's lovely, dear, but we're behind in the taxes.

MAGGIE: Used to say, I have one word written on my forehead. Why can't it be beautiful now? I get all that money next year.

QUENTIN: But you owe almost all of it—

MAGGIE: Don't hold the future like a vase—touch now, touch me! I'm here, and it's now!

She rushes into semi-darkness, where she is surrounded by Carrie, a dresser, and a secretary.

QUENTIN, *against himself, alone on the forestage:* Okay! Tear it down! Make it beautiful! Do it now! Maybe I *am* too cautious . . . Forgive me!

Her voice is suddenly heard in a recorded vocal number. He breaks into a genuine smile of joy and dances for a moment alone, as a group of executives surround Maggie. Now Maggie appears in a gold dress out of the group of cautiously listening executives. Quentin rushes to her.

QUENTIN: Maggie, sweetheart—that's magnificent!

MAGGIE, *worried, uncertain:* No! Tell me the truth! That piano's off, you're not listening!

A pianist, wearing sunglasses and smoking, emerges from the group listening to the record.

QUENTIN: But nobody'll ever notice that!

MAGGIE: I notice it. Don't you want me to be good? I *told* Weinstein I wanted Johnny Block, but they give me this fag and he holds back my beat!

The pianist walks away, silently insulted.

QUENTIN: But you said he's one of the best.

MAGGIE: I said Johnny Block was best, but they wouldn't pay his price. I make millions for them and I'm still some kind of a joke.

QUENTIN: Maybe I ought to talk to Weinstein. . . . *He hurries to a point upstage.*

MAGGIE, *calling after him:* No, don't get mixed up in my crummy business, you've got an important case—

QUENTIN: Weinstein, get her Johnny Block! *Turning back to her as a new version of the number comes on:* There now! Listen now! *She flies into his arms. The executives leave, gesturing their congratulations.* See? There's no reason to get upset.

MAGGIE: Oh, thank you, darling!

QUENTIN: Just tell me and I'll talk to these people any time you . . .

The music goes out.

MAGGIE: See? They respect you. Ask Ludwig Reiner, soon as you come in the studio my voice flies! Oh, I'm going to be a good wife, Quentin, I just get nervous sometimes that I'm . . . only bringing you my problems. But I want my stuff to be perfect, and all they care is if they can get rich on it. *She sits dejectedly.*

QUENTIN: Exactly, dear—so how can you look to them for your self-respect? Come, why don't we go for a walk? We never walk any more. *Sits on his heels beside her.*

MAGGIE: You love me?

QUENTIN: I adore you. I just wish you could find some joy in your life.

MAGGIE: Quentin, I'm a joke that brings in money.

QUENTIN: I think it's starting to change though—you've got a great band now, and Johnny Block, and the best sound crew—

MAGGIE: Only because I fought for it. You'd think somebody'd come to me and say: Look, Maggie, you made us all this money, now we want you to develop yourself, what can we do for you?

QUENTIN: Darling, they'd be selling frankfurters if there were more money in it; how can you look to them for love?

Pause. Her loneliness floods in on her.

MAGGIE: But where will I look?

QUENTIN, *thrown down:* Maggie, how can you say that?

MAGGIE—*she stands; there is an underlying fear in her now:* When I walked into the party you didn't even put your arms around me. I felt like one of those *wives* or something!

QUENTIN: Well, Donaldson was in the middle of sentence and I—

MAGGIE: So what? I walked into the room! I hire him, he doesn't hire me!

Louise appears upstage in dim light; she is cold-creaming her face.

QUENTIN: But he is directing your TV show, and I was being polite to him.

MAGGIE: You don't have to be ashamed of me, Quentin. I had a right to tell him to stop those faggy jokes at my rehearsal. Just because he's cultured? I'm the one the public pays for, not Donaldson! Ask Ludwig Reiner what my value is!

QUENTIN: I married you, Maggie. I don't need Ludwig's lecture on your value.

MAGGIE, *looking at him with strange, unfamiliar eyes:* Why—why you so cold?

QUENTIN: I'm not cold, I'm trying to explain what happened.

MAGGIE: Well, take me in your arms, don't explain. *He takes her in his arms, he kisses her.* Not like that. *Hold* me.

QUENTIN—*he tries to hold her tighter, then lets go:* Let's go for a walk, honey. Come on.

MAGGIE, *sinking:* What's the matter?

QUENTIN: Nothing.

MAGGIE: But Quentin—you should look at me, like I *existed* or something. Like you used to look—out of your *self.*

Maggie moves away into darkness, meets maid, and changes into negligee.

QUENTIN, *alone:* I adore you, Maggie; I'm sorry; it won't ever happen again. *Louise exits.* Never! You need more love than I thought. But I've got it, and I'll make you see it, and when you do you're going to astound the world!

A rose light floods the bed; Maggie emerges in a dressing gown.

MAGGIE, *indicating out front:* Surprise! You like it? See the material?

QUENTIN: Oh, that's lovely! How'd you think of that?

MAGGIE: All you gotta do is close them and the sun makes the bed all rose.

QUENTIN, *striving for joy, embracing her on the bed:* Yes, it's beautiful! You see? An argument doesn't mean disaster! Oh, Maggie, I never knew what love was!

MAGGIE, *kissing him:* Case during the day, like maybe you get the idea to come home and we make love again in daytime. *She ends sitting in a weakness; nostalgically.* Like last year, remember? In the winter afternoons? And once there was still snow on your hair. See, that's all I am, Quentin.

QUENTIN: I'll come home tomorrow afternoon.

MAGGIE, *half humorously:* Well, don't *plan* it.

He laughs, but she looks at him strangely again, her stare piercing. His laugh dies.

QUENTIN: What is it? I don't want to hide things any more, darling. Tell me, what's bothering you?

MAGGIE, *shaking her head, seeing:* I'm not a good wife. I take up so much of your work.

QUENTIN: No, dear. I only said that because you—*Striving to soften the incident*—you kind of implied that I didn't fight the network hard enough on that penalty, and I got it down to twenty thousand dollars. They had a right to a hundred when you didn't perform.

MAGGIE, *with rising indignation:* But can't I be sick? I was sick!

QUENTIN: I know, dear, but the doctor wouldn't sign the affidavit.

MAGGIE, *furious at him:* I had a pain in my side, for Christ's sake, I couldn't stand straight! You don't believe me, do you!

QUENTIN: Maggie, I'm only telling you the legal situation.

MAGGIE: Ask Ludwig what you should do! You should've gone in there roaring! 'Stead of a polite liberal and affidavits—I shouldn't have had to pay anything!

QUENTIN: Maggie, you have a great analyst, and Ludwig is a phenomenal teacher, and every stranger you meet has all the answers, but I'm putting in forty per cent of my time on your problems, not just some hot air.

MAGGIE: You're not putting forty per cent of—

QUENTIN: Maggie, I keep a log, I know what I spend my time on!

She looks at him, mortally wounded, goes upstage to a secretary, who enters with an invisible drink. Maid joins them with black dress, and Maggie changes.

I'm sorry, darling, but when you talk like that I feel a little like a fool. Don't start drinking, please.

MAGGIE: Should never have gotten married; every man I ever knew they hate their wives. I think I should have a separate lawyer.

QUENTIN, *alone on forestage:* Darling, I'm happy to spend my time on you; my greatest pleasure is to know I've helped your work to grow!

MAGGIE, *as a group of executives surrounds her:* But the only reason I went to Ludwig was so I could make myself an artist you'd be proud of! You're the first one that believed in me!

QUENTIN: Then what are we arguing about? We want the same thing, you see? *Suddenly to Listener:* Yes, power! To transform somebody, to save!

MAGGIE, *emerging from the group, wearing reading glasses:* He's a very good lawyer; he deals for a lot of stars. He'll call you to give him my files.

QUENTIN, *after a slight pause; hurt:* Okay.

MAGGIE: It's nothing against you; but like that girl in the orchestra, that cellist—I mean Andy took too much but he'd have gone in there and got rid of her. I mean you don't laugh when a singer goes off key.

QUENTIN: But she said she coughed.

MAGGIE, *furiously:* She didn't cough, she laughed!

QUENTIN: Now, Maggie.

MAGGIE: I'm not finishing this tape if she's in that band tomorrow! I'm entitled to my conditions, Quentin—and I shouldn't have to plead with my husband for my rights. I want her out!

The executives are gone.

QUENTIN: I don't know what the pleading's about. I've fired three others in three different bands.

MAGGIE: Well, so what? You're my husband. You're supposed to do that. Aren't you?

QUENTIN: But I can't pretend to enjoy demanding people be fired—

MAGGIE: But if it was your daughter you'd get angry, wouldn't you? Instead of apologizing for her?

QUENTIN, *envisioning it:* I guess I would, yes. I'm sorry. I'll do it in the morning.

MAGGIE, *with desperate warmth, joining him, sitting center:* That's all I mean. If I want something you should ask yourself why, why does she want it, not why she shouldn't have it. . . . That's why I don't smile, I feel I'm fighting all the time to make you *see.* You're like a little boy, you don't see the knives people hide.

QUENTIN: Darling, life is not all that dangerous. You've got a husband now who loves you.

Pause. She seems to fear greatly.

MAGGIE: When your mother tells me I'm getting fat, I know where I am. And when you don't do anything about it.

QUENTIN: But what can I do?

MAGGIE: Slap her down, that's what you do!

Secretary enters with imaginary drink, which Maggie takes.

QUENTIN: But she says anything comes into her head, dear—

MAGGIE: She insulted me! She's jealous of me!

QUENTIN: Maggie, she adores you. She's proud of you.

MAGGIE, *a distance away now:* What are you trying to make me think, I'm crazy? *Quentin approaches her, groping for reassurance.* I'm not crazy!

QUENTIN, *carefully:* The thought never entered my mind, darling. I'll . . . talk to her.

MAGGIE: Look, I don't want to see her any more. If she ever comes into this house, I'm walking out!

QUENTIN: Well, I'll tell her to apologize.

Secretary exits.

MAGGIE: I'm not going to work tomorrow. *She lies down on the bed as though crushed.*

QUENTIN: Okay.

MAGGIE, *half springing up:* You know it's not "okay"! You're scared to death they'll sue me, why don't you say it?

QUENTIN: I'm not scared to death; it's just that you're so wonderful in this show and it's a pity to—

MAGGIE, *sitting up furiously:* All you care about is money! Don't shit me!

QUENTIN, *quelling a fury, his voice very level:* Maggie, don't use that language with me, will you?

MAGGIE: Call me vulgar, that I talk like a truck driver! Well, that's where I come from. I'm for Negroes and Puerto Ricans and truck drivers!

QUENTIN: Then why do you fire people so easily?

MAGGIE, *her eyes narrowing—she is seeing him anew:* Look. You don't want me. What the hell are you doing here?

Father and Dan enter, above them.

QUENTIN: I live here. And you do too, but you don't know it yet. But you're going to. I—

FATHER: Where's he going? I need him! What are you?

QUENTIN, *not turning to Father:* I'm here, and I stick it, that's what I am. And one day you're going to catch on. Now go to sleep. I'll be back in ten minutes, I'd like to take a walk.

He starts out and she comes to attention.

MAGGIE: Where you going to walk?

QUENTIN: Just around the block. *She watches him carefully.* There's nobody else, kid; I just want to walk.

MAGGIE, *with great suspicion:* 'Kay.

Father and Dan exit.

He goes a few yards, halts, turns to see her taking a pill bottle and unscrewing the top.

QUENTIN, *coming back:* You can't take pills on top of whisky, dear. *He has reached for them. She pulls them away, but he grabs them again and puts them in his pocket.* That's how it happened the last time. And it's not going to happen again. Never. I'll be right back.

MAGGIE—*an intoxication weighs on her speech now:* Why you wear those pants? *He turns back to her, knowing what is coming.* I told you the seat is too tight.

QUENTIN: Well, they made them too tight, but I can take a walk in them.

MAGGIE: Fags wear pants like that; I told you. They attract each other with their asses.

QUENTIN: You calling me a fag now?

MAGGIE, *very drunk:* Just I've known fags and some of them didn't even know themselves that they were. . . . And I didn't know if you knew about that.

QUENTIN: That's a hell of a way to reassure yourself, Maggie.

MAGGIE, *staggering slightly:* I'm allowed to say what I see!

QUENTIN: You trying to get me to throw you out? Is that what it is? So life will get real again?

MAGGIE, *pointing at him, at his control:* Wha's that suppose to be, strong and silent? I mean what is it?

She stumbles and falls. He makes no move to pick her up.

QUENTIN, *standing over her:* And now I walk out, huh? And you finally know where you are, huh? *He picks her up angrily.* Is that what you want?

Breaking from him, she pitches forward. He catches her and roughly puts her on the bed.

MAGGIE: Wha's the angle? Whyn't you beat it? *She gets on her feet again.* You gonna wait till I'm old? You know what another cab driver said to me today? "I'll give you fifty dollars . . ." *An open, lost sob, wild and contradictory, flies out of her.* You know what's fifty dollars to a cab driver?

Her pain moves into him, his anger is swamped with it. Go ahead, you can go; I can even walk a straight line, see? Look, see? *She walks with arms out, one foot in front of the other.* So what is it, heh? I mean you want dancing? You want dancing? *Breathlessly she turns on the phonograph and goes into a hip-flinging caricature of a dance around him.* I mean what do you want? What is it?

QUENTIN: Please don't do that. *He catches her and lays her down on the bed.*

MAGGIE: You gonna wait till I'm old? Or what? I mean what is it? What is it?

She lies there, gasping. He stares down at her, addressing the Listener, as he sits beside the bed.

QUENTIN: It's that if there is love, it must be limitless; a love not even of persons but blind, blind to insult, blind to the spear in the flesh, like justice blind, like . . .

Felice appears behind him. He has been raising up his arms. Father appears, slumped in chair.

MOTHER'S VOICE, *off*: Idiot!

A dozen men appear on second level, under the harsh white light of a subway platform, some of them reading newspapers. Apart from them Mickey and Lou appear from each side, approaching each other.

MAGGIE, *rushing off unsteadily*: I mean whyn't you beat it?

QUENTIN, *his arms down, crying out to Listener*: But in whose name do you turn your back?

MICKEY: That we go together, Lou, and name the names! Lou!

Lou, staring at Quentin, mounts the platform where the men wait for a subway train.

QUENTIN: I saw it clear—in whose name you turn your back! I saw it once, I saw the name!

The approaching sound of a subway train is heard, and Lou leaps; the racking squeal of brakes.

LOU: Quentin! Quentin!

All the men look at Quentin, then at the "tracks." The men groan. Quentin's hands are a vise against his head. The tower lights as . . . Mother enters in prewar costume, sailboat in hand, bending toward the "bathroom door" as before.

QUENTIN: In whose name? In whose blood-covered name do you look into a face you loved, and say, Now you have been found wanting, and now in your extremity you die! It had a name, it . . .

MOTHER, *toward the "bathroom door":* Quentin? Quentin?

QUENTIN: Hah? *He hurries toward her, but in fear.*

MOTHER: See what we brought you from Atlantic City! From the boardwalk!

Men exit from subway platform. A tremendous crash of surf spins Quentin about, and Mother is gone and the light of the moon is rising on the pier.

QUENTIN: By the ocean. That cottage. That night. The last night.

Maggie in a rumpled wrapper, a bottle in her hand, her hair in snags over her face, staggers out to the edge of the pier and stands in the sound of the surf. Now she starts to topple over the edge of the pier, and he rushes to her and holds her in his hands. Maggie turns around and they embrace. Now the sound of jazz from within is heard, softly.

MAGGIE: You were loved, Quentin; no man was ever loved like you.

QUENTIN, *releasing her:* Carrie tell you I called? My plane couldn't take off all day—

MAGGIE, *drunk, but aware:* I was going to kill myself just now. *He is silent.* Or don't you believe that either?

QUENTIN, *with an absolute calm, a distance, but without hostility:* I saved you twice, why shouldn't I believe it? *Going toward her:* This dampness is bad for your throat, you oughtn't be out here.

MAGGIE—*she defiantly sits, her legs dangling:* Where've *you* been?

QUENTIN, *going upstage, removing his jacket:* I've been in Chicago. I told you. The Hathaway estate.

MAGGIE, *with a sneer:* Estates!

QUENTIN: Well, I have to pay some of our debts before I save the world. *He removes his jacket and puts it on bureau box; sits and removes a shoe.*

MAGGIE, *from the pier:* Didn't you hear what I told you?

QUENTIN: I heard it. I'm not coming out there, Maggie, it's too wet.

She looks toward him, gets up, unsteadily enters the room.

MAGGIE: I didn't go to rehearsal today.

QUENTIN: I didn't think you did.

MAGGIE: And I called the network that I'm not finishing that stupid show. I'm an artist! And I don't have to do stupid shows, no matter what contract you made!

QUENTIN: I'm very tired, Maggie. I'll sleep in the living room. Good night. *He stands and starts out upstage.*

MAGGIE: What *is* this?

Pause. He turns back to her from the exit.

QUENTIN: I've been fired.

MAGGIE: You're not fired.

QUENTIN: I didn't expect you to take it seriously, but it is to me; I can't make a decision any more without something sits up inside me and busts out laughing.

MAGGIE: That my fault, huh?

Slight pause. Then he resolves.

QUENTIN: Look, dear, it's gone way past blame or justifying ourselves, I . . . talked to your doctor this afternoon.

MAGGIE, *stiffening with fear and suspicion:* About what?

QUENTIN: You want to die, Maggie, and I really don't know how to prevent it. But it struck me that I have been playing with your life out of some idiotic hope of some kind that you'd come out of this endless spell. But there's only one hope, dear—you've got to start to look at what *you're* doing.

MAGGIE: You going to put me away somewhere. Is that it?

QUENTIN: Your doctor's trying to get a plane up here tonight; you settle it with him.

MAGGIE: You're not going to put *me* anywhere, mister. *She opens the pill bottle.*

QUENTIN: You have to be supervised, Maggie. *She swallows pills.* Now listen to me while you can still hear. If you start going under tonight I'm calling the ambulance. I haven't the strength to go through that alone again. I'm not protecting you from the newspapers any more, Maggie, and the hospital means a headline. *She raises the whisky bottle to drink.* You've got to start facing the consequences of your actions, Maggie. *She drinks whisky.* Okay. I'll tell Carrie to call the ambulance as soon as she sees the signs. I'm going to sleep at the inn. *He gets his jacket.*

MAGGIE: Don't sleep at the inn!

QUENTIN: Then put that stuff away and go to sleep.

MAGGIE—*afraid he is leaving, she tries to smooth her tangled hair:* Could you . . . stay five minutes?

QUENTIN: Yes. *He returns.*

MAGGIE: You can even have the bottle if you want. I won't take any more. *She puts the pill bottle on the bed before him.*

QUENTIN, *against his wish to take it:* I don't want the bottle.

MAGGIE: 'Member how used talk to me till I fell asleep?

QUENTIN: Maggie, I've sat beside you in darkened rooms for days and weeks at a time, and my office looking high and low for me—

MAGGIE: No, you lost patience with me.

QUENTIN, *after a slight pause:* That's right, yes.

MAGGIE: So you lied, right?

QUENTIN: Yes, I lied. Every day. We are all separate people. I tried not to be, but finally one is—a separate person. I have to survive too, honey.

MAGGIE: So where you going to put me?

QUENTIN, *trying not to break:* You discuss that with your doctor.

MAGGIE: But if you loved me . . .

QUENTIN: But how would you know, Maggie? Do you know any more who I am? Aside from my name? I'm all the evil in the world, aren't I? All the betrayal, the broken hopes, the murderous revenge? *She pours pills into her hand, and he stands. Now fear is in his voice.* A suicide kills two people, Maggie, that's what it's for! So I'm removing myself, and perhaps it will lose its point. *He resolutely starts out. She falls back on the bed. Her breathing is suddenly deep. He starts toward Carrie, who sits in semi-darkness, praying.* Carrie!

MAGGIE: Quentin, what's Lazarus?

He halts. She looks about for him, not knowing he has left.

Quentin?

Not seeing him, she starts up off the bed; a certain alarm . . .

Quen?

He comes halfway back.

QUENTIN: Jesus raised him from the dead. In the Bible. Go to sleep now.

MAGGIE: Wha's 'at suppose to prove?

QUENTIN: The power of faith.

MAGGIE: What about those who have no faith?

QUENTIN: They only have the will.

MAGGIE: But how you get the will?

QUENTIN: You have faith.

MAGGIE: Some apples. *She lies back. A pause.* I want more cream puffs. And my birthday dress? If I'm good? Mama? I want my mother! *She sits up, looks about as in a dream, turns and sees him.* Why you standing there? *She gets out of bed, squinting, and comes up to him, peers into his face; her expression comes alive.* You—you want music?

QUENTIN: All right, you lie down, and I'll put a little music on.

MAGGIE: No, you; you, sit down. And take off your shoes. I mean just to rest. You don't have to do anything. *She staggers to the machine, turns it on; jazz. She tries to sing, but suddenly comes totally awake.* Was I sleeping?

QUENTIN: For a moment, I think.

MAGGIE, *coming toward him in terror:* Was—was my—was anybody else here?

QUENTIN: No. Just me.

MAGGIE: Is there smoke? *With a cry she clings to him; he holds her close.*

QUENTIN: Your mother's dead and gone, dear, she can't hurt you any more, don't be afraid.

MAGGIE, *in the helpless voice of a child as he returns her to the bed:* Where you going to put me?

QUENTIN, *his chest threatening a sob:* Nowhere, dear—the doctor'll decide with you.

MAGGIE: See? I'll lay down. *She lies down.* See? *She takes a strange, deep breath.* You—you could have the pills if you want.

QUENTIN—*stands and, after a hesitation, starts away:* I'll have Carrie come in and take them.

MAGGIE, *sliding off the bed, holding the pill bottle out to him:* No. I won't give them to Carrie. Only you. You take them.

QUENTIN: Why do you want me to have them?

MAGGIE, *extending them:* Here.

QUENTIN, *after a pause:* Do you see it, Maggie? Right now? You're trying to make me the one who does it to you? I grab them; and then we fight, and then I give them up, and you take your death from me. Something in you has been setting me up for a murder. Do you see it? *He moves backward.* But now I'm going away; so you're not my victim any more. It's just you, and your hand.

MAGGIE: But Jesus must have loved her.

QUENTIN: Who?

MAGGIE: Lazarus?

Pause. He sees, he gropes toward his vision.

QUENTIN: That's right, yes! He . . . loved her enough to raise her from the dead. But He's God, see . . . and God's power is love without limit. But when a man dares reach for that . . . he is only reaching for the power. Whoever goes to save another person with the lie of limitless love throws a shadow on the face of God. And God is what happened, God is what is; and whoever stands between another person and her truth is not a lover, he is . . . *He breaks off, lost, peering, and turns back to Maggie for his clue.* And then she said. *He goes back to Maggie, crying out to invoke her.* And then she said!

MAGGIE: I still hear you. Way inside. Quentin? My love? I hear you! Tell me what happened!

QUENTIN, *through a sudden burst of tears:* Maggie, we . . . used one another!

MAGGIE: Not me, not me!

QUENTIN: Yes, you. And I. "To live" we cried, and "Now" we cried. And loved each other's innocence, as though to love enough what was not there would cover up what was. But there is an angel, and night and day he brings back to us exactly what we want to lose. So you must love him because he keeps truth in the world. You eat those pills to blind yourself, but if you could only say, "I have been cruel," this frightening room would open. If you could say, "I have been kicked around, but I have been just as inexcusably vicious to others, called my husband idiot in public, I have been utterly selfish despite my generosity, I have been hurt by a long line of men but I have cooperated with my persecutors—"

MAGGIE—*she has been writhing in fury:* Son of a bitch!

QUENTIN: "And I am full of hatred; I, Maggie, sweet lover of all life—I hate the world!"

MAGGIE: Get out of here!

QUENTIN: Hate women, hate men, hate all who will not grovel at my feet proclaiming my limitless love for ever and ever! But no pill can make us innocent. Throw them in the sea, throw death in the sea and all your innocence. Do the hardest thing of all—see your own hatred and live!

MAGGIE: What about your hatred? You know when I wanted to die. When I read what you wrote, kiddo. Two months after we were married, kiddo.

QUENTIN: Let's keep it true—you told me you tried to die long before you met me.

MAGGIE: So you're not even there, huh? I didn't even meet you. You coward! What about your hatred! *She moves front.* I was married to a king, you son of a bitch! I was looking for a fountain pen to sign some autographs. And there's his desk—*She is speaking toward some invisible source of justice now, telling her injury*—and there's his empty chair where he sits and thinks how to help people. And there's his handwriting. And there's some words. *She almost literally reads in the air, and with the same original astonishment.* "The only one I will ever love is my daughter. If I could only find an honorable way to die." *Now she turns to him.* When you gonna face that, Judgey? Remember how I fell down, fainted? On the new rug? That's what killed me, Judgey. Right? *She staggers up to him, and into his face:* 'Zat right?

QUENTIN, *after a pause:* All right. You pour them back, and I'll tell you the truth about that.

MAGGIE: You won't tell truth.

He tries to tip her hand toward the bottle, holding both her wrists.

QUENTIN, *with difficulty:* We'll see. Pour them back first, and we'll see.

She lets him pour them back, but sits on the bed, holding the bottle in both hands.

MAGGIE, *after a deep breath:* Liar.

QUENTIN, *in quiet tension against his own self-condemnation:* We'd had our first party in our own house. Some important people, network heads, directors—

MAGGIE: And you were ashamed of me. Don't lie, now! You're still playing God! That's what killed me, Quentin!

QUENTIN: All right. I wasn't . . . ashamed. But . . . afraid. *Pause.* I wasn't sure if any of them . . . had had you.

MAGGIE, *astounded:* But I didn't know any of those!

QUENTIN, *not looking at her:* I swear to you, I did get to where I couldn't imagine what I'd ever been ashamed of. But it was too late. I had written that, and I was like all the others who'd betrayed you, and I could never be trusted again.

MAGGIE, *with a mixture of accusation and lament for a lost life, weeping:* Why did you write that?

QUENTIN: Because when the guests had gone, and you suddenly turned on me, calling me cold, remote, it was the first time I saw your eyes that way—betrayed, screaming that I'd made you feel you didn't exist—

MAGGIE: Don't mix me up with Louise!

QUENTIN: That's just it. That I could have brought two women so different to the same accusation—it closed a circle for me. And I wanted to face the worst thing I could imagine—that I could not love. And I wrote it down, like a letter from hell.

She starts to raise her hand to her mouth, and he steps in and holds her wrist.

That's rock bottom. What more do you *want?*

She looks at him; her eyes unreadable.

Maggie, we were both born of many errors; a human being has to forgive himself! Neither of us is innocent. What more do you want?

A strange calm overtakes her. She lies back on the bed. The hostility seems to have gone.

MAGGIE: Love me, and do what I tell you. And stop arguing. *He moves in anguish up and down beside the bed.* And take down the sand dune. It's *not* too expensive. I want to hear the ocean when we make love in here, but we never hear the ocean.

QUENTIN: We're nearly broke, Maggie; and that dune keeps the roof from blowing off.

MAGGIE: So you buy a new roof. I'm cold. Lie on me.

QUENTIN: I can't do that again, not when you're like this.

MAGGIE: Just till I sleep!

QUENTIN—*an outcry:* Maggie, it's a mockery. Leave me *something.*

MAGGIE: Just out of humanness! I'm cold!

Holding down self-disgust, he lies down on her but holds his head away. Pause.

If you don't argue with me any more, I'll let you be my lawyer again. 'Kay? If you don't argue? Ludwig doesn't argue. *He is silent.* And don't keep saying we're broke? And the sand dune? *The agony is growing in his face, of total disintegration.* 'Cause I love the ocean sound; like a big mother—sssh, sssh, sssh. *He lifts himself off, stands looking down at her. Her eyes are closed.* You gonna be good now? *She takes a very deep breath.*

He reaches in carefully and tries to snatch the bottle; she grips it.

QUENTIN: It isn't my love you want any more. It's my destruction! But you're not going to kill me, Maggie. I want those pills. I don't want to fight you, Maggie. Now put them in my hand.

She looks at him, then quickly tries to swallow her handful, but he knocks some of them out—although she swallows many. He grabs for the bottle, but she holds and he pulls, yanks. She goes with the force, and he drags her onto the floor, trying to pry her hands open as she flails at him and hits his face—her strength is wild and no longer her own. He grabs her wrist and squeezes it with both his fists.

Drop them, you bitch! You won't kill me!

She holds on, and suddenly, clearly, he lunges for her throat and lifts her with his grip.

You won't kill me! You won't kill me!

She drops the bottle as from the farthest distance Mother rushes to the "bathroom door," crying out—the toy sailboat in her hand.

MOTHER: Darling, open this door! I didn't trick you!

Quentin springs away from Maggie, who falls back to the floor, his hands open and in air.

Mother continues without halt.

Quentin, why are you running water in there! *She backs away in horror from the "door."* I'll die if you do that! I saw a star when you were born—a light, a light in the world.

He stands transfixed as Mother backs into his hand, which of its own volition, begins to squeeze her throat. She sinks to the floor, gasping for breath. And he falls back in horror.

QUENTIN: Murder?

Maggie gets to her hands and knees, gasping. He rushes to help her, terrified by his realization. She flails out at him, and on one elbow looks up at him in a caricature of laughter, her eyes victorious and wild with fear.

MAGGIE: Now we both know. You tried to kill me, mister. I been killed by a lot of people, some couldn't hardly spell, but it's the same, mister. You're on the end of a long, long line, Frank.

As though to ward off the accusation, he reaches again to help her up, and in absolute terror she springs away across the floor.

Stay 'way! . . . No! No—no, Frank. Don't you do that. *Cautiously, as though facing a wild, ravening beast:* Don't you do that. . . . I'll call Quentin if you do that. *She glances off and calls quietly, but never leaving him out of her sight.* Quentin! Qu—

She falls asleep, crumpled on the floor. Now deep, strange breathing. He quickly goes to her, throws her over onto her stomach for artificial respiration, but just as he is about to start, he stands. He calls upstage.

QUENTIN: Carrie? Carrie! *Carrie enters. As though it were a final farewell:* Quick! Call the ambulance! Stop wasting time! Call the ambulance!

Carrie exits. He looks down at Maggie, addressing Listener.

No-no, we saved her. It was just in time. Her doctor tells me she had a few good months; he even thought for a while she was making it. Unless, God knows, he fell in love with her too. *He almost smiles; it is gone. He moves out on the dock.* Look, I'll say it. It's really all I came to say. Barbiturates kill by suffocation. And the signal is a kind of sighing—the diaphragm is paralyzed. And I stood out on that dock. *He looks up.* And all those stars, still so fixed, so fortunate! And her precious seconds squirming in my hand, alive as bugs; and I heard. Those deep,

unnatural breaths, like the footfalls of my coming peace—and knew . . .
I wanted them. How is that possible? I loved that girl!

Enter Lou, Mickey, Father, Dan, Carrie, and Felice at various points. Louise appears.

And the name—yes, the name! In whose name do you ever turn your
back—*He looks out at the audience*—but in your own? In Quentin's name.
Always in your own blood-covered name you turn you back!

Holga appears on the highest level.

HOLGA: But no one is innocent they did not kill!

QUENTIN: But love, is love enough? What love, what wave of pity
will ever reach this knowledge—I know how to kill? . . . I know, I
know—she was doomed in any case, but will that cure? Or is it
possible—*He turns toward the tower, moves toward it as toward a terrible
God*—that this is not bizarre . . . to anyone? And I am not alone, and
no man lives who would not rather be the sole survivor of this place
than all its finest victims! What is the cure? Who can be innocent again
on this mountain of skulls? I tell you what I know! My brothers died
here—*He looks from the tower down at the fallen Maggie*—but my brothers
built this place; our hearts have cut these stones! And what's the cure?
. . . No, not love; I loved them all, all! And gave them willing to failure
and to death that I might live, as they gave me and gave each other,
with a word, a look, a trick, a truth, a lie—and all in love!

HOLGA: Hello!

QUENTIN: But what will defend her? *He cries up to Holga:* That woman
hopes!

She stands unperturbed, resolute, aware of his pain and her own.

Or is that—*Struck, to the Listener*—exactly why she hopes, because she
knows? What burning cities taught her and the death of love taught me:
that we are very dangerous! *Staring, seeing his vision:* And that, that's why
I wake each morning like a boy—even now, even now! I swear to you,
I could love the world again! Is the knowing all? To know, and even
happily, that we meet unblessed; not in some garden of wax fruit and
painted trees, that lie of Eden, but after, after the Fall, after many, many
deaths. Is the knowing all? And the wish to kill is never killed, but with

some gift of courage one may look into its face when it appears, and with a stroke of love—as to an idiot in the house—forgive it; again and again . . . forever?

He is evidently interrupted by the Listener.

No, it's not certainty, I don't feel that. But it does seem feasible . . . not to be afraid. Perhaps it's all one has. I'll tell her that. . . . Yes, she will, she'll know what I mean.

He turns upstage. He hesitates; all his people face him. He walks toward Louise, pausing; but she turns her face away. He goes on and pauses beside Mother, who stands in uncomprehending sorrow; he gestures as though he touched her, and she looks up at him and dares a smile, and he smiles back. He pauses at his dejected Father and Dan, and with a slight gesture magically makes them stand. Felice is about to raise her hand in blessing—he shakes her hand, aborting her enslavement. He passes Mickey and Lou and turns back to Maggie; she rises from the floor, webbed in with her demons, trying to awake. And with his life following him he climbs toward Holga, who raises her arm as though seeing him, and with great love . . .

HOLGA: Hello!

He comes to a halt a few yards from her and walks toward her, holding out his hand.

QUENTIN: Hello.

He moves away with her as a loud whispering comes up from all his people, who follow behind, endlessly alive. Darkness takes them all.

THE AMERICAN CLOCK

A Vaudeville

Based in part on Studs Terkel's *Hard Times*.

CAST OF CHARACTERS

THEODORE K. QUINN

LEE BAUM

ROSE BAUM, Lee's mother

MOE BAUM, Lee's father

ARTHUR A. ROBERTSON

CLARENCE, a shoeshine man

FRANK, the Baums' Chauffeur

FANNY MARGOLIES, Rose's sister

GRANDPA, Rose's father

Financiers {
DR. ROSMAN
JESSE LIVERMORE
WILLIAM DURANT
ARTHUR CLAYTON
}

TONY, a speakeasy owner

DIANA MORGAN

HENRY TAYLOR, a farmer

IRENE, a middle-aged black woman

BANKS, a black veteran

JOE, a boyhood friend of Lee's

MRS. TAYLOR, Henry's wife

HARRIET TAYLOR, their daughter

Farmers {
BREWSTER
CHARLEY

JUDGE BRADLEY
FRANK HOWARD, an auctioneer
MISS FOWLER, Quinn's secretary
GRAHAM, a *New York Times* reporter
SIDNEY MARGOLIES, Fanny's son
DORIS GROSS, the landlady's daughter

Students {
RALPH
RUDY

ISABEL, a prostitute
ISAAC, a black café proprietor
RYAN, a federal relief supervisor

People at the relief office {
MATTHEW R. BUSH
GRACE
KAPUSH
DUGAN
TOLAND
LUCY

EDIE, a comic-strip artist
LUCILLE, Rose's niece
STANISLAUS, a seaman
BASEBALL PLAYER
WAITER
THIEF
FARMERS
BIDDERS
SHERIFF
DEPUTIES
MARATHON DANCERS
WELFARE WORKER
SOLDIERS

ACT ONE

The set is a flexible area for actors. The actors are seated in a choral area onstage and return to it when their scenes are over. The few pieces of furniture required should be openly carried on by the actors. An impression of a surrounding vastness should be given, as though the whole country were really the setting, even as the intimacy of certain scenes is provided for. The background can be sky, clouds, space itself, or an impression of the geography of the United States.

A small jazz band onstage plays "Million-Dollar Baby" as a baseball pitcher enters, tossing a ball from hand to glove. Quinn begins to whistle "Million-Dollar Baby" from the balcony. Now he sings, and the rest of the company joins in, gradually coming onstage. All are singing by the end of the verse. All form in positions onstage. The band remains onstage throughout the play.

ROSE: By the summer of 1929 . . .

LEE: I think it's fair to say that nearly every American . . .

MOE: Firmly believed that he was going to get . . .

COMPANY: Richer and richer . . .

MOE: Every year.

ROBERTSON: The country knelt to a golden calf in a blanket of red, white, and blue. *He walks to Clarence's shoeshine box.* How you making out, Clarence?

CLARENCE: Mr. Robertson, I like you to lay another ten dollars on that General Electric. You do that for me?

361

ROBERTSON: How much stock you own, Clarence?

CLARENCE: Well, this ten ought to buy me a thousand dollars' worth, so altogether I guess I got me about hundred thousand dollars in stock.

ROBERTSON: And how much cash you got home?

CLARENCE: Oh, I guess about forty, forty-five dollars.

ROBERTSON, *slight pause:* All right, Clarence, let me tell you something. But I want you to promise me not to repeat it to anyone.

CLARENCE: I never repeat a tip you give me, Mr. Robertson.

ROBERTSON: This isn't quite a tip, this is what you might call an untip. Take all your stock, and sell it.

CLARENCE: Sell! Why, just this morning in the paper Mr. Andrew Mellon say the market's got to keep goin' up. *Got* to!

ROBERTSON: I have great respect for Andrew Mellon, Clarence, know him well, but he's up to his eyebrows in this game—he's got to say that. You sell, Clarence, believe me.

CLARENCE, *drawing himself up:* I never like to criticize a customer, Mr. Robertson, but I don't think a man in your position ought to be carryin' on that kind of talk! Now you take this ten, sir, put it on General Electric for Clarence.

ROBERTSON: I tell you something funny, Clarence.

CLARENCE: What's that, sir?

ROBERTSON: You sound like every banker in the United States.

CLARENCE: Well, I should hope so!

ROBERTSON: Yeah, well . . . bye-bye.

He exits. Clarence exits with his shoeshine box. The company exits singing and humming "Million-Dollar Baby"; Quinn sings the final line.

Light rises on Rose at the piano, dressed for an evening out. Two valises stand center stage.

ROSE, *playing piano under speech:* Now sing, darling, but don't forget to breathe—and then you'll do your homework.

LEE, *starts singing "I Can't Give You Anything But Love,"* *then speaks over music:* Up to '29 it was the age of belief. How could Lindbergh fly the Atlantic in that tiny little plane? He believed. How could Babe Ruth keep smashing those homers? He believed. Charley Paddock, "The World's Fastest Human," raced a racehorse . . . and won! Because he believed. What I believed at fourteen was that my mother's hair was supposed to flow down over her shoulders. And one afternoon she came into the apartment . . .

Rose, at piano, sings a line of "I Can't Give You Anything But Love."

. . . and it was short!

Rose and Lee sing the last line together.

ROSE, *continuing to play, speaking over music:* I personally think with all the problems there was never such a glorious time for anybody who loved to play or sing or listen or dance to music. It seems to me every week there was another marvelous song. What's the matter with you?

Lee can only shake his head— "nothing."

Oh, for God's sake! Nobody going to bother with long hair anymore. All I was doing was winding it up and winding it down . . .

LEE: It's *okay*! I just didn't think it would ever . . . happen.

ROSE: But why can't there be something new!

LEE: But why didn't you *tell* me!

ROSE: Because you would do exactly what you're doing now—carrying on like I was some kind of I-don't-know-what! Now stop being an idiot and *sing*!

Lee starts singing "On the Sunny Side of the Street."

You're not breathing, dear.

Moe enters carrying a telephone, joins in song. Lee continues singing under dialogue.

ROSE: Rudy Vallee is turning green.

Frank enters in a chauffeur's uniform.

MOE, *into phone:* Trafalgar five, seven-seven-one-one. *Pause.* Herb? I'm just thinking, maybe I ought to pick up another five hundred shares of General Electric. *Pause.* Good. *He hangs up.*

FRANK: Car's ready, Mr. Baum.

Frank chimes in with Lee on the last line of "Sunny Side of the Street." Then Lee sits on the floor, working on his crystal set.

ROSE, *to Frank:* You'll drop us at the theatre and then take my father and sister to Brooklyn and come back for us after the show. And don't get lost, please.

FRANK: No, I know Brooklyn.

He exits with the baggage. Fanny enters—Rose's sister.

FANNY, *apprehensively:* Rose . . . listen . . . Papa really doesn't want to move in with us.

A slow turn with rising eyebrows from Moe; Rose is likewise alarmed.

ROSE, *to Fanny:* Don't be silly, he's been with us six months.

FANNY, *fearfully, voice lowered:* I'm telling you . . . he is not happy about it.

MOE, *resoundingly understating the irony:* He's not happy.

FANNY, *to Moe:* Well, you know how he loves space, and this apartment is so roomy.

MOE, *to Lee:* He bought himself a grave, you know. It's going to be in the cemetery on the aisle. So he'll have a little more room to move around, . . .

ROSE: Oh, stop it.

MOE: . . . get in and out quicker.

FANNY, *innocently:* Out of a grave?

ROSE: He's kidding you, for God's sake!

FANNY: Oh! *To Rose:* I think he's afraid my house'll be too small; you know, with Sidney and us and the one bathroom. And what is he going to do with himself in Brooklyn? He never liked the country.

ROSE: Fanny, dear, make up your mind—he's going to *love* it with you.

MOE: Tell you, Fanny—maybe we should *all* move over to your house and he could live here with an eleven-room apartment for himself, and we'll send the maid every day to do his laundry . . .

FANNY: He's brushing his hair, Rose, but I know he's not happy. I think what it is, he still misses Mama, you see.

MOE: Now *that's* serious—a man his age still misses his mother . . .

FANNY: No, *our* mother—*Mama. To Rose, almost laughing, pointing at Moe:* He thought Papa misses his own mother!

ROSE: No, he didn't, he's kidding you!

FANNY: Oh, you . . . ! *She swipes at Moe.*

ROSE, *walking her to the doorway:* Go hurry him up. I don't want to miss the first scene of this show; it's Gershwin, it's supposed to be wonderful.

FANNY: See, what it is, something is always happening here . . .

MOE, *into phone:* Trafalgar five, seven-seven-one-one.

FANNY: . . . I mean with the stock market and the business. . . . Papa just loves all this!

Grandpa appears, in a suit, with a cane; very neat, proper—and very sorry for himself. Comes to a halt, already hurt.

MOE, *to Grandpa:* See you again soon, Charley!

FANNY, *deferentially:* You ready, Papa?

MOE, *on phone:* Herb? . . . Maybe I ought to get rid of my Worthington Pump. Oh . . . thousand shares? And remind me to talk to you about gold, will you? *Pause.* Good. *He hangs up.*

FANNY, *with Rose, getting Grandpa into his coat:* Rose'll come every few days, Papa . . .

ROSE: Sunday we'll all come out and spend the day.

GRANDPA: Brooklyn is full of tomatoes.

FANNY: No, they're starting to put up big apartment houses now; it's practically not the country anymore. *In a tone of happy reassurance:* On some streets there's hardly a tree! *To Rose, of her diamond bracelet:* I'm looking at that bracelet! Is it new?

ROSE: For my birthday.

FANNY: It's gorgeous.

ROSE: He gave exactly the same one to his mother.

FANNY: She must be overjoyed.

ROSE, *with a cutting smile, to Moe:* Why not?

GRANDPA, *making a sudden despairing announcement:* Well? So I'm going! *With a sharp tap of his cane on the floor, he starts off.*

LEE: Bye-bye, Grandpa!

GRANDPA, *goes to Lee, offers his cheek, gets his kiss, then pinches Lee's cheek:* You be a good boy. *He strides past Rose, huffily snatches his hat out of her hand, and exits.*

MOE: There goes the boarder. I lived to see it!

ROSE, *to Lee:* Want to come and ride with us?

LEE: I think I'll stay and work on my radio.

ROSE: Good, and go to bed early. I'll bring home all the music from the show, and we'll sing it tomorrow. *She kisses Lee.* Good night, darling. *She swings out in her furs.*

MOE, *to Lee:* Whyn't you get a haircut?

LEE: I did, but it grew back, I think.

MOE, *realizing Lee's size:* Should you talk to your mother about college or something?

LEE: Oh, no, not for a couple of years.

MOE: Oh. Okay, good. *He laughs and goes out, perfectly at one with the world.*

Robertson appears, walks over to the couch, and lies down. Dr. Rosman appears and sits in a chair behind Robertson's head.

ROBERTSON: Where'd I leave off yesterday?

DR. ROSMAN: Your mother had scalded the cat.

Pause.

ROBERTSON: There's something else, Doctor. I feel a conflict about saying it . . .

DR. ROSMAN: That's what we're here for.

ROBERTSON: I don't mean in the usual sense. It has to do with money.

DR. ROSMAN: Yes?

ROBERTSON: Your money.

DR. ROSMAN, *turns down to him, alarmed:* What about it?

ROBERTSON, *hesitates:* I think you ought to get out of the market.

DR. ROSMAN: Out of the market!

ROBERTSON: Sell everything.

DR. ROSMAN, *pauses, raises his head to think, then speaks carefully:* Could you talk about the basis for this idea? When was the first time you had this thought?

ROBERTSON: About four months ago. Around the middle of May.

DR. ROSMAN: Can you recall what suggested it?

ROBERTSON: One of my companies manufactures kitchen utensils.

DR. ROSMAN: The one in Indiana?

ROBERTSON: Yes. In the middle of May all our orders stopped.

DR. ROSMAN: Completely?

ROBERTSON: Dead stop. It's now the end of August, and they haven't resumed.

DR. ROSMAN: How is that possible? The stock keeps going up.

ROBERTSON: Thirty points in less than two months. This is what I've been trying to tell you for a long time now, Doctor—the market represents nothing but a state of mind. *He sits up.* On the other hand, I must face the possibility that this is merely my personal fantasy . . .

DR. ROSMAN: Yes, your fear of approaching disaster.

ROBERTSON: But I've had meetings at the Morgan Bank all week, and it's the same in almost every industry—it's not just my companies. The warehouses are overflowing, we can't move the goods, that's an objective fact.

DR. ROSMAN: Have you told your thoughts to your colleagues?

ROBERTSON: They won't listen. Maybe they can't afford to—we've been tossing the whole country onto a crap table in a game where nobody is ever supposed to lose! . . . I sold off a lot two years ago, but when the market opens tomorrow I'm cashing in the rest. I feel guilty for it, but I can't see any other way.

DR. ROSMAN: Why does selling make you feel guilty?

ROBERTSON: Dumping twelve million dollars in securities could start a slide. It could wipe out thousands of widows and old people. . . . I've even played with the idea of making a public announcement.

DR. ROSMAN: That you're dumping twelve million dollars? That could start a slide all by itself, couldn't it?

ROBERTSON: But it would warn the little people.

DR. ROSMAN: Yes, but selling out quietly might not disturb the market quite so much. You *could* be wrong, too.

ROBERTSON: I suppose so. Yes. . . . Maybe I'll just sell and shut up. You're right. I could be mistaken.

DR. ROSMAN, *relieved:* You probably are—but I think I'll sell out anyway.

ROBERTSON: Fine, Doctor. *He stands, straightens his jacket.* And one more thing. This is going to sound absolutely nuts, but . . . when you get your cash, don't keep it. Buy gold.

DR. ROSMAN: You can't be serious.

ROBERTSON: Gold bars, Doctor. The dollar may disappear with the rest of it. *He extends his hand.* Well, good luck.

DR. ROSMAN: Your hand is shaking.

ROBERTSON: Why not? Ask any two great bankers in the United States and they'd say that Arthur A. Robertson had lost his mind. *Pause.* Gold bars, Doctor . . . and don't put them in the bank. In the basement. Take care, now. *He exits.*

A bar. People in evening dress seated morosely at tables. An atmosphere of shock and even embarrassment.

LIVERMORE: About Randolph Morgan. Could you actually see him falling?

TONY: Oh, yeah. It was still that blue light, just before it gets dark? And I don't know why, something made me look up. And there's a man flyin' spread-eagle, falling through the air. He was right on top of me, like a giant! *He looks down.* And I look. I couldn't believe it. It's Randolph!

LIVERMORE: Poor, poor man.

DURANT: Damned fool.

LIVERMORE: I don't know—I think there is a certain gallantry . . . When you lose other people's money as well as your own, there can be no other way out.

DURANT: There's always a way out. The door.

TONY: Little more brandy, Mr. Durant?

LIVERMORE, *raising his cup:* To Randolph Morgan.

Durant raises his cup.

TONY: Amen here. And I want to say something else—everybody should get down on their knees and thank John D. Rockefeller.

LIVERMORE: Now you're talking.

TONY: Honest to God, Mr. Livermore, didn't that shoot a thrill in you? I mean, there's a *man*—to come out like that with the whole market falling to pieces and say, "I and my sons are buying six million dollars in common stocks." I mean, that's a bullfighter.

LIVERMORE: He'll turn it all around, too.

TONY: Sure he'll turn it around, because the man's a capitalist, he knows how to put up a battle. You wait, tomorrow morning it'll all be shootin' up again like Roman candles!

Enter Waiter, who whispers in Tony's ear.

Sure, sure, bring her in.

Waiter hurries out. Tony turns to the two financiers.

My God, it's Randolph's sister. . . . She don't know yet.

Enter Diana, a young woman of elegant ease.

How do you do, Miss Morgan, come in, come in. Here, I got a nice table for you.

DIANA, *all bright Southern belle:* Thank you!

TONY: Can I bring you nice steak? Little drink?

DIANA: I believe I'll wait for Mr. Robertson.

TONY: Sure. Make yourself at home.

DIANA: Are you the . . . *famous* Tony?

TONY: That's right, miss.

DIANA: I certainly am thrilled to meet you. I've read all about this marvelous place. *She looks around avidly.* Are all these people literary?

TONY: Well, not all, Miss Morgan.

DIANA: But this is the speakeasy F. Scott Fitzgerald frequents, isn't it?

TONY: Oh, yeah, but tonight is very quiet with the stock market and all, people stayin' home a lot the last couple days.

DIANA: Is that gentleman a writer?

TONY: No, miss, that's Jake the Barber, he's in the liquor business.

DIANA: And these?

She points to Durant and Livermore. Durant, having overheard, stands.

TONY: Mr. Durant, Miss Morgan. Mr. Livermore, Miss Morgan.

DIANA, *in a Southern accent, to the audience:* The name of Jesse Livermore was uttered in my family like the name of a genius! A Shakespeare, a Dante of corporate finance.

Clayton, at the bar, picks up a phone.

LEE, *looking on from choral area:* And William Durant . . . he had a car named after him, the Durant Six.

MOE, *beside Lee:* A *car*? Durant had control of General Motors, for God's sake.

DIANA: Not *the* Jesse Livermore?

LIVERMORE: Afraid so, yes!

DIANA: Well, I declare! And sitting here just like two ordinary millionaires!

LEE: Ah, yes, the Great Men. The fabled High Priests of the never-ending Boom.

DIANA: This is certainly a banner evening for me! . . . I suppose you know Durham quite well.

LIVERMORE: Durham? I don't believe I've ever been there.

DIANA: But your big Philip Morris plant is there. You do still own Philip Morris, don't you?

LIVERMORE: Oh, yes, but to bet on a horse there's no need to ride him. I never mix in business. I am only interested in stocks.

DIANA: Well, that's sort of miraculous, isn't it, to own a place like that and never've seen it! My brother's in brokerage—Randolph Morgan?

LIVERMORE: I dealt with Randolph when I bought the controlling shares in IBM. Fine fellow.

DIANA: But I don't understand why he'd be spending the night in his office. The market's closed at night, isn't it?

Both men shift uneasily.

DURANT: Oh, yes, but there's an avalanche of selling orders from all over the country, and they're working round the clock to tally them up. The truth is, there's not a price on anything at the moment. In fact,

Mr. Clayton over there at the end of the bar is waiting for the latest estimates.

DIANA: I'm sure something will be done, won't there? *She laughs.* They've cut off our telephone!

LIVERMORE: How's that?

DIANA: It seems that Daddy's lived on loans the last few months and his credit stopped. I had no idea! *She laughs.* I feel like a figure in a dream. I sat down in the dining car the other day, absolutely famished, and realized I had only forty cents! I am surviving on chocolate bars! *Her charm barely hides her anxiety.* Whatever has become of all the money?

LIVERMORE: You mustn't worry, Miss Morgan, there'll soon be plenty of money. Money is like a shy bird: the slightest rustle in the trees and it flies for cover. But money cannot bear solitude for long, it must come out and feed. And that is why we must all speak positively and show our confidence.

ROSE, *from choral area:* And they were nothing but pickpockets in a crowd of innocent pilgrims.

LIVERMORE: With Rockefeller's announcement this morning the climb has probably begun already.

ROBERTSON, *from choral area:* Yes, but they also believed.

TAYLOR, *from choral area: What* did they believe?

IRENE and BANKS, *from choral area, echoing Taylor:* Yeah, what did they believe?

ROBERTSON: Why, the most important thing of all—that talk makes facts!

DURANT: If I were you, Miss Morgan, I would prepare myself for the worst.

LIVERMORE: Now, Bill, there is no good in that kind of talk.

ROBERTSON: And they ended up believing it themselves!

DURANT: It's far more dreamlike than you imagine, Miss Morgan.

MOE: There they are, chatting away, while the gentleman at the end of the bar . . .

DURANT: . . . That gentleman . . . who has just put down the telephone is undoubtedly steeling himself to tell me that I have lost control of General Motors.

DIANA: What!

Clayton, at the bar, has indeed put down the phone, has straightened his vest, and is now crossing to their table.

DURANT, *watching him approach:* If I were you, I'd muster all the strength I have, Miss Morgan. Yes, Clayton?

CLAYTON: If we could talk privately, sir . . .

DURANT: Am I through?

CLAYTON: If you could borrow for two or three weeks . . .

DURANT: From whom?

CLAYTON: I don't know, sir.

DURANT, *standing:* Good night, Miss Morgan.

She is looking up at him, astonished.

How old are you?

DIANA: Nineteen.

DURANT: I hope you will look things in the face, young lady. Shun paper. Paper is the plague. Good luck to you. *He turns to go.*

LIVERMORE: We have to talk, Bill . . .

DURANT: Nothing to say, Jesse. Go to bed, old boy. It's long past midnight.

MOE, *trying to recall:* Say . . . didn't Durant end up managing a bowling alley in Toledo, Ohio?

CLAYTON, *nods:* Dead broke.

LIVERMORE, *turns to Clayton, adopting a tone of casual challenge:* Clayton . . . what's Philip Morris going to open at, can they tell?

CLAYTON: Below twenty. No higher. If we can find buyers at all.

LIVERMORE, *his smile gone:* But Rockefeller. Rockefeller . . .

CLAYTON: It doesn't seem to have had any effect, sir.

Livermore stands. Pause.

I should get back to the office, sir, if I may.

Livermore is silent.

I'm very sorry, Mr. Livermore.

Clayton exits. Diana is moved by the excruciating look coming onto Livermore's face.

DIANA: Mr. Livermore? . . .

ROBERTSON, *entering:* Sorry I'm late, Diana. How was the trip? *Her expression turns him to Livermore. He goes to him.* Bad, Jesse?

LIVERMORE: I am wiped out, Arthur.

ROBERTSON, *trying for lightness:* Come on, now, Jesse, a man like you has always got ten million put away somewhere.

LIVERMORE: No, no. I always felt that if you couldn't have *real* money, might as well not have any. Is it true what I've heard, that you sold out in time?

ROBERTSON: Yes, Jesse. I told you I would.

LIVERMORE, *slight pause:* Arthur, can you lend me five thousand dollars?

ROBERTSON: Certainly. *He sits, removes one shoe. To audience:* Five weeks ago, on his yacht in Oyster Bay, he told me he had four hundred and eighty million dollars in common stocks.

LIVERMORE: What the hell are you doing?

Robertson removes a layer of five thousand-dollar bills from the shoe and hands Livermore one as he stands. Livermore stares down at Robertson's shoes.

By God. Don't you believe in anything?

ROBERTSON: Not much.

LIVERMORE: Well, I suppose I understand that. *He folds the bill.* But I can't say that I admire it. *He pockets the bill, looks down again at Robertson's shoes, and shakes his head.* Well, I guess it's your country now. *He turns like a blind man and goes out.*

ROBERTSON: Not long after, Jesse Livermore sat down to a good breakfast in the Sherry-Netherland Hotel and, calling for an envelope, addressed it to Arthur Robertson, inserted a note for five thousand dollars, went into the washroom, and shot himself.

DIANA, *staring after Livermore, then turning to Robertson:* Is Randolph ruined too?

ROBERTSON, *taking her hand:* Diana . . . Randolph is dead. *Pause.* He . . . he fell from his window.

Diana stands, astonished. Irene sings " 'Tain't Nobody's Bizness" from choral area. Fadeout.

ROSE, *calling as she enters:* Lee? Darling?

LEE, *takes a bike from prop area and rides on, halting before her:* How do you like it, Ma!

ROSE: What a beautiful bike!

LEE: It's a Columbia Racer! I just bought it from Georgie Rosen for twelve dollars.

ROSE: Where'd you get twelve dollars?

LEE: I emptied my savings account. But it's worth way more! . . .

ROSE: Well, I should say! Listen, darling, you know how to get to Third Avenue and Nineteenth Street, don't you?

LEE: Sure, in ten minutes.

ROSE, *taking a diamond bracelet from her bag:* This is my diamond bracelet. *She reaches into the bag and brings out a card.* And this is Mr. Sanders' card and the address. He's expecting you; just give it to him, and he'll give you a receipt.

LEE: Is he going to fix it?

ROSE: No, dear. It's a pawnshop. Go. I'll explain sometime.

LEE: Can't I have an idea? What's a pawnshop?

ROSE: Where you leave something temporarily and they lend you money on it, with interest. I'm going to leave it the rest of the month, till the market goes up again. I showed it to him on Friday, and we're getting a nice loan on it.

LEE: But how do you get it back?

ROSE: You just pay back the loan plus interest. But things'll pick up in a month or two. Go on, darling, and be careful! I'm so glad you bought that bike. . . . It's gorgeous!

LEE, *mounting his bike:* Does Papa know?

ROSE: Yes, dear. Papa knows . . .

She starts out as Joey hurries on.

JOEY: Oh, hiya, Mrs. Baum.

ROSE: Hello, Joey. . . . Did you get thin?

JOEY: Me? *He touches his stomach defensively.* No, I'm okay. *To Lee as well, as he takes an eight-by-ten photo out of an envelope:* See what I just got?

Rose and Lee look at the photo.

ROSE, *impressed:* Where did you get that!

LEE: How'd you get it autographed?

JOEY: I just wrote to the White House.

LEE, *running his finger over the signature:* Boy . . . look at that, huh? "Herbert Hoover"!

ROSE: What a human thing for him to do! What did you write him?

JOEY: Just wished him success . . . you know, against the Depression.

ROSE, *wondrously:* Look at that! You're going to end up a politician, Joey. *She returns to studying the photo.*

JOEY: I might. I like it a lot.

LEE: But what about dentistry?

JOEY: Well, either one.

ROSE: Get going, darling.

She exits, already preoccupied with the real problem. Lee mounts his bike.

LEE: You want to shoot some baskets later?

JOEY: What about now?

LEE, *embarrassed:* No . . . I've got something to do for my mother. Meet you on the court in an hour. *He starts off.*

JOEY, *stopping him:* Wait, I'll go with you, let me on! *He starts to mount the crossbar.*

LEE: I can't, Joey.

JOEY, *sensing some forbidden area, surprised:* Oh!

LEE: See you on the court.

Lee rides off. Joey examines the autograph and mouths silently, "Herbert Hoover . . ." He shakes his head proudly and walks off.

ROBERTSON, *from choral area:* To me . . . it's beginning to look like Germany in 1922, and I'm having real worries about the banks. There are times when I walk around with as much as twenty-five, thirty thousand dollars in my shoes.

Frank enters in a chauffeur's uniform, a lap robe folded over his arm. Moe enters, stylishly dressed in a fur-collared overcoat, as though on a street.

FRANK: Morning, Mr. Baum. Got the car nice and warmed up for you this morning, sir. And I had the lap robe dry-cleaned.

MOE, *showing Frank a bill:* What is that, Frank?

FRANK: Oh. Looks like the garage bill.

MOE: What's that about tires on there?

FRANK: Oh, yes, sir, this is the bill for the new tires last week.

MOE: And what happened to those tires we bought six weeks ago?

FRANK: Those weren't very good, sir, they wore out quick—and I want to be the first to admit that!

MOE: But twenty dollars apiece and they last six weeks?

FRANK: That's just what I'm telling you, sir—they were just no good. But these ones are going to be a whole lot better, though.

MOE: Tell you what, Frank . . .

FRANK: Yes, sir—what I mean, I'm giving you my personal guarantee on this set, Mr. Baum.

MOE: I never paid no attention to these things, but maybe you heard of the market crash? The whole thing practically floated into the ocean, y'know.

FRANK: Oh, yes, sir, I certainly heard about it.

MOE: I'm glad you heard about it, because I heard a *lot* about it. In fact, what you cleared from selling my tires over the last ten years . . .

FRANK: Oh, no, sir! Mr. Baum!

MOE: Frank, lookin' back over the last ten years, I never heard of that amount of tires in my whole life since I first come over from Europe a baby at the age of six. That is a lot of tires, Frank; so I tell ya what we're gonna do now, you're going to drive her over to the Pierce Arrow showroom and leave her there, and then come to my office and we'll settle up.

FRANK: But how are you going to get around!

MOE: I'm a happy man in a taxi, Frank.

FRANK: Well, I'm sure going to be sorry to leave you people.

MOE: Everything comes to an end, Frank, it was great while it lasted. No hard feelings. *He shakes Frank's hand.* Bye-bye.

FRANK: But what . . . what am I supposed to do now?

MOE: You got in-laws?

FRANK: But I never got along with them.

MOE: You should've. *He hurries off, calling:* Taxi!

FRANK, *cap in hand, throws down lap robe and walks off aimlessly:* Damn!

Irene enters with a pram filled with junk and sings a few lines of "'Tain't Nobody's Bizness," unaccompanied. She picks up robe and admiringly inspects it. Then:

IRENE: You got fired, you walked away to nothing; no unemployment insurance, no Social Security—just the in-laws and fresh air. *She tosses the robe in with her junk.*

Fadeout.

ROSE: Still . . . it was very nice in a certain way. On our block in Brooklyn a lot of married children had to move back with the parents, and you heard babies crying in houses that didn't have a baby in twenty years. But of course the doubling up could also drive you crazy . . .

With hardly a pause, she turns to Grandpa, who is arriving center with canes and hatboxes. He drops the whole load on the floor.

What are *you* doing?

GRANDPA, *delivering a final verdict:* There's no room for these in my closet . . .

ROSE: For a few *canes*?

GRANDPA: And what about my hats? You shouldn't have bought such a small house, Rose.

ROSE, *of the canes:* I'll put them in the front-hall closet.

GRANDPA: No, people step on them. And where will I put my hats?

ROSE, *trying not to explode:* Papa, what do you want from me? We are doing what we can do!

GRANDPA: One bedroom for so many people is not right! You had three bathrooms in the apartment, and you used to look out the window, there was the whole New York. Here . . . listen to that street out there, it's a Brooklyn cemetery. And this barber here is *very* bad—look what he did to me. *He shows her.*

ROSE: Why? It's beautiful. *She brushes some hairs straight.* It's just a little uneven . . .

GRANDPA, *pushing her hand away:* I don't understand, Rose—why does he declare bankruptcy if he's going to turn around and pay his debts?

ROSE: For his reputation.

GRANDPA: His reputation! He'll have the reputation of a fool! The reason to go bankrupt is *not* to pay your debts!

ROSE, *uncertain herself:* He wanted to be honorable.

GRANDPA: But that's the whole beauty of it! He should've asked me. When I went bankrupt I didn't pay *nobody!*

ROSE, *deciding:* I've got to tell you something, Papa. From now on, I wish you . . .

GRANDPA, *helping her fold a bed sheet:* And you'll have to talk to Lee— he throws himself around in his bed all night, wakes me up ten times, and he leaves his socks on the floor. . . . Two people in that bedroom is too much, Rose.

ROSE: I don't want Moe to get aggravated, Papa.

He is reached, slightly glances at her.

He might try to start a new business, so he's nervous, so please, don't complain, Papa. Please?

GRANDPA: What did I say?

ROSE: Nothing. *Suddenly she embraces him guiltily.* Maybe I can find an umbrella stand someplace.

GRANDPA: I was reading about this Hitler . . .

ROSE: Who?

GRANDPA: . . . He's chasing all the radicals out of Germany. He wouldn't be so bad if he wasn't against the Jews. But he won't last six months. . . . The Germans are not fools. When I used to take Mama to Baden-Baden this time of year . . .

ROSE: How beautiful she was.

GRANDPA: . . . one time we were sitting on the train ready to leave for Berlin. And suddenly a man gallops up calling out my name. So I says, "Yes, that's me!" And through the window he hands me my gold watch and chain: "You left it in your room, mein Herr." Such a thing could only happen in Germany. This Hitler is finished.

ROSE, *of the canes:* Please. . . . Put them back in your closet, heh? *He starts to object.* I don't want Moe to get mad, Papa! *She cuts the rebellion short and loads him with his canes and hatboxes.*

GRANDPA, *muttering:* Man don't even know how to go bankrupt.

He exits. Lee appears on his bike—but dressed now for winter. He dismounts and parks the bike just as Rose lies back in the chair.

LEE: Ma! Guess what!

ROSE: What?

LEE: Remember I emptied my bank account for the bike?

ROSE: So?

LEE: The bank has just been closed by the government! It's broke! There's a whole mob of people in the street yelling where's their money! They've got cops and everything! There is no more money in the bank!

ROSE: You're a genius!

LEE: Imagine! . . . I could have lost my twelve dollars! . . . Wow!

ROSE: That's wonderful. *She removes a pearl choker.*

LEE: Oh, Ma, wasn't that Papa's wedding present?

ROSE: I hate to, but . . .

LEE: What about Papa's business! Can't he . . .

ROSE: He put too much capital in the stock market, dear—it made more there than in his business. So now . . . it's not there anymore.

A Thief swiftly appears and rides off on the bike.

But we'll be all right. Go. You can have a jelly sandwich when you come back.

Lee stuffs the pearls into his pants as he approaches where the bike was; he looks in all directions, his bones chilling. He runs in all directions and finally comes to a halt, breathless, stark horror in his face. As though sensing trouble, Rose walks over to him.

Where's your bike?

He can't speak.

They stole your bike?

He is immobile.

May he choke on his next meal. . . . Oh, my darling, my darling, what an awful thing.

He sobs once but holds it back. She, facing him, tries to smile.

So now you're going to have to walk to the hockshop like everybody else. Come, have your jelly sandwich.

LEE: No, I'd like to see if I can trot there—it'd be good for my track. By the way, I've almost decided to go to Cornell, I think. Cornell or Brown.

ROSE, *with an empty congratulatory exclamation:* Oh! . . . Well, there's still months to decide.

Rose and Lee join the company as they stand up to sing the Iowa Hymn, Verse 1: "We gather together to ask the Lord's blessing, He chastens and hastens His will to make known: The wicked oppressing now cease from distressing, Sing praises to His name: He forgets not His own." The hymn music continues under the following.

ROBERTSON: Till then, probably most people didn't think of it as a system.

TAYLOR: It was more like nature.

MRS. TAYLOR: Like weather; had to expect bad weather, but it always got good again if you waited. And so we waited. And it didn't change. *She is watching Taylor as he adopts a mood of despair and slowly sits on his heels.* And we waited some more and it never changed. You couldn't hardly believe that the day would come when the land wouldn't give. Land always gives. But there it lay, miles and miles of it, and there was us wanting to work it, and couldn't. It was like a spell on Iowa. We was all there, and the land was there waitin', and we wasn't able to move. *The hymn ends.* Amen.

Brewster, followed by Farmers, comes front and calls to the crowd in the audience's direction.

BREWSTER: Just sit tight, folks, be startin' in a few minutes.

FARMER 1, *hitting his heels together:* Looks like snow up there.

FARMER 2, *laughs:* Even the weather ain't workin'.

Low laughter in the crowd.

BREWSTER, *heading over to Taylor:* You be catchin' cold sitting on the ground like that, won't you, Henry?

TAYLOR: Tired out. Never slept a wink all night. Not a wink.

Mrs. Taylor appears carrying a big coffeepot, accompanied by Harriet, her fifteen-year-old daughter, who has a coffee mug hanging from each of her fingers.

MRS. TAYLOR: You'll have to share the cups, but it's something hot anyway.

BREWSTER: Oh, that smells good, lemme take that, ma'am.

She gives the coffeepot to Brewster and comes over to Taylor. Harriet hands out the cups.

MRS. TAYLOR, *sotto voce, irritated and ashamed:* You can't be sitting on the ground like that, now come on! *She starts him to his feet.* It's a auction—anybody's got a right to come to a auction.

TAYLOR: There must be a thousand men along the road—they never told me they'd bring a thousand men!

MRS. TAYLOR: Well, I suppose that's the way they do it.

TAYLOR: They got guns in those trucks!

MRS. TAYLOR, *frightened herself:* Well, it's too late to stop 'em now. So might as well go around and talk to people that come to help you.

CHARLEY, *rushing on:* Brewster! Where's Brewster!

BREWSTER, *stepping forward from the crowd:* What's up, Charley?

CHARLEY, *pointing off:* Judge Bradley! He's gettin' out of the car with the auctioneer!

Silence. All look to Brewster.

BREWSTER: Well . . . I don't see what that changes. *Turning to all:* I guess we're gonna do what we come here to do. That right?

The crowd quietly agrees: "Right," "Stick to it, Larry," "No use quittin' now," etc. Enter Judge Bradley, sixty, and Mr. Frank Howard, the auctioneer. The silence spreads.

JUDGE BRADLEY: Good morning, gentlemen. *He looks around. There is no reply.* I want to say a few words to you before Mr. Howard starts the auction. *He walks up onto a raised platform.* I have decided to come here personally this morning in order to emphasize the gravity of the situation that has developed in the state. We are on the verge of anarchy in Iowa, and that is not going to help anybody. Now, you are all property owners, so you—

BREWSTER: Used to be, Judge, used to be!

JUDGE BRADLEY: Brewster, I will not waste words; there are forty armed deputies out there. *Slight pause.* I would like to make only one point clear—I have levied a deficiency judgment on this farm. Mr. Taylor has failed to pay what he owes on his equipment and some of his cattle. A contract is sacred. The National Bank has the right to collect on its loans. Now then, Mr. Howard will begin the auction. But he has discretionary power to decline any unreasonable bid. I ask you again, obey the law. Once law and order go down, no man is safe. Mr. Howard?

MR. HOWARD, *with a clipboard in hand, climbs onto the platform:* Well, now, let's see. We have here one John Deere tractor and combine, three years old, beautiful condition.

Three Bidders enter, and the crowd turns to look at them with hostility as they come to a halt.

I ask for bids on the tractor and combine.

BREWSTER: Ten cents!

MR. HOWARD: I have ten cents. *His finger raised, he points from man to man in the crowd.* I have ten cents, I have ten cents . . .

He is pointing toward the Bidders, but they are looking around at the crowd in fear.

BIDDER 1: Five hundred.

JUDGE BRADLEY, *calling:* Sheriff, get over here and protect these men!

The Sheriff and four Deputies enter and edge their way in around the three Bidders. The deputies carry shotguns.

MR. HOWARD: Do I hear five hundred dollars? Do I hear five . . .

BIDDER 1: Five hundred!

MR. HOWARD: Do I hear six hundred?

BIDDER 2: Six hundred!

MR. HOWARD: Do I hear seven hundred?

BIDDER 3: Seven hundred!

Disciplined and quick, the Farmers grab the Deputies and disarm them; a shotgun goes off harmlessly.

JUDGE BRADLEY: Brewster! Great God, what are you doing!

Brewster has pinned the Judge's arms behind him, and another man lowers a noose around his neck.

BREWSTER, *to Deputies:* You come any closer and we're gonna string him up! You all get back on that road or we string up the Judge! So help me Christ, he goes up if any one of you deputies interferes with this auction! Now, let me just clear up one thing for you, Judge Bradley . . .

TAYLOR: Let him go, Brewster—I don't care anymore, let them take it!

BREWSTER: Just sit tight, Henry, nobody's takin' anything. That is all over, Judge. Mr. Howard, just to save time, why don't you take a bid on the whole place? Do that, please?

MR. HOWARD, *turns to the crowd, his voice shaking:* I . . . I'll hear bids on . . . everything. Tractor and combine, pair of mules and wagon, twenty-six cows, eight heifers, farm and outbuildings, assorted tools . . . and so forth. Do I hear . . .

BREWSTER: One dollar.

MR. HOWARD, *rapidly:* I hear one dollar. One dollar, one dollar? . . . *He looks around.* Sold for one dollar.

BREWSTER, *handing him a dollar:* Now, will you just sign that receipt, please?

Mr. Howard scribbles and hands him a receipt. Brewster leaps off the platform, goes to Taylor, and gives him the receipt.

Henry? Whyn't you go along now and get to milkin'. Let's go, boys.

He waves to the crowd, and his men follow him out. Judge Bradley, removing the noose, comes down off the platform and goes over to Taylor, who is staring down at the receipt.

JUDGE BRADLEY: Henry Taylor? You are nothing but a thief!

Taylor cringes under the accusation. The Judge points to the receipt.

That is a crime against every law of God and man! And this isn't the end of it, either! *He turns and stalks out.*

HARRIET: Should we milk 'em, Papa?

MRS. TAYLOR: Of course we milk 'em—they're ours. *But she needs Taylor's compliance.* Henry?

TAYLOR, *staring at the receipt:* It's like I stole my own place.

Near tears, humiliated, Taylor moves into darkness with his wife. The Farmers disperse.

ROBERTSON, *from choral area:* Nobody knows how many people are leaving their hometowns, their farms and cities, and hitting the road. Hundreds of thousands, maybe millions of internal refugees, Americans transformed into strangers.

Banks enters in army cap, uniform jacket and jeans, carrying his little bundle of clothes and a cooking pot.

BANKS: I still hear that train.
                         Still hear that long low whistle.
                         Still hear that train, yeah.

He imitates train whistle: Whoo-ooo! *He sings the first verse of "How Long,"
then speaks over music, which continues.*

Nineteen twenty-nine was pretty hard. My family had a little old cotton farm, McGehee, Arkansas. But a man had to be on the road—leave his wife, his mother—just to try to get a little money to live on. But God help me, I couldn't get anything, and I was too ashamed to send them a picture, all dirty and ragged and hadn't shaved. Write a postcard: "Dear Mother, doin' wonderful and hope you're all fine." And me sleepin' on a Los Angeles sidewalk under a newspaper. And my ma'd say, "Oh, my son's in Los Angeles, he's doin' pretty fair." *He grins.* Yeah . . . "all the way on the Santa Fe." So hungry and weak I begin to see snakes through the smoke, and a white hobo named Callahan got a scissors on me, wrapped me 'tween his legs—otherwise I'd have fell off into a cornfield there. But except for Callahan there was no friendships in the hobo jungle. Everybody else was worried and sad-lookin', and they was evil to each other. I still hear that long low whistle . . . *whoo-ooo!*

Banks sings the second verse of "How Long." Then the music changes into "The Joint Is Jumpin' ": Marathon Dancers enter, half asleep, some about to drop. They dance. Fadeout.

Light comes up on Moe in an armchair. Lee enters with college catalogues.

MOE: When you say three hundred dollars tuition . . . Lee!

LEE: That's for Columbia. Some of these others are cheaper.

MOE: That's for the four years.

LEE: Well, no, that's one year.

MOE: Ah. *He lies back in the chair and closes his eyes.*

LEE, *flipping a page of a catalogue:* Minnesota here is a hundred and fifty, for instance. And Ohio State is about the same, I think. *He turns to Moe, awaiting his reaction.* Pa?

Moe is asleep.

He always got drowsy when the news got bad. And now the mystery of the marked house began. Practically every day you'd see the stranger coming down the street, poor and ragged, and he'd go past house after house, but at our driveway he'd make a turn right up to the back porch and ask for something to eat. Why us?

Taylor appears at one side of the stage in mackinaw, farm shoes, and peaked hunter's cap, a creased paper bag under his arm. Looking front, he seems gaunt, out of his element; now he rings the doorbell. Nothing happens. Then Lee goes to the "door."

LEE: Yes?

TAYLOR, *shyly, still an amateur at the routine:* Ah . . . sorry to be botherin' you on a Sunday and all.

ROSE, *enters in housedress and apron, wiping her hands on a dish towel:* Who is that, dear? *She comes to the door.*

LEE: This is my mother.

TAYLOR: How-de-do, ma'am, my name is Taylor, and I'm just passing by, wondering if you folks have any work around the place . . .

MOE, *waking up suddenly:* Hey! The bell rang! *He sees the conclave.* Oh . . .

ROSE, *ironically:* Another one looking for work!

TAYLOR: I could paint the place or fix the roof, electrical, plumbing, masonry, gardening . . . I always had my own farm, and we do all that, don't you know. I'd work cheap . . .

ROSE: Well, we don't need any kind of . . .

MOE: Where you from?

TAYLOR: State of Iowa.

LEE, *as though it's the moon: Iowa!*

TAYLOR: I wouldn't hardly charge if I could have my meals, don't you know.

MOE, *beginning to locate Taylor in space:* Whereabouts in Iowa?

ROSE: My sister's husband comes from Cleveland.

MOE: No, no, Cleveland is nowhere near. *To Taylor:* Whereabouts?

TAYLOR: You know Styles?

MOE: I only know the stores in the big towns.

TAYLOR, *giving a grateful chuckle:* Well! I never expected to meet a . . .

He suddenly gets dizzy, breaks off, and reaches for some support. Lee holds his arm, and he goes down like an elevator and sits there.

ROSE: What's the matter!

MOE: Mister?

LEE: I'll get water! *He rushes out.*

ROSE: Is it your heart?

TAYLOR: 'Scuse me . . . I'm awful sorry . . .

He gets on his hands and knees as Lee enters with a glass of water and hands it to him. He drinks half of it, returns the glass.

Thank you, sonny.

ROSE, *looks to Moe, sees his agreement, gestures within:* He better sit down.

MOE: You want to sit down?

Taylor looks at him helplessly.

Come, sit down.

Lee and Moe help him to a chair, and he sits.

ROSE, *bending over to look into his face:* You got some kind of heart?

TAYLOR, *embarrassed, and afraid for himself now:* Would you be able to give me something to eat?

The three stare at him; he looks up at their shocked astonishment and weeps.

ROSE: You're *hungry?*

TAYLOR: Yes, ma'am.

Rose looks at Moe whether to believe this.

MOE, *unnerved:* Better get him something.

ROSE, *hurrying out immediately:* Oh, my God in heaven!

MOE, *now with a suspicious, even accusatory edge:* What're you doing, just going around? . . .

TAYLOR: Well, no, I come east when I lost the farm. . . . They was supposed to be hiring in New Jersey, pickers for the celery? But I only got two days. . . . I been to the Salvation Army four, five times, but they only give me a bun and a cup of coffee yesterday . . .

LEE: You haven't eaten since *yesterday?*

TAYLOR: Well, I generally don't need too much . . .

ROSE, *entering with a tray, bowl of soup, and bread:* I was just making it, so I didn't put in the potatoes yet . . .

TAYLOR: Oh, beets?

ROSE: That's what you call borscht.

TAYLOR, *obediently:* Yes, ma'am.

He wastes no time, spoons it up. They all watch him: their first hungry man.

MOE, *skeptically:* How do you come to lose a farm?

TAYLOR: I suppose you read about the Farmers' Uprisin' in the state couple months ago?

LEE: I did.

MOE, *to Lee:* What uprising?

LEE: They nearly lynched a judge for auctioning off their farms. *To Taylor, impressed:* Were you in *that?*

TAYLOR: Well, it's all over now, but I don't believe they'll be auctioning any more farms for a while, though. Been just terrible out there.

ROSE, *shaking her head:* And I thought they were all Republicans in Iowa.

TAYLOR: Well, I guess they all are.

LEE: Is that what they mean by radical, though?

TAYLOR: Well . . . it's like they say—people in Iowa are practical. They'll even go radical if it seems like it's practical. But as soon as it stops being practical they stop being radical.

MOE: Well, you probably all learned your lesson now.

LEE: Why! He was taking their homes away, that judge!

MOE: So you go in a court and lynch him?

LEE: But . . . but it's all *wrong*, Pa!

ROSE: Shh! Don't argue . . .

LEE, *to Rose:* But *you* think it's wrong, don't you? Suppose they came and threw us out of *this* house?

ROSE: I refuse to think about it. *To Taylor:* So where do you sleep?

MOE, *instantly:* Excuse me. We are not interested in where you sleep, Mr. . . . what's your name?

TAYLOR: Taylor. I'd be satisfied with just my meals if I could live in the basement . . .

MOE, *to Taylor, but half addressing Rose:* There is no room for another human being in this house, y'understand? Including the basement. *He takes out two or three bills.*

TAYLOR: I wasn't asking for charity . . .

MOE: I'm going to loan you a dollar, and I hope you're going to start a whole new life. Here . . . *He hands Taylor the bill, escorting him to the door.* And pay me back, but don't rush. *He holds out his hand.* Glad to have met you, and good luck.

TAYLOR: Thanks for the soup, Mrs. . . .

ROSE: Our name is Baum. You have children?

TAYLOR: One's fifteen, one's nine. *He thoughtfully folds the dollar bill.*

Grandpa enters, eating a plum.

ROSE: Take care of yourself, and write a letter to your wife.

TAYLOR: Yes, I will. *To Moe:* Goodbye, sir . . .

MOE, *grinning, tipping his finger at Taylor:* Stay away from rope.

TAYLOR: Oh, yeah, I will . . . *He exits.*

LEE, *goes out on the periphery and calls to him as he walks away:* Goodbye, Mr. Taylor!

TAYLOR, *turns back, waves:* Bye, sonny!

He leaves. Lee stares after him, absorbing it all.

GRANDPA: Who was that?

MOE: He's a farmer from Iowa. He tried to lynch a judge, so she wanted him to live in the cellar.

GRANDPA: What is a farmer doing here?

ROSE: He went broke, he lost everything.

GRANDPA: Oh. Well, he should borrow.

MOE, *snaps his fingers to Lee:* I'll run down the street and tell him! He got me hungry. *To Rose:* I'm going down the corner and get a chocolate soda. . . . What do you say, Lee?

LEE: I don't feel like it.

MOE: Don't be sad. Life is tough, what're you going to do? Sometimes it's not as tough as other times, that's all. But it's always tough. Come, have a soda.

LEE: Not now, Pa, thanks. *He turns away.*

MOE, *straightens, silently refusing blame:* Be back right away. *He strolls across the stage, softly, tonelessly whistling, and exits.*

Grandpa, chewing, the plum pit in his hand, looks around for a place to put it. Rose sees the inevitable and holds out her hand.

ROSE, *disgusted:* Oh, give it to me.

Grandpa drops the pit into her palm, and she goes out with it and the soup plate.

LEE, *still trying to digest:* That man was starving, Grandpa.

GRANDPA: No, no, he was hungry but not starving.

LEE: He was, he almost fainted.

GRANDPA: No, that's not starving. In Europe they starve, but here not. Anyway, couple weeks they're going to figure out what to do, and you can forget the whole thing. . . . God makes one person at a time, boy—worry about yourself.

Fadeout.

ROBERTSON: His name is Theodore K. Quinn.

Music begins—"My Baby Just Cares for Me"—and Quinn, with boater and cane, sings and dances through Robertson's speech.

The greatest Irish soft-shoe dancer ever to serve on a board of directors. They know him at Lindy's, they love him at "21." High up on top of the American heap sits Ted Quinn, hardly forty years of age in 1932 . . .

QUINN, *continues singing, then breaks off and picks up the phone:* Ted Quinn. Come over, Arthur, I've got to see you. But come to the twenty-ninth floor. . . . I've got a new office.

ROBERTSON, *looking around, as at a striking office:* All this *yours?*

QUINN: Yup. You are standing on the apex, the pinnacle of human evolution. From that window you can reach out and touch the moustache of Almighty God.

ROBERTSON, *moved, gripping Quinn's hand:* Ted! *Ted!!*

QUINN: Jesus, don't say it that way, will ya?

ROBERTSON: President of General Electric!

QUINN: I'm not sure I want it, Arthur.

Robertson laughs sarcastically.

I'm not, goddammit! I never expected Swope to pick me—never!

ROBERTSON: Oh, go on, you've been angling for the presidency the last five years.

QUINN: No! I swear not. I just didn't want anybody else to get it . . .

Robertson laughs.

Well, that's not the same thing! . . . Seriously, Arthur, I'm scared. I don't know what to do. *He looks around.* Now that I'm standing here, now that they're about to paint my name on the door . . . and the *Times* sending a reporter . . .

ROBERTSON, *seriously:* What the hell's got into you?

QUINN, *searching in himself:* I don't know. . . . It's almost like shame.

ROBERTSON: For *what*? It's that damned upbringing of yours, that anarchist father . . .

QUINN: The truth is, I've never been comfortable with some of the things we've done.

ROBERTSON: But why suddenly after all these years . . .

QUINN: It's different taking orders and being the man who gives them.

ROBERTSON: I don't know what the hell you are talking about.

Pause. For Quinn it is both a confession and something he must *bring out into the open. But he sustains his humor.*

QUINN: I had a very unsettling experience about eighteen months ago, Arthur. Got a call from my Philadelphia district manager that Frigidaire was dropping the price on their boxes. So I told him to cut ours. And in a matter of weeks they cut, we cut, they cut, we cut, till I finally went down there myself. Because I was damned if I was going to get beat in Philadelphia . . . and I finally cut our price right down to our cost of production. Well—ting-a-ling-a-ling, phone call from New York: "What the hell is going on down there?" Gotta get down to Wall Street and have a meeting with the money boys. . . . So there we are, about ten of us, and I look across the blinding glare of that teakwood table, and lo and behold, who is facing me but Georgy Fairchild, head of sales for Frigidaire. Old friends, Georgy and I, go way back together, but he *is* Frigidaire, y'know—what the hell is he doing in a GE meeting? . . . Well, turns out that both companies are owned by the same money. And the word is that Georgy and Quinn are going to cut out this nonsense and get those prices up to where they belong. *He laughs.* Well, I tell you, I was absolutely flabbergasted. Here I've been fightin' Georgy from Bangkok to the Bronx, layin' awake nights thinkin' how to outfox him—hell, we were like Grant and Lee with thousands of soldiers out to destroy each other, and it's suddenly like all these years I'd been shellin' my own men! *He laughs.* It was farcical.

ROBERTSON: It's amazing. You're probably the world's greatest salesman, and you haven't an ounce of objectivity . . .

QUINN: Objectivity! Arthur, if I'm that great a salesman—which I'm far from denying—it's because I believe; I believe deeply in the creative force of competition.

ROBERTSON: Exactly, and GE is the fastest-growing company in the world because . . .

QUINN, *loves this point:* . . . because we've had the capital to buy up one independent business after another. . . . It's haunting me, Arthur—thousands of small businesses are going under every week now, and we're getting bigger and bigger every day. What's going to become of the independent person in this country once everybody's sucking off the same tit? How can there be an America without Americans—people not beholden to some enormous enterprise that'll run their souls?

ROBERTSON: Am I hearing what I think?

Quinn is silent.

Ted? You'd actually resign?

QUINN: If I did, would it make any point to you at all? If I made a statement that . . .

ROBERTSON: What statement can you possibly make that won't call for a return to the horse and buggy? The America you love is cold stone dead in the parlor, Ted. This is a corporate country; you can't go back to small personal enterprise again.

QUINN: A corporate country! . . . Jesus, Arthur, what a prospect!

Miss Fowler enters.

MISS FOWLER: The gentleman from the *Times* is waiting, Mr. Quinn . . . unless you'd like to make it tomorrow or . . .

QUINN, *slight pause:* No, no—it has to be now or never. Ask him in.

She exits.

Tell me the truth, Arthur, do I move your mind at all?

ROBERTSON: Of course I see your point. But you can't buck the inevitable.

Graham enters with Miss Fowler.

MISS FOWLER: Mr. Graham.

QUINN, *shakes hands, grinning:* Glad to meet you. . . . My friend Mr. Robertson.

GRAHAM, *recognizing the name:* Oh, yes, how do you do?

ROBERTSON: Nice to meet you. *To Quinn, escaping:* I'll see you later . . .

QUINN: No, stay . . . I'll only be a few minutes . . .

ROBERTSON: I ought to get back to my office.

QUINN, *laughs:* I'm still the president, Arthur—stay! I want to feel the support of your opposition.

Robertson laughs with Quinn, glancing uneasily at Graham, who doesn't know what's going on.

I'll have to be quick, Mr. Graham. Will you sit down?

GRAHAM: I have a few questions about your earlier life and background. I understand your father was one of the early labor organizers in Chicago.

QUINN: Mr. Graham, I am resigning.

GRAHAM: Beg your pardon?

QUINN: Resigning, I said.

GRAHAM: From the presidency? I don't understand.

QUINN: I don't believe in giant business, or giant government, or giant anything. And the laugh is . . . no man has done more to make GE the giant it is today.

GRAHAM: Well, now! *He laughs.* I think this takes us off the financial section and onto the front page! But tell me, how does a man with your ideas rise so high in a great corporation like this? How did you get into GE?

QUINN: Well, it's a long story, but I love to tell it. I started out studying law at night and working as a clerk in a factory that manufactured bulbs for auto headlights. Y'see, in those days they had forty or fifty makes of car and all different specifications for the lightbulbs. Now, say you got an order for five thousand lamps. The manufacturing process was not too accurate, so you had to make eight or nine thousand to come out with five thousand perfect ones. Result, though, was that we had hundreds of thousands of perfectly good lamps left over at the end of the year. So . . . one night on my own time I went through the records and did some simple calculations and came up with a new average. My figure showed that to get five thousand good bulbs we only had to make sixty-two hundred instead of eight thousand. Result was, that company saved a hundred and thirty thousand dollars in one year. So the boss and I became very friendly, and one day he says, "I'm selling out to General Electric," but he couldn't tell whether they'd be keeping me on. So he says to me, "Ted, tell you what we do. They're coming out from Wall Street"—these bankers, y'see—"and I'm going to let you pick them up at the depot." Figuring I'd be the first to meet them and might draw their attention and they'd rehire me, y'see. Well, I was just this hick-town kid, y'know, about to meet these great big juicy Wall Street bankers—I tell you, I hardly slept all night tryin' to figure how to make an impression. And just toward dawn . . . it was during breakfast—and I suddenly thought of that wall. See, the factory had this brick wall a block long; no windows, two stories high, just a tremendous wall of bricks. And it went through my mind that one of them might ask me how many bricks were in that wall. 'Cause I could answer any question about the company except that. So I got over to the plant as quick as I could, multiplied the vertical and horizontal bricks, and got the number. Well . . . these three bankers arrive, and I get them into the boss's limousine, and we ride. Nobody asks me anything! Three of them in those big fur-lined coats, and not one goddamn syllable. . . . Anyway, we round the corner, and doesn't one of them turn to me and say, "Mr. Quinn, how many bricks you suppose is in that wall!" And by God, I told him! Well, he wouldn't believe it, got out and counted himself—and it broke the ice, y'see, and one thing and another they made me manager of the plant. And that's how I got into GE.

GRAHAM, *astonished:* What are your plans? Will you join another company or . . .

QUINN: No. I've been tickling the idea I might set up an advisory service for small business. Say a fella has a concept, I could teach him how to develop and market it . . . 'cause I *know* all that, and maybe I could help—*To the audience:*—to keep those individuals coming. Because with this terrible Depression you hear it everywhere now—an individual man is not worth a bag of peanuts. I don't know the answers, Mr. Graham, but I sure as hell know the question: How do you keep everything that's

big from swallowing everything that's small? 'Cause when that happens
—God Almighty—it's not going to be much fun!

GRAHAM: Well . . . thanks very much. Good day. Good day, Mr. Robertson. I must say . . . ! *With a broken laugh and a shake of the head, he
hurries out.*

QUINN: He was not massively overwhelmed, was he?

ROBERTSON: He heard the gentle clip-clop of the horse and buggy
coming down the road.

QUINN: All right, then, damn it, maybe what you ought to be looking
into, Arthur, is horseshoes!

ROBERTSON: Well, you never did do things in a small way! This is
unquestionably the world record for the shortest presidency in corporate
history. *He exits.*

*Alone, Quinn stares around in a moment of surprise and fright at what he's
actually done. Soft-shoe music steals up, and he insinuates himself into it, dancing
in a kind of uncertain mood that changes to release and joy, and at the climax
he sings the last lines of "My Baby Just Cares for Me." As the lyrics end, the
phone rings. He picks up the receiver, never losing the beat, and simply lets it
drop, and dances off.*

Rose comes downstage, staring front, a book in her hand.

ROSE: Who would believe it? You look out the window in the middle
of a fine October day, and there's a dozen college graduates with ad-
vanced degrees playing ball in the street like children. And it gets harder
and harder to remember when life seemed to have so much purpose,
when you couldn't wait for the morning!

*Lee enters, takes a college catalogue off the prop table, and approaches her, turning
the pages.*

LEE: At Cornell there's no tuition fee at all if you enroll in bacteriology.

ROSE: Free *tuition*!

LEE: Maybe they're short of bacteriologists.

ROSE: Would you like that?

LEE, *stares, tries to see himself as a bacteriologist, sighs:* Bacteriology?

ROSE, *wrinkling her nose:* Must be awful. Is anything else free?

LEE: It's the only one I've seen.

ROSE: I've got to finish this before tomorrow. I'm overdue fourteen cents on it.

LEE: What is it?

ROSE: *Coronet* by Manuel Komroff. It's about this royal crown that gets stolen and lost and found again and lost again for generations. It's supposed to be literature, but I don't know, it's very enjoyable. *She goes back to her book.*

LEE, *closes the catalogue, looks at her:* Ma?

ROSE, *still reading:* Hm?

LEE, *gently breaking the ice:* I guess it's too late to apply for this year anyway. Don't you think so?

ROSE, *turns to him:* I imagine so, dear . . . for this year.

LEE: Okay, Ma . . .

ROSE: I feel so terrible—all those years we were throwing money around, and now when you need it—

LEE, *relieved, now that he knows:* That's okay. I think maybe I'll try looking for a job. But I'm not sure whether to look under "Help Wanted, Male" or "Boy Wanted."

ROSE: Boy! *Their gazes meet. She sees his apprehension.* Don't be frightened, darling—you're going to be wonderful! *She hides her feeling in the book.*

Fadeout. Light comes up on Fanny, standing on the first-level balcony. She calls to Sidney, who is playing the piano and singing "Once in a While."

FANNY: Sidney?

He continues singing.

Sidney?

He continues singing.

Sidney?

He continues singing.

I have to talk to you, Sidney.

He continues singing.

Stop that for a minute!

SIDNEY, *stops singing:* Ma, look . . . it's only July. If I was still in high school it would still be my summer vacation.

FANNY: And if I was the Queen of Rumania I would have free rent. You graduated, Sidney, this is not summer vacation.

SIDNEY: Mama, it's useless to go to employment agencies—there's grown men there, engineers, college graduates. They're willing to take anything. If I could write one hit song like this, just one—we wouldn't have to worry again. Let me have July, just July—see if I can do it. Because that man was serious—he's a good friend of the waiter who works where Bing Crosby's manager eats. He could give him any song I write, and if Crosby just sang it one time . . .

FANNY: I want to talk to you about Doris.

SIDNEY: What Doris?

FANNY: Doris! Doris from downstairs. I've been talking to her mother. She likes you, Sidney.

SIDNEY: Who?

FANNY: Her mother! Mrs. Gross. She's crazy about you.

SIDNEY, *not comprehending:* Oh.

FANNY: She says all Doris does is talk about you.

SIDNEY, *worried:* What is she talking about me for?

FANNY: No, nice things. She likes you.

SIDNEY, *amused, laughs incredulously:* Doris? She's thirteen.

FANNY: She'll be fourteen in December. Now listen to me.

SIDNEY: What, Ma?

FANNY: It's all up to you, Sidney, I want you to make up your own mind. But Papa's never going to get off his back again, and after Lucille's wedding we can forget about *her* salary. Mrs. Gross says—being she's a widow, y'know? And with her goiter and everything . . .

SIDNEY: What?

FANNY: If you like Doris—only if you like her—and you would agree to get married—when she's eighteen, about, or seventeen, even—if you would agree to it now, we could have this apartment rent-free. Starting next month.

SIDNEY, *impressed, even astounded:* Forever?

FANNY: Of course. You would be the husband, it would be your house. You'd move downstairs, with that grand piano and the tile shower . . . I even think if you'd agree she'd throw in the three months' back rent that we owe. I wouldn't even be surprised you could take over the bakery.

SIDNEY: The bakery! For God's sake, Mama, I'm a composer!

FANNY: Now listen to me . . .

Doris enters and sits on the floor weaving a cat's cradle of string.

SIDNEY: But how can I be a baker!

FANNY: Sidney, dear, did you ever once look at that girl?

SIDNEY: Why should I look at her!

FANNY, *taking him to the "window":* Because she's a beauty. I wouldn't have mentioned it otherwise. Look. Look at that nose. Look at her hands. You see those beautiful little white hands? You don't find hands like that everywhere.

SIDNEY: But Ma, listen—if you just leave me alone for July, and if I write one hit song . . . I know I can do it, Mama.

FANNY: Okay. Sidney, we're behind a hundred and eighty dollars. August first we're out on the street. So write a hit, dear. I only hope that four, five years from now you don't accidentally run into Doris Gross somewhere and fall in love with her—after we all died from exposure!

SIDNEY: But Ma, even if I agreed—supposing next year or the year after I meet some other girl and I really like her . . .

FANNY: All right, and supposing you marry *that* girl and a year after you meet another girl you like better—what are you going to do, get married every year? . . . But I only wanted you to know the situation. I'll close the door, everything'll be quiet. Write a big hit, Sidney! *She exits.*

Sidney begins to sing "Once in a While"; Doris echoes him timorously. They trade a few lines, Sidney hesitant and surprised. Then:

DORIS, *fully confident, ending the song:* ". . . nearest your heart."

SIDNEY, *sits on his heels beside her as she weaves the string:* Gee, you're really terrific at that, Doris.

He stands, she stands, and they shyly walk off together as he slips his hand into hers.

ROBERTSON, *from choral area:* I guess the most shocking thing is what I see from the window of my Riverside Drive apartment. It's Calcutta on the Hudson, thousands of people living in cardboard boxes right next to that beautiful drive. It is like an army encampment down the length of Manhattan Island. At night you see their campfires flickering, and some nights I go down and walk among them. Remarkable, the humor they still have, but of course people still blame themselves rather than the government. But there's never been a society that hasn't had a clock running on it, and you can't help wondering—how long? How long will they stand for this? So now Roosevelt's got in I'm thinking—boy, he'd better move. He'd better move fast. . . . And you can't help it; first thing every night when I get home, I go to the window and look down at those fires, the flames reflecting off the river through the night.

Lights come up on Moe and Rose. Moe, in a business suit and hat, is just giving her a peck.

ROSE: Goodbye, darling. This is going to be a good day—I know it!

MOE, *without much conviction:* I think you're right. G'bye. *He walks, gradually comes to a halt. Much uncertainty and tension as he glances back toward his house and then looks down to think.*

Lee enters, and Rose gives him a farewell kiss. He wears a mackinaw. She hands him a lunch bag.

ROSE: Don't squeeze it, I put in some cookies. . . . And listen—it doesn't mean you can *never* go to college.

LEE: Oh, I don't mind, Ma. Anyway, I like it around machines. I'm lucky I got the job!

ROSE: All the years we had so much, and now when you need it—

LEE, *cutting her off:* See ya!

He leaves her; she exits. He walks and is startled by Moe standing there.

I thought you left a long time ago!

MOE: I'll walk you a way.

He doesn't bother explaining, simply walks beside Lee, but at a much slower pace than Lee took before. Lee feels his unusual tension but can only glance over at him with growing apprehension and puzzlement. Finally Moe speaks.

Good job?

LEE: It's okay. I couldn't believe they picked me!

MOE, *nodding:* Good.

They walk on in silence, weaving all over the stage, the tension growing as Lee keeps glancing at Moe, who continuously stares down and ahead as they proceed. At last Moe halts and takes a deep breath.

How much money've you got, Lee?

LEE, *completely taken aback:* . . . money have I got?

MOE, *indicating Lee's pockets:* I mean right now.

LEE: Oh! Well, about . . . *he takes out change* . . . thirty-five cents. I'm okay.

MOE: . . . Could I have a quarter? . . . So I can get downtown.

LEE, *pauses an instant, astonished:* Oh, sure, Pa! *He quickly searches his pockets again.*

MOE: You got your lunch—I'll need a hotdog later.

LEE, *handing him a quarter:* It's okay. I have a dollar in my drawer. . . . Should I . . . *He starts to go back.*

MOE: No, don't go back. *He proceeds to walk again.* Don't, ah . . . mention it, heh?

LEE: Oh, no!

MOE: She worries.

LEE: I know. *To audience:* We went down to the subway together, and it was hard to look at one another. So we pretended that nothing had happened. *They come to a halt and sit, as though on a subway.* But something had. . . . It was like I'd started to support my *father*! And why that should have made me feel so happy, I don't know, but it did! And to cheer him up I began to talk, and before I knew it I was inventing a fantastic future! I said I'd be going to college in no more than a year, at most two; and that I'd straighten out my mind and become an A student; and then I'd not only get a job on a newspaper, but I'd have my own column, no less! By the time we got to Forty-second Street, the Depression was practically over! *He laughs.* And in a funny way it *was*—*He touches his breast*—in here . . . even though I knew we had a long bad time ahead of us. And so, like most people, I waited with that crazy kind of expectation that comes when there is no hope, waited for the dream to come back from wherever it had gone to hide.

A voice from the theatre sings the end of "In New York City, You Really Got to Know Your Line," or similar song.

End of Act One

ACT TWO

Rose, at the piano, has her hands suspended over the keyboard as the band pianist plays. She starts singing "He Loves and She Loves," then breaks off.

ROSE: But this piano is not leaving this house. Jewelry, yes, but nobody hocks this dear, darling piano. *She "plays" and sings more of the song.* The crazy ideas people get. Mr. Warsaw on our block, to make a little money he started a racetrack in his kitchen, with cockroaches. Keeps them in matchboxes with their names written on—Alvin, Murray, Irving . . . They bet nickels, dimes. *She picks up some sheet music.* Oh, what a show, that *Funny Face. She sings the opening of "'S Wonderful."* The years go by and you don't get to see a show and Brooklyn drifts further and further into the Atlantic; Manhattan becomes a foreign country, and a year can go by without ever going there. *She sings more of "'S Wonderful."* Wherever you look there's a contest; Kellogg's, Post Toasties, win five thousand, win ten thousand. I guess I ought to try, but the winners are always in Indiana somehow. I only pray to God our health holds up, because one filling and you've got to lower the thermostat for a month. Sing! *She sings the opening of "Do-Do-Do What You Done-Done-Done Before."* I must go to the library—I must start taking out some good books again; I must stop getting so stupid. I don't see anything, I don't hear anything except money, money, money . . . *She "plays" Schumann. Fadeout.*

ROBERTSON, *from choral area:* Looking back, of course, you can see there were two sides to it—with the banks foreclosing right and left, I picked up some first-class properties for a song. I made more money in the thirties than ever before, or since. But I knew a generation was coming of age who would never feel this sense of opportunity.

405

LEE: After a lot of jobs and saving, I did get to the university, and it was a quiet island in the stream. Two pairs of socks and a shirt, plus a good shirt and a mackinaw, and maybe a part-time job in the library, and you could live like a king and never see cash. So there was a distinct reluctance to graduate into that world out there . . . where you knew nobody wanted you.

Joe, Ralph, and Rudy gather in graduation caps and gowns.

Joey! Is it possible?

JOE: What?

LEE: You're a dentist!

RALPH: Well, I hope things are better when you get out, Lee.

LEE: You decide what to do?

RALPH: There's supposed to be a small aircraft plant still working in Louisville . . .

LEE: Too bad you picked propellers for a specialty.

RALPH: Oh, they'll make airplanes again—soon as there's a war.

LEE: How could there be another war?

JOE: Long as there's capitalism, baby.

RALPH: There'll always be war, y'know, according to the Bible. But if not, I'll probably go into the ministry.

LEE: I never knew you were religious.

RALPH: I'm sort of religious. They pay pretty good, you know, and you get your house and a clothing allowance . . .

JOE, *comes to Lee, extending his hand in farewell:* Don't forget to read Karl Marx, Lee. And if you're ever in the neighborhood with a toothache, look me up. I'll keep an eye out for your by-line.

LEE: Oh, I don't expect a newspaper job—papers are closing all over the place. Drop me a card if you open an office.

JOE: It'll probably be in my girl's father's basement. He promised to dig the floor out deeper so I can stand up . . .

LEE: What about equipment?

JOE: I figure two, three years I'll be able to open, if I can make a down payment on a used drill. Come by, I'll put back those teeth Ohio State knocked out.

LEE: I sure will! . . . So long, Rudy!

RUDY: Oh, you might still be seeing me around next semester.

JOE: You staying on campus?

RUDY: I might for the sake of my root canals. If I just take one university course I'm still entitled to the Health Service—could get my canals finished.

LEE: You mean there's a course in the Lit School you haven't taken?

RUDY: Yeah, I just found out about it. Roman Band Instruments.

JOE, *laughs:* You're kiddin'!

RUDY: No, in the Classics Department. Roman Band Instruments. *He pulls his cheek back.* See, I've still got three big ones to go on this side.

Laughter.

Well, if you really face it, where am I running? Chicago's loaded with anthropologists. Here, the university's like my mother—I've got free rent, wash dishes for my meals, get my teeth fixed, and God knows, I might pick up the paper one morning and there's an ad: "Help Wanted: Handsome young college graduate, good teeth, must be thoroughly acquainted with Roman band instruments"!

Laughter. They sing "Love and a Dime" accompanied by Rudy on banjo.

RALPH: I'll keep looking for your by-line anyway, Lee.

LEE: No, I doubt it; but I might angle a job on a Mississippi paddleboat when I get out.

RUDY: They still run those?

LEE: Yeah, there's a few. I'd like to retrace Mark Twain's voyages.

RUDY: Well, if you run into Huckleberry Finn—

LEE: I'll give him your regards.

Laughing, Ralph and Rudy start out.

RALPH: Beat Ohio State, kid!

JOE, *alone with Lee, gives him a clenched-fist salute:* So long, Lee.

LEE, *returning the salute:* So long, Joe! *With fist still clenched, he mimes pulling a whistle, dreamily imagining the Mississippi.* Toot! Toot!

He moves to a point, taking off his shirt, with which he wipes sweat off his face and neck as in the distance we hear a paddleboat's engines and wheel in water and whistle. Lee stares out as though from a deck. He is seeing aloud.

How scary and beautiful the Mississippi is. How do they manage to live? Every town has a bank boarded up, and all those skinny men sitting on the sidewalks with their backs against the storefronts. It's all stopped; like a magic spell. And the anger, the anger . . . when they were handing out meat and beans to the hungry, and the maggots wriggling out of the beef, and that man pointing his rifle at the butcher demanding the fresh meat the government had paid him to hand out . . . How could this have happened, is Marx right? Paper says twelve executives in tobacco made more than thirty thousand farmers who raised it. How long can they accept this? The anger has a smell, it hangs in the air wherever people gather. . . . Fights suddenly break out and simmer down. Is this when revolution comes? And why not? How would Mark Twain write what I have seen? Armed deputies guarding cornfields and whole families sitting beside the road, staring at that food which nobody can buy and is rotting on the stalk. It's insane. *He exits.*

ROSE, *from choral area, to audience:* But how can he become a sportswriter if he's a Communist?

Joe, carrying a large basket of flowers, crosses downstage to the sound effect of a subway train passing. He sings a verse of "In New York City, You Really Got to Know Your Line." He then breaks upstage and enters Isabel's apartment. She is in bed.

ISABEL: Hello, honey.

JOE: Could you start calling me Joe? It's less anonymous. *He starts removing his shoes and top pair of trousers.*

ISABEL: Whatever you say. You couldn't come later—hey, could you? I was just ready to go to sleep, I had a long night.

JOE: I can't, I gotta catch the girls before they get to the office, they like a flower on the desk. And later I'm too tired.

ISABEL: Ain't that uncomfortable—hey? Two pairs of pants?

JOE: It's freezing cold on that subway platform. The wind's like the Gobi Desert. The only problem is when you go out to pee it takes twice as long.

ISABEL: Sellin' books too—hey?

JOE: No, I'm reading that. Trying not to forget the English language. All I hear all day is shit, fuck, and piss. I keep meaning to tell you, Isabel, it's so relaxing to talk to you, especially when you don't understand about seventy percent of what I'm saying.

ISABEL, *laughs, complimented:* Hey!

JOE, *takes her hand:* In here I feel my sanity coming back, to a certain extent. Down in the subway all day I really wonder maybe some kind of lunacy is taking over. People stand there waiting for the train, talking to themselves. And loud, with gestures. And the number of men who come up behind me and feel my ass. *With a sudden drop in all his confidence:* What scares me, see, is that I'm getting too nervous to pick up a drill—if I ever get to practice dentistry at all, I mean. The city . . . is crazy! A hunchback yesterday suddenly comes up to me . . . apropos of nothing . . . and he starts yelling, "You will not find one word about democracy in the Constitution, this is a Christian Republic!" Nobody laughed. The Nazi swastika is blossoming out all over the toothpaste ads. And it seems to be getting worse—there's a guy on Forty-eighth Street and Eighth Avenue selling two hotdogs for seven cents! What can he make?

ISABEL: Two for *seven*? Jesus.

JOE: I tell you I get the feeling every once in a while that some bright morning millions of people are going to come pouring out of the buildings and just . . . I don't know what . . . kill each other? Or only the Jews? Or just maybe sit down on the sidewalk and cry. *Now he turns to her and starts to climb up on the bed beside her.*

ISABEL, *looking at the book:* It's about families?

JOE: No, it's just called *The Origin of the Family, Private Property, and the State*, by Friedrich Engels. Marxism.

ISABEL: What's that?

JOE, *his head resting on hers, his hand holding her breast:* Well, it's the idea that all of our relationships are basically ruled by money.

ISABEL, *nodding, as she well knows:* Oh, right—hey, yeah.

JOE, *raising himself up:* No, it's not what you think . . .

ISABEL: It's a whole book about *that*?

JOE: It's about socialism, where the girls would all have jobs so they wouldn't have to do this, see.

ISABEL: Oh! But what would the guys do, though?

JOE, *flustered:* Well . . . like for instance if I had money to open an office I would probably get married very soon.

ISABEL: Yeah, but I get married guys. *Brightly:* And I even get two dentists that you brought me . . . Bernie and Allan? . . . and they've got offices, too.

JOE: You don't understand. . . . He shows that underneath our ideals it's all economics between people, and it shouldn't be.

ISABEL: What should it be?

JOE: Well, you know, like . . . love.

ISABEL: Ohhh! Well that's nice—hey. You think I could read it?

JOE: Sure, try. . . . I'd like your reaction. I like you early, Isabel, you look so fresh. Gives me an illusion.

ISABEL: I'm sorry if I'm tired.

JOE, *kisses her, trying to rouse himself:* Say . . . did Bernie finish the filling?

ISABEL: Yeah, he polished yesterday.

JOE: Open.

She opens her mouth.

Bernie's good. *Proudly:* I told you, we were in the same class. Say hello when you see him again.

ISABEL: He said he might come after five. He always says to give you his best.

JOE: Give him my best, too.

ISABEL, *readying herself on the bed:* Till you I never had so many dentists.

He lowers onto her. Fadeout.

Lights come up on Banks, suspended in a painter's cradle, painting a bridge. He sings a verse of "Backbone and Navel Doin' the Belly Rub," then speaks.

BANKS: Sometimes you'd get the rumor they be hirin' in New York City, so we all went to New York City, but they wasn't nothin' in New York City, so we'd head for Lima, Ohio; Detroit, Michigan; Duluth, Minnesota; or go down Baltimore; or Alabama or Decatur, Illinois. But anywhere you'd go was always a jail. I was in a chain gang in Georgia pickin' cotton for four months just for hoboin' on a train. That was 1935 in the summertime, and when they set me free they give me thirty-five cents. Yes, sir, thirty-five cents is what they give me, pickin' cotton four months against my will. *Pause.* Yeah, I still hear that train, that long low whistle, *whoo-ooo!*

Fadeout. Lights come up on Rose, seated at the piano, playing. Two moving men in work aprons enter, raise her hands from the piano, and push the piano off.

ROSE, *half to herself, furious:* How stupid it all is. How stupid! *Prayerfully:* Oh, my dear Lee, wherever you are—believe in something. Anything. But believe. *She turns and moves off with the piano stool, as though emptied out.*

Lights come up on Lee, sitting at an open-air café table under a tree. Isaac, the black proprietor, brings him a watermelon slice.

ISAAC: You been workin' the river long? I ain't seen you before, have I?

LEE: No, this is my first trip down the river, I'm from New York City—I'm just kind of looking around the country, talking to people.

ISAAC: What you lookin' around *for?*

LEE: Nothing—just trying to figure out what's happening. Ever hear of Mark Twain?

ISAAC: He from round here?

LEE: Well, long time ago, yeah. He was a story writer.

ISAAC: Unh-unh. I ain't seen him around here. You ask at the post office?

LEE: No, but I might. I'm kind of surprised you can get fifteen cents a slice down here these days.

ISAAC: Ohhh—white folks *loves* watermelon. Things as bad as this up North?

LEE: Probably not quite. I sure wouldn't want to be one of you people down here . . . specially with this Depression.

ISAAC: Mister, if I was to tell you the God's honest truth, the main thing about the Depression is that it finally hit the white people. 'Cause us folks never had nothin' else. *He looks offstage.* Well, now—here come the big man.

LEE: He trouble?

ISAAC: He's anything he wants to be, mister—he the sheriff.

The Sheriff enters, wearing holstered gun, boots, badge, broad-brimmed hat, and carrying something wrapped under his arm. He silently stares at Lee, then turns to Isaac.

SHERIFF: Isaac?

ISAAC: Yes, sir.

SHERIFF, *after a moment:* Sit down.

ISAAC: Yes, sir.

He sits on a counter stool; he is intensely curious about the Sheriff's calling on him but not frightened. The Sheriff seems to be having trouble with Lee's strange presence.

LEE, *makes a nervous half-apology:* I'm off the boat. *He indicates offstage.*

SHERIFF: You don't bother me, boy—relax.

He sits and sets his package down and turns with gravity to Isaac. Lee makes himself unobtrusive and observes in silence.

ISAAC: Looks like rain.

SHERIFF, *preoccupied:* Mm . . . hard to know.

ISAAC: Yeah . . . always is in Louisiana. *Pause.* Anything I can do for you, Sheriff?

SHERIFF: Read the papers today?

ISAAC: I couldn't read my name if an air-o-plane wrote it in the sky, Sheriff, you know that.

SHERIFF: My second cousin Allan? The state senator?

ISAAC: Uh-huh?

SHERIFF: The governor just appointed him. He's gonna help run the state police.

ISAAC: Uh-huh?

SHERIFF: He's comin' down to dinner Friday night over to my house. Bringin' his wife and two daughters. I'm gonna try to talk to Allan about a job on the state police. They still paying the *state* police, see.

ISAAC: Uh-huh. Well, that be nice, won't it.

SHERIFF: Isaac, I like you to cook me up some of that magical fried chicken around six o'clock Friday night. Okay? I'll pick it up.

ISAAC, *noncommittal:* Mm.

SHERIFF: That'd be for . . . let's see . . . *counts on his fingers* . . . eight people. My brother and his wife comin' over too, 'cause I aim to give Allan a little spread there, get him talkin' real good, y'know.

ISAAC: Mm.

An embarrassed pause.

SHERIFF: What's that gonna cost me for eight people, Isaac?

ISAAC, *at once:* Ten dollars.

SHERIFF: Ten.

ISAAC, *with a little commiseration:* That's right, Sheriff.

SHERIFF, *slight pause; starts to unwrap radio:* Want to show you something here, Isaac. My radio, see?

ISAAC: Uh-huh. *He runs his hand over it.* Play?

SHERIFF: Sure! Plays real good. I give twenty-nine ninety-five for that two years ago.

ISAAC, *looks in the back of it:* I plug it in?

SHERIFF: Go right ahead, sure. You sure painted this place up real nice. Like a real restaurant. You oughta thank the Lord, Isaac.

ISAAC, *takes out the wire and plugs it in:* I sure do. The Lord and fried chicken!

SHERIFF: You know, the county ain't paid nobody at all in three months now . . .

ISAAC: Yeah, I know. Where you switch it on?

SHERIFF: Just turn the knob. There you are. *He turns it on.* They're still payin' the *state* police, see. And I figure if I can get Allan to put me on—

Radio music. It is very faint.

ISAAC: Cain't hardly hear it.

SHERIFF, *angrily:* Hell, Isaac, gotta get the aerial out! *Untangling a wire at the back of the set:* You give me eight fried chicken dinners and I let you hold this for collateral, okay? Here we go now.

The Sheriff backs away, stretching out the aerial wire, and Roosevelt's voice suddenly comes on strong. The Sheriff holds still, the wire held high. Lee is absorbed.

ROOSEVELT: Clouds of suspicion, tides of ill-will and intolerance gather darkly in many places. In our own land we enjoy, indeed, a fullness of life . . .

SHERIFF: And nice fat chickens, hear? Don't give me any little old scruffy chickens.

ISAAC, *of Roosevelt:* Who's that talkin'?

ROOSEVELT: . . . greater than that of most nations. But the rush of modern civilization itself has raised for us new difficulties . . .

SHERIFF: Sound like somebody up North.

ISAAC: Hush! *To Lee:* Hey, that's Roosevelt, ain't it?

LEE: Yes.

ISAAC: Sure! That's the President!

SHERIFF: How about it, we got a deal? Or not?

Isaac has his head close to the radio, absorbed. Lee comes closer, bends over to listen.

ROOSEVELT: . . . new problems which must be solved if we are to preserve to the United States the political and economic freedom for which Washington and Jefferson planned and fought. We seek not merely to make government a mechanical implement, but to give it the vibrant personal character that is the embodiment of human charity. We are poor indeed if this nation cannot afford to lift from every recess of American life the dark fear of the unemployed that they are not needed in the world. We cannot afford to accumulate a deficit in the books of human fortitude.

Sidney and Doris enter as lights fade on Lee, Isaac, and the Sheriff.

SIDNEY: What's the matter? Boy, you can change quicker than . . .

DORIS, *shaking her head, closing her eyes:* I can't help it, it keeps coming back to me.

SIDNEY: How can you let a dope like Francey bother you like this?

DORIS: Because she's spreading it all over the class! And I still don't understand how you could have said a thing like that.

SIDNEY: Hon . . . all I said was that if we ever got married I would probably live downstairs. Does that mean that that's the reason we'd get married? Francey is just jealous!

DORIS, *deeply hurt:* I just wish you hadn't said that.

SIDNEY: You mean you think I'd do a thing like that for an *apartment*? What must you think of me! . . .

DORIS, *sobs:* It's just that I love you so much! . . .

SIDNEY: If I could only sell a song! Or even pass the post office exam. Then I'd have my own money, and all this garbage would stop.

DORIS: . . . I said I love you, why don't *you* say something?

SIDNEY: I love you, I love you, but I tell ya, you know what I think?

DORIS: What?

SIDNEY: Honestly—I think we ought to talk about seeing other people for a while.

DORIS, *uncomprehending:* What other people?

SIDNEY: Going out. You're still a little young, honey . . . and even at my age, it's probably not a good idea for us if we never even went out with somebody else—

DORIS: Well, who . . . do you want to take out?

SIDNEY: Nobody! . . .

DORIS: Then what do you mean?

SIDNEY: Well, it's not that I *want* to.

DORIS: Yeah, but who?

SIDNEY: Well, I don't know . . . like maybe . . . what's-her-name, Margie Ganz's sister . . .

DORIS, *alarmed:* You mean Esther Ganz with the . . . ? *She cups her hands to indicate big breasts.*

SIDNEY: Then *not* her!

DORIS, *hurt:* You want to take out *Esther Ganz*?

SIDNEY: I'm not saying *necessarily*! But . . . for instance, you could go out with Georgie.

DORIS: Which Georgie?

SIDNEY: Georgie Krieger.

DORIS: You're putting me with *Georgie Krieger* and *you* go out with *Esther Ganz*?

SIDNEY: It was only an *example!*

DORIS, *with incredulous distaste:* But Georgie *Krieger!* . . .

SIDNEY: Forget Georgie Krieger! Make it . . . all right, *you* pick somebody, then.

DORIS, *stares, reviewing faces:* Well . . . how about Morris?

SIDNEY, *asking the heart-stopping question:* What Morris? You mean Morris from . . .

DORIS: Yeah, Morris from the shoe store.

SIDNEY, *glimpsing quite a different side of her: Really?*

DORIS: Well, didn't he go a year to City College?

SIDNEY: No, he did not, he went one semester—and he *still* walks around with a comb in his pocket. . . . I think maybe we just better wait.

DORIS: I don't know, maybe it would be a good idea . . . at least till I'm a little older . . .

SIDNEY: No, we'll wait, we'll think it over.

DORIS: But you know . . .

SIDNEY, *with high anxiety: We'll think it over,* hon! . . .

He goes to the piano, plays a progression. She comes to him, then runs her fingers through his hair.

DORIS: Play "Sittin' Around"?

SIDNEY: It's not any good.

DORIS: What do you mean, it's your greatest! Please!

SIDNEY, *sighs, sings:* You've got me
        Sittin' around
        Just watching shadows
        On the wall;
        You've got me
        Sittin' around,
        And all my hopes beyond recall;

> I want to hear
> The words of love,
> I want to feel
> Your lips on mine,

DORIS: And know
>   The days and nights
>   There in your arms.

SIDNEY and DORIS: Instead I'm . . .

> Sittin' around
> And all the world
> Is passing by,
> You've got me
> Sittin' around
> Like I was only
> Born to cry,

> When will I know
> The words of love,
> Your lips on mine—
> Instead of

> Sittin' around,
> Sittin' around,
> Sittin' around . . .

Fadeout. A large crowd emerges from darkness as a row of factory-type lights descend, illuminating rows of benches and scattered chairs. This is an emergency welfare office temporarily set up to handle the flood of desperate people. A Welfare Worker hands each applicant a sheet of paper and then wanders off.

MOE: I don't understand this. I distinctly read in the paper that anybody wants to work can go direct to WPA and they fix you up with a job.

LEE: They changed it. You can only get a WPA job now if you get on relief first.

MOE, *pointing toward the line:* So this is not the WPA.

LEE: I told you, Pa, this is the relief office.

MOE: Like . . . welfare.

LEE: Look, if it embarrasses you—

MOE: Listen, if it has to be done it has to be done. Now let me go over it again—what do I say?

LEE: You refuse to let me live in the house. We don't get along.

MOE: Why can't you live at home?

LEE: If I can live at home, I don't need relief. That's the rule.

MOE: Okay. So I can't stand the sight of you.

LEE: Right.

MOE: So you live with your friend in a rooming house.

LEE: Correct.

MOE: . . . They're gonna believe that?

LEE: Why not? I've got a few clothes over there.

MOE: All this for twenty-two dollars a week?

LEE, *angering:* What am I going to do? Even old-time newspapermen are out of work. . . . See, if I can get on the WPA Writers Project, at least I'd get experience if a real job comes along. I've explained this a dozen times, Pa, there's nothing complicated.

MOE, *unsatisfied:* I'm just trying to get used to it. All right.

They embrace.

We shouldn't look too friendly, huh?

LEE, *laughs:* That's the idea!

MOE: I don't like you, and you can't stand the sight of me.

LEE: That's it! *He laughs.*

MOE, *to the air, with mock outrage:* So he laughs.

They move into the crowd and find seats in front of Ryan, the supervisor, at a desk.

RYAN: Matthew R. Bush!

A very dignified man of forty-five rises, crosses, and follows Ryan out.

MOE: Looks like a butler.

LEE: Probably was.

MOE, *shakes his head mournfully:* Hmm!

ROBERTSON, *from choral area:* I did a lot of walking back in those days, and the contrasts were startling. Along the West Side of Manhattan you had eight or ten of the world's greatest ocean liners tied up—I recall the SS *Manhattan*, the *Berengaria*, the *United States*—most of them would never sail again. But at the same time they were putting up the Empire State Building, highest in the world. But with whole streets and avenues of empty stores who would ever rent space in it?

A baby held by Grace, a young woman in the back, cries. Moe turns to look, then stares ahead.

MOE: Lee, what'll you do if they give you a pick-and-shovel job?

LEE: I'll take it.

MOE: You'll dig holes in the streets?

LEE: It's no disgrace, Dad.

ROBERTSON: It was incredible to me how long it was lasting. I would never, never have believed we could not recover before this. The years were passing, a whole generation was withering in the best years of its life . . .

The people in the crowd start talking: Kapush, Slavonic, in his late sixties, with a moustache; Dugan, an Irishman; Irene, a middle-aged black woman; Toland, a cabbie.

KAPUSH, *with ferocious frustration:* What can you expect from a country that puts a frankfurter on the Supreme Court? Felix the Frankfurter. Look it up.

DUGAN, *from another part of the room:* Get back in the clock, ya cuckoo!

KAPUSH, *turning his body around angrily to face Dugan and jarring Irene, sitting next to him:* Who's talkin' to me!

IRENE: Hey, now, don't mess with me, mister!

DUGAN: Tell him, tell him!

Ryan rushes in. He is pale, his vest is loaded with pens and pencils, and a sheaf of papers is in his hand. A tired man.

RYAN: We gonna have another riot, folks? Is that what we're gonna have? Mr. Kapush, I told you three days running now, if you live in Bronx, you've got to apply in Bronx.

KAPUSH: It's all right, I'll wait.

RYAN, *as he passes Dugan:* Leave him alone, will you? He's a little upset in his mind.

DUGAN: He's a fascist. I seen him down Union Square plenty of times.

Irene slams her walking stick down on the table.

RYAN: Oh, Jesus . . . here we go again.

IRENE: Gettin' on to ten o'clock, Mr. Ryan.

RYAN: I've done the best I can, Irene . . .

IRENE: That's what the good Lord said when he made the jackass, but he decided to knuckle down and try harder. People been thrown out on the sidewalk, mattresses, pots and pans, and everything else they own. Right on A Hundred and Thirty-eighth Street. They goin' back in their apartments today or we goin' raise us some real hell.

RYAN: I've got no more appropriations for you till the first of the month, and that's it, Irene.

IRENE: Mr. Ryan, you ain't talkin' to me, you talkin' to Local Forty-five of the Workers Alliance, and you know what that mean.

DUGAN, *laughs:* Communist Party.

IRENE: That's right, mister, and they don't mess. So why don't you get on your phone and call Washington. And while you're at it, you can remind Mr. Roosevelt that I done swang One Hundred and Thirty-ninth Street for him in the last election, and if he want it swung again he better get crackin'!

RYAN: Holy Jesus.

He hurries away, but Lee tries to delay him.

LEE: I was told to bring my father.

RYAN: What?

LEE: Yesterday. You told me to—

RYAN: Get off my back, will ya? *He hurries out.*

DUGAN: This country's gonna end up on the top of the trees throwin' coconuts at each other.

MOE, *quietly to Lee:* I hope I can get out by eleven, I got an appointment with a buyer.

TOLAND, *next to Moe, with a* Daily News *open in his hands:* Boy, oh, boy, looka this—Helen Hayes gonna put on forty pounds to play Victoria Regina.

MOE: Who's that?

TOLAND: Queen of England.

MOE: She was so fat?

TOLAND: Victoria? Horse. I picked up Helen Hayes when I had my cab. Very small girl. And Adolphe Menjou once—he was small too. I even had Al Smith once, way back before he was governor. He was real small.

MOE: Maybe your cab was large.

TOLAND: What do you mean? I had a regular Ford.

MOE: You lost it?

TOLAND: What're you gonna do? The town is walkin'. I paid five hundred dollars for a new Ford, including bumpers and a spare. But thank God, at least I got into the housing project. It's nice and reasonable.

MOE: What do you pay?

TOLAND: Nineteen fifty a month. It sounds like a lot, but we got three nice rooms—providin' I get a little help here. What's your line?

MOE: I sell on commission right now. I used to have my own business.

TOLAND: Used-ta. Whoever you talk to, "I used-ta." If they don't do something, I tell ya, one of these days this used-ta be a country.

KAPUSH, *exploding:* Ignorance, ignorance! People don't know facts. Greatest public library system in the entire world and nobody goes in but Jews.

MOE, *glancing at him:* Ah-ha.

LEE: What're you, Iroquois?

DUGAN: He's a fascist. I seen him talking on Union Square.

IRENE: Solidarity, folks, black and white together, that's what we gotta have. Join the Workers Alliance, ten cents a month, and you git yourself some solidarity.

KAPUSH: I challenge anybody to find the word democracy in the Constitution. This is a republic! *Demos* is the Greek word for mob.

DUGAN, *imitating the bird: Cuckoo!*

KAPUSH: Come to get my money and the bank is closed up! Four thousand dollars up the flue. Thirteen years in hardware, savin' by the week.

DUGAN: Mental diarrhea.

KAPUSH: Mobocracy. Gimme, gimme, gimme, all they know.

DUGAN: So what're *you* doing here?

KAPUSH: Roosevelt was sworn in on a Dutch Bible! *Silence.* Anybody know that? *To Irene:* Betcha didn't know that, did you?

IRENE: You givin' me a headache, mister . . .

KAPUSH: I got nothin' against colored. Colored never took my store away. Here's my bankbook, see that? Bank of the United States. See that? Four thousand six hundred and ten dollars and thirty-one cents, right? Who's got that money? Savin' thirteen years, by the week. *Who's got my money?*

He has risen to his feet. His fury has turned the moment silent. Matthew Bush enters and sways. Ryan enters.

RYAN, *calls:* Arthur Clayton!

CLAYTON, *starts toward Ryan from the crowd and indicates Bush:* I think there's something the matter with—

Bush collapses on the floor. For a moment no one moves. Then Irene goes to him, bends over him.

IRENE: Hey. Hey, mister.

Lee helps him up and sits him in the chair.

RYAN, *calling:* Myrna, call the ambulance!

Irene lightly slaps Bush's cheeks.

LEE: You all right?

RYAN, *looking around:* Clayton?

CLAYTON: I'm Clayton.

RYAN, *Clayton's form in his hand:* You're not eligible for relief; you've got furniture and valuables, don't you?

CLAYTON: But nothing I could realize anything on.

RYAN: Why not?

IRENE: This man's starvin', Mr. Ryan.

RYAN: What're you, a medical doctor now, Irene? I called the ambulance! Now don't start makin' an issue, will you? *To Clayton:* Is this your address? Gramercy Park South?

CLAYTON, *embarrassed:* That doesn't mean a thing. I haven't really eaten in a few days, actually . . .

RYAN: Where do you get that kind of rent?

CLAYTON: I haven't paid my rent in over eight months . . .

RYAN, *starting away:* Forget it, mister, you got valuables and furniture; you can't—

CLAYTON: I'm very good at figures, I was in brokerage. I thought if I could get anything that required . . . say statistics . . .

IRENE: Grace? You got anything in that bottle?

Grace, in a rear row with a baby in her arms, reaches forward with a baby bottle that has an inch of milk at the bottom. She hands the bottle to Irene.

GRACE: Ain't much left there . . .

IRENE, *takes nipple off bottle:* Okay, now, open your mouth, mister.

Bush gulps the milk.

There, look at that, see? Man's starvin'!

MOE, *stands, reaching into his pocket:* Here . . . look . . . for God's sake. *He takes out change and picks out a dime.* Why don't you send down, get him a bottle of milk?

IRENE, *calls toward a young woman in the back:* Lucy?

LUCY, *coming forward:* Here I am, Irene.

IRENE: Go down the corner, bring a bottle of milk.

Moe gives her the dime, and Lucy hurries out.

And a couple of straws, honey! You in bad shape, mister—why'd you wait so long to get on relief?

BUSH: Well . . . I just don't like the idea, you know.

IRENE: Yeah, I know—you a real bourgeoisie. Let me tell you something—

BUSH: I'm a chemist.

IRENE: I believe it, too—you so educated you sooner die than say brother. Now lemme tell you people. *Addressing the crowd:* Time has come to say brother. My husband pass away and leave me with three small children. No money, no work—I's about ready to stick my head in the cookin' stove. Then the city marshal come and take my chest of drawers, bed, and table, and leave me sittin' on a old orange crate in the middle of the room. And it come over me, mister, come over me to get mean. And I got real mean. Go down in the street and start yellin' and howlin' like a real mean woman. And the people crowd around the marshal truck, and 'fore you know it that marshal turn himself around and go on back downtown empty-handed. And that's when I see it. I see the solidarity, and I start to preach it up and down. 'Cause I got me a stick, and when I start poundin' time with this stick, a whole lot of people starts to march, keepin' time. We shall not be moved, yeah, we shall in no wise be disturbed. Some days I goes to court with my brief-case, raise hell with the judges. Ever time I goes into court the cops commence to holler, "Here comes that old lawyer woman!" But all I got in here is some old newspaper and a bag of cayenne pepper. Case any cop start musclin' me around—that hot pepper, that's hot cayenne pepper. And if the judge happen to be Catholic I got my rosary layin' in there, and I kind of let that crucifix hang out so's they think I'm Catholic too. *She draws a rosary out of her bag and lets it hang over the side.*

LUCY, *enters with milk:* Irene!

IRENE: Give it here, Lucy. Now drink it slow, mister. Slow, slow . . .

Bush is drinking in sips. People now go back into themselves, read papers, stare ahead.

RYAN: Lee Baum!

LEE, *hurries to Moe:* Here! Okay, Dad, let's go.

Lee and Moe go to Ryan's desk.

RYAN: This your father?

MOE: Yes.

RYAN, *to Moe:* Where's he living now?

LEE: I don't live at home because—

RYAN: Let *him* answer. Where's he living, Mr. Baum?

MOE: Well, he . . . he rents a room someplace.

RYAN: You gonna sit there and tell me you won't let him in the house?

MOE, *with great difficulty:* I won't let him in, no.

RYAN: You mean you're the kind of man, if he rang the bell and you opened the door and saw him, you wouldn't let him inside?

MOE: Well, naturally, if he just wants to come in the house—

LEE: I don't want to live there—

RYAN: I don't care what *you* want, fella. *To Moe:* You will let him into the house, right?

MOE, *stiffening:* . . . I can't stand the sight of him.

RYAN: Why? I saw you both sitting here talking together the last two hours.

MOE: We weren't talking. . . . We were arguing, fighting! . . .

RYAN: Fighting about what?

MOE, *despite himself, growing indignant:* Who can remember? We were fighting, we're always fighting! . . .

RYAN: Look, Mr. Baum . . . you're employed, aren't you?

MOE: I'm employed? Sure I'm employed. Here. *He holds up the folded* Times. See? Read it yourself. R. H. Macy, right? Ladies' full-length slip, genuine Japanese silk, hand-embroidered with lace top and trimmings, two ninety-eight. My boss makes four cents on these, I make a tenth of a cent. That's how I'm employed!

RYAN: You'll let him in the house. *He starts to move.*

MOE: I will not let him in the house! He . . . he don't believe in anything!

Lee and Ryan look at Moe in surprise. Moe himself is caught off balance by his genuine outburst and rushes out. Ryan glances at Lee, stamps a requisition form, and hands it to him, convinced. Ryan exits.

Lee moves slowly, staring at the form. The welfare clients exit, the row of overhead lights flies out.

Lights come up on Robertson.

ROBERTSON: Then and now, you have to wonder what really held it all together, and maybe it was simply the Future: the people were still not ready to give it up. Like a God, it was always worshiped among us, and they could not yet turn their backs on it. Maybe it's that simple. Because from any objective viewpoint, I don't understand why it held.

The people from the relief office form a line as on a subway platform. Joe comes behind the line singing and offering flowers from a basket. There is the sound of an approaching train, its windows flashing light. Joe throws himself under it: a squeal of brakes. The crowd sings "In New York City, You Really Got to Know Your Line," one by one taking the lyrics, ending in a chorus. Fadeout.

Lights come up on Edie. Lee is in spotlight.

LEE, *to audience:* Any girl with an apartment of her own was beautiful. She was one of the dialogue writers for the *Superman* comic strip. *To her:* Edie, can I sleep here tonight?

EDIE: Oh, hi, Lee—yeah, sure. Let me finish and I'll put a sheet on the couch. If you have any laundry, throw it in the sink. I'm going to wash later.

He stands behind her as she works.

This is going to be a terrific sequence.

LEE: It's amazing to me how you can keep your mind on it.

EDIE: He's also a great teacher of class consciousness.

LEE: Superman?

EDIE: He stands for justice!

LEE: Oh! You mean under capitalism you can't . . .

EDIE: Sure! The implications are terrific. *She works lovingly for a moment.*

LEE: Y'know, you're beautiful when you talk about politics, your face lights up.

EDIE, *smiling:* Don't be such a bourgeois horse's ass. I'll get your sheet. *She starts up.*

LEE: Could I sleep in your bed tonight? I don't know what it is lately—I'm always lonely. Are you?

EDIE: Sometimes. But a person doesn't have to go to bed with people to be connected to mankind.

LEE: You're right. I'm ashamed of myself.

EDIE: Why don't you join the Party?

LEE: I guess I don't want to ruin my chances; I want to be a sportswriter.

EDIE: You could write for the *Worker* sports page.

LEE: The *Daily Worker* sports page?

EDIE: Then help improve it! Why are you so defeatist, hundreds of people are joining the Party every week.

LEE: I don't know why, maybe I'm too skeptical—or cynical. Like . . . when I was in Flint, Michigan, during the sit-down strike. Thought I'd write a feature story . . . all those thousands of men barricaded in the GM plant, the wives hoisting food up to the windows in baskets. It was like the French Revolution. But then I got to talk to them as individuals, and the prejudice! The ignorance! . . . In the Ford plant there was damn near a race war because some of the Negro workers didn't want to join the strike. . . . It was murderous.

EDIE: Well, they're still backward, I know that.

LEE: No, they're normal. I really wonder if there's going to be time to save this country from itself. You ever wonder that? You do, don't you.

EDIE, *fighting the temptation to give way:* You really want my answer?

LEE: Yes.

EDIE: We're picketing the Italian consulate tomorrow, to protest Mussolini sending Italian troops to the Spanish Civil War. Come! *Do* something! You love Hemingway so much, read what he just said—"One man alone is no fucking good." As decadent as he is, even *he's* learning.

LEE: Really, your face gets so beautiful when you . . .

EDIE: Anyone can be beautiful if what they believe is beautiful! I believe in my comrades. I believe in the Soviet Union. I believe in the working class and the peace of the whole world when socialism comes . . .

LEE: Boy, you really are wonderful. Look, now that I'm on relief can I take you out to dinner? I'll pay, I mean.

EDIE, *smiles:* Why must you pay for me, just because I'm a woman?

LEE: Right! I forgot about that.

EDIE, *working:* I've got to finish this panel. . . . I'll make up the couch in a minute. . . . What about the Writer's Project, you getting on?

LEE: I think so; they're putting people on to write a WPA Guide, it's going to be a detailed history of every section of the country. I might get sent up to the Lake Champlain district. Imagine? They're interviewing direct descendants of the soldiers who fought the Battle of Fort Ticonderoga. Ethan Allen and the Green Mountain Boys?

EDIE: Oh, yes! They beat the British up there.

LEE: It's a wonderful project; 'cause people really don't know their own history.

EDIE, *with longing and certainty:* When there's socialism everyone will.

LEE, *leaning over to look at her work:* Why don't you have Superman get laid? Or married even.

EDIE: He's much too busy.

He comes closer to kiss her; she starts to respond, then rejects.

What are you *doing?*

LEE: When you say the word "socialism" your face gets so beautiful . . .

EDIE: You're totally cynical, aren't you.

LEE: Why!

EDIE: You pretend to have a serious conversation when all you want is to jump into my bed; it's the same attitude you have to the auto workers . . .

LEE: I can't see the connection between the auto workers and . . . !

EDIE, *once again on firm ground:* Everything is connected! I have to ask you to leave!

LEE: Edie!

EDIE: You are not a good person! *She bursts into tears and rushes off.*

LEE, *alone, full of remorse:* She's right, too! *He exits.*

Grandpa enters from choral area, sits with his newspaper, and is immediately immersed. Then Rose's niece Lucille, her sister Fanny, and Doris, who wears a bathrobe, carry folding chairs and seat themselves around a table. Lucille deals cards. Now Rose begins speaking within the choral area, and as she speaks, she moves onto the stage proper.

ROSE: That endless Brooklyn July! That little wooden house baking in the heat. *She enters the stage.* I never smelled an owl, but in July the smell of that attic crept down the stairs, and to me it smelled as dry and dusty as an owl. *She surveys the women staring at their cards.* From Coney Island to Brooklyn Bridge, how many thousands of women waited out the afternoons dreaming at their cards and praying for luck? Ah, luck, luck . . .

DORIS: Sidney's finishing a beautiful new song, Aunt Rose.

ROSE, *sitting at the table, taking up her hand of cards:* Maybe this one'll be lucky for you. Why are you always in a bathrobe?

DORIS: I'm only half a block away.

ROSE: But you're so young! Why don't you get dressed and leave the block once in a while?

FANNY, *smugly:* All my girls love it home, too.

ROSE: It's you, isn't it?

FANNY, *brushing dandruff off her bosom and nervously examining her cards:* I'm trying to make up my mind.

ROSE: Concentrate. Forget your dandruff for a minute.

FANNY: It wasn't dandruff, it was a thread.

ROSE: Her dandruff is threads. It's an obsession.

LUCILLE: I didn't tell you; this spring she actually called me and my sisters to come and spend the day cleaning her house.

FANNY: What's so terrible! We used to have the most marvelous times the four of us cleaning the house . . . *Suddenly:* It's turning into an oven in here.

LUCILLE: I'm going to faint.

ROSE: Don't faint, all the windows are open in the back of the house. We're supposed to be away.

FANNY: But there's no draft. . . . For Papa's sake . . .

LUCILLE: Why couldn't you be away and you left a window open? . . . Just don't answer the door.

ROSE: I don't want to take the chance. This one is a professional collector, I've seen him do it; if a window's open he tries to listen. They're merciless. . . . I sent Stanislaus for lemons, we'll have cold lemonade. Play.

FANNY: I can't believe they'd actually evict you, Rose.

ROSE: You can't? Wake up, Fanny. It's a bank—may they choke after the fortune of money we kept in there all those years! Ask them for two hundred dollars now and they . . . *Tears start to her eyes.*

FANNY: Rose, dear, come on—something'll happen, you'll see. Moe's got to find something soon, a man so well known.

LUCILLE: Couldn't he ask his mother for a little?

ROSE: His mother says there's a Depression going on. Meantime you can go blind from the diamonds on her fingers. Which he gave her! The rottenness of people! I tell you, the next time I start believing in anybody or anything I hope my tongue is cut out!

DORIS: Maybe Lee should come back and help out?

ROSE: Never! Lee is going to think his own thoughts and face the facts. He's got nothing to learn from us. Let him help himself.

LUCILLE: But to take up Communism—

ROSE: Lucille, what do you know about it? What does anybody know about it? The newspapers? The newspapers said the stock market will never come down again.

LUCILLE: But they're against God, Aunt Rose.

ROSE: I'm overjoyed you got so religious, Lucille, but please for God's sake don't tell me about it again!

FANNY, *rises, starts to leave:* I'll be right down.

ROSE: Now she's going to pee on her finger for luck.

FANNY: All right! So I won't go! *She returns to her chair.* And I wasn't going to pee on my finger!

ROSE: So what're we playing—cards or statues?

Doris sits looking at her cards, full of confusion.

GRANDPA, *putting down his paper:* Why do they need this election?

ROSE: What do you mean, why they need this election?

GRANDPA: But everybody knows Roosevelt is going to win again. I still think he's too radical, but to go through another election is a terrible waste of money.

ROSE: What are you talking about, Papa—it's four years, they have to have an election.

GRANDPA: Why! If they decided to make him king . . .

ROSE: King!

FANNY, *pointing at Grandpa, agreeing and laughing:* Believe me!

GRANDPA: If he was king he wouldn't have to waste all his time making these ridiculous election speeches, and maybe he could start to improve things!

ROSE: If I had a stamp I'd write him a letter.

GRANDPA: He could be another Kaiser Franz Joseph. Then after he dies you can have all the elections you want.

ROSE, *to Doris:* Are you playing cards or hatching an egg?

DORIS, *startled:* Oh, it's my turn? *She turns a card.* All right; here!

ROSE: Hallelujah.

She plays a card. It is Lucille's turn; she plays.

Did you lose weight?

LUCILLE: I've been trying. I'm thinking of going back to the carnival.

Doris quickly throws an anxious look toward Grandpa, who is oblivious, reading.

FANNY, *indicating Grandpa secretively:* You better not mention . . .

LUCILLE: He doesn't have to know, and anyway I would never dance anymore; I'd only assist the magician and tell a few jokes. They're talking about starting up again in Jersey.

ROSE: Herby can't find anything?

LUCILLE: He's going out of his mind, Aunt Rose.

ROSE: God Almighty. So what's it going to be, Fanny?

FANNY, *feeling rushed, studying her cards:* One second! Just let me figure it out.

ROSE: When they passed around the brains this family was out to lunch.

FANNY: It's so hot in here I can't think!

ROSE: Play! I can't open the window. I'm not going to face that man again. He has merciless eyes.

Stanislaus, a middle-aged seaman in T-shirt and dungarees, enters through the front door.

You come in the front door? The mortgage man could come today!

STANISLAUS: I forgot! I didn't see anybody on the street, though. *He lifts bag of lemons.* Fresh lemonade coming up on deck. I starched all the napkins. *He exits.*

ROSE: Starched all the napkins . . . they're cracking like matzos. I feel like doing a fortune. *She takes out another deck of cards, lays out a fortune.*

LUCILLE: I don't know, Aunt Rose, is it so smart to let this man live with you?

DORIS: I would never dare! How can you sleep at night with a strange man in the cellar?

FANNY: Nooo! Stanislaus is a gentleman. *To Rose:* I think he's a little bit a fairy, isn't he?

ROSE: I hope!

They all laugh.

For God's sake, Fanny, play the queen of clubs!

FANNY: How did you know I had the queen of clubs!

ROSE: Because I'm smart, I voted for Herbert Hoover. I see what's been played, dear, so I figure what's left.

FANNY, *to Grandpa, who continues reading:* She's a marvel, she's got Grandma's head.

ROSE: Huh! Look at this fortune.

FANNY: Here, I'm playing. *She plays a card.*

ROSE, *continuing to lay out the fortune:* I always feed the vagrants on the porch, but Stanislaus, when I hand him a plate of soup he says he wants to wash the windows before he eats. *Before!* That I never heard. I nearly fell over. Go ahead, Doris, it's you.

DORIS, *desperately trying to be quick:* I know just what to do, wait a minute.

The women freeze, study their cards; Rose now faces front. She is quickly isolated in light.

ROSE: When I went to school we had to sit like soldiers, with backs straight and our hands clasped on the desk; things were supposed to be upright. When the navy came up the Hudson River, you cried it was so beautiful. You even cried when they shot the Czar of Russia. He was also beautiful. President Warren Gamaliel Harding, another beauty. Mayor James J. Walker smiled like an angel, what a nose, and those tiny feet. Richard Whitney, president of the Stock Exchange, a handsome, upright man. I could name a hundred from the rotogravure! Who could know that these upright handsome men would either turn out to be crooks who would land in jail or ignoramuses? What is left to believe? The bathroom. I lock myself in and hold on to the faucets so I shouldn't scream. At my husband, my mother-in-law, at God knows what until they take me away . . . *Returning to the fortune, and with deep anxiety:* What the hell did I lay out here? What is this?

Light returns to normal.

DORIS: "Gray's Elegy in a Country Churchyard."

ROSE: What?

FANNY, *touching her arm worriedly:* Why don't you lie down, Rose? . . .

ROSE: Lie down? . . . Why? *To Doris:* What Gray's "Elegy"? What are you . . .

Stanislaus enters rapidly, wearing a waist-length white starched waiter's jacket, a tray expertly on his shoulder, with glasses and rolled napkins. Rose shows alarm as she lays a card down on the fortune.

STANISLAUS: It's a braw bricht moonlicht nicht tonicht—that's Scotch.

FANNY: How does he get those napkins to stand up!

ROSE, *under terrific tension, tears her gaze from the cards she laid out:* What's the jacket suddenly?

The women watch her tensely.

STANISLAUS, *saluting:* SS *Manhattan.* Captain's steward at your service.

ROSE: Will you stop this nightmare? Take the jacket off. What're you talking about, captain's steward? Who are you?

STANISLAUS: I was captain's personal steward, but they're not sailing the *Manhattan* anymore. Served J. Pierpont Morgan, John D. Rockefeller, Enrico Caruso, lousy tipper, Lionel—

ROSE, *very suspiciously:* Bring in the cookies, please.

He picks up the pitcher to pour the lemonade.

Thank you, I'll pour it. Go, please.

She doesn't look at him; he goes out. In the silence she picks up the pitcher, tilts it, but her hand is shaking, and Fanny takes the pitcher.

FANNY: Rose, dear, come upstairs . . .

ROSE: How does he look to you?

FANNY: Why? He looks very nice.

LUCILLE: He certainly keeps the house beautiful, Aunt Rose, it's like a ship.

ROSE: He's a liar, though; anything comes into his head, he says; what am I believing him for? What the hell got into me? You can tell he's full of shit, and he comes to the door, a perfect stranger, and I let him sleep in the cellar!

LUCILLE: *Shhh!*

Stanislaus enters with a plate of cookies, in T-shirt again, determinedly.

ROSE: Listen, Stanislaus . . . *She stands.*

STANISLAUS, *senses his imminent dismissal:* I go down to the ship chandler store tomorrow, get some special white paint, paint the whole outside the house. I got plenty of credit, don't cost you.

ROSE: I thought it over, you understand?

STANISLAUS, *with a desperate smile:* I borrow big ladder from the hardware store. And I gonna make nice curtains for the cellar windows. Taste the lemonade, I learn that in Spanish submarine. Excuse me, gotta clean out the icebox. *He gets himself out.*

FANNY: I think he's very sweet, Rose. . . . Here . . . *She offers a glass of lemonade.*

LUCILLE: Don't worry about that mortgage man, Aunt Rose, it's after five, they don't come after five . . .

ROSE, *caught in her uncertainty:* He seems sweet to you?

GRANDPA, *putting the paper down:* What Lee ought to do . . . Rosie?

ROSE: Hah?

GRANDPA: Lee should go to Russia.

The sisters and Lucille turn to him in surprise.

ROSE, *incredulous, frightened:* To Russia?

GRANDPA: In Russia they need everything; whereas here, y'see, they don't need anything, so therefore, there's no work.

ROSE, *with an edge of hysteria:* Five minutes ago Roosevelt is too radical, and now you're sending Lee to Russia?

GRANDPA: That's different. Look what it says here . . . a hundred thousand American people applying for jobs in Russia. Look, it says it. So if Lee would go over there and open up a nice chain of clothing stores—

ROSE: Papa! You're such a big anti-Communist . . . and you don't know the government owns everything in Russia?

GRANDPA: Yeah, but not the *stores.*

ROSE: Of course the stores!

GRANDPA: The *stores* they own?

ROSE: Yes!

GRANDPA: Them bastards.

ROSE, *to Lucille:* I'll go out of my mind here . . .

DORIS: So who wrote it?

ROSE: Wrote what?

DORIS: "Gray's Elegy in a Country Churchyard." It was a fifteen-dollar question on the radio yesterday, but you were out. I ran to call you.

ROSE, *suppressing a scream:* Who wrote Gray's "Elegy in a Country Churchyard"?

DORIS: By the time I got back to the radio it was another question.

ROSE: Doris, darling . . . *Slowly:* Gray's "Elegy in a—

Fanny laughs.

What are you laughing at, do you know?

FANNY, *pleasantly:* How would I know?

LUCILLE: Is it Gray?

Rose looks at her, an enormous sadness in her eyes. With a certain timidity, Lucille goes on:

Well, it says "Gray's Elegy," right?

DORIS: How could it be Gray? That's the title!

Rose is staring ahead in an agony of despair.

FANNY: What's the matter, Rose?

DORIS: Well, what'd I say?

FANNY: Rose, what's the matter?

LUCILLE: You all right?

FANNY, *really alarmed, turning Rose's face to her:* What is the matter!

Rose bursts into tears. Fanny gets up and embraces her, almost crying herself.

Oh, Rosie, please . . . don't. It'll get better, something's got to happen . . .

A sound from the front door galvanizes them. A man calls from off: "Hello?"

DORIS, *pointing:* There's some—

ROSE, *her hands flying up in fury: Sssh! Whispering:* I'll go upstairs. I'm not home.

She starts to go; Moe enters.

DORIS, *laughing:* It's Uncle Moe!

MOE: What's the excitement?

ROSE, *going to him:* Oh, thank God, I thought it was the mortgage man. You're home early.

He stands watching her.

FANNY: Let's go, come on.

They begin to clear table of tray, lemonade, glasses, etc.

MOE, *looking into Rose's face:* You crying?

LUCILLE: How's it in the city?

ROSE: Go out the back, huh?

MOE: The city is murder.

FANNY: Will you get your bills together? I'm going downtown tomorrow. I'll save you the postage.

ROSE: Take a shower. Why are you so pale?

LUCILLE: Bye-bye, Uncle Moe.

MOE: Bye, girls.

DORIS, *as she exits with Fanny and Lucille:* I must ask him how he made that lemonade . . .

They are gone, Moe is staring at some vision, quite calm, but absorbed.

ROSE: You . . . sell anything? . . . No, heh?

He shakes his head negatively—but that is not what he is thinking about.

Here . . . *She gets a glass from the table.* Come drink, it's cold.

He takes it but doesn't drink.

MOE: You're hysterical every night.

ROSE: No, I'm all right. It's just all so stupid, and every once in a while I can't . . . I can't . . . *She is holding her head.*

MOE: The thing is . . . You listening to me?

ROSE: What? *Suddenly aware of her father's pressure on Moe, she turns and goes quickly to him.* Go on the back porch, Papa, huh? It's shady there now . . . *She hands him a glass of lemonade.*

GRANDPA: But the man'll see me.

ROSE: It's all right, he won't come so late, and Moe is here. Go . . .

Grandpa starts to go.

. . . and why don't you put on your other glasses, they're much cooler.

Grandpa is gone. She returns to Moe.

Yes, dear. What. What's going to be?

MOE: We are going to be all right.

ROSE: Why?

MOE: Because we are. So this nervousness every night is unnecessary, and I wish to God—

ROSE, *indicating the table and the cards spread out:* It's just a fortune. I . . . I started to do a fortune, and I saw . . . a young man. The death of a young man.

MOE, *struck:* You don't say.

ROSE, *sensing:* Why?

He turns front, amazed, frightened.

Why'd you say that?

MOE: Nothing . . .

ROSE: Is Lee . . .

MOE: Will you cut that out—

ROSE: Tell me!

MOE: I saw a terrible thing on the subway. Somebody jumped in front of a train.

ROSE: Aaaahhh—again! My God! You saw him?

MOE: No, a few minutes before I got there. Seems he was a very young man. One of the policemen was holding a great big basket of flowers. Seems he was trying to sell flowers.

ROSE: I saw it! *Her spine tingling, she points down at the cards.* Look, it's there! That's death! I'm going to write Lee to come home immediately. I want you to put in that you want him home.

MOE: I have nothing for him, Rose; how can I make him come home?

ROSE, *screaming and weeping:* Then go to your mother and stand up like a man to her . . . instead of this goddamned fool! *She weeps.*

MOE, *stung, nearly beaten, not facing her:* This can't . . . it can't go on forever, Rose, a country can't just die!

She goes on weeping; he cries out in pain.

Will you stop? I'm trying! God Almighty, I am trying!

The doorbell rings. They start with shock. Grandpa enters, hurrying, pointing.

GRANDPA: Rose—

ROSE: *Ssssh!*

The bell rings again. Moe presses stiffened fingers against his temple, his eyes averted in humiliation. Rose whispers:

God in heaven . . . make him go away!

The bell rings again. Moe's head is bent, his hand quivering as it grips his forehead.

Oh, dear God, give our new President the strength, and the wisdom . . .

Door knock, a little more insistent.

. . . give Mr. Roosevelt the way to help us . . .

Door knock.

Oh, my God, help our dear country . . . and the people! . . .

Door knock. Fadeout.

Lights come up on company as the distant sound of a fight crowd is heard and a clanging bell signals the end of a round. Sidney enters in a guard's uniform; he is watching Lee, who enters smoking a cigar stub, wearing a raincoat, finishing some notes on a pad, his hat tipped back on his head.

SIDNEY: Good fight tonight, Mr. Baum.

LEE, *hardly glancing at him:* Huh? Yeah, pretty good.

Sidney looks on, amused, as Lee slowly passes before him, scribbling away.

As Banks speaks, Soldiers appear and repeat italicized words after him.

BANKS: When the *war* came I was so *glad* when I got in the *army.* A man could be *killed* anytime at all on those trains, but with that uniform on I said, "Now I am safe."

SIDNEY: Hey!

LEE: Huh? *Now he recognizes Sidney.* Sidney!

SIDNEY: Boy, you're some cousin. I'm looking straight at you and no recognito! I'm chief of security here.

BANKS: I felt proud to salute and look around and see all the *good soldiers* of the United States. I was a good *soldier too*, and got five battle stars.

Other Soldiers repeat, "Five, five, five."

LEE: You still on the block?

SIDNEY: Sure. Say, you know who'd have loved to have seen you again? Lou Charney.

LEE: Charney?

RALPH: Hundred yard dash—you and him used to trot to school together . . .

LEE: Oh, Lou, sure! How is he!

SIDNEY: He's dead. Got it in Italy.

BANKS: Yeah, I seen all kinds of war—including the kind they calls . . .

COMPANY: . . . peace.

Four soldiers sing the beginning of "We're in the Money."

SIDNEY: And you knew Georgie Rosen got killed, didn't you?

LEE: Georgie Rosen.

RALPH: Little Georgie.

SIDNEY: Sold you his racing bike.

RALPH: That got stolen.

LEE: Yes, yes! God—Georgie too.

COMPANY, *whispering:* Korea.

RALPH: Lot of wars on that block.

One actor sings the first verse of "The Times They Are A-Changin'."

SIDNEY: Oh, yeah—Lou Charney's kid was in *Vietnam*.

The company says "Vietnam" with Sidney.

Still and all, it's a great country, huh?

LEE: Why do you say that?

SIDNEY: Well, all the crime and divorce and whatnot. But one thing about people like us, you live through the worst, you know the difference between bad and *bad*.

BANKS: One time I was hoboin' through that high country—the Dakotas, Montana—I come to the monument for General Custer's last stand, Little Big Horn. And I wrote my name on it, yes, sir. For the memories; just for the note; so my name will be up there forever. Yes, sir . . .

SIDNEY: But I look back at it all now, and I don't know about you, but it seems it was friendlier. Am I right?

LEE: I'm not sure it was friendlier. Maybe people just cared more.

SIDNEY, *with Irene singing "I Want to Be Happy" under his speech:* Like the songs, I mean—you listen to a thirties song, and most of them are so happy, and still—you could cry.

BANKS: But I still hear that train sometimes; still hear that long low whistle. Yes, sir, I still hear that train . . . *whoo-ooo!*

LEE: You still writing songs?

SIDNEY: Sure! I had a couple published.

RALPH: Still waiting for the big break?

SIDNEY: I got a new one now, though—love you to hear it. I'm calling it "A Moon of My Own." I don't know what happened, I'm sitting on the back porch and suddenly it came to me—"A Moon of My Own." I ran in and told Doris, she could hardly sleep all night.

Doris quietly sings under the following speeches: ". . . and know the days and nights there in your arms. Instead I'm sittin' around . . ."

LEE: How's Doris, are you still . . .

SIDNEY: Oh, very much so. In fact, we were just saying we're practically the only ones we know didn't get divorced.

LEE: Did I hear your mother died?

SIDNEY: Yep, Fanny's gone. I was sorry to hear about Aunt Rose, and Moe.

LEE, *over "Life Is Just a Bowl of Cherries" music:* After all these years I still can't settle with myself about my mother. In her own crazy way she was so much like the country.

Rose sings the first line of "Life Is Just a Bowl of Cherries." Through the rest of Lee's speech, she sings the next four lines.

There was nothing she believed that she didn't also believe the opposite. *Rose sings.* She'd sit down on the subway next to a black man—*Rose sings*—and in a couple of minutes she had him asking her advice—*Rose sings*—about the most intimate things in his life. *Rose sings.* Then, maybe a day later—

LEE and ROSE: "Did you hear! They say the colored are moving in!"

LEE: Or she'd lament her fate as a woman—

ROSE and LEE: "I was born twenty years too soon!"

ROSE: They treat a woman like a cow, fill her up with a baby and lock her in for the rest of her life.

LEE: But then she'd warn me, "Watch out for women—when they're not stupid, they're full of deceit." I'd come home and give her a real bath of radical idealism, and she was ready to storm the barricades; by evening she'd fallen in love again with the Prince of Wales. She was so like the country; money obsessed her, but what she really longed for was some kind of height where she could stand and see out and around and breathe in the air of her own free life. With all her defeats she believed to the end that the world was meant to be better. . . . I don't know; all I know for sure is that whenever I think of her, I always end up—with this headful of life!

ROSE, *calls, in a ghostly, remote way:* Sing!

Alternating lines, Lee and Rose sing "Life Is Just a Bowl of Cherries." The whole company takes up the song in a soft, long-lost tonality. Robertson moves forward, the music continuing underneath.

ROBERTSON: There were moments when the word "revolution" was not rhetorical.

Ted Quinn steps forward.

QUINN: Roosevelt saved them; came up at the right minute and pulled the miracle.

ROBERTSON: Up to a point; but what really got us out of it was the war.

QUINN: Roosevelt gave them back their belief in the country. The government belonged to them again!

ROBERTSON: Well, I'll give you that.

QUINN: Of course you will, you're not a damned fool. The return of that belief is what saved the United States, no more, no less!

ROBERTSON: I think that's putting it a little too . . .

QUINN, *cutting him off and throwing up his hands:* That's it! . . . God, how I love that music!

He breaks into his soft-shoe dance as the singing grows louder. He gestures for the audience to join in, and the company does so as well as the chorus swells . . .

End

THE LAST YANKEE

THE CAST

Leroy Hamilton	John Heard
John Frick	Tom Aldredge
Patricia Hamilton	Frances Conroy
Karen Frick	Rose Gregorio
Unnamed Patient	Charlotte Maier

Directed by John Tillinger. Opened January 21, 1993, Manhattan Theatre Club, New York City.

Scene One

The visiting room of a state mental hospital. Leroy Hamilton is seated on one of the half-dozen chairs, idly leafing through an old magazine. He is forty-eight, trim, dressed in subdued Ivy League jacket and slacks and shined brogans. A banjo case rests against his chair.

Mr. Frick enters. He is sixty, solid, in a business suit. He carries a small valise. He looks about, glances at Leroy, just barely nods, and sits ten feet away. He looks at his watch, then impatiently at the room. Leroy goes on leafing through the magazine.

FRICK, *pointing right:* Supposed to notify somebody in there?

LEROY, *indicating left:* Did you give your name to the attendant?

FRICK: Yes. 'Seem to be paying much attention, though.

LEROY: They know you're here, then. He calls through to the ward. *Returns to his magazine.*

FRICK, *slight pause:* Tremendous parking space down there. 'They need that for?

LEROY: Well a lot of people visit on weekends. Fills up pretty much.

FRICK: Really? That whole area?

LEROY: Pretty much.

FRICK: 'Doubt that. *He goes to the window and looks out. Pause.* Beautifully landscaped, got to say that for it.

LEROY: Yes, it's a very nice place.

FRICK: 'See them walking around out there it's hard to tell. 'Stopped one to ask directions and only realized when he stuck out his finger and pointed at my nose.

LEROY: Heh-heh.

FRICK: Quite a shock. Sitting there reading some thick book and crazy as a coot. You'd never know. *He sits in another chair. Leroy returns to the magazine. He studies Leroy.* Is it your wife?

LEROY: Yes.

FRICK: I've got mine in there too.

LEROY: Uh, huh. *He stares ahead, politely refraining from the magazine.*

FRICK: My name's Frick.

LEROY: Hi. I'm Hamilton.

FRICK: Gladamettu. *Slight pause.* How do you find it here?

LEROY: I guess they do a good job.

FRICK: Surprisingly well kept for a state institution.

LEROY: Oh, ya.

FRICK: Awful lot of colored, though, ain't there?

LEROY: Quite a few, ya.

FRICK: Yours been in long?

LEROY: Going on seven weeks now.

FRICK: They give you any idea when she can get out?

LEROY: Oh, I could take her out now, but I won't for a couple weeks.

FRICK: Why's that?

LEROY: Well this is her third time.

FRICK: 'Don't say.

LEROY: I'd like them to be a little more sure before I take her out again. . . . Although you can never *be* sure.

FRICK: That fairly common?—that they have to come back?

LEROY: About a third they say. This your first time, I guess.

FRICK: I just brought her in last Tuesday. I certainly hope she doesn't have to stay long. They ever say what's wrong with her?

LEROY: She's a depressive.

FRICK: Really. That's what they say about mine. Just gets . . . sort of sad?

LEROY: It's more like . . . frightened.

FRICK: Sounds just like mine. Got so she wouldn't even leave the house.

LEROY: That's right.

FRICK: Oh, yours too?

LEROY: Ya, she wouldn't go out. Not if she could help it, anyway.

FRICK: She ever hear sounds?

LEROY: She used to. Like a loud humming.

FRICK: Same thing! Ts. What do you know! —How old is she?

LEROY: She's forty-four.

FRICK: Is that all! I had an idea it had something to do with getting old . . .

LEROY: I don't think so. My wife is still—I wouldn't say a raving beauty, but she's still . . . a pretty winsome woman. They're usually sick a long time before you realize it, you know. I just never realized it.

FRICK: Mine never showed any signs at all. Just a nice, quiet kind of a woman. Always slept well . . .

LEROY: Well mine sleeps well too.

FRICK: Really?

LEROY: Lot of them love to sleep. I found that out. She'd take naps every afternoon. Longer and longer.

FRICK: Mine too. But then about six, eight months ago she got nervous about keeping the doors locked. And then the windows. I had to air-condition the whole house. I finally had to do the shopping, she just wouldn't go out.

LEROY: Oh I've done the shopping for twenty years.

FRICK: You don't say!

LEROY: Well you just never think of it as a sickness. I like to ski, for instance, or ice skating . . . she'd never come along. Or swimming in the summer. I always took the kids alone . . .

FRICK: Oh you have children.

LEROY: Yes. Seven.

FRICK: Seven!—I've been wondering if it was because she never had any.

LEROY: No, that's not it. —You don't have *any*?

FRICK: No. We kept putting it off, and then it got too late, and first thing you know . . . it's just too late.

LEROY: For a while there I thought maybe she had too *many* children . . .

FRICK: Well I don't have any, so . . .

LEROY: Yeah, I guess that's not it either.

Slight pause.

FRICK: I just can't figure it out. There's no bills; we're very well fixed; she's got a beautiful home. . . . There's really not a trouble in the world. Although, God knows, maybe that's the trouble . . .

LEROY: Oh no, I got plenty of bills and it didn't help mine. I don't think it's how many bills you have.

FRICK: What do you think it is, then?

LEROY: Don't ask me, I don't know.

FRICK: When she started locking up everything I thought maybe it's these Negroes, you know? There's an awful lot of fear around; all this crime.

LEROY: I don't think so. My wife was afraid before there were any Negroes. I mean, around.

FRICK: Well one thing came out of it —I finally learned how to make coffee. And mine's better than hers was. It's an awful sensation, though —coming home and there's nobody there.

LEROY: How'd you like to come home and there's seven of them there?

FRICK: I guess I'm lucky at that.

LEROY: Well, I am too. They're wonderful kids.

FRICK: They still very young?

LEROY: Five to nineteen. But they all pitch in. Everything's clean, house runs like a ship.

FRICK: You're lucky to have good children these days. —I guess we're both lucky.

LEROY: That's the only way to look at it. Start feeling sorry for yourself, that's when you're in trouble.

FRICK: Awfully hard to avoid sometimes.

LEROY: You can't give in to it though. Like tonight—I was so disgusted I just laid down and . . . I was ready to throw in the chips. But then I got up and washed my face, put on the clothes, and here I am. After all, she can't help it either, who you going to blame?

FRICK: It's a mystery—a woman with everything she could possibly want. I don't care what happens to the country, there's nothing could ever hurt her anymore. Suddenly, out of nowhere, she's terrified! . . . She lost all her optimism. Yours do that? Lose her optimism?

LEROY: Mine was never very optimistic. She's Swedish.

FRICK: Oh. Mine certainly was. Whatever deal I was in, couldn't wait till I got home to talk about it. Real estate, stock market, always interested. All of a sudden, no interest whatsoever. Might as well be talking to that wall over there. —Your wife have brothers and sisters?

LEROY: Quite a few, ya.

FRICK: Really. I even thought maybe it's that she was an only child, and if she had brothers and sisters to talk to . . .

LEROY: Oh no—at least I don't think so. It could be even worse.

FRICK: They don't help, huh?

LEROY: They *think* they're helping. Come around saying it's a disgrace for their sister to be in a public institution. That's the kind of help. So I said, "Well, I'm the public!"

FRICK: Sure! —It's a perfectly nice place.

LEROY: They want her in the Rogers Pavilion.

FRICK: Rogers! —that's a couple of hundred dollars a day minimum . . .

LEROY: Well if I had that kind of money I wouldn't mind, but . . .

FRICK: No-no, don't you do it. I could afford it, but what are we paying taxes for?

LEROY: So they can go around saying their sister's in the Rogers Pavilion, that's all.

FRICK: Out of the question. That's fifty thousand dollars a year. Plus tips. I'm sure you have to tip them there.

LEROY: Besides, it's eighty miles there and back, I could never get to see her . . .

FRICK: If they're so sensitive you ought to tell *them* to pay for it. That'd shut them up, I bet.

LEROY: Well no—they've offered to pay part. Most of it, in fact.

FRICK: Whyn't you do it, then?

LEROY, *holding a secret:* I didn't think it's a good place for her.

FRICK: Why?—if they'd pay for it? It's one of the top places in the country. Some very rich people go there.

LEROY: I know.

FRICK: And the top doctors, you know. And they order whatever they want to eat. I went up there to look it over; no question about it, it's absolutely first-class, much better than this place. You should take them up on it.

LEROY: I'd rather have her here.

FRICK: Well I admire your attitude. You don't see that kind of pride anymore.

LEROY: It's not pride, exactly.

FRICK: Never mind, it's a great thing, keep it up. Everybody's got the gimmes, it's destroying the country. Had a man in a few weeks ago to put in a new showerhead. Nothing to it. Screw off the old one and screw on the new one. Seventeen dollars an hour!

LEROY: Yeah, well. *Gets up, unable to remain seated.* Everybody's got to live, I guess.

FRICK: I take my hat off to you—that kind of independence. Don't happen to be with Colonial Trust, do you?

LEROY: No.

FRICK: There was something familiar about you. What line are you in?

LEROY, *he is at the window now, staring out. Slight pause:* Carpenter.

FRICK, *taken aback:* Don't say. . . . Contractor?

LEROY: No. Just carpenter. —I take on one or two fellas when I have to, but I work alone most of the time.

FRICK: I'd never have guessed it.

LEROY: Well that's what I do. *Looks at his watch, wanting escape.*

FRICK: I mean your whole . . . your way of dressing and everything.

LEROY: Why? Just ordinary clothes.

FRICK: No, you look like a college man.

LEROY: Most of them have long hair, don't they?

FRICK: The way college men used to look. I've spent thirty years around carpenters, that's why it surprised me. You know Frick Supply, don't you?

LEROY: Oh ya. I've bought quite a lot of wood from Frick.

FRICK: I sold out about five years ago . . .

LEROY: I know. I used to see you around there.

FRICK: You did? Why didn't you mention it?

LEROY, *shrugs:* Just didn't.

FRICK: You say Anthony?

LEROY: No, Hamilton. Leroy.

FRICK, *points at him:* Hey now! Of course! There was a big article about you in the *Herald* a couple of years ago. Descended from Alexander Hamilton.

LEROY: That's right.

FRICK: Sure! No wonder! *Holding out his palm as to a photo.* Now that I visualize you in overalls, I think I recognize you. In fact, you were out in the yard loading plywood the morning that article came out. My bookkeeper pointed you out through the window. It's those clothes— if I'd seen you in overalls I'd've recognized you right off. Well, what do you know? *The air of condescension plus wonder.* Amazing thing what clothes'll do, isn't it. —Keeping busy?

LEROY: I get work.

FRICK: What are you fellas charging now?

LEROY: I get seventeen an hour.

FRICK: Good for you.

LEROY: I hate asking that much, but even so I just about make it.

FRICK: Shouldn't feel that way; if they'll pay it, grab it.

LEROY: Well ya, but it's still a lot of money. —My head's still back there thirty years ago.

FRICK: What are you working on now?

LEROY: I'm renovating a colonial near Waverly. I just finished over in Belleville. The Presbyterian church.

FRICK: Did you do *that*?

LEROY: Yeah, just finished Wednesday.

FRICK: That's a beautiful job. You're a good man. Where'd they get that altar?

LEROY: I built that.

FRICK: That altar?

LEROY: Uh huh.

FRICK: Hell, that's first-class! Huh! You must be doing all right.

LEROY: Just keeping ahead of it.

FRICK, *slight pause:* How'd it happen?

LEROY: What's that?

FRICK: Well coming out of an old family like that—how do you come to being a carpenter?

LEROY: Just . . . liked it.

FRICK: Father a carpenter?

LEROY: No.

FRICK: What was your father?

LEROY: Lawyer.

FRICK: Why didn't you?

LEROY: Just too dumb, I guess.

FRICK: Couldn't buckle down to the books, huh?

LEROY: I guess not.

FRICK: Your father should've taken you in hand.

LEROY, *sits with magazine, opening it:* He didn't like the law either.

FRICK: Even so. —Many of the family still around?

LEROY: Well my mother, and two brothers.

FRICK: No, I mean of the Hamiltons.

LEROY: Well they're Hamiltons.

FRICK: I know, but I mean— some of them must be pretty important people.

LEROY: I wouldn't know. I never kept track of them.

FRICK: You should. Probably some of them must be pretty big. — Never even looked them up?

LEROY: Nope.

FRICK: You realize the importance of Alexander Hamilton, don't you?

LEROY: I know about him, more or less.

FRICK: More or less! He was one of the most important Founding Fathers.

LEROY: I guess so, ya.

FRICK: You read about him, didn't you?

LEROY: Well sure . . . I read about him.

FRICK: Well didn't your father talk about him?

LEROY: Some. But he didn't care for him much.

FRICK: Didn't care for *Alexander Hamilton?*

LEROY: It was something to do with his philosophy. But I never kept up with the whole thing.

FRICK, *laughing, shaking his head:* Boy, you're quite a character, aren't you.

Leroy is silent, reddening. Frick continues chuckling at him for a moment.

LEROY: I hope to God your wife is cured, Mr. Frick, I hope she never has to come back here again.

FRICK, *sensing the hostility:* What have I said?

LEROY: This is the third time in two years for mine, and I don't mean to be argumentative, but it's got me right at the end of my rope. For all I know I'm in line for this funny farm myself by now, but I have to tell you that this could be what's driving so many people crazy.

FRICK: What is!

LEROY: This.

FRICK: This what?

LEROY: This whole kind of conversation.

FRICK: Why? What's wrong with it?

LEROY: Well never mind.

FRICK: I don't know what you're talking about.

LEROY: Well what's it going to be, equality or what kind of country—I mean, am I supposed to be ashamed I'm a carpenter?

FRICK: Who said you . . . ?

LEROY: Then why do you talk like this to a man? One minute my altar is terrific and the next minute I'm some kind of shit bucket.

LEROY: Hey now, wait a minute . . . !

LEROY: I don't mean anything against you personally, I know you're a successful man and more power to you, but this whole type of conversation about my clothes—should I be ashamed I'm a carpenter? I mean everybody's talking "labor, labor," how much labor's getting; well if it's so great to be labor how come nobody wants to be it? I mean you ever hear a parent going around saying—*mimes thumb pridefully tucked into suspenders*—"My son is a carpenter"? Do you? Do you ever hear people brag about a bricklayer? I don't know what you are but I'm only a dumb swamp Yankee, but . . . *Suddenly breaks off with a shameful laugh.* Excuse me. I'm really sorry. But you come back here two-three more times and you're liable to start talking the way you were never brought up to. *Opens magazine.*

FRICK: I don't understand what you're so hot about.

LEROY, *looks up from the magazine. Seems to start to explain, then sighs:* Nothing.

He returns to his magazine. Frick shakes his head with a certain condescension, then goes back to the window and looks out.

FRICK: It's one hell of a parking lot, you have to say that for it.

They sit for a long moment in silence, each in his own thoughts.

Blackout.

Scene Two

Most of the stage is occupied by Patricia's bedroom. In one of the beds a fully clothed woman lies motionless with one arm over her eyes. She will not move throughout the scene.

Outside this bedroom is a corner of the Recreation Room, bare but for a few scattered chairs.

Presently . . . from just offstage the sound of a Ping-Pong game. The ball comes bouncing into the Recreation Room area and Patricia Hamilton enters chasing it. She captures it and with a sigh of boredom goes offstage with it.

We hear two or three pings and the ball comes onstage again with Patricia Hamilton after it. She starts to return to the game offstage but halts, looks at the ball in her hand, and to someone offstage . . .

PATRICIA: Why are we doing this? Come let's talk, I hate these games.

Mrs. Karen Frick enters. She is in her sixties, very thin, eyeglasses, wispy hair.

I said I'm quitting.

Karen stares at the paddle.

Well never mind. *Studies her watch.* You're very good.

KAREN: My sister-in-law taught me. She used to be a stewardess on the *Queen Mary*. She could even play when the ship was rocking. But she never married.

PATRICIA: Here, put it down, dear.

Karen passively gives up the paddle, then stands there looking uncomfortable.

I'm going to lie down; sit with me, if you like.

KAREN, *indicates Ping-Pong area:* Hardly anyone ever seems to come out there.

PATRICIA: They don't like exercise, they're too depressed.

Patricia lies down. The woman in the other bed does not stir and no attention is paid to her.

Don't feel obliged to say anything if you . . .

KAREN: I get sick to my stomach just looking at a boat. Does your husband hunt?

PATRICIA: Sit down. Relax yourself. You don't have to talk. Although I think you're doing a little better than yesterday.

KAREN: Oh, I like talking with you. *Explaining herself timorously; indicating offstage—and very privately* . . . I should go out—he doesn't like being kept waiting, don't y'know.

PATRICIA: Why are you so afraid? He might start treasuring you more if you make him wait a little. Come, sit.

Karen adventurously sits at the foot of the bed, glancing about nervously.

Men are only big children, you know—give them a chocolate soda every day and pretty soon it doesn't mean a thing to them. *Looks at her watch again.* Only reason I'm nervous is that I can't decide whether to go home today. —But you mustn't mention it, will you?

KAREN: Mention . . . ?

PATRICIA: About my pills. I haven't told anybody yet.

Karen looks a bit blank.

Well never mind.

KAREN: Oh! You mean not taking them.

PATRICIA: But you mustn't mention it, will you. The doctor would be very upset.

KAREN: And how long has it been?

PATRICIA: Twenty-one days today. It's the longest I've been clean in maybe fifteen years. I can hardly believe it.

KAREN: Are you Baptist?

PATRICIA: Baptist? No, we're more Methodist. But the church I'd really love hasn't been invented yet.

KAREN, *charmed, slavishly interested:* How would it be?

PATRICIA, *begins to describe it, breaks off:* I can't describe it. *A sign of lostness.* I was raised Lutheran, of course. —But I often go to the Marble Baptist Church on Route 91? I've gotten to like that minister. —You hear what I'm saying, don't you?

Karen looks at her nervously trying to remember.

I must say it's kind of relaxing talking to you, Karen, knowing that you probably won't remember too much. But you'll come out of it all right, you're just a little scared, aren't you. —But who isn't? *Slight pause.* Doctor Rockwell is not going to believe I'm doing better without medication but I really think something's clicked inside me. *A deep breath.* I even seem to be breathing easier. And I'm not feeling that sort of fuzziness in my head. —It's like some big bird has been hovering over me for fifteen years, and suddenly it's flown away.

KAREN: I can't stand dead animals, can you?

PATRICIA: Well just insist that he has to stop hunting! You don't have to stand for that, you're a *person.*

KAREN: Well you know, men like to . . .

PATRICIA: Not all—I've known some lovely men. Not many, but a few. This minister I mentioned?—he came one day this summer and sat with me on our porch . . . and we had ice cream and talked for over an hour. You know, when he left his previous church they gave him a Pontiac Grand Am. He made me realize something; he said that I seem to be in like a constant state of prayer. And it's true; every once in a while it stops me short, realizing it. It's like inside me I'm almost continually talking to the Lord. Not in words exactly . . . just—you know—communicating with Him. Or trying to. *Deeply excited, but suppressing it.* I tell you truthfully, if I can really come out of this I'm going to . . . I don't know what . . . fall in love with God. I think I have already.

KAREN: You're really beautiful.

PATRICIA: Oh no, dear, I'm a torn-off rag of my old self. The pills put ten years on my face. If he was a Jew or Italian or even Irish he'd be suing these doctors, but Yankees never sue, you know. Although I have to say the only thing he's been right about is medication.

KAREN: Your husband against pills?

PATRICIA: Fanatical. But of course he can stick his head out the window and go high as a kite on a breath of fresh air. *Looks at her watch.*

KAREN: I really think you're extremely attractive.

PATRICIA: No-no, dear, although I did win the county beauty pageant when I was nineteen. But if you're talking beauty you should have seen my mother. She only died two years ago, age eighty-nine, but I still haven't gotten over it. On the beach, right into her seventies, people would still be staring at her—she had an unbelievable bust right up to the end.

KAREN: I cut this finger once in a broken Coke machine. But we never sued.

PATRICIA: Did your conversation always jump around? Because it could be your pills, believe me; the soul belongs to God, we're not supposed to be stuffing Valium into His mouth.

KAREN: I have a cousin who went right through the windshield and she didn't get a cent. *Slight pause.* And it was five below zero out. *Slight pause.* Her husband's Norwegian.

PATRICIA: Look, dear, I know you're trying but don't feel you have to speak.

KAREN: No, I like speaking to you. Is he Baptist too, your husband?

PATRICIA: I said Methodist. But he's more Episcopal. But he'll go to any church if it's raining. *Slight pause.* I just don't know whether to tell him yet.

KAREN: What.

PATRICIA: That I'm off everything.

KAREN: But he'll like that, won't he?

PATRICIA: Oh yes. But he's going to be doubtful. —Which I am, too, let's face it—who can know for sure that you're going to stay clean? I don't want to fool myself, I've been on one medication or another for almost twenty years. But I do feel a thousand percent better. And I really have no idea how it happened. *Shakes her head.* Dear God, when I think of him hanging in there all these years . . . I'm so ashamed. But at the same time he's absolutely refused to make any money, every one of our children has had to work since they could practically write their names. I can't be expected to applaud, exactly. *Presses her eyes.* I guess sooner or later you just have to stand up and say, "I'm normal, I made it." But it's like standing on top of a stairs and there's no stairs. *Staring ahead.*

KAREN: I think I'd better go out to him. Should I tell your husband you're coming out?

PATRICIA: I think I'll wait a minute.

KAREN, *stands:* He seems very nice.

PATRICIA: —I'll tell you the truth, dear —I've put him through hell and I know it. . . . *Tears threaten her.* I know I have to stop blaming him; it came to me like a visitation two weeks ago, I-must-not-blame-Leroy-anymore. And it's amazing. I lost all desire for medication, I could feel it leaving me like a . . . like a ghost. *Slight pause.* It's just that he's got really well-to-do relatives and he simply will not accept anyone's help. I mean you take the Jews, the Italians, Irish—they've got their Italian-Americans, Irish-Americans, Hispanic-Americans—they stick together and help each other. But you ever hear of Yankee-Americans? Not on your life. Raise his taxes, rob him blind, the Yankee'll just sit there all alone getting sadder and sadder. —But I'm not going to think about it anymore.

KAREN: You have a very beautiful chin.

PATRICIA: Men with half his ability riding around in big expensive cars and now for the second Easter Sunday in a row his rear end collapsed.

KAREN: I think my license must have expired.

PATRICIA, *a surge of deep anger:* I refuse to ride around in a nine-year-old Chevrolet which was bought secondhand in the first place!

KAREN: They say there are only three keys for all General Motors cars. You suppose that's possible?

PATRICIA, *peremptorily now:* Believe me, dear, whatever they tell you, you have got to cut down the medication. It could be what's making your mind jump around . . .

KAREN: No, it's that you mentioned Chevrolet, which is General Motors, you see.

PATRICIA: Oh. . . . Well, let's just forget about it. *Slight pause.* Although you're probably right—here you're carefully locking your car and some crook is walking around with the same keys in his pocket. But everything's a fake, we all know that.

KAREN, *facing Patricia again:* I guess that would be depressing.

PATRICIA: No, that's not what depressed me . . .

KAREN: No, I meant him refusing to amount to anything and then spending money on banjo lessons.

PATRICIA: Did I tell you that?—I keep forgetting what I told you because I never know when you're listening. *Holds out her hand.* Here we go again. *Grasps her hand to stop the shaking.*

KAREN: —You sound like you had a wonderful courtship.

PATRICIA: Oh, Karen, everyone envied us, we were the handsomest pair in town; and I'm not boasting, believe me. *Breaks off; watches her hand shake and covers it again.* I just don't want to have to come back here again, you see. I don't think I could bear that. *Grips her hand, moving about.* I simply have to think positively. But it's unbelievable—he's seriously talking about donating his saw-and-chisel collection to the museum!—some of those tools are as old as the United States, they might be worth a fortune! —But I'm going to look ahead, that's all, just as straight ahead as a highway.

Slight pause.

KAREN: I feel so ashamed.

PATRICIA: For Heaven's sake, why? You've got a right to be depressed. There's more people in hospitals because of depression than any other disease.

KAREN: Is that true?

PATRICIA: Of course! Anybody with any sense has got to be depressed in this country. Unless you're really rich, I suppose. Don't let him shame you, dear.

KAREN: No . . . it's that you have so many thoughts.

PATRICIA: Oh. Well you can have thoughts, too—just remember your soul belongs to God and you musn't be shoving pills into His mouth.

Slight pause.

KAREN: We're rich, I think.

PATRICIA, *quickly interested:* . . . Really rich?

KAREN: He's got the oil delivery now, and of course he always had the fertilizer and the Chevy dealership, and of course the lumber yard and all. And Isuzu now.

PATRICIA: What's Isuzus?

KAREN: It's a Japanese car.

PATRICIA: . . . I'll just never catch up.

KAREN: We go to Arkansas in the spring.

PATRICIA: Arkansas?

KAREN: For the catfish. It's where I broke down. But I can't help it, the sight of catfish makes me want to vomit. Not that I was trying to . . . you know . . . do anything. I just read the instructions on the bottle wrong. Do you mind if I ask you something?

PATRICIA: I hope it's nothing personal, is it?

KAREN: Well I don't know.

PATRICIA: . . . Well go ahead, what is it?

KAREN: Do you shop in the A&P or Stop & Shop?

PATRICIA: . . . I'm wondering if you've got the wrong medication. But I guess you'll never overdose—you vomit at the drop of a hat. It may be your secret blessing.

KAREN: —He wants to get me out of the house more, but it's hard to make up my mind where.

PATRICIA: Well . . . A&P is good. Or Stop & Shop. More or less. Kroger's is good for fish sometimes.

KAREN: Which do you like best? I'll go where you go.

PATRICIA: You're very flattering. *Stands, inner excitement.* It's amazing— I'm really beginning to feel wonderful; maybe I ought to go home with him today. I mean what does it come down to, really?—it's simply a question of confidence . . .

KAREN: I wish we could raise some vegetables like we did on the farm. Do you?

PATRICIA: Oh, he raises things in our yard. Healthy things like salsify and collards—and kale. You ever eat kale?

KAREN: I can't remember kale.

PATRICIA: You might as well salt your shower curtain and chop it up with a tomato.

KAREN: —So . . . meats are . . . which?—A&P?

PATRICIA: No. Meats are Stop & Shop. I'm really thinking I might go home today. It's just not his fault, I have to remember that . . .

KAREN: But staples?

PATRICIA: What? —Oh. Stop & Shop.

KAREN: Then what's for A&P?

PATRICIA: Vegetables.

KAREN: Oh right. And Kroger's?

PATRICIA: Why don't you just forget Kroger's.

KAREN, *holds up five fingers, bends one at a time:* . . . Then Stop & Shop . . .

PATRICIA: Maybe it's that you're trying to remember three things. Whyn't you just do A&P and Stop & Shop.

Slight pause.

KAREN: I kind of liked Kroger's.

PATRICIA: Then go to Kroger's, for Heaven's sake!

KAREN: Well I guess I'll go out to him. *Moves to go. Halts.* I hope you aren't really leaving today, are you?

PATRICIA, *higher tension:* I'm deciding.

KAREN: Well . . . here I go, I guess. *Halts again.* I meant to tell you, I kind of like the banjo. It's very good with tap dancing.

PATRICIA: Tap dancing.

KAREN: There's a tap teacher lives on our road.

PATRICIA: You tap-dance?

KAREN: Well John rented a video of Ginger Rogers and Fred Astaire, and I kind of liked it. I can sing "Cheek to Cheek"? Would you like to hear it?

PATRICIA: Sure, go ahead—this is certainly a surprise.

KAREN, *sings in a frail voice:* "Heaven, I'm in heaven, and the cares that clung around me through the week . . ."

PATRICIA: That's beautiful, Karen! Listen, what exactly does Doctor Rockwell say about you?

KAREN: Well, he says it's quite common when a woman is home alone all day.

PATRICIA: What's common?

KAREN: Something moving around in the next room?

PATRICIA: Oh, I see. —You have any idea who it is?

KAREN: My mother. —My husband might bring my tap shoes and tails . . . but he probably forgot. I have a high hat and shorts too. And a walking stick? But would they allow dancing in here?

PATRICIA: They might. But of course the minute they see you enjoying yourself they'll probably try to knock you out with a pill.

Karen makes to go, halts again.

KAREN: Did your mother like you?

PATRICIA: Oh yes. We were all very close. Didn't yours?

KAREN: No. She left the whole farm to her cousin. Tell about your family, can you? Were they really all blond?

PATRICIA: Oh as blond as the tassels on Golden Bantam corn . . . everybody'd turn and look when we went by. My mother was perfection. We all were, I guess. *With a chuckle.* You know, we had a flat roof extending from the house over the garage, and mother and my sisters and me—on the first warm spring days we used to sunbathe out there.

KAREN, *covering her mouth:* No! You mean nude?

PATRICIA: Nudity doesn't matter that much in Sweden, and we were all brought up to love the sun. And we'd near die laughing because the minute we dropped our robes—you know how quiet a town Grenville is—you could hear the footsteps going up the clock tower over the Presbyterian church, and we pretended not to notice but that little narrow tower was just packed with Presbyterians.

KAREN: Good lord!

PATRICIA: We'd stretch out and pretend not to see a thing. And then my mother'd sit up suddenly and point up at the steeple and yell, "Boo!" And they'd all go running down the stairs like mice!

They both enjoy the laugh.

KAREN: I think your husband's very good-looking, isn't he.

PATRICIA: He is, but my brothers . . . I mean the way they stood, and walked . . . and their teeth! Charles won the All-New England golf tournament, and Buzz came within a tenth of an inch of the gold medal in the pole vault—that was in the Portugal Olympics.

KAREN: My! Do you still get together much?

PATRICIA: Oh, they're all gone now.

KAREN: Moved away?

PATRICIA: No . . . dead.

KAREN: Oh my. They overstrain?

PATRICIA: Buzz hung himself on his wife's closet door.

KAREN: Oh my!

PATRICIA: Eight days later Charles shot himself on the tractor.

KAREN, *softly*: Oh my. Did they leave a note or anything?

PATRICIA: No. But we all knew what it was.

KAREN: Can you say?

PATRICIA: Disappointment. We were all brought up expecting to be wonderful, and . . . *breaks off with a shrug* . . . just wasn't.

KAREN: Well . . . here I go.

Karen exits. Patricia stares ahead for a moment in a blankly reminiscent mood. Now she looks at her face in a mirror, smoothing wrinkles away . . .

Leroy enters.

PATRICIA: I was just coming out.

LEROY: 'Cause Mrs. Frick . . .

PATRICIA, *cuts him off by drawing his head down and stroking his cheek. And in a soft but faintly patronizing tone:* . . . I was just coming out, Leroy. You don't have to repeat everything. Come, sit with me and let's not argue.

LEROY: . . . How's your day been?

She is still moved by her brothers' memory; also, she hasn't received something she hoped for from him. She shrugs and turns her head away.

PATRICIA: I've had worse.

LEROY: Did you wash your hair?

PATRICIA, *pleased he noticed:* How can you tell?

LEROY: Looks livelier. Is that nail polish?

PATRICIA: M-hm.

LEROY: Good. You're looking good, Patty.

PATRICIA: I'm feeling better. Not completely but a lot.

LEROY, *nods approvingly:* Great! Did he change your medication or something?

PATRICIA: No.

LEROY: Something different about you.

PATRICIA, *mysteriously excited:* You think so?

LEROY: Your eyes are clearer. You seem more like you're . . . connecting.

PATRICIA: I am, I think. But I warn you, I'm nervous.

LEROY: That's okay. Your color is more . . . I don't know . . . vigorous.

PATRICIA: Is it? *She touches her face.*

LEROY: You look almost like years ago . . .

PATRICIA: Something's happened but I don't want to talk about it yet.

LEROY: Really? Like what?

PATRICIA, *instant resistance:* I just said I . . .

LEROY: . . . Okay. *Goes to a window.* —It looks like rain outside, but we can walk around if you like. They've got a beautiful tulip bed down there; the colors really shine in this gray light. Reds and purple and whites, and a gray. Never saw a tulip be that kind of gray.

PATRICIA: How's Amelia's leg? Are you getting her to change her bandage?

LEROY: Yes. But she'd better stop thinking she can drive a car.

PATRICIA: Well, why don't you tell her?

LEROY, *a little laugh:* That'll be the day, won't it, when she starts listening to her father.

PATRICIA, *a softness despite her language:* She might if you laid down the law without just complaining. And if she could hear something besides disappointment in your voice.

LEROY: She's learned to look down at me, Patty, you know that.

PATRICIA, *strongly, but nearly a threat of weeping:* Well, I hope you're not blaming me for that.

LEROY, *he holds back, stands silent. Then puffs out his cheeks and blows, shaking his head with a defensive grin:* Not my day, I see.

PATRICIA: Maybe it could have been.

LEROY: I was looking forward to telling you something.

PATRICIA: What.

LEROY: I got Harrelson to agree to twelve-thousand-five for the altar.

PATRICIA: There, you see!—and you were so glad to accept eight. I told you . . . !

LEROY: I give you all the credit. I finally got it through my thick skull, I said to myself, okay, you are slower than most, but quality's got a right to be slow. And he didn't make a peep—twelve thousand, five hundred dollars.

She looks at him, immensely sad.

—Well why do you look so sad?

PATRICIA: Come here. *Draws him down, kisses him.* I'm glad. . . . I just couldn't help thinking of all these years wasted trying to get you to charge enough; but I've decided to keep looking straight ahead, not back—I'm very glad you got the twelve. You've done a wonderful thing.

LEROY, *excited:* Listen, what has he got you on?

PATRICIA: Well, I'm still a long way from perfect, but I . . .

LEROY: Patty, nothing's perfect except a hot bath.

PATRICIA: It's nothing to joke about. I told you I'm nervous, I'm not used to . . . to . . .

LEROY: He changed your medication, didn't he.

PATRICIA: I just don't want you to think I have no problems anymore.

LEROY: Oh, I'd never think that, Patty. Has he put you on something new?

PATRICIA: *He* hasn't done anything.

Pause.

LEROY: Okay, I'll shut up.

She sweeps her hair back; he silently observes her. Then . . .

. . . This Mr. Frick handles oil burners; I don't know if I can trust him but he says he'd give me a good buy. We could use a new burner.

PATRICIA: What would you say if I said I'm thinking of coming home.

LEROY, *a pause filled with doubt:* You are? When?

PATRICIA: Maybe next Thursday. For good.

LEROY: Uh huh.

PATRICIA: You don't sound very positive.

LEROY: You know you're the only one can make that decision, Pat. You want to come home I'm always happy to take you home.

Slight pause.

PATRICIA: I feel if I could look ahead just the right amount I'd be all right.

LEROY: What do you mean?

PATRICIA: I realized something lately; when I'm home I have a tendency—especially in the afternoons when everybody's out and I'm alone—I look very far ahead. What I should do is only look ahead a little bit, like to the evening or the next day. And then it's all right. It's when I start looking years ahead . . . *slight pause* . . . You once told me why you think I got sick. I've forgotten . . . what did you say?

LEROY: What do I really know about it, Pat?

PATRICIA: Why do you keep putting yourself down?—you've got to stop imitating your father. There are things you know very well. — Remind me what you said . . . Why am I sick?

LEROY: I always thought it was your family.

PATRICIA, *fingers pressing on her eyes:* I want to concentrate. Go on.

LEROY: They were so close, they were all over each other, and you all had this—you know—very high opinion of yourselves; each and every one of you was automatically going to go to the head of the line just because your name was Sorgenson. And life isn't that way, so you got sick.

Long pause; she stares, nodding.

PATRICIA: You've had no life at all, have you.

LEROY: I wouldn't say that.

PATRICIA: I can't understand how I never saw it.

LEROY: Why?—it's been great watching the kids growing up; and I've had some jobs I've enjoyed . . .

PATRICIA: But not your wife.

LEROY: It's a long time since I blamed you, Pat. It's your upbringing.

PATRICIA: Well I could blame yours too, couldn't I.

LEROY: You sure could.

PATRICIA: I mean this constant optimism is very irritating when you're fifty times more depressed than I am.

LEROY: Now Patty, you know that's not . . .

PATRICIA: You are depressed, Leroy! Because you're scared of people, you really don't trust anyone, and that's incidentally why you never made any money. You could have set the world on fire but you can't bear to work along with other human beings.

LEROY: The last human being I took on to help me tried to steal my half-inch Stanley chisel.

PATRICIA: You mean you *think* he tried . . .

LEROY: I didn't think anything, I found it in his tool box. And that's an original Stanley, not the junk they sell today.

PATRICIA: So what!

LEROY: So what?—that man has three grandchildren! And he's a Chapman—that's one of the oldest upstanding families in the county.

PATRICIA, *emphatically, her point proved:* Which is why you're depressed.

LEROY, *laughs:* I'm not, but why shouldn't I be?—a Chapman stealing a chisel? I mean God Almighty, they've had generals in that family, secretaries of state or some goddam thing. Anyway, if I'm depressed it's from something that happened, not something I imagine.

PATRICIA: I feel like a log that keeps bumping against another log in the middle of the river.

LEROY: Boy, you're a real roller coaster. We were doing great there for a minute, what got us off on this?

PATRICIA: I can't be at peace when I know you are full of denial, and that's saying it straight.

LEROY: What denial? *Laughs.* You want me to say I'm a failure?

PATRICIA: That is not what I . . .

LEROY: Hey, I know what—I'll get a bumper sticker printed up—"The driver of this car is a failure!" —I betcha I could sell a hundred million of them . . . *A sudden fury:* . . . Or maybe I should just drive out on a tractor and shoot myself!

PATRICIA: That's a terrible thing to say to me, Leroy!

LEROY: Well I'm sorry, Patty, but I'm not as dumb as I look—I'm never going to win if I have to compete against your brothers!

PATRICIA, *chastened for the moment:* I did not say you're a failure.

LEROY: I didn't mean to yell; I'm sorry. I know you don't mean to sound like you do, sometimes.

PATRICIA, *unable to retrieve:* I said nothing about a failure. *On the verge of weeping.*

LEROY: It's okay, maybe I am a failure; but in my opinion no more than the rest of this country.

PATRICIA: What happened?—I thought this visit started off so nicely.

LEROY: Maybe you're not used to being so alert; you've been so lethargic for a long time, you know.

She moves; he watches her.

I'm sure of it, Pat, if you could only find two ounces of trust I know we could still have a life.

PATRICIA: I know. *Slight pause; she fights down tears.* What did you have in mind, exactly, when you said it was my upbringing?

LEROY: I don't know . . . I had a flash of your father, that time long ago when we were sitting on your porch . . . we were getting things ready for our wedding . . . and right in front of you he turns to me cool as a cucumber and says—*through laughter, mimicking Swedish accent*—"No Yankee will ever be good enough for a Swedish girl." I nearly fell off into the rosebushes.

PATRICIA, *laughs with a certain delight:* Well, he was old-fashioned . . .

LEROY, *laughing:* Yeah, a real old-fashioned welcome into the family!

PATRICIA: Well, the Yankees *were* terrible to us.

LEROY: That's a hundred years ago, Pat.

PATRICIA, *starting to anger:* You shouldn't keep denying this! —They paid them fifty cents a week and called us dumb Swedes with strong backs and weak minds and did nothing but make us ridiculous.

LEROY: But, Patty, if you walk around town today there isn't a good piece of property that isn't owned by Swedes.

PATRICIA: But that's now.

LEROY: Well when are we living?

PATRICIA: We were treated like animals, some Yankee doctors wouldn't come out to a Swedish home to deliver a baby . . .

LEROY, *laughs:* Well all I hope is that I'm the last Yankee so people can start living today instead of a hundred years ago.

PATRICIA: There was something else you said. About standing on line.

LEROY: On line?

PATRICIA: That you'll always be at the head of the line because . . . *breaks off.*

LEROY: I'm the only one on it.

PATRICIA: . . . Is that really true? You do compete, don't you? You must, at least in your mind?

LEROY: Only with myself. We're really all on a one-person line, Pat. I learned that in these years.

Pause. She stares ahead.

PATRICIA: That's very beautiful. Where'd you get that idea?

LEROY: I guess I made it up, I don't know. It's up to you, Pat—if you feel you're ready, let's go home. Now or Thursday or whenever. What about medication?

PATRICIA, *makes herself ready:* I wasn't going to tell you for another week or two, till I'm absolutely rock sure; —I've stopped taking anything for . . . this is twenty-one days.

LEROY: *Anything?*

She nods with a certain suspense.

My God, Patty. And you feel all right?

PATRICIA: . . . I haven't felt this way in—fifteen years. I've no idea why, but I forgot to take anything, and I slept right through till morning, and I woke up and it was like . . . I'd been blessed during the night. And I haven't had anything since.

LEROY: Did I tell you or didn't I!

PATRICIA: But it's different for you. You're not addictive . . .

LEROY: But didn't I tell you all that stuff is poison? I'm just flying, Patty.

PATRICIA, *clasps her hands to steady herself:* But I'm afraid about coming home. I don't know if I'm jumping the gun. I *feel* I could, but . . .

LEROY: Well, let's talk about it. Is it a question of trusting yourself? Because I think if you've come this far . . .

PATRICIA: Be quiet a minute! *She holds his hand.* Why have you stayed with me?

LEROY, *laughs:* God knows!

PATRICIA: I've been very bad to you sometimes, Leroy, I really see that now. *Starting to weep.* Tell me the truth; in all these years, have you gone to other women? I wouldn't blame you, I just want to know.

LEROY: Well I've thought of it but I never did anything.

PATRICIA, *looking deeply into his eyes:* You really haven't, have you.

LEROY: No.

PATRICIA: Why?

LEROY: I just kept hoping you'd come out of this.

PATRICIA: But it's been so long.

LEROY: I know.

PATRICIA: Even when I'd . . . throw things at you?

LEROY: Uh uh.

PATRICIA: Like that time with the roast?

LEROY: Well, that's one time I came pretty close. But I knew it was those damned pills, not you.

PATRICIA: But why would you be gone night after night? That was a woman, wasn't it.

LEROY: No. Some nights I went over to the library basement to practice banjo with Phil Palumbo. Or to Manny's Diner for some donuts and talk to the fellas.

PATRICIA, *slightest tinge of suspicion:* There are fellas there at *night?*

LEROY: Sure; working guys, mostly young single fellas. But some with wives. You know—have a beer, watch TV.

PATRICIA: And women?

LEROY, *a short beat:* —You know, Pat—and I'm not criticizing—but wouldn't it better for you to try believing a person instead of trying not to believe?

PATRICIA: I'm just wondering if you know . . . there's lots of women would love having you. But you probably don't know that, do you.

LEROY: Sure I do.

PATRICIA: You know lots of women would love to have you?

LEROY: . . . Well, yes, I know that.

PATRICIA: Really. How do you know that?

LEROY, *his quick, open laugh:* I can tell.

PATRICIA: Then what's keeping you? Why don't you move out?

LEROY: Pat, you're torturing me.

PATRICIA: I'm trying to find myself!

She moves in stress, warding off an explosion. There is angry resentment in his voice.

LEROY: I'd remember you happy and loving—that's what kept me; as long ago as that is now, I'd remember how you'd pull on your stockings and get a little makeup on and pin up your hair. . . . When you're positive about life there's just nobody like you. Nobody. Not in life, not in the movies, not on TV. *Slight pause.* But I'm not going to deny it—if it wasn't for the kids I probably *would* have gone.

She is silent, but loaded with something unspoken.

You're wanting to tell me something, aren't you.

PATRICIA: . . . I know what a lucky woman I've been.

LEROY, *he observes her:* —What is it, you want me to stop coming to see you for a while? Please tell me, Pat; there's something on your mind.

Pause. She forces it out.

PATRICIA: I know I shouldn't feel this way, but I'm not too sure I could stand it, knowing that it's never going to . . . I mean, will it ever change anymore?

LEROY: You mean—is it ever going to be "wonderful."

She looks at him, estimating.

Well—no, I guess this is pretty much it; although to me it's already wonderful—I mean the kids, and there are some clear New England mornings when you want to drink the air and the sunshine.

PATRICIA: You can make more out of a change in temperature than any human being I ever heard of—I can't live on weather!

LEROY: Pat, we're getting old! This is just about as rich and handsome as I'm ever going to be and as good as you're ever going to look, so you want to be with me or not?

PATRICIA: I don't want to fool either of us . . . I can't bear it when you can't pay the bills . . .

LEROY: But I'm a carpenter—this is probably the way it's been for carpenters since they built Noah's ark. What do you want to do?

PATRICIA: I'm honestly not sure I could hold up. Not when I hear your sadness all the time and your eyes are full of disappointment. You seem . . . *breaks off.*

LEROY: . . . How do I seem?

PATRICIA: I shouldn't say it.

LEROY: . . . Beaten. Like it's all gone by. *Hurt, but holding on:* All right, Patty, then I might as well say it—I don't think you *ever* had a medical problem; you have an attitude problem . . .

PATRICIA: My problem is spiritual.

LEROY: Okay, I don't mind calling it spiritual.

PATRICIA: Well that's a new note; I thought these ministers were all quacks.

LEROY: Not all; but the ones who make house calls with women, eating up all the ice cream, are not my idea of spiritual.

PATRICIA: *You* know what spiritual is?

LEROY: For me? Sure. Ice skating.

PATRICIA: Ice skating is spiritual.

LEROY: Yes, and skiing! To me spiritual is whatever makes me forget myself and feel happy to be alive. Like even a well-sharpened saw, or a perfect compound joint.

PATRICIA: Maybe this is why we can't get along—spiritual is nothing you can see, Leroy.

LEROY: Really! Then why didn't God make everything invisible! We are in this world and you're going to have to find some way to love it!

Her eyes are filling with tears.

Pounding on me is not going to change anything to wonderful, Patty.

She seems to be receiving him.

I'll say it again, because it's the only thing that's kept me from going crazy—you just have to love this world. *He comes to her, takes her hand.* Come home. Maybe it'll take a while, but I really believe you can make it.

Uncertainty filling her face . . .

All right, don't decide now, I'll come back Thursday and we'll see then.

PATRICIA: Where you going now?

LEROY: For my banjo lesson. I'm learning a new number. —I'll play it for you if you want to hear it.

PATRICIA, *hesitates, then kisses him:* Couldn't you do it on guitar?

LEROY: It's not the same on guitar. *He goes to his banjo case and opens it.*

PATRICIA: But banjo sounds so picky.

LEROY: But that's what's good about it, it's clean, like a toothpick . . .

Enter the Fricks.

LEROY: Oh hi, Mrs. Frick.

KAREN: He brought my costume. Would you care to see it? *To Frick:* This is her—Mrs. Hamilton.

FRICK: Oh! How do you do?

KAREN: This is my husband.

PATRICIA: How do you do?

FRICK: She's been telling me all about you. *Shaking Patricia's hand:* I want to say that I'm thankful to you.

PATRICIA: Really? What for?

FRICK: Well what she says you've been telling her. About her attitude and all.

KAREN, *to Patricia:* Would you like to see my costume? I also have a blue one, but . . .

FRICK, *overriding her:* . . . By the way, I'm Frick Lumber, I recognized your husband right away . . .

KAREN: Should I put it on?

PATRICIA: Sure, put it on!

Leroy starts tuning his banjo.

FRICK, *to Patricia:* All it is is a high hat and shorts, y'know . . . nothing much to it.

KAREN, *to Frick:* Shouldn't I?

PATRICIA: Why not, for Heaven's sake?

FRICK: Go ahead, if they want to see it. *Laughs to Patricia.* She found it in a catalogue. I think it's kinda silly at her age, but I admit I'm a conservative kind of person . . .

KAREN, *cutting him off, deeply embarrassed:* I'll only be a minute. *She starts out, and stops, and to Patricia:* You really think I should?

PATRICIA: Of course!

FRICK, *suppressing an angry embarrassment:* Karen, honey, if you're going to do it, do it.

Karen exits with valise. Leroy tunes his instrument.

FRICK: The slightest decision, she's got to worry it into the ground. — But I have to tell you, it's years since I've seen this much life in her, she's like day and night. What exactly'd you say to her? *To Leroy, thumbing toward Patricia:* She says she just opened up her eyes . . .

LEROY, *surprised:* Patricia?

FRICK: I have to admit, it took me a while to realize it's a sickness . . .

PATRICIA: You're not the only one.

FRICK: Looked to me like she was just favoring herself; I mean the woman has everything, what right has she got to start shooting blanks like that? I happen to be a great believer in self-discipline, started from way down below sea level myself, sixty acres of rocks and swampland is all we had. That's why I'm so glad that somebody's talked to her with your attitude.

PATRICIA, *vamping for time:* What . . . what attitude do you mean?

FRICK: Just that you're so . . . so positive.

Leroy looks up at Patricia, thunderstruck.

She says you made her realize all the things she could be doing instead of mooning around all day . . .

PATRICIA: Well I think being positive is the only way.

FRICK: That's just what I tell her . . .

PATRICIA: But you have to be careful not to sound so disappointed in her.

FRICK: I sound disappointed?

PATRICIA: In a way, I think. —She's got to feel treasured, you see.

FRICK: I appreciate that, but the woman can stand in one place for half an hour at a time practically without moving.

PATRICIA: Well that's the sickness, you see.

FRICK: I realize that. But she won't even go shopping . . .

PATRICIA: You see? You're sounding disappointed in her.

FRICK, *angering:* I am not disappointed in her! I'm just telling you the situation!

PATRICIA: Mr. Frick, she's standing under a mountain a mile high—you've got to help her over it. That woman has very big possibilities!

FRICK: Think so.

PATRICIA: Absolutely.

FRICK: I hope you're right. *To Leroy, indicating Patricia:* You don't mind my saying it, you could do with a little of her optimism.

LEROY, *turns from Patricia, astonished:* Huh?

FRICK, *to Patricia, warmly:* Y'know, she made me have a little platform built down the cellar, with a big full-length mirror so she could see herself dance . . .

PATRICIA: But do you spend time watching her . . .

FRICK: Well she says not to till she's good at it.

PATRICIA: That's because she's terrified of your criticism.

FRICK: But I haven't made any criticism.

PATRICIA: But do you like tap dancing?

FRICK: Well I don't know, I never thought about it one way or another.

PATRICIA: Well that's the thing, you see. It happens to mean a great deal to her . . .

FRICK: I'm for it, I don't mean I'm not for it. But don't tell me you think it's normal for a woman her age to be getting out of bed two, three in the morning and start practicing.

PATRICIA: Well maybe she's trying to get you interested in it. Are you?

FRICK: In tap dancing? Truthfully, no.

PATRICIA: Well there you go . . .

FRICK: Well we've got a lot of new competition in our fuel-oil business . . .

PATRICIA: Fuel oil!

FRICK: I've got seven trucks on the road that I've got to keep busy . . .

PATRICIA: Well there you go, maybe that's why your wife is in here.

FRICK, *visibly angering:* Well I can't be waked up at two o'clock in the morning and be any good next day, now can I. She's not normal.

PATRICIA: Normal! They've got whole universities debating what's normal. Who knows what's normal, Mr. Frick?

FRICK: You mean getting out of bed at two o'clock in the morning and putting on a pair of tap shoes is a common occurrence in this country? I don't think so. —But I didn't mean to argue when you're . . . not feeling well.

PATRICIA: I've never felt better.

She turns away, and Frick looks with bewildered surprise to Leroy, who returns him a look of suppressed laughter.

FRICK: Well you sure know how to turn somebody inside out.

Karen enters; she is dressed in satin shorts, a tailcoat, a high hat, tap shoes, and as they turn to look at her, she pulls out a collapsible walking stick, and strikes a theatrical pose.

PATRICIA: Well now, don't you look great!

KAREN, *desperate for reassurance:* You really like it?

LEROY: That looks terrific!

PATRICIA: Do a step!

KAREN: I don't have my tape. *Turns to Frick, timorously:* But if you'd sing "Swanee River . . ."

FRICK: Oh Karen, for God's sake!

PATRICIA: I can sing it . . .

KAREN: He knows my speed. Please, John . . . just for a minute.

FRICK: All right, go ahead. *Unhappily, he sings:* "Way down upon the Swanee River . . ."

KAREN: Wait, you're too fast . . .

FRICK, *slower and angering:* "Way—down—upon—the—Swanee River, Far, far away. That's where my heart is turning ever . . ." [etc.]

Karen taps out her number, laboriously but for a short stretch with a promise of grace. Frick continues singing . . .

PATRICIA: Isn't she wonderful?

LEROY: Hey, she's great!

Karen dances a bit more boldly, a joyous freedom starting into her.

PATRICIA: She's marvelous! Look at her, Mr. Frick!

A hint of the sensuous in Karen now; Frick, embarrassed, uneasily avoids more than a glance at his wife.

FRICK: ". . . everywhere I roam . . ."

PATRICIA: Will you look at her!

FRICK, *hard-pressed, explodes: I am looking at her, goddammit!*

This astonishing furious shout, his reddened face, stops everything. A look of fear is on Karen's face.

KAREN, *apologetically to Patricia:* He *was* looking at me . . . *To Frick:* She didn't mean you *weren't* looking, she meant . . .

FRICK, *rigidly repressing his anger and embarrassment:* I've got to run along now.

KAREN: I'm so sorry, John, but she . . .

FRICK, *rigidly:* Nothing to be sorry about, dear. Very nice to have met you folks.

He starts to exit. Karen moves to intercept him.

KAREN: Oh John, I hope you're not . . . [going to be angry.]

JOHN: I'm just fine. *He sees her despair coming on.* What are you looking so sad about?—you danced great . . .

She is immobile.

I'm sorry to've raised my voice but it don't mean I'm disappointed, dear. You understand? *A nervous glance toward Patricia. Stiffly, with enormous effort:* . . . You . . . you danced better than I ever saw you.

She doesn't change.

Now look here, Karen, I hope you don't feel I'm . . . disappointed or something, you hear . . . ? 'Cause I'm not. And that's definite.

She keeps staring at him.

I'll try to make it again on Friday. —Keep it up.

He abruptly turns and exits.

Karen stands perfectly still, staring at nothing.

PATRICIA: Karen?

Karen seems not to hear, standing there facing the empty door in her high hat and costume.

How about Leroy playing it for you? *To Leroy:* Play it.

LEROY: I could on the guitar, but I never did on this . . .

PATRICIA: Well couldn't you try it?—I don't know what good that thing is.

LEROY: Well here . . . let me see.

He picks out "Swanee River" on his banjo, but Karen doesn't move.

PATRICIA: There you go, Karen! Try it, I love your dancing! Come on . . . Sings:* "Way down upon the Swanee River . . ."

Karen now breaks her motionlessly depressed mode and looks at Patricia. Leroy continues playing, humming along with it. His picking is getting more accurate . . .

PATRICIA: Is it the right tempo? Tell him!

KAREN, *very very softly:* Could you play a little faster?

Leroy speeds it up. With an unrelieved sadness, Karen goes into her number, does a few steps, but stops. Leroy gradually stops playing. Karen walks out. Patricia starts to follow her but gives it up and comes to a halt.

Leroy turns to Patricia, who is staring ahead. Now she turns to Leroy.

He meets her gaze, his face filled with inquiry. He comes to her and stands there.

For a long moment neither of them moves. Then she reaches out and touches his face—there is a muted gratitude in her gesture.

She goes to a closet and takes a small overnight bag to the bed and puts her things into it.

Leroy watches her for a moment, then stows his banjo in its case, and stands waiting for her. She starts to put on a light coat. He comes and helps her into it.

Her face is charged with her struggle against her self-doubt.

LEROY, *laughs, but about to weep:* Ready?

PATRICIA, *filling up:* Leroy . . .

LEROY: One day at a time, Pat—you're already twenty-one ahead. Kids are going to be so happy to have you home.

PATRICIA: I can't believe it . . . I've had nothing.

LEROY: It's a miracle.

PATRICIA: Thank you. *Breaking through her own resistance, she draws him to her and kisses him. Grinning tauntingly:* . . . That car going to get us home?

LEROY, *laughs:* Stop picking on that car, it's all checked out!

They start toward the door, he carrying her bag and his banjo.

PATRICIA: Once you believe in something you just never know when to stop, do you.

LEROY: Well there's very little rust, and the new ones aren't half as well built . . .

PATRICIA: Waste not, want not.

LEROY: Well I really don't *go* for those new Chevies . . .

She walks out, he behind her. Their voices are heard . . .

PATRICIA: Between the banjo and that car I've certainly got a whole lot to look forward to.

His laughter sounds down the corridor.

The woman on the bed stirs, then falls back and remains motionless. A stillness envelops the whole stage.

End.

BROKEN GLASS

A Play in Two Acts

THE CAST

Phillip Gellburg	Ron Rifkin
Sylvia Gellburg	Amy Irving
Dr. Harry Hyman	David Dukes
Margaret Hyman	Frances Conroy
Harriet	Lauren Klein
Stanton Case	George N. Martin

Directed by John Tillinger. The original production was staged on March 1, 1994, at the Long Wharf Theater, in New Haven, Connecticut.

(Final Acting Version)

The Play takes place in Brooklyn in the last days of November 1938, in the office of Dr. Harry Hyman, the bedroom of the Gellburg house, and the office of Stanton Case.

ACT ONE

Scene One

A lone cellist is discovered, playing a simple tune. The tune finishes. Light goes out on the cellist and rises on. . . .

Office of Dr. Harry Hyman in his home. Alone on stage Phillip Gellburg, an intense man in his late forties, waits in perfect stillness, legs crossed. He is in a black suit, black tie and shoes, and white shirt.

Margaret Hyman, the doctor's wife, enters. She is lusty, energetic, carrying pruning shears.

MARGARET: He'll be right with you, he's just changing. Can I get you something? Tea?

GELLBURG, *faint reprimand:* He said seven o'clock sharp.

MARGARET: He was held up in the hospital, that new union's pulled a strike, imagine? A strike in a hospital? It's incredible. And his horse went lame.

GELLBURG: His horse?

MARGARET: He rides on Ocean Parkway every afternoon.

GELLBURG, *attempting easy familiarity:* Oh yes, I heard about that . . . it's very nice. You're Mrs. Hyman?

MARGARET: I've nodded to you on the street for years now, but you're too preoccupied to notice.

491

GELLBURG, *a barely hidden boast:* Lot on my mind, usually. *A certain amused loftiness.*—So you're his nurse, too.

MARGARET: We met in Mount Sinai when he was interning. He's lived to regret it. *She laughs in a burst.*

GELLBURG: That's some laugh you've got there. I sometimes hear you all the way down the block to my house.

MARGARET: Can't help it, my whole family does it. I'm originally from Minnesota. It's nice to meet you finally, Mr. Goldberg.

GELLBURG: —It's Gellburg, not Goldberg.

MARGARET: Oh, I'm sorry.

GELLBURG: G-e-l-l-b-u-r-g. It's the only one in the phone book.

MARGARET: It does sound like Goldberg.

GELLBURG: But it's not, it's Gellburg. *A distinction.* We're from Finland originally.

MARGARET: Oh! We came from Lithuania . . . Kazauskis?

GELLBURG, *put down momentarily:* Don't say.

MARGARET, *trying to charm him to his ease:* Ever been to Min-nesota?

GELLBURG: New York State's the size of France, what would I go to Minnesota for?

MARGARET: Nothing. Just there's a lot of Finns there.

GELLBURG: Well there's Finns all over.

MARGARET, *defeated, shows the clipper:* . . . I'll get back to my roses. Whatever it is, I hope you'll be feeling better.

GELLBURG: It's not me.

MARGARET: Oh. 'Cause you seem a little pale.

GELLBURG: Me?—I'm always this color. It's my wife.

MARGARET: I'm sorry to hear that, she's a lovely woman. It's nothing serious, is it?

GELLBURG: He's just had a specialist put her through some tests, I'm waiting to hear. I think it's got him mystified.

MARGARET: Well, I mustn't butt in. *Makes to leave but can't resist.* Can you say what it is?

GELLBURG: She can't walk.

MARGARET: What do you mean?

GELLBURG, *an overtone of protest of some personal victimization:* Can't stand up. No feeling in her legs.—I'm sure it'll pass, but it's terrible.

MARGARET: But I only saw her in the grocery . . . can't be more than ten days ago . . .

GELLBURG: It's nine days today.

MARGARET: But she's such a wonderful-looking woman. Does she have fever?

GELLBURG: No.

MARGARET: Thank God, then it's not polio.

GELLBURG: No, she's in perfect health otherwise.

MARGARET: Well Harry'll get to the bottom of it if anybody can. They call him from everywhere for opinions, you know . . . Boston, Chicago . . . By rights he ought to be on Park Avenue if he only had the ambition, but he always wanted a neighborhood practice. Why, I don't know—we never invite anybody, we never go out, all our friends are in Manhattan. But it's his nature, you can't fight a person's nature. Like me for instance, I like to talk and I like to laugh. You're not much of a talker, are you.

GELLBURG, *a purse-mouthed smile:* When I can get a word in edgewise.

MARGARET, *burst of laughter:* Ha!—so you've got a sense of humor after all. Well give my best to Mrs. Goldberg.

GELLBURG: Gellbu . . .

MARGARET, *hits her own head:* Gellburg, excuse me! —It practically sounds like Goldberg . . .

GELLBURG: No-no, look in the phone book, it's the only one, G-e-l-l . . .

Enter Dr. Hyman.

MARGARET, *with a little wave to Gellburg:* Be seeing you!

GELLBURG: Be in good health.

Margaret exits.

HYMAN, *in his early fifties, a healthy, rather handsome man, a determined scientific idealist. Settling behind his desk—chuckling:* She chew your ear off?

GELLBURG, *his worldly mode:* Not too bad, I've had worse.

HYMAN: Well there's no way around it, women are talkers . . . *Grinning familiarly:* But try living without them, right?

GELLBURG: Without women?

HYMAN, *he sees Gellburg has flushed; there is a short hiatus, then:* . . . Well, never mind. —I'm glad you could make it tonight, I wanted to talk to you before I see your wife again tomorrow. *Opens cigar humidor.* Smoke?

GELLBURG: No thanks, never have. Isn't it bad for you?

HYMAN: Certainly is. *Lights a cigar.* But more people die of rat bite, you know.

GELLBURG: Rat bite!

HYMAN: Oh yes, but they're mostly the poor so it's not an interesting statistic. Have you seen her tonight or did you come here from the office?

GELLBURG: I thought I'd see you before I went home. But I phoned her this afternoon—same thing, no change.

HYMAN: How's she doing with the wheelchair?

GELLBURG: Better, she can get herself in and out of the bed now.

HYMAN: Good. And she manages the bathroom?

GELLBURG: Oh yes. I got the maid to come in the mornings to help her take a bath, clean up . . .

HYMAN: Good. Your wife has a lot of courage, I admire that kind of woman. My wife is similar; I like the type.

GELLBURG: What type you mean?

HYMAN: You know—vigorous. I mean mentally and . . . you know, just generally. Moxie.

GELLBURG: Oh.

HYMAN: Forget it, it was only a remark.

GELLBURG: No, you're right, I never thought of it, but she is unusually that way.

HYMAN, *pause, some prickliness here which he can't understand:* Doctor Sherman's report . . .

GELLBURG: What's he say?

HYMAN: I'm getting to it.

GELLBURG: Oh. Beg your pardon.

HYMAN: You'll have to bear with me . . . may I call you Phillip?

GELLBURG: Certainly.

HYMAN: I don't express my thoughts very quickly, Phillip.

GELLBURG: Likewise. Go ahead, take your time.

HYMAN: People tend to overestimate the wisdom of physicians so I try to think things through before I speak to a patient.

GELLBURG: I'm glad to hear that.

HYMAN: Aesculapius stuttered, you know—ancient Greek god of medicine. But probably based on a real physician who hesitated about giving advice. Somerset Maugham stammered, studied medicine. Anton Chekhov, great writer, also a doctor, had tuberculosis. Doctors are very often physically defective in some way, that's why they're interested in healing.

GELLBURG, *impressed:* I see.

HYMAN, *pause, thinks:* I find this Adolf Hitler very disturbing. You been following him in the papers?

GELLBURG: Well yes, but not much. My average day in the office is ten, eleven hours.

HYMAN: They've been smashing the Jewish stores in Berlin all week, you know.

GELLBURG: Oh yes, I saw that again yesterday.

HYMAN: Very disturbing. Forcing old men to scrub the sidewalks with toothbrushes. On the Kurfürstendamm, that's equivalent to Fifth Avenue. Nothing but hoodlums in uniform.

GELLBURG: My wife is very upset about that.

HYMAN: I know, that's why I mention it. *Hesitates.* And how about you?

GELLBURG: Of course. It's a terrible thing. Why do you ask?

HYMAN, *a smile:* —I don't know, I got the feeling she may be afraid she's annoying you when she talks about such things.

GELLBURG: Why? I don't mind. —She said she's annoying me?

HYMAN: Not in so many words, but . . .

GELLBURG: I can't believe she'd say a thing like . . .

HYMAN: Wait a minute, I didn't say she said it . . .

GELLBURG: She doesn't annoy me, but what can be done about such things? The thing is, she doesn't like to hear about the other side of it.

HYMAN: What other side?

GELLBURG: It's no excuse for what's happening over there, but German Jews can be pretty . . . you know . . . *Pushes up his nose with his forefinger.* Not that they're pushy like the ones from Poland or Russia but a friend of mine's in the garment industry; these German Jews won't take an ordinary good job, you know; it's got to be pretty high up in the firm or they're insulted. And they can't even speak English.

HYMAN: Well I guess a lot of them were pretty important over there.

GELLBURG: I know, but they're supposed to be *refugees*, aren't they? With all our unemployment you'd think they'd appreciate a little more.

Latest official figure is twelve million unemployed you know, and it's probably bigger but Roosevelt can't admit it, after the fortune he's pouring into WPA and the rest of that welfare *mishugas*. —But she's not *annoying* me, for God's sake.

HYMAN: . . . I just thought I'd mention it; but it was only a feeling I had . . .

GELLBURG: I'll tell you right now, I don't run with the crowd, I see with these eyes, nobody else's.

HYMAN: I see that. —You're very unusual— *Grinning.* —you almost sound like a Republican.

GELLBURG: Why?—the Torah says a Jew has to be a Democrat? I didn't get where I am by agreeing with everybody.

HYMAN: Well that's a good thing; you're independent. *Nods, puffs.* You know, what mystifies me is that the Germans I knew in Heidelberg . . . I took my M.D. there . . .

GELLBURG: You got along with them.

HYMAN: Some of the finest people I ever met.

GELLBURG: Well there you go.

HYMAN: We had a marvelous student choral group, fantastic voices; Saturday nights, we'd have a few beers and go singing through the streets. . . . People'd applaud from the windows.

GELLBURG: Don't say.

HYMAN: I simply can't imagine those people marching into Austria, and now they say Czechoslovakia's next, and Poland. . . . But fanatics have taken Germany, I guess, and they can be brutal, you know . . .

GELLBURG: Listen, I sympathize with these refugees, but . . .

HYMAN, *cutting him off:* I had quite a long talk with Sylvia yesterday, I suppose she told you?

GELLBURG, *a tensing:* Well . . . no, she didn't mention. What about?

HYMAN, *surprised by Sylvia's omission:* . . . Well about her condition, and . . . just in passing . . . your relationship.

GELLBURG, *flushing: My* relationship?

HYMAN: . . . It was just in passing.

GELLBURG: Why, what'd she say?

HYMAN: Well that you . . . get along very well.

GELLBURG: Oh.

HYMAN, *encouragingly, as he sees Gellburg's small tension:* I found her a remarkably well-informed woman. Especially for this neighborhood.

GELLBURG, *a pridefully approving nod; relieved that he can speak of her positively:* That's practically why we got together in the first place. I don't exaggerate, if Sylvia was a man she could have run the Federal Reserve. You could talk to Sylvia like you talk to a man.

HYMAN: I'll bet.

GELLBURG, *a purse-mouthed grin:* . . . Not that talking was all we did —but you turn your back on Sylvia and she's got her nose in a book or a magazine. I mean there's not one woman in ten around here could even tell you who their Congressman is. And you can throw in the men, too. *Pause.* So where are we?

HYMAN: Doctor Sherman confirms my diagnosis. I ask you to listen carefully, will you?

GELLBURG, *brought up:* Of course, that's why I came.

HYMAN: We can find no physical reason for her inability to walk.

GELLBURG: No physical reason . . .

HYMAN: We are almost certain that this is a psychological condition.

GELLBURG: But she's numb, she has no feeling in her legs.

HYMAN: Yes. This is what we call an hysterical paralysis. Hysterical doesn't mean she screams and yells . . .

GELLBURG: Oh, I know. It means like . . . ah . . . *Bumbles off.*

HYMAN, *a flash of umbrage, dislike:* Let me explain what it means, okay?—Hysteria comes from the Greek word for the womb because it was thought to be a symptom of female anxiety. Of course it isn't, but that's where it comes from. People who are anxious enough or really frightened can imagine they've gone blind or deaf, for instance . . . and they really can't see or hear. It was sometimes called shell-shock during the War.

GELLBURG: You mean . . . you don't mean she's . . . crazy.

HYMAN: We'll have to talk turkey, Phillip. If I'm going to do you any good I'm going to have to ask you some personal questions. Some of them may sound raw, but I've only been superficially acquainted with Sylvia's family and I need to know more . . .

GELLBURG: She says you treated her father . . .

HYMAN: Briefly; a few visits shortly before he passed away. They're fine people. I hate like hell to see this happen to her, you see what I mean?

GELLBURG: You can tell it to me; is she crazy?

HYMAN: Phillip, are you? Am I? In one way or another, who isn't crazy? The main difference is that our kind of crazy still allows us to walk around and tend to our business. But who knows?—people like us may be the craziest of all.

GELLBURG, *scoffing grin:* Why!

HYMAN: Because we don't know we're nuts, and the other kind does.

GELLBURG: I don't know about that . . .

HYMAN: Well, it's neither here nor there.

GELLBURG: I certainly don't think *I'm* nuts.

HYMAN: I wasn't saying that . . .

GELLBURG: What do you mean, then?

HYMAN, *grinning:* You're not an easy man to talk to, are you.

GELLBURG: Why? If I don't understand I have to ask, don't I?

HYMAN: Yes, you're right.

GELLBURG: That's the way I am—they don't pay me for being easy to talk to.

HYMAN: You're in . . . real estate?

GELLBURG: I'm head of the Mortgage Department of Brooklyn Guarantee and Trust.

HYMAN: Oh, that's right, she told me.

GELLBURG: We are the largest lender east of the Mississippi.

HYMAN: Really. *Fighting deflation.* Well, let me tell you my approach; if possible I'd like to keep her out of that whole psychiatry rigmarole. Not that I'm against it, but I think you get further faster, sometimes, with a little common sense and some plain human sympathy. Can we talk turkey? *Tuchas offen tisch,* you know any Yiddish?

GELLBURG: Yes, it means get your ass on the table.

HYMAN: Correct. So let's forget crazy and try to face the facts. We have a strong, healthy woman who has no physical ailment, and suddenly can't stand on her legs. Why?

He goes silent. Gellburg shifts uneasily.

I don't mean to embarrass you . . .

GELLBURG, *an angry smile:* You're not embarrassing me. —What do you want to know?

HYMAN, *sets himself, then launches:* In these cases there is often a sexual disability. You have relations, I imagine?

GELLBURG: Relations? Yes, we have relations.

HYMAN, *a softening smile:* Often?

GELLBURG: What's that got to do with it?

HYMAN: Sex could be connected. You don't have to answer . . .

GELLBURG: No-no it's all right. . . . I would say it depends—maybe twice, three times a week.

HYMAN, *seems surprised:* Well that's good. She seems satisfied?

GELLBURG, *shrugs; hostilely:* I guess she is, sure.

HYMAN: That was a foolish question, forget it.

GELLBURG, *flushed:* Why, did she mention something about this?

HYMAN: Oh no, it's just something I thought of later.

GELLBURG: Well, I'm no Rudolph Valentino but I . . .

HYMAN: Rudolph Valentino probably wasn't either.—What about before she collapsed; was that completely out of the blue or . . .

GELLBURG, *relieved to be off the other subject:* I tell you, looking back I wonder if something happened when they started putting all the pictures in the paper. About these Nazi carryings-on. I noticed she started . . . staring at them . . . in a very peculiar way. And . . . I don't know. I think it made her angry or something.

HYMAN: At you.

GELLBURG: Well . . . *Nods, agreeing.* In general. —Personally I don't think they should be publishing those kind of pictures.

HYMAN: Why not?

GELLBURG: She scares herself to death with them—three thousand miles away, and what does it accomplish! Except maybe put some fancy new ideas into these anti-Semites walking around New York here.

Slight pause.

HYMAN: Tell me how she collapsed. You were going to the movies . . . ?

GELLBURG, *breathing more deeply:* Yes. We were just starting down the porch steps and all of a sudden her . . . *Difficulty; he breaks off.*

HYMAN: I'm sorry but I . . .

GELLBURG: . . . Her legs turned to butter. I couldn't stand her up. Kept falling around like a rag doll. I had to carry her into the house. And she kept apologizing . . . ! *He weeps; recovers.* I can't talk about it.

HYMAN: It's all right.

GELLBURG: She's always been such a level-headed woman. *Weeping threatens again.* I don't know what to do. She's my life.

HYMAN: I'll do my best for her, Phillip, she's a wonderful woman. — Let's talk about something else. What do you do exactly?

GELLBURG: I mainly evaluate properties.

HYMAN: Whether to grant a mortgage . . .

GELLBURG: And how big a one and the terms.

HYMAN: How's the Depression hit you?

GELLBURG: Well, it's no comparison with '32 to '36, let's say—we were foreclosing left and right in those days. But we're on our feet and running.

HYMAN: And you head the department . . .

GELLBURG: Above me is only Mr. Case. Stanton Wylie Case; he's chairman and president. You're not interested in boat racing.

HYMAN: Why?

GELLBURG: His yacht won the America's Cup two years ago. For the second time. The *Aurora*?

HYMAN: Oh yes! I think I read about . . .

GELLBURG: He's had me aboard twice.

HYMAN: Really.

GELLBURG, *the grin:* The only Jew ever set foot on that deck.

HYMAN: Don't say.

GELLBURG: In fact, I'm the only Jew ever worked for Brooklyn Guarantee in their whole history.

HYMAN: That so.

GELLBURG: Oh yes. And they go back to the 1890s. Started right out of accountancy school and moved straight up. They've been wonderful to me; it's a great firm.

A long moment as Hyman stares at Gellburg, who is proudly positioned now, absorbing his poise from the evoked memories of his success. Gradually Gellburg turns to him.

How could this be a mental condition?

HYMAN: It's unconscious; like . . . well take yourself; I notice you're all in black. Can I ask you why?

GELLBURG: I've worn black since high school.

HYMAN: No particular reason.

GELLBURG, *shrugs:* Always liked it, that's all.

HYMAN: Well it's a similar thing with her; she doesn't know why she's doing this, but some very deep, hidden part of her mind is directing her to do it. You don't agree.

GELLBURG: I don't know.

HYMAN: You think she knows what she's doing?

GELLBURG: Well I always liked black for business reasons.

HYMAN: It gives you authority?

GELLBURG: Not exactly authority, but I wanted to look a little older. See, I graduated high school at fifteen and I was only twenty-two when I entered the firm. But I knew what I was doing.

HYMAN: Then you think she's doing this on purpose?

GELLBURG:—Except she's numb; nobody can purposely do that, can they?

HYMAN: I don't think so. —I tell you, Phillip, not really knowing your wife, if you have any idea why she could be doing this to herself . . .

GELLBURG: I told you, I don't know.

HYMAN: Nothing occurs to you.

GELLBURG, *an edge of irritation:* I can't think of anything.

HYMAN: I tell you a funny thing, talking to her, she doesn't seem all that unhappy.

GELLBURG: Say!—yes, that's what I mean. That's exactly what I mean. It's like she's almost . . . I don't know . . . enjoying herself. I mean in a way.

HYMAN: How could that be possible?

GELLBURG: Of course she apologizes for it, and for making it hard for me—you know, like I have to do a lot of the cooking now, and tending to my laundry and so on . . . I even shop for groceries and the butcher . . . and change the sheets . . .

He breaks off with some realization. Hyman doesn't speak. A long pause.

You mean . . . she's doing it against me?

HYMAN: I don't know, what do *you* think?

Stares for a long moment, then makes to rise, obviously deeply disturbed.

GELLBURG: I'd better be getting home. *Lost in his own thought.* I don't know whether to ask you this or not.

HYMAN: What's to lose, go ahead.

GELLBURG: My parents were from the old country, you know,—I don't know if it was in Poland someplace or Russia—but there was this woman who they say was . . . you know . . . gotten into by a . . . like the ghost of a dead person . . .

HYMAN: A dybbuk.

GELLBURG: That's it. And it made her lose her mind and so forth. — You believe in that? They had to get a rabbi to pray it out of her body. But you think that's possible?

HYMAN: Do I think so? No. Do you?

GELLBURG: Oh no. It just crossed my mind.

HYMAN: Well I wouldn't know how to pray it out of her, so . . .

GELLBURG: Be straight with me—is she going to come out of this?

HYMAN: Well, let's talk again after I see her tomorrow. Maybe I should tell you . . . I have this unconventional approach to illness, Phillip. Especially where the mental element is involved. I believe we get sick in twos and threes and fours, not alone as individuals. You follow me? I want you to do me a favor, will you?

GELLBURG: What's that.

HYMAN: You won't be offended, okay?

GELLBURG, *tensely:* Why should I be offended?

HYMAN: I'd like you to give her a lot of loving. *Fixing Gellburg in his gaze.* Can you? It's important now.

GELLBURG: Say, you're not blaming this on me, are you?

HYMAN: What's the good of blame? —from here on out, *tuchas offen tisch*, okay? And Phillip?

GELLBURG: Yes?

HYMAN, *a light chuckle:* Try not to let yourself get mad.

Gellburg turns and goes out. Hyman returns to his desk, makes some notes. Margaret enters.

MARGARET: That's one miserable little pisser.

He writes, doesn't look up.

He's a dictator, you know. I was just remembering when I went to the grandmother's funeral? He stands outside the funeral parlor and decides who's going to sit with who in the limousines for the cemetery. "You sit with him, you sit with her . . ." And they obey him like he owned the funeral!

HYMAN: Did you find out what's playing?

MARGARET: At the Beverly they've got Ginger Rogers and Fred Astaire. Jimmy Cagney's at the Rialto but it's another gangster story.

HYMAN: I have a sour feeling about this thing. I barely know my way around psychiatry. I'm not completely sure I ought to get into it.

MARGARET: Why not?—She's a very beautiful woman.

HYMAN, *matching her wryness:* Well, is that a reason to turn her away? *He laughs, grasps her hand.* Something about it fascinates me—no disease and she's paralyzed. I'd really love to give it a try. I mean I don't want to turn myself into a post office, shipping all the hard cases to specialists, the woman's sick and I'd like to help.

MARGARET: But if you're not getting anywhere in a little while you'll promise to send her to somebody.

HYMAN: Absolutely. *Committed now: full enthusiasm.* I just feel there's something about it that I understand.—Let's see Cagney.

MARGARET: Oh, no Fred Astaire.

HYMAN: That's what I meant. Come here.

MARGARET, *as he embraces her:* We should leave now . . .

HYMAN: You're the best, Margaret.

MARGARET: A lot of good it does me.

HYMAN: If it really bothers you I'll get someone else to take the case.

MARGARET: You won't, you know you won't.

He is lifting her skirt.

Don't, Harry. Come on.

She frees her skirt, he kisses her breasts.

HYMAN: Should I tell you what I'd like to do with you?

MARGARET: Tell me, yes, tell me. And make it wonderful.

HYMAN: We find an island and we strip and go riding on this white horse . . .

MARGARET: Together.

HYMAN: You in front.

MARGARET: Naturally.

HYMAN: And then we go swimming . . .

MARGARET: Harry, that's lovely.

HYMAN: And I hire this shark to swim very close and we just manage to get out of the water, and we're so grateful to be alive we fall down on the beach together and . . .

MARGARET, *pressing his lips shut:* Sometimes you're so good. *She kisses him.*

Blackout.

Scene Two

The lone cellist plays. Then lights go down . . .

Next evening. The Gellburg bedroom. Sylvia Gellburg is seated in a wheelchair reading a newspaper. She is in her mid-forties, a buxom, capable, and warm woman. Right now her hair is brushed down to her shoulders, and she is in a nightgown and robe.

She reads the paper with an intense, almost haunted interest, looking up now and then to visualize.

Her sister Harriet, a couple of years younger, is straightening up the bedcover.

HARRIET: So what do you want, steak or chicken? Or maybe he'd like chops for a change.

SYLVIA: Please, don't put yourself out, Phillip doesn't mind a little shopping.

HARRIET: What's the matter with you, I'm going anyway, he's got enough on his mind.

SYLVIA: Well all right, get a couple of chops.

HARRIET: And what about you. You have to start eating!

SYLVIA: I'm eating.

HARRIET: What, a piece of cucumber? Look how pale you are. And what is this with newspapers night and day?

SYLVIA: I like to see what's happening.

HARRIET: I don't know about this doctor. Maybe you need a specialist.

SYLVIA: He brought one two days ago, Doctor Sherman. From Mount Sinai.

HARRIET: Really? And?

SYLVIA: We're waiting to hear. I like Doctor Hyman.

HARRIET: Nobody in the family ever had anything like this. You feel *something*, though, don't you?

SYLVIA, *pause, she lifts her face:* Yes . . . but inside, not on the skin. *Looks at her legs.* I can harden the muscles but I can't lift them. *Strokes her thighs.* I seem to have an ache. Not only here but . . . *She runs her hands down her trunk.* My whole body seems . . . I can't describe it. It's like I was just born and I . . . didn't want to come out yet. Like a deep, terrible aching . . .

HARRIET: Didn't want to come out yet! What are you talking about?

SYLVIA, *sighs gently, knowing Harriet can never understand:* Maybe if he has a nice duck. If not, get the chops. And thanks, Harriet, it's sweet of you.—By the way, what did David decide?

HARRIET: He's not going to college.

SYLVIA, *shocked:* I don't believe it! With a scholarship and he's not going?

HARRIET: What can we do? *Resignedly.* He says college wouldn't help him get a job anyway.

SYLVIA: Harriet, that's terrible!—Listen, tell him I have to talk to him.

HARRIET: Would you! I was going to ask you but with this happening. *Indicates her legs.* I didn't think you'd . . .

SYLVIA: Never mind, tell him to come over. And you must tell Murray he's got to put his foot down—you've got a brilliant boy! My God . . . *Picks up the newspaper.* If I'd had a chance to go to college I'd have had a whole different life, you can't let this happen.

HARRIET: I'll tell David . . . I wish I knew what is suddenly so interesting in a newspaper. This is not normal, Sylvia, is it?

SYLVIA, *pause, she stares ahead:* They are making old men crawl around and clean the sidewalks with toothbrushes.

HARRIET: Who is?

SYLVIA: In Germany. Old men with beards!

HARRIET: So why are you so interested in that? What business of yours is that?

SYLVIA, *slight pause; searches within:* I don't really know. *A slight pause.* Remember Grandpa? His eyeglasses with the bent sidepiece? One of the old men in the paper was his spitting image, he had the same exact glasses with the wire frames. I can't get it out of my mind. On their knees on the sidewalk, two old men. And there's fifteen or twenty people standing in a circle laughing at them scrubbing with toothbrushes. There's three women in the picture; they're holding their coat collars closed, so it must have been cold . . .

HARRIET: Why would they make them scrub with toothbrushes?

SYLVIA, *angered:* To humiliate them, to make fools of them!

HARRIET: Oh!

SYLVIA: How can you be so . . . so . . . ? *Breaks off before she goes too far.* Harriet, please . . . leave me alone, will you?

HARRIET: This is not normal. Murray says the same thing. I swear to God, he came home last night and says, "She's got to stop thinking about those Germans." And you know how he loves current events. *Sylvia is staring ahead.* I'll see if the duck looks good, if not I'll get chops. Can I get you something now?

SYLVIA: No, I'm fine, thanks.

HARRIET, *moves upstage of Sylvia, turns:* I'm going.

SYLVIA: Yes.

She returns to her paper. Harriet watches anxiously for a moment, out of Sylvia's sight line, then exits. Sylvia turns a page, absorbed in the paper. Suddenly she turns in shock—Phillip is standing behind her. He holds a small paper bag.

SYLVIA: Oh! I didn't hear you come in.

GELLBURG: I tiptoed, in case you were dozing off . . . *His dour smile.* I bought you some sour pickles.

SYLVIA: Oh, that's nice! Later, maybe. You have one.

GELLBURG: I'll wait. *Awkwardly but determined:* I was passing Greenberg's on Flatbush Avenue and I suddenly remembered how you used to love them. Remember?

SYLVIA: Thanks, that's nice of you. What were you doing on Flatbush Avenue?

GELLBURG: There's a property across from A&S. I'm probably going to foreclose.

SYLVIA: Oh that's sad. Are they nice people?

GELLBURG, *shrugs:* People are people—I gave them two extensions but they'll never manage . . . nothing up here. *Taps his temple.*

SYLVIA: Aren't you early?

GELLBURG: I got worried about you. Doctor come?

SYLVIA: He called; he has the results of the tests but he wants to come tomorrow when he has more time to talk to me. He's really very nice.

GELLBURG: How was it today?

SYLVIA: I'm so sorry about this.

GELLBURG: You'll get better, don't worry about it. Oh!—there's a letter from the captain. *Takes it out of his jacket.*

SYLVIA: Jerome?

GELLBURG, *terrific personal pride:* Read it.

She reads; his purse-mouthed grin is intense.

That's your son. General MacArthur talked to him twice.

SYLVIA: Fort Sill?

GELLBURG: Oklahoma. *He's going to lecture them on artillery! In Fort Sill!* That's the field-artillery center.

She looks up dumbly.

That's like being invited to the Vatican to lecture the Pope.

SYLVIA: Imagine. *She folds the letter and hands it back to him.*

GELLBURG, *restraining greater resentment:* I don't understand this attitude.

SYLVIA: Why? I'm happy for him.

GELLBURG: You don't seem happy to me.

SYLVIA: I'll never get used to it. Who goes in the army? Men who can't do anything else.

GELLBURG: I wanted people to see that a Jew doesn't have to be a lawyer or a doctor or a businessman.

SYLVIA: That's fine, but why must it be Jerome?

GELLBURG: For a Jewish boy, West Point is an honor! Without Mr. Case's connections, he never would have gotten in. He could be the first Jewish general in the United States Army. Doesn't it mean something to be his mother?

SYLVIA, *with an edge of resentment:* Well, I said I'm glad.

GELLBURG: Don't be upset. *Looks about impatiently.* You know, when you get on your feet I'll help you hang the new drapes.

SYLVIA: I started to . . .

GELLBURG: But they've been here over a month.

SYLVIA: Well this happened, I'm sorry.

GELLBURG: You have to occupy yourself is all I'm saying, Sylvia, you can't give in to this.

SYLVIA, *near an outburst:* Well I'm sorry—I'm sorry about everything!

GELLBURG: Please, don't get upset, I take it back!

A moment; stalemate.

SYLVIA: I wonder what my tests show.

Gellburg is silent.

That the specialist did.

GELLBURG: I went to see Doctor Hyman last night.

SYLVIA: You did? Why didn't you mention it?

GELLBURG: I wanted to think over what he said.

SYLVIA: What did he say?

With a certain deliberateness, Gellburg goes over to her and gives her a kiss on the cheek.

SYLVIA, *she is embarrassed and vaguely alarmed:* Phillip! *A little uncomprehending laugh.*

GELLBURG: I want to change some things. About the way I've been doing.

He stands there for a moment perfectly still, then rolls her chair closer to the bed on which he now sits and takes her hand. She doesn't quite know what to make of this, but doesn't remove her hand.

SYLVIA: Well what did he say?

GELLBURG, *he pats her hand:* I'll tell you in a minute. I'm thinking about a Dodge.

SYLVIA: A Dodge?

GELLBURG: I want to teach you to drive. So you can go where you like, visit your mother in the afternoon. —I want you to be happy, Sylvia.

SYLVIA, *surprised:* Oh.

GELLBURG: We have the money, we could do a lot of things. Maybe see Washington, D.C. . . . It's supposed to be a very strong car, you know.

SYLVIA: But aren't they all black?—Dodges?

GELLBURG: Not all. I've seen a couple of green ones.

SYLVIA: You like green?

GELLBURG: It's only a color. You'll get used to it. —Or Chicago. It's really a big city, you know.

SYLVIA: Tell me what Doctor Hyman said.

GELLBURG, *gets himself set:* He thinks it could all be coming from your mind. Like a . . . a fear of some kind got into you. Psychological.

She is still, listening.

Are you afraid of something?

SYLVIA, *a slow shrug, a shake of her head:* . . . I don't know, I don't think so. What kind of fear, what does he mean?

GELLBURG: Well, he explains it better, but . . . like in a war, people get so afraid they go blind temporarily. What they call shell-shock. But once they feel safer it goes away.

SYLVIA: What about the tests the Mount Sinai man did?

GELLBURG: They can't find anything wrong with your body.

SYLVIA: But I'm numb!

GELLBURG: He claims being very frightened could be doing it. —Are you?

SYLVIA: I don't know.

GELLBURG: Personally. . . . Can I tell you what I think?

SYLVIA: What.

GELLBURG: I think it's this whole Nazi business.

SYLVIA: But it's in the paper—they're smashing up the Jewish stores . . . Should I not read the paper? The streets are covered with broken glass!

GELLBURG: Yes, but you don't have to be constantly . . .

SYLVIA: It's ridiculous. I can't move my legs from reading a newspaper?

GELLBURG: He didn't say that; but I'm wondering if you're too involved with . . .

SYLVIA: It's ridiculous.

GELLBURG: Well you talk to him tomorrow. *Pause. He comes back to her and takes her hand, his need open.* You've got to get better, Sylvia.

SYLVIA, *she sees his tortured face and tries to laugh:* What is this, am I dying or something?

GELLBURG: How can you say that?

SYLVIA: I've never seen such a look in your face.

GELLBURG: Oh no-no-no . . . I'm just worried.

SYLVIA: I don't understand what's happening . . . *She turns away on the verge of tears.*

GELLBURG: . . . I never realized . . . *Sudden sharpness* . . . look at me, will you?

She turns to him; he glances down at the floor.

I wouldn't know what to do without you, Sylvia, honest to God. I . . . *Immense difficulty.* I love you.

SYLVIA, *a dead, bewildered laugh:* What is this?

GELLBURG: You have to get better. If I'm ever doing something wrong I'll change it. Let's try to be different. All right? And you too, you've got to do what the doctors tell you.

SYLVIA: What can I do? Here I sit and they say there's nothing wrong with me.

GELLBURG: Listen . . . I think Hyman is a very smart man . . . *He lifts her hand and kisses her knuckle; embarrassed and smiling.* When we were talking, something came to mind; that maybe if we could sit down with him, the three of us, and maybe talk about . . . you know . . . everything.

Pause.

SYLVIA: That doesn't matter anymore, Phillip.

GELLBURG, *an embarrassed grin:* How do you know? Maybe . . .

SYLVIA: It's too late for that.

GELLBURG, *once launched he is terrified:* Why? Why is it too late?

SYLVIA: I'm surprised you're still worried about it.

GELLBURG: I'm not worried, I just think about it now and then.

SYLVIA: Well it's too late, dear, it doesn't matter anymore. *She draws back her hand.*

Pause.

GELLBURG: . . . Well all right. But if you wanted to I'd . . .

SYLVIA: We did talk about it, I took you to Rabbi Steiner about it twice, what good did it do?

GELLBURG: In those days I still thought it would change by itself. I was so young, I didn't understand such things. It came out of nowhere and I thought it would go the same way.

SYLVIA: I'm sorry, Phillip, it didn't come out of nowhere.

Silent, he evades her eyes.

SYLVIA: You regretted you got married.

GELLBURG: I didn't "regret" it . . .

SYLVIA: You did, dear. You don't have to be ashamed of it.

A long silence.

GELLBURG: I'm going to tell you the truth—in those days I thought that if we separated I wouldn't die of it. I admit that.

SYLVIA: I always knew that.

GELLBURG: But I haven't felt that way in years now.

SYLVIA: Well I'm here. *Spreads her arms out, a wildly ironical look in her eyes.* Here I am, Phillip!

GELLBURG, *offended:* The way you say that is not very . . .

SYLVIA: Not very what? I'm here; I've been here a long time.

GELLBURG, *a helpless surge of anger:* I'm trying to tell you something!

SYLVIA, *openly taunting him now:* But I said I'm here!

Gellburg moves about as she speaks, as though trying to find an escape or a way in.

I'm here for my mother's sake, and Jerome's sake, and everybody's sake except mine, but I'm here and here I am. And now finally you want to talk about it, now when I'm turning into an old woman? How do you want me to say it? Tell me, dear, I'll say it the way you want me to. What should I say?

GELLBURG, *insulted and guilty:* I want you to stand up.

SYLVIA: I can't stand up.

He takes both her hands.

GELLBURG: You can. Now come on. Stand up.

SYLVIA: I can't!

GELLBURG: You can stand up, Sylvia. Now lean to me and get on your feet.

He pulls her up; then steps aside, releasing her; she collapses on the floor. He stands over her.

What are you trying to do? *He goes to his knees to yell into her face: What are you trying to do, Sylvia!*

She looks at him in terror at the mystery before her.

Blackout.

Scene Three

The lone cellist plays. Then lights go down . . .

Dr. Hyman's office. He is in riding boots and a sweater. Harriet is seated beside his desk.

HARRIET: My poor sister. And they have everything! But how can it be in the mind if she's so paralyzed?

HYMAN: Her numbness is random, it doesn't follow the nerve paths; only part of the thighs are affected, part of the calves, it makes no physiological sense. I have a few things I'd like to ask you, all right?

HARRIET: You know, I'm glad it's you taking care of her, my husband says the same thing.

HYMAN: Thank you . . .

HARRIET: You probably don't remember, but you once took out our cousin Roslyn Fein? She said you were great.

HYMAN: Roslyn Fein. When?

HARRIET: She's very tall and reddish-blond hair? She had a real crush . . .

HYMAN, *pleased:* When was this?

HARRIET: Oh—NYU, maybe twenty-five years ago. She adored you; seriously, she said you were really *great. Laughs knowingly.* Used to take her to Coney Island swimming, and so on.

HYMAN, *laughs with her:* Oh. Well give her my regards.

HARRIET: I hardly see her, she lives in Florida.

HYMAN, *pressing on:* I'd like you to tell me about Sylvia; —before she collapsed, was there any sign of some shock, or anything? Something threatening her?

HARRIET, *thinks for a moment, shrugs, shaking her head:* Listen, I'll tell you something funny—to me sometimes she seems . . . I was going to say happy, but it's more like . . . I don't know . . . like this is how she wants to be. I mean since the collapse. Don't you think so?

HYMAN: Well I never really knew her before. What about this fascination with the Nazis—she ever talk to you about that?

HARRIET: Only this last couple of weeks. I don't understand it, they're in *Germany*, how can she be so frightened, it's across the ocean, isn't it?

HYMAN: Yes. But in a way it isn't. *He stares, shaking his head, lost.* . . . She's very sensitive; she really sees the people in those photographs. They're alive to her.

HARRIET, *suddenly near tears:* My poor sister!

HYMAN: Tell me about Phillip.

HARRIET: Phillip? *Shrugs.* Phillip is Phillip.

HYMAN: You like him?

HARRIET: Well he's my brother-in-law . . . You mean personally.

HYMAN: Yes.

HARRIET, *takes a breath to lie:* . . . He can be very sweet, you know. But suddenly he'll turn around and talk to you like you've got four legs and long ears. The men—not that they don't respect him—but they'd just as soon not play cards with him if they can help it.

HYMAN: Really. Why?

HARRIET: Well, God forbid you have an opinion—you open your mouth and he gives you that Republican look down his nose and your brains dry up. Not that I don't *like* him . . .

HYMAN: How did he and Sylvia meet?

HARRIET: She was head bookkeeper at Empire Steel over there in Long Island City . . .

HYMAN: She must have been very young.

HARRIET: . . . Twenty; just out of high school practically and she's head bookkeeper. According to my husband, God gave Sylvia all the brains and the rest of us the big feet! The reason they met was the company took out a mortgage and she had to explain all the accounts to Phillip—he used to say, "I fell in love with her figures!" *Hyman laughs.* Why should I lie?—personally to me, he's a little bit a prune. Like he never stops with the whole Jewish part of it.

HYMAN: He doesn't like being Jewish.

HARRIET: Well yes and no—like Jerome being the only Jewish captain, he's proud of that. And him being the only one ever worked for Brooklyn Guarantee—he's proud of that too, but at the same time . . .

HYMAN: . . . He'd rather not be one.

HARRIET: . . . Look, he's a mystery to me. I don't understand him and I never will.

HYMAN: What about the marriage? I promise you this is strictly between us.

HARRIET: What can I tell you, the marriage is a marriage.

HYMAN: And?

HARRIET: I shouldn't talk about it.

HYMAN: It stays in this office. Tell me. They ever break up?

HARRIET: Oh God no! Why should they? He's a wonderful provider. There's no Depression for Phillip, you know. And it would kill our mother, she worships Phillip, she'd never outlive it. No-no, it's out of the question, Sylvia's not that kind of woman, although . . . *Breaks off.*

HYMAN: Come, Harriet, I need to know these things!

HARRIET: . . . Well I guess everybody knows it, so . . . *Takes a breath.* I think they came very close to it one time . . . when he hit her with the steak.

HYMAN: Hit her with a *steak*?

SYLVIA: It was overdone.

HYMAN: What do you mean, hit her?

SYLVIA: He picked it up off the plate and slapped her in the face with it.

HYMAN: And then what?

HARRIET: Well if my mother hadn't patched it up I don't know what would have happened and then he went out and bought her that gorgeous beaver coat, and repainted the whole house, and he's tight as a drum, you know, so it was hard for him. I don't know what to tell you. —Why?—you think *he* could have frightened her like this?

HYMAN, *hesitates:* I don't know yet. The whole thing is very strange.

Something darkens Harriet's expression and she begins to shake her head from side to side and she bursts into tears. He comes and puts an arm around her.

HYMAN: What is it?

HARRIET: All her life she did nothing but love everybody!

HYMAN, *reaches out to take her hand:* Harriet.

She looks at him.

What do you want to tell me?

HARRIET: I don't know if it's right to talk about. But of course, it's years and years ago . . .

HYMAN: None of this will ever be repeated; believe me.

HARRIET: Well . . . every first of the year when Uncle Myron was still alive we'd all go down to his basement for a New Year's party. I'm talking like fifteen, sixteen years ago. He's dead now, Myron . . . he was . . . you know . . . *Small laugh* . . . a little comical; he always kept this shoebox full of . . . you know, these postcards.

HYMAN: You mean . . .

HARRIET: Yes. French. You know, naked women, and men with these great big . . . you know . . . they hung down like salamis. And everybody'd pass them around and die laughing. It was exactly the same thing every New Year's. But this time, all of a sudden, Phillip . . . we thought he'd lost his mind . . .

HYMAN: What happened?

HARRIET: Well Sylvia's in the middle of laughing and he grabs the postcard out of her hand and he turns around screaming—I mean, really screaming—that we're all a bunch of morons and idiots and God knows what, and throws her up the stairs. Bang! It cracked the bannister, I can still hear it. *Catches her breath.* I tell you it was months before anybody'd talk to him again. Because everybody on the block loves Sylvia.

HYMAN: What do you suppose made him do that?

HARRIET, *shrugs:* . . . Well if you listen to some of the men—but of course some of the dirty minds on this block . . . if you spread it over the backyard you'd get tomatoes six feet high.

HYMAN: Why?—what'd they say?

HARRIET: Well that the reason he got so mad was because he couldn't . . . you know . . .

HYMAN: Oh really.

HARRIET: . . . anymore.

HYMAN: But they made up.

HARRIET: Listen, to be truthful you have to say it—although it'll sound crazy . . .

HYMAN: What.

HARRIET: You watch him sometimes when they've got people over and she's talking—he'll sit quietly in the corner, and the expression on that man's face when he's watching her—it could almost break your heart.

HYMAN: Why?

HARRIET: He adores her!

Blackout.

Scene Four

The cellist plays, and is gone.

Stanton Case is getting ready to leave his office. Putting on his blazer and a captain's cap and a foulard. He has a great natural authority, an almost childishly naive self-assurance. Gellburg enters.

CASE: Good!—you're back. I was just leaving.

GELLBURG: I'm sorry. I got caught in traffic over in Crown Heights.

CASE: I wanted to talk to you again about 611. Sit down for a moment.

Both sit.

We're sailing out through the Narrows in about an hour.

GELLBURG: Beautiful day for it.

CASE: Are you all right? You don't look well.

GELLBURG: Oh no, I'm fine.

CASE: Good. Have you come to anything final on 611? I like the price, I can tell you that right off.

GELLBURG: Yes, the price is not bad, but I'm still . . .

CASE: I've walked past it again; I think with some renovation it would make a fine annex for the Harvard Club.

GELLBURG: It's a very nice structure, yes. I'm not final on it yet but I have a few comments . . . unless you've got to get on the water right away.

CASE: I have a few minutes. Go ahead.

GELLBURG: . . . Before I forget—we got a very nice letter from Jerome.

No reaction from Case.

My boy.

CASE: Oh yes!—how is he doing?

GELLBURG: They're bringing him out to Fort Sill . . . some kind of lecture on artillery.

CASE: Really, now! Well, isn't that nice! . . . Then he's really intending to make a career in the army.

GELLBURG, *surprised Case isn't aware:* Oh absolutely.

CASE: Well that's good, isn't it. It's quite surprising for one of you people—for some reason I'd assumed he just wanted the education.

GELLBURG: Oh no. It's his life. I'll never know how to thank you.

CASE: No trouble at all. The Point can probably use a few of you people to keep the rest of them awake. Now what's this about 611?

GELLBURG, *sets himself in all dignity:* You might recall, we used the ABC Plumbing Contractors on a couple of buildings?

CASE: ABC? —I don't recall. What have they got to do with it?

GELLBURG: They're located in the neighborhood, just off Broadway, and on a long shot I went over to see Mr. Liebfreund—he runs ABC. I was wondering if they may have done any work for Wanamaker's.

CASE: Wanamaker's! What's Wanamaker's got to do with it?

GELLBURG: I buy my shirts in Wanamaker's, and last time I was in there I caught my shoe on a splinter sticking up out of the floor.

CASE: Well that store is probably fifty years old.

GELLBURG: Closer to seventy-five. I tripped and almost fell down; this was very remarkable to me, that they would leave a floor in such condition. So I began wondering about it . . .

CASE: About what?

GELLBURG: Number 611 is two blocks from Wanamaker's. *A little extra-wise grin.* They're the biggest business in the area, a whole square block, after all. Anyway, sure enough, turns out ABC does all Wanamaker's plumbing work. And Liebfreund tells me he's had to keep patching up their boilers *because they canceled installation of new boilers last winter.* A permanent cancellation.

Pause.

CASE: And what do you make of that?

GELLBURG: I think it could mean they're either moving the store, or maybe going out of business.

CASE: *Wanamaker's?*

GELLBURG: It's possible, I understand the family is practically died out. Either way, if Wanamaker's disappears, Mr. Case, that neighborhood in my opinion is no longer prime. Also, I called Kevin Sullivan over at Title Guarantee and he says they turned down 611 last year and he can't remember why.

CASE: Then what are you telling me?

GELLBURG: I would not touch Number 611 with a ten-foot pole—unless you can get it at a good defensive price. If that neighborhood starts to slide, 611 is a great big slice of lemon.

CASE: Well. That's very disappointing. It would have made a wonderful club annex.

GELLBURG: With a thing like the Harvard Club you have got to think of the far distant future, Mr. Case, I don't have to tell you that, and the future of that part of Broadway is a definite possible negative. *Raising a monitory finger:* I emphasize "possible," mind you; only God can predict.

CASE: Well I must say, I would never have thought of Wanamaker's disappearing. You've been more than thorough, Gellburg, we appreciate it. I've got to run now, but we'll talk about this further . . . *Glances at his watch.* Mustn't miss the tide . . . *Moves, indicates.* Take a brandy if you like. Wife all right?

GELLBURG: Oh yes, she's fine!

CASE, *the faint shadow of a warning:* Sure everything's all right with you—we don't want you getting sick now.

GELLBURG: Oh no, I'm very well, very well.

CASE: I'll be back on Monday, we'll go into this further. *Indicates.* Take a brandy if you like.

Case exits rather jauntily.

GELLBURG: Yes, sir, I might!

Gellburg stands alone; with a look of self-satisfaction starts to raise the glass.

Blackout.

Scene Five

The cello plays, and the music falls away.

Sylvia in bed, reading a book. She looks up as Hyman enters. He is in his riding clothes. Sylvia has a certain excitement at seeing him.

SYLVIA: Oh, doctor!

HYMAN: I let myself in, hope I didn't scare you . . .

SYLVIA: Oh no, I'm glad. Sit down. You been riding?

HYMAN: Yes. All the way down to Brighton Beach, nice long ride—I expected to see you jumping rope by now.

Sylvia laughs, embarrassed.

I think you're just trying to get out of doing the dishes.

SYLVIA, *strained laugh:* Oh stop. You really love riding, don't you?

HYMAN: Well there's no telephone on a horse.

She laughs.

Ocean Parkway is like a German forest this time of the morning—riding under that archway of maple trees is like poetry.

SYLVIA: Wonderful. I never did anything like that.

HYMAN: Well, let's go—I'll take you out and teach you sometime. Have you been trying the exercise?

SYLVIA: I can't do it.

HYMAN, *shaking a finger at her:* You've *got* to do it, Sylvia. You could end up permanently crippled. Let's have a look.

He sits on the bed and draws the cover off her legs, then raises her nightgown. She inhales with a certain anticipation as he does so. He feels her toes.

You feel this at all?

SYLVIA: Well . . . not really.

HYMAN: I'm going to pinch your toe. Ready?

SYLVIA: All right.

He pinches her big toe sharply; she doesn't react. He rests a palm on her leg.

HYMAN: Your skin feels a little too cool. You're going to lose your muscle tone if you don't move. Your legs will begin to lose volume and shrink . . .

SYLVIA, *tears threaten:* I know . . . !

HYMAN: And look what beautiful legs you have, Sylvia. I'm afraid you're getting comfortable in this condition . . .

SYLVIA: I'm not. I keep trying to move them . . .

HYMAN: But look now—here it's eleven in the morning and you're happily tucked into bed like it's midnight.

SYLVIA: But I've tried . . . ! Are you really sure it's not a virus of some kind?

HYMAN: There's nothing. Sylvia, you have a strong beautiful body . . .

SYLVIA: But what can I do, I can't feel anything!

She sits up with her face raised to him; he stands and moves abruptly away. Then turning back to her . . .

HYMAN: I really should find someone else for you.

SYLVIA: Why!—I don't want anyone else!

HYMAN: You're a very attractive woman, don't you know that?

Deeply excited, Sylvia glances away shyly.

HYMAN: Sylvia, listen to me . . . I haven't been this moved by a woman in a very long time.

SYLVIA: . . . Well, you mustn't get anyone else.

Pause.

HYMAN: Tell me the truth, Sylvia. Sylvia? How did this happen to you?

SYLVIA, *she avoids his gaze:* I don't know. *Sylvia's anxiety rises as he speaks now.*

HYMAN: . . . I'm going to be straight with you; I thought this was going to be simpler than it's turning out to be, and I care about you too much to play a game with your health. I can't deny my vanity. I have a lot of it, but I have to face it—I know you want to tell me something and I don't know how to get it out of you. *Sylvia covers her face, ashamed.* You're a responsible woman, Sylvia, you have to start helping me, you can't just lie there and expect a miracle to lift you to your feet. You tell me now—what should I know?

SYLVIA: I would tell you if I knew! *Hyman turns away defeated and impatient.* Couldn't we just talk and maybe I could . . . *Breaks off.* I like you. A lot. I love when you talk to me . . . couldn't we just . . . like for a few minutes. . . .

HYMAN: Okay. What do you want to talk about?

SYLVIA: Please. Be patient. I'm . . . I'm trying. *Relieved; a fresher mood:* —Harriet says you used to take out our cousin Roslyn Fein.

HYMAN, *smiles, shrugs:* It's possible, I don't remember.

SYLVIA: Well you had so many, didn't you.

HYMAN: When I was younger.

SYLVIA: Roslyn said you used to do acrobatics on the beach? And all the girls would stand around going crazy for you.

HYMAN: That's a long time ago. . . .

SYLVIA: And you'd take them under the boardwalk. *Laughs.*

HYMAN: Nobody had money for anything else. Didn't you used to go to the beach?

SYLVIA: Sure. But I never did anything like that.

HYMAN: You must have been very shy.

SYLVIA: I guess. But I had to look out for my sisters, being the eldest . . .

HYMAN: Can we talk about Phillip?

Caught unaware, her eyes show fear.

I'd really like to, unless you . . .

SYLVIA, *challenged:* No!—It's all right.

HYMAN: . . . Are you afraid right now?

SYLVIA: No, not . . . Yes.

Picks up the book beside her.

Have you read *Anthony Adverse*?

HYMAN: No, but I hear it's sold a million copies.

SYLVIA: It's wonderful. I rent it from Womraths.

HYMAN: Was Phillip your first boyfriend?

SYLVIA: The first serious.

HYMAN: He's a fine man.

SYLVIA: Yes, he is.

HYMAN: Is he interesting to be with?

SYLVIA: Interesting?

HYMAN: Do you have things to talk about?

SYLVIA: Well . . . business, mostly. I was head bookkeeper for Empire Steel in Long Island City . . . years ago, when we met, I mean.

HYMAN: He didn't want you to work?

SYLVIA: No.

HYMAN: I imagine you were a good businesswoman.

SYLVIA: Oh, I loved it! I've always enjoyed . . . you know, people depending on me.

HYMAN: Yes. —Do I frighten you, talking like this?

SYLVIA: A little. —But I want you to.

HYMAN: Why?

SYLVIA: I don't know. You make me feel . . . hopeful.

HYMAN: You mean of getting better?

SYLVIA: —Of myself. Of getting . . . *Breaks off.*

HYMAN: Getting what?

She shakes her head, refusing to go on.

. . . Free?

She suddenly kisses the palm of his hand. He wipes her hair away from her eyes. He stands up and walks a few steps away.

HYMAN: I want you to raise your knees.

She doesn't move.

Come, bring up your knees.

SYLVIA, *she tries:* I can't!

HYMAN: You can. I want you to send your thoughts into your hips. Tense your hips. Think of the bones in your hips. Come on now. The strongest muscles in your body are right there, you still have tremendous power there. Tense your hips.

She is tensing.

Now tense your thighs. Those are long dense muscles with tremendous power. Do it, draw up your knees. Come on, raise your knees. Keep it up. Concentrate. Raise it. Do it for me.

With an exhaled gasp she gives up. Remaining yards away . . .

Your body strength must be marvelous. The depth of your flesh must be wonderful. Why are you cut off from yourself? You should be dancing, you should be stretching out in the sun. . . . Sylvia, I know you know more than you're saying, why can't you open up to me? Speak to me. Sylvia? Say anything.

She looks at him in silence.

I promise I won't tell a soul. What is in your mind right now?

A pause.

SYLVIA: Tell me about Germany.

HYMAN, *surprised:* Germany. Why Germany?

SYLVIA: Why did you go there to study?

HYMAN: The American medical schools have quotas on Jews, I would have had to wait for years and maybe never get in.

SYLVIA: But they hate Jews there, don't they?

HYMAN: These Nazis can't possibly last— Why are you so preoccupied with them?

SYLVIA: I don't know. But when I saw that picture in the *Times*—with those two old men on their knees in the street . . . *Presses her ears.* I swear, I almost heard that crowd laughing, and ridiculing them. But nobody really wants to talk about it. I mean Phillip never even wants to talk about being Jewish, except—you know—to joke about it the way people do . . .

HYMAN: What would you like to say to Phillip about it?

SYLVIA, *with an empty laugh, a head shake:* I don't even know! Just to talk about it . . . it's almost like there's something in me that . . . it's silly . . .

HYMAN: No, it's interesting. What do you mean, something in you?

SYLVIA: I have no word for it, I don't know what I'm saying, it's like . . . *She presses her chest.*—something alive, like a child almost, except it's a very dark thing . . . and it frightens me!

Hyman moves his hand to calm her and she grabs it.

HYMAN: That was hard to say, wasn't it. *Sylvia nods.* You have a lot of courage.—We'll talk more, but I want you to try something now. I'll stand here, and I want you to imagine something. *Sylvia turns to him, curious.* I want you to imagine that we've made love.

Startled, she laughs tensely. He joins this laugh as though it is a game.

I've made love to you. And now it's over and we are lying together. And you begin to tell me some secret things. Things that are way down deep in your heart. *Slight pause.* Sylvia—

Hyman comes around the bed, bends, and kisses her on the cheek.

Tell me about Phillip.

Sylvia is silent, does not grasp his head to hold him. He straightens up.

Think about it. We'll talk tomorrow again. Okay?

Hyman exits. Sylvia lies there inert for a moment. Then she tenses with effort, trying to raise her knee. It doesn't work. She reaches down and lifts the knee, and then the other and lies there that way. Then she lets her knees spread apart . . .

Blackout.

Scene Six

The cellist plays, then is gone.

Hyman's office. Gellburg is seated. Immediately Margaret enters with a cup of cocoa and a file folder. She hands the cup to Gellburg.

GELLBURG: Cocoa?

MARGARET: I drink a lot of it, it calms the nerves. Have you lost weight?

GELLBURG, *impatience with her prying:* A little, I think.

MARGARET: Did you always sigh so much?

GELLBURG: Sigh?

MARGARET: You probably don't realize you're doing it. You should have him listen to your heart.

GELLBURG: No-no, I think I'm all right. *Sighs.* I guess I've always sighed. Is that a sign of something?

MARGARET: Not necessarily; but ask Harry. He's just finishing with a patient. —There's no change, I understand.

GELLBURG: No, she's the same. *Impatiently hands her the cup.* I can't drink this.

MARGARET: Are you eating at all?

GELLBURG, *suddenly shifting his mode:* I came to talk to *him*.

MARGARET, *sharply:* I was only trying to be helpful!

GELLBURG: I'm kind of upset, I didn't mean any . . .

Hyman enters, surprising her. She exits, insulted.

HYMAN: I'm sorry. But she means well.

Gellburg silently nods, irritation intact.

HYMAN: It won't happen again. *He takes his seat.* I have to admit, though, she has a very good diagnostic sense. Women are more instinctive sometimes . . .

GELLBURG: Excuse me, I don't come here to be talking to her.

HYMAN, *a kidding laugh:* Oh, come on, Phillip, take it easy. What's Sylvia doing?

GELLBURG, *it takes him a moment to compose himself:* . . . I don't know what she's doing.

Hyman waits. Gellburg has a tortured look; now he seems to brace himself, and faces the doctor with what seems a haughty air.

I decided to try to do what you advised. —About the loving.

HYMAN: . . . Yes?

GELLBURG: So I decided to try to do it with her.

HYMAN: . . . Sex?

GELLBURG: What then, handball? Of course sex.

The openness of this hostility mystifies Hyman, who becomes conciliatory.

HYMAN: . . . Well, do you mean you've done it or you're going to?

GELLBURG, *long pause; he seems not to be sure he wants to continue. Now he sounds reasonable again:* You see, we haven't been really . . . together. For . . . quite a long time. *Correcting:* I mean specially since this started to happen.

HYMAN: You mean the last two weeks.

GELLBURG: Well yes. *Great discomfort.* And some time before that.

HYMAN: I see. *But he desists from asking how long a time before that. A pause.*

GELLBURG: So I thought maybe it would help her if . . . you know.

HYMAN: Yes, I think the warmth would help. In fact, to be candid, Phillip—I'm beginning to wonder if this whole fear of the Nazis isn't because she feels . . . extremely vulnerable; I'm in no sense trying to blame you but . . . a woman who doesn't feel loved can get very disoriented you know? —lost. *He has noticed a strangeness.*—Something wrong?

GELLBURG: She says she's not being loved?

HYMAN: No—no. I'm talking about how she may feel.

GELLBURG: Listen . . . *Struggles for a moment; now firmly.* I'm wondering if you could put me in touch with somebody.

HYMAN: You mean for yourself?

GELLBURG: I don't know; I'm not sure what they do, though.

HYMAN: I know a very good man at the hospital, if you want me to set it up.

GELLBURG: Well maybe not yet, let me let you know.

HYMAN: Sure.

GELLBURG: Your wife says I sigh a lot. Does that mean something?

HYMAN: Could just be tension. Come in when you have a little time, I'll look you over. . . . Am I wrong?—you sound like something's happened . . .

GELLBURG: This whole thing is against me . . . *Attempting a knowing grin.* But you know that.

HYMAN: Now wait a minute . . .

GELLBURG: She knows what she's doing, you're not blind.

HYMAN: What happened, why are you saying this?

GELLBURG: I was late last night—I had to be in Jersey all afternoon, a problem we have there—she was sound asleep. So I made myself some spaghetti. Usually she puts something out for me.

HYMAN: She has no problem cooking.

GELLBURG: I told you—she gets around the kitchen fine in the wheel-chair. Flora shops in the morning—that's the maid. Although I'm beginning to wonder if Sylvia gets out and walks around when I leave the house.

HYMAN: It's impossible.—She is paralyzed, Phillip, it's not a trick—she's suffering.

GELLBURG, *a sideways glance at Hyman:* What do you discuss with her? —You know, she talks like you see right through her.

HYMAN, *a laugh:* I wish I could! We talk about getting her to walk, that's all. This thing is not against you, Phillip, believe me. *Slight laugh.*—I wish you could trust me, kid!

GELLBURG, *seems momentarily on the edge of being reassured and studies Hyman's face for a moment, nodding very slightly:* I would never believe I could talk this way to another person. I do trust you.

Pause.

HYMAN: Good!—I'm listening, go ahead.

GELLBURG: The first time we talked you asked me if we . . . how many times a week.

HYMAN: Yes.

GELLBURG, *nods:* . . . I have a problem sometimes.

HYMAN: Oh.—Well that's fairly common, you know.

GELLBURG, *relieved:* You see it often?

HYMAN: Oh very often, yes.

GELLBURG, *a tense challenging smile:* Ever happen to you?

HYMAN, *surprised:* . . . Me? Well sure, a few times. Is this something recent?

GELLBURG: Well . . . yes. Recent and also . . . *breaks off, indicating the past with a gesture of his hand.*

HYMAN: I see. It doesn't help if you're under tension, you know.

GELLBURG: Yes, I was wondering that.

HYMAN: Just don't start thinking it's the end of the world because it's not—you're still a young man. Think of it like the ocean—it goes out but it always comes in again. But the thing to keep in mind is that she loves you and wants you.

Gellburg looks wide-eyed.

You know that, don't you?

GELLBURG, *silently nods for an instant:* My sister-in-law Harriet says you were a real hotshot on the beach years ago.

HYMAN: Years ago, yes.

GELLBURG: I used to wonder if it's because Sylvia's the only one I was ever with.

HYMAN: Why would that matter?

GELLBURG: I don't know exactly—it used to prey on my mind that . . . maybe she expected more.

HYMAN: Yes. Well that's a common idea, you know. In fact, some men take on a lot of women not out of confidence but because they're afraid to lose it.

GELLBURG, *fascinated:* Huh! I'd never of thought of that. —A doctor must get a lot of peculiar cases, I bet.

HYMAN, *with utter intimacy:* Everybody's peculiar in one way or another but I'm not here to judge people. Why don't you try to tell me what happened? *His grin; making light of it.* Come on, give it a shot.

GELLBURG: All right . . . *Sighs.* I get into bed. She's sound asleep . . . *Breaks off. Resumes; something transcendent seems to enter him.* Nothing like it ever happened to me, I got a . . . a big yen for her. She's even more beautiful when she sleeps. I gave her a kiss. On the mouth. She didn't wake up. I never had such a yen in my life.

Long pause.

HYMAN: And?

Gellburg silent.

Did you make love?

GELLBURG, *an incongruous look of terror, he becomes rigid as though about to decide whether to dive into icy water or flee:* . . . Yes.

HYMAN, *a quickening, something tentative in Gellburg mystifies:* How did she react? —It's been some time since you did it, you say.

GELLBURG: Well yes.

HYMAN: Then what was the reaction?

GELLBURG: She was . . . *Searches for the word.* Gasping. It was really something. I thought of what you told me—about loving her now; I felt I'd brought her out of it. I was almost sure of it. She was like a different woman than I ever knew.

HYMAN: That's wonderful. Did she move her legs?

GELLBURG, *unprepared for that question:* . . . I think so.

HYMAN: Well did she or didn't she?

GELLBURG: Well I was so excited I didn't really notice, but I guess she must have.

HYMAN: That's wonderful, why are you so upset?

GELLBURG: Well let me finish, there's more to it.

HYMAN: Sorry, go ahead.

GELLBURG: —I brought her some breakfast this morning and—you know—started to—you know—talk a little about it. She looked at me like I was crazy. She claims she doesn't remember doing it. It never happened.

Hyman is silent, plays with a pen. Something evasive in this.

How could she not remember it?

HYMAN: You're sure she was awake?

GELLBURG: How could she not be?

HYMAN: Did she say anything during the . . . ?

GELLBURG: Well no, but she's never said much.

HYMAN: Did she open her eyes?

GELLBURG: I'm not sure. We were in the dark, but she usually keeps them closed. *Impatiently:* But she was . . . she was groaning, panting . . . she had to be awake! And now to say she doesn't remember?

Shaken, Hyman gets up and moves; a pause.

HYMAN: So what do you think is behind it?

GELLBURG: Well what would any man think? She's trying to turn me into nothing!

HYMAN: Now wait, you're jumping to conclusions.

GELLBURG: Is such a thing possible? I want your medical opinion— could a woman not remember?

HYMAN, *a moment, then:* . . . How did she look when she said that; did she seem sincere about not remembering?

GELLBURG: She looked like I was talking about something on the moon. Finally, she said a terrible thing. I still can't get over it.

HYMAN: What'd she say?

GELLBURG: That I'd imagined doing it.

Long pause. Hyman doesn't move.

What's your opinion? Well . . . could a man imagine such a thing? Is that possible?

HYMAN, *after a moment:* Tell you what; supposing I have another talk with her and see what I can figure out?

GELLBURG, *angrily demanding:* You have an opinion, don't you?—How could a man imagine such a thing!

HYMAN: I don't know what to say . . .

GELLBURG: What do you mean you don't know what to say! It's impossible, isn't it? To invent such a thing?

HYMAN, *fear of being out of his depth:* Phillip, don't cross-examine me, I'm doing everythig I know to help you! —Frankly, I can't follow what you're telling me—you're sure in your own mind you had relations with her?

GELLBURG: How can you even ask me such a thing? Would I say it unless I was sure? *Stands shaking with fear and anger.* I don't understand your attitude! *He starts out.*

HYMAN: Phillip, please! *In fear he intercepts Gellburg.* What attitude, what are you talking about?

GELLBURG: I'm going to vomit, I swear—I don't feel well . . .

HYMAN: What happened . . . has she said something about me?

GELLBURG: About you? What do you mean? What could she say?

HYMAN: I don't understand why you're so upset with me!

GELLBURG: What are you doing!

HYMAN, *guiltily:* What am *I* doing! What are you talking about!

GELLBURG: She is trying to destroy me! And you stand there! And what do you do! Are you a doctor or what! *He goes right up to Hyman's face.* Why don't you give me a straight answer about anything! Everything is in-and-out and around-the-block! —Listen, I've made up my mind; I don't want you seeing her anymore.

HYMAN: I think she's the one has to decide that.

GELLBURG: I am deciding it! It's decided!

He storms out. Hyman stands there, guilty, alarmed. Margaret enters.

MARGARET: Now what? *Seeing his anxiety:* Why are you looking like that?

He evasively returns to his desk chair.

Are *you* in trouble?

HYMAN: Me! Cut it out, will you?

MARGARET: Cut what out? I asked a question—are you?

HYMAN: I said to cut it out, Margaret!

MARGARET: You don't realize how transparent you are. You're a pane of glass, Harry.

HYMAN, *laughs:* Nothing's happened. *Nothing has happened!* Why are you going on about it!

MARGARET: I will never understand it. Except I do, I guess; you believe women. Woman tells you the earth is flat and for that five minutes you're swept away, helpless.

HYMAN: You know what baffles me?

MARGARET: . . . And it's irritating.—What is it—just new ass all the time?

HYMAN: There's been nobody for at least ten or twelve years . . . more! I can't remember anymore! You know that!

MARGARET: What baffles you?

HYMAN: Why I take your suspicions seriously.

MARGARET: Oh that's easy. —You love the truth, Harry.

HYMAN, *a deep sigh, facing upward:* I'm exhausted.

MARGARET: What about asking Charley Whitman to see her?

HYMAN: She's frightened to death of psychiatry, she thinks it means she's crazy.

MARGARET: Well, she is, in a way, isn't she?

HYMAN: I don't see it that way at all.

MARGARET: Getting this hysterical about something on the other side of the world is sane?

HYMAN: When she talks about it, it's not the other side of the world it's on the next block.

MARGARET: And that's sane?

HYMAN: I don't know what it is! I just get the feeling sometimes that she *knows* something, something that . . . It's like she's connected to some . . . some wire that goes half around the world, some truth that other people are blind to.

MARGARET: I think you've got to get somebody on this who won't be carried away, Harry.

HYMAN: I am not carried away!

MARGARET: You really believe that Sylvia Gellburg is being threatened by these Nazis? Is that real or is it hysterical?

HYMAN: So call it hysterical, does that bring you one inch closer to what is driving that woman? It's not a word that's driving her, Margaret—she *knows* something! I don't know what it is, and she may not either—but I tell you it's real.

A moment.

MARGARET: What an interesting life you have, Harry.

Blackout.

Intermission.

ACT TWO

Scene One

The cellist plays, music fades away.

Stanton Case is standing with hands clasped behind his back as though staring out a window. A dark mood. Gellburg enters behind him but he doesn't turn at once.

GELLBURG: Excuse me . . .

CASE, *turns:* Oh, good morning. You wanted to see me.

GELLBURG: If you have a minute I'd appreciate . . .

CASE, *as he sits:* —You don't look well, are you all right?

GELLBURG: Oh I'm fine, maybe a cold coming on . . .

Since he hasn't been invited to sit he glances at a chair then back at Case, who still leaves him hanging—and he sits on the chair's edge.

I wanted you to know how bad I feel about 611 Broadway. I'm very sorry.

CASE: Yes. Well. So it goes, I guess.

GELLBURG: I know how you had your heart set on it and I . . . I tell you the news knocked me over; they gave no sign they were talking to Allan Kershowitz or anybody else . . .

CASE: It's very disappointing—in fact, I'd already begun talking to an architect friend about renovations.

GELLBURG: Really. Well, I can't tell you how . . .

CASE: I'd gotten a real affection for that building. It certainly would have made a perfect annex. And probably a great investment too.

GELLBURG: Well, not necessarily, if Wanamaker's ever pulls out.

CASE: . . . Yes, about Wanamaker's—I should tell you—when I found out that Kershowitz had outbid us I was flabbergasted after what you'd said about the neighborhood going downhill once the store was gone— Kershowitz is no fool, I need hardly say. So I mentioned it to one of our club members who I know is related to a member of the Wanamaker board. —He tells me there has never been any discussion whatever about the company moving out; he was simply amazed at the idea.

GELLBURG: But the man at ABC . . .

CASE, *impatience showing:* ABC was left with the repair work because Wanamaker's changed to another contractor for their new boilers. It had nothing to do with the store moving out. Nothing.

GELLBURG: . . . I don't know what to say, I . . . I just . . . I'm awfully sorry . . .

CASE: Well, it's a beautiful building, let's hope Kershowitz puts it to some worthwhile use. —You have any idea what he plans to do with it?

GELLBURG: Me? Oh no, I don't really know Kershowitz.

CASE: Oh! I thought you said you knew him for years?

GELLBURG: . . . Well, I "know" him, but not . . . we're not personal friends or anything, we just met at closings a few times, and things like that. And maybe once or twice in restaurants, I think, but . . .

CASE: I see. I guess I misunderstood, I thought you were fairly close.

Case says no more; the full stop shoots Gellburg's anxiety way up.

GELLBURG: I hope you're not . . . I mean I never mentioned to Kershowitz that you were interested in 611.

CASE: Mentioned? What do you mean?

GELLBURG: Nothing; just that . . . it almost sounds like I had something to do with him grabbing the building away from under you. Because I would never do a thing like that to you!

CASE: I didn't say that, did I. If I seem upset it's being screwed out of that building, and by a man whose methods I never particularly admired.

GELLBURG: Yes, that's what I mean. But I had nothing to do with Kershowitz . . .

Breaks off into silence.

CASE: But did I say you did? I'm not clear about what you wanted to say to me, or have I missed some . . . ?

GELLBURG: No-no, just that. What you just said.

CASE, *his mystification peaking:* What's the matter with you?

GELLBURG: I'm sorry. I'd like to forget the whole thing.

CASE: What's happening?

GELLBURG: Nothing. Really. I'm sorry I troubled you!

Pause. With an explosion of frustration, Case marches out. Gellburg is left open mouthed, one hand raised as though to bring back his life.

Blackout.

Scene Two

The cellist plays and is gone.

Sylvia in a wheelchair is listening to Eddie Cantor on the radio, singing "If You Knew Susie Like I Know Susie." She has an amused look, taps a finger to the rhythm. Her bed is nearby, on it a folded newspaper.

Hyman appears. She instantly smiles, turns off the radio, and holds a hand out to him. He comes and shakes hands.

SYLVIA, *indicating the radio:* I simply can't stand Eddie Cantor, can you?

HYMAN: Cut it out now, I heard you laughing halfway up the stairs.

SYLVIA: I know, but I can't stand him. This Crosby's the one I like. You ever hear him?

HYMAN: I can't stand these crooners—they're making ten, twenty thousand dollars a week and never spent a day in medical school. *She laughs.* Anyway, I'm an opera man.

SYLVIA: I never saw an opera. They must be hard to understand, I bet.

HYMAN: Nothing to understand—either she wants to and he doesn't or he wants to and she doesn't. *She laughs.* Either way one of them gets killed and the other one jumps off a building.

SYLVIA: I'm so glad you could come.

HYMAN, *settling into chair near the bed:*—You ready? We have to discuss something.

SYLVIA: Phillip had to go to Jersey for a zoning meeting . . .

HYMAN: Just as well—it's you I want to talk to.

SYLVIA:—There's some factory the firm owns there . . .

HYMAN: Come on, don't be nervous.

SYLVIA: . . . My back aches, will you help me onto the bed?

HYMAN: Sure.

He lifts her off the chair and carries her to the bed where he gently lowers her.

There we go.

She lies back. He brings up the blanket and covers her legs.

What's that perfume?

SYLVIA: Harriet found it in my drawer. I think Jerome bought it for one of my birthdays years ago.

HYMAN: Lovely. Your hair is different.

SYLVIA, *puffs up her hair:* Harriet did it; she's loved playing with my hair since we were kids. Did you hear all those birds this morning?

HYMAN: Amazing, yes; a whole cloud of them shot up like a spray in front of my horse.

SYLVIA, *partially to keep him:* You know, as a child, when we first moved from upstate there were so many birds and rabbits and even foxes here —Of course that was *real* country up there; my dad had a wonderful general store, everything from ladies' hats to horseshoes. But the winters were just finally too cold for my mother.

HYMAN: In Coney Island we used to kill rabbits with slingshots.

SYLVIA, *wrinkling her nose in disgust:* Why!

HYMAN, *shrugs:*—To see if we could. It was heaven for kids.

SYLVIA: I know! Brooklyn was really beautiful, wasn't it? I think people were happier then. My mother used to stand on our porch and watch us all the way to school, right across the open fields for—must have been a mile. And I would tie a clothesline around my three sisters so I wouldn't have to keep chasing after them! —I'm so glad—honestly . . . *A cozy little laugh.* I feel good every time you come.

HYMAN: Now listen to me; I've learned that these kinds of symptoms come from very deep in the mind. I would have to deal with your dreams to get any results, your deepest secret feelings, you understand? That's not my training.

SYLVIA: But when you talk to me I really feel my strength starting to come back . . .

HYMAN: You should already be having therapy to keep up your circulation.

A change in her expression, a sudden withdrawal which he notices.

You have a long life ahead of you, you don't want to live it in a wheelchair, do you? It's imperative that we get you to someone who can . . .

SYLVIA: I could tell you a dream.

HYMAN: I'm not trained to . . .

SYLVIA: I'd like to, can I?—I have the same one every night just as I'm falling asleep.

HYMAN, *forced to give way:* Well . . . all right, what is it?

SYLVIA: I'm in a street. Everything is sort of gray. And there's a crowd of people. They're packed in all around, but they're looking for me.

HYMAN: Who are they?

SYLVIA: They're Germans.

HYMAN: Sounds like those photographs in the papers.

SYLVIA, *discovering it now:* I think so, yes!

HYMAN: Does something happen?

SYLVIA: Well, I begin to run away. And the whole crowd is chasing after me. They have heavy shoes that pound on the pavement. Then just as I'm escaping around a corner a man catches me and pushes me down . . . *Breaks off.*

HYMAN: Is that the end of it?

SYLVIA: No. He gets on top of me, and begins kissing me . . . *Breaks off.*

HYMAN: Yes?

SYLVIA: . . . And then he starts to cut off my breasts. And he raises himself up, and for a second I see the side of his face.

HYMAN: Who is it?

SYLVIA: . . . I don't know.

HYMAN: But you saw his face.

SYLVIA: I think it's Phillip. *Pause.* But how could Phillip be like . . . he was almost like one of the others?

HYMAN: I don't know. Why do you think?

SYLVIA: Would it be possible . . . because Phillip . . . I mean . . . *A little laugh* . . . he sounds sometimes like he doesn't like Jews? *Correcting.* Of course he doesn't *mean* it, but maybe in my mind it's like he's . . . *Breaks off.*

HYMAN: Like he's what. What's frightening you? *Sylvia is silent, turns away.* Sylvia?

Hyman tries to turn her face towards him, but she resists.

Not Phillip, is it?

Sylvia turns to him, the answer is in her eyes.

I see.

He moves from the bed and halts, trying to weigh this added complication. Returning to the bedside, sits, takes her hand.

I want to ask you a question.

She draws him to her and kisses him on the mouth.

SYLVIA: I can't help it.

She bursts into tears.

HYMAN: Oh God, Sylvia, I'm so sorry . . .

SYLVIA: Help me. Please!

HYMAN: I'm trying to.

SYLVIA: I know!

She weeps even more deeply. With a cry filled with her pain she embraces him desperately.

HYMAN: Oh Sylvia, Sylvia. . . .

SYLVIA: I feel so foolish.

HYMAN: No-no. You're unhappy, not foolish.

SYLVIA: I feel like I'm losing everything, I'm being torn to pieces. What do you want to know, I'll tell you!

She cries into her hands. He moves, trying to make a decision . . .

I trust you. What do you want to ask me?

HYMAN: —Since this happened to you, have you and Phillip had relations?

SYLVIA, *open surprise:* Relations?

HYMAN: He said you did the other night.

SYLVIA: We had *relations* the other night?

HYMAN: But that . . . well he said that by morning you'd forgotten. Is that true?

She is motionless, looking past him with immense uncertainty.

SYLVIA, *alarmed sense of rejection:* Why are you asking me that?

HYMAN: I didn't know what to make of it. . . . I guess I still don't.

SYLVIA, *deeply embarrassed:* You mean you believe him?

HYMAN: Well . . . I didn't know what to believe.

SYLVIA: You must think I'm crazy, —to forget such a thing.

HYMAN: Oh God no!—I didn't mean anything like that . . .

SYLVIA: We haven't had relations for almost twenty years.

The shock pitches him into silence. Now he doesn't know what or whom to believe.

HYMAN: Twenty . . . ? *Breaks off.*

SYLVIA: Just after Jerome was born.

HYMAN: I just . . . I don't know what to say, Sylvia.

SYLVIA: You never heard of it before with people?

HYMAN: Yes, but not when they're as young as you.

SYLVIA: You might be surprised.

HYMAN: What was it, another woman, or what?

SYLVIA: Oh no.

HYMAN: Then what happened?

SYLVIA: I don't know, I never understood it. He just couldn't anymore.

She tries to read his reaction; he doesn't face her directly.

You believe me, don't you?

HYMAN: Of course I do. But why would he invent a story like that?

SYLVIA, *incredulously:* I can't imagine. . . . Could he be trying to . . . *Breaks off.*

HYMAN: What.

SYLVIA: . . . Make you think I've gone crazy?

HYMAN: No, you mustn't believe that. I think maybe . . . you see, he mentioned my so-called reputation with women, and maybe he was just trying to look . . . I don't know—competitive. How did this start? Was there some reason?

SYLVIA: I think I made one mistake. He hadn't come near me for like—I don't remember anymore—a month maybe; and . . . I was so young . . . a man to me was so much stronger that I couldn't imagine I could . . . you know, hurt him like that.

HYMAN: Like what?

SYLVIA: Well . . . *Small laugh.* I was so stupid, I'm still ashamed of it . . . I mentioned it to my father—who loved Phillip—and he took him aside and tried to suggest a doctor. I should never have mentioned it, it was a terrible mistake, for a while I thought we'd have to have a divorce . . . it was months before he could say good morning, he was so furious. I finally got him to go with me to Rabbi Steiner, but he just sat there like a . . . *She sighs, shakes her head.* —I don't know, I guess you just gradually give up and it closes over you like a grave. But I can't help it, I still pity him; because I know how it tortures him, it's like a snake eating into his heart. . . . I mean it's not as though he doesn't like me, he does, I know it. —Or do you think so?

HYMAN: He says you're his whole life.

She is staring, shaking her head, stunned.

SYLVIA, *with bitter irony:* His whole life! Poor Phillip.

HYMAN: I've been talking to a friend of mine at the hospital, a psychiatrist. I want your permission to bring him in; I'll call you in the morning.

SYLVIA, *instantly:* Why must you leave? I'm nervous now. Can't you talk to me a few minutes? I have some yeast cake. I'll make fresh coffee . . .

HYMAN: I'd love to stay but Margaret'll be upset with me.

SYLVIA: Oh. Well call her! Ask her to come over too.

HYMAN: No-no . . .

SYLVIA, *a sudden anxiety burst, colored by her feminine disappointment:* For God's sake, why not!

HYMAN: She thinks something's going on with us.

SYLVIA, *pleased surprise—and worriedly:* Oh!

HYMAN: I'll be in touch tomorrow . . .

SYLVIA: Couldn't you just be here when he comes. I'm nervous—please—just be here when he comes.

Her anxiety forces him back down on the bed. She takes his hand.

HYMAN: You don't think he'd do something, do you?

SYLVIA: I've never known him so angry. —And I think there's also some trouble with Mr. Case. Phillip can hit, you know. *Shakes her head.* God, everything's so mixed up! *Pause. She sits there shaking her head, then lifts the newspaper.* But I don't understand—they write that the Germans are starting to pick up Jews right off the street and putting them into . . .

HYMAN, *impatience:* Now Sylvia, I told you . . .

SYLVIA: But you say they were such nice people—how could they change like this!

HYMAN: This will all pass, Sylvia! German music and literature is some of the greatest in the world; it's impossible for those people to suddenly change into thugs like this. So you ought to have more confidence, you see?—I mean in general, in life, in people.

She stares at him, becoming transformed.

HYMAN: What are you telling me? Just say what you're thinking right now.

SYLVIA, *struggling:* I . . . I . . .

HYMAN: Don't be frightened, just say it.

SYLVIA, *she has become terrified:* You.

HYMAN: Me! What about me?

SYLVIA: How could you believe I forgot we had relations!

HYMAN, *her persistent intensity unnerving him:* Now stop that! I was only trying to understand what is happening.

SYLVIA: Yes, And what? What is happening?

HYMAN, *forcefully, contained:* . . . What are you trying to tell me?

SYLVIA: Well . . . what . . .

Everything is flying apart for her; she lifts the edge of the newspaper; the focus is clearly far wider than the room. An unbearable anxiety . . .

What is going to become of us?

HYMAN, *indicting the paper:* —But what has Germany got to do with . . . ?

SYLVIA, *shouting; his incomprehension dangerous:* But how can those nice people go out and pick Jews off the street in the middle of a big city like that, and nobody stops them . . . ?

HYMAN: You mean *I've* changed? Is that it?

SYLVIA: I don't know . . . one minute you say you like me and then you turn around and I'm . . .

HYMAN: Listen, I simply must call in somebody . . .

SYLVIA: No! You could help me if you believed me!

HYMAN, *his spine tingling with her fear; a shout:* I do believe you!

SYLVIA: No!—you're not going to put me away somewhere!

HYMAN, *a horrified shout:* Now you stop being ridiculous!

SYLVIA: But . . . but what . . . what . . . *Gripping her head; his uncertainty terrifying her:* What will become of us!

HYMAN, *unnerved:* Now stop it—you are confusing two things . . . !

SYLVIA: But . . . from now on . . . you mean if a Jew walks out of his house, do they arrest him . . . ?

HYMAN: I'm telling you this won't last.

SYLVIA, *with a weird, blind, violent persistence:* But what do they do with them?

HYMAN: I don't know! I'm out of my depth! I can't help you!

SYLVIA: But why don't they run out of the country! What is the matter with those people! Don't you understand . . . ? *Screaming:* . . . This is an *emergency*! What if they kill those children! Where is Roosevelt! Where is England! Somebody should do something before they murder us all!

Sylvia takes a step off the edge of the bed in an hysterical attempt to reach Hyman and the power he represents. She collapses on the floor before he can catch her. Trying to rouse her from her faint . . .

HYMAN: Sylvia? Sylvia!

Gellburg enters.

GELLBURG: What happened!

HYMAN: Run cold water on a towel!

GELLBURG: What happened!

HYMAN: Do it, goddam you!

Gellburg rushes out.

Sylvia!—oh good, that's it, keep looking at me, that's it dear, keep your eyes open . . .

He lifts her up onto the bed as Gellburg hurries in with a towel. Gellburg gives it to Hyman, who presses it onto her forehead and back of her neck.

There we are, that's better, how do you feel? Can you speak? You want to sit up? Come.

He helps her to sit up. She looks around and then at Gellburg.

GELLBURG, *to Hyman:* Did *she* call *you*?

HYMAN, *hesitates; and in an angry tone:* . . . Well no, to tell the truth.

GELLBURG: Then what are you doing here?

HYMAN: I stopped by, I was worried about her.

GELLBURG: You were worried about her. Why were you worried about her?

HYMAN, *anger is suddenly sweeping him:* Because she is desperate to be loved.

GELLBURG, *off guard, astonished:* You don't say!

HYMAN: Yes, I do say. *To her:* I want you to try to move your legs. Try it.

She tries; nothing happens.

I'll be at home if you need me; don't be afraid to call anytime. We'll talk about this more tomorrow. Good night.

SYLVIA, *faintly, afraid:* Good night.

Hyman gives Gellburg a quick, outraged glance. Hyman leaves.

GELLBURG, *reaching for his authority:* That's some attitude he's got, ordering me around like that. I'm going to see about getting somebody else tomorrow. Jersey seems to get further and further away, I'm exhausted.

SYLVIA: I almost started walking.

GELLBURG: What are you talking about?

SYLVIA: For a minute. I don't know what happened, my strength, it started to come back.

GELLBURG: I knew it! I told you you could! Try it again, come.

SYLVIA, *she tries to raise her legs:* I can't now.

GELLBURG: Why not! Come, this is wonderful . . . ! *Reaches for her.*

SYLVIA: Phillip, listen . . . I don't want to change, I want Hyman.

GELLBURG, *his purse-mouthed grin:* What's so good about him?—you're still laying there, practically dead to the world.

SYLVIA: He helped me get up, I don't know why. I feel he can get me walking again.

GELLBURG: Why does it have to be him?

SYLVIA: Because I can talk to him! I want *him. An outburst:* And I don't want to discuss it again!

GELLBURG: Well we'll see.

SYLVIA: We will not see!

GELLBURG: What's this tone of voice?

SYLVIA, *trembling out of control:* It's a Jewish woman's tone of voice!

GELLBURG: A Jewish woman . . . ! What are you talking about, are you crazy?

SYLVIA: Don't you call me crazy, Phillip! I'm talking about it! They are smashing windows and beating children! I am talking about it! *Screams at him:* I am talking about it, Phillip!

She grips her head in her confusion. He is stock still; horrified, fearful.

GELLBURG: What . . . "beating children"?

SYLVIA: Never mind. Don't sleep with me again.

GELLBURG: How can you say that to me?

SYLVIA: I can't bear it. You give me terrible dreams. I'm sorry, Phillip. Maybe in a while but not now.

GELLBURG: Sylvia, you will kill me if we can't be together . . .

SYLVIA: You told him we had relations?

GELLBURG, *beginning to weep:* Don't, Sylvia . . . !

SYLVIA: You little liar!—you want him to think I'm crazy? Is that it? *Now she breaks into weeping.*

GELLBURG: No! It just . . . it came out, I didn't know what I was saying!

SYLVIA: *That I forgot we had relations?! Phillip?*

GELLBURG: Stop that! Don't say anymore.

SYLVIA: I'm going to say anything I want to.

GELLBURG, *weeping:* You will kill me . . . !

They are silent for a moment.

SYLVIA: What I did with my life! Out of ignorance. Out of not wanting to shame you in front of other people. A whole life. Gave it away like a couple of pennies—I took better care of my shoes. *Turns to him.* —You want to talk to me about it now? Take me seriously, Phillip. What happened? I know it's all you ever thought about, isn't that true? *What happened?* Just so I'll know.

A long pause.

GELLBURG: I'm ashamed to mention it. It's ridiculous.

SYLVIA: What are you talking about?

GELLBURG: But I was ignorant, I couldn't help myself. —When you said you wanted to go back to the firm.

SYLVIA: What are you talking about?—When?

GELLBURG: When you had Jerome . . . and suddenly you didn't want to keep the house anymore.

SYLVIA: And? —You didn't want me to go back to business, so I didn't.

He doesn't speak; her rage an inch below.

Well what? I didn't, did I?

GELLBURG: You held it against me, having to stay home, you know you did. You've probably forgotten, but not a day passed, not a person could come into this house that you didn't keep saying how wonderful and interesting it used to be for you in business. You never forgave me, Sylvia.

She evades his gaze.

So whenever I . . . when I started to touch you, I felt that.

SYLVIA: You felt what?

GELLBURG: That you didn't want me to be the man here. And then, on top of that when you didn't want any more children . . . everything inside me just dried up. And maybe it was also that to me it was a miracle you ever married me in the first place.

SYLVIA: You mean your face?

He turns slightly.

What have you got against your face? A Jew can have a Jewish face.

Pause.

GELLBURG: I can't help my thoughts, nobody can. . . . I admit it was a mistake, I tried a hundred times to talk to you, but I couldn't. I kept waiting for myself to change. Or you. And then we got to where it didn't seem to matter anymore. So I left it that way. And I couldn't change anything anymore.

Pause.

SYLVIA: This is a whole life we're talking about.

GELLBURG: But couldn't we . . . if I taught you to drive and you could go anywhere you liked. . . . Or maybe you could find a position you liked . . . ?

She is staring ahead.

We have to sleep together.

SYLVIA: No.

Gellburg drops to his knees beside the bed, his arms spread awkwardly over her covered body.

GELLBURG: How can this be?

She is motionless.

Sylvia? *Pause.* Do you want to kill me?

She is staring ahead, he is weeping and shouting.

Is that it! Speak to me!

Sylvia's face is blank, unreadable. He buries his face in the covers, weeping helplessly. She at last reaches out in pity toward the top of his head, and as her hand almost touches . . .

Blackout.

Scene Three

Case's office. Gellburg is seated alone. Case enters, shuffling through a handful of mail. Gellburg has gotten to his feet. Case's manner is cold; barely glances up from his mail.

CASE: Good morning, Gellburg.

GELLBURG: Good morning, Mr. Case.

CASE: I understand you wish to see me.

GELLBURG: There was just something I felt I should say.

CASE: Certainly. *He goes to a chair and sits.* Yes?

GELLBURG: It's just that I would never in this world do anything against you or Brooklyn Guarantee. I don't have to tell you, it's the only place I've ever worked in my life. My whole life is here. I'm more proud of this company than almost anything except my own son. What I'm trying to say is that this whole business with Wanamaker's was only because I didn't want to leave a stone unturned. Two or three years from now I didn't want you waking up one morning and Wanamaker's is gone and there you are paying New York taxes on a building in the middle of a dying neighborhood.

Case lets him hang there. He begins getting flustered.

Frankly, I don't even remember what this whole thing was about. I feel I've lost some of your confidence, and it's . . . well, it's unfair, I feel.

CASE: I understand.

GELLBURG, *he waits, but that's it:* But . . . but don't you believe me?

CASE: I think I do.

GELLBURG: But . . . you seem to be . . . you don't seem . . .

CASE: The fact remains that I've lost the building.

GELLBURG: But are you . . . I mean you're not still thinking that I had something going on with Allan Kershowitz, are you?

CASE: Put it this way—I hope as time goes on that my old confidence will return. That's about as far as I can go, and I don't think you can blame me, can you. *He stands.*

GELLBURG, *despite himself his voice rises:* But how can I work if you're this way? You have to trust a man, don't you?

CASE, *begins to indicate he must leave:* I'll have to ask you to . . .

GELLBURG, *shouting:* I don't deserve this! You can't do this to me! It's not fair, Mr. Case, I had nothing to do with Allan Kershowitz! I hardly know the man! And the little I do know I don't even like him, I'd certainly never get into a deal with him, for God's sake! This is . . . this whole thing is . . . *Exploding:* I don't understand it, what is happening, what the hell is happening, what have I got to do with Allan Kershowitz, just because he's also a Jew?

CASE, *incredulously and angering:* What? What on earth are you talking about!

GELLBURG: Excuse me. I didn't mean that.

CASE: I don't understand . . . how could you say a thing like that!

GELLBURG: Please. I don't feel well, excuse me . . .

CASE, *his resentment mounting:* But how could you say such a thing! It's an outrage, Gellburg!

Gellburg takes a step to leave and goes to his knees, clutching his chest, trying to breathe, his face reddening.

CASE: What is it? Gellburg? *He springs up and goes to the periphery.* Call an ambulance! Hurry, for God's sake! *He rushes out, shouting:* Quick, get a doctor! It's Gellburg! Gellburg has collapsed!

Gellburg remains on his hands and knees trying to keep from falling over, gasping.

Blackout.

Scene Four

Sylvia in wheelchair, Margaret and Harriet seated on either side of her. Sylvia is sipping a cup of cocoa.

HARRIET: He's really amazing, after such an attack.

MARGARET: The heart is a muscle; muscles can recover sometimes.

HARRIET: I still can't understand how they let him out of the hospital so soon.

MARGARET: He has a will of iron. But it may be just as well for him here.

SYLVIA: He wants to die here.

MARGARET: No one can know, he can live a long time.

SYLVIA, *handing her the cup:* Thanks. I haven't drunk cocoa in years.

MARGARET: I find it soothes the nerves.

SYLVIA, *with a slight ironical edge:* He wants to be here so we can have a talk, that's what it is. *Shakes her head.* How stupid it all is; you keep putting everything off like you're going to live a thousand years. But we're like those little flies—born in the morning, fly around for a day till it gets dark—and bye-bye.

HARRIET: Well, it takes time to learn things.

SYLVIA: There's nothing I know now that I didn't know twenty years ago. I just didn't say it. *Grasping the chair wheels.* Help me! I want to go to him.

MARGARET: Wait till Harry says it's all right.

HARRIET: Sylvia, please—let the doctor decide.

MARGARET: I hope you're not blaming yourself.

HARRIET: It could happen to anybody—*To Margaret.* Our father, for instance—laid down for his nap one afternoon and never woke up. *To Sylvia.* Remember?

SYLVIA, *a wan smile, nods:* He was the same way all his life—never wanted to trouble anybody.

HARRIET: And just the day before he went and bought a new bathing suit. And an amber holder for his cigar. *To Sylvia*—She's right, you mustn't start blaming yourself.

SYLVIA, *a shrug:* What's the difference? *Sighs tiredly—stares. Basically to Margaret.* The trouble, you see—was that Phillip always thought he was supposed to be the Rock of Gibraltar. Like nothing could ever bother him. Supposedly. But I knew a couple of months after we got married that he . . . he was making it all up. In fact, I thought I was stronger than him. But what can you do? You swallow it and make believe you're weaker. And after a while you can't find a true word to put in your mouth. And now I end up useless to him . . . *starting to weep*, just when he needs me!

HARRIET, *distressed, stands:* I'm making a gorgeous pot roast, can I bring some over?

SYLVIA: Thanks, Flora's going to cook something.

HARRIET: I'll call you later, try to rest. *Moves to leave, halts, unable to hold back.* I refuse to believe that you're blaming yourself for this. How can people start saying what they know?—there wouldn't be two marriages left in Brooklyn! *Nearly overcome.* It's ridiculous!—you're the best wife he could have had!—better! *She hurries out. Pause.*

MARGARET: I worked in the pediatric ward for a couple of years. And sometimes we'd have thirty or forty babies in there at the same time. A day or two old and they've already got a personality; this one lays there, stiff as a mummy . . . *mimes a mummy, hands closed in fists*, a regular banker. The next one is throwing himself all over the place . . . *wildly flinging her arms*, happy as a young horse. The next one is Miss Dreary, already worried about her hemline drooping. And how could it be otherwise—each one has twenty thousand years of the human race backed up behind him . . . and you expect to change him?

SYLVIA: So what does that mean? How do you live?

MARGARET: You draw your cards face down; you turn them over and do your best with the hand you got. What else is there, my dear? What else can there be?

SYLVIA, *staring ahead:* . . . Wishing, I guess . . . that it had been otherwise. Help me! *Starts the chair rolling.* I want to go to him.

MARGARET: Wait. I'll ask Harry if it's all right. *Backing away.* Wait, okay? I'll be right back.

She turns and exits. Alone, Sylvia brings both hands pressed together up to her lips in a sort of prayer, and closes her eyes.

Blackout.

Scene Five

The cellist plays, the music falls away.

Gellburg's bedroom. He is in bed. Hyman is putting his stethoscope back into his bag, and sits on a chair beside the bed.

HYMAN: I can only tell you again, Phillip,—you belong in the hospital.

GELLBURG: Please don't argue about it anymore! I couldn't stand it there, it smells like a zoo; and to lay in a bed where some stranger died . . . I hate it. If I'm going out I'll go from here. And I don't want to leave Sylvia.

HYMAN: I'm trying to help you. *Chuckles.* And I'm going to go on trying even if it kills both of us.

GELLBURG: I appreciate that. I mean it. You're a good man.

HYMAN: You're lucky I know that. The nurse should be here around six.

GELLBURG: I'm wondering if I need her—I think the pain is practically gone.

HYMAN: I want her here overnight.

GELLBURG: I . . . I want to tell you something; when I collapsed . . . it was like an explosion went off in my head, like a tremendous white light. It sounds funny but I felt a . . . happiness . . . that funny? Like I suddenly had something to tell her that would change everything, and we would go back to how it was when we started out together. I couldn't wait to tell it to her . . . and now I can't remember what it was. *Anguished, a rushed quality; suddenly near tears.* God, I always thought there'd be time to get to the bottom of myself!

HYMAN: You might have years, nobody can predict.

GELLBURG: It's unbelievable—the first time since I was twenty I don't have a job. I just can't believe it.

HYMAN: You sure? Maybe you can clear it up with your boss when you go back.

GELLBURG: How can I go back? He made a fool of me. It's infuriating. I tell you—I never wanted to see it this way but he goes sailing around on the ocean and meanwhile I'm foreclosing Brooklyn for them. That's what it boils down to. You got some lousy rotten job to do, get Gellburg, send in the Yid. Close down a business, throw somebody out of his home. . . . And now to accuse me . . .

HYMAN: But is all this news to you? That's the system, isn't it?

GELLBURG: But to accuse me of double-crossing the *company*! That is absolutely unfair . . . it was like a hammer between the eyes. I mean to me Brooklyn Guarantee—for God's sake, Brooklyn Guarantee was like . . . like . . .

HYMAN: You're getting too excited, Phillip . . . come on now. *Changing the subject:* —I understand your son is coming back from the Philippines.

GELLBURG, *he catches his breath for a moment:* . . . She show you his telegram? He's trying to make it here by Monday. *Scared eyes and a grin.* Or will I last till Monday?

HYMAN: You've got to start thinking about more positive things—seriously, your system needs a rest.

GELLBURG: Who's that talking?

HYMAN, *indicating upstage:* I asked Margaret to sit with your wife for a while, they're in your son's bedroom.

GELLBURG: Do you always take so much trouble?

HYMAN: I like Sylvia.

GELLBURG, *his little grin:* I know . . . I didn't think it was for my sake.

HYMAN: You're not so bad. I have to get back to my office now.

GELLBURG: Please if you have a few minutes, I'd appreciate it. *Almost holding his breath.* Tell me—the thing she's so afraid of . . . is me isn't it?

HYMAN: Well . . . among other things.

GELLBURG, *shock:* It's me?

HYMAN: I think so . . . partly.

Gellburg presses his fingers against his eyes to regain control.

GELLBURG: How could she be frightened of me! I worship her! *Quickly controlling:* How could everything turn out to be the opposite—I made my son in this bed and now I'm dying in it . . . *Breaks off, downing a cry.* My thoughts keep flying around—everything from years ago keeps coming back like it was last week. Like the day we bought this bed. Abraham & Straus. It was so sunny and beautiful. I took the whole day off. (God, it's almost twenty-five years ago!) . . . Then we had a soda at Schrafft's—of course they don't hire Jews but the chocolate ice cream is the best. Then we went over to Orchard Street for bargains. Bought our first pots and sheets, blankets, pillowcases. The street was full of pushcarts and men with long beards like a hundred years ago. It's funny, I felt so at home and happy there that day, a street full of Jews, one Moses after another. But they all turned to watch her go by, those fakers. She was a knockout; sometimes walking down a street I couldn't believe I was married to her. Listen . . . *Breaks off, with some diffidence:* You're an educated man, I only went to high school—I wish we could talk about the Jews.

HYMAN: I never studied the history, if that's what you . . .

GELLBURG: . . . I don't know where I am . . .

HYMAN: You mean as a Jew?

GELLBURG: Do you think about it much? I never . . . for instance, a Jew in love with horses is something I never heard of.

HYMAN: My grandfather in Odessa was a horse dealer.

GELLBURG: You don't say! I wouldn't know you were Jewish except for your name.

HYMAN: I have cousins up near Syracuse who're still in the business— they break horses. You know there are Chinese Jews.

GELLBURG: I heard of that! And they look Chinese?

HYMAN: They are Chinese. They'd probably say you don't look Jewish.

GELLBURG: Ha! That's funny. *His laugh disappears; he stares.* Why is it so hard to be a Jew?

HYMAN: It's hard to be anything.

GELLBURG: No, it's different for them. Being a Jew is a full-time job. Except you don't think about it much, do you. —Like when you're on your horse, or . . .

HYMAN: It's not an obsession for me . . .

GELLBURG: But how'd you come to marry a shiksa?

HYMAN: We were thrown together when I was interning, and we got very close, and . . . well she was a good partner, she helped me, and still does. And I loved her.

GELLBURG: —a Jewish woman couldn't help you?

HYMAN: Sure. But it just didn't happen.

GELLBURG: It wasn't so you wouldn't seem Jewish.

HYMAN, *coldly:* I never pretended I wasn't Jewish.

GELLBURG, *almost shaking with some fear:* Look, don't be mad, I'm only trying to figure out . . .

HYMAN, *sensing the underlying hostility:* What are you driving at, I don't understand this whole conversation.

GELLBURG: Hyman . . . Help me! I've never been so afraid in my life.

HYMAN: If you're alive you're afraid; we're born afraid—a newborn baby is not a picture of confidence; but how you deal with fear, that's what counts. I don't think you dealt with it very well.

GELLBURG: Why? How did I deal with it?

HYMAN: I think you tried to disappear into the goyim.

GELLBURG: . . . You believe in God?

HYMAN: I'm a socialist. I think we're at the end of religion.

GELLBURG: You mean everybody working for the government.

HYMAN: It's the only future that makes any rational sense.

GELLBURG: God forbid. But how can there be Jews if there's no God?

HYMAN: Oh, they'll find something to worship. The Christians will too—maybe different brands of ketchup.

GELLBURG, *laughs:* Boy, the things you come out with sometimes . . . !

HYMAN: —Some day we're all going to look like a lot of monkeys running around trying to figure out a coconut.

GELLBURG: She believes in you, Hyman . . . I want you to tell her—tell her I'm going to change. She has no right to be so frightened. Of me or anything else. They will never destroy us. When the last Jew dies, the light of the world will go out. She has to understand that—those Germans are shooting at the sun!

HYMAN: Be quiet.

GELLBURG: I want my wife back. I want her back before something happens. I feel like there's nothing inside me, I feel empty. I want her back.

HYMAN: Phillip, what can I do about that?

GELLBURG: Never mind . . . since you started coming around . . . in those boots . . . like some kind of horseback rider . . . ?

HYMAN: What the hell are you talking about!

GELLBURG: Since you came around she looks down at me like a miserable piece of shit!

HYMAN: Phillip . . .

GELLBURG: Don't "Phillip" me, just stop it!

HYMAN: Don't scream at me Phillip, you know how to get your wife back! . . . don't tell me there's a mystery to that!

GELLBURG: She actually told you that I . . .

HYMAN: It came out while we were talking. It was bound to sooner or later, wasn't it?

GELLBURG, *gritting his teeth:* I never told this to anyone . . . but years ago when I used to make love to her, I would almost feel like a small baby on top of her, like she was giving me birth. That's some idea? In bed next to me she was like a . . . a marble god. I worshipped her, Hyman, from the day I laid eyes on her.

HYMAN: I'm sorry for you, Phillip.

GELLBURG: How can she be so afraid of me? Tell me the truth.

HYMAN: I don't know; maybe, for one thing . . . these remarks you're always making about Jews.

GELLBURG: What remarks?

HYMAN: Like not wanting to be mistaken for Goldberg.

GELLBURG: So I'm a Nazi? Is Gellburg Goldberg? It's not, is it?

HYMAN: No, but continually making the point is kind of . . .

GELLBURG: Kind of what? What is kind of? Why don't you say the truth?

HYMAN: All right, you want the truth? Do you? Look in the mirror sometime!

GELLBURG: . . . In the mirror!

HYMAN: You hate yourself, that's what's scaring her to death. That's my opinion. How it's possible I don't know, but I think you helped paralyze her with this "Jew, Jew, Jew" coming out of your mouth and the same time she reads it in the paper and it's coming out of the radio day and night? You wanted to know what I think . . . that's what I think.

GELLBURG: But there are some days I feel like going and sitting in the *schul* with the old men and pulling the *talles* over my head and be a full-time Jew the rest of my life. With the sidelocks and the black hat, and settle it once and for all. And other times . . . yes, I could almost kill them. They infuriate me. I am ashamed of them and that I look like them. *Gasping again:* —Why must we be different? Why is it? What is it for?

HYMAN: And supposing it turns out that we're *not* different, who are you going to blame then?

GELLBURG: What are you talking about?

HYMAN: I'm talking about all this grinding and screaming that's going on inside you—you're wearing yourself out for nothing, Phillip, absolutely nothing! —I'll tell you a secret—I have all kinds coming into my office, and there's not one of them who one way or another is not persecuted. Yes. *Everybody's* persecuted. The poor by the rich, the rich by the poor, the black by the white, the white by the black, the men by the women, the women by the men, the Catholics by the Protestants, the Protestants by the Catholics—and of course all of them by the Jews. Everybody's persecuted—sometimes I wonder, maybe that's what holds this country together! And what's really amazing is that you can't find anybody who's persecuting anybody else.

GELLBURG: So you mean there's no Hitler?

HYMAN: Hitler? Hitler is the perfect example of the persecuted man! I've heard him—he kvetches like an elephant was standing on his pecker! They've turned that whole beautiful country into one gigantic kvetch! *Takes his bag.* The nurse'll be here soon.

GELLBURG: So what's the solution?

HYMAN: I don't see any. Except the mirror. But nobody's going to look at himself and ask what am *I* doing—you might as well tell him to take a seat in the hottest part of hell. Forgive her, Phillip, is all I really know to tell you. *Grins:* But that's the easy part—I speak from experience.

GELLBURG: What's the hard part?

HYMAN: To forgive yourself, I guess. And the Jews. And while you're at it, you can throw in the goyim. Best thing for the heart you know.

Hyman exits. Gellburg is left alone, staring into space. Sylvia enters, Margaret pushing the chair.

MARGARET: I'll leave you now, Sylvia.

SYLVIA: Thanks for sitting with me.

GELLBURG, *a little wave of the hand:* Thank you Mrs. Hyman!

MARGARET: I think your color's coming back a little.

GELLBURG: Well, I've been running around the block.

MARGARET, *a burst of laughter and shaking her finger at him:* I always knew there was a sense of humor somewhere inside that black suit!

GELLBURG: Yes, well . . . I finally got the joke.

MARGARET, *laughs, and to Sylvia:* I'll try to look in tomorrow. *To both:* Good-bye!

Margaret exits.

A silence between them grows self-conscious.

GELLBURG: You all right in that room?

SYLVIA: It's better this way, we'll both get more rest. You all right?

GELLBURG: I want to apologize.

SYLVIA: I'm not blaming you, Phillip. The years I wasted I know I threw away myself. I think I always knew I was doing it but I couldn't stop it.

GELLBURG: If only you could believe I never meant you harm, it would . . .

SYLVIA: I believe you. But I have to tell you something. When I said not to sleep with me . . .

GELLBURG: I know . . .

SYLVIA, *nervously sharp:* You don't know!—I'm trying to tell you something! *Containing herself:* For some reason I keep thinking of how I used to be; remember my parents' house, how full of love it always was? Nobody was ever afraid of anything. But with us, Phillip, wherever I looked there was something to be suspicious about, somebody who was going to take advantage or God knows what. I've been tip-toeing around my life for thirty years and I'm not going to pretend—I hate it all now. Everything I did is stupid and ridiculous. I can't find myself in my life.

She hits her legs.

Or in this now, this thing that can't even walk. I'm not this thing. And it has me. It has me and will never let me go.

She weeps.

GELLBURG: Sshh! I understand. I wasn't telling you the truth. I always tried to seem otherwise, but I've been more afraid than I looked.

SYLVIA: Afraid of what?

GELLBURG: Everything. Of Germany. Mr. Case. Of what could happen to us here. I think I was more afraid than you are, a hundred times more! And meantime there are Chinese Jews, for God's sake.

SYLVIA: What do you mean?

GELLBURG: They're *Chinese*!—and here I spend a lifetime looking in the mirror at my face!—Why we're different I will never understand but to live so afraid, I don't want that anymore. I tell you, if I live I have to try to change myself.—Sylvia, my darling Sylvia, I'm asking you not to blame me anymore. I feel I did this to you! That's the knife in my heart.

Gellburg's breathing begins to labor.

SYLVIA, *alarmed:* Phillip!

GELLBURG: God almighty, Sylvia forgive me!

A paroxysm forces Gellburg up to a nearly sitting position, agony on his face.

SYLVIA: Wait! Phillip!

Struggling to break free of the chair's support, she starts pressing down on the chair arms.

There's nothing to blame! There's nothing to blame!

Gellburg falls back, unconscious. She struggles to balance herself on her legs and takes a faltering step toward her husband.

Wait, wait . . . Phillip, Phillip!

Astounded, charged with hope yet with a certain inward seeing, she looks down at her legs, only now aware that she has risen to her feet.

Lights fade.

THE END.

TIMEBENDS: A LIFE

FOR THREE DAYS WE WENT OUT and climbed the hillside, planting the hundreds of seedlings out of the pail, and finally, with some help, six thousand of them. Inge, pregnant then but hardly showing it—she would be photographing from a high crane in the Brooklyn Navy Yard four hours before the labor pains began—carefully set roots in the slits I was cutting with a flat spade. From the middle of Europe she has brought this reverence for the consecration of such moments in life when the consciousness of time's flow is supreme. And twenty-five years later our ankle-high seedlings are dense sixty-foot trees with stems thicker than telephone poles, and Rebecca is a young woman, a painter and actress, and her brother Robert is working in film in California, and her sister Jane is a weaver and busy sculptor's wife, and I have heard the word "Grandpa!" from a girl of two, a boy of six, and girl of fourteen, Bob's kids.

There was no denying the resistance to that word—my God, I had hardly begun! What are these small persons doing on my lap lovingly repeating that terrible accusation with all its finality? How confidently they imagine I am Grandpa. And this makes me wonder who I imagine I am.

And then the pleasure of growing accustomed to it and even getting to where I can call it into a phone—"Hello? This is Grandpa!"—as though I am not an impersonator trying to show some kind of fatuous procreative accomplishment.

The shocks are there but feel more distant. At a recent town meeting in the high school on the nuclear freeze issue, people standing up to make their comments had stated their names and the number of years they had lived here: "John Smith; I've lived here seven years," as though this gave their opinions more authority. The longest period of residence was around twelve years, except for one young woman whose family had settled here in 1680. I felt a slight unwillingness to announce that I had lived here forty years. Heads turned. I was the old man. Okay, but who was I?

I have lived more than half my life in the Connecticut countryside, all the time expecting to get some play or book finished so I can spend more time in the city, where everything is happening. There is something about this forty-year temporary residence that strikes me funny now. If only we could stop murdering one another we could be a wonderfully humorous species. My contentment discontents me when I know that little happens here that I don't make happen, except the sun coming up and going down and the leaves emerging and dropping off and an occasional surprise like the recent appearance of coyotes in the woods. There is more unbroken forest from Canada down to here than there was even in Lincoln's youth, the farms having gradually vanished, and there is even the odd bear, they say, a wanderer down from the north, and now these coyotes. I have seen them. They have a fixed smug grin, as though they just stole something. And they cannot be mistaken for dogs, whom they otherwise resemble, because of their eyes, which look at you with a blue guilt but no conscience, a mixture of calculation and defensive distrust that domestication cured in dogs thousands of years ago.

And so the coyotes are out there earnestly trying to arrange their lives to make more coyotes possible, not knowing that it is my forest, of course. And I am in this room from which I can sometimes look out at dusk and see them warily moving through the barren winter trees, and I am, I suppose, doing what they are doing, making myself possible and those who come after me. At such moments I do not know whose land this is that I own, or whose bed I sleep in. In the darkness out there they see my light and pause, muzzles lifted, wondering who I am and what I am doing here in this cabin under my light. I am a mystery to them until they tire of it and move on, but the truth, the first truth, probably, is that we are all connected, watching one another. Even the trees.

BIBLIOGRAPHY OF WORKS
OF ARTHUR MILLER

Plays (*The date in parentheses is of the first production*)

That They May Win (1943), in *The Best One-Act Plays of 1944,* Margaret Mayorga, ed. New York: Dodd, Mead, 1945, pp. 45–59.

The Man Who Had All the Luck (1944), in *Cross-Section,* Edwin Seaver, ed. New York: L. B. Fischer, 1944, pp. 486–552. (This is a pre-production version of the play.)

All My Sons (1947), in *Collected Plays.* New York: Viking, 1957, pp. 57–127.

Death of a Salesman (1949), in *Collected Plays,* pp. 130–222.

An Enemy of the People (1950). New York: Viking, 1951. (Adaptation of Henrik Ibsen's play.)

The Crucible (1953), in *Collected Plays,* pp. 223–330.

A Memory of Two Mondays (1955), in *Collected Plays,* pp. 331–376.

A View from the Bridge (1955). New York: Viking, 1955.

A View from the Bridge (1956). Revised version; in *Collected Plays,* pp. 377–439.

After the Fall (1964). New York: Viking, 1964.

Incident at Vichy (1964). New York: Viking, 1965.

The Price (1968). New York: Viking, 1968.

The Creation of the World and Other Business (1972). New York: Viking, 1973.

The Golden Years (written 1939–40) and *The Man Who Had All the Luck* (1944). London: Methuen, 1989.

The Archbishop's Ceiling (1977) and *The American Clock* (1980). New York: Grove Press, 1989.

Two-Way Mirror (1982). London: Methuen, 1984. As *Elegy for a Lady* (1982) and *Some Kind of Love Story* (1982). New York: Dramatists' Play Service, 1984.

Playing for Time (1985). Chicago: Dramatic Publishing Company, 1985.

Danger: Memory! Two Plays (1987). New York: Grove Press, 1987.

The Ride Down Mount Morgan (1990). London: Methuen, 1991.

The Last Yankee (1993). New York: Dramatists' Play Service, 1991.

Broken Glass (1994). New York: Penguin, 1994.

Radio Plays

The Pussycat and the Expert Plumber Who Was a Man, in *One Hundred Non-Royalty Radio Plays,* William Kozlenko, ed. New York: Greenberg, 1941, pp. 20–30.

William Ireland's Confession, in *One Hundred Non-Royalty Radio Plays*, pp. 512–521.
Grandpa and the Statue, in *Radio Drama in Action*, Erik Barnouw, ed. New York: Farrar and Rinehart, 1945, pp. 267–281.
The Story of Gus, in *Ralph's Best Plays*, Joseph Liss, ed. New York: Greenberg, 1947, pp. 303–319.

Screenplays

Everybody Wins (1990). New York: Grove Weidenfeld, 1990.

Fiction and Reportage

Situation Normal. New York: Reynal and Hitchcock, 1944.
Focus. New York: Reynal and Hitchcock, 1945.
The Misfits. New York: Viking, 1961.
I Don't Need You Any More, Stories by Arthur Miller. New York: Viking, 1967.
"Kidnapped," *Saturday Evening Post*, CCXLII (January 25, 1969), 40–42, 78–82.
In Russia. New York: Viking, 1969. (With Inge Morath.)
"Bees," *Michigan Quarterly Review*, Spring 1990, pp. 153–57.
Homely Girl: A Life. New York: Peter Blum, 1992.

Articles

"Tragedy and the Common Man," *The New York Times*, February 27, 1949, II, pp. 1, 3.
"Arthur Miller on 'The Nature of Tragedy,' " *The New York Herald Tribune*, March 27, 1949, V, pp. 1, 2.
"Journey to 'The Crucible,' " *The New York Times*, February 8, 1953, II, p. 3.
"University of Michigan," *Holiday*, XIV (December 1953), 68–70, 128–143.
"A Modest Proposal for Pacification of the Public Temper," *Nation*, CLXXIX (July 3, 1954), 5–8.
"The American Theater," *Holiday*, XVII (January 1955), 90–104.
"A Boy Grew in Brooklyn," *Holiday*, XVII (March 1955), 54–55, 117–124.
"On Social Plays," Preface to *A View from the Bridge*. New York: Viking, 1955, pp. 1–15.
Untitled comment, *World Theatre*, IV (Autumn 1955), 40–41.
"The Family in Modern Drama," *The Atlantic Monthly*, CXCVII (April 1956), 35–41.
"Global Dramatist," *The New York Times*, July 21, 1957, II, p. 1.
"The Writer's Position in America," *Coastlines*, II (Autumn, 1957), 38–40.
"The Shadow of the Gods," *Harper's*, CCXVII (August 1958), 35–43.
"Bridge to a Savage World," *Esquire*, L (October 1958), 185–190.
"The Playwright and the Atomic World," *Tulane Drama Review*, V (June 1961), 3–20.
"The Bored and the Violent," *Harper's*, CCXXV (November 1962), 50–56.

"On Recognition," *Michigan Quarterly Review*, II (Autumn 1963), 213–220.

"Lincoln Repertory Theatre—Challenge and Hope," *The New York Times*, January 19, 1964, II, pp. 1, 3.

"Our Guilt for the World's Evil," *The New York Times Magazine*, January 3, 1965, pp. 10–11, 48.

"The Role of P.E.N.," *Saturday Review*, XLIX (June 4, 1966), 16–17.

"It Could Happen Here—And Did," *The New York Times*, April 30, 1967, II, p. 17.

"Arthur Miller Talks," *Michigan Quarterly Review*, VI (Summer 1967), 153–184.

"Broadway from O'Neill to Now," *The New York Times*, December 21, 1969, pp. 1, 7.

"Arthur Miller in Russia," *Harper's*, September 1969, pp. 37–78.

"A Genuine Countryman," *Country Journal*, January 1978, pp. 34–38.

"The Sin of Power," *Index on Censorship*, May–June 1978, pp. 3–6.

"In China," *The Atlantic Monthly*, March 1979, pp. 90–103.

"A Kind of Despair," *Index on Censorship*, June 1981, pp. 31–32.

"The Night Ed Murrow Struck Back," *Esquire*, December 1983, pp. 460–67.

"Arthur Miller Speaks Out on the Election," *Literary Cavalcade*, November 1984, pp. 4–5.

"A Note from Arthur Miller," *The New Theatre Review*, Winter 1988, p. 2.

"Arthur Miller on Rushdie and Global Censorship," *Authors' Guild Bulletin*, Summer 1989, p. 5.

"Death in Tiananmen," *The New York Times*, September 10, 1989.

"Uneasy About the Germans," *The New York Times Magazine*, May 6, 1990, pp. 46, 77, 84, 85.

"Get It Right: Privatize Executions," *The New York Times*, May 8, 1992, p. A31.

"Last Word," *American Theatre*, July–August 1992, p. 68.

"Ibsen and the Drama of Today," in *The Cambridge Companion to Arthur Miller*, James McFarlane, ed. Cambridge: 1994, pp. 227–32.

Interviews

Schumach, Murray, "Arthur Miller Grew Up in Brooklyn," *The New York Times*, February 6, 1949, II, pp. 1, 3.

Wolfert, Ira, "Arthur Miller, Playwright in Search of His Identity," *New York Herald Tribune*, January 25, 1953, IV, p. 3.

Griffin, John and Alice, "Arthur Miller Discusses *The Crucible*," *Theatre Arts*, XXXVII (October 1953), 33–34. (The interview introduces the published play, pp. 35–67.)

Samachson, Dorothy and Joseph, in *Let's Meet the Theatre*. New York: Abelard-Schuman, 1954, pp. 15–20.

United States House of Representatives, Committee on Un-American Activities, Investigation of the Unauthorized Use of United States Passports, Part 4, June 21, 1956. Washington: United States Government Printing Office, November, 1956. ("Interview" is not exactly the word for this item.)

Gelb, Philip, "Morality and Modern Drama," *Educational Theatre Journal*, X (October 1958), 190–202.

Allsop, Kenneth, "A Conversation with Arthur Miller," *Encounter*, XIII (July 1959), 58–60.

Brandon, Henry, "The State of the Theatre: A Conversation with Arthur Miller," *Harper's*, CCXXI (November 1960), 63–69.

Gelb, Barbara, "Question: 'Am I My Brother's Keeper?' " *The New York Times*, November 29, 1964, II, pp. 1, 3.

Feron, James, "Miller in London to See 'Crucible,' " *The New York Times*, January 24, 1965, p. 82.

Morley, Sheridan, "Miller on Miller," *Theatre World*, LXI (March 1965), 4, 8.

Gruen, John, "Portrait of the Playwright at Fifty," *New York*, October 24, 1965, pp. 12–13.

Carlisle, Olga, and Styron, Rose, "The Art of the Theatre II: Arthur Miller, an Interview," *Paris Review*, X (Summer 1966), 61–98.

Miller, Arthur, "The Contemporary Theatre," *Michigan Quarterly Review*, VI (1967), 153–63.

Evans, Richard I., *Psychology and Arthur Miller*. New York: Dutton, 1969, pp. 85–116.

Martin, Robert A., "Arthur Miller: Tragedy and Commitment," *Michigan Quarterly Review*, VIII (1969), 176–78.

Miller, Arthur, and Styron, William, "Conversation," *Audience*, I (November–December 1971), 4–21.

Martin, Robert A., and Richard D. Meyer, "Arthur Miller on Plays and Playwriting," *Modern Drama*, IXX (1976), 375–84.

Martine, James J., *Critical Essays on Arthur Miller*. Boston: G. K. Hall, 1979, pp. 177–88.

Moss, Leonard, *Arthur Miller*. Boston: Twayne, 1980, pp. 107–22.

Centola, Steve, "The Will to Live: An Interview with Arthur Miller," *Modern Drama*, XXVII (1984), 345–60.

Roudané, Matthew C., "An Interview with Arthur Miller," *Michigan Quarterly Review*, XXIV (1985), 373–89.

Lamos, Mark, "An Afternoon with Arthur Miller," *American Theatre*, III (1986), 18–23.

Roudané, Matthew C., *Conversations with Arthur Miller*. Jackson: University of Mississippi, 1987.

Bigsby, Christopher, ed., *Arthur Miller and Company*. London: 1990.

Centola, Steve, *Arthur Miller in Conversation*. Dallas: 1993.

A bibliography of works about Arthur Miller will be found in the Viking Critical Library editions of *Death of a Salesman* and *The Crucible*, both volumes edited by Gerald Weales, to whom grateful acknowledgment is made for his substantial contribution to the bibliography printed here. The bibliography here has been updated by Christopher Bigsby.

CLICK ON A CLASSIC
www.penguinclassics.com

The world's greatest literature at your fingertips

Constantly updated information on more than a thousand titles,
from Icelandic sagas to ancient Indian epics, Russian drama to
Italian romance, American greats to African masterpieces

•

The latest news on recent additions to the list, updated
editions, and specially commissioned translations

•

Original essays by leading writers

•

A wealth of background material, including biographies
of every classic author from Aristotle to Zamyatin, plot
synopses, readers' and teachers' guides, useful web links

•

Online desk and examination copy assistance for academics

•

Trivia quizzes, competitions, giveaways, news on
forthcoming screen adaptations

Available in Penguin Classics editions:

All My Sons
Told against the setting of a suburban backyard in the 1940s, Miller's play is a classic American drama about the idealization of a father, the loss of a son, and the secrets that destroy a family. Winner of the Drama Critics Circle Award for Best New Play in 1947, *All My Sons* was the work that established Arthur Miller as the new voice in the American theater. *ISBN 0-14-118546-5*

The Crucible
"I believe the reader will discover here the essential nature of one of the strangest and most awful chapters in human history," Arthur Miller wrote in an introduction to *The Crucible*, his classic play about the witch-hunts and trials in seventeenth-century Salem, Massachusetts. Based on historical people and actual events, Miller's drama is a thinly veiled indictment of the McCarthy trials of the early 1950s. *ISBN 0-14-243733-6*

Death of a Salesman
All his life Willy Loman has been a traveling salesman who made a decent living— but not more. Dreams and evasions have kept him from seeing himself as he is. He has learned the American go-getter philosophy by heart, and passed it on to his sons, to their undoing. And then, at sixty-three, finally forced to face reality, Willy turns away, down the only road open to him. Out of this simple human situation, Arthur Miller has fashioned the winner of the Pulitzer Prize and Drama Critics Circle Award in 1949 and one of the greatest dramas of our time.
ISBN 0-14-118097-8

All of the above include an introduction by Christopher Bigsby

Available in Penguin Plays editions

After the Fall
Arthur Miller has set this devastating play inside a mind. The mind belongs to Quentin, a lawyer with a lofty reputation and a prosecutor's zeal for pursuing the finest threads of guilt. Yet the guilt that most obsesses Quentin is his own: his guilt as a son and husband, friend, lover, and man. And in the course of his plunge through the labyrinths of consciousness and conscience, Quentin will be joined by several hostile witnesses—from the partner he abandoned to the beautiful, childlike wife he couldn't save. Masterly in its orchestration, searing in its candor, *After the Fall* is a victory of the moral imagination. *ISBN 0-14-048162-1*

A View from the Bridge
Longshoreman Eddie Carbone struggles with his predictable life, the arrival of two of his wife's relatives from Italy, and his true feelings for his niece Catherine.
ISBN 0-14-048135-4

Also available from Arthur Miller in Penguin Plays editions

Broken Glass   ISBN 0-14-024938-9
The Crucible   ISBN 0-14-048138-9
Death of a Salesman   ISBN 0-14-048134-6
An Enemy of the People   ISBN 0-14-048140-0
Incident at Vichy   ISBN 0-14-048193-1
Mr. Peters' Connections   ISBN 0-14-048245-8
The Price   ISBN 0-14-048194-X
The Ride Down Mt. Morgan   ISBN 0-14-048244-X

Also by Arthur Miller:

Timebends
A Life
With passion, wit, and candor, Arthur Miller recalls his childhood in Harlem and Brooklyn during the 1920s and the Depression; his successes and failures in the theater and in Hollywood; the formation of his political beliefs that, two decades later, brought him into confrontation with the House Committee on Un-American Activities; and his later work on behalf of human rights as the president of PEN International. He writes with astonishing perception and tenderness of Marilyn Monroe, his second wife, as well as the host of famous and infamous that he has intersected with during his adventurous life. *Timebends* is Miller's love letter to the twentieth century: its energy, its humor, its chaos and moral struggles.

ISBN 0-14-024917-6

Echoes Down the Corridor
Collected Essays: 1944–2000
"A fascinating collection that reminds us that Miller's chief concern and great subject has always been the citizen in his world."—*Los Angeles Times*
Witty and wise, rich in artistry and insight, *Echoes Down the Corridor* gathers together a dazzling array of more than forty previously uncollected essays and works of reportage, reaffirming Arthur Miller's standing as one of the greatest writers of our time.

ISBN 0-14-200005-1

Homely Girl, A Life and Other Stories
This is a stunning collection of brilliant short fiction from the Pulitzer Prize–winning dramatist and one of the twentieth century's greatest writers. All three prose works in *Homely Girl, A Life* demonstrate all the insight, precision, and greatness of spirit of Miller's classic plays.

ISBN 0-14-025279-7